THE

PUBLICATIONS

OF THE

Lincoln Record Society

FOUNDED IN THE YEAR

1910

VOLUME 89

ISSN 0267-2634

LINCOLN WILLS

1532–1534

EDITED BY

DAVID HICKMAN

The Lincoln Record Society

The Boydell Press

First published 2001

A Lincoln Record Society Publication
published by The Boydell Press
an imprint of Boydell & Brewer Ltd
PO Box 9, Woodbridge, Suffolk IP12 3DF, UK
and of Boydell & Brewer Inc.
PO Box 41026, Rochester, NY 14604–4126, USA
website: http://www.boydell.co.uk

ISBN 0 901503 66 5

A catalogue record for this book is available
from the British Library

Details of other Lincoln Record Society volumes are available
from Boydell & Brewer Ltd

This publication is printed on acid-free paper

Typeset by Joshua Associates Ltd, Oxford
Printed in Great Britain by
St Edmundsbury Press Ltd, Bury St Edmunds, Suffolk

CONTENTS

MAPS, TABLES AND FIGURES

For Richard and Susan Hickman

for their help and support during the preparation of this edition

ACKNOWLEDGEMENTS

I would like to thank the following for their assistance in the preparation of this volume. Professor David Smith and Dr Nicholas Bennet of the Lincoln Record Society for initially commissioning the project and for their continuing help and advice thereafter. The staff of Lincolnshire Archives for their help in providing ready access to the manuscript collections in their care. The British Academy, the Department of History at the University of Nottingham, and the School of Cultural and Community Studies at the University of Sussex for providing the time and resources necessary to transcribe and index the wills. Above all, I would like to thank my wife Cairo for her patience and encouragement during the course of this project.

ABBREVIATIONS

BIHR	*Bulletin of the Institute of Historical Research.*
Chantry Certificates (1923)	'The Chantry Certificates for Lincoln and Lincolnshire returned under the Act of Parliament of 1 Edward VI', ed. C.W. Foster and A. Hamilton-Thompson, *Reports and Papers of the Associated Architectural Societies*, 36 (1923), 183–294.
Chantry Certificates (1926)	Foster and Hamilton-Thompson (eds.), *Reports and Papers of the Associated Architectural Societies*, 37 (1926), 18–106, 247–75.
DC	Court of the Dean and Chapter of Lincoln Cathedral.
HJ	*Historical Journal.*
JEH	*Journal of Ecclesiastical History.*
L	Henry Litherland, bachelor in decrees, commissary and official of the archdeacon of Stow.
LCC	Lincoln Consistory Court.
LRS	Lincoln Record Society.
P	John Pryn, official of the archdeaconry of Lincoln.
P2	John Pope, official of the archdeaconry of Lincoln.
Stow	Court of the Archdeaconry of Stow.
TRHS	*Transactions of the Royal Historical Society.*
VCH Lincolnshire	*The Victoria History of the County of Lincoln*, ed. W. Page, 2 vols (London, 1906).

INTRODUCTION

THE PUBLICATION OF LINCOLNSHIRE WILLS

In 1914 the Lincoln Record Society published the first of three volumes of Lincolnshire wills. Edited for publication by Canon C.W. Foster, these wills ranged chronologically from 1271 to March 1532, and were drawn from the probate records of the Lincoln Consistory Court (incorporating the Archdeaconry Court of Lincoln) and the Archdeaconry Court of Stow.[1] Canon Foster's intention was the systematic publication of all extant Lincolnshire wills, with the exception of those proved in the Prerogative Court of the Archbishop of Canterbury, and he edited the wills as a single, chronological series, arranged by date of composition. Foster and his assistants prepared abstracts of wills as far as 1547,[2] but the Canon's death prevented further publication until the appearance of the present edition, which continues the series up to the end of October 1534.

By the time the first LRS volumes of wills were published a number of other printed editions of Lincolnshire wills had already appeared, providing abstracts and calendars of a significant sample of medieval and early modern wills from the county.[3] This reflected an increasing contemporary interest in historical probate documents nationally, principally fuelled by a growing demand for accessible genealogical and local historical sources. Indeed, in this respect, the purpose of such publications has changed significantly from eighteenth-century antiquarian preoccupations, which, when directed towards probate material, had focussed essentially on the wills of the monarchy and the nobility alone.[4] While the demands of local history continue to provide an important impetus behind the publication of wills, developments in social and cultural history from the 1950s onwards have led to a considerably wider use of probate material for historical

---

[1] C.W. Foster (ed.), *Lincoln Wills Registered in the District Probate Registry at Lincoln, I: 1271–1526* (LRS, 5, 1914); *Lincoln Wills II: 1505 – May 1530* (LRS, 10, 1918); *Lincoln Wills III: 1530–1532* (LRS, 24, 1930).

[2] L.A. F.L.b, 1–36.

[3] A. Gibbons (ed.), *Early Lincoln Wills: an Abstract of all the Wills and Administrations Recorded in the Episcopal Registers of the Old Diocese of Lincoln, 1280–1547* (Lincoln, 1888); A.R. Maddison, *Lincolnshire Wills, 1500–1617*, 2 vols. (Lincoln, 1888–91).

[4] See, for example, J. Nichols, *A Collection of all the Wills Known to be Extant of the Kings and Queens of England, Princes and Princesses of Wales, and every branch of the Blood Royal from the Reign of William the Conqueror to that of Henry the Seventh, exclusive* (London, 1780); W.P.W. Phillimore, *A Calendar of Wills relating to the Counties of Northampton and Rutland, Proved in the Court of the Archdeacon of Northampton, 1510–1652* (London, 1888); R.R. Sharpe, *Calendar of Wills Proved and Enrolled in the Court of Husting, London, A.D. 1258 – A.D. 1688*, 2 vols. (London, 1889–90); R. White, *Calendar of Nottinghamshire Wills in the York Registry, A.D. 1514 to 1619* (Worksop, 1890); H.R. Plomer, *Abstracts from the Wills of English Printers and Stationers, from 1492 to 1630* (London, 1903); J.W. Clay and E.W. Crossley, *Halifax Wills: Being Abstracts and Translations of the Wills Registered at York from the Parish of Halifax* (Halifax, 1904); E.A. Fry, *Calendars of Wills and Administrations Relating to the Counties of Devon and Cornwall, Proved in the Principal Registry of the Bishop of Exeter, 1559–1799* (British Record Society, 35, 36, 1908–14).

purposes.[5] Developments in the study of the English Reformation, in particular, have played a significant role in refining methodologies for the use of probate documentation as a historical source in relation to changing patterns of religious belief and practice in early modern England.[6]

In taking account of these developments the present edition adopts slightly different conventions from the former volumes, in that many items previously considered insignificant or too repetitive for publication purposes are now routinely included. The most important new inclusion is that of the preamble, the initial bequest of the soul to God, which has been used extensively, albeit with increasing caution, in charting the development of testators' religious beliefs during the period of the English Reformation. At the same time the opportunity has been taken to include the numerous small and repetitive bequests of pots, pans, cows and carts which can provide useful indications of the material culture of early modern testators. Finally, it has also been decided to include the initial declaration of the state of health of the testator, since this can provide anecdotal evidence for the immediate circumstances surrounding the making of a will.

In most other respects, however, the format adopted in the previous volumes has been retained. The 585 wills published in this volume are arranged chronologically by date of composition. Although some earlier wills not included in the earlier publications preface the main series, this edition commences where volume III finished, at 25 March 1532, the beginning of the year in the Old Style calendar. Based principally on the manuscript register LCC 1532–34, the present edition ends at 30 October 1534, the date of the latest will in the register. Following previous practice it has been decided to include all Lincolnshire wills written during this period, and appropriate documents have been published from the registers of the two other main probate courts exercising jurisdiction over the county. Equally, wills contained in later registers because of a later date of probate, but written in the period covered here, have also been included.

LCC 1532–34

The vast majority of the wills presented here were proved in the Lincoln Consistory Court and the Archdeaconry Court of Lincoln, and entered together in a single series of probate registers. The core of this edition is therefore register LCC 1532–34, which provides 533 (91%) of the wills made and proved in this period.[7] The register itself is a volume of 338 folios, bound, in common with the other early modern registers in the LCC series, in hard vellum. The arrangement of the wills

[5] See, for example, M. Spufford, *Constrasting Communities: English Villagers in the Sixteenth and Seventeenth Centuries* (Cambridge, 1974); K. Wrightson and D. Levene, *Poverty and Piety in an English Village: Terling 1525–1700*, 2nd edn. (Oxford, 1995).

[6] For recent discussions of the relevant literature see E. Duffy, *The Stripping of the Altars: Traditional Religion in England 1400–1580* (New Haven and London, 1992), 504–23; D. Hickman, 'From Catholic to Protestant: the Changing Meaning of Testamentary Religious Provisions in Elizabethan London', in N. Tyacke (ed.), *England's Long Reformation 1500–1800* (London, 1998), 117–39; C. Marsh, *Popular Religion in Sixteenth-Century England: Holding their Peace* (Basingstoke, 1998), 128–38.

[7] LCC 1535–37 provides 23 (4%) of the wills, LCC 1534 andc. provides 7 (1.2%), the Stow Archdeaconry records 17 (3%) and the Dean and Chapter records 5 (0.8%).

within the volume is loosely chronological by date of probate, but consists of a series of bundles not always consecutive in their dating, reflecting the origin of the records in two probate courts that were theoretically distinct although employing the same officials. As would be expected, therefore, it would appear that the documents were copied into the registers at a slightly later date, as the originals became available to the scribe.

The probate procedures of early sixteenth-century ecclesiastical courts are reasonably well known, yet historical interpretations placed on the impact and significance of their activities for contemporaries have varied considerably.[8] In rejecting earlier views that represented medieval and early sixteenth-century church courts as cumbersome burdens to the majority of the English population, scholars since the later 1970s have tended to lay greater stress on the flexibility and responsiveness of the courts to the populations they served.[9] While some recent studies have adopted a more cautious approach in this regard, it remains the case that most church courts operated with some degree of efficiency, and with considerable co-operation and support from the populations under their jurisdiction.[10]

The wills from Lincolnshire would support this position in a number of respects. Above all, it is apparent from the recorded locations of the court when granting probate that ecclesiastical officials made frequent journeys over considerable distances in the course of their business. This aspect of ecclesiastical court administration has not received sufficient attention, and is worth examining in some detail. The mobility of the court officials is most easily demonstrable in the case of the officials of the Lincoln consistory and archdeaconry courts, largely because their jurisdiction provides the majority of wills in the present edition. The smaller number of wills originating from the jurisdiction of the Stow archdeaconry court makes it difficult to demonstrate an equal level of mobility there, as does the frequent failure of Stow wills to record the location of the court at the time of probate. Nevertheless instances of the court conducting business at Belton, in the north-west of the county, and Waddingham, somewhat to the west of Caistor, would tend to indicate a similarly peripatetic approach.[11] Indeed, of the seventeen Stow wills proved in the whole period March 1532–October 1534, three were certainly proved at Lincoln, two at Belton, one at Waddingham and the remaining eleven do not record a place of probate, although it is likely that this was Lincoln. The peculiar court of the Dean and Chapter of Lincoln Cathedral is only attested sitting in the cathedral itself, although only one of the five wills that it handled in our period was made by a resident of the city, in this case a vicar of the cathedral.[12]

---

[8] Foster, *Lincoln Wills II*, xiv–xxii; R. Houlbrooke, *Church Courts and the People during the English Reformation, 1520–1570* (Oxford, 1979), 89–116.

[9] C. Kitching, 'The Prerogative Court of Canterbury from Warham to Whitgift', in R. O'Day and F. Heal (eds.), *Continuity and Change: Personnel and Administration of the Church of England 1500–1642* (Leicester, 1976), 191–213; S. Lander, 'Church Courts and the Reformation', in O'Day and Heal, *Continuity and Change*, 215–37; M. Ingram, *Church Courts, Sex and Marriage in England, 1570–1640* (Cambridge, 1987). For older, less optimistic views of contemporary attitudes towards the pre-Reformation church courts and the clergy as a whole see C. Hill, *Economic Problems of the Church: From Archbishop Whitgift to the Long Parliament* (Oxford, 1956); A.G. Dickens, *The English Reformation*, 2nd edn. (London, 1989).

[10] C. Marsh, *Popular Religion*, 107–12.

[11] See wills nos. 27, 70, 75.

[12] See wills nos. 180 (Thomas Hawe, vicar of Glentham), 245 (John Rose of Strubby), 298 (Robert

The geographical range of the probate activities of Lincolnshire's ecclesiastical courts is represented in Map 1, summarising the data for the single year January to December 1533. While not showing every individual journey, the map does attempt to indicate the direct journeys taken from place to place, and the number of wills proved at each location during this year.

Table 1 provides a more detailed breakdown of the movement of the Lincoln consistory and archdeaconry courts during the year, which may be compared with the map to indicate the most frequently travelled routes.

The most immediately striking aspects of the data are the frequency of travel, and the distances that the court officials were prepared to cover in order to prove a relatively small number of wills. The grants of probate from May illustrate this particularly well, with the court travelling widely across the archdeaconry, and stopping at various locations to prove very small numbers of wills in each locality. To that extent, it would appear that executors did not necessarily have to travel far, or wait excessively long periods, before being able to present a will for probate.

Ralph Houlbrooke has suggested that it is possible to provide a general impression of the relative efficiency of ecclesiastical court probate procedures by calculating the time elapsing between the date on which a will was made and that on which it was proved. By taking a sufficiently large body of wills, and allowing for the fact that precise dates of death are usually unavailable, it is thereby possible to make a rough estimate of the time taken by a particular court to prove the wills coming before it. Houlbrooke took samples of fifty wills from each of the archdeaconry courts of Norfolk and Surrey, and the consistory court of Norwich, in the periods 1516–17, 1522–25 and 1520–21 respectively. His figures indicate that in the Norfolk archdeaconry court 54% of the wills were proved within two months, 88% within a year, while 12% took a year or longer to prove. In the Surrey archdeaconry 82% of the wills were proved within two months, suggestive perhaps of excessive speed in expediting probate procedures, 98% were proved within a year, and only 2% took longer. The Norwich consistory was rather slower, proving some 50% of its wills within two months, 76% within a year, and taking a year or longer to prove the remaining 22%.[13]

Using the same method, the Lincolnshire courts compare reasonably well with this record. Of the total 585 wills 21 (3.6%) could not be used in this way, since they lack precise dates either of composition or of probate. However, of the remaining 564 wills 227 (40%) were proved within two months of writing, and a further 320 (57%) were proved before the end of a year. Hence 97% of the wills were proved within a year of composition, leaving only 17 (3%) that took a year or longer to prove. This would suggest that the Lincolnshire courts were operating at a reasonably high level of efficiency for the period, particularly when the size of the area under their jurisdiction, compared with the much smaller archdeaconries examined by Houlbrooke, is taken into consideration.

Indeed, a comparison of the movements of the court officials through the county, with the geographical distribution of will composition, further reinforces the impression of a considerable degree of responsiveness on the part of the ecclesiastical courts towards local demand. Map 2 shows the Lincolnshire parishes that

West, vicar of Lincoln Cathedral), 437 (Stephen Chapman of Skillington), 452 (Robert Gage of Skillington).
[13] Houlbrooke, *Church Courts and the People*, 95–7.

Belton (1)

Grimsby (6)

Caistor (7)

Market Rasen (2)

Louth (10)

Gayton le Marsh (1)

Wragby (2)

Muckton (2)

LINCOLN (48)

Baumber (2)

Alford (8)

South Hykeham (2)

Horncastle (10)

Partney (27)

Navenby (6)

Leadenham (3)

Heckington (1)

Boston (12)

Ancaster (2)

Great Hale (5)

Skirbeck (5)

Swineshead (3)

Kirton in Holland (2)

Grantham (9)

Pickworth (3)

Donington in Holland (14)

Bitchfield (4)

Bourne (6)

Spalding (9)

Cowbit (4)

10 miles

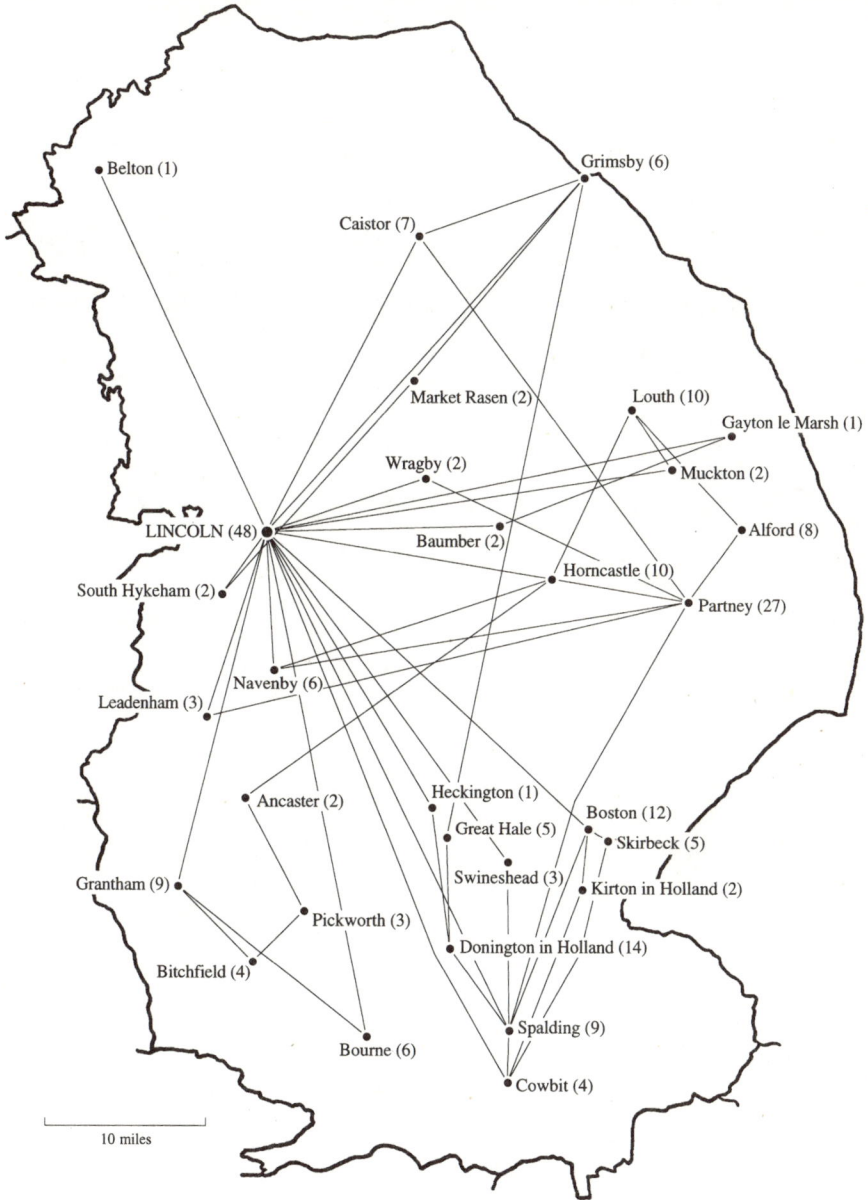

Map 1. Lincolnshire probate locations 1533
showing the number of wills proved at each location, and the movements of
the Lincoln consistory and archdeaconry courts

Table 1. Locations of Lincoln consistory/archdeaconry court probate in 1533

Date	Location	Number	Date	Location	Number
9 Jan.	Lincoln	1	17 May	Navenby	2
13 Jan.	Grantham	6	23–25 May	Lincoln	3
15 Jan.	Bourne	6	26 May	Lincoln & Boston	3 & 3
18–19 Jan.	Lincoln	2	27 May	Spalding	3
3 Feb.	Horncastle	1	28 May	Donington in Holland	10
4 Feb.	Partney	6	29 May	Heckington	1
5 Feb.	Alford	3	3–24 June	Lincoln	6
6 Feb.	Louth & Muckton	4 & 1	15 July	Gayton le Marsh	1
9 Feb.	Lincoln	1	17 July	Baumber	2
10 Feb.	Caistor	2	18–29 July	Lincoln	5
11 Feb.	Grimsby	1	1 Aug.	Cowbit	1
16–17 Feb.	Great Hale	5	5 Aug.	Skirbeck & Boston	5 & 1
18 Feb.	Donington in Holland	4	6 Aug.	Kirton in Holland	2
19 Feb.	Spalding	2	7 Aug.	Cowbit & Spalding	3 & 1
20 Feb.	Boston	8	21 Aug.– 26 Sept.	Lincoln	9
4–16 Apr.	Lincoln	3	9 Oct.	Swineshead	3
28 Apr.	Horncastle	4	10 Oct.	Spalding & Partney	3 & 1
29 Apr.	Partney	6	14 Oct.	Caistor	4
30 Apr.	Wragby	2	15 Oct.	Grimsby	3
1–2 May	Lincoln	2	17 Oct.	Lincoln	1
4 May	Horncastle	1	20 Oct.	Grantham	3
5 May	Louth	3	21 Oct.	Bitchfield	4
6 May	Alford & Partney	2 & 1	23 Oct.	Pickworth	3
8 May	Leadenham	3	24 Oct.	Ancaster	2
9 May	Lincoln	2	29 Oct.	Horncastle	4
12 May	Caistor	1	4 Nov.	Navenby	4
13 May	Grimsby	2	10 Nov.	Partney	13
14 May	Market Rasen	2	11 Nov.	Alford	3
15 May	South Hykeham	2	12 Nov.	Louth & Muckton	4 & 1
16 May	Lincoln	1	15 Nov. – 9 Dec	Lincoln	9

produced wills during the whole period 25 March 1532–31 October 1534, and it will be observed that the locations showing the greatest levels of probate activity outside Lincoln itself broadly correspond to geographical concentrations of will-making.

At the same time, the chronological distribution of the wills suggests that while patterns of probate activity do not directly coincide with the pattern of will-making, they do bear some relation to the broad national pattern of seasonal variations in mortality rates. This, in itself, helps to confirm the suggestion that the probate services of the ecclesiastical courts were generally available fairly quickly after the death of a testator.

The seasonal mortality pattern for England as a whole in the early sixteenth century, as estimated by Wrigley and Schofield, peaks from the end of February to the beginning of April, drops fairly sharply during May and June and reaches its lowest point in July. It then climbs slowly again during August, September, October and November, before accelerating over December and January to peak again at the end of the following February.[14] It is apparent that, in Lincolnshire, peaks of probate activity do occur in the early months of each year, being concentrated in February and May of 1533, and March, May and June of 1534, possibly in response to the higher mortality rates expected for February to April.

There are also, however, peaks in October 1532, November and December of 1533, and October 1534. These peaks may represent a backlog of probate business arising from a gradual increase in mortality over the preceding few months, and it is clear that in 1533 at least, the Summer and early Autumn was a period during which the consistory court carried out relatively little probate business. Nevertheless, it is evident that the pattern of probate activity does not correspond precisely with national mortality rate fluctuations, and it should be emphasised that the present sample is probably too small, and too geographically restricted, to demonstrate a closer overall correspondence. Indeed, it is likely that local mortality rates varied substantially throughout England, and it is difficult to take into account unknown variables such as the length of time that might elapse between the composition and probation of any particular will. This latter variable in particular will have a significant impact on a local sample of wills of the present size, and it is perhaps more surprising to find a considerable degree of conformity to the national pattern than it is to find divergences from it.

Similar problems exist with any analysis of the pattern of will composition revealed by the present sample. While there does appear to be a tendency for more wills to be written just before, or during, periods of expected higher mortality, variations in individual circumstances will impact strongly on a local sample of this nature. The most important difficulty is the fact that although early modern testators usually made their last wills and testaments within months, weeks or days of their deaths, this was not always the case. Nor was it always possible to be certain that what appeared to be a last illness, and hence a compelling circumstance for settling an estate, would actually prove fatal. Indeed, only 50 (8.5%) of the testators in the present collection declare themselves 'sick of body' in their wills, while a few even state themselves to be 'of good helthe', or 'of perfyte helthe'.[15] Moreover it has been estimated that by the later sixteenth century only around a

[14] E.A. Wrigley and R.A. Schofield, *The Population History of England 1541–1871* (London, 1981), 285–355, esp. 293 (fig. 8.2).
[15] Thomas Wenslay of Grimsby, describing himself as 'of good helthe', made his will on 26 March 1534, and it was not proved until 20 October 1534 (will no. 448). Edward Humble, of Roughton,

10 miles

Map 2. Lincolnshire parishes producing wills 1532–34

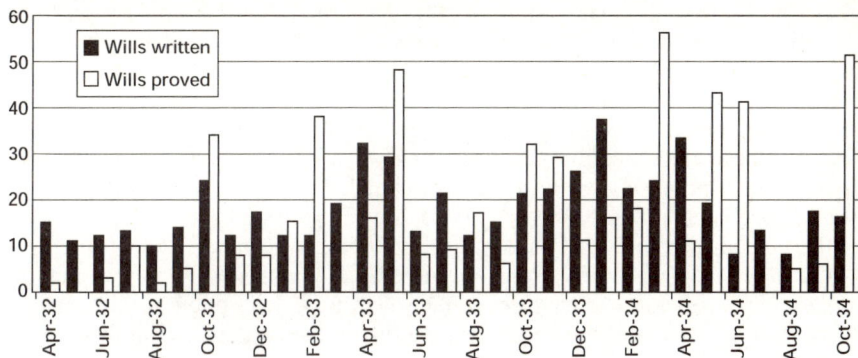

Fig. 1. Wills written and proved April 1532 – October 1534

half of adult males and a tenth of adult females actually came to the attention of the probate courts, and these proportions were probably lower in the early part of the century. It is, therefore, apparent that we do not have here a truly random cross-section of Lincolnshire society as a whole.[16] Above all, the population represented in the wills, being necessarily endowed with some degree of property, is inherently less likely to have been affected by short-term mortality crises brought on by poor harvests, or, to some extent, the seasonal fluctuations caused by poorer weather and meagre food supplies.[17]

Bearing these limitations in mind, then, it is striking that the evidence we do have still bears some relationship to expected patterns of mortality for the English population as a whole. To this extent, it would appear that probate activity on the part of the church courts was surprisingly sensitive to periods of higher mortality, and this, again, would suggest a generally high level of availability of probate services to the Lincolnshire population. Yet, as has been suggested above, it is important to consider exactly what sort of population is represented in the wills if we are to make any further assessment of their potential as a historical source.

THE TESTATORS

Any large sample of early modern English probate documents will usually exclude from consideration most of the poor, most women, except for reasonably wealthy widows, and the substantial numbers of individuals who normally would fall within the will-making class but who died intestate. The Lincolnshire wills conform closely to this basic pattern, the overwhelming majority of testators being male, 523 (89.4%), as opposed to the 62 female testators (10.6%). These proportions seem fairly typical for a predominantly rural population in the early sixteenth century. A sample of 919 London wills made between 1529 and 1546 reveals a somewhat

---

however, 'of . . . perfyte helthe', made his will on 15 April 1534 and clearly declined rapidly thereafter, since it was proved three weeks later on 4 May (will no. 471).

[16] M.L. Zell, 'The Social Parameters of Probate Records in the Sixteenth Century', *BIHR*, 57 (1984), 107–13.

[17] See below, 'The testators'.

higher proportion of female testators, 21% of the total, but this would seem to be exceptional, a peculiarity of a city with a higher literacy rate and a higher number of independently propertied women.[18]

In terms of the social range of the testators, it is difficult to reach definitive conclusions for the entire sample, since only 108 (20.6%) of male and 28 (45%) of female testators recorded their status in their wills. Furthermore, of the 108 males giving a description of their status, 35 individuals (32.4%) belonged to the clergy. Some broad conclusions, however, may be drawn regarding the social composition of the Lincolnshire testators, based on the information summarised in Table 2.

The largest single status group among the lay male testators was that of husbandman, providing thirty-three of the wills with a description of the testator's occupation or status. Although ranging considerably in wealth and in local social standing and influence, these were individuals regarded as among those 'who do not rule' in sixteenth-century political theory, although clearly higher in the social scale than Henry Weste of Great Coates, the only testator to describe himself as a labourer.[19] The five yeomen occupied a slightly more exalted social position, although the only lay testators of substantial rank are represented by three esquires, four gentlemen and an alderman of Lincoln.[20] Indeed, with the exception of these latter individuals, all of the male testators who gave their occupations belonged to the lower ranks of the social spectrum, albeit above that of the landless poor.[21] Most of those who described themselves as following an occupation other than husbandry tended to come from the towns, particularly Lincoln and Boston. In these cases the occupations stated are predominantly in manufacturing roles such as tanning, while there is only a single example of a 'professional' role in the form of Richard Lambeson, a notary from Swineshead.[22]

The clergy are represented by 35 testators, providing 6% of the total will-making population or 6.7% of the total male will-making population. It has been estimated that the priesthood as a whole comprised about 4% of the total male population of England on the eve of the Reformation.[23] If we take into account the fact that a higher proportion of the male clergy are likely to have made wills than the male laity, it would appear that Lincolnshire's clerical population as a proportion of the of overall county population was not untypical of the country as a whole. Even so, certain features of the clerical wills would suggest that a potentially large body of serving clergy may well be underrepresented in the probate record, in that the wills of beneficed priests greatly outnumber those of chantry priests and curates. Although considerably more numerous than beneficed clergy, such priests were often poorly paid and, disposing of smaller estates, are less likely to make an impact

---

[18] S. Brigden, *London and the Reformation* (Oxford, 1989), 414–16.

[19] Will no. 182.

[20] Wills nos. 8 (John Thomson, yeoman), 49 (John Snarry, yeoman), 141 (Henry Weste, yeoman), 344 (William Boston, yeoman), 550 (Richard Burton, yeoman), 139 (Nicholas Upton, esquire), 239 (John Langton, esquire), 519 (John Upton, esquire), 91 (Christopher Haghus, gentleman), 145 (Godfrey Bolles, gentleman), 204 (Thomas Overton, gentleman), 229 (Nicholas Wymbyshe, gentleman), 421 (George Browne, alderman of Lincoln).

[21] The wills of higher status individuals from Lincolnshire were proved in the Prerogative Court of the Archbishop of Canterbury, which exercised jurisdiction over all probate causes over a certain value, or involving property ownership in more than one county.

[22] Will no. 463.

[23] C. Haigh, *English Reformations: Religion, Politics and Society under the Tudors* (Oxford, 1993), 5–6.

Table 2. Status and occupations recorded in Lincolnshire wills 1532–34

M/F	Lay or clergy	Designation	Number
Male	Clergy	Parson	11
		Priest	7
		Rector	1
		Vicar	16
	Lay	Alderman of Lincoln	1
		Barber	1
		Barber & fishmonger	1
		Brazier	1
		Cordwainer	1
		Draper	1
		Esquire	3
		Fisherman	1
		Fishmonger	2
		Freemason	1
		Gentleman	4
		Glover	2
		Husbandman	33
		Labourer	1
		Mariner	1
		Mercer	1
		Netherlander	1
		Notary	1
		Pewterer	1
		Roper	1
		Saddler	1
		Servant	2
		Single man	1
		Tanner	3
		Tiler	1
		Weaver	1
		Yeoman	5
Female	Lay	Widow	28
			136

in the probate record.[24] Indeed, while only one clerical testator held the rank of rector,[25] twenty-seven of the rest exercised cure of souls in their parishes. Only seven, describing themselves simply as 'priest', were chantry or stipendiary priests.

[24] In the diocese of Lincoln unbeneficed clergy may have been twice as numerous as their beneficed contemporaries: M. Bowker, 'The Henrician Reformation and the Parish Clergy', in C. Haigh, *The English Reformation Revised* (Cambridge, 1987), 80–2.

[25] William Ashton, rector of Belton: will no. 27.

The most glaring gap in the testamentary record, however, is the married female population of the county, and those women who died before they married, or never did marry. It is immediately noticeable that those female testators who give a status description all designate themselves as widow, reflecting the fact that married women or those still under the authority of a parent or guardian were not considered in law as owning property. Women generally would have estates to dispose of only in the event of remaining unmarried following the death of a spouse, and it is highly likely that the majority of female testators in the present sample who failed to indicate their social status would also be in this position. Unfortunately, none of the female testators provide any further indication of the social status of their households, although it is clear that a number of them possessed estates equivalent to those of the wealthier husbandmen and yeomen in the present sample.

A final consideration in exploring the population of testators represented in these wills is their geographical spread within the county. As shown in Map 2 above, the parishes producing wills in the period 1532–34 cluster noticeably in the south-east of the county, in the Fenlands particularly, in the centre of the county to the south-east of Lincoln itself, and along the coast. The north-western parts of the county are somewhat underrepresented, while the large numbers of small parishes in the central-eastern parts, inland from the coast, present a similarly uneven distribution. In many respects the biases in the geographical distribution arise from the relatively small size of the sample itself, covering a limited chronological range. This in itself might well explain the anomalous lack of wills from towns such as Stamford, which produced only one will in the entire period under consideration, while Gainsborough produced only two. At the same time, factors of population distribution and geographical variation in the local mortality rate have played some part in influencing the overall pattern. A higher mortality rate, and hence a greater degree of testamentary activity, might be expected from less healthy areas such as the Fens, although such long-term demographic factors are difficult to assess through a source that excludes a substantial section of the population. Moreover, despite some anomalies, the locations that produced the largest number of wills in the period were among the more heavily populated parts of the county. To that extent, population density is probably the overriding factor in determining the levels of testamentary activity.[26]

It will be apparent, therefore, that the interpretation of a will, or group of wills, is far from a straightforward matter. Yet it remains the case that in many instances the last will is the single most informative source we possess about most individuals in the later medieval and early modern periods, particularly from the social groups below the 'middling sort'. For this reason, while it is essential to allow for the 'missing' elements of society, a great part of the historical value of early modern wills lies in the fact that they provide detailed information across a broader social range than many other classes of source material. Moreover, handled sensitively,

---

[26] The parishes producing the highest densities of testators (counting Lincoln as one location) were: Boston (18), Lincoln (15), Gosberton (14), Kirton in Holland (14), Pinchbeck (14), Burgh in the Marsh (9), Swineshead (9), Spalding (9), Donington in Holland (7), Horbling (7), Wigtoft (7), Benington in Holland (6), Leake (6), Ingoldmells (6), Moulton (6), Swaton (5), Tetney (5), Wrangle (5), Wyberton (5). These parishes provided 30% of all the wills in the present edition. A further thirteen parishes produced 4 wills each (Bardney, Barrow, Barton on Humber, Billinghay, Frampton, Grantham, Holbeach, Horncastle, Huttoft, Mumby, Sibsey, Skirbeck and Tattershall). In total, 12% of the 266 parishes represented in the sample produced 39% of the county's wills.

the evidence for patterns of belief and practice contained within testamentary documents remains among the richest and most voluminous sources for this period.

WILLS AS A HISTORICAL SOURCE

The use of wills as historical documents in recent decades has made questions of exclusivity and representation particularly significant. Indeed demographic history has tended to eschew wills as a statistical source for many of the reasons discussed above.[27] Yet the enormous body of potentially useful data contained in the probate registers of the early modern period has made a significant impact, especially on approaches to social and cultural history. Used individually for anecdotal evidence, or in quantity when studying large populations over a period of time, wills have made an important contribution to our understanding of the material culture of the late medieval and early modern periods, as well as broader developments in religious and cultural practices and beliefs.

In many respects the bequests found in the Lincolnshire wills reflect what might be expected of a predominantly rural society. Agricultural implements and livestock feature prominently, with sheep and cattle forming the most common type of livestock bequest. The higher value of particular animals is reflected in bequests specifically giving a wether sheep to a named individual. It is also fairly common to find a clear distinction made between the generality of cattle and the family bull or milk cow, to the point that such animals are sometimes distinguished by name. William Copeland of Ruskington, for example, bequeathed 'a redde cowe cromplehornyd' to his wife Helen, while Thomas Bretfelde of Braceby, left 'a cowe namyd Chery' to the churchwardens of his parish in order to provide an annual obit for his and his wife's souls.[28] The same applies to horses, which are often identified by a brief description or by name, as befitting a more valuable animal. Decisions on the allocation of livestock to particular persons were made on a similar basis as bequests of inanimate objects, individuals of greater significance to the testator being given animals of greater worth or in greater number. Robert Burwell, a husbandman of West Keal, stipulated precisely how his sixty ewes were to be divided when he made his will in March 1533: 'I will that all my yowys togyther schall be pute in holde and lette runne, and xx yowys with ther lammys that runne firste and other xx of the laste runnynge owte of the holde schall bee delyverid to Johanne my wyffe, and iff ther bee ij or iij of the yowys that sche lyke not, I will better yowis schall be delyverid to hir for them.'[29]

The significance of such bequests should not be underestimated in a society whose wealth was largely tied up in livestock, and it is noticeable that considerably more wills provide more details about livestock than about material possessions or household goods. Nevertheless, bequests of furniture, bedding and clothing are

[27] E.g. D.E.C. Eversley, P. Laslett and E.A. Wrigley, *An Introduction to English Historical Demography from the Sixteenth to the Nineteenth Century* (London, 1966); E.A. Wrigley and R.S. Schofield, *The Population History of England 1541–1871: a Reconstruction* (London, 1981); E.A. Wrigley, R.S. Davies, J.E. Oeppen and R.S. Schofield, *English Population History from Family Reconstitution 1580–1837* (Cambridge, 1997).
[28] Wills nos. 301, 374.
[29] Will no. 169.

often specified in great detail, reflecting the relative scarcity of ownership of quantities of furniture. Brass cooking vessels were particularly prized and were disposed of carefully, but testators frequently allocated specific items of clothing or furniture to specific beneficiaries with equal care. The will of Gilbert Tylson of Pinchbeck provides a good, but by no means unique, example of a testator detailing every piece of furniture, plate, bedding, clothing and every animal to be given to each of his beneficiaries, and the age they would have to be before receiving their bequests. Other testators added further details in terms of the provisions that were made in the event of the premature death of one or more beneficiaries.[30]

Disposal of land and real estate tends to follow a fairly typical pattern for the early sixteenth century, copyhold being the most common form of holding, with rather fewer individuals bequeathing freehold property. These latter tend to belong to the upper strata of society, although the problems inherent in identifying social status through wills make a rigorous correlation difficult. At the same time local custom clearly retained some significance in determining the disposal of lands and goods, several testators referring to the custom of the manor or lordship when dividing the bulk of their estates.

RELIGIOUS BEQUESTS

In terms of historical research, wills have made their greatest impact as a class of source material in the field of religious history. Historical interest has increasingly focussed on the practical impact and course of religious and cultural change on the population as a whole, as opposed to viewing it through the partial lens of official legislation and proclamation. For this reason, wills have been extensively quarried for the information they contain about the religious investment made by testators. Indeed, despite some scepticism regarding the sensitivity of a will as an indicator of the faith of a particular individual, especially as the pressures of the Reformation period intensified, wills still provide one of the most important large-scale forms of source material for general patterns of pious expenditure.[31]

The cornerstone of pre-Reformation Catholicism was, for most of the English population, the belief that, except in the case of truly egregious sinners, good works and prayer could materially affect one's chances of salvation in the afterlife. It was assumed that the vast majority of ordinary Christians would eventually attain heaven, provided that appropriate sincere penance and purgation was performed for their sins, both before and after physical death. The doctrine of purgatory had developed since the twelfth century as a rationalisation of such beliefs, and posited an intermediate stage between heaven and hell where all but the sainted and the irrevocably damned would undergo purging torment for their sins before release into paradise. Prayers and good works by, or on behalf of the deceased, could induce the Virgin and the saints to intercede for those in purgatory, and effectively shorten their time in this intermediate state. Since the twelfth century a multiplicity of practices had been elaborated in order to provide such intercession, and probate records, reflecting the final disposition of an individual's wealth and property in the face of death, necessarily provides an especially rich source for such practices.

---

[30] Will no. 249.
[31] Duffy, *Stripping of the Altars*, 504–23.

Much of our evidence for inner belief, therefore, derives from outward investment in the practices through which belief was expressed. This circumstance leads to
particular difficulties of interpretation in periods of significant religious change such
as the Reformation, in terms of relating widespread popular practices to specific,
often unstated, beliefs and doctrines. For example, before the Reformation certain
forms of testamentary bequest offer a very secure indication of a testator's religious
inclinations. Endowments of prayers for the dead, anniversary masses, trentals of
masses and obits, together with most donations to religious houses, were inextric-
ably linked to the doctrine of purgatory, and their presence in a will virtually
guarantees that the testator held at least some level of belief in the doctrine. In the
middle years of the sixteenth century, however, against a background of rapid and
confusing doctrinal change involving successive abolitions and restorations of many
longstanding practices, testators frequently abandoned older forms of bequest that
explicitly linked pious investment with the concept of intercession for souls in
purgatory.

Under these circumstances, a testator failing to make such bequests might be
expressing a truly evangelical rejection of the associated beliefs. On the other hand,
even a testator whose religious opinions were impeccably Catholic in nature would
be understandably reluctant to risk the consequences of investing in, or stating a
strong belief in, doctrines and practices that were prone to official abolition. Nor is
it necessarily a simple task to interpret the meaning of those forms of religious
practice that were acceptable across the doctrinal spectrum, and continued to
appear in wills throughout the Reformation. Charitable benefaction, for example,
was understood by both Catholics and evangelicals as a fundamental religious duty
and was encouraged as such. Without an explicit statement of a testator's motiva-
tion, however, it is impossible to distinguish between a bequest reflecting intercessory concerns and one representing a more evangelical interpretation that
eschewed all notions of the direct efficacy of good works in influencing the salvation
or damnation of the individual soul.

In many respects then, the present sample of Lincolnshire wills is particularly
interesting, in that it covers the very last years of papal authority in England and the
period in which Henry VIII established the royal supremacy over what was to
become an independent Church of England. At the same time, the sample dates
from the period before official action attenuated the range of avenues available to
the testator for pious investment. Hence it offers a direct comparison with other
studies which have used wills from the same period in order to weigh the strength of
popular commitment to the traditional religion against signs of developing evangelical tendencies. The probate records of many localities have revealed traces of
evangelical sentiment by the 1530s, including London, Kent, Yorkshire, Gloucestershire and other parts of the realm.[32] Lincolnshire itself is known to have
harboured groups of evangelicals in the coastal regions involved in direct trade
with the continent.[33] Yet one of the most striking aspects of the wills in the present
collection is the complete absence of indications of evangelical leanings on the part

---

[32] A.G. Dickens, *Lollards and Protestants in the Diocese of York 1509–1558* 2nd. edn. (London,
1982); P. Clark, *English Provincial Society from the Reformation to the Revolution: Religion, Politics
and Society in Kent, 1500–1640* (Brighton, 1977); Brigden, *London and the Reformation*; C.
Litzenburger, *The English Reformation and the Laity: Gloucestershire 1540–1580* (Cambridge,
1997).
[33] Dickens, *Lollards and Protestants*; Dickens, *English Reformation*, 325–34.

of any the testators. Indeed, the pattern of religious bequests in these wills would tend to suggest an extremely strong commitment to the traditional belief system, despite occasional suggestions of anxiety over the future of pious investment, and this may reflect the vigour of Bishop Longland's drive against heresy in his diocese.[34]

A survey of the religious bequests contained in these wills provides a very powerful impression of the strength of the traditional belief system in the county. The will preambles, the opening clauses leaving the testators' souls to God, are nearly all wholly traditional in character, leaving the soul to God, the Virgin and the saints. It is now widely accepted that the formulaic nature of the preamble makes it a very insecure indicator of individual religious belief, although it would appear that most testators were unlikely to use a formula that directly contradicted the general tenor of their faith. The influence of a local scribe or clergyman in providing preamble wording has been identified as a particular problem in this regard, and is well illustrated by the two wills from the parish of Barnoldby. Both are distinctive in being among the very few to use Latin for their preambles, and both were witnessed by the parish priest, Sir Robert Lodyngton, who probably wrote them using an existing formula.[35]

It is, of course, possible to find more individualistic preambles that do suggest something of the beliefs of the individual concerned. Thomas Staynborn, parson of Thornton, bequeathed his soul 'into the mercyfull handes of my savior Criste Jhesus, and into the handes of Hys blessyd mother Mary, and into the handes of all the angellys and archangellys, and to the holy patryaches and prophetes, appostelles, martyrs, confessors, virgins, with all the celestyall congregacion of heven'.[36] A number of testators' preambles are explicit enough to make their statements of faith more than merely mechanical rehearsals of conventional piety. Thomas Hawe, vicar of Glentham, left his soul to God 'besechyng Our Blessyd Lady and all the holly cumpeny of heven to pray for me', while Sir Robert Weste, vicar of Lincoln Cathedral, made his will 'fermly trustyng and belevyng in the fathe catholike', and Godfrey Bolles, gentleman of Gosberton, did likewise 'trustyng in God and in the sacramentes off holy churche and therby to be savyd'.[37] It is also possible to find examples of preambles which evangelicals certainly were using at the time, and which would provide the basis for most forms of preamble after the 1550s. Hugh Wylkynson, barber, of St. Paul's in the Bailey, Lincoln, left his soul 'to God allmyghtty' alone, yet he went on to bequeath 2s. to his curate 'to pray for me', suggestive of a thoroughly orthodox faith on his part.[38]

Indeed, when attention is paid to the religious bequests in the main body of the wills, the evidence for deeply entrenched intercessory belief is overwhelming. Although the actual word 'purgatory' is only used once,[39] 207 (35%) of the testators endowed masses to be celebrated for their souls, or for the souls of others, while 86 (17%) made provisions explicitly for prayers for the departed. These figures might

---

[34] Bowker, 'Henrician Reformation and the Parish Clergy', 77–8.

[35] M. Spufford, 'The Scribes of Villagers' Wills in the Sixteenth and Seventeenth Centuries and their Influence', *Local Population Studies*, 7 (1971), 28–43; J.D. Alsop, 'Religious Preambles in Early Modern English Wills as Formulae', *JEH*, 40 (1989), 19–27; wills nos. 221, 232.

[36] Will no. 407.

[37] Wills nos. 180, 298, 145.

[38] Will no. 411.

[39] Will no. 181.

seem rather low in comparison with other parts of the country, but a clearer picture is revealed when we take other bequests into account, such as the very common bequest of the residue of an estate to be used for charitable works 'for the health of my soul'.[40] In total 466 (79%) of the wills contain bequests explicitly linked to the concept of providing intercession for the dead, whether in the form of bequests 'for the health of my soul', or in the form of intercessory masses, trentals of masses and obits. Of the remaining 119 wills all but 32 contain some form of bequest strongly implying intercessory belief, such as the provision of lights to burn on the altar of a saint, bequests to religious fraternities, donations to religious houses, or the provision of mass equipment and ornaments to a parish church. Thus slightly over 5% of the wills in the present collection do not contain deliberate investment in religious practices overtly indicative of the central aspects of pre-Reformation Catholic belief.

An examination of these remaining thirty-two wills, however, reveals no obvious sign of non-Catholic sentiment. On the contrary, it is clear that in most cases a lack of funds, rather than specific doctrinal scruples, prevented the testators from making the kind of overt pious gesture that would find its way into a written testamentary document. Indeed thirty of these wills contain at least a bequest of funds to the repairs of Lincoln Cathedral or to the cathedral generally, over and above bequests to their own parish churches. Several of the testators, furthermore, made benefactions to more than one parish church in their locality besides their local parish clergy. This would tend to suggest at least a conventional piety, centred on the established church and its existing practices. Only two testators, Robert Wynter, parson of Sedgebrook,[41] and Agnes Myddylton, of Ludborough,[42] failed to provide even this level of pious investment. In both of these cases it would be very difficult to argue that religious heterodoxy caused the deviation from the more normal pattern, and it seems more likely that financial constraints were the dominant factor. Agnes Myddylton, for instance, left only 6s. 8d. to her daughter Catherine, and the same sum to her parish priest 'desyeryng hym to be good frende to my executor, John Burman', while Robert Wynter detailed only two cows, a colt and two beehives to be divided between his beneficiaries.

Within this broadly traditional pattern of belief a number of trends may be observed, mirroring national developments but also highlighting the distinctiveness of the county. In the first place it is clear that devotion to local religious houses remained relatively strong in Lincolnshire, with 169 (29%) of the testators leaving bequests to religious houses, usually in order to provide for some form of long-standing intercession for their souls. As would be expected for the period, the Lincolnshire wills suggest that the orders of friars were considerably more popular than the older religious houses, attracting the bequests of more than twice as many testators. It is still striking, however, that 59 (10%) of the testators left bequests to these older houses. Indeed one of these, Roger Robynson of Swineshead, was living within Swineshead Abbey when he made his will in May 1533, and requested burial in the conventual church. Several other testators requested the services of the monks of more than one abbey, as well as burial within a conventual church, or posthumous enrolment as a lay brother in order to provide

---

[40] Haigh, *English Reformations*, 36–7.
[41] Will no. 120.
[42] Will no. 280.

for sufficient post-mortem intercession.[43] While these more striking bequests tend to belong to clerical rather than lay testators, it remains significant that a relatively large number of socially diverse laymen continued to exhibit signs of devotion to the older houses.

In other respects the pattern of devotional bequests from Lincolnshire bears broad similarities with the national picture. At least 103 testators (18%) demonstrated their membership of religious gilds or fraternities gilds through bequests directly to them, or through requests that a particular gild administer an endowment of land or livestock to provide for obits and other masses.[44] A similar observation might be made of the more general indications of devotion to the particular saints revered by the gilds and by individual testators. In Lincolnshire, as in other parts of England, the Virgin was by far the most popular saint as a vehicle for intercession, since her aid on behalf of souls in purgatory was considered particularly effective. 157 testators (27%) made bequests implying the invocation of her aid specifically. St. John the Baptist was next most popular (5%), with St. Catherine coming third with slightly fewer invocations. One of the interesting features of the wills is an apparently low level of devotion to local saints, paralleling devotional patterns in most other regions of the country.[45]

Lincolnshire testators also reflect national trends in their endowment of older devotional forms such as pilgrimages. While lengthy pilgrimages had declined in popularity since the fifteenth century, particularly those to shrines outside England, local and regional shrines continued to attract offerings. Only one of the Lincolnshire wills makes explicit reference to the pilgrimage as a source of intercessory grace. Henry Weste, labourer of Great Coates, left an ox to his son Alan on condition that he undertake a pilgrimage to the tomb of King Henry VI at Windsor, the focus of a popular, though unofficial, cult since the later fifteenth century.[46] However, there were two other bequests to Henry VI, while ten testators left bequests to the famous shrine of Our Lady at Walsingham and two remembered the shrine of St. John at Beverley.

At the same time it is clear that the presence of the cathedral at Lincoln continued to exercise a profound hold over the spiritual loyalties of the Lincolnshire population. The shrine of St. Hugh, or more specifically his head, attracted donations from seven individuals, making it the second most popular shrine among Lincolnshire testators.[47] More telling, however, is the prevalence of bequests to the cathedral itself. Next to the customary offering to the high altar of a parish church in recompense for forgotten tithes, found in 98% of the wills, offerings to the cathedral were the most common form of pious bequest. Nearly two thirds of the testators made such bequests couched in various terms, either to the high altar of the Cathedral, to 'Our Lady's works', or simply to 'Our Lady of Lincoln'. Such bequests demonstrate a strong sense of the cathedral as a religious centre second only to the parish church at the centre of the local community, to the point that bequests to 'Our Lady's works' were actually more common than local bequests towards the repair and maintenance of parish churches.

[43] Wills nos. 224, 387, 431, 496, 510, 560.
[44] E.g. wills nos. 282, 374.
[45] Duffy, *Stripping of the Altars*, 157.
[46] Will no. 182.
[47] Wills nos. 27, 66, 212, 284, 298, 481.

The strength of devotion to the cathedral, however, should not mask a more general lack of evidence for devotion to other, more strictly parochial devotional foci. Indeed, other than bequests linked specifically to the cathedral, the most popular practices tended to be those found throughout England, rather than those limited to Lincolnshire itself. A good example of such a devotion is the endowment of masses 'at Scala Coeli'. Originally referring to masses performed at the church of St. Mary at Scala Coeli in Rome, in honour of a vision of the ascension of saved souls into heaven, the term quickly came to mean the papal indulgence attached to the masses. From the early sixteenth century the indulgence was granted to other churches throughout Europe, Boston acquiring it in 1510 and building a Scala Coeli chapel dedicated to the observance.[48] This chapel provided the focus of the devotion in Lincolnshire, and the wills provide some evidence of the popularity of the indulgence among those who could afford it. Like the more general devotion to the Virgin, the Scala Coeli indulgence was of obvious significance for those making intercessory arrangements, and some sixteen of the Lincolnshire testators requested masses 'at Scala Coeli'. This indulgence was one of the forms of Catholic piety specifically singled out for attack by evangelical reformers in the 1520s and 1530s, precisely because its wide distribution was due to popular demand rather than official promotion.[49]

In many respects, then, the evidence of these wills places Lincolnshire's religious position at the very beginning of the Reformation firmly within a broader, national pattern of belief and practice. Much of the evidence for pious activity resembles the picture obtained from other regions and counties, including broad changes in the early sixteenth century to the overall pattern of devotional foci and forms of practice. Within these wider similarities there are a number of aspects peculiar to Lincoln itself, not least the significance of the cathedral in providing a religious focus over and above that of the parish church and community. Moreover, the level of investment in friaries and the older religious houses would tend to place the county's spiritual life on the more conservative side of the spectrum for the 1530s. While it would be unwise to draw too sharp a dichotomy between conservative North and West and more radical South and East, it is clear that where comparisons can be made Lincolnshire was notably less inclined to religious change than London and parts of the South-East. In this respect, the county offers a valuable insight into the range of religious practices existing among a relatively traditional population on the eve of a period of rapid and far-reaching transition.

EDITORIAL METHOD

As mentioned above, the conventions adopted in preparing the present edition of wills for publication closely follow those used for the previous LRS volumes. In the interests of retaining as much of the flavour, vocabulary and orthography of the original register copy wills as possible, Canon Foster's practice of compression has

---

[48] D.M. Owen, *Church and Society in Medieval Lincolnshire* (Lincoln, 1971), 127; Duffy, *Stripping of the Altars*, 375–6.
[49] M. Aston, 'Popular Religious Movements in the Middle Ages', in M. Aston, *Faith and Fire: Popular and Unpopular Religion, 1350–1600* (London, 1993), 1–26.

been retained.[50] Hence, the bequests are presented as they appear in the original with the omission of highly repetitive formulae such 'Item, I bequeath . . .'. Equally, provision for the transferal of a bequest to another individual in the event of the death of the initial legatee often involved the repetition of lengthy phrases which, in themselves, do not add to the meaning or understanding of the will. In these cases the phrase [remainder to] has been substituted to indicate the abbreviation, and to assist the readability of the document. Additional explanatory material in the text has been similarly indicated in square brackets, as have expansions of unusual abbreviations. Common abbreviations, such as w^t (with), w^{ch} (which), th^t (that) have been expanded silently, while the use of 'þ' (often indistinguishable from 'y') and 'ð', the archaic forms of 'th' have been regularised as 'th' in the interests of readability.

The principal departure from Canon Foster's policy has been an expansion of the items included in the transcriptions, with the aim of anticipating the requirements of readers in the context of a continually expanding use of probate material as a historical source. Hence, as previously mentioned, preambles have been quoted in full, as have declarations of the state of health and mind of the testator. Furthermore, whereas previously many bequests of mundane items such as pots and pans were not recorded in full, it has been decided that the new edition should contain a complete listing of all such bequests. This is essentially because these items often constituted important family heirlooms and in the case of poorer testators might well represent the most important single elements of their estate. Their inclusion is therefore essential for a full representation of the material culture and wealth of all the individuals whose wills are included here, as well as for a better general impression of the wide range of wealth and property ownership found among the will-making population. While Canon Foster's own transcripts have proved extremely useful initial guides to the practical problem of compressing original documents while still retaining their essential form and language, the copy-text throughout has been provided by the probate registers themselves.

It has been decided to keep footnoting to a minimum, partly to avoid duplication of material contained in the introduction, but also because most archaic or rare terms have been fully detailed in the glossaries provided by Canon Foster in the previous three volumes.[51] A glossary specific to the present edition has not been deemed necessary, since the vast majority of potentially unfamiliar terms are already explained there. Furthermore, since the present edition contains very few new terms beyond those defined in the former volumes, it seems sufficient to deal with them as part of the textual footnoting.

---

[50] For an alternative approach see M.E. Allen, *Wills of the Archdeaconry of Suffolk, 1625–1626* (Suffolk Records Society, 37, 1995), where every bequest is included, but orthography has been modernised and compression of length has been achieved by providing a précis of each bequest.
[51] *Lincoln Wills I, 1271–1526* (LRS, 5, 1914), 243–62; *Lincoln Wills II, 1505 – May 1530* (LRS, 10, 1918), 293–300.

LINCOLN WILLS, 1532–1534

1. MARGARET MICHILL [OF BARDNEY]
   [LCC 1532–34, fo. 78v]

4 October 1500. I, Margaret Michil of Bardeney, hole of mynde and good memory, make thys my last will. Fyrst I bequeth my soule to God, Our Lady and to all the saintes of heven, and my body to be buryed in the parysh churche of Bardeney. To Our Lady warke of Lincoln vjd. To the high altare of Our Lady of Lincoln vjd. To the iiij orders of frerys of the same xvjd. To the commune lighttes in Bardeney churche xxd, one towell, one candylstyk and ij pewter dyshes. I will ther be done at the day of my buryall one pryncipall dirige and messe off requiem with note. To my sonne Sir William one matteres, one pare of lyn schetes, one coverlyd, one pillow, one chaffyng dyshe and one pewter dyshe. To my sonne Edmund one yowe, and to hys eldest doughter my best brasse pott, one matteres, and a burlyng calffe. To hys secund doughter my secund panne. To hys thurde doughter my kettyll. To William Mylforthe one off my best yowys with her lamme and my fether bed. To Jenet my doughter ij of my best pannys, my secund brasse pott, my lytyll pott, my payntyd clothe, my best gowne, one matteres and ij partes of my glasse wyndoys. To my sonne Laurence Mylforth my best coveryng and all my beyff and bacon, and aftyr my decesse one trentall off messys. To Jenet my servant one schepe. To Sir Edmunde Watson xxd and one yowe. To my lorde and the convent of Bardeney vjs viijd. The resydue of my goodes I gyff and bequeth fully to Laurence Mylforthe, whome I make my executor for to order and dispose as he thynkes most expedyent for the helthe of my soule and all my good frendes soulys. Thes wytnes; Sir Edmund Watson, vicar, John Godsalffe, John Walshe, with other.

   Proved before P at Wragby, 17 October 1532.

2. WILLIAM TEDDE [OF HUNDLEBY]
   [LCC 1532–34, fo. 59]

20 January 1531/2. I, William Tedde of Hundylby, hole of mynde and of good remembraunce, makes my testament with my last will. Fyrst I bequeth my soule to allmyghtty God, to Hys blessyd mother St. Mary and to all the holy cumpeny in heven, and my [fo. 59v] body to be buryed in the churche of Hundylby aforesayd with that that the law doth assygne to be my mortuary.[1] To the high altare of Hundylby iiijd. To Our Lady within the high quere of Hundylby aforesayd ijd. To Our Lady warke of Lincoln viijd. To every one of the v lighttes in Hundilby churche iijd. To Jenet my wyff iiij kye, iij heder burlynges, ij marys, a colte fole, all my schepe and an ambre. I will the sayd Jenet my wyff have all the houshold stuff that she brought unto me. To Libeas my sonne a fedder bed, a pare of schetes, a counter, ij chystes, a blak borde and a chaffer. To the sayd Libeas my sonne, vjs viijd and a blak dowed yeryng calffe. To Catheryne my doughter a red dowyd yong calffe and my led. To Thomas Benton a red calff now beyng a yeryng. To every one of my godchylder iijd. To Jenet my wyff xxxiijs iiijd. To Libeas my sonne a close lying at

---

[1] Mortuary payments, arguably one of the more contentious issues between the laity and the clergy, were regulated on a strict scale by an Act of 1529, passed by the Reformation Parliament of 1529–36. No mortuary was owed by anyone worth less than 10 marks (£6 13s. 4d.), 3s. 4d. was payable by anyone worth over 10 marks and under £30, 6s. 8d. by those worth between £30 and £40, and payments were not to be more than 10s. for anyone worth over £40: *Statutes of the Realm*, 21 Henry VIII, c.6; S.E. Lehmberg, *The Reformation Parliament, 1529–1536* (Cambridge, 1970), 91–2.

the Olde Ee, and another close callyd Wydale, to hym and hys heyres and hys assygnes for ever. I will that Mr. Libeas Alcoke have the house that I dwell in and the crofte that longes to the sayd house, and he to pay for the house and the crofte with the appurtenances vij markes. The resydue of all my goodes I gyff to Jenet my wyff and to Libeas my sonne, whome I make executors. Wytnes herof; Sir Robert Dawson, vicar of Hundylby, Robert Jenkynson, Libeas Smyth and John Sadler, with other moy.

Proved before P2 at Partney, 2 October 1532.

3.   WILLIAM COME [OF HORBLING]
      [LCC 1532–34, fo. 170]

26 February 1531/2. I, William Come of Horblyng, seke of body, hole of mynde and good remembraunce, makes thys my last will and testament. Fyrst I bequethe my soule to God allmyghtty and to Our Lady St. Mary, and to all the holy cumpeny of heven. My body to be buryd in the churcheyerde of St. Andro in Horblyng. To Our Lady of Lincoln iij*d.* To Our Lady workes of Lincoln iij*d.* [fo. 170v] To the pore chylder at St. Catheryn's ij*d.*[2] To the high altare in Horblyng churche viij for forgottyn tythys. To St. Catheryne in Horblyng churche iiij*d.* I will that my wyff cause vij messys to be sayd for me of the whiche I will v messys of the v woundes[3] be sayd at St. Catheryne altare and ij at the high altare, and I will my gostly father Sir John Hill say them for me. To Sir John a lamme. I gyff my mother halffe a skore yowes. To Richerde my broder my russyt cote. To John Come my broder my sleveles tawny cote and my worstyt dooblet and best cappe. I make Agnes my wyff my sole executrix. All the resydue of my goodes, bothe moveable and unmoveable, I gyff to Agnes my wyff, and she to pay my dettes savyng a cowe and iiij yowes I gyff to William Come my sun. I make Henry Atwyk and William Somerbe oversears, that may be plesure to God and the helthe to my soule, and helpe and succure to my wyff. Thes wytnesses; Sir John Hyll, Richerde Bawdwyn, Roger Preston, with other mo.

Proved before P at Lincoln, 16 June 1532. Adm. granted to the executor.

---

[2] Originally founded by Bishop Robert Bluet of Lincoln (1094–1123), the hospital was placed in the custody of the Gilbertine priory of St. Catherine, founded soon after 1148 by Bishop Robert de Chesney. By 1535 the hospital was staffed by five lay sisters caring for orphans and the sick poor, at an annual cost of £21 10s. The last years of the hospital and priory were turbulent. Prior Robert Holgate was cited by his successor, Prior William Griffiths, to appear before the king's commissioners for misappropriation of funds. Griffiths himself is said to have been deprived of office for promoting the Lincolnshire rebellion in 1536, and for dissipating the goods of the house. Refusing to accept dismissal, he re-entered the priory by force, expelled his replacement, and remained as effective head until the surrender and dissolution of the house on 14 July 1538, at which point he was provided with an annual pension of £40. Nevertheless the hospital remained the singular most popular institution for charitable donations, being mentioned in some 159 (27%) of the wills in the present edition: *VCH Lincolnshire*, II, 188–90; D. Knowles and R.N. Hadcock, *Medieval Religious Houses, England and Wales*, 2nd edn. (London, 1971), 371.

[3] Found in 15 (2.5%) of the wills presented here, the mass of the Five Wounds of Christ was particularly associated with obit provisions and with funerary commemoration: Duffy, *Stripping of the Altars*, 242–4.

4.   JOHN AWSTYN [OF MOULTON]
      [LCC 1532–34, fos. 73r–74r]

28 February 1531/2. I, John Awstyn of Multon, hole of mynde and seke off bedy, make thys my testament and last will. Fyrst I bequeth my soule unto almyghtty God, Our Lady St. Mary and to all the compeny in heven, and my body to be buryed in the churchyerde of All Halloys in Multon, and for my mortuary as the law will require. To the high altare in Multon for tythys and [fo. 73v] oblacions forgottyn iiij*d*. To the church warke of Multon viij*d*. To the thre lighttes iij*d*. To the stonys light ij*d*. To Our Lady warke of Lincoln ij*d*. To the fatherles chyldren j*d*. Thys is the last will of John Austyn of Multon mayd the day and yere above wryttyn. To Anne Austyn my wyff fyve acres of arable land lying at Grevy's Holt in ffee symple. To Anne Austyn my wyff a house that was Gylberd Burdun's for the terme of her lyff. And aftyr her decesse I will the house remayn to Christofer Austyn my sonne and to the heyres of hys body laufully begottyn [remainder to] Isabell Austyn my doughter and to her heyres of her body laufully begottyn. I wyll that yff my sonne Christofer and my doughter Isabell dye without heyres of ther bodys laufully begottyn, then I will that the forsayd house remayn to the next of the kyn. To Anne Austyn my wiff iiij acres of arable lande that was Baldyn's for the space of vj yeres. And aftyr the vj yeres be comm yn, then I will that the forsayd iiij acres of arable lande do remayn to Christofer Austyn my sonne, and to hys heyres of hys body laufully begottyn. And yff Christofer Austyn my sonne dy without heyres of hys body [remainder to] Isabell Austyn my doughter and to her heyres of her body. And yff my sonne Christofer and my doughter Isabell dye withowt heyres of ther bodys, [remainder to] the nexte of the same kyn. To Christofer Austyn my sonne one acre of pasture grounde lying in Gunesfelde and to hys heyres of hys body. To [fo. 74r] Isabell my doughter ij acres of arable lande that was Watkyn's lying in Gunesfelde and to her heyres of her body laufully begottyn. And yff my sun Christofer and my doughter Isabell dye withowt heyres of ther bodys, [remainder to] the next of the kyn. I will that iij acres of pasture grounde that lyeth in Gunesfelde and ij acres of arable lande lying in the same felde be solde for to pay my dettes withall. Also I, John Austyn of Multon aforesayd, do make surrender of all my copyholdes landes and fee into the handes off Thomas Strowtyng, tenant of the sayd lordschip, he for to certify the lorde or hys officers as the law will. To Christofer Austyn my sone a mare. To Isabell Austyn my doughter a calffe. To Anne Austyn my wyff iij marys, iij kye and all my householde stuff. The resydue of my goodes I gyff to Anne Austyn my wyff, whome I mak my hole executrix to dispose for the helthe of my soule and all Christen soulys. In wytnes herof; Thomas Trowtyng, William Wolsay, William Kyrton, with other moy.
      Proved before P at Spalding, 10 October 1532.

5.   THOMAS TILE [OF WHAPLODE]
      [LCC 1532–34, fo. 73r]

25 March 1532. I, Thomas Tyle of Whaplode, in good mynde and hole remembraunce, makes thys my last will. Fyrst I bequeth my soule to God allmyghtty, to Our Lady St. Mary, and to all the holy cumpeny of heven, and my body to be buryed within the churchyerde of Whaplode. To the high altare of Whaplode for tithys forgottyn ij*s*. To every altare in the sayd churche ij*d*. To the reparacions of the

churche of Whaplode viij*d*. To our mother churche of Lincoln vj*d*. To the orphans of St. Catheryn's of Lincoln ij*d*. I will that ther be a trentall sung in Whaplode churche for the helthe off my soule, be Sir Thomas Ceyton, or at hys synyng. To the reparacion of St. Catheryn chapell in Whaplode iij*s* iiij*d*. The resydue of all my goodes I put to the disposicion of Johanne my wyff, whome I make my full executrix. Wytnes therof; Sir Thomas Ceyton, Charlys Male, Oliver Waltur, with other moy.

Proved before P at Spalding, 10 October 1532.

6.   **RICHARD MOLLER [OF PINCHBECK]**
      [LCC 1532–34, fos. 5r–6v]

26 March 1532. I, Richerd Moller of Pynchbek, beyng hole in mynde and off good remembraunce, makes my testament and last will. Fyrst I bequethe my soule to God allmyghtty, Our Lady St. Mary, and to all the celestyall cumpeny in heven. My body to be buryd in the churcheyerde of Our Lady of Pynchbek. To the high altare of Pynchbek for tithys and oblacions negligently forgottyn xvj*d*. To every altare in the same churche xij*d*. To Our Lady of Lincoln xij*d*. To St. Catheryn's withowt the wallys of Lincoln vj*d*. To Helene Moller my wyff all my housholde stuff and iiij of my best kyne, and my mayres, plugh and carte with all the implementes therto belongyng, [fo. 5v] the cowe, burlynges and iiij calves, iiij*l* of good and laufull money of Ynglande. To Elizabethe Fowlle xl*s*. To Cecily Collet xl*s*. To Johan Reyde xl*s*. I will that vj*l* be distrybutyd in the dedes of charite in the towne off Pynchbek immediatly aftyr the receyvyng of the money for my lande. And also the forsayd vj*l* gyffyn to Elizabeth Fowlle, Cecily Collet and Johan Reyd to be payd aftyr the receyvyng of the forsayd money, and also the iiij*l* gyffyn to Helene my wyff to be payd in lyke maner. I will that a preste syng for me and my good frendes in the churche of Pynchbek duryng the space of halff a yere. To Thomas Mason a lyttyll dun mare. The resydue of my goodes I put them to the disposicion of Rayff Whyte, to dispose for the welthe of my soule as he thynkes best, whome I orden my executor, and he to have for hys labor xx*s*. Thes beyng wytnes; Sir Robert Gee, Richerd Tylson, William Tylson, Thomas Mason, and other mo, the day and yere abovesayd. Thys scedule mayd xxxj^ty Marche, xxiij^ty Henry VIII,[4] and annexyd to the will aforesayd, wytnesseth, that where I, the fornamyd Richerd Moller have gyffyn by the same will to Elizabeth Fowlle xl*s*, to Cecily Collet xl*s* and to Johanne Reyd xl*s*, I ferther will that yff the persons abovenamyd, or eny of them or ther executors, or the executors of eny of them at any tyme heraftyr vexe, troble, sowe inquiete, or disturbe myn executor or one William Wesylhed off Wynthorpe, who bought of me my landes in Wynthorpe, I will that my gifte to them mayd [fo. 6r] be utterly voyd, and I will that my executor shall not pay to eny of the sayd persons eny parte of the sayd bequeste to the tyme that they and every of them shall seale suche acquietance as shall be devisyd by my good frende Mr. Richerd Ogle to myne executor or to the sayd William Weshilhed, or to bothe of them as to the sayd Mr. Ogle shall seme good.

Proved before P at Spalding, 19 February 1532/3.

---

4 1531/2.

7.   WILLIAM SPURNE [OF HOLBEACH]
     [LCC 1532–34, fo. 20]

2 April 1532. I, William Spurne of the paryshe of Holbeche, seke of body and hole of mynde, makes my testament and my last will. Fyrste I gyff and wyt my soule unto allmyghtty God, unto the Blessyd Virgyn Our Lady St. Mary and to all the holly cumpeny of heven, and my body to be buryd within the churcheyerde of the blessyd All Hallo of Holbeche. To the high altare for my forgottyn tithes xij*d*. To Our Lady altare iiij*d*. To Saint Stephyn altare iiij*d*. To every altare within the sayd churche ij*d*. To the roode light vj*d*. To the sepulcre vj*d*. To the reparacions of our mother churche of Lincoln vj*d*. To the orphans chylder at Saint Catheryn's at Lincoln ij*d*. To Margaret my doughter ij kye and a gret potte of brasse. To Robert Spurne my sune ij kye whyche he hase in hys kepyng. To Elizabethe my doughter one cowe. To Thomas Spurne, the sun of Robert Spurne, one calve. To iche of my chylder one calve. To Margaret my wyff my house and a holte of woode, and all my landes and emolumentes belongyng therto duryng her lyffe, and the said Margaret my wyff for [fo. 20v] to occupy or sell the woode to the moste proffet that she can duryng the terme. And aftyr her decesse, I will my house and landes and emolumentes belongyng therto for to remayn to Robert Sporne and to Margaret hys syster, equally to be devydyd betwyxte them and to ther assignes for evermore. The resydue of all my goodes I gyff to Margaret my wyff whome I make my executrix, and she for to dispose for my soule to the pleasure of God and helthe of my soule, at the discrecion of John Lesse, whome I make my supervisor. Whytnes theroff; Sir Robert Browne, my curet, John Lessy, Nicholes Rance, John Rance, Robert Spurne, wyth other mo.

    Proved before P at Spalding, 10 October 1532, by the executrix.

8.   JOHN THOMSON [OF FOSDYKE]
     [LCC 1532–34, fo. 44]

5 April 1532. I, John Thomson of Fossedyke in Hollande, yoman, of good mynde and perfyte remembraunce, make, orden and constitute my testament and last will. Fyrste I gyff and bequeth my soule to God allmyghtty, to Our Lady St. Mary and to all the cumpeny of heven, and my body to be buryed within the churcheyerde of Saintes Peter and Paule th'appostellys at Algarkyrke, with my mortuary accordyng to the statute that now is. To the high altare ther for tithys forgottyn xij*d*. To the light before the rode ther iiij*d*. To every accomptable light in the churche ther j*d*. To the sepulcre light att Fossedyke ij*d*. To Our Lady of Lincoln ij*d*. To St. Catheryn's ij*d*. To Richerde my brother, in recompence of suche dettes as I owe unto hym, and for the payment of all suche dettes as I owe to dyverse other persones, all my landes and tenementes in Algarkyrke to hym, hys heyres and assygnes for ever. I will my feoffes now seasyd therof to my use, make immediatly aftyr my decease a laufull estate therof to the sayd Richerde my brother and hys heyres, or to other persones and ther heyres, to the use of my sayd brother and hys heyres for evermore. All my dettes payd, I gyff unto Isabell my wyff xx*l*, to be payd unto her by the handes of the same Richerde my brother at thes tymes foloyng: fyrste at Candylmes[5] nexte aftyr the date herof x*l*, and at Candilmes then iij yeres nexte aftyr the same, other x*l*. To

---

[5] Candlemas fell on 2 February.

Isabell my wyff a fether bed, ij bolsters, a cupborde, iiij coverlydes, all my shetes, iiij brasse pottes, iiij pannys. To Marciall my doughter iij pewter platters, a basyn of lattyn, a bras pot, a chare, a fether bed, a matteres, a cownter and a gret hutche. Yff my wyff be with chylde I gyff unto it iij pewter platters, a basyn of lattyn, a bras pot, a chare and iij matteres. I will gyff other of dye before the other that then the deade's parte to be gyffyn to the qwyk. I will yff they bothe dye or they cum to laufull age, that then Isabell my wyff ther mother to have bothe ther partes. To Isabell my wyff the yren hangynges in the chimnay, the better pece of clothe of iiij yerdes, a treyfete, ij hutches and ij chares. To Richerde my brother my best gowne, my dooblet and a worstyd jakyt. To my uncle Roger Bosy my best jerkyn. To Wyllyngham my gray cote. To John my servante my best violet cote and my whyte fustyan dooblet. To John Keston a violet cote. To Jenet my servante a peace of marbell for her lyveray.[6] To William my servante my jerkyn of motlay. To Thomas Shypparde an olde chamlet jerkyn and a pare of doble [fo. 44v] solyd shoys. To John Grice a pare of whyte hose. To William Manby my violet hose. To John Percy my best cappe. To William Percy my russyt cappe. To Thomas Percy my hatte. I will yff my wyff clame any manner of thynges at any tyme heraftyr of my executors, salve onely thys my bequest and legacy, that then she shall stande to that thyng that my executors will rewarde her. I will that my executors be bounden in an obligacion to Isabell my wyff and to her assygnes for sure payment of the same xx*l*, to be payd unto her or her assygnes at the termes above wryttyn. The resydue of all my goodes I gyff to Richerde my brother and to Agnes my mother, whome I make executors, and Roger Bosy of Sutterton, supervisor. Thes wytnesses; Sir Thomas Pytfelde my gostly father, Robert Bosye, Thomas Felde of Fossedyke, Adam Hunt and Lambert Bayly of Walpoll. Geven at Fossedyke, the day, moneth, the yere and place abovesayd.

Proved before P at Lincoln, 11 July 1532.

9.   THOMAS CRYAR [OF FENHOUSE IN PARISH OF WIGTOFT]
       [LCC 1532–34, fo.70]

10 April 1532. I, Thomas Cryar off Fenhouse in Wygtofte parysh, makes my testament and last will. Fyrst I bequeth my soule to allmyghtty God, to Our Lady Hys mother, and to all the holly cumpeny of heven. My body to be buryd in the churcheyerde of the appostellys Peter and Paule of Wygtofte. To the high altare of Wygtofte ij*d*. To Robert Cryer my sonne one qwye burnyng and one calve. All the resydue of my goodes I bequeth them to Alyson Cryar my wyff, whome I make my executrix. Wytnes heroff; Roger Hunt, Lambert Warryngton and Jamys Cryar, with mo.

Proved before P at Boston, 9 October 1532.

10.   ROGER ROWCE [OF BOSTON]
       [LCC 1532–34, fos. 70r–71v]

13 April 1532, 23 Henry VIII. I, Roger Rowce of Boston in the county of Lincoln, of a hole mynde and perfyte remembraunce, make thys my testament and last will. Fyrst I bequeth my soule to God allmyghtty, to Our Lady St. Mary and all the holy cumpeny in heven. My body to be buryed within the Whyte Frerys' churche in

---

[6] A piece of dyed cloth for her servant's attire.

Boston. To my mortuary as the lawe requiryth. To Our Lady of Lincoln vj*d*. To the orphans at St. Catheryn's withowt the barrys at Lincoln iij*d*. To the reparacion of the high altare in Boston vj*d*. To the churche in Kyrton iij*s* iiij*d*. To the high altare ther for tithys forgottyn xij*d*. To Isabell my doughter ij sylver sponys, a chare, ij matterys, ij pare of flaxyn schetes, ij pare of hardyn schetes, my best coveryng, a coverlet, thre brasse pottes, my byggest panne [fo. 70v] viij pecys of pewder, iiij semyd pylloys and a red arke, ij towellys flaxen, ij salte sellers, ij sawssers and ij candylstykes. To Robert my sone a fether bed, a matres, a pare of flaxyn schetes, a coverlyd, my best brasse pot, a panne next the best, iiij pewter platters and ij sylver sponys. To Alice my wyff iiij kye and a gray horse. The resydue of my goodes I gyff them holy to Alice my wyff, whome I make my executrix, and I will she have the possession of them. I will that Robert Cony of Boston, Merchaunt of the Staple at Calice, be my executor joyntly with my wyff, to se thys my testament and last will fullyd and performyd and also my dettes payd, and he to have for hys labor and payne vj*s* viij*d*. Thys is the last will of me Roger Rowce, wrytten and mayd the day and yere abovesayd. I will that Isabell my doughter have a lytill cotage liyng betwyxt the landes of Thomas Stawarde and John Thomson, in Wyllyngton in Kyrton, immediatly aftyr my decesse, with one acre and a halff of land arable lying in Hammertofte in Kyrton aforesayd, to her and her heyres and assignes. I will that Robert my sonne have all my landes and tenementes, rentes, revercions and services, with all and syngler ther appurtenances beyng and lying in Kyrton aforesayd, or ellyswhere in the countie of Lincoln immediatly aftyr my decesse, to hym, hys heyres and assygnes excepte the cotage and land arable before to my doughter bequethyd. And I will he be in the custody of Alice my wyff as long as she is wydoy. And yff she mary agane, yff her husband and she be good unto hym, they to have hym styll, till he cum to laufull age or unto suche tyme he be maryed, and to have the orderyng of hys landys and the proffyttes of the same duryng the sayd tyme. And yff they be not good to my sayd sonne and kepe hym as he ought to be kepte, then I will that the abovenamyd Robert Cony have hym in hys custody aftyr maner and forme as is aforesayd. I will yff Isabell my doughter decesse or she cum to laufull age [fo. 71r] or before she be maryed, I will the cotage and the lande arable before to her bequethyd, with all other thynges before in my testament to her gyffyn, remayn unto Robert my sonne. And in lykewysse yff the sayd Robert decesse before he cum to laufull age, then I will all the landes, tenementes and other premisses with the legaces to hym before bequethyd, remayn to Isabell my doughter and her heyres, so that I will ether of them be other heyres bothe of landes and goodes. I will that yff bothe Isabell my doughter and Robert decesse before they cum to laufull age, then I will all my landes and tenementes, rentes, revercions and services, with all and synguler the appurtenances, remayn to the next heyre of my blode and hys heyres for ever upon thys condicion, I will have one obbyt or aniversary kept yerly within the parysh churche of Kyrton with placebo and dirige and messe be note, wyth ryngyng of bellys, to the valew of v*s*. And also I will ther be gyffyn and disposyd the same day in allmys emong pore people, for my soule, my good frendes' soulys and all other Christen soulys, other v*s*. And yff ther be none of my blode alyve at that tyme, then I will all my sayd landes and tenementes and other premisses be solde be my executors, or the executors of them, to the uttermost valew, and the money therof receyvyd to be disposyd in charitable warkes within Kyrton, as the churche warkes or suche other as it shall be thought best be my sayd executors, or other to whose disposicion the sayd money shall cum, always reservyng my obbyt which I will be kepte yerly in maner and forme as is aforesayd, whosoeover shall have the sayd landes. Provydyd always that yff ther be anythyng in thys my testament and last will conteynyd and wryttyn contrary to the due forme and order of the lawe, then I will my sayd executors, with suche councell lernyd as they shall take to them, shall reforme wher nede is, changeyng not the effecte and intent of my mynde. Thes beyng wytnes; John Huchenson, Richerd Soresby and William Colman, with other moy.

Proved before P at Boston, 9 October 1532.

11.   JOHN KNOTTE [OF ALGARKIRK]
       [LCC 1532–34, fo. 19]

14 April 1532. I, John Knott the elder off Algarkyrk in Holand, husbandman, gud off mynd and hole off remembraunce, do make my testament and last will. Fyrst I bequeythe my sowle to allmyghtty God, to Hys blessyd moder Our Lady Sant Mary and to all the holly sayntes off hevyn, and my body to be buryed in the churcheyard off the holy appostyles Peter and Paule off Algarkyrke, and for my mortuarye accordyng to the ackes off our soferant lord Kyng Henry the heght. To our mother chyrche off Lincoln ij*d* and to Saynt Katherin's extra portas Lincoln ij*d*, and to the reparacions off the parych chyrche off Allgarkyrke viij*d*. To the light of Sent Sunday[7] ther ij*d*, to the light off the broun roud ther ij*d*, and to the reparacions off the hyght auter ther ij*d*. To John Knott my sone, imediatly after my decese, my howse with on acar and a halff off grownd under the sayd howse duryng the lyff off the sayd John my sone, and after his decesse I will it do remayn to whiche of hys chylder as shall please hym best, and to the heyres of the body of the sayd chylde. And for lacke of suche heyres I will it do remayn from one to another of the chylder of the sayd John Knotte my sun, [fo. 19v] so that the sayd house and grounde, aftyr the decesse of the aforesayd chylde and heyres of the body, shall discende from the eldeste to the nexte and to the heyres of ther bodys so long as any of the chylder of the sayd John Knotte my sun, or the heyres of ther bodyes, shall be founde onlyve. And [if] it shulde fortune the sayd John Knotte my sun or hys chylder to dye withowt heyres of ther bodyes, then I will the sayd house and grounde shall remayn to Robert Knotte my sun and to the heyres off hys body. I will that John Knotte and Robert Knotte my chylder do fynde one preste one quarter off a yere to pray for my soule, the soule of Elizabethe my wyff, with all other that God will have prayd for.[8] To John Knotte my sun ij acres lande lying in Oxham Felde, to gyff and sell at hys plesure. To John Knotte sun of Roger Knotte x yowes and ther increse att mydsomer nexte foloyng aftyr my decesse. Also ij brasse pottes, a bygger one and a lesse, and iij brasse pannes, every one bygger then other, ij matteresses, ij pare schettes, the one pare flaxen and the other myng towe, and viij*s* laufull money of Ynglande. The resydue of my goodes I do gyff to John Knotte and to Robert Knotte my chylder, whome I have ordenyd my executors. Thes beyng testes; Nicholes Braye, William Alenson, William Hawker and Thomas Gull, preste.

Proved before P at Boston, 9 October 1532.

---

[7] A literal translation of *Sanctum Sabbatum*, 'holy Sabbath'.
[8] A strong statement of belief in intercessory prayers for the dead, diametrically opposed to the contention of evangelicals that such practices were of human invention, and hence derogatory to the glory of God. It suggests an implicit assumption on the part of the testator that prayers for the dead were not only beneficial for their souls, but were of divine institution.

12. ELIZABETH STOKELAY [OF GOSBERTON]
[LCC 1532–34, fo. 71v]

15 April 1532. I, Elizabeth Stokeley, vidoy, beyng hole of mynde and of perfyte remembraunce, dothe make, orden and dispose thys my present testament and last will. Fyrst I bequeth my soule to God allmyghtty, to Our Lady St. Mary, and to all the holy cumpeny of heven, and my body to be buryed in the sowthe yle within the parysh churche of the holy appostelles St. Peter and St. Paule in Gosberchurche. I gyff for my buryall ther to the reparacion of the same churche vjs viijd. To the high altare for my tithys forgottyn or negligently withholdyn iiijd. To every gylde in the churche iiijd. To the yomens' and maydens' light of the churche envyntyn⁹ iiijd. To all Christen soulys' light ijd. To the gyldhall one table clothe. To Our Lady of Lincoln offeryng ijd. To the fatherles chyldren of St. Catheryn's withowt Lincoln ijd. To John Vassell one matteres, one bolster, one pilloy, one pare of flaxen schetes, one coverlyt and one eshe planke. To William Hogson my starlyt. All the resydue of my goodes I gyff them unto John Thorpe my sonne, whome I make my executer. Thes beryng wytnes; Syr Henry Topplys, paryshe preste, Richerd Dyat and William Olyver, with other moy.

    Proved before P at Spalding, 10 October 1532.

13. RICHARD PYNDER [OF DONINGTON IN HOLLAND]
[LCC 1532–34, fos. 71v–72r]

16 April 1532. I, Richerde Pynder of Donyngton in Holland, within the countie of Lincoln, beyng of hole mynde and good remembraunce at thys tyme, lovyd be God, make my testament and last will. Fyrst I bequeth my soule to God allmyghtty and to Our Lady St. Mary, and to all the saintes in heven. My body to the churchyerde of Donyngton. To the high altare of Donyngton for tithynges forgottyn iiijd. To every altare within the same churche ijd. To the bellys viijd. To every light that standes abowt my herse¹⁰ at my buryall day ijd. To Our Lady warke of Lincoln [fo. 72r] iiijd. To the fatherles chyldren at St. Catheryn's withowt the wallys of Lincoln ijd. Thys is my will that Thomas Pender, my sonne, have my plugh with all that longes to hit, and my carte with all the harnes that belong to hit. Also I will that he have my yong balde mare, a gray mare, a dapuld gray mare, a bay geldyng, iij ij yere olde felys, a fely fole red coloryd, ij kye, a gowne, ij cotes, an elve of worstyd. To John Wright a sukyng calff. The resydue of all my goodes I gyff them to Catheren Pender my wyff, whome I make my executrix, to bring me furthe and pay my dettes, and Sir John Gybson vicar of Donyngton to be oversear, and to have for hys labor iijs iiijd. Thes beyng wytnes; Robert Pulvertofte, Henry Wryght, Rayff Stafesaker, Thomas Wright, with other mo.

    Proved before P at Spalding, 10 October 1532.

---

⁹ Presumably 'each one'.
¹⁰ The hearse was a metal stand or cart enclosing the coffin. Draped with a hearse cloth, it formed the focus for the overnight Office of the Dead: C. Daniell, *Death and Burial in Medieval England, 1066–1550* (London and New York, 1997), 47; Duffy, *Stripping of the Altars*, 301–76.

14.   ROGER WALKER [OF BASSINGHAM]
[LCC 1532–34, fo. 157v]

20 April 1532. I, Roger Walker off Bassyngham, of good mynde and will, makes my
testament. Fyrst I bequethe my soule unto allmyghtty God and to Our Lady St.
Mary, and to all the saintes in heven, and my body to be buryd in the churcheyerde
of St. Michel th'archaungell off Bassyngham, and my mortuary to be gyffyn aftyr
the custome of the cuntry. To Our Lady warke of Lincoln viij*d*. To the high altare
off Bassyngham vj*d*. To Thomas Everyngham a fylly of a yere age. To the churche
of Bassyngham ij*s*. To Margaret Gregory my wyff best bonnet and her best kyrtyll.
Also I make to my executors William Walker my sun and Helene my doughter, for
to dispose the resydue off my goodes for the well of my soule. I make supervisors of
my will Sir Robert Stanley and Thomas Everyngham, for to se that my dettes be
payd and my will ffulfyllyd, as it is before wryttyn. Then beyng wytnes; Sir Robert
Stanley, preste, Robert Arosmyth, Thomas Dente, John Hunter with other mo.
    Proved before P at South Hykeham, 15 May 1533, Helen Walker an
    executrix being underage.

15.   RICHARD DENYS [OF WISPINGTON]
[LCC 1532–34, fos. 56r–57r]

22 April 1532. I, Richerd Denys off Wyspyngton, hole off mynde and memory, do
make and order thys my last will and testament. Fyrst I bequeth and commit my
soule to God allmyghtty and my body to be buryed within the parysh churche of
Wyspyngton, and to gyff for the same accordyng to the auncient custome ther usyd.
To the high altare of Wyspyngton xij*d*. To our mother churche of Lincoln towardes
the workes theroff xij*d*. To the high altare of the same [fo. 56v] mother churche xij*d*.
To the parysh churche off Edlyngton iiij*d*. To the high altare of the same churche
iiij*d*. To the parysh churche of Horsyngton xij*d*. To the parysh church of Bamburgh
ij*s*. To the parysh church off Gawdby iij*d*. To the parysh church of Wadyngworth
iiij*d*. To the parysh church of Myntyng iiij*d*. To the parysh church of Buknall xij*d*.
To the parysh church of Wylseby xij*d*. To the parysh church of Wood Enderby ij*s*.
To the high altare of the same iij*d*. To the parysh church of Marom iiij*d*. To the
parysh church of Haltham iiij*d*. To the parysh church of Screvelesby xij*d*. To the
convent of the monastery of Revesby xij*d*. I will ther be done for my soule, my
father's and mother's, and for all my frendes' soulys iiij trentalles at the discrestion
of my executors. I will that Margaret my wyff have all my hole messuage with
th'appurtenaunces set lying and beyng within the towne and feldes of Wyspygnton
duryng her lyff naturall [remainder to] the use of my laufully begottyn chyldren that
then shall fortune to be alyve for the terme and space onely of syx yeres next
ensuyng the decesse naturall of the sayd Margaret my wyff, [remainder to] the lorde
abbot and convent of the monastery of Our Blessyd Lady of Kyrksted and to ther
successors, and the same to have and holde to ther propre use converte for the terme
and space of xx^ty yeres. And at the ende of the sayd xx^ty yeres I will that the lord
abbot of the monastery off Our Blessyd Lady aforesayd for the tyme beyng do make
or cause to be mayd sale of my sayd messuage wyth th'appurtenaunces in
Wyspyngton, and distribute the money therfore takyn emong the convent aforesayd, to the entent that the sayd convent may pray for my soule, [fo. 57r] my
father's and mother's and all my frendes' soulys in ther holy suffragys, when and so

oftyn as shall seme to the sayd lorde of the tyme beyng convenient and expedyent. All the resydue of my goodes I holy gyff to Margaret my wyff and John my sonne, whome I make myne executers. I will that my chyldern have the thyrde parte of my goodes equally devydyd emong them. And yff it fortune any of my sayd chyldren to decease or they cum to the yeres of discrestion then I will that the parte of that chylde or chyldren so deceasyd remayn equally emong the rest of my chyldren that do supervive. I will that the house and lande of John Hogeson, late of Enderby, be solde be my executers and the executers of the sayd John Hogeson, and the money therfore taken to be disposyd accordyng to the tenor of the last will of the sayd John Hogeson. Moreover I will that yff any chylde naturall of the sayd John Hogeson will by the sayd house and lande that they or any of them shall have the sayd house and lande xxs cheper then any other persone shall have. In wytnes of thys my last will and testament I do take and desyre Dayn Richerd Sutton, curate of Wyspyngton aforesayd, William Chapman, Christofer Jonson, William Haltham and John Kydeson of the sayd towne of Wyspyngton.

Proved before P at Horncastle, 1 October 1532. Adm. granted to the executrix, the said John, the son and co-executor, being under age.

16.   SIR JOHN YONG [PARSON OF SKINNAND]
       [LCC 1532–34, fos. 44v–45r]

22 April 1532. I, John Yong clerke, parsone of Skynnande in the countie of Lincoln, of hole mynde and reasone, makes my last will and testament. Fyrst I bequethe my soule to God allmyghtty, and to Our Lady Saynt Mary, and to all the holy cumpeny of heven, and my body to be buryed in the parysh kyrke of Brant Broughtton. I bequeth for my mortuary as the lawe dothe require. To William Snaynton, my syster sone, xl to hys fyndyng at the universite, iij yeres.[11] To Richerd Greswell hys wyff and hys chylder, to every one of them, one hyve of bees at Skynnande, and the resydue of bees at Skynnande I gyff to my brother Kellum and my syster. To my brother Kellum chylder one cowe at Skynnande each. To Elizabeth Kellum one counter at Broughton. I will that Richerde Snaynton, my syster sone, have my house in Broughton for terme of hys lyff. To my brother William Yong ij chylder, ij stokes of bees at Broughton [fo. 45r] and the resydue I gyff to my brother and my syster. To Broughton kyrke xxvjs viijd in price of one booke that standyth me in fyve marke, so that the townschip pay to my executers xls betwyxte thys and the feste of Saynt Martyn in wynter nexte foloyng.[12] I will ther be disposyd for me peny dole at my buryeng and x yeres aftyr, every yere xxs to be disposyd at Broughtton kyrke and one preste wagys iij yeres, and further as my goodes may do it, and the same x yeres peny dole to be done at Skynnande. I make my executers John Kellum, gent., and William Yong my brother. Thes beryng wytnes; Sir Robert Lewty, Richerd Greswell, John Naler, with other moy.

Proved before P at Lincoln, 12 July 1532, by the executors.

---

[11] There is no record of a William Snaynton at either Oxford or Cambridge in this period. The bequest was probably provisional upon Snaynton's gaining admission, presumably to Cambridge given the geographical proximity.
[12] The Winter feast of St. Martin fell on 11 November. The feast celebrating his ordination and translation fell on 4 July.

17. JOHN CRYAR [OF WIGTOFT]
[LCC 1532–34, fo. 67v]

23 April 1532. I, John Cryar of Wigtoft, of a hole mynd and gud remembrance, makeith my testament and last will. Firste I bequeth my soull to allmighty God, to Our Lady Sainct Mary and to all the holly companye of hevyn, and my bodie to be beureid in the chircheyard of Sainct Petir and Paull of Wigtoft. To Ower Ladie of Lincoln iiij*d*. To the fatherles children of Sainct Kateryne ij*d*. The residew of my gudes I gif them to Margaret my wif whom I maike myne executrix, she to bryng up my children and paie my dettes to the high plessour of God and to the welth of my soull. Thies being witnes; William Freman, John Baker, Thomas Pasmer, Sir Robert the parisse preste, with other mo.
Proved before P at Boston, 9 October 1532.

18. JOHN CHAPMAN [OF TATTERSHALL]
[LCC 1532–34, fos. 98v–99r]

24 April 1532. I, John Chapman of the paryshe of Tateshale, of a hole mynde and good memory, makyth my last will and testament. Fyrst I bequethe my soule unto God allmyghtty, to Our Lady St. Mary and unto all the cumpeny in heven, and my body to be buryed within the holy churcheyerde of Tatheshale. To the high altare of Tateshale for forgottyn tithys xij*d*. To the paryshe altare and to the mayntenance of the bellys viij*d*. To [fo. 99r] Our Lady of Lincoln iiij*d*. To Thomas Themylby a calve and my best dooblet. To William Themylby my best hosen. To Margaret my wyff bothe my copyes duryng her lyff. And aftyr her decesse I will that Alyson Grenewoode have the copy of the hed house and Roger Grenewoode to have the copy of the house that hys father dyd dwell in. The reste of my goodes I gyff unto Margaret my wyff, and she to be my executryx to dispose it for the helthe of my soule. Also I will that sir Edwarde Flynt, paryshe preste of Tateshale, and Thomas Themylby be the supervisors, and other of them to have for ther payns ij*s*. Thes wytnes; Robert Sergeande, John Nodyll, Jamys Dune, cum ceteris.
Proved before P at Horncastle, 28 April 1532.

19. RICHARD STOWYNG [OF BOSTON]
[LCC 1532–34, fos. 18v–19r]

25 April 1532. I, Rychard Stowyng of Boston, beyng of hole mynde and gud remembraunce, makes thys my last wyll and on the same concludes my testament. Fyrst I bequeythe my sowle to God allmyghty, to Our Lady Sant Mary, and to all the holy company off hevyn, and my body to be buryed wher God shall be best plesyd. To Our Lady off Lincoln xij*d*. To Our Lady off Manton xij*d*. To Tymberland chyrche xij*d*. To the hyght auter off Boston viij*d*. To Our Lady's frerys in Boston iij*s* iiij*d*. To my moder xl*s*. To Agnes my syster vj*s* viij*d*. To Elesabethe my syster ij*s* iiij*d*. To my syster Janett Stowyng ij*s* iiij*d*. To Frere John Leydes to say a trentall of xxx messes at Scala Celi for the sowle off me Rychard Stowyng, my father sowle, our benefactors' sowlys and all Crysten sawles,[13] and he to have for hys labor x*s*, and for drowyng off this my last wyll xij*d*. [fo. 19r] To John Stowyng, my brother

---

[13] See Introduction, p. xxvii.

sone, iijs iiijd. The resydew off my guddes remanyng in the handes off my mayster John Dayle, I geve unto John Rawghton off Fosdyke, whom I do ordaine my executor. And yff anythyng fortune to me or I cum home off the sey, I wyll that John Rawghton take all my guddes into hys handes within iij quarters off a yer then next folowyng, and he to distren William Bell and Robert Synte's suertes for ytt yff thei wyll not pay ytt. Theys beyng wyttnes; Sir Jhon Markby, prest and n[ota]rie, John Leydes, frear, John Dayle hys master, Sir Thomas Cersy, curate off Sant Botalphe chyrche Boston, with other mo.

Proved before P at Boston, 9 October 1532.

20.   WILLIAM HUBBERT [OF WAINFLEET ALL SAINTS]
       [LCC 1532–34, fos. 168v–169v]

26 April 1532. I, William Hubbert of Waynflet All Halloys, of an good mynde and hole memory, makes my testament. Fyrste I bequethe my soule to allmyghtty God and to Hys moder Mary and to all the saintes in heven, and my body to be buryed in the churche off All Halloys in Waynflet, in the medle ale as ny Margaret my wyff as may be. To the hy altare in the same churche for tentes forgottyn ijs. To the reparacions of the same churche for my buryall and all togyders xs. To the bellys ijs. To Our Lady's gylde xxd. To St. Jamys' gylde xijd. To the light burnyng before Our Lady of Bethelen xxd. To the same churche for an owrment of the blessyd sacrament a towyll of diaper. To the mayntenance or anournyng of St. John chapell to the altare iijs iiijd. To the parsone of St. Thomas churche in Northolm for tentes forgottyn ijs. To the manetenance of the same churche xijd. To the high altare in the churche off Crofte for tentes forgottyn xxd. To the high altare in the churche of Thorpe for the same use [fo. 169r] xvjd. To Our Lady of Lincoln xxd and to her warkes xijd. To the faderles chylder at St Catheryn's at Lincoln xijd. To the iiij orders of frerys in Boston, iche of them, xxd. To the lady ancrys of Boston vjd.[14] To Margaret Hubbert my doughter, to her promocion and goode fortherans of her mariage, forty poundes. To Anne my doughter to pray for me xxs. To Cassandra her doughter xs. To Margaret her oder doughter xs. To my brother John Hubbert at Lundon vjs viijd. To my brother George Hubbert at Calis xs. To Addelarde Hubbert xls to pray for me. To Clement Hubbert hys broder iijs iiijd. To iche of ther systers Elizabeth and Alice iijs iiijd. To William Hubbert my kynsman vjs viijd. To Robert Alger my servant iijs iiijd. To Agnes Herryson my kynswoman xxs. To Jane Lincoln my kynswoman vjs viijd. To Elizabeth Relay iijs iiijd. To Margaret Lowman at Lundon xxd. To iche of my godchyler viijd. I will also that my sun John Hubbert do fynde an obbyt yerely for hys lyff tyme to the value of iijs iiijd, takyn owt of ij acres of the high toftes aftyr the best discrescion of my executors, to be spente of messe and dirige, bed rolle and oblacions, iij messe pennys for my soule, my wyves, my father and my mother soulys. To the mayntenaunce and reparacions of the highway or stight to the churche of All Halloys xs. To my executors for ther true labors, iche of them, xls, sum betwyxte them bothe iiijl. The resydue of my goodes not gyffyn nor bequethyd I will that they be at the disposicion and good order of my sun John Hubbert and Sir Richerde Ranson, parson of All Halloys in the same towne, whiche I make my executors to se truly the performance and

---

[14] A hermit. Such individuals were not uncommon in major towns before the Reformation, frequently receiving similar bequests and pious donations.

fulfyllyng of thys my last testament, and to occupy the forsayd resydue in warkes of pety and charite for the helthe of my soule, my wyvys, my fader and my moder, with all Crysten soulys, so as they will make answer and discharge ther owne conscience. Thes beyng wytnes; John Crake, John Cawdra, William Crake, Simon Grebbe, with other mo. This is the last will of me [fo. 169v] William Hubbert of Waynflet in the paryshe of All Halloys, wryttyn the xxvj[th] day of Apryll 1532. I will that John Hubbert my sun have all my landes in Crofte and all my landes lying in Bawmborow felde, and my mansion house that I dwell in in Waynflet with all the appurtenances, with ij housys callyd the store house and the thake house annext to it, wyth thyes landes foloyng; fyrst one acre pasture under my house, ij acre in the high tofte, ij acre in Redeberd and one pece arable lande lying on the toftes callyd Bent Hyll, and one acre and one halffe pasture in Newcroftes, and iiij acre arable lande lying in Newcroftes, to hym and to hys heyres of hys body laufully begottyn. I will also to have aftyr the same maner vij acre pasture lying in Thorpe. I will also that my sun John Hubbert have my house in Sutterton in Fyshmer Ende with one acre grounde under it, and iiij acre and one halffe arable lande, and ij acre and one halffe pasture, and oder ij acre and one halffe pasture, all lying in Sutterton, to hym and to hys heyres of hys body. I will also that ix acre lande pasture and arable lying in Sutterton, whiche I purchesyd of one John Wiche and Anthony Lucas, be solde be my executors to and for the performance of my laste will and testament. I will also that my house that John Lodde dwellys in, lying in Sutterton, and all the landes lying under the same with ther appurtenances, and iiij acre and one halffe of pasture and arable lande lying in Algarkyrke be solde lykewyse by myn executors to and for the performance of thys my laste will and testament. I will also that my house agenst the market stede in Waynflet, lately purchased of one John Wheteley with all and singler the appurtenances, and the lytyll house lately purchased of Henry Spicer in Waynflet, and my fyshinges with my mooses and all that I have in the thowes in Waynflet,[15] be solde lykewyse by my executors to and for the performance of thys my last will and testament.

Proved before P at Lincoln, 3 June 1533. Adm. granted to the executors.

21.   ROBERT TURNER [OF DOWSBY]
       [LCC 1532–34, fo. 26v]

27 April 1532. I, Robert Turner the elder of Dowesby, hole of mynde and good remembraunce, make my testament and last will. Fyrst I bequeth my soule to God allmyghtty, to Our Lady St. Mary and to all the holly cumpeny of heven, and my body to be buryed in the churcheyerde off St. Andro within the towne of Dowesby. I bequethe for my mortuary as the lawe hath determynyd. To the high altare of Dowesby j bushyll of barly. To the reparacions of the same churche of Dowesby vj*d*. To the reparacions of our mother churche of Lincoln iiij*d*. To Our Lady offerynges of Lincoln iiij*d*. To John Turner my sun iiij oxen, a mayr, a carte body, a plowe, ij qwyes, iij yowes and iiij lammys, one table borde, a pare of bed bordes, a be hyeff and all the corne of the hall lande that is sowyn in the felde excepte one acre of peys and one acre of barly. To Edmunde Turner my sonne ij sterys, iiij yowes and iiij lammys, one be hyeff, one table. To Johanne Turner my wyff all the goodes that I

---

[15] Fishing rights and access to peat in the wetlands of the parish.

had with her and one cowe, ij swyne and a seame malte, one acre barly, an acre pees, ij lode woode, iij olde schepe, one lamme and a qwye. To the churche aforesayd one lampe, the price vjs viijd. And one schepe to the sayd churche for to fynde the sayd lampe light with. To John Turner the yonger one schepe and one lamme. To Robert Turner and Elizabeth Turner one yowe and one lamme each, and every one of them other heyres yff they dye within the age of xv yeres. The resydue of my goodes I gyff to Robert Turner my sonne, whome I make my full executor to pay my dettes and to dispose of my goodes as he shall thynke best, to the pleasur of God and helthe of my soule. Wytnes herof; Robert Wyghed and John Carter.

Proved before P at Bourne, 15 January 1532/3.

22.   JOHN HELVYSHE [OF TOTHILL]
      [LCC 1532–34, fos. 152v–153r]

1 May 1532. I, John Helvysh of the paryshe of Tottyll in the countie of Lincoln and dicise of the same, beyng hole of mynde and of good remembrance, makes thys testament and last will. Fyrst and before all other thynges I commende my soule unto allmyghtty God through the gloriose intercession of the Blessyd Virgyn and mother of mercy, Our Lady St. Mary, and all the holly cittizens off heven, and my body to be buryed within the paryshe churche yerde of Our Lady of Tottyll aforesayd. To the high altare of Totyll aforesayd for all my tithys negligently payd or forgottyn iiijd. I will also that Elizabeth my wyff, the day of my buryall, shall se my body honestly brought into the sepulture and that day to cause placebo and dirige with messe of requiem to be sung by note for my soule and all Crysten soulys, with the preste and viij clerkes. And I will that the preste shall have vjd and every clerke ijd. The resydue of all my goodes not gyven nor grauntyd I gyff to the forsayd Elizabethe my wyff and to my chyldren. And the sayd Elizabeth my wyff I do make my sole executrix, that she may pay my dettes and se thys my last wyll fulfyllyd to the laude and singler praysyng of God onely, and to the helthe of my soule. And in dyscharge of her conscience in that behalff my gostly father Sir Thomas Taylboys, curate ther, herin beryng wytnes. To William my sun a yow and a lambe and [fo. 153r] halff a seame wheate. To Agnes my doughter a yong qwy of ij yere olde and a yowe and a lambe. To Alson my doughtter a yowe and a lambe. To Margaret Helvyse halffe a seame wheate and a yowe and a lambe.

Proved before P at Alford, 6 May 1533.

23.   JOHN FORLOWE [OF KIRKBY ON BAIN]
      [LCC 1532–34, fo. 57]

4 May 1532. I, John Forlowe off Kyrkby Bayn in the county of Lincoln, husband-man, off good and hole mynde, makes my last will. Fyrst I bequethe my soule to our Lord Ihesu Cryst, Our Lady St. Mary and to all the saintes in heven, and my body to be buryed in the church yerde of Our Lady at Kyrkby. To the high altare [fo. 57v] of Kyrkby for forgottyn or withholdyn tithys iiijd. To Our Lady of Lincoln warke iiijd. To Margery my wyff iiij oxsyn, iij kye, ij qwyes, a horse, a mare and halff a skore olde schepe with ther lamys. Also all my crop sawyn in the felde. To Richerd Buknall my whyt horse. To Alice Buknall one potte and a kettyll. To Johanne Buknall a pott and a kettell. To Robert Buknall a calff. To Sir William Longcaster

xx*d* to say v messys off the fyve principall woundes of Our Lorde for the helthe of my soule. The resydue of my goodes I bequeth to Margery my wyff, whome I make my executrix to dispose for the helthe of my soule as shall be moste nedefull, and Sir Thomas Forlowe to be supervisor, and he to have for hys labor iij*s* iiij*d* and a panne. Thes wytnes; Sir Thomas Banester parysh preste, William Dafte and Thomas Burghe, with other moy.

Proved before P at Horncastle, 16 October 1532.

24.   SIR ROBERT LYNDELEY [VICAR OF BILSBY]
       [LCC 1532–34, fos. 2r–3v]

5 May 1532. I, Robert Lyndeley, preste, and of Billesby the vicare, of hole mynde and good memory, ordens and makes my testament and last will. Fyrst I bequethe my soule to allmyghtty God, Our Blessyd Lady St. Mary, and to all the saintes in heven, and my body to be buryed in the chauncell of the churche of Billesby afore the blessyd trinite. To the steple warke of the sayd Billesby xx*s*, to be takyn in the handes of John Skynner of Mabylthorp. To Our Lady warke of Lincoln iij*s* iiij*s*. To the pore chyldren at St. Catheryn's iiij*d*. To the steple warke off Alforde vj*s* viij*d*. To the churche of Hoggesthorp iij*s* iiij*d* to by ij altare clothes, one for the high altare and another for Our Lady altare within the same churche. [fo. 2v] To an honest preste iiij*l* xiij*s* iiij*d* to syng one hole yere in the churches of Billesby and Thurlby for my soule and all Crysten soules. To Bryan Coldecolle ij sterys. To Malde Baston ij qweys, one brasse potte, one panne, halff a dosen puter, one feder bedde that Sir Robert Lyndelay liethe apon, one bolster, one pare of schetes, and one coverlyd. To Sir Robert Lindeley my beste feder bed, one matteres, one pare of blankyttes, ij pare of schetes, ij coverlyds, one coveryng with all the hangynges over the bed, ij gret tabylls, a cownter, a cupborde, a spruse chyste in the chamber, one carvyd chyste in the hall, a bruyng leade, a mashe fat with other vessellys necessary, my best gowne, my best jaket, my best dooblet, ij brasse pottes, iiij dooblers, iiij puter dyshes, ij podyshers, ij sawssers, one salte seller, ij candylstykes, ij chares, ij formes, one maser, one chaffer to warme water in, one chaffyng dyshe, my blak horsse, my sadle, my brydle, my bootes, my spurrys, all my bookes and also in money iiij*l*. To John Lindelay my beste matteres, on pare of schetes and one coverlyd. To Thomas Lyndelay my secund feder bed, one pare of schetes, one coverlyd, one coveryng of a bed and one brasse potte. To the prior of Markeby x*s*, and to the convent of the same xxvj*s* viij*d*. To th'abbot off Hagneby and to the convent of the same for to make me brother in the chapter house x*s*.[16] To Elizabeth Oldefelde xij*s* viij*d*, to be takyn of Richerd Lyndeley. To Richerd Lyndley all my harnes, my beste bowe, my qwyver and all my arroys, and I forgyff hym x*l* of dettes in recompense of hys charges when I was last seke, and that he troble not my executors. To Christofer Richerdson an acre of barly to be at the order of my executors. To John Oldefelde one pare of bedstokes, one matteres, one pare of schetes and one coverlyd. To the vicare of Alforde my best sylver spone. To John Stevenson iij*s* iiij*d*. To Catheryne, wyff of Robert Johnson of Alforde, one cowe. I will that as towchyng my landes

---

[16] This was a further aspect of intercessory provision for the soul, posthumous membership of the monastic community ensuring a permanent source of prayers on behalf of the testator's soul after death. Among the laity similar assumptions often led to posthumous enrolment in a religious fraternity.

which I bought off William Mykylbarowe in Hotofte, wherin the prior of Markeby, Andrewe Billesby, Edwarde Forcet and Robert Lyndeley be seassyd off, to my use and for the performance of my will as in a dede of foeffement mayd to them beryng date 5 Marche 24 Henry [fo. 3r] VII,[17] as in the same dede more playnly dothe appere, I will that they and other ther sayd coeffeoffes ther heyres and ther assygnes schall stande and be seassyd in the sayd landes to the use and intent foloyng: the sayd prior of Markeby, Andrew Byllesby and other ther sayd coeffeoffes, ther heyres and assygnes, shall stande and be seassyd of and in the sayd landes and pasturys for the terme of xl yeres then nexte immediatly foloyng after the date of thys my last will, and my executors theyr deputes or the churchewardens of the trinite churche of Billesby for the tyme beyng, to receyve the yerely rentes of the sayd landes and pasture duryng the sayd xl yeres, to make or cause to be mayd an obyt, to be done in the sayd churche of Byllysby yerely duryng the sayd xl yeres for my soule, my fader and moder soulys, and all Crysten soulys, with placebo and dirige over the nyght and messe of requiem in the mornyng, with ij prestes. And ether of the prestes to have iiij*d* for ther labor and v*d* to be gyffyn to pore folkes apon the sayd day. And the sayd obyt to be done and kepte the vij[th] day of May yerely duryng the sayd xl yeres, or within a monyth nexte immediatly foloyng the same day yff it may be done be the lawe of holly churche. And the resydue of the rentes of the sayd landes duryng the sayd xl yeres to go to by a tenor bell to the other ij bellys that be nowe in the sayd churche off Byllesby, and for the cariage and hangyng of the sayd bell, and for the buyldyng of the steple of the sayd churche of Billesby and other reparacions of the same churche. And yff my executors, there deputes, or the churchewardens of the sayd churche of Billesby for the tyme beyng do not kepe and performe all thys my will for the sayd lande, than I will that the heyres of William Mykelbarowe aforesayd shall have the sayd landes. And yff they do performe and kepe thys my laste will for the sayd lande as is above specifyed, I will then that the sayd my feoffes, ther heyres and assygnes, injoy the sayd landes to th'uses aforesayd duryng the sayd xl yeres. Also I will that yff all my sayd feoffes dye excepte ij or iij, that then the sayd ij or thre that overlyffes the other to make a new estate to fowre, sex, eight or mo aftyr the discrecion of the sayd feoffes that overlyffes, to th'uses above rehersyd. And then at th'ende of the sayd [fo. 3v] xl yeres to make an astate of the sayd landes to th'eyres of the sayd William Mykylbarow and their heyres for ever. I make John Lyndley and Thomas Lyndeley of Billesby my executors, and I desyre Sir Andrewe Billesby, knyght, to be supervisor, and I bequethe to hym for hys labor xls. Thes wytnes; Sir Robert Lyndley, preste, Edwarde Sandon, William Cracrofte, John Stevenson, Jamys Sellers, John Sutton and John Oldefelde, with other mo.

Proved before P at Alford, 5 February 1532/3, by the executors.

25.   ROBERT BRYG [OF WIGTOFT]
       [LCC 1532–34, fos. 65r–66r]

6 May 1532. I, Robert Bryg off Wygtofte, of good mynde and hole memory beyng, make my testament and last will. Fyrst I bequeth my soule to allmyghtty God, to Our Lady St. Mary and to all the holy cumpeny off heven, and my body to be buryed in the churche of the appostellys Peter and Paule of Wygtofte with my

[17] 1509.

mortuary aftyr the custome of the lawe. To our Lady warke of Lincoln viij*d*. To the fatherles chyldren of St Catheryn's ther iiij*d*. To the high altare in the sayd churche of Wygtofte ij*s*. To Our Lady altare ther xij*d*. To St. Nicholes altare ther viij*d*. To the rode lyght ther xij*d*. To the hogners' light ther xij*d*. To the plough light ther xij*d*.[18] To the warke of the sayd churche of Wygtofte xx*s*. Towarde the gyltyng of the ymage of St. Paule ther xx*s*. To every cumpeny and covent of the iiij housys of frerys in Boston x*s* and one wether schepe, on condicion that they, or xxx^{ty} prestes of them, joyntly all together syng or say iiij trentallys for my soule iiij days together and immediatly foloyng, that is to say in every of ther conventuall chyrches on trentall till all the sayd trentallys be so sungen sayd and done, and thys to be done so shortely aftyr my decease as convenyently may be. I bequeth and will that one honest and well disposyd preste do syng for me and my good frendes one yere in Wygtofte churche as sone aftyr my decease as conveniently may be. To Cecill my doughter one fether bed, one coverlyd, one pare of flaxyn schetes, one bolster and ij pilloys. To Anne my doughter one matteres, one coverlyd, one pare of flaxyn schetes, one bolster and ij pilloys. To Barbara my doughter one matteres, one coverlyd, one pare of flaxyn schetes, one bolster and ij pilloys. And also to every of the sayd Cecill, Anne and Barbara my doughters x net bestes, that is to say iij kye, iij calvys, iij burnynges and one of ij yere olde, and also to every of them, xx^{ty} schepe, that is to say xvj schepe and iiij lambys. To every one of my godchylder one lambe. To Alice Peerson my servant one lambe. To Margaret Storer my servant one lambe. To John Sheperde my cosyn one bay mare of ij yere olde. To Jenet Browne my syster one baye mare of ij yere olde. To Alice Stokdale my syster one gryssylde [fo. 65v] colte. To Richerde Brandon one blak geldyng of iij yeres olde. The resydue of my goodes I bequeth to Margaret my wyff whome I orden myne executrice. I will that Thomas Halgh and Richerd Wolmer of Wygtofte, gentylmen, be the supervisors, and I will that either of them have for ther labors x*s*. Thys is the last will of me the sayd Robert Bryg. I will that my feoffys that be seasyd of and in my talyd landes shall stande seassyd from the day of my decessyng to the ende and terme of xv yeres then next foloyng, to the use of Margaret my wyff. And aftyr the ende of the sayd terme to the use of the laste willes of Thomas Bryg my grandfather and of Richerd Brig hys father. I will that the sayd Margaret my wyff have my messys nyghe the churche of Wygtofte, iij roodes of lande, iij acres and j roode off pasture in Wigtofte, and the messe in Fyshmere Ende within the parysh off Sutterton, by me purchesyd of Richerde Brandon, and the iij acres and a halffe of lande and iiij acres and a halffe of pasture to the sayd messe in Sutterton belongyng. And also one acre and a ryg of lande in Wygtofte, purchessyd of John Grene, with all ther appurtenances for the hole terme of her lyffe, fyndyng and honestly brynyng up all my chyldren and reparyng all the premisses. And aftyr her decease I will that all

---

[18] Gatherings of 'hogglers', known as 'hognels', are recorded as early as the 1450s, and may be older. In Lincolnshire, according to Hutton, they are found only in two neighbouring parishes in the Fens while, more widely, they are attested in only nineteen rural parishes across Gloucestershire, Somerset, Devon, Surrey, Sussex and Kent. The 'hognel time', during which these gatherings occurred, varied from place to place, usually occurring at Easter or Christmas. The function of the gatherings, however, beyond collecting for it, is unknown. The maintenance of the plough light, particularly widepread in Lincolnshire, was closely associated with the rites and religious rituals that accompanied the opening of the ploughing season on Plough Monday, celebration of which is first recorded in 1413, but may be considerably older. See R. Hutton, *The Rise and Fall of Merry England: the Ritual Year 1400–1700* (Oxford, 1996), 12–13, 16–17.

my sayd purchest landes and tenementes remayn to Cecill, Anne and Barbara my doughters to ther heyres and assygnes for ever. I will that the sayd Margaret my wyffe have for the terme of her lyffe one roode of lande lying in Bullholme in the parysh of Wygtofte and one acre and iij roodes of pasture callyd Slye Land lying in redy hyrnes within the sayd parysh of Wygtofte, beyng now of the yerly valewe of vj*s*, on condicion that the sayd Margaret with iiij*s* therof do kepe one obbyt for my soule all my good frendes soulys and all crysten soulys yerly duryng the sayd terme of her lyff, that is to say the fyrst day of Aprill within the parysh churche of Wygtofte. [fo. 66r] And aftyr the decesse of my sayd wyff I will that the sayd roode of lande in Bullholme and the sayd acre and iij roodes of pasture in redy hirnes remayn to Cecill my doughter and to the heyres of her body laufully begottyn, kepyng the sayd obbyt as is above specifyed. And for defawtte of suche issue to remayn to Anne my doughter, [remainder to] Barbara my doughter and to the heyres of her body laufully begottyn. And yff it fortune the sayd Barbara to dye withowt heyres of her body laufully begottyn, then I will that the sayd roode of lande and the acre and iij roodes of pasture be solde be my feoffys of the same, the survivors or the heyres of them then lyffyng, and the money for the same to be receyvyd to be by them disposyd in prayers and other dedes of almys in the parysh of Wigtofte for the helthe of my soule and the soulys of my wyff, my chyldren and all Crysten soulys. Wytnes heroff; Sir Robert Walker, parysh preste of Wygtofte, Sir Robert Leedes of the same, preste, John Atkynson, John Howsson and John Felde of the same, with other moy. Dated the day and yere above wryttyn.

Proved before P at Boston, 9 October 1532.

26.   JOHN BURBECHE [OF BARROWBY]
       [LCC 1532–34, fos. 46r–47v]

11 May 1532. I, John Burbeche of Barughbe, husbandman, seke in body, hole in mynde and of good remembraunce, makes my testament and last will. Fyrst I bequeth my soule to God allmyghtty, Our Lady St. Mary and to all the holy cumpeny in heven, and my body to be buryed in the churcheyerde of All Saints in Barughby. To the high altare for tithys forgottyn xij*d*. To the parsone of Barughby a schere schepe. To the red arke for the mayntenance of Our Lady warke of the cathedrall churche of Lincoln xij*d*. To the reparacions of Barughby churche all my gret tymber. To the same churche the best kyrchyff save one to make a corporax of.[19] To Harlaxtone churche ij*s* iiij*d*. To Gonwarby churche ij*s*. To the frerys in Grantham v*s* to say halff a trentall of messes. I will ther be delte at my buryall halpeny brede. To Laurence of Merys a yow and a lamme. To John a Burton of Grantham ij quarters barly ij halff landes of rye. To John Gosse my father-in-lawe v landes of pease, ij landes [fo. 46v] of barly, iiij yowes and iiij lammys and my lether dooblet, ij lodes off wood. To John Gosse wyff my wyffe's gowne and her red kyrtell. I bequeth vj yowys and vj lammys and a cowe to kepe a yerely obbyt withall for my soule and all my good frendes soulys. And the sayd yowys lammys and cowe to be in custody of the churchewardyns of Barughby for ther tymys beyng, and they to dispose at the same obbyt ij*s*, and the reste or the overplus to go to the mayntenance of the sayd stoke. Also a yowe and a lamme to the fyndyng of a

---

[19] The corporass was a cloth on which the Host was consecrated: Duffy, *Stripping of the Altars*, 96.

light afore the blessyd sacrament. To my lorde of Newbo xij*d* and to every preste of the same house iiij*d* and to every novisse ij*d*. To the parsone of Alyngton xij*d*. To Sir William Maysone viij*d*. To Sir Gabriel Kyrke viij*d*. To Sir John Coe a bushyll barly. To Henry Hadlar a bushyll barly. To Henry Scherpe one stryke of rye. To Robert Smyth a stryke of barly. To Robert Torkyngton a stryke of barly. To Robert Trayn a bushyll malte. To Crele my brother-in-lawe a bushyll of rye. To Crane wyff a cappe. To Raffe Forde a lamme. To Richerd Wryght wyff a lamme. To William Robson a lamme. To Gregory my servant a lamme. To William my brother a dowe cowe, a brendyd cowe, a dowe stere and a flecte stere, a red qwe and a blak qwye, a colte, a mare, a bownde wane and lx woollyd schepe, accordyng to my father will and dischargyng of my conscience. To Thomas my brother a blake stere, a red stere, a blak qwe and a tagyd qwy, a gray fely and a bay fely, a bounde wayn and lx wollyd schepe. Also yff it shall happyn my brother William to departe thys worlde before he cum to laufull age, that is to say the age of xiiij yere, then I will that my sun William shall have the halff of hys parte of his goodes and the other halff to Thomas my brother withe the halff of my housholde stuff. And I will that the sayd Thomas and hys goodes be in the custody of John a Burton of Grantham untill he be xv yere of age. And yff he departe the worlde before he cum to laufull age then I will it be disposyd for the helthe of ther soulys and all Christen soulys at the discrestion of John Burton. I will that Rayff Forthe and Richerd Wright of Barughby do make the best of my ferme in Barughby to the best use and moste proffyt of William my sonne, which ferme I have for [fo. 47r] certen yeres by lease of the abbot and convent of Newbo. The resydue of my goodes I gyff them to William my sonne and to Richerd my sonne, to be devydyd bewtyxst them be eyvn porcions. And I will that Rayff Forthe have the custody of William my sonne and hys parte to he cum to the age of xiij yere. I will that Richerd Wryght shall have the custody of Richerde my sonne to he cum to the age aforesayd. Yff Richerde my sonne departe before he cum to laufull age, I will hys parte remayn to my sonne William. And I will the sayd William and all hys goodes be at the putting and governaunce of the sayd Rayff and the sayd Richerde to he cum to xiij yere of age, and then I will he have the sayd goodes delyveryd to hym. And yff it happyn hym to dye I will it to be disposyd for the welthe of my soule and all Christen soulys at the discrestion of the sayd Rayff Forthe and the sayd Richerde Wryght whome I make my executors, and other of them to have for ther labor vj*s* viij*d* and Thomas Burton of Grantham to be supervisor. Thes wytnesses; Sir William Meyson my gostly father, John a Burton of Grantham, William Robson, Robert Oxsone, with other moy.

Proved before P at Lincoln, 11 July 1532. Adm. granted to Richard Wright as executor reserving power to grant to Ralph Forthe the co-executor.

27. WILLIAM ASHTON [RECTOR OF BELTON]
[Stow 1530–52, fos. 10v–11v]

12 May 1532. I, William Ashton, preste, the parson of Belton in the Ile of Axholm within the diocese and countie of Lincoln, beyng of holl mynde and gud remem-braunce, make my testament. First I bequeth my saull to almyghty God, Owr Lade Saynt Marire and to all his sayntes, and my body to be buryed in the chauncell of Belton aforsaid. Also in the name of my mortuarye, myne awmlynge hors, the wiche

I last rode upon. I bequeth for my benefice of Whyttington in the name of my mortuary there on grey awmlynge geldinge. To the churche warke of Belton aforsaid xxs. To the churche warke of Whyttington aforsaid xxs. To the churche warke of Crolle xxs. To the Gray Freers of Yorke xxs. To the Gray Freers of Dancaster xxs. To the Austen Freers of Theckill xxs. To the Blake Freers of Pounfrett xxs. To the Whyt Freers of Douncaster xs. To the makinge of elande calsey xs. To the makinge of ferye calsey xls.[20] To Our Lady warke of Lincoln xijd. To Saynt Hugh ther xijd. I bequeth that on preste [fo. 11r] synge ij yeres next after my decesse for my saull and all Cristen saulles, and he to have therefore xiijl vjs viijd. To the mariage of v maiddes within the parish of Whittington aforsaid vl, that is to sey, to every on of them, xxs. To Syr Myles Huddilston, the parson of Normanton, xxl. To Sir Richard Ledett, my chaplen, for on quarter servys next after my decesse, xxvjs viijd. To William Draper my servant, John Hudson and Ranold Kaykwicke, on quarter wages each. To Thomas Wikes my servant on quarter wages and every on of them iiij to have therfore xxs. To Elen Batie my servant on cowe. To Sir Christofer Ashton, the parson of Kighley, on teaster with the curtayns of sarconytt havinge the rawmpinge lion uppon. Also on feder bede, the better of ij now beinge at Yorke, on carpett of Turkye now beynge in the parloour at Belton, on bedde coverynge, the better of twoe at Yorke, also on pare of launde yrens now beynge at Belton, to th'entent that at his decesse he bequeth the launde yerns to on of his kynsfolke.[21] To Jamys Ashton the best feder bedd now beinge at Belton with the bolster and beadde coverynge and all the hangynges in the parloure at Belton, on teaster of velvytt red and grene, with gardes of cloth of gold with the sparner of sarcenet grene and yalow. Also on trussinge bedd with the feder bed, bolster and coverynge called the grene bedd, now beinge in the chambr over the parlour at Belton. Also my best table clothe. Also on dosyn of my best napkyns and ij payr of my best shetes. [fo. 11v] To Cristoffer Ashton on testour with the sperner and on fedder bed, the coverynges, bolster and blankyttes with all thinge pertenynge therto now beynge at Yorke. Also the better feder bed beinge in Sir Roberte's chawmber with the tester and sperner, redd and yalow blankittes and bolster therto pertenynge. Also iijl vjs viijd sterlinge beinge in the handes of th'abbott of Selby, delyveryd to hym for the income of the howse in Estoft in wiche now Robert Smyth dothe dwell. To Isabell, the wyffe of John Pecoke, all my right and titill in the mylne called Belton Mylne in Norcroft. To Christofer Gradell, prest, on gowne furred with blake lame. To Sir Robert Taliour on gowne furred with shenkes. I will that all the residew of my howshold stuff and rement be distributed emonge my kynsfolke after the discrestion of myne executours, provydyd alway that iff any of my kynnesfolke in tyme to come do aske, chalange, or clame bi sute or plee, or bi any other mean, eny of my said howshold stuffe or rement, then I will the said askar, chalenger or clamer, askars, chalangers or claymers, shall have no part of my said howshold stuffe and rement. The residew off my goodes I giffe to Sir Robert Taliour, prest of Haxey, and William Standish, whome I orden my executors. Thies

---

[20] This refers to the reinforcement of causeways in the parish, made necessary by the low-lying, wet nature of the ground in this part of the county.

[21] Christopher Ashton was presented to the living of Keighley by its patron, William Ashton, on 14 April 1524. He died in September 1555, having been instituted to the rectory of All Saints, York, in June of the same year: *Fasti Parochiales*, IV, ed. N.K.M. Gurney and C. Clay (Yorkshire Archaeological Society Record Series, 1971), 70.

beynge wytnesse; Richard Poplewell, Thomas Wikes, John Holand, Thomas Awdhous and John Kechyn off Braken.

Proved before Edward Darby, archdeacon of Stow in the parish church of Belton, 24 June 1532. Adm. granted to the executors.

28.   ROGER BELL [OF BUTTERWICK]
      [LCC 1532–34, fos. 15v–16r]

12 May 1532. I, Roger Bell off Butterwyke in Holland, husbandman, beyng off hoole mynd and good remembrance att this tyme, lovyd be God, mayke thys my last will and testament. Fyrst I bequethe my sowle to God allmyghtty and to Oure Blyssed Lady Saynt Mare and to all the santtes in hevyn, and my body to be buryed within the churcheyard off Butterweke, and the ryght off the churche to be payd accordyng to the law. To the hye auter viijd. To Oure Lady's auter iiijd and to Sant Katerine auter iiijd. To oure mother churche off Lincoln vjd. I will that Isabell Fowle, the wyffe of John Fowle, have all my landes and tenimenttes, medewse and pasturs within the townes and feldes of Butterweke and Freston duryng hyr lyffe naturall, and after the dethe off hyr I will that Rychard Smythe, the sone off Thomas Smyth, have v acres arable land callyd Brygcroft, also iiij akars pasturs callyd Brascott Pastur, also iiij akars medew ground callyd Dayn John Dyke, to hym and to hys heres off hys body after the dysses off hys mother. I wyll that Rychard Smyth pay unto Margarett Fowle, dowghter off John Fowle, xls within thre yeres immediately folowyng that he doyth entre the sayde landdes. To John Fowle my brother-in-law [fo. 16r] the howse that he dwells in duryng the terme off hys lyff with ij akars pastur and a wod, be yt more or lesse, yff ytt fortune hym to over lyve my sister hys wyffe. Also I will that the forsayd John have ij akars medew ground lying in Freston callyd Bastyngcroft, also ij akars medew ground lying by Swangape and an akar ing ground callyd Bowleryge. Also I wyll that John Fowle, sone off John Fowle, that ys the younger John Fowle, have all the landes and tenementtes and medew ground that hys fayer hathe by this my wyll after the dysses of hys father. I wyll that if ytt happen Rychard Smyth do dye withote heres off hys body lawfully begotten then I wyll that the foresayd John Fowle the yonger have the forsayd landes, payng Margarett hys sister xls. Also I will that if yt happen John Fowle to dye afore Rychard Smythe withote heres off hys body lawfully bygotton, then I wyll that the sayd Rychard Smythe have all the hole land as ys aforsayd. To Dorothe Smythe on pese of land callyd Puddybryge, contenyng v roodes in fe semple, and all the resydew off my guddes I geve them to Isabell Fowle my syster whyche I do mayke myne executor, and she to dyspose them for the welthe off my soule. Thyse beryng wytnesse; Peter Blakester, John Blake, John Symson, John Dockyn, John Kechen, John Worme, Jamys Jacson, with other mo.

Proved before P at Lincoln, 26 June 1532.

29.   RICHARD FENTON [OF BASSINGHAM]
      [LCC 1532–34, fo. 157v]

18 May 1532. I, Richerde Fenton off Bassyngham, off good mynde and will, makes my testament. Fyrste I bequethe my soule unto allmyghtty God, and to Our Lady St. Mary and to all the saintes in heven, and my body to be beryed in the

churcheyerde of St. Michel the archaungell. And my mortuary to be gyffyn aftyr the custome of the cuntry. To Our Lady warke of Lincoln viij*d*. To the high altare of Bassyngham xij*s*. To the iiij orders of freres, to every of them, iiij*d*. I make my executrix Margaret my wyff, to dispose the resydue of my goodes for the well of my soule and to se that my chylder have ther barne parte. I make supervisor of my will William Clattercotes to se that my will be fulfyllyd as it is before wryttyn, and to have a balde horse for hys labor. Thes beyng wytnes; Sir Robert Stanley prest, Robert Coke, Henry Carnell, John Kente, with other.

Proved before P at South Hykeham, 15 May 1533.

30.   JOHN ALCOKSON [OF FRISKNEY]
      [LCC 1532–34, fo. 49r]

20 May 1532. I, John Alcokeson of Fryskeney, beyng of hole mynde and good remembraunce, makyth thys my last will and testament. Fyrst I bequeth my soule to God allmyghtty, to Our Lady St. Mary and to all the holy compeny of heven, and my body to be buryed in the churche porche or in the churcheyerde of All Halloys of Fryskney by the discrestion of my executors, with that that right requyryth to be my mortuary. To Our Lady of Lincoln xij*d*. To Our Lady warkes ther iiij*d*. To the high altare in Frysknay churche for tithes forgottyn xij*d*. To the high altare in the churche of Saynt Mary in Waynfleet for tithes forgottyn vj*d*. To the reparacions of Fryskeney churche xij*d*. To every gylde in the sayd churche of Fryskeney iiij*d*. To every altare in the sayd churche of Fryskeney iiij*d*. To every one of my godchylder iiij*d*. To John, Catheryne and Robert Cowton my doughter chyldren, ich of them, vj*s* viij*d*. To John, Humfray, Catheryne, Dorethe, Thomas and Ann my sonne chyldren, ich of them, a yowe and a lamme. To Alice my sone wyff a yowe and a lamme. To the iiij orders of frerys in Boston, iche of them, xij*d*. To Catheryne my wyff xx^ty yowes. The resydue of my goodes not wytt I gyff to Catheryne my wyff and Richard Alcokeson my sone, whom I make my executors of thys my testament. Thyes beyng wytnes; Roger Stevenson, Thomas Godfrey, Simon Esterby and Robert Gose of Fryskeney. Thys is my last will mayd the day and yere above wryttyn. To Catheryne my wyff my house that I dwell in with the garthens and kytcrofte therto belongyng, and a pece of red grounde late purchasyd of John Bodde the terme of her lyff [remainder to] Richerde my sonne. To the sayd Richerd my sone all my other landes, medoys, pasturys, fedynges and marshes in Waynflet and Fryskeney to hym and hys heyres males accordyng to my father will. I will that my executors have one acre of lande lying in Smalney in Fryskney therwyth to fynde the obyt of Richard Hode and Margaret hys wyff accordyng to the laste will of the sayd Margaret to them and ther heyres for ever. Wytnes Roger Stevenson and other abovenamyd.

Proved before P at Lincoln, 29 July 1532. Adm. granted to Richard Alcokeson the natural son of the deceased and an executor, reserving power to grant to Catherine the relict.

31.   RICHARD MAYSON [OF GUNBY ST. PETER]
        [LCC 1532–34, fo. 60v]

20 May 1532. I, Richard Mayson, off holle mynd and gud remembraunce, makes
this my last wyll and testament. In primis I bequeyth my solle to allmyghty God and
Our Lord [sic] Sanct Mary, and to all the sanctes in heven. My body to be beryyd in
the cherchyerd of Sanct Peter of Gunby. To Our Laydy warke of Lincoln viij*d*. To
the hyy auter in Sanct Peter cherch in Gunby iij*s* iiij*d*. To Robert my son ij sterrys,
an amblynge mare, a cowe with a kafe, iiij hogges, a wane with new whelles and all
that belongys to yt, a ploghe harow with all that belongys to thame, a gret poot. To
Agnes Gren a feder beed and a calfe. To John Barker a scheder hogg. I beqwyth
x*s* to a prest to syng a trentall for my soll and all Cresten solles in the cherch of
Sanct Peter of Gunby. To Myllyer sell hawff an aker weyth.[22] The ressydew of my
gewddes I put to the desspoyscson of John Mayson and Richard Mayson my
sonnys, qwome I make myn executors, thayt may desposs for the helth of my soll
and all Cresten solles as thay thynk best for the helth of my solles and all Cresten
solles. I will Robert Wylliamson be the supervizour, and he to have for his labor ij*s*.
Thys wettnes; Robert Wylliamson, Thomas Say, William Symkenson, with odder.
        Proved before P2 at Partney, 26 October 1532.

32.   CECILY PEDDER [OF KIRTON IN HOLLAND]
        [LCC 1532–34, fos. 68v–69r]

26 May 1532. I, Cecill Pedder of Kyrton in Holland, hole in mynd and good
memory, makes my testament and last will. Fyrst I bequeth my soule to God
allmyghtty, Our Lady St. Mary, and to all the celestiall cumpeny in heven, and my
body to be buryed in the churcheyerde of St. Peter and Paul in Kyrton in Holand.
To the principall altare in Kyrton churche for tithys forgottyn ij*d*. To the iij Marys
in the sayd churche ij*d*. To Our Lady altare in the sayd churche ij*d*. To the sayd
churche warkes iiij*d*. To Our Lady of Lincoln ij*d*. To the fatherles chylder ij*d*. To
Robert Typler, sonne of Roger, one you. To Jenet Typler my doughter my best
gowne. To Margaret my doughter my best panne and my best kyrtyll and my best
kyrchyff. To Jenet Overton, the doughter of John Overton of Frampton, j lamme.
[fo. 69r] I will that my sonne do sell vj yowys to bryng me to the grounde. I will that
my sonne sell one cowe to kepe my husband yere day, and myne. To Jenet Typler
one towell of iij yerdes and one kyrdhyff. To ether of my doughters one sylver ring.
The resydue of my goodes I gyff them to John my sonne, whome I make my
executor. Thes wytnes; Sir Richerd Thomson, curate, Roger Typler, Edward
Broughton, Alan Lamberd, with other mo.
        Proved before P at Boston, 9 October 1532.

33.   ROBERT TAMWORTHE [OF SILK WILLOUGHBY]
        [LCC 1532–34, fo. 75]

[1 June 1532] I, Robert Tamworthe of Sylke Willoby, of good mynd and
remembraunce, makes my testament and last will. Fyrst I bequeth my soule to
allmyghtty God, Our Lady, and to all the holy cumpeny in heven, and my body to

---

[22] Presumably 'sell half an acre's weight [of grain] to the miller'.

the erthe and to be buryed in the churcheyerde of Sylk Willobe. To the churche warke of Sylke Willobe xl*d*. To the high altare of the same for discharge of conscience, my best beaste. To the churche warke of Our Lady at Lincoln iiij*d*. To Helene Tamworthe my wyff, my messuage in Sylke Willowbe with all the appurtenances therto belongyng for terme of her lyff. And aftyr her I will and gyff to John Tamworthe, my sone, the sayd messuage with the appurtenances therto belongyng, [fo. 75v] and to hys heyres laufully brought forthe. And in defawte of heres of the sayd John, I gyff the sayd messuage with the appurtenances to Robert Tamworthe, my sonne. The resydue of my goodes I gyff to Helene my wyff, John and Robert my sonnys, whome I make my executors. Wryttyn at Sylke Willobe aforesayd the fyrst day of June 1532. Thes wytnes; Robert Cottyngham, prest, William Samer, William Bery, with diverse other.

Proved before P at Bloxholm, 11 October 1532. Adm. granted to John and Robert, the natural sons and executors of the deceased, reserving power to grant to Helen the relict.

34.   SIR RICHARD WHYTE [PARSON OF STAIN]
       [LCC 1532–34, fos. 48v–49r]

1 June 1532. I, Richerde Whyte, parsone of Stane, beyng of hole mynde, make thys my testament and last will. Fyrste I bequethe my soule to allmyghtty God, Our Lady St. Mary, and to all the saintes in heven. My body to be buryed within the churche of St. John in Stane. Also my mortuary as the law will. To Our Lady at Lincoln vj*d* and to her churche warke ther vj*d*. To Our Lady of Walsyngham xij*d*. To Sir John Hall in Kestwyn xij*d*. To the churche of Byllyngburgh to by ij candylstykes to stand afore the high altare xxvj*s* viij*d*. [fo. 49r] To the sayd churche of Byllyngsburgh iiij*l* to by a vestiment acordyng to the best cope. To Alice Baker my syster x*s*. To John Baker, sonne of Robert Baker, vj*s* viij*d*. To Sir John Newcom, vicare of Strubby, iij*s* iiij*d*. To Sir Thomas Shepparde iij*s* iiij*d*. To the frerys of Grantham to say a trentall x*s*. To Our Lady Frerys of Boston to syng a trentall x*s*. To the prior and convent of Sempyngham xx*s*. I will have v trentalles of messys to be done be one able preste, ij of them at Dunesby and other ij at Byllyngburgh and one at Stane. To the churche of Stane xxvj*s* viij*d*, to the payntyng off the rode lofte. To the churche of Strubby vj*s* viij*d*. To the churche of Dunesby vj*s* viij*d*. To Our Lady Frerys off Lincoln iij*s* iiij*d*. To the Blak Frerys in Lincoln iij*s* iiij*d*. To the Gray Frerys of Grymesby iij*s* iiij*d*. To the Augustyn Frerys of the same iij*s* iiij*d*. To the churche of Thedylthorpe to the buyldyng of a steple x*s*. The resydue of my goodes I bequeth to Sir William Whyte off Thedylthorpe, Sir Richerd Saneborne of Mablethorpe and to Thomas Whyte of Thedylthorpe, whome I make my executors. Thes beyng wytnesses; John Whyte, Richerd Broune, Robert Garbra, William Cooke, with other mo.

Proved before P at Lincoln, 29 July 1532.

35.   THOMAS SPALDYNG [OF TOFT BY NEWTON]
       [LCC 1532–34, fo. 16]

14 June 1532. I, Thomas Spaldyng off Toft juxta Newton, beyng hole off mynd and gud remembraunce, makyng this my last wyll. Fyrst I bequeyth my sowle to God

almyghty and to Our Lady Sant Mare and to all the holy company off hevyn, and my body to be buryed within the chyrche off Sant Peter and Paule off the forsayd Toft. To Mayster Parson off the sayd chyrche xij*d* to pray for me. To the chyrche off Toft aforesayd a ornament cald a cope, the price xxvj*s* viij*d*. To Our Lady warke off Lincoln xij*d* [fo. 16v]. To Newton chyrche viij*d*. To every order of freyrs within the cyte off Lincoln vj*d*. To Medyll Rasyn Drax viij*d*. To Medyll Tuphom xij*d*. To Necholas my servand a cowe and halff an acar off barly. To Sysly Stykney a cowe. To Modyll Durrans a yowe and a lam. To Durrans Robertson a yowe hoge. To Esabell Eldale a qwye calff. To Sir Marmaduce Constable, to be gud mayster to my whyffe, vj*s* viij*d*. To Esabell my wyf my hows and all my land, medows, pasturs, fedyng grundes belongyng to the same house within the towne and feld off Toft and Newton. And whereas Rychard Nayler and Wylliam Hopkyng my feoffers stand feoffyd and seasses off a mesuege with all and syngular landes, tenementes, medowes, pasturs and fedyng groundes within the town and feld off Toft and Newton to the use and performans off this my last wyll, I wyll that my sayd feoffers stand feffed and seassed off a mesuage and other the premysses to the ese off Esabell my wyffe dewryng the terme off hyr lyffe. And after the decesse off hyr to remayn to Wylliam Spaldyng the yongar for the terme off hys lyffe. And after hys decesse to remayn to Robert Spaldyng, sone off Wylliam Spaldyng, and to hys heres and hys assyners for ever. And yff it happen the forsayd Wylliam Spaldyng or Robert Spaldyng hys sone, or eyther off them, hereafter do medyll or interup the forsayd Esabell my wyffe off the foresayd mes[uage] and premisses, then I wyll that my sayd feffers stand feoffed to the use off my sayd wyf for the performacion off hyr laste wyll, qwyeche I mayke executor for to dyspose for the helthe off my sowle. Theys wyttnesses; Sir Robert Langlay, parson off the same chyrche, Wylliam Spaldyng, Wylliam Baw, Durrans Robertson, Rychard Naylor, Rychard Netlam, Wylliam Hopkyn, with other mo.

Proved before P at Lincoln, 25 July 1532, by the executrix.

36.   AMEE SWAGGE [OF FRISKNEY]
       [LCC 1532–34, fo. 48v]

14 June 1532. I, Ame Swagge of Fryskeney, of a hole mynde and good remembraunce, makes my testament. Fyrste I bequethe my soule to allmyghtty God, to Our Lady St. Mary, and to all the holy cumpeny of heven. My body to be buryed in the churcheyerde of All Halloys of Fryskeney. To Our Lady of Lincoln a pare of gret beades and viij*d* of money. To the fatherles chyldren of Saynt Catheryn's iiij*d*. To every order of frerys in Boston iiij*d*. To the ornamentes of the high altare off Fryskeney vj*d*. To the rode gylde vj*d*, and to every gylde in the same churche iiij*d*. To the churche warkes xx*d*, and to the bellys iiij*d*. To William my sun a cowe, a blak mare and a fole, a fether bed, a matterys, v schetes, ij pilloys, a coverlyd, a towell, a pott and a panne. To Walter my sonne a cowe, vij yowys and vij lammys, a potte, a panne, a matterys, a coverlyd, iiij schetes, ij pilloys and a towell. To Richerde my sonne a cowe, v yowes and v lammys, a potte, a gret panne, a matteres, a coverlyd, iiij schetes, ij pilloys and a towell. To John my sonne a cowe, ij yowes and ij lammys, a gryssylde mare and a fole, a new potte, a panne, a materes, a coverlyd, iiij schetes, ij pilloys and a table clothe. To Simon Esterbe my sone a cowe, a bay mare, ij yowes and ij lammys. To Agnes Cadbe my servant one lamme. I will have ij trentalles sung

for me and my fyrst husband, Simon Esterbe. The resydue of my goodes I gyff to Simon Esterby and John Swagge my sonnys, whome I make my executors by the advice and councell of Mr. Thomas Kyme, esqwyer, whome I make supervisor. Thes wytnes; Sir Robert Westmellys, preste, Walter Swag and Richerd Swag, with many other.

Proved before P at Lincoln, 29 July 1532. Adm. granted to Simon Esterby and executor, reserving right to grant to John Swagge, the co-executor.

37. BRIAN CRYAR [OF SWINESHEAD]
[LCC 1532–34, fo. 50v]

18 June 1532. I, Bryan Cryer of Swyneshed, in hole mynde and good remembraunce, makyth my last will. I bequeth my soule to God allmyghtty and till Hys blessyd mother Our Lady St. Mary, and to all the celestiall cumpeny of heven. My body to be buryed in the churchyerde of Our Blessyd Lady in Swyneshed. To the high altare for tithys forgottyn viijd. To Our Lady altare ther iiijd. To the kyrke warke ther xijd. To Our Lady of Lincoln iiijd. To the fatherles chylder of St. Catheryn's at Lincoln iiijd. To the covent of Swyneshed Abbay till a pot with ale xxd. To Richerd Cryer my sonne, Thomas Cryer my sun, Jenet my doughter and Christabell my doughter ij burlyngs each, and yf any of them dye or that they be habyll to have the gydyng of the said nette, ich to be other heyres. The resydue of my goodes I gyff unto Elizabeth my wyff, whome I make my executrix to dispose for the helth of my soule and all crystyn soulys. Wytnes heroff; William Cryer, Robert Heryson and Richerd Carter, with other moy.

Proved before P at Lincoln, 14 September 1532.

38. THOMAS HUDSON [OF APPLEBY]
[Stow 1530–52, fo. 12]

18 June 1532. I, Thomas Hudson, holl of mynde and of gud remembrance, makes my will. First I bequeth my saull to God almyghty and to his blessyd moder Saynt Marye and to all the holly compeny of hevyn, and my body to buryed in the churche of Saynt Barthollmew off Appulby. To Awer Lady of Lincoln xijd. To the hye awter of Appulby xijd. To the roode leight xijd. To the Trinite gilde viijd. To Ower Lady gilde viijd. Also half a trentall of messes to be done at Thornholm. Also half a trentall of messys to be done at Appulby. To Johanne my wiffe my indenture of this howse with the yeres for the terme of her liffe, and after the terme of her liffe, it to remayn to Robert my sonne and he be onliffe. To Agnes Lyndsey the indenture of Glaunforth brigges, and if she dye John Cockrell to have it for the yeres. To Agnes Lyndsey in guddes and catalles, to the valew of xls. I giff Syr Edwarde my sonne on bay hors and vj quarters barley. To Syr Robert Baxter iiij silver sponys and a foyll next to Syr Edwarde. I forgiffe my sister Cokrell xvs wiche she dothe owe me. To Richard Cokrell on silver broche, silver and gilt. To John Selby all my shop geres with a packe sadell and ij hampers with my rosell and tallow and all my shoyne for vs a dosen, and all my botes and legges for [fo. 12v] vjs viijd, and my shop on yere for nothynge. To ij prentessys iijs iiijd if he will tary with my wiff and help her to gett harvest. To Lucye on cowe and a calfe at her fote, and on white horse. To John Hudson on jakett that is at makyng and all my hoyse and my fustean jakett and my

kelter coytt and my ledder cote and my bonett. To Thomas Sell on quye that I bought of Clement Grene. To Jenytt Hopper iiij quarters barley that I bowght of olde William Hill. To Robert Bromby my chamlett gyrken. I will that my wiffe be myne executrice. To the kirke porche viijd. To Agnes Lyndsey on peyr of bedes, on gerdill with silver penner and bockell, and on counter and on grett chest. I bequeth Mr. Vicar of Appulby iij quarters barley. Witnesse Mr. Vicar, Sir Robert Baxter, John Hooton, Robert Hooton, Thomas Atkynson.

Proved before L, 24 September 1532. Adm. granted to the executrix.

39.   JOHN STELE [OF EVEDON]
        [LCC 1532–34, fo. 47]

19 June 1532. I, John Stele of Evedon, hole of mynde and memory, makes my testament and last will. Fyrste I bequethe my soule to allmyghtty God, to Our Lady St. Mary, and to all the cumpeny of heven. My body to be buryed in the churcheyerde of Our Blessyd Lady of Evedon. To the high altare of Evedon for tithys forgottyn xijd. To my curate halff an acre of the best arable. To Our Lady warke of Lincoln viijd. To the nonnys of Catley viijd. To Our Lady of Grace in Evedon churche a cowe to fynde a light afore her yerely. And the same cowe to be in the churchewardens handes, and they to let her for xvjd by yere, of the whiche I bequeth viijd to fynde the sayd light and vd to the curate for dirige and messe to be done at the syght [fo. 47v] of my executors and supervisors. To Our Lady of Pety in Dygby churche iiijs vjd to fynde a light afore her evermore. To Mr. William Harbe the best lande of wheate. To Mr. John Harbe an amblyng fole. To my curate xxd to pray for me. To my wyff iiij of the best oxene, iiij of the best kye, iiij of the best marys withowt folys, x schepe, all the housholde stuff, a wayn with that that longyth therto, a pare off new whelys, the plughe and that that longyth therto, and halff my croppe aftyr that Jenet Pechel be payd her legacy her foloyng, that is to say, to the sayd Jenet Pechel iij kye the price xxxs, and so muche of my corne in the felde as shall make up iiij markes with the sayd xxxs, ij yowes and ij lammes, a qwy callyd Rose. To Robert my sone ij bullokes, a gray balde stag, a qwye of the same age that Jenet Pechel qwy is, and a seme barly. To William my sonne a bullok calffe of thys yere and a seame barly. To John my sonne ij bullokes, a blake fely of ij yere olde, a qwy of the same age that Jenet Pechet qwy is and a seame barly. To Margaret my doughter a sternye qwy, a brandyd yeryng calffe. To Alice my doughter a qwy calffe of thys yere and a seame barly. To my brother William my sored horse and my best cote. To William hys sonne a dun fole. To Emote hys doughter a lamme. To William, my brother Richerd sonne a lamme. To Margaret Perte halff an acre barly. To her chylderyn John and Parenell a yeryng qwy calffe. To Richerd Wryght my whyte petycote. To William Gylys my russyt cote. To Alice, my brother William wyff a lamme. To Maryon a lamme. To Richerde my brother a gray stag. The resydue of my goodes, all funerall chargys of buryall day, vij day and xxx^{ty} day deducte, I will that William my brother and Alice my wyff, whome I make my executores, shall cause to be kepte yerly so long as the sayd residue of goodes will therto extende dirige and messe in the sayd churche of Evedon, for my soule and all Christen soulys at the oversight of Sir Bartilmew Ingoldesby, parsone of Evedon, whome I make supervisor. Thes wytnes; Sir Bartilmew Ingoldesby, parsone of Evedon, John Harby, gentleman,

Henry Jay, Richerd Wetell, Rayff Screnschawe, William Gilys, Richerd Wryght, with other mo.

Proved before P at Lincoln, 9 July 1532. Adm. granted to William, executor, Alice the relict and executrix being prevented by death.

40. RICHARD TROWTHE [OF SPALDING]
[LCC 1532–34, fos. 161v–162v]

20 June 1532. I, Richerde Trowthe off Spaldyng in the countie of Lincoln, beyng hole in mynde and good remembraunce, dothe make my testament and last will. Fyrste I bequethe my soule to allmyghtty God and Hys mother St. Mary, and to all the celestiall cumpeny in heven, and my body to be [fo. 162r] buryed within the paryshe churche of Spaldyng, beyng of Our Lady and St. Nicholes, by the holy water stok, and my mortuary as the lawe requiryth. To the high altare in the same churche for all thynges forgottyn xij*d*. To the Trinite gylde ther xij*d*. To the gylde of Our Lady ther xij*d*. To every devocion within the same churche iiij*d*. To the reparacionyng of the same churche xx*d*. To our mother churche of Lincoln xij*d*. To St. Catheryn's ther, helpyng the motherlesse chyldren xx*d*. I will have an hable preste to syng and rede for me and my wyffes Johanne and Margery with all Crysten soules in the parysh churche of Spaldyng, the space of halff a yere, and he to have for hys labor liij*s* iiij*d*. To Richerd my sun, immediatly aftyr my decesse, a house which is now in the holdyng of Thomas Ymmyngham, lying nexte to the Bull in Spaldyng callyd Keedy's house, with a pasture callyd Keede's pasture conteynyng xij acres, and iij acres pasture lying next unto Whetlie's, and one pasture in the holdyng of Richerd Lynsay, to hym and hys assygnes, which pastures dothe holde upon the prior of Spaldyng by coppy. Also iiij mares with ij foles, a violet gowne lynyd with blak cotton, a cote with a patlet of velvet apon it, a kendall cote, ij dooblettes of chamlet, ij jerkens of chamlet, the other kendall, a tawny jaket with all my hose and schose, a swerde, a bukler, a hole harnes for a man, ij ferther beddes with the bolsters, one matteres, ij coverlyddes, ij pare flaxen schetes, ij pilloys, a potte, a panne, halffe a dosyn puter, ij candylstykes, a basen, a laver, a cupborde, a folden table, a forme, a chare and vj poundes of lefull money, which he shall have payd by my executrix within a yere aftyr my decesse. I gyff the same Richerde aftyr the decesse of my wyff a maser and sex sylver sponys. And yff he dy before her, she to have them at her plesure. To Margery my wyff all my goodes within my house, iij mylke kye, a bay mare, ij yerynges, iij mylne horsse and a copy of a pasture callyd iij acre, lying nexte to Henry Percy. To Hugh Ordyng a chamlet chaket, and to Addelarde Byller a gray marbyll cote and x*s* of money. I will that my executrix do cause my grave stone to be layd upon my grave, and it to be mayd a yerde high above the grounde, as nygh the piller as can be.[23] The resydue off all my goodes not [fo. 162v] bequethyd nor gyffyn, I gyff unto Margery my wyff, whome I make my sole executrix, to bryng me unto the grounde, to pay my dettes and fulfyll my legaces, and receyve the dettes owyng to me, and so to dispose at her pleasure. I make Mr. Haryngton, esquyer, supervisor, and I gyff hym a sorrell amblyng geldyng for hys pane. Thes wytnes; Richerde Ogle the elder, gentilman,

---

[23] This would suggest a fairly substantial stone inside the church and in proximity to a specific location of significance to the testator, possibly near to the image of a particular saint.

Thomas Smyth, paryshe preste, Hugh Ordyng, Oswolde Stor, Robert Isaak, with other.

Proved before P at Spalding, 27 May 1533.

41.   JOHN BROWNE [OF LONG BENNINGTON]
[LCC 1532–34, fo. 153]

27 June 1532. I, John Browne of Long Benyngton, of a hole mynde and good remembraunce, under thys maner foloynge makes my testament and last will. Fyrste I bequethe my soule to God allmyghtty, and to Our Lady St. Mary and to all the holy cumpeny of heven. My body to be buryd in the churcheyerde of St. Swythune of Benyngton. To the high altare of Benyngton for forgottyn tithis xx*d* and a cowe. To Our Lady warke of Lincoln vj*d*. To the cawsy xx*d.* To the fen bryg iiij*d*. To the yong men gylde iiij*d*. To the churche of Benyngton vj*s* viij*d*. To Isabell Browne a qwye. To Thomas Browne a wane. [fo. 153v] To Isabell Parys a cowe. To Jenet Robynson a panne. To William Robynson a pare of yren galloys. To every one of Richerde Browne chylder a schepe. To every one of Robert Parys chylder a schepe. To Stephen Day ij bullokes, iiij quarter of barly and iiij horsse and marys. To Isabell my wyff ij oxgan of lande and a halff. The resydue of my goodes not gyvyn nor bequethyd I will it be devydyd in ij partes, one parte to my wyff and anoder parte to my selffe, and suche legaces as I have rehersyd afore and all my dettes to be payd of my parte. And the resydue of my parte I gyff and graunt to Stephyn Day. I will that Isabell my wyff and Richerde Browne and Robert Parys be my faythfull executors, that they may se my will be fullfyllyd and my dettes payd. I will that Richerd Browne and Robert Parys have for ther labors other of them iij*s* iiij*d*. Thes wytnes; Sir Robert Browne paryshe preste, William Pateman, Richerd Browne, with other mo.

Proved before P at Leadenham, 8 May 1533.

42.   ROBERT PAGE [OF BRATOFT]
[LCC 1532–34, fos. 34v–35r]

27 June 1532. I, Robert Page of Braytofte, with a hole and full mynde, makes thys my last will. Fyrst I bequethe my soule to allmyghtty God and Our Lady St. Mary and to all the saintes in heven, and my body to be buryed where it please allmyghty God and as the law will in the name of my mortuary. To Our Lady warke of Lincoln vj*d*. To the high altare of Gretham viij*d*. To the churche warkes of Wragby xx*d*. To [fo. 35r] the churche warke of Parteney xij*d*. To the churche of Tetforthe xij*d*. To the churche of Bag Enderby xij*d*. The resydue of all my goodes I put them to the disposicion of Thomas Page and John Page my bretherne, whome I make my executors. Thes beyng wytnes; Agnes Cowper, Catheryne Jakson.

Proved before P at Partney, 4 February 1532/3.

43.   JANE WRYGHT [OF GRIMOLDBY]
[LCC 1532–34, fo. 171r]

28 June 1532. I, Jane Wryght of Grymolby within the countie of Lincoln, beyng in hole mynde and good remembraunce, makes thys my testament and last will. Fyrst

I bequeth my soule to allmyghtty God, to Our Lady St. Mary and to all the cumpeny in heven, and my body to be buryd in the high ally of the churche of St. Edithe of Grymolby. And therfore the churche masters for the proffyt of the same churche to have vj*s* viij*d*. To Our Lady of Lincoln viij*d* and to her warke viij*d*. To the churche of Thurstrop xij*d*. To the churche of Sutton xij*d*. To the churche off Mablethorp xij*d*. To Agnes Wyat, doughter to Robert Wyat of Grymolby, a cofer, a sylver spone, a sylke rybbon. The resydue of my goodes I bequethe and gyff them to Sir Jamys Wryght, my brother, that he may order them as he thynkes moste necessary for the helthe of my soule. The whiche Sir Jamys Wright I constitute and make sole executor to thys my last will. In wytnes wheroff thes beyng present; John Kynyerby of Grymylby, Thomas Martyn of the same, Margaret Ranyarde of the same, Catheryne Thomson of the same, with other mo.

Proved before P at Gayton le Marsh, 15 July 1533.

44.   ALICE STELE [OF EVEDON]
       [LCC 1532–34, fo. 48r]

29 June 1532. I, Alice Stele of Evedon, hole of mynde and memory, makyth my testament and last will. Fyrst I bequethe my soule to allmyghtty God, to Our Lady St. Mary and to all the saintes in heven, and my body to be buryed in the churcheyerde of Evedon. To the high altare of Evedon for tithys forgottyn viij*d*. To Our Lady assumpsion in the high qwere a kowe to kepe a light before her every messe tyme, and the sayd cowe to be every yere at the lettyng of the churchewardons for xvj*d* be yere, be the oversight of my executor and supervisor. To Our Lady of Lincoln viij*d*, and to Our Lady warke ther viij*d*. To my curate halffe one acre wheate and also to the sayd curate to pray for me xx*d*. To Jenet Pechell my doughter ij coverlyttes, a matterys, iiij pilloys, vj schetes, ij borde clothys, ij brasse pottes, a gret panne and ij lyttyll pannys, v pewter dyshes, ij candylystykes, a hoche, a red chyste, a coffer, a table, a forme of led, a tob, a so, ij pelys the best and bygest, a kerne, a dyshe bynke, ij oxen, on flekyd and another brandyd, a cowe, a blak amblyng mare, a browne mare withowt felys, a seame wheate, ij seame barly, a seame peays and iiij schepe. To Margaret Stele a pare lyn schetes, a fombell schete, iiij yerdes lyn clothe, iiij schepe, a brokyn brasse potte, one olde panne, a lyttyll potte, a seame barly. To Alice Stele halff a seame barly. To Robert Stele the plugh and that that longyth therto, and ij seame barly. To John Stele a wayn and that that longyth therto, ij seames barly and a sallet. To William Stele a seame barly. To Richerd Stele my brother halffe a seame barly. To my syster Margaret my beste gowne, my beste kyrtell and a bushyll of wheate. To Richerd Gefferay ij stryke wheate and a bushyll barly. To my syster Alice Stele a seame wheate. I bequeth iij yerdes and a half clothe, to make a sepulchre clothe of. To Maryon my russyt gowne and my russyt kyrtell. To Jenet Pechell, Robert Stele and John Stele a pece of clothe to make every one of them a garment of. To Margaret Stele one garment bought. I will that ij oxin and ij marys be solde, and the money for them takyn I will be disposyd in one trentall doyng and other charitable dedes for my soule and all my frendes soulys. And with the resydue of all my goodes I will ther be yerely, so long as the sayd goodes shall laste, one obbyt kepte in the parysh churche of Evedon for the soulys of me and my husbande, at the discrestion and oversight of William Stele my brother, whome I make executor, and Bartilmew Ingoldesby, my curate, supervisor.

Thes wytnes; Sir Bartilmew Ingoldesby, parsone of Evedon, Richerd Stele, Robert Gregbe, William Gylys, Robert Merys, with other mo.

Proved before P at Lincoln, 9 July 1532, by the executor.

45.   ROBERT GAMMYLL [OF SWATON]
       [LCC 1532–34, fo. 80]

1 July 1532. I, Robert Gammyll of the parysh of Swaton in the countie of Lincoln, of good mynde and remembraunce, makes my last will. Fyrst I bequeth my soule to God allmyghtty and to the Gloriose Virgyn St. Mary, Hys mother, and to the holy cumpeny in heven, and my body to be buryed in the churche yerde of Swaton. To the high altare in Swaton iiij*d*. To Our Lady warke in Lincoln iiij*d* and towarde the mendyng of the way off Brygdyke iiij*d*. To Wylliam my sun a quarter barly and a qwye of ij yere olde. To Thomas my sun a quarter barly and a qwye of ij yere olde. I will the barly shall be delyveryd at Crystenmes and the qwyes att May Day to Robert Hosborneby, and he to put them furthe to ther moste proffyt unto the tyme that they be xviij yeres of age. I will that Robert Hosburneby have the garret chamber for to lay ther barly in, as long as my wyffe dwellys in the ferme of Mr. Wyllyamson's in Swaton. To Alice my doughter halff a quarter of barly, a ewe and a lambe. To Helene my doughter halffe a quarter of barly and a ewe and a lambe. To Johanne my doughter halffe a quarter of barly, a ewe and a lambe. I will that my wyff have the gydyng of my doughters and also of ther partes. I wyll that yff any of my chylder dye that the parte shall be devydyd emong them that lyffyth; and yff it chaunce that they all dye I will then that ther partes shall be delyveryd to the churche masters of Swaton chyrche, and they to kepe a yerely obyt [fo. 80v] for me and my chylder and all Crysten soulys, as Robert Hosborneby thynkes best. To Elizabeth my wyff the indenture of Loonsyon Lande, as long as she remaynys and dwellys in the towne of Swaton, but yff she flyt or be maryed owt of the towne of Swaton I wyll then that the indenture of the forsayd lande be solde and the money to be devydyd emong my chylder, the one halffe to my sonnys and the other halffe to my doughters. The resydue of my goodes not spokyn of before I wyt to Elizabeth my wyff, that she may dispose for the helthe of my soule as she thynkes best, and I make my wyff and Robert Parker of Screkynton full executors. Thes men beyng wyttenesses; Sir Thomas Smale, vicar, William Gammyll, Richerde Spynke, John Parker, Robert Hosburneby.

Proved before P at Laughton, 5 November 1532.

46.   WILLIAM LEE [OF ALGARKIRK]
       [LCC 1532–34, fos. 16v–17r]

4 July 1532. I, Wylliam Lee off Algarkyrke, husbandman, off hole mynd and good remembraunce, make, ordayn and constitute my last wyll and testament. Fyrst I geve and bequeythe my sowle to God almyghty, to Our Lady Sant Mary and to all the holy company off hevyn, and my body to be buryed in the chyrcheyeard off th'appostles Peter and [fo. 17r] Paule at Algarkyrke, with my mortuarye accordyng to the statute that now ys. To the hyght alter ther for tythes forgootton iiij*d*. To fower countible lyghtes ther viij*d*. To Our Lady off Lincoln iiij*d*. To the fatherles chyldren at Sant Katheryse ther ij*d*. Also yff Agnes my wyffe be with chyld I geve to

hyr my mensyon howse with the purtenance to the chyld and the heres of the body lawfully begootton, for ever. Yff nott I wyll that the forsayd howse with the mensyon remayn to the next off blode. Also I wyll that whose ever have my forsayd howse with the purtenance shal bestowe xij*d* yearly at Algarkyrke for my sowle and all Crystyn sowles, aftyr the dyscresyon off my executors. To Agnes my wyffe towe mylke ky and on fenne cowe att hyr electyon, and on mayre and a fole, also thre yoys with ther lames. Also all and syngular my howsehold stuff, on sawe, on stryke off berande wheytt, towe stryke off barly, towe stryke benys. To every on off my godbarnes on lame to be delyveryd att the Natyvitie of Saynt John Baptyst.[24] To Sybell my syster on calff, on lame, on royssett coyt and on smoke to be mayde to hyr bayke. To my mother Gryce on shepe hoge. To every on off my brother chyldryn on lame. The residue of all my guddes I geve to Jhon and Robert whome I make me executors, and other off them to have iij*s* iiij*d* for ther labar. Thyes wytnessys; Sir James Dugdayle, my gostly father, Thomas Baeke, Lambert Pantre off the same towne.

Proved before P at Lincoln, 26 July 1532, by the executors.

47.   BEATRICE WHITYNG [OF BURGH LE MARSH]
        [LCC 1532–34, fo. 37]

4 July 1532. I, Beatryx Whytyng of Burgh makyth my last [will]. Fyrst I bequethe my soule to allmyghtty God and to Our Lady St. Mary, and to all the hole cumpeny of heven, and my body to be buryed in the churcheyerde of St. Peter in Burgh. To the high altare of Burgh viij*d*. To Our Lady of Lincoln iiij*d*. To Henry Cokson of Burgh, for paying of my dettes, a fether bed, a coveryng, a pare of blankytes, a bolster, two pilloys, a pare of schetes and the bed stokes as they stand, too of the best brasse pottes and v schepe and three lammys, xij powndes of wolle, the best materys and the best coverlyd with the hyngyng laver. To Christofer Whytyng my sone thre quarters of wollyn clothe, the best posnet, a laver and a candylstyk and a chaffyng dyshe, a cownter, the best whyte coverlyd and a pare of schetes. To Isabell my doughter a pare of tonges and a pare of shetys, a materys, a red coverlyd and my best gowne, a kyrchyff, an appurne and fowre yerdes of hardyn clothe, a lyttyll spytt and a pare of cobbardes, and a candylstyk. To Jenet my doughtter all my hardyn garne and halffe my flakes, my best russyt gowne, my blak rybyn with sylver aglyttes, my best kyrchyff and my best aporne, my best spyt and a candylstyk, and my best slevys.[25] To Margaret my doughtter my best kyrtyll, a sylver spone, a kyrchyff and an appurne and the best rale, a lyttyll posnyt, a spruce coffer and halffe my flaxe, and iiij cushyns. To Jenet Whytyng a russyt gowne, a kyrchyff. To Dorothe her doughter a tawny kyrtill, a candylstyk and ij puter dooblers. To Mary Hall my best beades and my best gyrdell, a fether bed, a cobbarde and a chare and halff a dosyn of the best puter and all the payntyd clothys, too of the best candylstykes and my best cappe. Also yff ought cum to her within age then I will that Laurence Hall and Thomas Halle have it to devyd betwyxt them. To Elizabeth Carter a chyste, a borde and a forme, halffe a dosyn dyshes, halffe a dosyn trenschers and a pare of schetes, a materys, a pare of blak geate beades, a cappe and a kyrchyff, a panne, a brandryth and a candylstyk, and the thyrde brasse potte.

[24] 24 June.
[25] The sleeves of outer female costume were often made as separate pieces to facilitate cleaning.

To Thomas Hall a lyttyll chyste. To John Carter the fowrte brasse potte. To Austyn Carter a gret platter, a puter dyshe and a sawsser. To Laurence Hall a gret charger and a lattyn basyn. To William Meltham a lattyn laver and a sawsser. To Robert [fo. 37v] Symson a puter dyshe and too sawssers. The resydue of my goodes I will it be disposyd for the helthe of my soule and all my good frendes soulys, and to bryng me to the grounde by the oversyght of Christofer Whytyng whome I make my executor. These being witnesses; William Meltam, William Rysyll and John Thomson with other mo.

Proved before P at Alford, 5 February 1532/3.

48.   THOMAS HARDE [OF NORTH SOMERCOTES]
       [LCC 1532–34, fo. 77]

8 July 1532. I, Thomas Harde of Somercotes, mar[i]ne[r], hole of mynde and good memory beyng, makes my will. Fyrst I gyff my soule to God allmyghtty, to Hys mother St. Mary and to all saintes of heven. My body to be buryed in the kyrkeyerde of North Somercotes. To Our Lady warke of Lincoln xijd. To the high altare of North Somercotes for oblacions viijd. To the kyrke of North Somercotes iijs iiijd. To the kyrke of Cokryngton nexte Alvyngham vjd. I will ij trentall of messys be celebrat for the helthe of my soule and all my frendes soulys in North Somercotes kyrke. I will Agnes my wyff have ten yeres in the copy of my house that I wone in, with pasture and landes to it belongyng and all my stok of catall, she to bryng up and fynde my chylder the sayd ten yeres. And then aftyr the sayd ten yeres be fully endyt I will the forsayd coppy remayn to Thomas my sonne, and yff he decesse then to hys brother Edwarde. To Agnes my wyff the thyrde parte of my goodes. To Thomas my sonne my plough, my wayn, harroys and all suche thynges to the plough belongyng, one ambry, a bed stok beyng in the chamber, a gret brasse potte: he to have thes thynges when he cumys at lefull age. To Richerde Haryit one lamme. To every godbarne of myne beyng onelyve iiijd. All the resydue of my goodes not wytt nor gyffyn, I will they be equally devydyd to my iiij chylder, they to have ther partes when they cum at leful age. And yff any of the sayd chylder decesse or they cum at lefull age, then I will that chylde parte be devydyd to them onelyve, alowance to be takyn of that chylde parte for beryall. Executors of thys my hole and laste will I make Agnes my wyff and John Gunnylde of Strete. Thes wytnes; Sir William Hornse, chapland, Thomas Langton, Thomas Hornse.

   Proved before P at Louth, 15 October 1532. Adm. granted to Agnes, the relict, reserving power to grant to John Gunnylde, co-executor.

49.   JOHN SNARRY [OF SOUTH SOMERCOTES]
       [LCC 1532–34, fos. 80v–81v]

8 July 1532. I, John Snarrey of South Somercotes Peter, yoman, beyng hole of mynde and good remembraunce, makyth thys my last will. Fyrst I gyff my soule to God allmyghtty, to Our Lady St. Mary, and to all the saintes in heven, and my body to be buryed in the churche of St. Peter of Somercotes. To the high altare xijd. To Our Lady altare xijd. To St. Thomas altare viijd. To the cathedrall churche of Lincoln xxd. To Mr. Parsone of Somercotes Peter xxs. To the churche of Somercotes Peter xls. To the reparacion of the caussys to the same churche xls. I

will that one honest prest syng and say messe in the churche of Somercotes at St. Thomas altare the space of one yere, and he to have for hys stipende, to bred, wyne and wax, v*l*, and he to say iij days in the weke duryng the hole yere, *de profundis* at my grave for my soule and all Crysten soulys.[26] I will that penny dole be delte for my soule the day of my buryng, at my vijth day fyve markes, at my thyrty day fyve markes, and at my yere day fyve markes. To Agnes my wyff xx^{ty} markes, iij kye, xx^{ty} schepe beyng yowys, one bay amblyng mere with her fole, with halffe my housholde stuff and one acre off wheate, one acre of barly and one acre of benys. And she to have her dwellyng where John Foddyll dwellyth so long as she [fo. 81r] kepeth her sole. And yff she will not dwell in that house, my heyres to gyff her vj*s* viij*d* yerly, she beyng sole. To Alice my doughter xl^{ty} poundes, ij waynes, ij yren harroys, one plough and all the gere that to them belongyth with the other halffe of my housholde stuff and iiij oxen, ij mares, iiij kye, x acres of wheate, x acres of benys and iij acres of barly. To Roger Mylner xl*s*. To John Foddyll one acre of benys, to hys wyff vj*s* viij*d*, and to every one of hys chylder one schepe. To Jennet my syster and Thomas her sone xiij*s* iiij*d*. To my syster wyff to Thomas Lee vj*s* viij*d*. To the sayd Thomas and hys doughter ij schepe. To William Elvys ij yowys. To Helene hys syster one yowe. To Henry Mylner and Margaret hys syster ij yowys. To John Garman one schepe. To John Crosbe ij yewes and ij lammys and my lether dooblet. To Alice hys doughter ij yowes and ij lammys. To John Cole and William Plome xx^{ty} schepe that is at Belcheforthe. To William Andarson v yewes, fyve lammys. To Robert Whyte ij yowes, ij lammys. To Jenet my servant one yowe and one lamme. To every one of my godchyldren one schepe. To William Watson, sone of John, one schepe. To iij sonnys of Thomas Cole iij schepe. To hys iiij doughters iiij lammys. To Thomas Cole and Brydgyd hys syster ij schepe. To ij sonnys of Jenet Frankes ij lammys. To William Cole and hys wyff iiij schepe, one dooblet of woorstyd with my best lether jerkyn. To John Horsfaull vj*s* viij*d*, and xx*s* for hys father Wytwoode. To George and Anthony, sonnys to Master Edward Madyson, xxvj*s* viij*d*. To the churche of Somercotes Mary viij*d*. To the churche of Skydbroke xx*d*. To the churche of Conysholm iiij*d*. To the churche of Garnethorp vj*d*. To the churche of Grymylbe iiij*d*. To the churche of St. Leonerde of Cokryngton iiij*d*. To the churche of Cokryngton Mary iiij*d*. To the churche of Barton viij*d*. To the churche of Owsbe iiij*d*. To the churche of Brokelesbe iiij*d*. To the churche of Keleby iiij*d*. To the churche of Asby iiij*d*. To the churche of Howerby iiij*d*. To the churche of Cawthorp iiij*d*. To the churche of Conham iiij*d*. To the churche of Yerburgh iiij*d*. To the churche of Alvyngham iiij*d*. The resydue of my goodes [fo. 81v] I gyff frely to Alice my doughter, Thomas Dente and Edmunde Kendall, whome I make my full executors. And Master Edwarde Madyson to be supervisor of the same, to se it fullfyllyd, and he to have xx*d*. And ether executor, Thomas and Edmunde, for ther labor to have vj*s* viij*d*. Thes whytnes; Sir Robert Anderton, preste, John Fraunces, Walter Graunt and Thomas Lee, with other mo. Thys is the last will of me John Snarry, mayd the day and yere abovesayd. To Alice my doughter all my landes with my coppyholdes and my indenturys that I have in the lordeschyps of Somercotes and Skydbroke, to her and the heyres of her body laufully begottyn. And in defawte of heyres of her body laufully begottyn, I will it remane to the next of my blode accordyng to the custome of the cuntry. Also I will my heyres deale, or cause to be

---

[26] *De Profundis*, 'from the depths', was one of the seven penitential psalms, and formed a central part of the Office of the Dead: Duffy, *Stripping of the Altars*, 369.

delte, every Fryday in Lent for evermore, v*d* in bred to be gyffyn to pore folke, and the parysh preste for sayng dirige and messe iiij*d*, with one messe penny. And the churchewardons to se it done, and it to be takyn of one close of iij acres lying at the fenhouse. Also I will that Alice my doughter gyff to Agnes Snarrey, my mother, every yere duryng her lyff, viij*s*, with house rowme where sche dwellyth. And for lak of that payment I will that she or her assygnes strene of my grounde that she hathe that I am now possessyd off. Geven the day and yere abovesayd.

Proved before P at Lincoln, 7 November 1532.

50.　　　HELEN HOWET [OF INGOLDSBY]
　　　　　[LCC 1532–34, fo. 53v]

9 July 1532. I Helene Howet, seke in body and hole in mynde, make my last will and testament. Fyrst I bequeth my soule to allmyghtty God, to Hys blessyd mother St. Mary and to all the holy cumpeny of heven, and my body to be buryed wythin the paryshe churcheyarde of St. Androy of Ingoldesby. To our mother churche of Lincoln vj*d*. To the high altare of Ingoldesby vj*d*. I will to be done for me v messys att Scala Celi. To the chylder of Thomas Howet emong them one schepe. To Elizabeth my doughter the best panne. To Helene my doughter the best potte. To Margaret my doughter the myddell potte. I bequethe for to kepe one obbyt yerly for the soulys of Robert Howet and Helene at the Visitacion of Our Lady x*s*.[27] And to be payd at thys obbyt to the paryshe preste for dirige and messe iiij*d*, the clerk ij*d*, the offeryng ij*d*. To the reparacion of the bellys iiij*d* and the ryngers ij*d*. And all the resydue of my goodes I putt them in the handes of William Elsam, Simon Elsam and Thomas Howet, whome I make my full executors, and to have for ther pannys and labor xx*s*. Thes beryng wytnes; Sir Thomas Hacton, William Wylmore, John Tode, with many other.

Proved before P at Lincoln, 23 August 1532, by the executors.

51.　　　JOHN STOTTE [VICAR OF LISSINGTON]
　　　　　[LCC 1532–34, fo. 53r]

13 July 1532. I, John Stotte off Lyssyngton, vicare, of a hole mynde savyng seke in body, makes my testament. Fyrst I bequethe my soule to God allmyghtty, to Our Lady St. Mary, and to all the gloriose cumpeny in heven. My body to be buryed in the quere afore St. John Baptiste in Lyssyngton. To Our Lady warke of Lincoln xij*d*. To the high altare of the same place xij*d*. To the iiij orderes of frerys of the same, iche on off them singulerly, a bushyll of barly. To Howton kyrke, to Wykynby kyrke, to Lynwoode kyrke, to Leggesby kyrke, iche on of them singulerly, xij*d*. To Kelsay kyrke Nicholes iij*s* iiij*d*. To St. Mary kyrke of the same xij*d*. To Westburgh kyrke ij*s*. To ych on of my godchylder iiij*d*. To Dane William Holme of Louth Parke, my godsun, xij*d*. To Margaret Hamonde in peny and penyworthe xl*s*. To Mr. Commissary a yong horse. To Jenet Stotte a yowe and a lamme, and to Elizabeth her syster a yowe, Robert Stotte doughters. To ich on of my systers a schepe. To Robert Lowdon a schepe. To William Neyffe, Thomas Neyffe sonne a schepe. To Alice Mylner in penny and pennyworthe xx*s*. To

Elizabeth Mylnes a schepe. To John Mylnes and William hys brother other of them a schepe. To Robert Mylnes a yowe and a lamme. To John Grenesmyth vj*s* viij*d*, a quarter malte and a lamme. To Robert Yerburgh vj*s* viij*d* and a quarter of malte. To the parsone of Teryngton a sylver spone and a tepyt. To William Lowdon and Thomas Neyff, other of them, a quarter of malte. To the vicare of Westburgh my better blake gowne. I will have a prest to syng for me ij yere and it may be borne. To the kyrke off Lyssyngton a quarter of malte. The resydue of my goodes, I bequeth them to Thomas Wollerdby of North Wyllyngham, vicare, and to Robert Lesyng of Westeryngton, yoman, whome I orden my executors. Thes beyng wytnes; Sir Thomas Davyson, prest, Thomas Neyff the elder, Thomas Goderson and Henry Toynton, with other mo.

Proved before P at Lincoln, 2 August 1532, by the executors.

52. WILLIAM SWALLYS [OF MUMBY]
[LCC 1532–34, fo. 77v]

17 July 1532. I, William Swallys of Mumby, with my hole mynde and good remembraunce, make my testament. Fyrste I bequethe my soule to allmyghtty God, to Our Lady St. Mary, and to all the holy cumpeny in heven, and my body to be buryed in the churchyerde of the churche of Mumby, with my mortuary that the lawe will. To Our Lady of Lincoln xx*d*. To the churche of Mumby xx*d*. To the chapell of St. Leanerde iij*s* iiij*d*. To the churche of Hoggesthorpe xij*d*. To Catheryne and Rose my doughters xiij*l* vj*s* viij*d*. To every one of my godchyldren iiij*d*. I bequeth xxvj*s* viij*d* to a preste to pray for my soule. To Margaret Swete a yowe and to iij of her chyldren iij lammys. To Helene Swalys a yowe and to her iiij chyldren iiij lammys. To Agnes Barbur a yowe and to her iij chyldren iij lammys. To Isabell Wellys a yowe and to ij of her chyldren ij lammys. To Richerd Swallys ij lammys. To George Swallys ij lammys. To Christofer Yong a lamme. To Catheryne Yong a lamme. To my wyff halffe my goodes within and withowt the costes and chargys of my will fulfyllyd yff she mary, and yff she mary not, she shall have all at her liberte. And yff she do mary then the other parte of my goodes shall be disposyd for my soule, to have a preste a quarter of a yere. And that that dothe remayn further I bequeth to my vj chyldren, every one elyke muche. To my sonne Robert Swallys my horse mylne, of that condicion that he shall not sell it. And yff he sell it I will that Thomas Swallys have it for xxxiij*s* iiij*d*. Also I make my ij sonnys Thomas Swallys and Robert Swallys my executors. Thes men beyng wytnes; Sir William Huntte, Robert Swete and John Smyr, and other.

Proved before P at Alford, 16 October 1532.

53. THOMAS GUDSON [OF GREAT HALE]
[LCC 1532–34, fo. 91v]

18 July 1532. I, Thomas Gudson of Gret Hale, of a hole mynde and good remembraunce, makes my last will. Fyrst I bequethe my soule to God allmyghtty, and Our Lady St. Mary and to all the holy cumpeny of heven, and my body to be buryed within the churcheyerde of St. John Baptiste of Gret Hale, and for my mortuary that at the lawe dothe admyt. To the altare for tithys forgottyn xij*d*. To Mr. Vicare to pray for me ij*s*. To St. John Baptist light xij*d*. To St. Catheryn altare

vj*d*. To Our Lady's altare vj*d*. To St. Margaret vj*d*. To Ihesus light iiij*d*. To our Lady's warke of Lincoln iiij*d*. The resydue of my goodes I gyff to Alyson my wyff, whome I make my full executrix that she may dispose for the helthe of my soule as she thynkes the best. Thes beyng wytnes; Mr. Vicar, Sir John Johnson, William a Kyrton, Thomas a Kyrton, with other mo.

Proved before P at Donington, 18 February 1532/3.

54.   RICHARD FEWE [OF ASTERBY]
        [LCC 1532–34, fo. 54]

25 July 1532. I, Richerd Few off Asterby, of good and hole mynde do make my last [fo. 54v] will. Fyrst I bequeth my soule to almyghtty God and to Our Blessyd Lady St. Mary, and to all the holy cumpeny of heven, and my body to be buryd within the churcheyerde of St. Peter of Asterby. To the high altare ij schepe. To the churche one schepe. To Our Lady of Lincoln warke iiij*d*. The residue of my goodes I gyff to Jenet my wyff whome I make myn executrix and the parsone to be oversear, and they to dispose them for my soule, my father soule, my mother soule and all Crysten soulys. Wytnes; Dominus Robertus Halsal, rector, Willelmus Gebun, Johannes Stutt.

Proved before P at Horncastle, 1 October 1532.

55.   WILLIAM ALCOCKE [OF UTTERBY]
        [LCC 1532–34, fo. 39r]

26 July 1532. I, William Alcoke of Utterby, beyng of hole mynde and good remembraunce, make my testament and last will. Fyrste I bequethe my soule to God allmyghtty, Our Lady St. Mary and to all the holy compeny of heven. My body to be buryed in the churcheyerde of Utterby. To Our Lady's warke of Lincoln vj*d*. To Our Lady of Lincoln vj*d*. To the paryshe churche of Utterby iij*s*. To the high altare in the same churche iiij*d*. To the paryshe of Foterby viij*d*. To the paryshe church of South Somercotes vj*d*. To the high altare in the same churche vj*d*. To the paryshe churche of North Somercotes vj*d*. To the high altare in the same churche vj*d*. To Our Lady of Pety in Louthe churche iiij*d*. To Jenet my wyff all my ferme, bothe felde and towne, and she to bere all the charges therof. Also one plughe and vj bestes therto as one cople oxen and iiij marys with all thyng therto belongyng. And also all my housholde stuff within dorys, and she to gyff my ij chylder, Agnes and Dorothe, xx*s* for ther parte of the householde. To Thomas my sonne one plough and one waine, one yren harrowe and one cople oxen and ij marys and ther folys, and x schepe, also x quarters barly and one chalder beanys. To Agnes my doughter iij*l*, and unto my doughtter Dorothy iij*l* to be takyn of Bramton wyff of Louthe. To Agnes my doughtter one cowe in the holdyng of William Patryk and ij*s* viij*d* of the cowe hyer. To William Westerne one cople sterys and one quarter barly, and one quarter beanys. To the churche of Utterby one cowe. To the bying off one banner clothe to the churche of Utterby one quarter wheate and to Our Lady gylde in the same churche one quarter barly in the handes of John Grave. To William Marchande ij schepe and ij*s* iiij*d* in the handes of John Northe of Marche Chapell. To the doyng for me and my frendes one trentall x*s*. To John Croftes my sonne-in-lawe a quarter barly remanyng in the handes of John Grayff of South Ormesby. To

Agnes and Dorothe my douthers one cople oxen remayng in the handes of John Croftes and he to kepe them to the behoyff off my doughtters iij yeres aftyr my decesse yff he do well to them. The resydue of my goodes I will that my brother Roger and my sonne Thomas, whome I make my executors, dispose for the helthe of my soule by the syght of Sir John Smyth supervisor; and my brother Roger to have for hys labor iijs iiijd and Sir John Smyth iijs iiijd. Thes men beyng wytnes; John Brege, Gilbarde Croftes and John Crofftes, with other mo.

Proved before P at Louth, 6 February 1532/3.

56.   JOHN BURTON [OF GRANTHAM]
[LCC 1532–34, fo. 85]

28 July 1532. I, John Burton of Grantham, holle of mynde and of good remembraunce, make my testament. Firste I beqwerre my soll to allmyghty God, Our Lady Saynte Mary, and to all the cumpeny of heven. My body to be buriyd in the churcheyarde of Grantham. To the hye auter of Saynt Wulfrane in Grantham xijd. To Our Lady of Lincoln iiijd. To Our Lady [fo. 85v] warke in Lincoln iiijd. To thei hye auter of Harlaston xijd. To thei hye auter of Spraxton xijd. To thei frerys of Grantham ijs. I wyll that Alys my wyffe have all hyr one goods and stuffe that schee had afor I marryd hyr or ellys the valur thereof, and the thirde parte of all my goodes both croppe and catell. To Thomas Burton a cartte, ij bullokes, iij horsis, a mare with all the harnys and a plowe. I beqwerr to Androwe Burton iiij sterrys, iij horsys, a wayne and a plowe with all the gerres. I wyll that William Amor have the oversyght and gydyng of Thomas Burbage, son and eyre of Thomas Burbage lately decessid, at Barrobe, with all maner goodes freely gyffen unto hym by the last wyll and testament of thei sayd Thomas Burbage hys father for thei space of vij yeres after my decesse immediatly. Thei residue of my goodes not beqwerid I gyff them to Alis my wyffe and Thomas Burton whome I make my executors, and William More supervisor. Thes beryng wittnesse; Sir Richard Shepard, Sir Thomas Newton, with moo.

Proved before P at Lincoln, 13 December 1532.

57.   SIR ROBERT LEEDES [OF WIGTOFT]
[LCC 1532–34, fo. 1]

31 July 1532. I, Robert Leedes, priest, of Wygtofte in the countie of Lincoln, hole of remembraunce, make my testament and last will. Fyrste I bequethe my soule to allmyghtty God, Our Lady St. Mary, and all the angellys and saintes of heven. My body to be buryed in the paryshe churche where it shall please God. I bequethe for my mortuary as the lawe requiryth. To the high altare of Swyneshed iiijd. To the bellys where it shall please God that I lye xijd. To Our Lady warkes of Lincoln xijd. To every servant of Master Thomas Hollande, my master, beyng in wages of meate and drynke, xijd. To every godchylde a lambe or xvjd. To the churche in Thurlby in Morelande xxd. To the paryshe preste of the same to say dirige and messe of requiem for my soule and to reherse my soule in hys bead rowlle the space of one yere, viijd. To every house in the same towne not kepyng husbandry iiijd. To the paryshe of Bassyngham xxd. To the paryshe preste of the same viijd. To every house of the same towne not kepyng husbandry iiijd. To the paryshe churche of Carleton

in Morelande iij*s* iiij*d*. To the curate of the same to say dirige and messe of requiem for my soule, and to reherse my soule in hys bead rowlle the space of one yere, viij*d*. To every house in the same towne not kepyng husbandry iiij*d*. To the paryshe churche of Brant Broughtton x*s*. To the paryshe preste of the same to say dirige and messe of requiem for my soule, and to reherse my soule in hys beade rowlle the space of one yere, viij*d*. To every house in the same towne not kepyng husbandry iiij*d*. The resydue of my goodes not gyffyn nor bequethyd I gyff to Willum Clerke and Robert Maver of Carleton in Morelande, whome I make my executors, that they may dispose them for the helthe of my soule. And the sayd Willum and Robert and ether of them to have for there paynstakyng xj*s* iij*d*, and my master, Mr. Thomas Hollande to be supervisor, and to have for hys labor the red colte that cam of my bay mare. Also I will that they have all ther expenses and charges allowyd of the hole whatsoever they be. I gyff my house, hempelande and pasture in Quadryng Edyke, which that my master Thomas Hollande dyd bye for me off Robert Wright of Donyngton, whiche is in the yere the clere valure xiij*s* j*d*, to Robert Mawer [fo. 1v] of Carleton in Morelande and to hys heyres of hys body laufully begottyn, to kepe one obyt for me and for the soule of Richerde Ledes and Alice, with Richard Colson and Jenet, yereley to the value of iij*s* ij*d*, and the other ij*s* vj*d* to be disposyd emonges pore people of Good Fryday. And the resydue, vj*s* v*d* to go to reparacions of the sayd house and to hys use. And yff the sayd Robert Mawer dye withowt issue of hys body laufully begottyn, then I will that it remayn to the use of Agnes Mawer, hys syster, and to the heyres of her body laufully begottyn, kepyng the sayd obyt as is aforesayd. Also I gyff and bequethe to Masterys Isabell Herdeby my lesse qwye that I have. To Thomas Bell a yong colte of ij yere olde which was of my blake meyre. To Richerde Shepperde of Quadryng xij*d*. Moreover I will that my sayd tenemente, lande and pasture with ther appurtenances in Quadryng Edyke shall remayn in the handes of my feoffees, to ther heyres and assygnes, and to the use and performacion of thys my last will; and for the sure kepyng of my sayd obyt, expendyng theruppon as is aforesaid, to be kepte in the paryshe churche off Brant Broughtton the xx^{ty} day of Apryll or within iij days foloyng yerely duryng the lives of the sayd Robert Mawer and hys heyres, and the sayd Agnes Mawer and her heyres. And yff it fortune the sayd Robert or any of hys heyres, or the sayd Agnes or any of her heyres, negligently to fall in kepyng of my sayd obyt any yere here aftyr within the forsayd vij days, I will that then the alderman of the gylde of the Holy Trinite foundyd in the sayd churche of Brant Broughtton and hys succesor for the tyme beyng, shall entre in my sayd tenement, lande and pasture with ther appurtenances, and there to take the rentes and proffyttes therof that yere, and therwith to kepe my obyt in forme aforesayd, and so to do yerely as ofte as the sayd Robert Mawer and Agnes, or eny of theyr heyres shall fale in kepyng of my sayd obyt, withowt any let or gaynstandyng of theym or any of theyr heyres hereaftyr. Thes beyng wytnes; Sir Robert Smyth, Robert Knot, Richerde Carter and Richerd Whytlame.

Proved before P at Grantham, 13 January 1532/3. Adm. granted to the executors.

58. THOMAS TEDDE [OF CONINGSBY]
[LCC 1532–34, fo. 51]

4 August 1532. I, Thomas Tedde of Conesby, beyng of an hole mynde and perfyte remembraunce, make my testament and last will. Fyrst I gyff and bequeth my soule to allmyghtty God, to Our Lady St. Mary and to all the blessyd cumpeny in heven, and my body to be buryed in the churche of St. Michel in Conesby. To Our Lady warke of Lincoln vj*d*, and to St. Anne vj*d*. To the high altare of Conesby for ungottyn tithis vj*d*. To Our Lady altare of the same churche vj*d*. To All Soulys' light vj*d*. To Ihesus qwere one punde wax. To the light of St. Anne vj*d*. To the light of St. Margarete vj*d*. To the light of St. Catheryne ij*d*. To the light of St. Helene ij*d*. To the light of St. Sithe ij*d*. To the light of St. Anthony ij*d*. To the light of St. Jamys iiij*d*. To every gylde in the sayd churche of Conesby vj*d*. I wyll that Sir John Cooke and Thomas Cottes, myn executors, shall fynde one prest to syng for my soule and all Crsyten soulys one quarter of one yere in the parysh churche of Hyndelby. I gyff towarde one dirige the day of my buryeng v*s*. To the sustentacion of Ihesus preste in Conesby iij*s* iiij*d*. To my wyff ij kye and all the housholde stuff that was her awne, x yowes and one gray amblyng mare. To William Freston of Conesby my carte and one red mare with a colte fole, and x yowes. To every chylde of the sayd William Freston vj*s* viij*d*. To Alice Freston my mayd one burlyng. To Isabell Pepper my syster vj*s* viij*d*, and to Agnes Smyth xl*s*. To Libeus Tedde one burlyng, and to every one of my godchyldren iiij*d*. To yong Scherpe of Grebby, my kynsman, vj*s* viij*d*, and to every chylde of my wyffe's ij*s*. The resydue of my goodes I committ to the discrecion of Sir John Cooke and Thomas Cottes, whome I have mayd my executors, that they, for my soule helthe and all other of my benefactors, dispose the reste of my goodes in charitable warkes, to the pleasur of God and proffyt of my soule, and off my benefactor soulys, as they shall juge beste to be disposyd. I make Mr. William Mason supervisor, and to every one of them for ther paynes vj*s* viij*d*. [fo. 51v] And of thys my last will and testament I desyre and take to wytnes Mr. Thomas Hughetson, Sir William Porter, John Askewe and Thomas Waryng, with all other wych all the tyme of thys my last will and testament where present.

Proved before P at Lincoln, 20 September 1532, by the executors.

59. WILLIAM BLYSBERY [OF BROTHERTOFT IN PARISH OF KIRTON IN HOLLAND]
[LCC 1532–34, fos. 69v–70r]

8 August 1532. I, William Blysbery off Brothertofte and off the parysh of Kyrton,[28] makes my last will. Fyrst I bequeth to allmyghtty God, to Our Lady St. Mary and to all the holy cumpeny of heven my soule, and my body to be buryed in the parysh churcheyerde of St. Peter of Kyrton. To our holy mother churche of Lincoln iiij*d*. To the fatherles chylder of St. Catheryn's ij*d*. To the high altare of Kyrton xij*d*. To Maryon my wyff the copy of my house for vj yere, and she to kepe it in reparacions and to leve it as good as she doth fynde it, and aftyr to remayn to Richerd my sun. I will that John my brother be oversear to my sonne comme to laufull age, and yff

---

[28] The wills produced by testators dwelling in Brothertoft would suggest that the area was divided between the parishes of Kirton in Holland, Frieston and Wyberton.

ought cum at my sun that then the cope to remayn to John my brother. To Richerd my sonne my browne mere and her fole, and a stagge and v schepe, and a yong qwye. To Agnes my doughter a burlyng and iiij schepe. To Margaret my doughter a calve and ij schepe. To my brother John my best gowne. To nevue Richerd my best dooblet. The resydue off my goodes I gyff to Marion my wyff [fo. 70r] whome I make my executrice for to dispose for the welthe of my soule and to bryng up my chylder. Wytnes theroff; Richerd Blysbery and Michel Tunerde, Dane Otewell, chanon.

Proved before P at Boston, 9 October 1532.

60. ROGER WALKWID [OF LUDDINGTON]
[Stow 1530–52, fo. 14r]

9 August 1532. I, Roger Walkwid, of hol mynd and gud remembrans, make my will. Fyrst I gyffe and wytt my saule to almyghty God and to Our Blissit Lade Sant Mare and to all the blissit compane in hevyn, and my bode to be beryd in the churcheyarde of Luddyngton. To the hye alter in Luddyngton for forgettyn tithes xijd, and to Our Lade of Lincoln viijd. To the vicar of Luddyngton the best cowe that I have in my clows that he may pray for me. To Agnes my wyffe foure of my beste marys as she will take ande the best plugh and the best cart with the gere to tham besyd executor part. The residew I gyffe to Agnes my wiffe and to Thomas and Elsabeth my childer, whom I make myn executors. Wytnes herof; Sir Robert Clerke, vicar of Luddington, Sir George Jonson, William Walkewyd and Richard Uttyng.

Proved before L, 17 December 1532. Adm. granted to the executors.

61. THOMAS CARTER [OF ASTERBY]
[LCC 1532–44, fo. 54r]

10 August 1532. I, Thomas Carter of Asterby, good and hole of mynde, do make my laste will. Fyrst I bequeth my soule to allmyghtty God, and to Our Blessyd Lady and to all the holy cumpeny of heven, and my body to be buryed within the churche of St. Peter of Asterby. To Our Lady of Lincoln xijd. To the high altare in Asterby churche one schepe. To the sayd churche iiij schepe. To Calkewell churche viijd. To Asterby churche vjs viijd. To Scamelesby churche viijd. To Golceby churche iiijd. To Stanygote churche iiijd. To Henry my sonne viij schepe, one cople sterys, one horse and iiij quarters barly. To Alice my doughter one cowe and x schepe. To John my sonne one cople sterys and x schepe. To Elizabeth my doughter one cowe and x schepe. To Agnes my doughter one cowe and x schepe. To Thomas my sonne ij calvys and x schepe. To Henry my brother one horse. To Margaret my syster iij schepe. To Margery Halyfax one calffe. To Richerd Rysse ij quarters barley. To John my brother iijs iiijd. I will that yff any of my chyldren dye within laufull age then hys parte or hers to be devydyd emong the other. The resydue of my goodes I gyff to Alice my wyff. I make my executors John my brother, Alice my wyff and Richerd Rysse, they to dispose them for the helthe of my sone,[29] my father soule, my mother soule and all Crysten soulys, and the parsone to be supervisor. Wytnes;

---

[29] Read 'soule'.

Dominus Robertus Halsall, rector, Richard Risse, John Carter, William Barton, William Frysnay, with other moo.

Proved before P at Horncastle, 1 October 1532.

62. WILLIAM FORESTE [OF BROTHERTOFT IN PARISH OF WYBER-TON]
[LCC 1532–34, fos. 19v–20r]

11 August 1532. I, William Foreste of Brotherstofte and off the paryshe of Wyberton, with a hole mynde, makes my testament and last will. Fyrste I bequethe my soule to allmyghtty God, to Our Lady St. Mary, and to all the saintes in heven. My body to be buryd in St. Leogerde churcheyerde of Wyberton. To the high altare of Wyberton churche for all forgottyn tithes xijd, and to St. Leogerde iiijd. To Our Lady of Lincoln iiijd. To the fatherles chylder of St. Catheryn's ijd. To John my sun a colte fole that is of burde, my mayr and my best saddyll and brydyll, and my best cotte and dooblet, and my best cappe. To Helene my daughter iij kye and a blak mayr and her fole. To John my brother my russyt cote and my russyt hose, and my warkyn day [fo. 20r] dooblet, and my russyt felte hatte. To my wyff the copy of my house for the terme of her lyffe, and aftyr her decesse to dispose it to my ij doughters, that is for to say Alice and Helene. I will that Helene, my doughter, yff she mary with a yong man that have no house of hys owne to bryng her to, she for to have the house and for to gyff Alice my doughter xls. Also yff she mary with a yong man that have a house of hys owne to bryng her to, then Alice my doughter for to be in chose wether she will take the house and gyff Helene xls, or forsake the house and take xls of Helene and be discharged. To my wyff my lande frely to gyff or sell and for to do with it what she will. The resydue of my goodes not set I put them to the disposicion of Jenet my wyff, whome I do orden my executor for to dispose to the moste plesure of god and proffyt of my soule and all my good frende soulys, and for to do for me as she wolde and shulde do for her. Wytnes therof; John Skynner, Jenkyn Laurenson, Richerde Mableson.

Proved before P at Boston, 9 October 1532.

63. THOMAS GRANGE [OF HIGH TOYNTON]
[LCC 1532–34, fo. 55]

19 August 1532. I, Thomas Grange of Over Tynton in the countie of Lincoln, beyng hole of mynde and off good remembraunce, makes thys my last will and testament. In the fyrst I gyff and bequeth my soule unto allmyghtty God and to Our Lady St. Mary, and to all the saintes in heven, and my body to be buryd in the churchyerd of St. John Baptist of Over Tynton. To the high altare of the same churche for oblacions forgottyn xxd. To Our Lady of Lincoln xijd. To Our Lady warkes of Lincoln viijd. To the church warkes of Over Tynton iijs iiijd. To the church of Nether Tynton xijd. To the churche of Maryng xijd. To the churche of Scrafelde iiijd. To the churche of Gretham iiijd. I will and bequeth to Sir Martyn Rose, my curate, xs to pray for my soule and all my frende soulys. To Margaret my wyff iiij oxen, ij horsse, ij kye and xxty schepe. To Agnes my doughter iiij oxen, ij horsse, ij kye, xxxty schepe. To Isabell my syster vjs viijd. To Thomas Stor vjs viijd. To John Tole my servant a qwy, a yoke, a teame, and a pare of horsse gerys. To as many

godchyldren as I have onlyff, to every one of them a lamme. To every wyff that was
with me thys nyght, every one of them iiij*d*. To Humfray wyff xij*d*. To Margaret my
wyff the convent seale that I holde of the house of Revesby duryng the terme of her
lyff, and aftyr her decease I will that Agnes my doughter have it to hyr and her
heyres of her body laufully begottyn. And yff the sayd Agnes departe thys worlde
withowt suche issue, I will that it be solde and disposyd [fo. 55v] for the helthe of my
soule and all Crysten soulys. To Sir Martyn Rose, my curate, xx*d*, whome I put in
trust to se that thys my last will be well fulfyllyd. The resydue of all my goodes I gyff
to Margaret my wyff and Agnes my doughter, evenly to be devydyd betwyxt them
too at the sight of Sir Martyn Rose my curate, and the sayd Margaret my wyff and
Agnes my doughter I make my executors to dispose and performe thys my last will
to the helthe of my soule and all Crysten soulys. In wytnes heroff; Sir Martyn Rose,
my curate, Simon Eve, William Hurd and Thomas Umfray, with other mo.

Proved before P at Horncastle, 1 October 1532.

64.   ROBERT GUNNYLL [OF SPALDING]
          [LCC 1532–34, fos. 17v–18r]

22 August 1532. I, Robert Gunylle of Spaldyng, beyng holle off mynde and off gud
remembraunce, make this my testament and last will. Fyrst I bequethe my sowle to
God almyghty, to Our Lady Sant Mary and to all the celestyall company in hevyn,
my body to be buryed in the chyrche off our Lady off Sant Nycholas in Spaldyng,
befoore Sent Gorge auter. To the high auter of Spaldyng for tithys forgottyn xij*d*. To
Sant Kateryn's withoute the walles off Lincoln viij*d*. To every gyld and devocion in
Spaldyng iiij*d*. I wyll have a prest syng for me and my wyffe a yere in the chyrche off
Spaldyng wythein the space of x yeres folowyng. To the chyrche warke off Cowbytt
iij*s* iiij*d*. To John Gunyll my sone my howse att Cowbytt chyrche with ij acars pastur
therto belongyng paying yerly to Agnes Gunyll my wyffe xx*s* the terme off hyr lyffe,
and after her dethe ytt to remeyn frely to John Gunyll my sone. I wyll that John
Gunylle have my howse att Drove's End in Cowbytt with ij acars pastur therto
belongyng callyd Eggys, also a pastur at Skes Hylle off vj acars, and an halffe acare
in Spaldyng Drove and a pastur of v acars in the same Drove, and in Tharnam
Drove a pastur off iij acars, and in Stonne Gatte a pastur off iij acars and a howltt off
wode in Mylln Gatte, to hym and hys heres off hys body laufully begootton. And yff
ytt so happen the forsayd John to dy withoute heres off hys body, then the howsys
and pastures shall be solde by the wyll off my executors or elles by ther executors,
and the mony theroff takyn to be disposyde in chyrche warkes, hyyways, prestys
syngyng and other dedys off charyte in the towne off Spaldyng and Cowbytt. To
James Hydone my howse att Drove's End in Cowbytt with the purtynans that was
sumtyme John Herys'. To Agnes Gunylle my wyffe v mylke kyne and v burlyng
calves with a mare, and all syche stooffe as was hyr awne. To Jone Blanke my
doughtter xl*s*, and yt to be payd in x yers. To Elsabeth Blanke, the dowghtter off
John [fo. 18r] Blanke, xx*s* whan she ys att the age off xx^{ti} yers, and yff she dye within
the forsayd age then I wyll ytt remane to hyr brother or syster, and in defowtte off
brother or syster then I wyll yt be dysposyd for my sawle by myn executors or else by
ther executors. To Robert Blanke a boote[30] that Robert Alynson hath in ferme. To

---

[30] I.e. 'a boat'.

John Gunyll my sone all my boottes and troulles, and all my harsys and nettes, savyng an best that Robert Alynson shall have. The resydue off my guddes I put them to the dyspocysyone off John Gunyll and Robert Blanke to dyspoce for the helthe of my sowle, whome I ordane my executors. Wyttnes hereoff; Sir Robert Gee, Rychard Trothe, Rychard Lynsaye, Wylliam Payn, with other mo.

> Proved before P at Lincoln, 3 September 1532. Adm. granted to John Gunnyll an executor, reserving power to grant to Robert Blanke, co-executor. Afterwards the said Robert appeared and renounced.

65. WILLIAM WILLIAMSON [OF WHAPLODE]
     [LCC 1532–34, fos. 72v–73r]

27 August 1532. I, William Williamson off Whaplode, beyng of hole mynde and perfyte memory, makes thys my last will and testament. Fyrst I bequeth my soule to allmyghtty God, Our Lady St. Mary, and to all the holy cumpeny of heven. My body to be buryed within the churchyerde of St. John in Whaplode Drove. To the high altare for tithynges forgottyn xij*d*. To St. John within the same churche iij*s* iiij*d*. To the churche of Our Lady xij*d*. I bequeth toward the warkes of Our Lady of Lincoln viij*d*. To Our Lady of Lincoln viij*d*. I bequeth x*s* to have a trentall of messys sung for me and my frendes. To Margaret my wyff my house and my lande as long as she kepys her my wyff and aftyr her to remayn to my chylder. To William my sonne my house that I dwell in and iij acre of lande and a burlyng. To Richerd my sun a house and iiij acre of lande callyd Pertre Lande and a burlyng. To Robert my sun iij acre of lande a cowe and bullok. To Bartilmew my sun iij acres of lande in Holbych Drove and a mare. To Nicholes hys sun a calve. To Luce my doughter a cowe, a burlyng, a coverlyd and a pare of schetes. The resydue off my goodes I gyff to Margaret my [fo. 73r] wyff, whome I make my sole executrice. Wytnes heroff; Sir Robert Tharolde, Robert Hake, Wylliam Mayn and Robert Hoke, with other diverse mo.

> Proved before P at Spalding, 10 October 1532.

66. THOMAS HERTE [OF ST MARGARET IN THE CLOSE, LINCOLN]
     [LCC 1532–34, fo. 86]

28 August 1532. I, Thomas Herte of the parysche of St. Margaret within the Close of Lincoln, of good and hole remembraunce and memory, makyth my testament. Fyrst I gyff and bequethe my soule to allmyghtty God, to the Gloriose Virgyn Our Lady St. Mary, and to all the cumpeny in heven, and my body to be buryed within the churcheyerde of St. Margarete beforesayd by the porche ther. To the high altare ther xij*d*. To the high altare within the mynster xij*d*. To Our Lady warke xij*d*. To the hed of St. Hugh vj*d*. I will that a trentall of messys be done for the helthe off my soule as sone aftyr my departyng furthe of thys worlde as may be done convenyently. To every one of the foure closters of frerys within Lincoln xij*d*. To olde Agnes somme tyme my servant viij*d*. To Jennet Lyttyll iiij*d*. To my sonne Henry Herte too fether beddes with too bolsters, fowre pilloys, one blanket, fowre pare of lynyn schetes, one sylver pece weyng ix unces, one sylver salte weyng eyghten unces and fyve marke in redy money. To Elizabeth Herte my doughter too fether beddes with too bolsters, fowre pilloys, too blanketes, fowre pare lynyn schetes, one brasse

potte, one panne, one lattyn ladell, fowre platters, fowre dyshes, fowre sawssers, one cople of candylstykes, one sylver pece, three sylver spones, one maser with a gylte bande and fyve marke in redy money. I will that the sayd goodes bequethyd to my forsayd chylder be in the kepyng of my wyff Alice yf so be that she can fynde sewerty obligatory to the ordinary for the tyme beyng, and to Mr. Henry Sapcotes and suche other as they shall thynke best for the delyveraunce of the sayd goodes or the trewe valewe of the same when the sayd chylder comme to ten yere of age. And my forsayd chylder comme to the age of ten yeres aforesayd, then I will that ther goodes be put furthe to increste for ther use and proffyttes, by the councell and oversight of my supervisors. And yff ether of my forsayd chylder departe owt of thys worlde before the sayd ten yeres be comme, then I will the longer lyffer of them have bothe partes. And yff it fortune that both they departe thys worlde before the sayd age, as God forbyd, then [fo. 86v] I will that the sayd goodes be disposyd for the helthe of my soule, my chylder soules and all Crysten soules, by the oversight of Mr. Sapcotes aforesayd, Mr. John Smyth and Sir John Coke, clerkes, whom I make supervisors. To Mr. Sapcotes for hys labors vj*s* viij*d*. To Richerde Fax my servant one of my lyttyll horsse whiche he will chose. To Robert my servant xij*d*. To every one of thre mayd servants xij*d*. The resydue of my goodes I gyff to Alice my wyff, whome I make my full executrix for to dispose them to the pleasure of allmyghtty God and the helthe of my soule and all Crysten soules as sche shall thynke best. Thes men beyng wytnes; Sir Thomas Ingle curate, Rayff Wallys, Robert Gowllande and John Myllet, with other.

Proved before P at Lincoln, 14 December 1532. Adm. to Alice the relict and executrix.

67.   JOHN BEYLE [OF BICKER]
        [LCC 1532–34, fo. 163]

29 August 1532. I, John Beyle of Byker, with hole mynde and good remembraunce declare and make my testament and last will. Fyrst I bequethe my soule to God my maker, to Hys mother St. Mary and to all saintes. My body to be buryd in the holy grounde wher it shall please God to orden it. To my mortuary as the law limyttes. To the high altare in Byker iiij*d*. To Our Lady's altare ther ij*d*. To St. Nicholes altare ther ij*d*. To the churche warke ther xvj*d* that I promysyd in the churche. To the high altare in our mother churche of Lincoln iiij*d*. To the fatherles chyldren at St. Catheryn's withowt the gates off Lincoln ij*d*. Thys is the last will of me, the sayd John Beyle, the day and yere aforesayd. To John Bytam my doughter sun my elder plough, iij gray marys and a yeryng fylly, ij rogulyd dowyd qwyes. To Crystyne Bytam a red cowe. To [fo. 163v] John Lynsay and William Lynsay my other plough with all the gerys therto belongyng, with my carte and harnes for v horssys and a whyte meyr, a blak amblyng meyr and a red balde meyr. I wyll that all theys sayd bestes be kepte together thys wynter unto Mayday on my ferme. To the sayd John Lynsay and William ij kye that I bought of Cowper ber brede.[31] To Jenet Lynsay and William ij kye with v*s* iiij*d* rent on them, now in the ferme off the wever in Wolsondyke. To Cristine Bytam a blake dowyd burnyng with whyte mane. To William Bytam a red rogulde burnyng by himselff. To Isabell my doughter a blak

---

[31] This phrase is obscure. Possibly 'Cowper, barber'.

dowyd cowe that standyth with whyte mane. To William Lynsay my red geldyng. To Robert Bytham my gryssylde geldyng, and they to helpe my wyff in her besynes thys Wynter. The resydue of my goodes I gyff to Cristine my wyff, whome I orden my sole executrix to pay my dettes, performe thys my last will and to dispose for my soule as she thynkes good and plesyng to God, and resydue to remayn to her withowt scropull of conscience. I make Mr. John Lyttylbery, esquyre, off Hagworthyngham supervisor, to whome I gyff vj*s* viij*d*. Thes wytnesses; Syr Robert Johnson, preste, Nicholes Jakson, John Osse, with other mo.

Proved before P at Donington, 28 May 1533.

68. THOMAS MYLLET [OF LEVERTON]
[LCC 1532–34, fo. 96r]

1 September 1532. I, Thomas Milleitt of Leverton, holl myndeid and gud remembraunce, makeith my testament concludyng therin my last will. Firste I bequeth my soull to God allmyghtty, to Our Ladie Sainct Marye, and to all the sainctes of hevyn, and my bodie to be beureid in the chercheyard of Sainct Helyn in Leverton. To the honourmentes of the highe aulter in Leverton chirche iiij*d*. To the highe awter of Ouer Ladie and Sainct Thomas awter ther viij*d*. For tithynges and oblacions foryetyn ij*d*. To Ouer Ladie of Lincoln ij*d*. To the chirche wark of Leverton xx*d*. To John Milleitt my son v calfes tyen, vj calfes, ij qye burlyng, vj horses, ij folles, viij sheip, vj swyne, one plowghe and a cartt with all thynges to theym belongyng, and all my croppe. To William Milleitt my son one quee, one ewe and a lame. To Alice my doughter one que, one ewe and a lame, one greitt arke and a pare of flaxen sheittes. To Margaret my sister a ewe lame. The residew of all my guddes I gif it to John Milliett my son, whom I maike my executour, to paie my dettes and legacys and for my funerall charges, to dispoisse the residew for the helthe of my soull as he schall thinke beste, so that he cause halffe a trentall to be done in Leverton churche for my soule and all Crysten soulys. Thes wytnes; Sir John Fendyke the yonger, paryshe preste, Sir John Fendyke the elder, chauntre preste, and Robert Myllet of Leverton, with other mo.

Proved before P at Boston, 20 February 1532/3.

69. WILLIAM WILSON [OF THORESBY]
[LCC 1532–34, fos. 77v–78r]

2 September 1532. I, William Wylson off Thoresby, with hole will and mynde and good remembraunce, makes my laste will. Fyrst I witt my soule to God allmyghtty, Our Lady St. Mary, and all the hole cumpeny of heven, and my body to be buryed in the churchyerde [fo. 78r] of St. Andro in Thoresby. I wit to our mother churche of Lincoln xij*d*. I wit to Our Lady of Walsyngham xij*d*. To the churche off Thoresby xij*d*. To Calceby churche vj*d*. To Borwell churche vj*d*. I will that ther be done a trentall of messys for my soule and all Crysten soulys. The resydue of my goodes not wyt nor gyffyn I gyff to Margaret my wyff, whome I make my executrix that she may dispose for the helthe of my soule and all Cristen soulys. I will that Sir John Hill, the parsone of Thoresby, to be supervisor. Hiis testibus; John Tennande, William Procter, John Freman cum multis aliis.

Proved before P at Alford, 16 October 1532.

70.   ISABELL YALENCE [OF EPWORTH]
       [Stow 1530–52, fo. 17v]

2 September 1532. I, Isabell Yalence of Epworth, holl in mynde and gud remembraunce, makes my testament. First I bequeth my saull to almyghty God, to Owr Lady Saynt Mare and to all the holly compeny of hevyn, and my body to be buryed in the churcheyarde of Saynt Androwe in Epworth. I bequeth my varyn[32] hors to be my mortuary. To the highe awter iiij*d*. To Our Lady of Lincoln warke iiij*d*. I will that my executors shall cause iij diriges to be donne for my saull and all Cristen saulles, on at my buryall, the secunde at my vij day, the thyrde at my thyrty day. I will my executors cause on trentall of messes to be celebrate for my saull at Lancaster at the Feres Minors. To William my sonne vj*s* viij*d* when he shall come into the countre. The reste of my guddes not wytt, I giffe to Thomas Collen my sonne, whom I make my executor. This is my last will and mynde, that the saide Thomas my sonne shall have ne occupye no part off my guddes to his one use to this my will be truly performyde, but thatt my supervisors, Syr Thomas Thew, Robert Kelsay and Nicolas More, whom I putt in trust to see all performyde fully or he occupie any part theroff. Thies men beringe witnesse; Thomas Maw, Nicolas Halyfax, Edward Byrde, Adam Decon, with other moo.

   Proved before L at Belton [All Saints], 3 July 1533. Adm granted to the executor.

71.   ROBERT SPENDYLOVE [OF WHAPLODE]
       [LCC 1532–34, fo. 72v]

6 September, 1532. I, Robert Spendloffe of Whaplode, in good and hole mynde and with perfyte remembraunce, makes thys my last will. Fyrst I bequeth my soule to God allmyghtty, to Our Lady St. Mary, and to all the cumpeny of heven, and my body to be buryed in the churcheyerde of Whaplode. To the high altare of Whaplode viij*d*. To every altare in the sayd churche ij*d*. To our mother churche of Lincoln iiij*d*. To the orphans of St. Catheryn's ij*d*. To Robert Baynthorp iij*s* iiij*d*. The resydue of all my goodes I put them to the disposicion of Elizabeth my wyff whome I make my full executrix, and Edward Baynthorp supervisor of my will, havyng for hys labor iij*s* iiij*d*. Whytnes therof; Sir Thomas Ceyton, John Mayrs, John Buklay, with other moy.

   Proved before P at Spalding, 10 October 1532.

72.   ALAN DYKYNSON [OF WIGTOFT]
       [LCC 1532–34, fo. 69]

7 September 1532. I, Alen Dyconson of Wygtofte, in good mynde and hole memory makes my testament and last will. Fyrst I bequeth my soule to allmyghtty God, to Our Lady St. Mary and to all the holy cumpeny in heven, my body to be buryed within the churcheyerde of St. Peter and Paule the appostelles, of Wygtofte. My mortuary aftyr the custome of the lawe. To the high altare in Wygtofte churche iiij*d*. To Our Lady altare ij*d*. To St. Nicholes altare ij*d*. To Our Lady of Lincoln iiij*d*. To the fatherles chyldren of St. Cateryn's ij*d*. To the churche warke off [fo. 69v]

---

[32] 'Varon': wall-eyed.

Wygtofte iiij*d*. To Agnes my doughter one yong cowe, one bay mere, ij schepe, one brasse pot, one brasse panne, one materes, one coverlyd, one pare of schetes and ij pilloys at xv yere of age. Also yff it so be that my wyff do dye afore the date heroff I will that Richerd my brother have my doughter with her goodes at hys kepyng. To Richerd my brother one yow and one wether lamme. To William Hawdell one yowe. To Steven Dyckynson one lamme. All my goodes I bequeth them to Jenet my wyff whome I make my executrix. Whytnes heroff; John Greve, John Cressy, William Hawdell, with moy.

Proved before P at Boston, 9 October 1532.

73.   WILLIAM WIGHTMAN [OF BOSTON]
       [LCC 1532–34, fos. 20v–21r]

7 September 1532. I, William Wyghtman of Boston, hole of mynde and of good remembraunce, makes my will and last testament. Fyrst I bequethe my soule to God allmyghtty, to Hys mother St. Mary, and to all the saintes in heven, and my body to be buryed in the churcheyerde of Boston. To the high altare of Boston xij*d*. To Our Lady warke at Lincoln xij*d*. To the fatherles and motherles chyldren at St. Catheryn's at Lincoln xij*d*. To the gyltyng of St. Botulphe of Boston xvj*d*. To the vj martyrs gylde xvj*d*.[33] To Our Lady gylde of the same viij*d*. To the roode gylde of Boston vj*d*. To the gylde of the Assumption of Our Lady of the same vj*d*. To every order of frerys in Boston xx*d*. To my lady ancores of the same ij*s*. I will have halffe a trentall done afore the good roode at the Augustyn Frerys in Boston. Also halff a trentall at Scala Celi within the paryshe churche of Boston. I will that vj*s* viij*d* be disposyd in farthyng breade emonges pore people at the day of my buryall. I gyff to mendyng highways abowt Boston x*s*. To Richard Wyghtman my sonne v markes in money, my gowne, my best dooblet, my whyte nagge, halff a dosyn of pewter vessell of the nexte best, a brasse potte of xvj*li*. To John Wayd my brother-in-lawe xl*s*. To the same John, [fo. 21r] for a matterys, iij*s* iiij*d*. To John Fox and Jenet hys wyff to ether of them v*s*. To Jenet Foxe a brasse potte of xij*li*. To Andro Stubbys iij*s* iiij*d*. To Helene Stubbys a panne of x*li* weyght. To Stubbys wyff a kettyll of vj*li*. To Thomas Turner iij*s* iiij*d*. To Luce Fysher x*s* and my mantyll. To Robert Taylor my bedde as it standes. To Robert Whyte iij*s* iiij*d*. To John Johnson iiij*s*. To Isabell Twede a kettyll of iiij*li*. To the wyffe of John Johnson's a panne of vj*li*. To Sir Thomas Cersy iij*s* iiij*d*. To Agnes Blancherde a panne of x*li*. To the chylder of Richerde Olyver xviij pownde of newe puter equally to be devydyd emong them. To Catheryne Grene a panne of ix*li*. The resydewe of all my goodes I putte them in the handes of my executors whome I make Sir George Garner and Robert Taylor, they to pay my dettes, fulfyll my will and dispose for the helthe of my soule as my truste is in them. And I gyff to ether of them for ther labor xij*s*. Thes beyng wytnes; Sir Thomas Cersy, Richerde Smyght, Richerde Grene and Nicholes Mylner with other mo.

Proved before P at Lincoln, 17 November 1532. Adm. granted to executors.

---

[33] The Seven Martyrs were an early cult, whose legend revolved around the execution of seven brothers for refusing to apostatise in the second century A.D. They were supposedly the sons of St. Felicity, who was executed at the same time for the same offence. Until 1969 the Seven Martyrs' feast day fell on 10 July. The Boston gild, one of the more popular objects of devotion in these wills, was one of ten smaller, unincorporated gilds in St. Botolph's church. Nothing is known of it beyond what exists in testamentary evidence: P. Thompson, *The History and Antiquities of Boston* (Boston, 1856, repr. 1997), 154.

74. RICHARD VASSELL [OF MARKET RASEN]
[LCC 1532–34, fo. 50r]

9 September 1532. I, Richerde Vassell of Est Rasen, beyng of good mynd and hole memory makes my last wyll. Fyrst I bequeth my soule to God allmyghtty, to Our Blessyd Lady St. Mary and to all the cumpeny off heven, and my body to be buryed in the churche of St. Thomas in the forsayd Rasyn. To the high altare off the same churche xijd. To Our Lady altare in the same churche xijd. To St. Anthony altare in the same churche xijd. To the vicare of the sayd Rasyn for tithys forgottyn vjs viijd. To the high altare of our mother churche in Lincoln xijd. To every one of the iiij orders of frerys of the sayd Lincoln xijd. To Margaret Soirby alias Orrey halff of my housholde stuff. To Johan Skyll my servant my house which I holde by copy of the thre cheyff lordes of Rasyn aforesayd, and the house that I hold of John Wright, duryng her lyff. And aftyr her lyff I will that my executors shall dispose for my soule helthe the rente of bothe the sayd houses for the tyme and yeres that I have in them. To Agnes Clerke a cownter and a payntyd chyst. To Sir Hugh Belclyff, to syng St. Gregory trentall off messys one hole yere, vl vjs viijd.[34] I will that my executors make peny dole to every one that cumys to my buryeng the day of my buryall. The resydue of my goodes I gyff to Sir Thomas Feyldhouse, Richerde Clerke and John Skyll my servant, whome I make my executors. And I will that every one of them have for hys labor xiijs iiijd. I make Sir Hugh Belclyff my supervisor. Wytnesses; Sir Hugh Belclyff, Laurence Rawlet, with other mo.

Proved before P at Lincoln, 12 September 1532. Adm. granted to the executors.

75. HENRY FOOLLER [OF BRUMBY IN PARISH OF FRODINGHAM]
[Stow 1530–52, fo. 13]

10 September 1532. I, Henry Fooller of Bremby in the parishe of Frodingham in the countie of Lincoln, beinge in holl mynde and gud memory, do make my will and testament. First I bequeth my saull to almyghty God, Awr Lady Saynt Mary and to all the celestiall compeny in hevyn, and my body to be buryed within the parishe church of Ower Blessyd Lady in Frodingham, with my mortuary accostomed and as the law requiryth. To the hye awter of Our Lady in the cathedrall churche of Lincoln xijd. To the churche warke of Lincoln iiijd. To the hye awter of Froding-ham xijd. To the lady Gyrlington viijd. To the parishe churche of Frodingham a white cowe for this intent, to have messe and dirige yerely of the proufittes of the said cowe, the on half of the profittes to be giffyn to the use and prouffitt of the churche, and the other halff to performe and uphold messe and dirige withe ryngynge for my saull and all Criston saulles. And after the discesse of my wiff, she to be remembred in the said messes and dirige. To the churche warke of Frodingham vs xd wiche dothe remayn in the handes of Robert Hall of Crosby and xd wiche dothe remayn in the handes of Thomas Hall his fader [fo. 13v] ffor this intent, to have a serge leighted before Saynt Kateryn in the northe syde of the

---

[34] The St. Gregory Trental, or Pope Trental, was inspired by Pope Gregory the Great's vision of his mother who, tormented by the pains of purgatory, pleaded with him to pray for her unconfessed sins. The trental was regarded as theologically unsound by strict Catholic opinion as well as evangelical: R.W. Pfaff, 'The English Devotion of St. Gregory's Trental', *Speculum 49* (1974), 75–90; Duffy, *Stripping of the Altars*, 293–4.

churche in servys tyme on the holyday, and the saide money to be upstandinge yerely and Henry Fouler to giff a pounde wax to the makinge of the said serge. I will that a prest have wages on half yere to synge for my saull and all Criston saulles. To Thomas my sonne a toftestede buylded that I dwell in, a kylne house and the garth and a dowffcott,[35] a gret house except in the said garth, a tofte unbuylded in the west ende of Scomthorp and half the arable lande as it dothe lye in the feldys of Frodingham and Scomthorp with half more and myddows therto belongynge for the space of xxxix yeres. To the said Thomas Foller xxs and x yewes and x lammes. To Henry Fouller my sonne a tofte buylded that he dwellyth in, and a tofte unbuylded of the southe syde of wey, and the other half of the arable lande lyinge in the ffeldes of Frodingham and Scomthorp more and myddowes, and a long house fre except to remove at his owne plesur for the space of xxxix yeres. Also xxs, ten yowes and ten lammes. To William Fouler my sonne a house at Trent syde that John Grey dwellyth in, with landes, mores and myddows therto belongynge for the space of xxxix yeres. To the aforesaid Henry Fouler a tofte buylded, lyinge beside Robert Kendall. The residew I giffe to Syr Thomas Foller and to Elizabeth my wiffe whom I do make myne executors. Thies wytnesse; John Jonson, Roger Fooller, John Stampe and Robert Fooller, with other moo beinge present.

Proved before L at Wadingham, 4 November 1532. Adm. granted to Sir Thomas Fooller the executor, reserving power to grant to Elizabeth, the relict and executor.

76.   ROBERT PEYCOKE [OF KIRKBY ST. PETER]
        [LCC 1532–34, fos. 186v–187v]

12 September 1532. I, Robert Peycoke of Kyrkby Peter, make and conclude my testament. Fyrste I bequethe my soule to allmyghtty God, to Our Lady St. Mary, and to all the saintes in heven, and my body to be buryd in the churche of the holy appostyll St. Peter of Kyrkby beforesayd, and my mortuary as the lawe will. To the sacrament in the sayd churche of Kyrkby Peter for tithys forgottyn iijs iiijd. To the reparacions of our mother churche of Lincoln xijd. To the reparacions of the churche of Hekyngton viijd. To the churches of Burton, Kyrkby Dionys[36] and Asgarby iiijd each. To Margaret my wyff ij kye of the beste, one qwy, a gray mare and her fole, xij seamys corne, that is to say ij seamys wheate, ij seamys rye, iiij seamys barly, iij seamys pease and one seame oyttes, and the housholde stuffe lefte unspente that was her owne when I maryd her. To Thomas and to Jamys my sonnys x horssys, a carte, a wayn, ij plowys and the tyrementes of them, and xxx^{ty} acres corne: that is to say iij acres wheate, ij acres rye, xiij acres barly, x acres peasse and ij acres oyttes, to be delyveryd and equally shyftyd betwyxte them at Mayday nexte foloyng. To Robert Peycok a [fo. 187r] table callyd a cownter, a long spyt, a gryndstone with the bryg of yren, to be delyveryd at the day of hys mariage. And yff the foresayd Robert dye or he be maryed, then I will that John hys brother be hys heyr. To Margaret my doughter a calve, a hutche and a yren whele. To Alice my doughter the beste qwye, the grettyst brasse potte, a bason, a laver and the grettyst arke. To Agnes, the chylde that I bryng up, a red cowe, a

---

[35] I.e. 'a dovecote'.
[36] Kirkby Laythorpe.

red qwye, a yowe and a lamme, a ambre, a gret brasse potte, a basyn, a laver, a candylstyk and iij puter dyshes to be delyveryd at the day of her mariage. To every one of my godchyldren a stryke barly. To the yong freres of the iiij orders in the towne of Boston iiij strykes wheate. I will that the churchwardens of the paryshe of St. Peter of Kyrkby beforesayd have one house and the close therto belongyng, lying in the same towne nexte the churche mese of the northe and the mese of Mr. Stanley of the sowthe the space of iij^{xx} xiij yeres nexte foloyng aftyr my decesse, yff the kynge's lawes will suffer it, of thys condicion foloyng: fyrste that they kepe and leyff the sayd house in good and sufficient reperell all the forsayd yeres, and to pay the prior and convent of Haverholme yerely at Michelmas[37] vj*d*, and to kepe my yerely obbyt within the octaves off the Nativite of Our Blyssyd Lady[38] in thys forme foloyng, that is to say: to the curate to pray for my soule, for the saulys of my father and mother, for the soulys of my wyffes, for the soulys of all my good frendes and all Crysten soulys vj*d*, to dispose the same day in the dedes of charite as they thynke beste ij*s,* to dispose of All Saulys' Nyght vj*d*, the Tuysday in rogacion weke to refreshe them that go in procession wyth bred and ale xij*d*.[39] The reste of the rente of the sayd house to go to the reparacions of the churche. And yff so be the sayd churchewardens dispose not the yerely rent of the sayd house as is before rehersyd, it shall be lefull for the prior and convent of Haverholme to kepe my yerely obbyt within ther monastery, and to have the rente of the sayd house distrybutyd emong them to pray for my soule and for the soulys of all other before rehersyd. The rest of all my goodes moveable and unmoveable her not gyffyn nor bequethyd I put to the disposicion of Sir Robert Peycok my sone, vicare of Burton, whome I make my sole executor [fo. 187v] to pay my dettes, my legaces and my funerall charges. Thes wytnes; Sir Christopher Robynson, vicar of Kyrkby beforesayd, Simon Dawson, John Thomson, William Gyldyn, and other mo.

Proved before P at Lincoln, 21 August 1533.

77.   STEPHEN HUDSON [OF BARROW UPON HUMBER]
[LCC 1532–34, fo. 88]

20 September 1532. I, Stephyn Hudson of Barrow, hole of mynde and full memory, makyth thys my will and testament. Fyrst I gyff and bequethe my soule to allmyghtty God, to Our Blessyd Lady St. Mary, and to all the saintes in heven. My body to be buryed in the churche of Our Lady in Barrowe. To Mr. Vicare xxj*s* to pray for me. [fo. 88v] To the high altare of the sayd churche in Barro xx*d*. To Our Lady warke of Lincoln xij*d*. To Our Lady gylde in Barrow halff a quarter barly. To the Trinite gylde halff a quarter barly. To Jamys my brother viij yowes and a cowe. To William Hudson and to Anne Hudson, the chylder of my brother Jamys, other of them a yowe. To Robert Jakson my servant a quarter barly and a yowe, and to William Jakson hys sun a yowe. To Benedicte Tenby ij yowes. To Robert Hansay ij yowes. To Robert Hudson and John Hudson my chylder, ether of them, xij*l*. I will that a preste shall syng for my soule and all Crysten soulys halffe a yere. The reste of

---

[37] 29 September.

[38] 8 September–14 September.

[39] All Souls' Night was the night of 2 November. Rogation week began on the Monday before Ascension Day and lasted until the fifth Sunday after Easter Day.

my goodes I gyff to Johanne Hudson my wyff, whome I make my executrix. Thes men wytnes; Benedicte Tenby, Robert Hanshay, Robert Jakson, with other mo. Jamys Hudson my brother to be supervisor.

Proved before P at Caistor, 10 February 1532/3.

78.   WILLIAM MANNE [OF WIGTOFT]
      [LCC 1532–34, fo. 282]

20 September 1532. I, William Manne of Wygtofte, roper, beyng in good mynde and hole memory, makys my testament and laste wyll. First I bequethe my sawle to allmyghty God, to Owr Lady Saynt Mary and to all the holy company of heven. My body to be buryed in the churcheyarde of the appostolles Saynt Peter and Pawle of Wygtofte. To my mortuary as the lawe requerythe. To the hye aulter of Wygtofte vj*d*. To Ower Lady aulter ij*d*. To Saynt Nycolas aulter ij*d*. To the ploghe lyght iiij*d*. To the churche warke vj*d*. To Ower Lady of Lincoln vj*d*. To the fatherlesse chyldryn of Saynt Kateryne nye Lyncolln iij*d*. To John Manne my sonne ij marys wheche he wyll choce, x yowes, all my tolys whyche I wyrke withall, on karte, on ploghe yf it may be sparyd, [fo. 282v] and my beste bras potte. To Margarett my doghter ij queys. To John Vyrley on blacke horse. To John Bayly my servand on blacke colte goyng in the fenne. Also all my goodes unbequethyd I bequethe them to Jenette Manne, my wyffe, whome I make myne executryx. Wytnes heroff; Sir Robert Walker, William Bennet, William Manne and John Vyrlay, with mo.

Proved before P at Swineshead, 8 June 1534.

79.   JOHN SYGRAVE [OF HELPRINGHAM]
      [LCC 1532–34, fos. 74v–75r]

20 September 1532. I, John Sygrave of Helpryngham, husband[man], beyng in hole mynde, makes my last will and testament. Fyrst I bequeth my soule to allmyghtty God, Our Lady St. Mary and all the cumpeny of heven, and my body to be buryed in the churchyard of Helpryngham. To the high altare off Helpryngham for tithys forgottyn iiij*d*. To Our Lady warke of Lincoln ij*d*. To Our Lady of Lincoln ij*d*. To George my sonne on seame and a half of barly [fo. 75r] and one you and a lambe. To Helene my doughter one qwye, one seame barly. To John my sonne, the elder, and to John the yonger, and to Robert my chyldren, every one of them, one you and one lambe, and one seame barly. To Alyson my doughter one you and one lambe, and one seame barly. I gyff one cow and ij acres of my best falloys sawn with my owne barly to be departyd emong all my chylder. And every one of them to be heyres of other yff that ought happyn them afore the age of xviij yeres. To Agnes my syster one bushyll of barly. To Elizabeth Norice my goddoughter iiij*d*. The resydue of my goodes I gyff them to Catheryne my wyff and to Robert Cryar, whome I make my executors. Wytnes herof; Sir Robert Wyham, vicar of Helpryngham, Robert Grene, Richerd Robertson, with other moy.

Proved before P at Bloxholm, 11 October 1532.

80. ROBERT BASTON [OF STICKNEY]
[LCC 1532–34, fos. 57v–58r]

26 September 1532. I, Robert Baston of Stykney, beyng in hole mynde and good remembraunce, makyng my testament and will. Fyrst I witt my soule to allmyghtty God, and Our Blessyd Lady St. Mary Hys mother and to all the saintes in heven, and my body to be buryed in the churchyerde of St. Luce the Evangelist. To the high altare pro decimis oblitis[40] viij*d*. To Our Lady altare and St. Nicholes altare viij*d*. To Our Lady warke of Lincoln vj*d* and to the fatherles chylder at St. Catheryn's iiij*d*. To Jenet a cople of oxyn and iiij of my best kye, and ij of my best marys and all the hustylment of house. To William my sonne a blak colte stag, a amblyng fely and ij sheder calves. To Helyn my doughter a cowe [fo. 58r] and to Margaret my doughter a cowe. To Isabell my doughter a qwe. To Thomas Gannok a blak horsse and ij heder calvys. Thys is the last will of me Robert Baston. To Jenet my wyff my house with the buyldynges therapon and viij gaddes of medoy lying in Thornedalys the terme of her lyff and she kepe her unmaryed, and yff that she do mary then I will that the forsayd house and viij gaddes of medoy remayn to William my sonne and to hys heyres of hys body laufully begotten everlastyng. And yff it happyn William my sonne dy withowt heyres, then I will that the forsayd house and the viij gaddes of medoy remayn to my thre doughters Helyn, Margaret and Isabell, to them and ther heyres of ther bode laufully begottyn everlastyng [remainder to] Thomas Gannok to hym and hys heyres of hys body laufully begottyn everlastyng. Also I will that the foresayd Thomas Gannok have ingate and owtgate with all maner of cariage of my grounde to hym and hys heyres everlastyng of thys condicion, that my heyres get water at the forsayd Thomas Gannok dyke everlastyng. The resydue of all my goodes not wytt nor gyffyn to Jenet my wyff and William Baston my sonne, for to pay my dettes and for to dispose for the helthe of my soule and all Crysten soulys. Thes men wytnes; Alan Harde of Stykney, William Beyr of the same and William Baston senior of the same, et aliis.

Proved before P2 at Partney, 2 October 1532.

81. RICHARD OSGODBY [OF WEST RASEN]
[LCC 1532–34, fo. 83]

28 September 1532. I, Richerde Osgodby off West Rasyn, beyng of good and hole mynde with perfyte remembraunce, ordenyth and makes my last will and testament. Fyrste I bequeth my soule to God allmyghtty and unto Our Lady the Blessyd Virgyn Mary, and unto all the holy hevenly citezyns, and my body to be buryed in the churche off All Saintes of West Rasyn. To Our Lady warke of Lincoln viij*d*. To the high altare of West Rasyn for tithys forgottyn viij*d*. To the iiij orders of frerys of Lincoln, to every order of them iiij*d*. To the high altare off Kyrkby churche iiij*d*. To the high altare of Tofte Newton iiij*d*. To the high altare of [fo. 83v] Newton churche iiij*d*. I will that my hole housholde goodes be devydyd in ij partes, the one halff parte I will that Jenet my wyff shall have, and the other halff of the sayd housholde goodes I will that Beatrix my doughter shall have. And over the sayd halff parte of goodes I will the sayd Beatrix have one yong qwye and one gret chyst. To Olyver my sonne one yong blak stag. To Steven my sone one soryd stag. To Robert my sonne a

[40] 'For tithes forgotten'.

yong qwye and a yong fely. I will that the day of my funerall ther shall be one hole trentall song for my soule and all Crysten soulys. The resydue of my goodes not wit I will they shall be devydyd into iij partes, whereof I will that one parte thereof go to Jenet my wyff. The secund parte I will be devydyd emonges my fyve sonnys holy be equal partes, and the thyrde parte also I will that it be devydyd betweene my sayd fyve sonnys, and of the same parte I will that yff any of them departe before the age of xvij yeres, that all hys parte be devydyd emonges the other iiij my sonnys. And yff there shall remayn over and above the premisses and legaces at any tyme heraftyr any goodes, I will the sayd goodes to be at the order and disposicion of Sir Oliver Osgodby and Jenet Osgodby my wyff, and John Osgodby my brother, whome I make my trewe and juste executors, that they may order and se orderyd thys my last and trewe will, to be fulfyllyd as they will make answer before the high juge of heven. Thies wytnesses; William Rowthe, William Awlaye and William Frere, with other mo.

Proved before P at Kirkby, 13 November 1532.

82.   SIR JOHN FRESMORE [OF HUTTOFT]
        [LCC 1532–34, fo. 36]

2 October 1532. I, John Fresmore, preste, and of Hotofte the vicare, of hole mynde and good memory, ordence and makes my testament and last will. Fyrste I bequethe my soule to allmyghtty God, to Our Blessyd Lady St. Mary and to all the saintes in heven, and my body to be buryed in the chauncell of the churche of Hotofte. To Our Lady of Lincoln vij*s* and one pare of beades of awmber. To Our Lady warke of Lincoln xij*d*. To Our Lady of Walsyngham vj*d*.[41] To the churches of Anderby, Strubby and Mablethorp xij*d* each. To the convent of Markeby for celebratyng of one trentall for my soule and all Crysten soulys x*s*. To the convent of Hagneby for celebratyng one trentall for my soule and all Christen soulys x*s*. To an honest preste for to celebrate one hole yere in the churche of Hotofte for my soule and all Christen soulys, to brede wyne and wax, v*l* vj*s* viij*d*. I will that ther shall be a peny dole at my buryall day. I will that at my xxx^ty day ther shall be disposyd emong pore people wher moste nede is in the townys abowte the sayd Hotofte xx*s*. I will that my executors cause to be done ij trentallys for all those soulys that I have faryd better by, or have had anythyng of any man or woman that is now owt of my mynde, to make restitucion agane. To an honest preste for celebratyng halff a yere for all those soulys that I have faryd better by liij*s* iiij*d*. To William Weste vj*s* viij*d*, one chamlet dooblet and my best blak jaket. To John Weste iij*l* vj*s* viij*d*, my best cownter, my best bed, one chare, one pare of schetes, one coverlyd, one bolster, my wane, my carte, my ploughe and all that longeth therto, my best cobborde, my worstyd dooblet, my best gowne, vj cushyns, halff a dosyn off sylver sponys, one cowe, one mayr with her fole, my bruyng leade, my mash fat with other vessels for bruyng necessary. To Sir William Rannolde my table that standyth in my parlour, my chamlet chakkyt, my best short gowne, my typpyt furryd with cony, a lytle golde ryng with a stone. To Sir Richerde Scherwoode xij*d,* my typpyt furryd with

----

[41] The famous shrine of Our Lady at Walsingham, Norfolk, was a major pilgrimage centre in later medieval England. Just before its dissolution in 1536 it was reported to have attracted offerings worth at least £6 13s. 4d. on one Saturday and Sunday alone: Duffy, *Stripping of the Altars*, 377–8, 385.

fomarde.[42] To Sir William Steper xij*d*. To Sir John Hoope one syde gowne. To John Wryght my servant one cownter, one chare, one cowe that is with hys brother. To my lady Billesby one sylver spone. To lytyll Andro Billesby one sylver spone. To Ursula Billesby one sylver spone. To Alice Rannolde one sylver spone, one bed that standyth in my parlour [fo. 36v] with all that belongyth therto. To John Jakson vj*s* viij*d* and I forgyff hym all that he awyth unto me. To Elizabeth Jakson one feder bed with all that belongyth therto. To my awnt Jakson vj*s* viij*d* and I forgyff her all that she awyth unto me. To John Swyne one sylver spone. To John Atkyn my Lundon sadle. To William Hogson xx*d*. To Jenet Bocher iij*s* iiij*d*. To Robert Richerdson all that he dothe awe me excepte vij*s* vj*d* whiche I lent hym the last. To Robert Wryght v*s*. To every chylde of Henry Swyne and William Swyne xij*d*. To every one of my godchyldren iiij*d*. To Dorothe Elande x yardes of lynyn clothe. To Jenet Temper and Jenet Bocher all my colys. To Catheryne Cawthorn iij puter dyshes, one brasse potte, vj yardes of lyn clothe and one candylstyk. To Thomas Jakson one cownter. To Anne Mykylbarow one pare of schetes. To the amendyng of the churche ways and brygges in Hotofte xx*s*. To the bying of a suyt of blak vestmentes for the churche of Hotofte liij*s* iiij*d* or iij*l* yff it nede. I will that my executors do or cause to be done one obyt in the churche off Hotofte yerly duryng the space of xviij yeres next immediatly foloyng aftyr the day of my buryall, with placebo and dirige over the night, and messe of requiem one the morowe with one preste, and the sayd preste to have vj*d* for hys labor, and the ryngers of the bellys to have iiij*d* for ther labors, and to be bestowyd in bred and ale to the people beyng in the churche at the sayd obyt xvij*d*. I will that ther shalbe xiij pennce delte emong the pore people dwellyng in the sayd paryshe of Hotofte every Good Fryday yerely duryng the sayd xviij yeres, for my soule and all Christen soulys. I make Sir William Raynolde, preste and John Weste of Hotofte my executors. I pray Sir Andro Billesby, knyght, to be supervisor and I bequethe to hym for hys labor myn amblyng geldyng. Thyse wytnes; Sir John Hoope, William West, Sir John Croxston, with other mo.

Proved before P at Alford, 5 February 1532/3.

83.   WILLIAM HARYSON [OF CAREBY]
       [LCC 1532–34, fo. 199]

4 October 1532. I, William Hareson of Careby, hole of mynde, make and orden my last will. Fyrste I gyff my soule to allmyghtty God and to Our Lady St. Mary and to all the cumpeny of heven, and my body to be buryd in the churcheyerde of St Stephyn of Careby and my principall after the lawe of the realme. To the high altare in Careby churche xij*d*. To the churche of Lincoln [blank]. To my Syster Syssely Hareson a hecfor. To the bellys iiij strykes of barly. To Our Lady light iiij strykes of barly. To St. John light in the roode lofte ij strykes of barly. To the mendyng of the Spur Bryg xiij*s* iiij*d* to be payd with in the yere foloyng to the handes of the churchewardens. To John Hareson my eldeste sonne a hecfor, a ewe, a lambe and a seame of barly. To Henry Hareson ij sterys of ij yeres olde. To Alice my doughter a hecfor, a ewe and a lambe. To Laurence my sun a cowe with a calve, a ewe and a lambe hog. To Robert Hareson my sun a seame off barly, a ewe, a lambe hog and a

---

[42] 'Foumart': polecat.

bullok calve. To my wyff all my copys till the tyme that my sun John be complete xx^{ty} yeres olde, and John Hareson my sun to enter and to have all my copys with the proffyttes of them when he is complete the age abovesayd. I will that my executors shall gyff for my soule at my buryall fyve dosyn of brede. Also apon my seventh day v dosyn of brede and apon my xxx^{ty} dosyn of brede aftyr the rate abovesayd. To the mendyng of the churche royff vj*s* viij*d*. To the iiij orders of frerys in Stamforde, every house, ij strykes [fo. 199v]of barly. To the Frerys Augustyns ij strykes of barly and a stryke of rye. I make my wyff and John Hareson my sonne myne executors for to distribute and order thys my will and my goodes as my truste is in yow. I make Richerde Myller of Stamforde my supervisor to susteyne and ayd myne executors, and I gyff hym for hys payntaking vj*s* viij*d*. Thes beyng wytnes; Sir Richerde Warner, frer Austyn, Richarde Staworthe, Robert Tomson and other mo.

Proved before P at Bitchfield, 21 October 1533. Adm. granted to relict and executrix, John Hareson the co-executor having died in the meantime.

84.　　HENRY ELWARDE [OF HAGWORTHINGHAM]
　　　　[LCC 1532–34, fo. 32r]

7 October 1532. I, Henry Elwarde, beyng of Hagworthyngham, hole of mynde and of good memory, ordyns and makes my testament and last will. Fyrst I bequethe my soule to allmyghtty God, to Our Blessyd Lady St. Mary and to all the holy cumpeny of heven, my body to be buryed in the holy churchyerde of the Holy Trinite of Hagworthyngham. To the high altare of Our Lady of Lincoln xij*d*, and to her warke vj*d*. To the high altare of Hagworthyngham xij*d*. To the high altare of Wynceby churche xij*d*. To the churches of Gretham, Wynceby, Scrafelde, Hameryngham, Asgarby and Luceby iiij*d* each. To the bellys off Hagworthyngham iiij*d*, and to the gylde of Our Lady off Hagworthyngham xij*d*. To every one of my godbarns iiij*d*. To Richerde Elwarde iiij*d*. To Agnes Elwarde iiij*d*. To Thomas Charlys the yonger iiij*d*. To Thomas Burton a quarter barly. To Henry Bleytt a quarter barly. To Jenet Burwell a bushyll barly. To Thomas Barryt and hys wyff vj quarters barly. To Thomas Chelys ij quarters barly. The resydue of my goodes I gyff to Alyson my wyff whome I make my executrix, that she may ordyn and dispose all weyll for the helthe of my soule and all Crysten soulys. And I orden and make Thomas Barryt and Thomas Cheles to be supervisors of the same. Thes beyng wytnes; Thomas Hygdon, John Grene, Sir John Philipson, with other mo.

Proved before P at Horncastle, 3 February 1532/3.

85.　　THOMAS WYATSON [OF BURGH LE MARSH]
　　　　[LCC 1532–34, fo. 35v]

7 October 1532. I, Thomas Wyatson of Burgh in Marshe makes my will and testament. Fyrst I bequeth my soule to the mercy of allmyghtty God, Our Lady St. Mary, and to all the saintes in heven, and my body to be buryd in the churcheyerde of St. Peter in Burgh. To the high altare for tithys forgottyn xij*d*. To the churche warke xx*d*. To Peter gylde viij*d*. To the warke of Our Lady of Lincoln x*d*, and to her offeryng x*d*. I will that one trentall be done for my soule and all my frende soulys at Boston, and one trentall in the churche of St. Peter in Burgh. To every godchylde iiij*d*. To every one of my brother chylder viij*d*. To Henry Parenyll xij*d*. To George

Gluffer xij*d*, to help to sell my alam[43] at the best. To Robert Smyth iij*s* iiij*d*, and hys wyff iij*s* iiij*d*. To Malde Clerke a lame. To Agnes Clerke a lamme. I will that the house that was Robert Dar's that I have be copyholde be solde to pay my dettes. The resydue of my goodes, housys and lande taken for yeres, I gyff it to Elizabeth my wyff, wo I make my executrix, and William Pecok to be executor with her and to make the best of all thynges, and he to have for hys labor iij*s* iiij*d*, and Mr. William Quadryng to be supervisor, and for to have for hys labor iij*s* iiij*d*. Wytnes to the same; Sir John Pechell, John Waydes, Thomas More, Henry Dawson with other mo.

Proved before P at Partney, 4 February 1532/3.

86.   JOHN BUSTARDE [OF FISHTOFT]
        [LCC 1532–34, fo. 7]

8 October 1532. I, John Bustarde the yonger of the paryshe of St. Guthlak in Toft, beyng in hole mynde and good remembraunce, makyth [fo. 7v] my laste will. Fyrste and principally I bequethe my soule to God allmyghtty, to Hys blessyd mother St. Mary and to all the cumpeny of heven, and my body to be buryed in the churcheyerde of St. Guthlake aforesayd, and for my mortuary that the lawe and the custome of the kyng shall require. To the high altare of St. Guthlak in Tofte vj*d*. To Our Lady of Lincoln iiij*d*. To Our Lady chapell in Tofte ij*d*. To the Trinitie altare ij*d*. To St. John altare ij*d*. To Cecily my wyff fyve roodes of lande lying in Bendlam the terme of her lyff, and aftyr her decesse I will that the lande remayn to John my sun to hym and to hys heyres of hys body [remainder to] Robert Bustarde my sun [remainder to] the nexte of the blode forever. To John my sun iij schepe, a blake cowe calve, a coverlyd, a pare of schetes one of flaxen another of hardyn, and a pilloy with the coveryng. To Agnes Westmellys ij schepe. To Cecily my wyff an acre of lande lying of lay gayst the terme of her lyff [remainder to] Robert Bustarde to hym and to hys heyres forever. To Robert Bustarde my sun ij schepe. The resydue of my goodes I gyff them to Cecily my wyff, whome I make my executrix to dispose for the helthe of my soule and all Crsyten soulys. Thes beyng wytnes; Sir Nicholes Kytlok, Robert Bate, Thomas Kyrke, Willum Dawson, with other mo yff nede require.

Proved before P at Boston, 20 February 1532/3.

87.   JOZIAN COOKE [OF BURGH LE MARSH]
        [LCC 1532–34, fos. 32v–33r]

8 October 1532. I, Jozian Cooke, makes my will. Fyrste I bequethe my soule to God allmyghtty, Our Lady St. Mary and all the saints in heven, my body to be buryed in the churcheyerde of St. Peter in Burgh. I bequeth that a trentall be done at Boston for my husband soule, my soule and Isabell soule, with all Crysten soulys. To Our Lady of Lincoln ij*d*, and ij*d* to her warke. To my father v*s*. To my brother Sir Thomas hys beades, ij rynges, a materes and my best coverlyd and a pare schetes. To my syster Elizabeth my best gowne, my gret cawdrun and my best rebon. To my syster Margaret my best orege gowne, my best kyrtyll, the secund reban, my best

---

[43] 'Alan': wolf hound.

candylstyk and my best salte. To my brother Richerde my husbande's gowne. To Jenet Felypson my thyrde oryge gowne and my nexte best kyrtyll and my beste kyste. To my mother my best kettyll, my wollyn [fo. 33r] wele and my best kyrchyff. To Dame Hall my best apron. To Jamys Felipson ij yerdes of lyn clothe. To Jenet Mell, Alice Malteby, Agnes Baker to every one of them a kyrchyff or a apron. To Thomas Selby a sherte. To Alan Mell a scherte. To Robert Todde a sherte. To Sir John Pychell a pare of new schetes. To John Wade my husbande's best cappe. To Sir Thomas Jordan xijd, who I make my executor. The resydue of all my goodes I will that he dispose it for my soule and all Crysten soulys, and Sir Thomas my brother to be the supervisor. Wytnes; Sir John Pechell, John Wade, Mylys Bendlay.

Proved before P at Partney, 4 February 1532/3.

88. WILLIAM YONG [OF CAREBY]
    [LCC 1532–34, fo. 27]

8 October 1532. I, William Yong of Careby, beyng syk in body and hole in mynde, make thys my last will and testament. Fyrst I bequethe my soule to allmyghtty God, to Our Lady St. Mary, and to all the saintes of heven, and my body to be buryed in the churcheyerde of St. Stephyn of Careby. To Our Lady at Lincoln iiijd. To the churche of Careby halff a quarter of barly. To Sir Richerd Coterell a mare and a fole to syng a trentall of messys for my soule. To Agnes Harwolde my wyff doughtter a gret potte, a ketyll and a chaffyng dyshe. I bequeth [fo. 27v] a cowe in the handes of William Harwolde to be delte emonges pore people in the paryshe of Careby. To John Newton a cowe, ij yowes and ij lambys. To William Harwolde of Brasborow the thyrde cowe to dispose for the helthe of my soule. To my ij chylder xijd. To Sir Richerd Cotterell to pray for my soule vjs viijd. I will that my ij bullokes shalbe solde, and the money therof cumyng to be gyffyn to a preste to pray for my soule and all my frende soulys as long as it will last. To Margaret my wyff halff a seame of wheate and halff a seame of barly, with all her housholde stuff whiche she brought to me, so sche will be good to my soule and to fulfyll thys my last will. To John Colyn of Careby one ewe and a lambe to se my will performyd, which John, and Margaret my wyff, I make my executors. Thes wytnes; William Barnys, William Harwolde, Thomas Haulle, Robert Leacye, John Runton, Robert Eteson, John Gylham and all.

> Proved before P at Bourne, 15 January 1532/3. Adm. granted to John Colyn, an executor, reserving power to grant to Margaret the relict, being an executor.

89. JOHN YONG [OF PINCHBECK]
    [LCC 1532–34, fo. 93]

9 October 1532. I, John Yong of Pynchbek, beyng seke in body and hole in mynde, makes my last testament and will. Fyrst I bequethe my soule to God allmyghtty, to Our Lady and to all the saintes of heven, and my body to be buryed in the churcheyerde of Pynchbek. To the high altare within Pynchbek churche xijd. To the churche warke of Pynchbek vjs viijd. To the churche warke of Lincoln viijd. To the pupils or orphans withowt the wallys of Lincoln vjd. I will have disposyd at my buryall day of messe and dirige and to pore folkes xs, and at my vij[th] day vjs viijd. I

will that my executrix schall kyll, or cause to be kyllyd, a red dowyd stere, and to bake or cause to be bakyd halff a seame of grende, that is to say of wheat, rye and barly, and thys to be disposyd to pore folkes within the towne of Pynchbek by the discrescion of my executrix at my xxx^{ty} day. I will that my executrix shall cause v messys to be sayd at Scala Celi. I will that my executrix shall gyff to Sir Thomas Walpull vj*s* viij*d*, yff he will go to the universite, towardes hys exhibicion.[44] And iff he go not to the universite then I will my executrix schall dispose it to pore folkes within the towne of Pynchbek ther as moste nede shall be. To Margaret my doughtter ij kye and ij burlynges, a blak fely and a mare, v schepe. To William Yong my brother xij*d*. To every one of William Yonge's chyldren a lamme at clyppyng tyme. To Agnes Clare my syster a schepe hog. To John Yong my brother a schepe hog. To every godchylde that I have ij*d*. To my mother a stryke of wheate, a pek of rye and a pek of barly. The reste of my goodes and catallys not gyffyn nor bequethyd, I gyff to Agnes my wyff, whome I make my sole executrix with John Clare and John Yong to be my supervisors. Also I make my will in the same day and date above namyd. I surrender all my copyholde lande to the handes of John Wythe aftyr the order of the lorde's courte and custome of the cuntre to the performance and use of thys my last will. [fo. 93v] To Agnes my wyff one house with the appurtenances longyng therto be it more or lesse, lying in Hygate, the terme of her lyff. And aftyr her decesse I will the abovenamyd house with the appurtenances be solde, and William Clare the sun of Agnes Clare my syster, to have xx*s* of the mony takyn for the sayd house, and John Yong, the sun of John my brother, to have xx*s*. The reste of the money takyn for the same house I will that John Clare and John Yong my brother shall have it. To every one of the iiij chyldren that war Robert Yonge's my brother's, iij*s* iiij*d*, and any one, ij, or thre of them dye, then I will that they that lyvys shall be heyres in the money to them that be ded. And yff they all dye or they cum to laufull age then I will the abovenamyd marke shall be disposyd for my soule, ther soulys, and all Crysten soulys. To Agnes my wyff my house that I toke owt of the lorde's handes of Spaldyng, the terme of her lyff. And aftyr her decesse I will that Margaret my doughter shall have the abovenamyd house the date of my yeres. I will that Margaret my doughter shall have my house beyng copyholde and all my copyholde landes to her, to her heyres, and to her assygnes for ever. Thes beyng wytnesses; Sir Thomas Hill, preste, William Yong, John Withe, Richerd Storer, with other mo.

Proved before P at Spalding, 19 February 1532/3.

90.   RICHARD PAGE [OF GRANTHAM]
        [LCC 1532–34, fo. 85r]

11 October 1532. I, Richard Page of Grantham, beyng hoolle of mynd and of good remembrans, make my testament. Firste I beqwere my soll to allmyghty God, Our Lady Saynt Mary, and to all thei holy cumpeny of heven. My body to be buriyd in the churcheyarde of Grantham. To the blessid sacrament viij*d*. To Our Lady of Lincoln ij*d*. To Our Lady warke of Lincoln ij*d*. To Sibille Page on qwye. Thei residue of my goodes not beqwerid, I gyffe them to Margarete my wyffe, whome I

---

[44] There is no record of Thomas Walpull at either university.

make my executrice, and John Page my brother thei supervisor. Thes beryng wytnesseth; William Peyrtre, Robert Barge, with moo.

Proved before P at Lincoln, 13 December 1532.

91.   CHRISTOPHER HAGHUS [OF EAST KEAL]
       [LCC 1532–34, fos. 33r–34v]

12 October 1532. I, Christofer Haghus of Ester Kell, gentylman, beyng hole of mynde and of good memory, makes my testament and last will. Fyrst and principally I gyff and bequeth my soule to allmyghtty God, Our Lady St. Mary and to all the saintes in heven, and my body to be buryed in the churche of the Invencion of the Holy Crosse of Ester Kell, and the churche to have for my buryall vjs viijd with that the law requiryth to be my mortuary. To the blessyd sacrament of the same for tithys forgottyn xiijs iiijd. To the churche warkes of the same vjs viijd. To Our Lady light of the same xijd. To St. Christofer light of the same xijd. To all Crysten soulys' light of the same xijd. To Our Lady warke of Lincoln xijd. I will that Thomas Haghus my sonne be founde of my goodes at the gramer scole and to have all thynges necessary as schall becum a scholer to have, unto suche tyme that the sayd Thomas Haghus my sonne be fully xxiiij yeres of age, and then yff hys mynde will serve hym with cummyng to be a preste [fo. 33v] he to have, when he shall syng hys fyrst messe, iijl vjs viijd and ij sylver spones; and thys to be payd hym at the sayd age off xxiiij yeres be he preste be he none. To William Haghus my sonne vl to by horsse harness and honeste apparell to hys bak. To Alice Laughtton my syster xxs and one gowne that was my wyffes. To Christofer Haghus my sonne vjl xiijs iiijd or ellys the valure thereof and thys to be payd hym at the xxj yeres of hys age [remainder] to be at the disposicion of my executors. I will that Anne Claymonde and Cassander Claymonde, doughters of late of John Claymonde of Frampton in Hollande, ether of them, to have a harnest gyrdell, and the sayd gyrdellys to be delyveryd unto them at the day of ther maryage. To John Walker my servant on cowe and vj schepe, and thys to be delyveryd hym immedyatly aftyr my decesse. To Beatrix Barbar my servant a qwy and a shedder hog. To Christofer Nicolson my godsun a cowe that is in Robert Palmer handes. To Margaret Nicolson my servant a cowe and a qwy and sex schepe hogges. To Jenet Richerdson my servant ij schepe hogges. To John Gray my servant, for the good service he hath done me, xls and sex schepe hogges. To the iiij orders of frerys in Boston to pray for me xiijs iiijd, that is to wyt ich of the housys iijs iiijd. I will that ther be delte for me at my obbit day xiijd to xiij pore folkes duryng the terme of iij yeres. To viij townys nexte adjonyng unto me that is to say Ester Kell, Wester Kell, Bolyngbrok, Enderby Malvis,[45] Raythby, Hundylby, Spillesby and Toynton iijl iijs iiijd, [fo. 34r] to be delte for the helthe of my soule to the indigent people at the discrecion of the curates, so that ther be delte in every towne as is aforesayd vjs viijd, Ester Kell, Wester Kell and Toynton onely excepte, for in ich those townys I will that xs be delte for me. To Thomas Burton parson my gostly father, for hys paynes, iijs iiijd. Thys is the laste will of me, afore wryten, Christofer Haghus, mayd the day and yere afore specifyed. I will that John Haghus my sonne have and take the yerely proffyt of the rent of the ferme that Sylvester Haghus dwellys in, which of late was John Grygby's, the space of viij yeres

---

[45] Mavis Enderby.

nexte immediatly foloyng aftyr my decesse, to the performyng of thys my last will. And aftyr the sayd viij yeres be fully expyred then I will that the sayd ferme with all the appurtenance do remayn to William Haghus my sonne, to hys heyres and assygnes in fe simple for ever, with one rig lying in the est felde of Ester Kell aforesayd, in a place callyd Mylne Styght. I will that all other my landes, tenementes, and other hereditamentes, with all the appurtenances that I am seasyd in or any other man to my use, beyng and lying within the townys and feldes of Ester Kell aforesayd and Wester Kell, to John Haghus aforesayd my sonne and to the heyr male of hys body laufully begottyn. And yff that the sayd John Haghus my sone do dy withowt heyr male of hys body laufully begottyn [remainder to] William Haghus my sonne and to the heyr male of hys body laufully begottyn [remainder to] Thomas Haghus my sonne and to the heyr male of hys body laufully begottyn [remainder to] Christofer Haghus my sonne and to the hyr male of hys body laufully begottyn [remainder to] the right heyres of me the forsayd Christofer Haghus. The resydue of my goodes I will that they be at the disposicion of John Haghus my sonne and John Tayllor the elder, draper, whome I make my executors, and Mr. John Reede esquier to be supervisor, with thes wytnes; Thomas Burton, parson, my gostly father, Michel Gybson, preste, and Christofer Haghus, with other mo.

> Proved before P at Partney, 4 February 1532/3. Adm. granted to John Haghus the son, an executor, reserving power to grant to John Tayllor the co-executor.

92. EDMUND WILLOWBE [OF TIMBERLAND]
[LCC 1532–34, fo. 2r]

14 October 1532. I, Edmunde Willowbe off Tymberlande, hole of mynde and good remembraunce, makes my testament and laste will. Fyrste I bequethe my soule to allmyghtty God, Our Lady, and to all the cumpeny of heven. My body to be buryed in the churcheyarde of Tymberlande. To the high altare in the churche of Tymberlande iiijd. To Our Lady warke of Lincoln iijd. To the high altare of Our Lady of Lincoln iijd. To the prior of Nocton xijd. To Nocton churche viijd. To Isabell my doughter one cowe, one qwye, ij yong bullokes, ij calves, one quarter wheate, ij quarters barly and a olde wayn, a dun mare and halffe my housholde stuff. The resydue of my goodes I gyff them to Margaret my wyff, whome I make my executrix, and Richerde Warde supervisor. Thes beryng wytnes; Sir Robert Dowke, Anthony Kyrke, with mo.

> Proved before P at Grantham, 13 January 1532/3. Adm. granted to executrix.

93. WILLIAM TUCKE [OF HORBLING]
[LCC 1532–34, fos. 27v–28r]

15 October 1532. I, William Tuk of Horblyng, with a hole mynde and good remembruaunce makes thys my testament and last will. Fyrst I bequethe my soule to God allmyghtty, and to Our Lady St. Mary, and to all the holy cumpeny in heven. My body to be buryed in the churcheyerde of St. Andro in Horblyng. To the mother churche off Our Lady in Lincoln iijs iiijd. To the churche off Horblyng iijs iiijd. To

every one off my brether v*s*. To a prest to pray for me ij*s*, and more as it plesses my executor when sche seys [fo. 28r] my dettes payd. I make Elizabeth my wyff my sole executor, and Mr. Richerd Denton my supervisor. Thes wytnesses; Mr. Richerd Denton, Thomas Heveryngham, John Gybson, Thomas Haston, with other moy.

Proved before P at Bourne, 15 January 1532/3.

94.   ROBERT PARSONS [OF DORRINGTON]
        [LCC 1532–34, fo. 145r]

16 October 1532. I, Robert Parsons, of and in good and hole mynde, makyth my last will. I bequeth my soule to allmyghtty God, Hys mother Mary, and to all the cumpeny in heven, and my body to be buryed within the churcheyerde of St. Wolfray in Diryngton, and my mortuary as the lawe will. To the reparacion of the same paryshe churche x*s*. To the high altare of the same paryshe churche vj*s* viij*d*. To the sepulcre light iij*s* iiij*d*. To the reparacion of our moder churche of Lincoln xij*d*. To the fatherles chyldren at St. Catheryn's xij*d*. To John Parsons the elder the copy of the grange. To Johanne my wyff one house in the Hurne, and aftyr the dethe of her I gyff the sayd house to John Parsons my sun, the yonger. To John my sun hys chyldren, every one of them, a lamme. To my shepperde one lamme. To Robert my godsun one lamme. The resydue of my goodes I gyff to the disposicion of Johanne my wyff, which I make my full executrix, and she to dispose it as she thynkes best, and John my sun, the elder, for to help her in neyd, and he to have for hys labor vj*s* viij*d*. Wytnes of thys my last will; Sir William Tyngell, John Parsons, John Wryght, with other mo.

Proved before P at Lincoln, 23 May 1533.

95.   MARGARET ROMFORTHE [OF WYBERTON]
        [LCC 1532–34, fo. 94v]

16 October 1532. I, Margaret Romfforth of Wyberton, of hole mynd and gud remembranes, mayke my testament and last wyll. Firste I bequeth my soull to God allmighty and to Our Ladie Saint Marie, and to all the holly company of hevyn. My bodye to be bureid in the chircheyard of Sainct Leadegar. To Ouer Lady of Lincoln iiij*d*. To the fatherles children of Sainct Kateryn in Lincoln ij*d*. To the parson for my tithes forgetun iij*d*. To Ouer Ladie auter ij*d*. To Sainct Kateryn auter in the sam chirche ij*d*. To Sainct Anne auter ij*d* and iij yardes of lynen clothe. To Ouer Ladie awlter a awter cloith. I will that their schall be xx*s* bestoweid of me in iij daeis. I will have a trentall song at the chapill. To the chirche warkes of Wiberton iiij markes. To Richard Wilkynson a sprews chiste, a long spytt, a payr of bed sides, a borden char, a par lynen scheittes, a fether bed, a bolster, a pillawe and ij of the worste queshons. To Mawde Wilkynson a sprews chiste, a pare of the best lynen schettes, a ketill, a candilstake and a pewter dische. To the iiij orders of freers to be devideid equally vj*s* viij*d*. To Sir Richard Stephynson iij*s* iiij*d*. To George Wilkynson iij*s* iiij*d*. The residew of my gudes I putt theym to the dispossyng of Elisabeth Clymson, whom I make myn executrice. George Wilkynson to be supervisor. Thies being witnes; Sir Richard Stephynson, George Wilkynson, Richard Wilkynson, Richard Pacharnes, withe other mo.

Proved before P at Boston, 20 February 1532/3.

96.   RALPH SHOTTON [OF BILLINGBOROUGH]
       [LCC 1532–34, fos. 25v–26r]

16 October 1532. I, Rayff Schotton off the paryshe of Billyngburgh, beyng in good mynde and perfyte remembraunce, makes my last will and testament. Fyrste I bequethe my soule to allmyghtty God and to Our Blessyd Lady St. Mary, and to all the holy cumpeny of hevyn. And I will my body be buryed in the churcheyerde of Byllyngburgh be my wyff other husbande. To the high altare there for my tithys forgottyn viij*d*. To the offeryng off Our Lady of Lincoln iiij*d*. To the chylder of St. Catheryn's ij*d*. To the woman that kepys the same chylder iiij*d*. To the reparacion of Our Lady altare in Billyngburgh churche vj*d*. To the rode light vj*d*. To the churche warke xij*d*. To William Shotton my brother, the use and kepyng of one fether bed, [fo. 26r] one pare of flaxyn schetes, one pare of hardyn schetes and ij coverlydes for the terme of hys lyff. And aftyr the decesse of the sayd William I will the sayd goodes remayn to Richerde Shotton hys sun, hys heyres and assygnes. To William Shotton viij sylver sponys and ij kyne. To Richerde Shotton, sun of the sayd William my bond carte, ij marys and ij qwyes. To Thomas Gustert the younger iij seame barly, my brand and my pyche. To Thomas Gustert the elder one blake colte of ij yere olde. To Richerde Sop wyff one cowe. To Catheryne her doughter one qwye calffe. To every one of my godchylder iiij*d*. To John Metton one qwye calffe and one lamme. To Agnes Alen one yowe. To Sir John Cotes one qwater borde. To Jenet my wyff vj kyne, ij qwys, x quarter barly, ij quarter pees, one seame wheate, vj seame malte and all my housholde stuff not gyffyn nor bequethyd. I will that Jenet my wyff have the use and proffet of my house lying in Westgate for terme of her lyff, so that she kepe the sayd house in good reparacion. And aftyr her decesse I will that William Shotton my brother have the proffet of the sayd house for terme of hys lyff, and aftyr hys decesse I gyff the forsayd house with the purtenances therto perteynyng to Richerde Shotton, sun of the forsayd William. And aftyr hys decesse I will it remayn to Richerde Soppe wyff and to her chyldren evermore. The resydue of all my goodes I gyff them to William Schotton my brother and to Thomas Gusterde the yunger, the whiche I make my executors. Wytnes heroff; Sir John Cottes, William Batte, Thomas More, with other mo.
       Proved before P at Bourne, 15 January 1532/3.

97.   JOHN ROUTON [OF HORBLING]
       [LCC 1532–34, fo. 90v]

19 October 1532. I, John Routon of Horbelyng, with a hole mynde and good remembraunce, makes thys my last will and testament. Fyrst I bequeth my soule to God allmyghtty and to Our Lady St. Mary, and to all the holy cumpeny in heven. My body to be buryed in the churcheyerde of St. Andro in Horblyng. To Our Lady of Lincoln xx*d*. To the high altare of Horblyng xx*d*. To the fatherles chylder viij*d*. To my chylde that my wyff goyth withall xx^ty schepe, ij kye, ij calves and vj seame barly and a seame wheate. To my fader ij cotes and a qwy and a seame of bred corne, and halff a seame malte. I will a trentall be done for me and my moder for the helthe of our soulys. To Thomas Applegarthe a cowe and a qwy, and a score schepe. To Thomas Routon a score schepe. To Richerd Crale halff a score schepe. To William Banton vj schepe. To John Gypson halffe a seame peys. To Adam Paldyng a yowe and a lamme. To John Paldyng my godsun a yow and a lamme. To Robert

Crale a yow and a lamme. To William Skynner a yow and a lamme. To Richerd Bawdwyn xij*d*. All the resydue of my goodes I gyff to Agnes my wyff, whome I make my sole executor. And the same power and strenkyth that I am in, I put her in all maner of causys, and William Somerby I make my supervisor, and to have for hys labor vj*s* viij*d*. Thes wytnes; Sir John Kyrslay, Christofer Routon, Thomas Routon, Richerd Crale, Adam Paldyng, William Skynner, with other mo.

Proved before P at [Great] Hale, 17 February 1532/3.

98. ROGER HUNTE [OF KIRTON IN HOLLAND]
[LCC 1532–34, fo. 92]

20 October 1532. I, Roger Hunte of Kyrton in Holland, of hole mynde and memory, makyth my testament concludyng with my last will. Fyrst I bequethe my soule to God allmyghtty, Our Lady St. Mary, and to all the celestiall cumpeny of heven. My body to be buryed in the churchyerde of Kyrton, and for my mortuary aftyr the forme of the statutes. To the high altare of Kyrton for necligent tithys ij*d*, and to every altare in the sayd churche ij*d*. To the reparacion of our mother churche of Lincoln ij*d*. To the orphans of St Catheryn's ij*d*. To my wyff my messuage wyth the appurtenances, the which I dwell in, the terme of her lyff, and aftyr her decesse I will that same mesuage remayn to Edwarde my sonne and to hys heyres of hys body. And yff the sayd Edwarde departe thys worlde withowt heyres then I will the sayd mesuage with the purtenances remayn to Jamys my sonne and to hys heyres of hys body, [remainder to] Thomas my sonne and to hys heyres [remainder to] the reste off my kyn. I will that ij acres in fen landes and one acre lying in Kyrton yng remayn to my wyff the terme of her lyff, and aftyr her decesse to remayn to Thomas my sonne and to hys heyres of hys body [fo. 92v] [remainder to] Edwarde my sonne and the heyres of hys body [remainder to] the nexte of my kyn in maner before namyd. To my wyff ij acres lande lying in Mores and one acre lande lying at Halgate the terme of her lyff, and aftyr her decesse [remainder in succession to] Jamys, Thomas and Edwarde my sonnes and the heyres of their bodies [remainder to] the nexte of my kyn in maner before rehersyd. I gyff my copy of my house to my wyff. To Elizabeth and Agnes my doughters iij*l* vj*s* viij*d* each at the age of xx^ty yeres, and ether of them one yong cowe to be delyveryd be my executrix or her assigners. And yff ether of the sayd my doughters departe before the age aforesayd then I will the sayd iij*l* vj*s* viij*d* and one cowe remayn at the disposicion off my executrix. And yff bothe my doughtters departe before the age of xx^ty yeres, then I will all the hole remayn to my executrix. The resydue of my goodes I put them to the disposicion off Agnes my wyff whome I make my executrix to dispose my goodes to the pleasure of God and helthe of my soule. Wytnes; Sir Thomas Est, paryshe prest, Thomas Cony the elder, with other.

Proved before P at Donington, 18 February 1532/3.

99. THOMAS GREGBY [OF SCREMBY]
[LCC 1532–34, fo. 35]

22 October 1532. I, Thomas Gregby of Scremby, hole of mynde, makyth my testament and last will. Fyrst I bequethe my soule to God allmyghtty, to Our Lady and to all the saintes in heven, and my body to be buryed in the churcheyerde of St

Peter in Scremby. To Our Lady warke of Lincoln xij*d*. To the high altare of Scremby churche vj*d*. To the bying of a new crosse to Scremby churche xxvj*s* viij*d*. To Jenet my wyff ij oxen, ij marys, iiij kye, xxx^{ty} schepe, with all my croppe in the barne and all the croppe that is sawyn and to be sawyn in Gregby thys yeare, and one acre wheate, j acre barly and one acre beanys of my ferme in Scremby. Also my wayn, my plugh with all the geres therto belongyng, and all my housholde stuff. To Thomas my sun ij oxen, one balde fylly, ij qwyes, xx^{ty} of the best lammys and a bras pot. To John my sonne ij sterys and x lammys. To ich on of my iij doughters xx^{ty} yowes and a qwye. To my mother xx*s*. The resydue of my goodes I put to the disposicion of John Carter and Richerd Atkynson, whome I make my executors for fulfyllyng of my testament and paying my dettes, and the overdele that remayneth to the bryngyng up of my yong chyldren, and therfore I bequethe ether of them for ther labor x*s*. Thes wytnes; Sir William Torner, John Hawarde with other.

Proved before P at Partney, 4 February 1532/3.

100.   WILLIAM JOLANDE [OF WEST RASEN]
       [LCC 1532–34, fos. 83v–84r]

23 October 1532. I, William Jolande off West Rasyn, husbandman, of hole mynde and good remembraunce, makes my testament and last will. Fyrst I wyt my soule to God allmyghtty and to Our Lady St. Mary and to all the holy cumpeny of heven, and my body to be buryed within the churchyerde of All Halloys in West Rasyn. To Mr. Parsone xx*d* to pray for me. To Sir Edmunde [fo. 84r] Walkyngton viij*d*. To Our Lady warke of Lincoln xij*d*. To the frerys, every house iiij*d*. To the church body of West Rasyn xij*d*. To the churche of Kynyerby iiij*d*. A brannyd cowe to my doughter dwellyng in the towne of Kyrkby. To Agnes my doughter a blak qwye. To Richerd my sonne and Alyson my doughter, other of them, a schepe hog. To Elizabeth my wyff all the housholde stuff. I will that my goodes not wyt be departyd into iij partes, one parte to Elizabeth my wyff and Thomas my sonne whome I make my executors, the secunde parte to be devydyd emonges my chyldren the which is unwede, the thyrde parte to be disposyd for my soule. The resydue of my parte not wit nor bequeste I will that it be devydyd emonges my chyldren whose names is Thomas, Edon, Margaret, Robert, Isabell, William, Cristofor, aftyr the cownsell of Thomas my brother, whome I make the supervisor, and he to have for hys labor iij*s* iiij*d*. Thes wytnes; John Lammyng, William Frer, Thomas Jolande, with other mo.

Proved before P at Kirkby [cum Osgodby], 13 November 1532.

101.   ROBERT BARKER [OF DUNSTON]
       [LCC 1532–34, fo. 21]

24 October 1532. I, Robert Barker of Dunston, with a hole mynde and beyng of goode remembraunce, make and conclude my testament. Fyrste I bequethe my soule to allmyghtty God, to Our Lady St. Mary and to all the saintes in heven, and my body to be buryd in the churcheyerde of St. Peter in Dunston beforesayd, and my mortuary as the lawe dothe assygne. To the reparacions of the churche of Dunston xij*d*. To the reparacions of our mother churche of Lincoln xij*d.* To the churche of Rowston iij*s* iiij*d,* and to the high altare in the same churche for tithys

forgottyn xij*d*. To the iiij orders of frerys in the towne of Lincoln, every one of them, a halffe stryke wheate and a halffe stryke barly. To the pore orphans of St. Catheryn's a bushyll wheate. To the pore people of Rowston a halffe quarter off wheate to be distrybutyd emong them. Also I will that ther be v messys sayd of the v woundes of Our Lorde for me and my chyldren, and one messe for my brother Rawlande. To my chyldren that lyff to they be at laufull age [fo. 21v] xl*s*, and yff none of them lyff then I will that it be disposyd for our soulys by the discrecion of my executors. The rest of my goodes her not gyffyn I put to the disposicion of Johanne my wyff and Sir Charlys Wellys my brother, whome I make my executors to dispose for my soule, to pay my dettes, my legacies and my funerall charges. And the sayd Sir Charles to have for hys labor iij*s* iiij*d*. Also I desyre Richerde Wellys and John Lane to se that the hole legacy of thys my testament be well and truly fulfyllyd and they to have for ther labor equally shyftyd betwyxte them vj*s* viiij*d*. Thes wytnes; Sir William Whyte, vicar, and William Purgyn, with other mo.

Proved before P at Lincoln, 13 December 1532. Adm. granted to Sir Charles Wellys as executor, Joan Barker the relict and co-executor meanwhile having died.

102. JOHN BRODELEY [OF APPLEBY]
[Stow 1530–52, fos. 12v–13r]

26 October 1532. I, John Brodley of Appulby makes my testament. First I bequeth my saull to almyghty God and to Owr Saynt Mary and to all the sayntes of hevyn, and my body to be buryed in the churchyarde off Saynt Bartilmew in Appulby. To the high awtur iiij*d*. To Ower Lady of Lincoln iiij*d*. To Ower Lady of haly breid awter iiij*d*. To [fo. 13r] the rode litht ij*d*. To All Hallows light ij*d*. To William my sonn on mylke cowe and iij quarters barley and a bey stag with a sterne in the forhed. To Agnes my doughter on mylk cowe, iij quarters barley and on dune ffilly. I make my wiff executrix. Wetnesse of the same; Master Vicar Sir William Bayns, parish preste, Robert Hoton, William Brodley, William Norffolke, and other moo.

Proved before L, 9 January 1532/3. Adm. granted to the executrix.

103. JOHN DALBY [OF LITTLE PONTON]
[LCC 1532–34, fo. 24v]

28 October 1532. I, John Dalby of Panton the Lesse, off hole mynde and good remembraunce, do make thys my last will and testament. Fyrst I bequethe my soule to allmygtty God, Our Lady and Hys saintes, and my body to be buryed in the churcheyerde of St. Michel of Paunton aforesayd. To the high altare I bequethe xij*d*. I will have done for my soule and all Christen soulys v messys. The resydue of all my goodes I gyff to Agnes my wyff and my chyldren at her discrestion. I make Agnes my wyff my full executrix and Thomas Bell supervisor. Thes wytnesses; Sir Robert Hornby, Hugh Osberner, with other mo.

Proved before P at Grantham, 13 January 1532/3.

104. TESTAMENT OF OLIVER ASHLAY [OF WALCOT]
[LCC 1532–34, fo. 24r.]

30 October 1532. I, Oliver Ashlay of Walcot, of a hole mynde and good rememberaunce, make my will and full testament. Fyrst I will my soule to allmyghtty God, to the Virgyn Mary and to all the saintes in heven, my body to be buryed in the churche of St. Andro off Walcot. I will for my mortuary that the law doyth admyt. To the high altare of Walcot xij*d*. To the churche of Walcot iij*s* iiij*d*. To Our Lady warke of Lincoln xij*d*. To St. John gylde one yowe. To All Halloy lyght one lamme. To every one of my chylder severall be themselffe viij*l*. And yff it fortune any of the sayd chylder to departe within the age of xvj yeres then I will the sayd viij*l* be devydyd emong the other. To William my sun one bun carte. To Thomas my sun one cownter aftyr the dethe of hys mother. To Christofer my sun one gray amblyng stag. To Margery my doughter one prasser aftyr the dethe of her mother. To Elizabethe my doughter a pare of amber beades gawdyd with sylver aftyr the dethe of her mother. To Mr. Prior of Sempyngham vj*s* viij*d*. To the subprior viij*d*. To every one of the chanons iiij*d*. To one preste to say a trentall for my soule and all christen soulys x*s*. To Peter Ashlay my brother my best cote. To Margaret Qwynsy vj*s* viij*d*. To Mr John Blak of Grantham x*s*. To Sir Thomas Pell x*s*. To Robert Armestrong of Oykham x*s*. The resydue off my goodes I gyff to Jenet my wyff, whome I make my full executrix for to dispose for the helthe off my soule. And Mr. John Blak and Sir Thomas Pell supervisors. Thes wytnesses; Edmunde Qwynsy, William Fysher, William Ashlay, with other mo.

Proved before P at Grantham, 13 January 1532/3.

105. TESTAMENT OF MARGARET AWVERAY [OF BECKINGHAM]
[LCC 1532–34, fo. 61v]

31 October 1532. I, Margaret Awveray of the paryshe of Bekkyngham, vidue, of a good remembraunce and a hole mynde, make my testament and my last will. Fyrst I bequethe my soule unto God allmyghtty, to Our Lady St. Mary and to all the holy saintes in heven. My body to be buryed in the churcheyerde off All Halloys off Bekkyngham. To Our Lady warkes at Lincoln iiij*d*. To the high altare of Bekkyngham iiij*d*. To the churche off Stapulfurthe iiij*d*. To the churche of Stragilthorpe iiij*d*. To the chapell of St. Margaret iiij*d*. To Richerde my sonne a brasse potte and to hys chyldren, ij schepe hogges. To Thomas my sonne ij schepe hogges. To William hys sun on schepe hog, and to Robert hys sonne one schepe hog, and to hys wyff a russyt gowne. To Helene Sutton a schepe hog. To Elizabeth Carter one schepe hog. The resydue of my goodes I gyff to William my sonne, the whiche I make my executor that he may dispose it for the helthe of my soule to the plesure of allmyghtty God. I will that Richerde my sonne be supervisor. Thes wytnesses; Sir Thomas Hyrde, curat, Thomas Holforthe, John Burtte.

Proved before P at Lincoln, 30 December 1532.

106. ROBERT MANNYNG [OF MAREHAM]
[LCC 1532–34, fo. 149]

1 November 1532. I, Robert Mannyng of Marom, with a hole mynde and of a good remembraunce makyth my will. In primis I gyff my soule to God allmyghtty, to Our

Lady St. Mary and to all the saintes in heven, and my body to by buryd in the churcheyerde of St. Helene in Marom. To Our Lady's warke of Lincoln vj*d*. To the high altare of Our Lady of Lincoln vj*d*. To the high altare of Marom viij*d*. To the churche warke of Marom xx*d*. To every gylde halffe a quarter barly or ellys malte. To Ame my doughter the best matteres save one, one qwye and a lytyll lande of barly. To Isabell my doughter the coverlet that I bought at Staynton, one stere and halffe a lande of barly. To John my sun my best cote, iij bushylls of barly and a bushyll of whete. To William Howcam of Conesby my worstyd dooblet. I will that ther be done iij trentallys at St. Catheryn altare. I will that ther be takyn vj*s* viij*d* of my goodes to fynde a lyght afore St. Catheryne, and the aldermen to have the rule of it. To Thomas Toly a lyttyll lande of barly, and to John Wylson my servant another lyttyll lande of barly. The resydue of my goodes not gyffyn, my dettes payd, I gyff to Margarete my wyff. I will that William Watson of Tomby and Margaret my wyff be my executors for to dispose my goodes for the helthe of my soule, and the sayd William Watson to have a blak stag for hys labor. I will that Thomas, Richerde and Agnes my chylder have payd owt of all my landes and tenementes in Marom, the whiche I bought of Michell Bower otherwayse callyd Paronyll, iij*l* emong them, that is to say to every off them xx*s*. And yff any of them dye before the age of mariage then I will the other of them lyffyng have the parte of hym or them so departyd. Also I will that my iij doughters, that is to say Ame, Isabell and Margarete, have other iij*l* owt of the sayd landes and tenementes, that is to say every of them xx*s*. And yff any of them dye before the age of mariage then I will the other of them survyvyng have the parte of hym or them so departyd. And lykewise [fo. 149v] off all the foresayd legaces. Also I will that as sone as the sayd vj*l* is payd, that all the sayd landes and tenementes be lattyn for the value that they can be by the space of ij yeres, and the value therof to be gyffyn to Michel Bower or to hys heyres, provydyd alway that duryng the takyng up of the sayd vj*l*, and also after that the takyng up the sayd ij yeres value, sufficient reparacions be done yerely apon the sayd house continually unto hit comme unto the use of my sayd sone John Mannyng. Also I will that as sone as the sayd vj*l* is payd and the sayd ij yeres be expyred and passyd, I will that my sonne John have all the sayd landes and tenementes to hym and hys heyres, uppon thys condicion, that he shall not sell it excepte that he do sell it to one of hys iij systers, Ame, Isabell and Margaret, or ellys to Michel Bower, or to somme of hys heyres, and uppon thys condicion, that my wyff Margaret have yerely owt of it duryng her lyff vj*s* viij*d* aftyr my sayd lande comme to the use of my sayd sun John. Also I will that the medo grounde that I bought of John Bower that lyes in the northe yges fynde a lyght before Our Lady in the high qwere. Thes beyng wytnes; Sir Thomas Snydall, Richerde Whalley, Thomas Johnson and Dennys Appley.

Proved before P at Lincoln, 20 June 1533. Adm. granted to the executors.

107. THOMAS FISHER [OF LEAKE]
[LCC 1532–34, fo. 94r]

6 November 1532. I, Thomas Fysher of Leeke, beyng in hole mynde and off good remembraunce makes my testament. Fyrst I bequethe my soule to allmyghtty God, to Hys moder St Mary, and to all the saintes beyng in heven. My body to be buryed in the kyrkeyerde of Our Lady of Leeke. To the parsone for forgottyn tithys viij*d*.

To the anowrnement of Our Lady of Leeke. To every altare in the same kyrke iiij*d*. To the high altare of Our Lady of Lincoln vj*d*. To Our Lady warkes ther vj*d*. I bequeth x*s* to one preste for to syng one trentall in the kyrk off Leeke for my soule, the soulys of my fader and moder, and all Christen soulys. To Thomas, Henry and Michel my sonnys ij sterys and ij horses each, and Thomas and Henry to have the iiij eldest sterys, and Michel ij yonger sterys and one qwye of the same age. To Thomas my sonne one colte stag of ij yere olde and one fely of one yere olde. To Henry my sonne a dun stag and a fely of ij yeres olde. To Michel my sonne one blak balde mare with her fole. To Jenet Fysher one whyte blakkyd cowe. To Elizabethe Fysher one pyed cowe. To John Fysher one quarter barly. To John Wasteler yonger one yow and one lamme. To John Fysher, sonne of Richerde Fysher, ij yowes. To Jenet Fysher ij yowes. To Elizabeth Fysher one yowe. The resydue of my goodes I gyff to Beatrix my wyff and William Wasteler, whome I make my executors to pay my dettes and my legaces and to dispose for my soule as they thynke shall be moste plesur to God. To William Wasteler for hys labor one cowe with calve of iij yere olde. I make Mr John Thamworthe supervisor. And I gyff hym for hys labor iij*s* iiij*d*. To my masterys hys wyff iij*s* iiij*d*. Thes wytnes; Frere Thomas Camook, William Whetley, John Pekeryng and John Wytton, with other mo.

Proved before P at Boston, 20 February 1532/3.

108.   THOMAS PHILIP [OF BARDNEY]
       [LCC 1532–34, fo. 84]

9 November 1532. I, Thomas Philip of Bardeney, hole of mynde and memory, makes thys my last will. Fyrst I bequeth my soule to God, Our Lady and to all saintes of heven, and my body to be buryed in the parysh churche of Bardeney. To Our Lady warke of Lincoln iiij*d*. To the high altare of the same iiij*d*. To the Trinite light of Sotheray iiij*d*. To the plow light of Sotheray ij*d*. To Our Lady light off Bardeney ij*d*. To the soule light of the same ij*d*. To Roger my sonne a browne geldyng oxe and a gray mere. To Robert my sonne one oxe and a yong meyr. To Alexander my sonne ij kye. To Alice Pecok a yong meyr. To Richerde my sonne ij of my best oxen and a cowe. To William my sonne ij oxe calves and an ambre. [fo. 84v] To my lorde of Bardeney one oxe calffe. To Sir Edmunde Watson on hog schepe. To Lenten chylder ij yeryng calffys. To Alice Couverley one hog schepe and one rye lande. I bequethe for v messys in the woorschip of the v woundes of Jesus Cryst xx*d*. I will that all my housholde stuff be devydyd to Richerde my sonne and to Lenten chylder in equall porcions. The resydue of my goodes I will that Roger my sonne and Robert my sonne, whome I make my executors, distribute emong all my chylder in equall porcions. Thes wytnes; Sir Edmunde Watson, vicar, Robert Wauker, Richerde Bunbe, with other.

Proved before P at Lincoln, 9 December 1532.

109.   THOMAS ROOSSE [VICAR OF RIBY]
       [LCC 1532–34, fo. 83r]

10 November 1532. I, Sir Thomas Roosse, vicar of Ryby, beyng hole of mynde and of good memory, makyth my testament and last will. Fyrst I bequeth my soule unto God allmyghtty, unto the Virgine Mary, and to all the hevenly citezyns. My body to

be buryed in the monastery of St. Augustyn and St. Olyve of Welhoo. To Our Lady of Lincoln iiij*d*. To Our Lady warkes of Lincoln iiij*d*. To the high altare of St. Edmunde of Ryby vj*d*. To the churche warke of the sayd Ryby vj*d*. I bequeth xl*s* to the convent of Welhoo to kepe one obyt for my soule, my father and my mother and all my frendes soulys. To Sir Thomas Lincoln one cote, one ratchet, one kyrchyff. To Sir William Yorke one ratchet, one kyrchyff. To the iiij nonys iiij ratchetes, iiij kyrchyffes. To John Hemperyngham one lamme. To John Whythode one lamme. The resydue of my goodes not wyt I will that they shall be orderyd and disposyd be the mynde and order of Sir Robert Whytgyfte, abbot of Welhoo,[46] whome I make my trewe executor, that he may order and dispose for my soule and all Crysten soulys. Thes whytnes; Steven Est, Henry Whythode, Henry Thomson, with other moo.

Proved before P at Grimsby, 12 November 1532.

110.   THOMAS ROUTON [OF HORBLING]
       [LCC 1532–34, fo. 91r]

12 November 1532. I, Thomas Routon of Horblyng, makes my last will and testament. Fyrst I bequethe my soule to God allmyghtty and to Our Lady St. Mary and to all the holy cumpeny of heven, and my body to be buryed in the churcheyerde of St. Andro in Horblyng. To Our Lady of Lincoln xij*d*. To the churche of Horblyng a noble. To the pore chyldren at St. Catheryn's iiij*d*. I will a prest syng a trentall of messes for me and my frendes. To Laurence my servant a yow and a lamme. To Jenet my servant a pese of russyt clothe and a pese of whyte, and ij ewes and ij lammys. To William Skynner my russyt cote. To Sir John the curat at thys tyme xij*d*. To Christofer Routon, my sonne, a cowe and a score schepe with the increse to he be at age, and yff Christofer Routon my sonne departe thys worlde I will that t'oder halff be doyn for hym, and the toder halff remayn agayn to my wyff. To Richerd Bawdwyn xij*d*. To Edmunde Tillot iiij*d*. Also I make Marion my wyff sole executor, and Richerd Palmer supervisor with the syght of Mr. Prior of Sempyngham and Wyssemend, to dispose my goodes to the pleasure of God and the helthe of my soule. Wytnes wherof; Sir John Kyrslay the curate, Richard Palmer, Richard Bawdwyn, Jamys Therylbe, Nicholes Carre, Edmunde Tyllot, with other mo.

Proved before P at [Great] Hale, 17 February 1532/3.

111.   ROBERT GOODRYK [OF MUMBY]
       [LCC 1532–34, fos. 217v–218r]

15 November 1532. I, Robert Goodryk of Mumby, of hole mynde and good remembraunce, make my testament with my laste will. Fyrste I bequethe my soule unto allmyghtty God, to the Blessyd Virgyn Our Lady and to all the holy cumpeny in heven, and my body to be buryd in the churcheyerde of Mumby with a mortuary yff the lawe will. To Our Lady of Lincoln iiij*d*. To the high altare of Mumby churche iiij*d*. To the other ij altares iiij*d*. To Our Lady of Grace and Our Lady of

---

[46] Robert Whitgift was elected abbot of Wellow, near Grimsby, in 1525. The last abbot of the house, he signed the acknowledgement of Henry VIII's royal supremacy in 1534, and on the dissolution of the house in 1536 received a pension of £16 per annum: *VCH Lincolnshire*, II, 161–3.

Pety ij lammys. To the bellys iij*s* iiij*d*. To Agnes my wyff ij ky, ij marys and xxx^{ty} schepe, and all my housholde stuff. To my chyldren the iij fatte oxen, and other of them ij kye and x schepe. To John Morre vj*s* viij*d* to be good and specyall frende to my chyldren. To [fo. 218r] my godchylder, everyche of them, ij*d*. The resydue of all my goodes not bequethyd from my rent and dettes be payd, I gyff to my ij chylder Mathew Goodryk and Lenarde, aftyr the disposicion of John Morre, whome I make my executor that he shall bryng me to the grounde and pay my dettes and save the remayne to the well of my chylder, to be shyfte aftyr hys discrecion and one of them to be other heyr. Thes men beyng wytnes; Richerde Cartewryght, curate, John Lafelde, Richerde Thomson, and other mo. Wryttyn att Mumby the day and the yere above wryttyn.

Proved before P at Alford, 11 November 1533.

112.   WILLIAM PALLYNG [OF HUNDLEBY]
        [LCC 1532–34, fos. 58v–59r]

17 November 1532. I, William Pallyng of Hundylby, hole of mynde and of good remembraunce, makes my testament with my last will. Fyrst I bequeth my soule to allmyghtty God, to Our Blessyd Lady St. Mary, and to all the holly cumpeny in heven, and my body to be buryed in the churchyerde off Hundylby with that that the lawe doyth assigne to be my mortuary. To Our Lady of Lincoln iiij*d*. To Our Lady within the high quere of Hundylby iiij*d*. To the commune in Hundylby ij*d*. To All Halloys' light ij*d*. To the yong meny's light ij*d*. To the [fo. 59r] mades' light ij*d*. To Agnes my wyff ij kye and all my houshold stuff, to bring up my chyldren withall. To Robert my sonne a cople heder burlynges now yerynges. To Jamys my sonne my best cople heder burlynges now yerynges. To Jane my doughter my whyte bakkyd cowe. And yf it fortune the sayd Jane my doughter to dy before she be xv yere of age, then I will that her parte remayn to Agnes my wyff. And yff it fortune any of all my other chylder to dy before they be xv yere of age, then I will that the parte or the partes of them that be ded remayn holy to Agnes my wyff, and she for to cause halff a trentall of messys to be done for my soule and my frendes soulys. To Jenet my doughter a dowed qwe. To Robert my sonne my best cote. To John my sonne ij yowes. To the master of the chauntry of Spyllesby viij*d*. To Sir Thomas Peper iiij*d*. To Sir Jamys iiij*d*. To Sir Thomas Smyth iiij*d*. To Sir Thomas Arnolde iiij*d*. To the wyff of the chauntry iiij*d*.⁴⁷ I will that my yong horse and my mare be solde be Agnes my wyff and Robert my sonne, to pay withall my dettes and my rentes. The resydue of my goodes I gyff to Agnes my wyff and Robert my sonne, whome I make my executors, and I will desyre William Bordon to be supervisor, and to be good to my wyff and my chylder, and he to have for hys labor iij*s* iiij*d*. Wytnes herof; Sir Robert Dawson, vicar of Hundylby, John Hotofte, Libeus Smyth and Thomas Anton, with other.

Proved before P2 at Partney, 2 October 1533.

---

⁴⁷ The college of chantry priests at Spilsby was founded in 1347 by John Willoughby, Lord de Eresby. By the time the chantry certificates for the county were compiled in 1548 the college had already been dissolved the previous year, when it had been worth a clear value of £40 19s. 11d. in lands. Its last master, Thomas Maltby, was presented in 1532: *VCH Lincolnshire*, II, 236; Chantry Certificates (1923), 183–6.

113. JOHN WILLIAMSON [OF FRAMPTON]
[LCC 1532–34, fos. 162v–163r]

17 November 1532. I, John Williamson off Frampton, in hole mynde and good remembraunce beyng, makyth my testament with my last will. Fyrst I bequethe my soule to allmyghtty God, Our Lady St. Mary and to all the blessyd cumpeny of heven, and my body to be buryed in the churcheyerde [fo. 163r] off Our Lady off Frampton. To the high altare off Frampton for tithys forgottyn vjd. To every altare of the sayd churche ijd. To Our Lady gylde of Frampton one yowe. To the churche warke ijd. To Our Lady of Lincoln box iijd. To the orphans without the wallys of Lincoln ijd. For one messe doyng a Scala Celi vd. I will that Jenet my wyff have all my housholde stuff with my mylke kye, one gray meyr with xviij schepe. I will that Walter my sun have one yong gray meyr and a fole. To Mary my doughtter one qwye. To Isabell my doughter one qwye and one calve and oder of my doughtters one platter and one dyshe. To Edwarde my sun one olde gray meyr and one fole. To Thomas my sun one red meyr and one fole. To my father ij swyne schotrelles with iij bushyll benys. To Thomas my sun v stong arable lande. To Walter my sun, Mary my doughtter, and Isabell my doughter every one of them one chyste. The resydue of all my goodes not disposyd, I put to the disposicion of Walter Williamson my fader and Jenet Williamson my wyffe, whome I make my executors. Thes beyng wytnes; Sir John Lee, prest, John Dun and many mo. I will that Edwarde Cuthberde be the supervisor.

Proved before P at Donington, 28 May 1533.

114. CECILY JOHNSON [OF SWATON]
[LCC 1532–34, fo. 200v]

19 November 1532. I, Cecily Johnson of the paryshe of Swaton, of goode mynde and remembraunce, makes my laste will. Fyrste I bequethe my soule unto allmyghtty God and to the Gloriose Virgyn St. Mary Hys mother, and to all the holy cumpeny in heven. My body to be buryed in the churcheyerde of the blessyd apostill St. Andro in Swaton. To the high altare in Swaton for forgottyn tithes iiijd. To Our Lady's warke in Lincoln iiijd. To the pore chyldren in Saynt Catheryn's in Lincoln iiijd. To the paryshe churche of Swaton a lynene schete and my best lynen towell, and also to the paryshe churche of Swaton towarde the fyndyng of the light afore the roode, my best be hyve. To Sir Thomas Smale, the vicare of Swaton, to pray for me, a qwye, a lynen schete and a lynen towell. To Sir William Saunderson a lyttyll foldyng table. To Thomas Hurste my secunde be hyve. To Robert Hosborneby my thyrde be hyve. To John Hurst a bullok calve and a lyttyll panne. To Jamys Mylner a matteres whiche I ly on and a greene coverlet and a pare of harden schetes, and to hys wyff a red kyrtyll, and to every one of hys chylder a jd. To Rayff Harys a femble schete and a scherte clothe. To Thomas Hurste wyffe iiij puter platters, a pare of schetes, one lynen and one hardyn, a long spyt, a gret flackyt and my thirde kyrchyff. To Agnes Spynk my secunde kyrchyff. To Cecily Carnell my best kyrchyff, a hoode and ryppill comme, and a candylstyk stok to mak candyls in. To every godchylde that I have jd. I make Thomas Hurste and John Carnell my full executors. I will that my executors kepe my buryall day and my vij day, and I will they shall cause a trentall to be done for me and all Christen soulys within the paryshe churche of Swaton, and more yff it may be sparyd. The resydue of my

goodes not spokyn of before I will it shall be disposyd for the helthe of my husbande soule and myne and all Christen soulys, as my executors thynkes best. Thes men beryng wytnes; Sir Thomas Small, vicar of Swaton, Nicholas Woodburne and John Harosmyth, with other mo.

Proved before P at Pickworth, 23 October 1533.

115.   THOMAS STOWE [OF THE CITY OF LINCOLN]
        [LCC 1532–34, fo. 147r]

22 November 1532. I, Thomas Stowe of the citie of Lincoln, cordwainer, seke in body and of good remembraunce, ordeyne my last will and mynd. Fyrst I bequeth my soule to God almyghtie, Our Lady St. Marie and to all the hole company of heven, and my body to be buried within the pariche churche of St. John's the Evangeliste in Wykford. To Our Lady of Lincoln vj*d*. The resydue of my goodes, my dettes paied, I give them to Alice Stowe my wif, whome I do make myne executrix to fulfil my will and pay my dettes and to dispose my goodes for the helth of my soule, as she thinkes best. Witnes wherof thys my last mynde and will; Sir William Grene, Sir John Henryson, prestes, and George Henryson, with other mo.

Proved before P at Lincoln, 26 May 1533. Adm. granted to the executor.

116.   JOHN THOMSON [OF WRANGLE]
        [LCC 1532–34, fo. 95v]

26 November 1532. I, John Thomson of Wrangle, husbandman, beyng of hole mynde and good remembraunce, make my last will and testament. Fyrst I bequethe my soule to allmyghtty God, to Our Lady St. Mary and to all the cumpeny of heven, and my body to be buryed within the churcheyerde of Wrangle. To the high altare in Wrangle and to Our Lady altare, ether of them, a altare clothe. To the vicare or hys proctor for tithys forgottyn ij*s*. To Our Lady of Lincoln xij*d*. To St. Catheryn's iiij*d*. I will that my executors cause me to have iij diriges with note at the day of my buryall, and vij day and xxx^{ty} day. To my wyff my house with the garthe sted duryng her lyff, she makyng no waste. And aftyr her decesse I will that Walter Hopster my godsun have it yff he be alyff. And yff he fortune to dye before my wyff, then I will that my executors sell it and dispose the money in warkes of charite within the churche of Wrangle. To Walter Hopster my gowne and my fustian dooblet, and yff he be dede I will that my executors sell them and dispose the money. To Jenet Hopster my servant a bed and a brasse potte. To Agnes Hopster a flaxen schete. To Jenet Hopster my russet cote. To John Whytneyff a blak jaket and a new ele net. To John Hopster all the resydue of my fyshyng geare, a pare hose and my hattes and cappys, he payng ij*s* viij*d*. To my wyff ij kye, one calve, one fylly fole, iij swyne and all my barly, and all my housholde stuff that is nott before bequethyd. To Sir Thomas Potter and to John Grene, whome I make my executors, ether of them, vj*s* viij*d*. Thes beyng wytnes; Hugh Lekke, William Scryme and John Hopster.

Proved before P at Boston, 20 February 1532/3.

117. MARTIN WYGHT [OF COWBIT IN PARISH OF SPALDING]
[LCC 1532–34, fos. 241v–242r]

27 November 1532. I, Martyn Wyght of Cowbyt in the paryche of Spaldyng, gud remembrance havyng, lovyd be God, and belevyng in the faythe of holy churche lyke a Crysten man, do declare my testament and last wyll. Fyrst I bequeythe my sowle to almyghtie God, Owr Lady, and all the company of hevyn. My body to be buryed in the churcheyard of Cowbyt. To the hye awter in Cowbyt for tithys forgotton viij*d*. To the churche warke in Spaldyng iiij*d*. To the churche warke in Cowbyt xx*d*. To Owr Lady's warke in Lincoln vj*d*. To Our Lady off Wallsyngam viij*d*. To Mary off the wall viij*d*. To Margaret my wyffe all the houshold stuffe that she brought in suche reypeyr as it ys nowe and also the howse I dwell in for the terme of ij yeres, or elles xxvj*s* and viij*d*, whedder she wyll, and after the terme of ij yeres be expyred I will the howse be laten to ferme for the most profytt by myne executors to the tyme that John Wyght my sone cum to lawfull age, and the mony therof cummyng to be devydyd in forme folowyng: that ys to say, I wyll that John Wyght have halff the rent yerely when he cum to lawfull age, and the other half I wyll remayne to Johanne and Agnes my doughters att the same tyme, allwhey provydyd yff any of my chyldren deceasse within the sayd tyme that the parte and porcyon of the yerly rente of the howse remayne to the other beyng alyve. I [will]that John Wyght have my howse with the apurtinance when he is xxj yers of age to hym and to hys heyres lawfully begotton, and yff he deceasse before the sayd yers, I wyll it remayne to my dowghters in lyke forme. And yf they all deceasse withowt heres before ther mother, I wyll she have it the terme of her lyffe so that she kepe it wythe dew reparacyons, and after I wyll it be sold by myne executors or elles be the churche masters of Cowbyt then beyng, and the mony therof cumyng to be ordered in forme folowyng: fyrst I wyll they provyde an honest prest to pray att Cowbytt halff a yere for my sowle, my benefactors and all Chrysten sowles, and he to have for hys stypend vij nobulles; to Robert Smythe, Oswald Smythe, Rychard Calow, Robert Calow, Martyn Calow, Wylliam Calford the yonger, xx*s* each; and the rest to be bestoyd in repayryng the churche at Cowbytt. To Margaret my [fo. 242r] wyffe a pece of erable land that lyethe att my yardys ende and the crope therupon the terme off her lyffe, and after I wyll it remayne to John my sone and hys heyreys. To the sayd Margaret a lyttyll botte and halffe my fyschyng nettes, and the other halffe I gyffe to John Wyght. To Agnes Wyght my dowghter a foldyng table and a turnyd chayre. To Johanne Wyght a table standyng in my howse. The residew of my gudys nott bequested I gyffe to the dysposicion of Thomas Smythe and John Wyght whome I make my executors, for the helthe of my sowle and profytt of my chyldren, with the discret counsyll and oversyght off Mr. Antony Irby whome I make supervisor, and he to have for hys payn and labor x*s*. Thes beyng wyttnessys; Sir Thomas Shreve, prest, Robert Harrys, prest, Renold Horner, Rychard Sander, and many mo.
    Proved before P at Spalding, 4 March 1533/4.

118. CATHERINE CARLETON [OF STUBTON]
[LCC 1532–34, fos. 96v–97r]

2 December 1532. I, Catheryne Carleton of Stubton, vidoy, with hole mynde and memory ordyn and make thys my laste will and testament. Fyrste and principally I

bequethe my soule unto allmyghtty God my creator, to Hys Blessyd mother Our Lady St. Mary and to all the holy cumpeny in heven, my body to be buryed in the churche of St. Martyn in Stubton. To the high altare in the same churche viij*d*. To Our Lady of Lincoln viij*d*. To St Catheryne altare in Stubton churche xij*d*. To the Trinitie light in the same churche vj*s* viij*d* and one pounde waxe for evermore to sustayne the sayd light. To Margaret Cantyng my gret brasse potte and all my best puter uppon the high shelffe and my best candylstyk, fyve hede of kyne and qwyes, that is to say ij kyne and iij qwyes, iij pare schetes, iij quarters wheate. To Anne Scathe one cowe and ij pare schetes, one of lyn and the other of hardyn, iiij strykes of wheate and one fatte hogge. To Robert Yong one yren bounde wane and all the gere that longyth to the same, iiij strykes of wheate and ij bullokes. To William Yong of Grantham xx*s*. To John Mylner my servant one qwye grym-faceyt.[48] To Thomas Staythe one calve of one yere age. The resydue of my goodes I gyff unto Thomas Yong of Muscam, husbandman, my cosyn, and Thomas Cantyng, and I make the sayd Thomas Yong and Thomas Cantyng myn executors and I bequethe to them xx*s* a pece for ther labors. I will that they do make peny dole at the day of my buryall. I wyll that they do fynde a preste callyd Sir Nicholes Chapman to syng and pray for my soule, my frendes soulys and [fo. 97r] all Crysten soulys duryng the space of ij yeres nexte foloyng aftyr my decesse, and he for to have yerely for hys stipende iiij*l* xiij*s* iiij*d*. And I will that the sayd sir Nicholes be supervisore, to whome I gyff xiij*s* iiij*d* for hys labor. Thes testes; Syr Nicholes Chapman, Robert Petty, John Patman, Richerde Chapman, Rayff Auve, Robert Yong and William Parseval, with other mo.

Proved before P at Lincoln, 4 April 1533.

119. JOHN GRENE [OF LITTLE PONTON]
[LCC 1532–34, fo. 24v]

2 December 1532. I, John Grene of Panton the Lesse, of hole mynde and good remembraunce, do make thys my last will and testament. Fyrste I bequethe my soule to God allmyghtty, Our Lady, and Hys saintes, and my body to be buryed in the churcheyerde of St. Michel of Panton aforesayd. To Our Lady of Lincoln ij*d*. I will have done for my soule and all Christen soulys v messys of the v woundes off Our Lorde God. I will that my mother-in-lawe have my wyff best gowne, and Alice my doughter to have my wyff best red kyrtyll and her best cappe. To Agnes Bygley halff a quarter barly. The resydue of all my goodes I will that they be devydyd emong all my chyldren, aftyr my funerall expenses and my dettes to be done and payd. I make my mother Alice Grene my executrix and William Holme my executor. I will that my gostly father Sir Robert Hornby be supervisor. Thes wytnesses; Sir Robert Hornby, Godfray Atkinson and Hugh Osberner, with other mo.

Proved before P at Grantham, 13 January 1532/3.

---

[48] 'Grim-faced'.

120. SIR ROBERT WYNTER [PARSON OF SEDGEBROOK]
[LCC 1532–34, fo. 29r]

2 December 1532. I, Sir Robert Wynter, parsone off Segbroke, hole of mynde and good memory, make my testament and laste will. Fyrste I bequethe my soule to allmyghtty God, Our Lady St. Mary, and to all the cumpeny of heven. My body to be buryed in the chapell of St. Jamys in Est Alyngton. To the sayd chapell for my buryall one cowe. To Rayff my brother one cowe. To Thomas Barber of Grantham one colte. To Marc Marshall one be hyve. To Robert Kellam one be hyve. The resydue of my goodes I gyff them to Thomas Wynter, William Wynter and Hugh Renolde, for to helpe to fynde one Rayff Wynter till he be able to fynde hymselffe. The which Thomas Wynter, William Wynter and Hugh Renolde I make executors. Thes beyng wytnessys; Sir Gabriell Kyrke, William Richeman, wyth mo.
Proved before P at Lincoln, 19 January 1532/3, by the executors.

121. MAUD GILLIOTHE [OF BIGBY]
[LCC 1532–34, fo. 88r]

3 December 1532. I, Malde Gylliothe of Thorpe within the paryshe of Bekeby, vidoy, consyderyng the feblenes of my mortall body, in a hole and a perfecte mynde makes my will. Fyrst I wyt my soule unto God allmyghtty, my saviour Criste Jhesu and Hys mother Mary, and my body to be buryed in the churche off All Halloys in Bekeby. To Our Lady's warke at Lincoln iijs iiijd. To the high altare at Bekeby xijd. To Barnetby churche iijs iiijd. I wyt xiijs iiijd to fynde ij perpetuall lighttes in Bekeby churche, one before the ymage of Our Lady vjs viijd, another before the image of St. Catheryne vjs viijd. To every one of my chyldren barne a yowe. To Robert my sun a cople oxen, a bay mare and a bay fole. I wyt till every one of my godchyldren a gose. To Helen Malton ij gese. To Isabell my doughter my best gowne. To Helene my doughter my secund gowne. To Agnes Whytefote my best kyrtell. To Jenet Stall my red sylke belte. I will that a preste be hyered to syng for me and all Crysten soulys a halffe yere, yff it may be sparyd, my dettes and will fulfyllyd in other thynges. The reste of my goodes in thys my will not wyt, my dettes payd, I will be at the disposicion of Thomas Whytfote and Robert Gilliothe my sonnys, whome I make my executors to dispose and occupy as they thynke moste expedient and necessary to the pleasure of god and the well of my soule. Thes persons bearyng wytnes; Sir William Swallo, Henry Cottyngham, John Barton, Henry Scotte, with diverse other.
Proved before P at Caistor, 10 February 1532/3.

122. ROBERT BULLE [OF SWINESHEAD]
[LCC 1532–34, fos. 225r–228v]

7 December 1532. I, Robert Bulle of Swyneshed, of hole mynde and good rememberaunce beyng, ordeyn, establyshe and make my testament and last will in forme articulary foloyng. Fyrste I commyt and bequethe my soule to allmyghtty God my maker and redemer, humbely besechyng Hym to accepte it to hys gret mercy and grace thrugh the merytes of Hys gloriose passyon, and by the meke intercessions off Hys blyssyd moder and Virgyn Saynt Mary and off all the sayntes in heven. And I bequethe my symple body to be buryed wythin the paryshe churche

off Our Blessyd Lady Saynt Mary in Swyneshed, for the whiche buryall and my wyff buryall and for a grave stone lying in the high alye ther for me and my wyff, xls. To the churche warke of Swyneshed ijs. To the high altare ther for tithys forgottyn ijs. To the altare of the gylde of Our Lady in the sayd churche xijd. To every other altare in the sayd churche xijd. To Our Lady's warke of Lincoln xijd. To the pupillys and orphans in the house off Saynt Catheryn's nyghe Lincoln iiijd. To the priors and conventes of the fowre orders of frerys in Boston xxs, that is to say to every order vs to thys intente; that they schall emonge them syng and say too trentallys callyd Saynt Gregory trentall of diriges and messys, to be sayd and done in the conventuall churchys within vij days nexte aftyr my decessyng. I bequethe to a sufficient preste [fo. 225v] that can do good service in the qwere to syng and pray wythein the sayd churche, at the altare of Saynt Jamys and Saynt Mathewe, for the soulys of me, my wyffe, my parenttes, my benefactors and all Crysten soulys, by the space of ij yeres immediatly aftyr my decesse, and he to have for hys stipende for sayd too yeres xl xiijs iiijd, to be payd to hym quarterly by myne executors by evyn porcions. I will that every housholde wythin the paryshe off Swynneshed that nede to have schall have, at the day off my decessyng affore my buryeng, ijd, and then to be expendyd to prestes and clerkes in the qwere and in the churche, to them that be strangers, xs at my buryng day. And at my vijth day and at my thyrty day in lyke maner in every thyng. To the gyldyng off the highe crucifyx and Mary and John and the egle in the sayd churche iiijl.[49] I will that all my feoffys off and in all my messes landes and tenementes stande seassyd off and in them from hensforthe to the use off thys my last will. Also I will that Johanne my wyff have my capytall messe and all the housys therto perteynyng, my pasture and an acre of hemplande togeder, lying nyghe my sayd messe wyth all ther appurtenances duryng the hole terme of her lyffe. And aftyr her deceasse I will that the sayd messe, lande and pasture wyth ther appurtenances shall be solde by my feoffys and the vicare off Swynneshed for the tyme [fo. 226r] beyng. And the money therfore to be receyvyd I will it be devydyd into thre partes, that is to say oone parte theroff to Thomas my sone or to hys chyldren then beyng onlyve, another parte theroff to Gilbert Dale of Boston and to Isabell hys wyff my doughter or to ther chyldren yff they have any then lyffyng, and the thirde parte theroff to Robert my sonne and to Alice my doughter or to ther chyldren. And yff it fortune any of my sayd chyldren or there heyres off there bodys laufully begottyn to dy afore my sayd wyff I will that then ther parte of the sayd money so deceassyng schall remayn to my other chyldren then beyng onlyve or to ther heyres of ther bodyes laufully begotten. And yff it fortune all my sayd chyldren to dye wythowt heyres of ther bodyes laufully begotten afore my sayd wyffe, I will then the sayd money be disposyd in the churche and towne off Swynneshed by my feoffys and the vicare in forme foloyng; that is to say to be devydyd into thre partys wheroff one parte to the moste necessaries of the churche of Swynneshed, and another parte of the sayd money to pore people in Swynneshed, and the thyrde parte therof to the reparacion of the causay there. Also I will that the sayd Thomas my sone, and Gylbert Dale and Isabell hys wyff schall have my tenemente in Barthorpe, one pece of lande and a pyngle lying in the [fo. 226v] Chapell Felde,

[49] The great crucifix, or rood, flanked by figures of the Virgin Mary and St. John the Baptist, stood on the rood beam, above the rood screen, in pre-Reformation parish churches. The eagle probably refers to the lectern. See e.g. 'The State of Melford Church as I, Roger Martyn, did know it', in W. Parker, *The History of Long Melford* (London, 1873), 70–3.

ande one pece of lande lying in Galowe Felde to them, ther heyres and assyngnes. Also I will that the sayd Thomas my sonne have my tenement that was of late Robert Browne. And the tenemente that Alice Fletcher dwellyth in aftyr her decesse wythe ther appurtenances to hym, hys heyres and assygnes. Also I will that the sayd Gylbert Dale and Isabell hys wyff have my tenemente which was late of Steven Laurenson wyth appurtenances to them, theyr heyres and assygnes. Also I will that Robert my sone and Alice my doughter have all suche money whych remanyth in the handes off John Harrys off Connyngton in the countie of Cambryge, husband-man, equally to be devydyd betwene them. Also I will that Johanne my wyff have my tenemente with the appurtenances sette and lying in Swynneshed in the whiche Robert Rogerson dwellyth, to her and to her heyres and assygnes wyth thys condicion; that sche her heyres and assygnes shall pay yerely to the cheyff lorde theroff for rente assyse iiij*d* and a half, and also to distrybute yerly xv kyrffes off good peattes uppon Crystenmes Evyn to pore people in Swynneshed. Also I will that halffe an acre of hemplande callyd Barker Lande in Swynneshed lying, and a garden and my tenemente nexte the sayd garden, wythe ther appurtenances, schall immediatly afftyr my decesse remayn in the handes off my feoffys and ther heyres and assygnes, to th'use and behoyff off the alderman and bredren and ther successors of the gylde off Our Lady off Swynneshed, unto [fo. 227r] the proffyt of the sayd gylde clerely wythowt paying off any owtt rentes doyng the servicys therfore due to the cheyff lordes theroff, so long as the lawe will gyff licence therto. The whych sayd tenemente, garden and lande I have lattyn it for the rente of xij*s* by yere. Wheruppon I will that the sayd alderman and bredren and successors for the tyme beyng shall kepe in the qwere off the sayd gylde a yerely obit solemply for my soule, the soulys off my wyff, my parentes, my benefactors and all Crysten soulys expendyng theruppon yerely vj*s* in forme foloyng; that is to say to the vicare or the chauntry preste ther, wheder off them dothe synge the messe off requiem, he to have vj*d* to ij prestys beyng diacon and subdiacon, either of them, v*d*, to a monke off the abbay of Swynneshed to come and se that my sayd obyt be suerly kepte he to have vj*d* for hys labor and for sayng dirige and messe. And the alderman and the monke to offre ij*s* at the messe. And for ij sergys iiij*d* to burne at my dirige and messe. And to the belman to go thorowe the towne to pray for the soules aforesayd j*d*. And for ryngyng off all the bellys and for drynke v*d*. And for bred and ale for them that shall offer iiij*d* when the obyt is done. Also to pore people beyng at [fo. 227v] the sayd obyt xij*d*. Also to other prestys and clerkes beyng at the sayd obit xxij*d*. And over that I will that the sayd alderman and bredren shall have xx*s* at the fyrste day that they shall kepe my sayd obyt to the intente that they shall not grutche to kepe my sayd obyt surely. And the resydue off the proffyttes cumyng of the sayd tenemente garden and lande to remane yerely to the moste proffyt of the sayd gylde so that myne obyt be surely kepte. To every on of my godchylder iiij*d*. To Helene my syster a gowne and x*s*. To Johanne her doughter iij*s* iiij*d*. To Johanne my wyff all my housholde stuffe and my qwyk catall and my corne that is uppon my chambre that is payd for and all my plate and x*l*. Also I will that my sayd wyff schall make for me at my buryng day vij^th day and xxx^ty day, every off them, a brekefaste for them that offre. Also I will that Robert my sonne have x*l* beyng in the handes of John Martyn off Saynt Ives. To Alice my doughter other x*l* beyng in the handes of the sayd John Martyn. I will that yff Robert my sonne be not contente wyth the gyfte to hym in thys my laste will then I will that he have nothyng off my goodes. To Thomas Hall my best dooblet. To Gylbert Dale my best jaket. [fo. 228r] To Thomas my sonne my nexte beste dooblet. To Richerde Bull my brother the thyrde dooblet. To Thomas Hunne of Wygtoffte my russyt gowne furryd. To Robert my sonne my violet gowne furryd. I wyll that myne other goodes not afore gyffyn nor bequethyd, as golde and sylver hempsede and hempe, shall remayne to the fulfyllyng off thys my last will. The residue of all my goodes not afore gyffyn nor bequethyd, fyrst my dettes and funerall expenses payd and thys my laste will trewly fullfyllyd, I gyff to be devydyd equally into thre partes, wheroff the fyrste parte I will that myne executors distrybute to pore people in the paryshe of Swynneshed wher moste nede is. Also the secunde parte therof I will myne executors expende it uppon the makyng of the causy thorowe the towne of Swynneshed so far as it may extende. And the thyrde parte theroff I will that my executors have it equally to be devydyd emonge them for ther labors wheroff I make Johanne my wyffe, Thomas my sonne and Gylbert Dale of Boston to be my faythfull executors, that they pay my dettes and dispose as to the honor of god and the helthe of my soule to them better shall be sene to be expedyent [fo. 228v] as they will make answer theroff afore God at the day off dome. I will that Richerde Wolmer of Swynneshed, gentilman, be super-visor off all the premisses. And he to have for hys goode helpe and councell xls. Thyes wytnesses; Syr Thomas Garton, vicare of Swynneshed, Syr Roberte Smythe, Syr John Webster of the same, prestys, and other moy. Dated the day and yere aforesayd.

Proved before P at Lincoln, 23 December 1532. Adm. granted to the executors.

123.   AGNES HAYLANDE [OF KIRTON IN HOLLAND]
        [LCC 1532–34, fos. 3v–4r]

8 December 1532. I, Agnes Haylande of Kyrton in Hollande, beyng in good mynde and remembraunce, dothe make my testament therwith concludyng my last will. Fyrste I commende my soule to God allmyghtty, to Our Lady St. Mary and to all the celestiall cumpeny of heven, and my body to be buryd in the churche of the appostellys Peter and Paule of Kyrton, and in the name of my mortuary I bequethe accordyng to the kyng statutes. To the high altare xijd. To every altare in the sayd churche of Kyrton iiijd. To the churche warke vjs viijd. To Our Lady's warke of Lincoln vjd. To the orphans at St Catheryn's iiijd. To the high altare of Kyrton one towell and to Our Lady altare in the same churche one towell. To every order of frerys in Boston xxd and to the ancorys of Boston viijd, and to the Trinitie gylde off Kyrton xijd. To Umfray Haylande my best materes, one coverlyd, one feder bed with the hangyng of blewe, one of the best schetes, one basyn, one laver and one gret platter, and one candylstyk. To Umfray Ordyng my bed that I ly in with the hanges, one coverlyd and one pare of schetes. To Jenet Garrat one gowne purfelyd with shankes. To Isabell Hoode my gowne purfelyd with velvet. To Isabell Lanrake my russyt gowne. To Robert Bray wyff one panne. [fo. 4r] To Thomas Hubbarde wyff one cowe. To Jenet my syster my best furryd gowne and my worstyt kyrtyll. To Agnes my mayd one brade panne, one materes, iiijs of money, one pare of flaxen schetes and one pare of harden schetes. To Richerd Haylande the sun of Humfray Haylande one cupborde. The resydue of my goodes not gyffyn nor bequethyd I gyff and bequethe to Humfray Haylande whome I make executor to pay my dettes and dispose my goodes to the moste plesur of god and helthe of my soule, and I will that

Sir John Bruster be supervisor. Thes wytnesses; Sir George Lincoln off Kyrton and Robert Butler of the same, with other mo.

    Proved before P at Donington, 18 February 1532/3.

124.   JOHN WATERFALL [OF CAWTHORPE IN PARISH OF BOURNE]
        [LCC 1532–34, fo. 25]

12 December 1532. I John Waterfall of Cowthorp within the parysh of Burne, hole of mynde and good remembraunce, make my testament and last will. Fyrst I bequethe my soule to God allmyghtty, to Our Lady St. Mary, and to all the holly cumpeny of heven, and my body to be buryed in the churcheyerde of the Holly Appostell Peter within the towne of Burne. To our mother churche of Lincoln vj*d*. To the high altare off Burne for offerynges and tithynges forgottyn vj*d*. To the Trinite gylde xij*d*. To St. John gylde iiij*d*. To the bellys iiij*d*. To John Waterfall my sone a carte and a plowe with all carte and plowe gerys to them belongyng, and all my catell, as horse and marys, oxon [fo. 25v] or kye, and also all suche money, corne or other thynges that I have takyn or lent to hym in tyme past. Also a pare of malte quernys. To Margaret Stokkes a lamme, a potte off brasse, a panne, a coverlet and a pare of schetes. To John Warner a flaxen schete. To iij chyldren of John my sun's, to every one of them a lamme. To Sir Thomas Waterfall and Simon my sonnys all my housholde stuff to be devydyd betwyxte them, and Sir Thomas to have the cheyff theroff, also xx*s*. I will that parte of my schepe be solde to bere the charges off my buryall day, my seventh day and my xxx^ty day, and other chargys concernyng the probacion of my will. And the resydue of my goodes I gyff to Sir Thomas Waterfall and John Waterfall my sonnes, whome I make my executors. Wytnes; John Botery, Richerd Smyth, Arthure Thomson.

    Proved before P at Bourne, 15 January 1532/3, by the executors.

125.   JOHN CLEY [OF HACCONBY]
        [LCC 1532–34, fo. 89v]

13 December 1532. I, John Cley of Hacconby, hole the mynde [sic] and perfite of memory, make my will and testament. Fyrst I bequethe my soule to God allmyghtty, to the Virgyn Our Lady St. Mary and to all the holy cumpeny of heven, and my body to be buryed in the churchyerde of St. Andro in Hacconby. To the high altare for forgottyn tithys xij*d*. To Our Lady off Lincoln viij*d*. To the manetenaunce of the churche of Hacconby v*s*. To Alice my doughter one seame barly and a qwy. To Thomas my sonne a quarter of barly and a stere. To Edwarde my sonne a quarter barly and a fole. To Elizabeth my doughter a quarter barly and a qwy. To Henry my sonn a quarter barly. To Isabell my doughter a quarter barly. To Thomas Cley a stryke barly. The resydue of all my goodes I gyff unto Margaret my wyff, whome I make my executrix with the helpe and succur of Robert Cley and Robert Atkyn, gyffyng to ether a bushyll barly yff she kepe her sole and marry not. And yff she mary then I will my goodes be devydyd in thre partes and that my chylder shall have the thyrde parte theroff. Thes beryng wytnes; Thomas Clyff, vicare, John Jakson the yonger, Richerde Doddes, with other.

    Proved before P at [Great] Hale, 16 February 1532/3.

126. **JOHN THOMSON [OF NORMANBY ON THE WOLD]**
[LCC 1532–34, fos. 61v–62r]

17 December 1532. I, John Thomson of Normanbe, syk of body, hole of mynde, seyng the perelles of dethe drawyng nere, makes thys my testament and last will. Fyrste I bequethe my soule to allmyghtty God, to Our Lady St. Mary and to all the holy cumpeny in heven, and my body to be buryed in the churche of Irforde, yff I fortune to decesse ther. To the high altare of Normanby for tithys forgottyn and to be prayd for xiijs iiijd. To the churche warke of the same iijs iiijd. To Our Lady of Lincoln xijd. To Our Lady warke off the same xijd. To the churche of Staynton xxd. To the churche of Claxby iiijd. To Thomas Hetton ij sterys of iiij yere olde, with ij lyttyll calvys, x yowes. To every godchylde of myne one lamme. To every chylde of my ij systers one yowe. I will ther be a trentall of messys for my soule, to be sung within the yere. To the convent of Yrforthe vjs viijd. To my syster Mawde vjs viijd. The resydue of all my goodes I gyff into the handes of Jenet my wyff, whome I make my executrix. I make the parsone of Normanby the supervisor. Thes beyng wytnesses; Sir Thomas Hanserde, the parsone of Kelsay Marie, Olyver Morelay and John Hetton, with other mo.

Proved before P at Lincoln, 9 January 1532/3.

127. **JOHN CLYMSON [OF WYBERTON]**
[LCC 1532–34, fos. 6r–7r]

20 December 1532. I, John Clymson of Wyberton, of a hole mynde and good remembraunce beyng, makyth thys my testament and herin conclude my last will. Fyrste I bequethe my soule to God allmyghtty, to Our Lady St. Mary the moder of marcy and to all the saintes in heven, and my body to be buryed in the churche of St. Leogerde of Wyberton, and my mortuary accordyng to the order of the lawe accustomyd and usyd. To our mother churche of Lincoln iiijd. To the fatherles chyldren at St Catheryn's without the barre at Lincoln iiijd. To the high altare in Wyberton churche vjd. To Our Lady's altare iiijd. To St Catheryn's altare iiijd. To St. Anne altare iiijd. To the reparacion and buyldyng of the churche of Leeke vjs viijd. To the churche of Wrangle iijs iiijd. To the churche of Leverton iijs iiijd. I will that Elizabeth Clymson my wyff have vj acre pasture grounde lying in Leeke in Haigate the terme of her lyff naturall, or xxs of redy money off annuite and yerely rente be takyn owt of all my landes and tenementes as well in Leeke, Wrangle and Leverton, to be payd by myn heyre, executors and assygnes when it shall be requyryd. And for lak of suche payment she to distrayn at all tymes, to suche tyme all arregagies be contentyd and payd at the costes and charges of me John Clymson, myn heyre, executors and assignes. And aftyr her decesse I will the forsayd landes remayn to Roger my sun and to the heyres of hys body. And yff [fo. 6v] it fortune the forsayd Roger Clymson to decesse or he cum to possession of the landes withowt heyres of hys body, then I will the forsayd landes remayn to John Clymson my sun and to the heyres of hys body. The resydue of all my landes and tenementes lying in Leeke and Leverton I gyff them to John Clymson my sun, to hym and the heyres of hys bodye, and yff it fortune the forsayd John Clymson to dye withowt heyres of hys body then I will that Roger my sun have all the forsayd landes and tenementes to hym and to the heyres of hys body, and so every one of them to be other heyre. And yff they bothe departe thys worlde, as God defende it so shulde be,

then I will they discende to Beatrix and Alice Clymson my ij doughters and the heres of ther ij bodyes. To Beatrix Clymson my doughter x*l* at the age of xviij yeres. To Alice Clymson my doughter x*l* at the age of xviij yeres. To Mawd Wylkynson x*l* at the age of xviij yeres. And yff any of my doughters dye or they cum to xviij yeres every one of them to be other heyre. And yff they all departe or they cum to xviij yeres the money shall remayn to John Clymson and Roger Clymson my ij sunys. And yff they all decesse then I will it be disposyd by the executor of me, the executors of them to the highe pleasure of God, the welthe of my soule, my father and mother soules, all our parentes, benefactors and frendes soules whith all other Crysten soules. I will that vj acre of lande lying in Wrangle be solde be my executors Elizabeth Clymson and John Clymson, and the money therof cumyng to be payd to the performance of my wyff mariage money and the mariage of my ij doughters. To John Clymson my eldest sun my swanne marke. The resydue of all my [fo. 7r] goodes I gyff to Elizabeth Clymson my wyffe and John Clymson my son, whome I make executors to bryng me furthe, pay my dettes, legaces, bequestes and to dispose the reste to the high plesure of God and the welthe of my soule. I make Master Nicholes Robertson surveer, and he to have for hys labors xx*s*. Thes beyng wytnes; Sir Richerd Stevenson, curate and paryshe preste off Wyberton, John Whendon, clerke, Richerde Dyconson, Nicholes Hudson, with other mo.

Proved before P at Boston, 20 February 1532/3.

128.   SIR ROBERT GANESBORO [VICAR OF KIRMOND LE MIRE]
        [LCC 1532–34, fo. 28]

23 December 1532. I, Sir Robert Ganesboro, vicare of Kyrmonde, hole of mynde and in good remembraunce, do make my testament and last will. Fyrste I bequethe my soule to allmyghtty God, to Our Lady St. Mary and to all the holy cumpeny in heven, and my body to be buryed within the quere of St. Martyn within the churche of Kyrmonde. To the high altare of Our Lady of Lincoln viij*d*. To Our Lady warke ther viij*d*. To ether of the churches off Ludfurthe viij*d*. To fyve chyldren of my brother William Ganesboro, every of them, x schepe suche as my executor schall sett owt for them. To John, Robert, William, Thomas and Johanne, my brother Thomas Ganesboro chyldren, every of them, x schepe. To the sayd John, my brother Thomas sun, xx*s* whiche he awyth me. Also I will that the schepe whiche I have gyffyn to the sayd Thomas Ganesboro, my brother Thomas sun, and to Johanne hys syster, be in the custody of Robert Gaynesboro ther brother, my executor, unto suche tyme as they shall be maryed or ellys cum to the age of xx^{ty} yeres. And yff the sayd schepe dy or they be maryed or cum to the sayd age of xx^{ty} yeres, then I will that sayd Robert shall gyff to ether of them for ther schepe xx*s* in money. To the same Thomas, my brother Thomas sun, iij*l* and one house in Kyrmund callyd Malkyn house wyth th'appurtenances therto belongyng the terme of hys lyff. Also I will the same Thomas shall have vj*l* xiij*s* iiij*d* whiche was hys father bequeste, which vj*l* xiij*s* iiij*d* with hys other legaces I will be in the custody of the sayd Robert Ganesboro, hys brother, my executor, to the tyme he be maryed or cum to the age aforesayd. [fo. 28v] And yff it fortune the sayd Thomas to departe owt of thys worlde before he be maryed or cum to the age off xx^{ty} yeres, then I will the sayd Robert my executor shall sell the sayd house, and the money for it receyvyd to be delte for my soule, my frendes soulys and all Crysten soulys. I will that a

pryste shall syng for my soule ij yeres in the paryshe churche of Kyrmunde. To Mr Charlys Gudhand xx*s* to the intent that he se that no man do my executor wrong, and to testify of my mowth that I awe no man nought. And also to se that no man medle with my goodes but my executor. To Masterys Goodhande hys wyffe x*s* to pray for me. To Thomas Hall x*s* to pray for me. To John Woode a quarter barly. I will that x of my beste schepe be kyllyd and gyffyn to pore people as sone aftyr my dethe as conveniently may be. To Elizabeth Burwell vj schepe, a chalder barly and a chalder malte. And I will also that she schall dwell within my sayd house in Kyrmunde whiche before I have gyffyn to Thomas, my brother sun, unto suche tyme as sche may provyde her of a service. Also I will that my ij men servantes shall have vj acres of tillyd lande evenly betwyxte them which for thys yere I have hyryd in Kyrmund felde and also to ether of them ij schepe. To my schepperde one schepe. To Kyrmunde churche xl*s* to by a vestment with. I will that the sayd Robert Ganesboro my executor have the proffyttes of the house which before I have gyffyn to Thomas Ganesboro, unto the tyme that the same Thomas shall be maryed or ellys cum to the age of xx^{ty} yeres as is aforesayd, and he to fynde yerely, with the proffyttes cumyng of the same house, fyve sergys to burne before the sacrament in the sayd churche of Kyrmunde. And also I will that the sayd Robert shall kepe the sayd house in good and sufficient reparacion, and he so to delyver it to the sayd Thomas Ganesboro at the tyme before lymytyd. The resydue of my goodes I put to the disposicion of the forsayd Robert Ganesboro whome I make my executor, he to dispose them for the well of my soule and proffyt for the sayd Thomas Ganesboro, my brother sun. Thes wytnesses; Mr. Charlys Goodhande, Thomas Hall, William Browne, John Woode, and many other mo.

Proved before P at Lincoln, 18 January 1532/3, by the executor.

129.　　WILLIAM HARBRED [OF BOSTON]
　　　　[LCC 1532–34, fo. 7r]

24 December 1532. I, William Harbred of Boston, hole of mynde and of good remembraunce, makes my will and last testament. Fyrst I bequethe my soule to God allmyghtty, to Our Lady St. Mary and to all the holly cumpeny off heven, and my body to be buryed in the churcheyerde of St. Botulphe of Boston. To the high altare of Boston viij*d*. To Our Lady of Lincoln xvj*d*. To the vij martyrs gylde vj*d*. I will have a trentall of messys done for me in Boston churche. To Simon and Jude gylde xx*d*. The resydue of all my good I gyff them unto Elizabeth my wyff, whome I make my executrix by the oversyght of Richerd Tonner whome I make supervisor, and to have for hys labor ij*s*. Thes beryng wytnes; Sir Thomas Cersy, preste, John Nuball and Thomas Pope, with other mo.

Proved before P at Boston, 20 February 1532/3.

130.　　RICHARD HORSARDE [OF ALVINGHAM]
　　　　[LCC 1532–34, fo. 38]

25 December 1532. I, Richerd Horsarde, husbandman, hole of mynde and in good memory beyng, ordens and makes thys my last will and testament. The fyrst I bequethe my soule to allmyghtty God and to Our Blessyd Lady and to all the blessyd saintes in heven, and my body to be buryed in the paryshe churcheyerde of

Alvyngham Adelwald. To the same churche a cowe, and to our Lady of Lincoln in oblacion viij*d*. To Cokryngton Marie, to Kedyngton, to Yarburghe, to Cauthorpe, to Covenam, to Conysholm, to every one of thes churches iiij*d*. To Mr. Prior a stag and a qwye in dischargeyng of my conscience. To the churche aftyr the decesse of George my sonne a kyst, and to Corpus Christi gylde a gret brasse pot, and to every one of my godchylder *j*d. To Richerd Horsard a yowe. The resydue of all my goodes I gyff to my wyff Helene Horsard and to George my sonne, whome I orden my executors for to do and dispose as they shall thynke moste expedyent for the helthe of my soule and in dischargeyng of my conscience. Wytnes theroff; Henry Forman, Thomas Yarburgh, Richerd Hard, William Yarburgh, with other mo.

Proved before P at Louth, 6 February 1532/3.

131.   ALICE WESTREN [OF SAUSTHORPE]
       [LCC 1532–34, fos. 12v–13r]

26 December 1532. Ego, Alice Westren, vidua, of Sawsthorp, compos mentis et sane memorie, meam ultimam voluntatem facio. In primis lego animam meam omnipotenti Deo creatori meo, et beate Marie virgini et omnibus sanctis eius.[50] My body to be buried in the cemetery of the church of St. Andrew of Sawsthorpe. To the fabric of the church of the Blessed Mary of Lincoln iiij*d*. To the red ark of the same iiij*d*. To the high altar of Sawsthorpe for forgotten tithes xij*d*. To a table to St. Jamys altare iij*s* iiij*d*. To the bellys iiij*d*. To John Button my sun one cowe and one meyr and one stere, and vj schepe, and a panne, a mete borde and one stong ryg off rye. To Catherine Ruke one cowe and iiij schepe and my best gowne and my best kyrtyll. To John Ruke one stong ryg of rye. To Isabell Ruke one schepe hog and a matterys. To Thomas Westren a basen, a ewre, a matterys, one pare of schetes [fo. 13r] and a bed coveryng. To Alice Westren one pare of schetes. To Elizabeth Westren and to Jane Westren one schete each. To Jenet my servant one matteres and one pare of schetes and a towyll, and one schepe hog. To every one of my godbarnes iiij*d*. I will that Robert Button my sun have all the other resydue of my goodes. Thes wytnesses sir John Slator, Sir John Pynder and John Westren with many other.

Proved before P at Partney, 15 April 1533.

132.   WILLIAM SKALFLETE [OF INGOLDMELLS]
       [LCC 1532–34, fos. 211v–212r]

28 December 1532. I, William Skalflet of Ingolmellys Adelthorpe, beyng of hole mynde and perfyte of remembraunce, knawyng that every man is mortall and nothyng so uncertain as dethe is, dothe make my last will and testament. Fyrste I bequethe my soule to allmyghtty God, Our Lady St. Mary and to all the holly cumpeny of heven, and my body to be buryd in the churche of St. Nicholes of Adelthorpe. To Our Lady's warke of Lincoln iiij*d*. To the fatherless chyldren of St. Catheryn's withowt Lincoln iiij*d*. To the churche warke of Ingolmellys Adylthorp vj*s* viij*d*. To Our Lady's altare within the sayd paryshe churche of Adylthorp xx*d*. To the Trinite altare within the sayd churche of Adylthorp xx*d*. To the high altare

---

[50] 'I, Alice Westren, widow, of Sausthorpe, whole of mind and of good memory, make my last will. First I bequeath my soul to almighty God my creator, and to the Blessed Virgin Mary and all His saints.'

gyltyng within the sayd churche of Adylthorpe iiij*l*. [fo. 212r] To Alyson my wyffe forty yowes, xx^{ty} weders, xx^{ty} hogges, ij olde horsses and one fole, one cople oxen, iiij kye, ij beystes of ij yere olde, the one of them a heder and the other a sheder, and all my hole housholde stuff within the house. To Jenet Hunt my servant vj yowes and a qwe of ij yeres olde, to be delyveryd unto the sayd Jenet by myn executors aftyr th'end and terme of ij yeres be endyd nexte insuyng the date aftyr my decesse. To George Temper xl*s* to be delyveryd hym by myn executors when he cumys to the age of xx^{ty} yeres. And yff the sayd George dye before the sayd age of xx^{ty} yeres, that parte of the sayd xl*s* go to hys buryall, and other parte to the relevyng of John Temper hyss father, yff the sayd John do lyff than. And yff the sayd John be ded, to be distrybutyd in charytable dedes by the advyce and discrescion of myne executors. To William Wylson thre yowes and thre hogges, to remane in the handes of my executors to he cum at laufull age, yff he do not go to no occupacion. To William Storyman my servant a yowe. To Elizabethe Kaye a yowe. To every one of my godchylder a lamme to be delyveryd at Relique Sonday[51] nexte insuyng aftyr my decesse. To William Gernewyk the yonger ij schepe. To William Temper my syster sonne ij schepe. The resydue of my goodes not gyffyn I gyff them to John Skalflet my brother and John Besouthen, whome I make my executors to be disposyd and orderyd by the discrecion of the sayd John Skalflet. I bequethe the sayd John Skalflet vj*s* viij*d*, and to the sayd John Besouthen for hys labor vj*s* viij*d*. Thes wytnes; Sir John Cokson, prest, William Skegnes, Robert Orby, Robert Boston, Robert More, Robert Goshauke and Robert Gybson, with other mo.

Proved before P at Partney, 10 November 1533.

133.   JOHN HOPSTER [OF WRANGLE]
[LCC 1532–34, fo. 95r]

30 December 1532. I, John Hopster of Wrangle, beyng in good remembraunce and hole of mynde, makes thys my testament. Fyrst I bequethe my soule to allmyghtty God, to Our Lady St. Mary, and to all the holy cumpeny of heven. My body to be buryed in the churcheyerde of St. Peter and Palle of Wrangle. I bequethe for my mortuary as lawe and custome requiryth now. I bequethe for tithys forgottyn viij*d*. To the high altare iiij*d*. To Our Lady altare iiij*d*. To St. John altare iiij*d*. To Our Lady of Lincoln to the red arke iiij*d* and to be prayd for to the high altare ther iiij*d*. To Alice my wyff my best cowe and my mare. I will my wyff have the governaunce and rule of all my goodes and catallys her lyff to bryng up my chyldren with. And after her decesse I will that John my sonne have a cowe nexte the beste that I have now, or ellys another as good as she is now. I will a seame barly be solde and the money therof to be waryd of a burlyng calve to the behove of John my sonne. To Agnes my doughter a flekyd cowe, a gret panne and a bed. To Grace my doughter the browne cowe or ellys another as good as she is now and my best keverlet, a pare of schetes, one sewyd with sylke, ij bolsters and a table. To Jenet my doughter a arke, a puter platter and a pare of schetes, and a calve of Agnes' cowe. To William my sonne a calve and a qwye of the prove of iij yeres olde. To Edmunde my sonne a calve and my foule. I will yff any off my chyldren dye before ther mother that then ther parte shall remayn and be gyffyn to the yongest beyng alyve. To Sir Robert

---

[51] Generally the first Sunday after 7 July, although this could vary. At Lincoln Cathedral it was the first Sunday after 10 July.

Symson vj*d*. To Thomas Wyberde of Leverton, whome I make my executor with my wyff, iij*s* iiij*d*. The resydue of my goodes I gyff them to my wyff. Thes beyng wytnes; Sir Thomas Potter, Sir Robert Symson, John Ape.

Proved before P at Boston, 20 February 1532/3.

134.   SIR WILLIAM CROSSE [VICAR OF HAGNABY]
        [LCC 1532–34, fo. 32]

31 December 1532. I, Sir William Crosse, vicare of Hagneby nygh Bollyngbroke, beyng in hole mynde and good remembraunce, makyng my last will and testament. Fyrst I bequethe my soule to allmyghtty God and to Our Lady Saynt Mary and to all the holy cumpeny of heven, and my body to be buryed within the churche of St. Andro of Hagneby, and that to my mortuary that the lawe requiryth. [fo. 32v] To the high altare of St. Andro vj*d*. To Our Lady warke of Lincoln vj*d*. To a preste for to syng a trentall in the parysche churche of Hagneby x*s*. To every one of my pore neburs that hath no corne a stryke corne or ellys malte. To John Bere and Isabell Perot, my servantes, my wayn and ij sterys of iij yere olde, and they to pay for them xxiij*s* iij*d* and they to be founden of my costes and charges to Mayday nexte commyng. To the churche of Hagneby a cople of oxsun and they to be founden of my costes and charges to Mayday. The resydue of my goodes I gyff to Richerd Lincoln and John Stonys of Hagneby, whome I make my executors to pay my dettes and for to dispose for the helthe of my soule and all Crysten soulys. Thes men wytnes; Sir William Herryson, John Richerdson and Henry Salter, and other mo.

Proved before P at Partney, 4 February 1532/3.

135.   WILLIAM HOLSAM [OF LITTLE PONTON]
        [LCC 1532–34, fo. 25r]

1 January 1532/3. I, William Holsam of Paunton the Lesse, of hole mynde and good remembraunce, do make thys my last will and testament. Fyrst I bequethe my soule to God, Our Lady and all Hys saintes, and my body to be buryed in the churcheyerde of St. Michel of Paunton aforesayd. To the high altare there, to be prayd for, xij*d*. To Our Lady warke of Lincoln iiij*d*. To the churche of Paunton xij*d*. To the churche of Gret Paunton xij*d*. I will have done for my soule and all Christen soulys hallff a trentall, and my gostly father to provyde for the preste as he thynkes best. The resydue of my goodes I gyff to Margaret my wyff and to her chyldren at her discression, and the sayd Margaret to be my full executrix, and my father John Helsam of Gret Paunton to be supervisor. Thes beyng wytnes; Sir Robert Hornby, Godfray Atkynson and Hugh Osberner, with other mo.

Proved before P at Grantham, 13 January 1532/3.

136.   WILLIAM MAYSERT [OF PICKWORTH]
        [LCC 1532–34, fos. 89v–90r]

2 January 1532/3. I, William Maysert of Pykworthe in the countie of Lincoln, husbandman, makyth my last will. Fyrst I bequethe my soule to allmyghtty God, Our Lady St. Mary and to all the holy saintes in heven, and my body to be buryed in the churcheyerde of Pykworthe, night the crosse on the est syde. To the high altare

in Pykworthe churche xij*d*. To Our Blessyd Lady in Lincoln mynster iij*s*. I bequethe a cowe namyd Levill with the proffet that may cum of her to kepe an obyt in Pykworthe churche yerely, to continue for my fader soule, my mother soule, the soulys of me, my wyff and chyldren, and all Crysten soulys. It is my will that my wyff and Thomas my sonne have the forsayd cowe in ther kepyng [fo. 90r] as long as they be contentyd to answer and pay yerely to the churche the proffet theroff to the use aforesayd. And when they be not so contentyd to do, then it is my wyll that the sayd cowe to be delyveryd to the churche graves of Pykworthe for the tyme beyng, and they to put her to be kept for the same use as afore is wrytten for ever. To the upholdyng of the bellys of Pykworthe xij*d*. To Thomas my sonne one bullok namyd Swanne. To too of hys chyldren, ether of them, to have of my goodes a schepe, and to George Baker a schepe. And the sayd schepe to be delyveryd to theym by discrecion of Alice my wyff. I make my sayd wyff and Thomas my sonne my executors, to whome I give all my goodes not bequethyd, my dettes payd, and they to do therwith for the helthe of my soule as they thynke best. Whytnes herof; Christofer Hogekynson, John Tayllor, John Fysher and Robert Bradschaw.

Proved before P at [Great] Hale, 17 February 1532/3.

137.   ROBERT THEKER [OF SIBSEY]
       [LCC 1532–34, fo. 213]

2 January 1532/3. I, Robert Theker, makes thys my last will. Fyrste I gyff my soule to God allmyghtty, Our Lady St. Mary, and to all the saintes in heven. My body to be buryd in the churcheyerde of St. Margaret off Sybsay. To the high altare in Sybsay churche iiij*d*. To St. Margaret light ij*d*. To the roode light ij*d*. To Our Lady warke of Lincoln iiij*d*. I will that my heed house in Westhorp, with an acre lande lying in Well Felde that was late John Herde's, remane to Robert Theker after the decesse of Margaret my wyff, and to hys heyres laufully begottyn of hys body. And yff the sayd Robert decesse withowt heyres, it to remayn to Stephyn Theker and hys heyres [remainder to] Thomas Theker and hys assygnes. To Robert Theker one acre of yng lying in Sudland Dalys, to hym and to hys assygnes, also halffe one acre yng, buttyng of Hyldayk, and to hys assyners. To Steven Theker a house that he wonnys in Southorp, to hym and to all heyres males of hys body laufully begottyn [remainder to] Thomas Theker and hys assygnes. I gyff the sayd Stephyn Theker iij stong tyll lande lying in Northcrofte with iij stong tyll lande lying in south west felde that was Jenet Theke's, with halffe an acre that was late Jenet Pygge's, to the sayd Stephyn and hys heyres malys. And yff so be the sayd Stephyn decesse withowt heyr male, then I will the iiij last pecys namyd remane to John Theker and hys assygners. To the sayd Stephyn ij yong sterys. To the sayd Stephyn a rood and a half of tyll lande lying in the sowth west felde. And yff the sayd Stephyn decesse withowt heyr male, it to remane to Thomas Theker and to hys assygnes. I wyll, yff so be that Stephyn Theker my sun do not occupy thes presentes my bequestes, the landes and the ij sterys sumthyng lying to get hys lyffyng by, and then I will that Thomas Theker my sun have all landes and goodes that I have gyffyn to the sayd Stephyn Theker my sun, chargeyng Thomas Theker my sun to gyff the sayd Stephyn aftyr hys conscience to gyff yerly sumthyng to hys lyffyng and hys wyffe's. To John Theker an acre of tyll lande lying in Welfelde that was Jenet Pygge's, with halff one acre tyll lande lying in sowth este felde [fo. 213v] by the

highway syde, and a roode and a halffe in the same felde that was Jenkyn Wrytte's, with halffe an acre att Benyngton Brygges, to hym and hys assygnes. To Thomas Theker iij stong of tyll lande lying in Northcrofte that was John Redde's, with an acre tyll lande lying in the south west felde lying at Scharpe Willose, with halffe one acre tyll lande Hyserecrofte, with iij stong lying in Mosseheade and half one acre lying by it. I will the forsayd Thomas have the sayd iij stong with the halffe acre by it, to hym and hys assygnes for my buryall. To Margaret Theker my wyff all the landes her lyffe afore gyffyn and bequest, exepte iij stong and a half, an acre of till lande lying in the Moshed. To Thomas Theker ij acres of medo grounde lying at Hyll Dyke Hed, and he to have it at thys present day, doyng for me and all my frendes one trentall. The resydue of my goodes and landes not gyffyn, I gyff them to Margaret my wyff and Thomas Theker my sun, whome I make my executers. Thes beryng wytnes; Henry West, John Copper, Thomas Topper, Sir Adam Pottes, with ther many mo. To Stephyn Theker aforesayd an acre of medo grounde lying in Southsyke, and it to be orderyd as is afore notyd.

Proved before P at Partney, 10 November 1533.

138. ROBERT MAWER [OF CAWTHORPE IN PARISH OF COVENHAM ST. BARTHOLOMEW]
[LCC 1532–34, fos. 37v–38r]

6 January 1532/3. I, Robert Mawer of Cawthorpe Bartilmew, in good mynde and will, makes thys my last testament. Fyrst I bequeth my soule to allmyghtty God and to Our Lady St. Mary and to all the hole cumpeny in heven, and my body to be buryed in the churcheyerde of Covenham Bartilmew. To Our Lady of Lincoln vj*d*. To Our Lady warke of Lincoln vj*d*. To the high altare of Covenham Bartilmew viij*d*. To the churche warke of Covenham Bartilmew iij*s* iiij*d*. To the churche warke of Covenham Marie xij*d*. To the churche warke of St. Laurence of Fulstow viij*d*. To Agnes Mawer my doughter ij kye, v yow schepe, a matteres and a coverlet, and a pare of lyn schetes, a pillow and a brasse pot, and iij puter doblers. To Margaret Mawer my doughter ij kye and v yowys and hogges, a materes, a coverlyt, a pare of lyn schetes, a pillo and a brasse potte, and iij puter doblers. To John Cooke my godsun my russyt cote. To every godbarne that I have ij*d*. To John Mawer, the sonne of Richerd Mawer a filly fole. To Elizabeth Mawer, the doughter of Thomas Mawer a qwy calve of a yere olde. To Thomas Robertson a yowe hog. To John Mawer my brother xij*d*. To Jenet Robertson a yowe hog. To Mathe my servant a yong lamme. To Agnes Robertson a lamme. To Thomas Mawer my godsun a yow hog. To Alen Paryshe a stryke wheate. To Agnes Bate a stryke wheate. To Elizabeth Robertson a stryke wheate. To Thomas [fo. 38r] Mawer wyffe a caye schepe. I will that Jenet my wyff and Thomas my sonne have my house and my lande yff it please my master William Skypwyth esquyer. To Richerd Mawer my sonne a baye mare and a mydyl teame of yrne. To Thomas Mawer my sun a blak mare. Thomas my sun shall have a wane, a plugh and all the gerys that longes to them, so long as hys mother and he dose agre. And yff they agre not, I will that my wyffe have it remaynyng to her agane. I will Thomas my sonne and Rycherde have ij apys, v wymbyls, a handesaw, ij yryn chyssyls, a hammer. The resydue off my goodes I gyff it to Jenet my wyff for to dispose for the helthe of my soule, whome I make my executrix, and Thomas my sun and Richerd my sun to be executers with

her. Wytnes Robert Drowry, Robert Frende, Roger Awcok, Uter Wylson, Richerd
Woode, with other mo.

Proved before P at Muckton, 6 February 1532/3.

139.   NICHOLAS UPTON [OF NORTHOLME BY WAINFLEET]
        [LCC 1532–34, fos. 210v–211v]

8 January 1532/3, 24 Henry VIII. I, Nicholes Upton th'elder, esqwyer, of Northolme besyde Waynflete in the countie of Lincoln, beyng of hole mynde and of good
remembraunce, made my wyll. Fyrst I bequethe my soule to allmyghtty God and to
Our Lady St. Mary and to all the holly cumpeny of heven, and my body to be buryd
where it pleasyth God. To Our Lady warke of Lincoln iijs iiijd. To the iiij orders of
frerys in Boston xls, that is to say, for every one of them xs. To the chauntry prestes
of Corporis [sic] Christi in Boston xs for a trentall.[52] I bequethe xs to the frerys in
Boston to syng a trentall for me at Scala Celi by the discrecion of my executors. To
the churche of Northolme vjs viijd, and to the churche of All Halloys in Waynflete
iijs iiijd. To the churche of St. Mary's in Waynflete iijs iiijd. To Nicholes my sonne
my swanne marke with thre halffe barrys for terme of hys lyffe. And aftyr hys
decesse the remaner over to John my sun for ever. To Hamonde my sun my swanne
marke with ij halffe mounes for ever. To my sun John my swanne marke with the
barre and iij nykkes for ever. The resydue of my goodes not bequethyd I [fo. 211r]
gyff to John my sun. Also I will that my executors have xls apece and my supervisor
other xls. I will that my sun John pay xxx[ty] pownndes equally to Isabell and Barbara,
doughters of Robert Barret, when they shall cum to laufull age; yff one of theym
dye, the other to have the hole xxx[ty] pownndes. And yff they bothe dye before they be
maryed, or at they cum at laufull age, then I will that the sayd xxxl go to makyng of
the highway betwene Waynflete and Spyllesby. Wytnes thes men foloyng; John
Lytylbery, esqwyer, Richerde Wolmer, esqwyer, John Upton, gent[leman], Thomas
Lytylbery, gent[leman], John Skupholm, preste, John Johnson, preste, William
Vavasore, gent[leman]. Thys is the last will of me Nicholes Upton th'elder, esqwyer,
mayd at Netherholme besyde Waynflete the 8 day of January, 24 Henry VIII.[53] I
will that all my landes and tenementes within the partes of Lyndesey in the countie
of Lincoln, as well fee symple landes as other, to my sun John Upton and to the
heyres of hys body laufully begottyn, uppon condicion that he fynde a preste of my
fe symple landes to syng for my soule, bothe my wyffe soulys and my father and
mother soulys, and all Christen soulys, for the terme of xx[ty] yeres. And for defawtte
of suche issue, the remaner over to Hamonde my sonne and to the heyres of hys
body laufully begottyn uppon lyke condicion. And for defawtte of such issue, the
remaner over to Isabell and Dorothe excepte my fee symple landes and to the heyres
of ther bodyes laufully begottyn. Also I will, yff John and Hamonde dy withowt
heyres of ther bodyes laufully begottyn, then I will all my fe symple landes, as well
by purchase or that dissendyt to me by my unkyll George Upton, remayn in my

---

[52] Corpus Christi gild was one of five incorporated gilds in St. Botolph's, Boston. Having received
incorporation in 1349–50, by the time of the compilation of the *Valor Ecclesiasticus* in 1535 it was
staffed by six chaplains, each paid £5 6s. 8d. annually. Dissolved in 1548, the chantry certificates
record its gross income at £114 16s. 7d.: Chantry Certificates (1926), 260, 265.
[53] 8 January 1532/33.

feoffys handes and executors for the terme of xx^{ty} yeres, to th'entent that my sayd feoffes and executors shall take the issues and proffyttes theruppon duryng the sayd yeres for the makyng and reparyng of the highway betwene Wyanflete and Spyllesby. And aftyr the ende of the sayd xx^{ty} yeres, I will all my sayd fe symple landes remayn to Richerde Welmer and Isabell my doughter, and to the heyres of ther bodys laufully begottyn. Also I will that my sun Nicholes have x markes yerely payd be me sayd feoffys and executors owt of my maner of Frampton, unto suche season as he be promotyd by the religion of St. John and take the profettes theruppon.[54] Also I will my sun Hamonde have x*l* yerely payd be my sayd feoffes owt of my maner [fo. 211v] of Frampton for the terme of hys lyffe in full satisfaction of Richmonde fee. Also I will, yff my sun John dye withowt heyres of hys body laufully begottyn and the lande dissende to my sun Hamonde, then I will my said feoffes pay to my sun Nicholes xx markes over and besyde xx^{ty} nobles to he be promotyd as it is above sayd. Also I will, my will performyd, all my landes in Hollande remayn to John my sun and to the heyres of hys body laufully begottyn. And for defawtte of suche issue, the remaner over to Hamonde my sun and to the heyres of hys body laufully begottyn, and for defawtte of suche issue, the remaner over to my right heyres. To Adryan Upton my brother xl*s* yerely for the terme of hys lyff, and thys to be takyn of my landes in Frampton. I make my executors my sun John Upton and Mr. Doctor Smythe, warden of the Gray Frerys in Lincoln, and my supervisor my cosyn John Lytilbery.

Proved before P at Partney, 10 November 1533. Adm. granted to John Upton an executor, reserving power to grant to Dr. Smyth, the co-executor.

140.   SIR JOHN GARNET [PARSON OF SALTFLEETBY ST. PETER]
        [LCC 1532–34, fo. 151r]

10 January 1532/3. I, Sir John Garnet, parson off Saltefletby Peter, hole of mynde and good remembraunce, makes thys my last will. Fyrste I bequethe my soule to allmightty God, Our Lady St. Mary and all the saintes in heven, and my body to be buryed in the chauncell of St. Peter in Saltfletby, with my mortuary due to the same as the lawe and custome requiryth. To Our Lady warkes of Lincoln iij*s* iiij*d*. To the churche warkes of St. Peter in Saltefletby xl*s*. To the churche of St. Peter in Saltefletby v*s*. To the churche of St. Clement in Saltefletby v*s*. To the churche of Turnstall vj*s* viij*d*. To Mellyng churche vj*s* viij*d*. To Jenet Towns vj*s* viij*d*. To Isabell Fargwat vj*s* viij*d*. To Margery Burton vj*s* viij*d*. To Nicholes Cawtrop vj*s* viij*d*. To William Thornton one cowe. To the convent of Legborne ij*s*. To Elizabeth Necommen one yowe. To Parnell Mers one yowe. To Isabell my servant one hog lamme. To Agnes my servant one lamme. To Mabell Long one lamme. To Sir Nicholes Garnet my furde gowne. To Gylys Thornton my chamblet dooblet. I will to Sir William Hunt, one yere to syng for my soule, my fader and moder soulys, Nicholes Garnet and Margery. For thys my laste will to be performyd fulfyllyd and kepte I make Sir Nicholes Garnet, Thomas Spendlove, Gylys Thorneton, John Cawthorp my executors. The resydue of my goodes not bequethyd, my will and all

---

[54] This refers to presentation to a benefice by the order of the Knights Hospitaller, which maintained several houses in Lincolnshire, formerly the property of the Knights Templar: *VCH Lincolnshire*, II, 163–4.

other thynges or charges discharged, I will that they be devydyd equally to Sir Nicholes Garnet, Thomas Spendlove, Gylys Thorneton, John Cawthorp. Thies wytnes; Robert Burgh off Saltefletby Peter, Richerde Manfelde of the same, John Sparke of Grymylby, Sir William Hount, Richerde Grantham.

Proved before P at Louth, 5 May 1533.

141.   HENRY WESTE [OF SIBSEY]
        [LCC 1532–34, fos. 220v–221v]

12 January 1532/3. I Henry Weste of Sybsay in the countye of Lincoln, yeman, beyng of hole mynde and good remembraunce, makes thys my last will and testament. Fyrste I bequethe my soule to God and to Our Lady St. Mary, and to all the holy cumpeny of heven, and my body to be buryed in the churcheyerde of St. Margaret of Sybsay, and that the churche to have that is duety by the lawe. To the sacrament viij*d.* To Our Lady viij*d.* To St. Anne xij*d.* To St. Margaret light viij*d.* To Our Lady of Lincoln viij*d.* To the orphans at St. Catheryn's withowt Lincoln xij*d.* To Margaret my wyff syx kye. To her iij doughters, to every of them, ij kye a pece. I will that my wyff have a wane and a cople of oxen of the best, iij marys of the best and a plough, and the tyre that longes therto, xx^ty ewes with ther lammes by ther sydys of the beste. Also I will that she have all my housholde stuff to her and to my chyldren. Also I will that she shall have malte, barly and pease so muche as shall fynde her and her iij doughters a hole yere, and as long as she kepes her vydoy, yff she do sawe no croppe nor no man for her, and that croppe to be payd and delyveryd by Jamys my sun. To every one of my iij doughters when they cum at the age of xxj^ty yeres yff that then eny of them be alyve. And they will release ther title and interest to Jamys my sun in ther mother's joyntry then they to have xx^ty marke apece. And yff they wil not release ther titill then they not to have the money. And yff they mary afore the age of xxj^ty yeres, yff they can fynde sufficient suerty to release ther tityll and interest that they have in ther mother's joyntry unto Jamys my sun, when they cum to the age of xxj^ty yeres. And yff they can fynde no suerty that is sufficient, that [fo. 221r] then they shall tary unto suche tyme as they cum to the age of xxj yeres, and yff they will not release then I will that Jamys my sun injoy ther money as is aforesayd. To Stephyn my sun my hed mansion wherin I do dwell and the house that was Bedlemy's and the mylne therin uppon thys condicion, that he will release hys tityll unto Jamys hys brother in thes parcellys that lyes in the crofte of the northe syde of the Hayell Gote nexte of all, or ellys and he will not release, Jamys to have Bedlem House with the mylne. To Stephyn my sun the wrayes with all the landes that longyth therto and the house that Thomas Saule dwellys in, and all the landes that longes therto in the felde and in the fellandes by thos Henry Dale syde and the cote rigge of thys syde of the mylne, and the sette crofte with all other that was geven to me and to my heyres. To Jamys my sun all those tenementes and parcellys of landes, pasturys and fedynges, the which I purcheste excepte suche as is geven or ellys hereaftyr shalbe geven to hym and to hys assygnes. And he to have my indenture and ferme of the parsonage duryng my yeres and my copy of St. John's of Jerusalem. Also I will that Stephyn my sun have the bakehouse which longes not to the gret copy, payng yerely to St. John's viij*d*, at the feste of Michelmes, and a rigge which was Agnes Bray's. Also I will that Stephyn my sun have the ferme of the gylde of Conesby duryng my yeres. To John my sun a fether

bedde with an over se tyke[55] and a coverlet, a bolster and a pilloy with a pare of good schetes and my best horse that I have at the day of my departyng. To Jamys my sun a wane and a plough with all the tyrys that longes therto and iiij oxen and vj marys. To John my sun a swanne marke when he cumys at the age of xxj^{ty} yeres with the too V V.[56] Also I will that a preste shall be founde immediatly aftyr my departyng to syng for my soule and all Christen soulys the space of a hole yere. The resydue of my goodes not bequethyd nor gyffyn I will that they be disposyd at the discrecion of Jamys my sun and John my sun whome I make my executers, and [fo. 221v] Stephyn my sun to be supervisor, and he to have for hys pane and labor xv$s$. To Stephyn my sun a swanne marke whiche is callyd the Cressent. To Jamys my sun the resydue of all my swanne markes ungeven and unbequethyd, and he to gyff Margaret my wyff yerely too swanne burdes. Thes beryng wytnes; William Baven, Thomas Suttell and other mo.

Proved before P at Lincoln, 18 November 1533. Adm. granted to the executers.

142. ALICE BAKER [OF SALTFLEETBY ALL SAINTS]
[LCC 1532–34, fo. 38v]

18 January 1532/3. I, Alison Baker, vidoy, of the paryshe of All Halloys of Saltfletby, hole of mynde and good memory, make thys my last will and testament. Fyrst I bequeth my soule unto allmyghtty God, to Our Lady St. Mary and to all the celestiall compeny of heven, and my body to be buryed in the churche of All Halloys aforesayd, and my mortuary to be payd aftyr the rate and substance of my goodes. To Our Lady of Lincoln vj$d$. To Our Lady warke off Lincoln vj$d$. To the high altare of All Halloys aforesayd for oblacions forgottyn xij$d$. To the churche warke of All Halloys aforesayd ij$s$. To the churche of St. Mary of Mabylthorpe xij$d$. I will have a trentall done for me, xs. To every one of my godchyldren iiij$d$. To my brother John Pacok viij$s$. To my brother John Pacok wyff xx$d$. To every one of my brother John Pacoke chyldren vj$d$. To my syster Jenet Mawer chyldren vj$d$. To my sun Walter wyff xx$d$. To Richerd Baker my servant xij$d$. To Mary Moyd my servant xij$d$. The rest of my goodes I gyff them to Walter my sone, whome I make my executor, and my brother John Pacok supervisor. Wytnes therof; Mr. Raythby, Sir John Gybson, curat, Thomas Brown, John Cayd, wyth other mo.

Proved before P at Louth, 6 February 1532/3.

143. JOHN JAKSON [OF KIRTON IN HOLLAND]
[LCC 1532–34, fos. 4r–5r]

20 January 1532/3. I, John Jakson off the paryshe of Kyrton in Holande, of hole mynde and perfyte remembraunce, makyth my testament concludyng with my last will. In the fyrste I bequethe my soule to God allmyghtty, Our Lady St. Mary and to all the celestiall cumpeny of heven, and my body to be buryed in the churcheyerde of the blessyd appostellys Peter and Paule of Kyrton before namyd, and for my mortuary aftyr the forme of the statutes. To the high altare off Kyrton beforesayd

---

[55] A covering of foreign manufacture.
[56] An official mark of ownership cut on the bill of a swan, at the ceremony of swan-upping. Often a hereditary privilege.

xij*d*. To every altare in the sayd churche ij*d*. To the reparacion of our mother churche of Lincoln iiij*d*. To the orphans of St Catheryn's ij*d*. To the reparacion of the sayd churche of Kyrton v*s*. I will that Margaret my wyffe have my house with the appurtenances to Thomas my sun be of the age of xviij yeres, so that she kepe or cause to be kepte the sayd house with the appurtenances in sufficient reparell duryng the sayd tyme. And then I will the sayd house with the appurtenances remayn to the sayd Thomas my sun in fe symple. And yff the sayd Thomas departe thys worlde before the age of xviij yeres [remainder to] George my sun in fe simple. And yff the sayd George departe thys worlde before the age of xviij yeres [remainder to] Alice and Agnes my doughters at the age of xviij yeres [fo. 4v] in fe symple evenly betwyxt them to be devydyd. And yff ether of the sayd my doughters departe thys worlde before the age prenominate, then I will the sayd house remayn to her that survyves. And yff bothe the sayd my doughters departe thys worlde before the age of xviij yeres, then I will the sayd house remayn to the disposicion of my executrix or her assygnes. To Margaret my wyff vj of the beste milke kye and xl^{ty} ewes. I will that Thomas my sun have delyveryd by myn executrix or hyr assignes, at the age of xviij yeres, xx*s*, one silver spone, one cowe, iij ewes, one materes with a bolster, one pare of schetes, one coverlyd with the best harnest gyrdyll the whiche was hys grandam's [remainder to] George my sun. I will that George my sun have delyveryd by the sayd myn executrix or her assignes at the age of xviij yeres, xl*s*, one silver spone, one cowe, iij ewes, one materes with a bolster, one pare of schetes and one colverlyd [remainder to] Thomas my sun. And yff so be that bothe the sayd Thomas and George my suns departe before the age of xviij yeres, that then bothe ther parte and porcions remayn to Alice and Agnes my doughters at the age before namyd, evenly betwyxte them by equall porcions. And yff ether of them departe thys worlde before the sayd age [remainder to] her that survyves. I will that Alice and Agnes my doughters have delyveryd by my sayd executrix or her assynges at the age of xviij yeres either of them xxvj*s* viij*d*, one cowe, iij ewes, one brasse potte, one brasse panne, vj pecys of puter, the one halff platters and the other halff dyshes, one bed and all thynges thereto belongyng, and either of them iij pare of schetes, the one halff lynen and the other halff harden, and either of them ij towellys. And yff ether of them departe before the sayd age [fo. 5r] then I will ther porcions remayn to her that survyves at the age before namyd [remainder to] Thomas and George my sunys [remainder to] hym that survyves. Moreover, yff all the sayd my chyldren departe owt of thys worlde before the age of xviij yeres, then I will all ther sayd porcions of money remayn all hole to the disposcion of myn executrix or her assygnes. I will that Jenet Thalker have immediatly aftyr my decesse, by the legacy and gyft of Clemence Stalworthe my mother, iiij brasse pottes, one kettyl and ij lyttyll pannys, ij chystes, one materes, one coverlyd, iij pare of schetes, ij borde clothes, the one flaxen and the other harden, and ij towellys. The resydue of all my goodes, I gyff them to Margaret my wyff whome I constitute my executrix, to dispose my goodes to the most pleasure of God and helthe of my soule. I make Richerd Brice of Swyneshed supervisor. Wytnessyth; Sir Thomas Este, Mr Cheney, Sir George Lincoln, with other.

Proved before P at Donington, 18 February 1532/3.

144.   SIR HENRY GOSLYNG [VICAR OF EDLINGTON]
        [LCC 1532–34, fos. 106v–108r]

25 January 1532/3. I, Henry Goslyng, preste and vicare of the paryshe of Edlyngton within the countie of Lincoln, hole of mynde and memory, makyth and ordenyth thys my last will or testament. Fyrst I bequethe my soule to God allmyghtty, to Our Lady St. Mary and to all the holly cumpeny off heven, and my body to be buryed within the quere of St. Helene of Edlyngton. To our mother churche of Lincoln and towarde the warkes therof xij*d*. To the high altare of the same mother churche xij*d*. I bequeth for and towarde the buyldyng of the churche stepyll of Edlyngton vij*l*. To the churchewardens of the same x*s*. And the sayd churchwardens for the tyme beyng yerely, with the incresse of the same, to fynde fyve smale tapers before an ymage of Our Blessyd Lady in the high quere of Edlyngton for ever. To the churche off Bamburgh xij*d*. To the churches of Thymolby xij*d*, Thorneton xij*d*, Marton xx*d*, Langton xij*d*, Woodhall x*s*, Horsyngton xij*d*, Wyspyngton xij*d*. To every house of freres of Lincoln xx*d*. I will that my executors do cause a preste to syng and pray for my soule within the paryshe churche of Edlyngton duryng the space of ij yeres aftyr thys forme foloyng; every quarter the sayd preste to say a hole trentall for the helthe of and welthe of my soule, my father and mother soule and all my frende soules, and myn executors duryng the sayd ij yeres [fo. 107r] yerely to pay to the sayd preste for hys stipende or salary v poundes, and he also to syng and pray the reste of the sayd ij yeres at hys plesure, so that it be within the sayd paryshe churche and also for the helthe of my soule. To the lorde abbot of Bardeney xx^{ty} wedders. To the convent of the same xxvj*s* viij*d*. To Jenet Hall my syster xij yowes and x yerdes of lynnyn clothe, and x yerdes of hardyn. To Isabell Elsen sex schepe and x yerdes. To Alice Nicolson sex schepe, x yerdes clothe. To John Goslyng, my brother sun, xij yowes schepe, iiij oxen, one horsse and one mare, one plugh and one wane and a borden carte. To the chyldren of Thomas Pape viij schepe. To Jenet Goslyng, doughter of Thomas Goslyng my brother, x schepe, ij kye and a yong mare, a bed with that that therto belonges, a brasse potte, iiij dyshes of puter and xx^{ty} yerdes of clothe, x of lynyn and x of harden, and a hutche that is in my chamber. To Nicholes Goslyng her brother iij quarters barly and vj schepe. To Helene Goslyng syster to the sayd Nicholes one qwye brandyd, ij schepe. To every one of my godchyldren viij*d*. To Jenet Smyth a qwye ij yere olde, v schepe and viij yerdes of clothe. To John Browne iiij schepe. To Roger Webster ij schepe. To Thomas Foston one schepe. To Henry Johnson iij schepe and a sylver spone. I bequethe by thys my last will or testament and gyffys to the within namyd Nicholes and to the heres of hys body laufully begottyn for ever one messuage, set lying and beyng within the towne of Thorneton, callyd South Thyng, now in the holdyng of John Balerston and viij landes arable within the feldes of Edlyngton as they be knawn by ther bowndes, the which viij landes I the sayd Henry testator dyd by off one John Edlyngton, as more playnly dothe appere by a dede of feoffment mayd to the use of thys my last will, doyng the dutys to the lordes of bothe fees, and payng yerely to the churchewardens of Edlyngton ij*s*, and to the churchewardes of Woodhall [fo. 107v] xij*d*. To the churchewardens of Thorneton ij*s* for thre annuall obyttes for ever, to be done in the sayd churches for the helthe of my soule, my father and mother soules, and all my good frende soules aftyr thys maner and forme foloyng: the obbyt at Edlyngton ever to be done at my yere day, and the vicare for the tyme beyng to have for the messe and dirige iiij*d*. For the bed rolle iiij*d,* and the messe penny to be offeryd by one of the sayd churchewardens, and

the ryngers to have iij*d*. The reste of the sayd ij*s* I will it shall go to the use of the sayd churche for ever. I will also that the other ij obbyttes be orderyd aftyr the same forme and facion the same day. And yff it happen the sayd Nicholes to decesse withowt heyres off hys body, then I will the sayd house in Thorneton with the landes arable within the feldes of Edlyngton remayn to John Goslyng, my brother sun, and to the heyres of hym for ever, doyng and payng also as is before specyfyed. To John Pape my syster sun my house in Langton to hym and to hys heyres for ever, callyd Plummer Thyng, payng to th'abbot of Kyrksted and to the convent of the same xij*d*. I will that myn executors have the order and lettyng of the sayd house unto suche tyme as the sayd John cum to laufull age, the proffet theroff, reparacions and owt rent allowyd, to remayn to the use of the sayd John for and towardes makyng hym a stok. And it happen the sayd John to dye withowt issue, then I will the sayd house remayn to the nexte of hys brethren or systers for ever. To Sir Leonerde Nurse, my syster sun, vj oxen, iiij kye, iij horsses, one mare wyth all other implementes of housholde not gyffyn nor before bequethyd. The resydue of my goodes I gyff holy to Sir Leonerde Nurse, Robert Palfreman and Thomas Johnson, which I make my executors that they may do and dispose [fo. 108r] for the helthe of my soule as they shall thynke moste meritoriouse and nedefull, and also to se that everythyng herin conteynyd be done accordyng to my will. And the sayd Robert to have for hys labor and payn xx*s,* and Robert Johnson also to have x*s*. I will that Robert Bennet, prior of Bardeney,[57] be supervisor with the licence of hys master, that he may se everything in the same done and disposyd by my within namyd executors. And he to have for hys labors, oversight and payn xx*s*. In wytnes of all thes premises callyd and desyryd; Sir John Wylkynson, Gyles Smertwyth, Robert Marshall, John Ryshby and William Dycson, with other mo.

> Proved before P at Wragby, 30 April 1533. Adm. granted to Leonard Nurse, executor, in the presence of Thomas Johnson, co-executor, who renounced; reserving power to grant to Robert Palfreyman, executor.

145. GODFREY BOLLES [OF GOSBERTON]
[LCC 1532–34, fos. 41v–43r]

26 January 1532/3. I, Godfray Bolles of Gosberkyrk, gent[leman], beyng of hole mynde and good remembraunce, trustyng in God and in the sacramentes off holy churche and therby to be savyd, make my last will and testament. Fyrst I commende my soule to allmyghtty God, Our Lady St Mary and to all the celestiall cumpeny of heven, and my body to be buryed in the qwere of Our Lady within the churche of holy appostellys Peter and Paule in Gosbarkyrke. I gyff in the name of my mortuary as the lawe and acte of parliament dothe limite and require. I gyff for my tithys by negligence or obliviosnes of mynde forgottyn vj*s* viij*d*. To every gylde in the same churche xij*d*. To the reparacion of Our Lady's altare xij*d*. To the churche warke xij*d*. To the other iiij altares in the same churche every one of them iiij*d*. To the reparacion of our mother churche of Lincoln xij*d*. To the offeryng of Our Lady of

---

[57] Bardney Abbey was one of the oldest in the county, founded before 697. William Marton, its last abbot (Robert Bennet's master), was elected in 1507. Following the Lincolnshire rising of 1536, six monks from Bardney were executed for complicity in the rebellion. The house was dissolved soon afterwards: *VCH Lincolnshire*, II, 97–104; F.A. Gasquet, *Henry VIII and the English Monasteries*, 2 vols. (London, 1889), II, 81–2.

Lincoln xij*d*. To the pore chyldren of St Catheryn's without the gates of Lincoln xij*d*. I will that John Bolles my sonne have one pasture of too acres and a haff callyd Chappell Grene and one acre and a stonge, sumtyme Richerde Erkyllys', to hym hys heyres and assygnes of thys condicion, that is to say that sayd John hys heyres and assygnes schall kepe, or cause to be kepte, within the churche of Gosberkyrk one obyt with placebo and dirige and messe of requiem solemply celebratyd, to somme of x*s* yerely for the space and terme of lxxxxix yeres for my soule, my father and my mother soules, and all crysten soules. And yff the sayd John Bolles do not kepe or cause to be kepte the sayd obyt, then I will by thys my last will that it shall be laufull to the churche masters of Gosberkyrk for tyme beyng yerley to entre and distrayne the sayd ij pecys off pasture and the sayd stresse to retayne and kepe till the sayd somme of x*s* be fully contentyd and payd. To the reparacions of the gylde hall xij*d*. I will that my executors do gyve or cause to be gyffyn to the iiij orders of frerys in Boston, every one of them, iij*s* iiij*d* for to syng messe of requiem, placebo and dirige for my soule and all my frendes' soulys. Thys is the last will of me the forsayd Godfrey Bolles mayd the day and yere abovesayd. [fo. 42r] I will that John my sonne have all suche landes and tenementes as afore is covenantith by indenture betwyxte me the sayd Godfrey Bolles on the one partie, and Anthony Irby of Gosberton, gentilman, on the other partie [remainder to] Rankyn Bolles [remainder to] Thomas Bolles my sonne [remainder to] Godfrey Bolles my sonne [remainder to] Richerd Bolles my sonne [remainder to] George Bolles my sonne. To Thomas Bolles my sonne a pasture callyd Walys Tofte and iij stong pasture lying in Throt Polys and halff an acre of pasture in the holdyng of the wyff of Thomas Adam, with ij acres of pasture in the holdyng of John Pott and one messuage lying in Pynchbek [remainder to] Godfrey my sonne [remainder to] lenyall discendyng from one of my chyldren to another. To John my sonne halff a hundreth schepe, my marke of swannys, ij marys, one pare of fustyan blankyttes, ij rede stakkes, my mes boke and challys with a vestiment therto perteyning, iij sylver sponys, my nutte of sylver and gylte, and I will that aftyr the decesse of John my sonne that Godfrey Bolles sun of the sayd John have the forsayd nutte of sylver and gylte. To Margaret Bolles, Godfrey Bolles, Thomas Bolles and Anne Bolles, chyldren of the sayd John Bolles, every one of them a yong cowe of the age of iij yeres. To Rose, wyff of John Bolles, one cowe. To Rankyn Bolles my sonne xl^{ty} wedders, xl^{ty} yowes, xl^{ty} [fo. 42v] hogges, my best carte and my plough and the geres therto perteynyng with the geldynges and marys therto peteynyng, v kyne gyffyng mylke and one yong cowe, iiij sylver spones, one salte of sylver gylte with a coveryng. To the same Ranykn vj bestes of ij yere of age, iiij burnynges and one swanne marke sumtyme Sir John Adams', iiij runnyng kyne. I will John my sonne gyff to Rankyn hys brother x yong swannys to mayntene hys marke. To Catheryne Bolles wyff of Rankyn Bolles one cowe with a calffe. To Rankyn my sonne one pare of fustyan blankyttes. To Thomas my sonne xl^{ty} yowes, xl^{ty} wedders, xx^{ty} hogges, xx^{ty} runyng bestes of diverse ages, sum yong, sum olde, iiij marys, one yong horsse of dun color, iij sylver sponys, one sylver salte gylte. To Godfrey my sonne xl^{ty} yowes, lxxx wedders, xx^{ty} runyng bestes of diverse ages, iij yeryng coltes one fylly, iiij sylver sponys, one sylver goblet with a cover, one sylver bokell with a pendyll therto belongyng. To Thomas and Godfrey my sonnys the ferme which I have be indenture of the monastery of Swynneshed. To Richerd my sonne a hundrethe schepe, xx^{ty} runyng bestes, one gray mare, iij sylver sponys. To George my sonne a hundreth schepe, xiiij runyng bestes and vj kyne gyffyng mylke and iij sylver sponys. I will my executors cause and hyre a laufull and honest preste to celebrate and syng within the churche of Gosberton at Our Lady altare the space of one hole yere for my soule, my father and mother soulys, and all Crysten soulys. And I will the sayd preste have to hys wages viij marke. I will that my obyt be kepte the Tuysday aftyr Allowmas Day.[58] To Elizabeth Brodchawe a cowe of ij yere olde. To Thomas Tofte a runyng calffe. To William Coke a runyng calffe. To Edward Ballarde a runyng calffe. To Robert Herryson my shepparde a runyng calffe. To Godfrey, Richerd, Thomas and George my chyldren every one of them a feder bed, ij pare schetes and one pare blankyttes. To Thomas my best coveryng and to Godfrey my nexte beste coveryng and to George and Richerde either a coverlet. I will the resydue of all my householde [fo. 43r] stuff be devydyd by equall porcions to my chyldren. I will that my executors deale and gyff or cause to be gyffyn in almys dedes the day of my buryall vl. I will that my executors cause one gravestone to be layd on my grave. I will that all my goodes be solde be my executors to the beste price, and I will that the money therof commyng to be disposyd in good warkes off charyte for the helthe of my soule and all my good frendes soulys. To Rankyn, Thomas, Godfrey and every one of them a folden table, one spyt with a pare of coberdes, v puter platters, v puter dyshes, v puter sawssers, one lattyn candylstyk, one chaffyng dyshe, ij seame wheate, iiij seame malte, ij seame maslen corne, one puter charger. To Richerd and George and either of them v puter platters, v puter dyshes, iiij puter sawssers, one lattyn candylstyk. To George my sonne one long table with ij trestyllys perteynyng therto, one gret iren spyt, a pare of cobordes. To John my sonne the counter in the hall uppon condicion he gyff Godfrey a folden table. I will that John Bolles, Rankyn and Thomas and Godfrey my sonnes be my executors. Thes beryng wytnes; Robert Dethe, Sir Herry Toppliche, preste, William Beste, William Osburnbe, William Cade, Thomas Mylner, wyth diverse moo.

Proved before P at Lincoln, 9 February 1532/3. Adm. granted to the executors.

146.   JOHN MASON [OF ITTERBY IN PARISH OF CLEE]
       [LCC 1532–34, fos. 88v–89r]

28 January 1532/3. I, John Mason of Itterby in the paryshe of Cle, hole of mynde and off good remembraunce, makes my testament and last will. Fyrste I bequethe my soule unto allmyghtty God and to Our Blessyd Lady and to all the fare compeny off heven, and my body to be buryed in the churchyerde of the Holy Trinite of Clee. To the warke of Our Lady of Lincoln viijd. To the high altare of the Holy Trinite of Clee for tithys forgottyn xijd. To the upholdyng of the bellys of my paryshe churche of Clee iiijd. To John Mason my eldest sonne iiij schepe. To the sayd John Mason a quartron of a v man cooke.[59] To the sayd John Mason and Helene, my wyff, the thyrde parte of a cog,[60] and the [fo. 89r] sayd Helene to have halffe of her gettynges with the sayd John Mason to her socurre and her chylders upholdyng and beryng halffe the charges of the sayd cog. To the sayd John ij hawvares. To Sibille Mason my doughter a yong qwye, the elder, and a bed, that is to say a materes, a coverlet, a

---

[58] 1 November.
[59] A fishing vessel of substantial size.
[60] A fishing vessel, smaller than a 'cooke', but still capable of coastal, rather than riverine, operations.

pare of schetes, a pillo bere. To Ellys Mason my doughter another yong qwye, the yonger of the sayd qwyes, and a bed aftyr the forme of her other syster. To Andro Mason my sonne iij fysher nettes. To Herry Mason my sonne ij schepe. To John Mason my brother sonne a yowe and a lamme. To William Mason my sonne ij schepe. To Jenet Mason, my brother Thomas doughter, a yowe and a lamme. To Sibill Mason my doughter a potte and ij puter dooblers. To Ellys Mason a potte and ij puter dooblers. To Martyn Mason my russyt jaket. To Thomas Mason my worstyt dooblet. The resydue of my goodes not wyt, I gyff and I wyt to Helene Mason my wyff, whome I make my full executor for to dispose for the helthe of my soule and bryngyng up of her chyldren as she will make answer before the high juge in heven. I will that Henry Redhed be supervisor. Thes wytnesses; Sir Robert Lanam, curat, Henry Jekyll of Clee, Henry Redhed of Itterby, John Sele of Howell, with other mo.

Proved before P at Grimsby, 11 February 1532/3.

147. LAWRENCE ROWNE [OF CONISHOLME]
[LCC 1532–34, fo. 218v]

31 January 1532/3. I, Laurence Rowne of Conysholm, beyng of hole mynde and good remembraunce, makes my last will and testament. Fyrste I bequethe my soule to God allmyghtty, Our Lady St. Mary and to all the holy cumpeny off heven. My body to be buryd in the churcheyerde of St. Peter in Conysholm. To the high altare in Conysholm churche. To the churche of Conysholm xij*d*. To Our Lady's warke of Lincoln iiij*d*. To my sun Rayff one cowe and ij schepe. To my sun Peter on cowe and ij schepe. To my doughter Catheryn on cowe and ij schepe. To my doughter Agnes one cowe and ij schepe, and unto my doughter Alice one cowe and ij schepe. Yff my wyffe Isabell be with chylde, I will that chylde have one cowe and ij schepe. And yff any of thes my chylder departe thys worlde under age, I will every one of them be other ayr. To Rayff and Peter my sonnys one bayd fole. To Peter my sonne one red qwe. To my sun Rayff one lamme. To one preste for doyng halffe a trentall v*s*. To Sir John Smyth, my curate, xij*d*. To Sir Thomas Martyn iiij*d*. To Margaret my mayd one lamme. To my sonnys Rayff and Peter one acre of medo grounde and halff a acre of arable lande lying in Northe Somercotes lordeschyp, also my wane with all the gerys longyng unto it. I will that my wyff Isabell have all my chylder wytworde to my sonnys be xviij yere of age and my doughters xv yeres of age, and my wyff Isabell to be bownde in obligacion unto Evone Throndyke for my chylder parte. The resydue of my goodes not bequethyd, I bequethe them to my wyff Isabell, whome I make my hole executrix. Evone Throndyke and Thomas Symson supervisors. Wytnes heroff; Rollande Colynwoode, Peter Phylipson, John Harde, with other mo. The day and yere above namyd.

Proved before P at Louth, 12 November 1533.

148. LAWRENCE MYLNER [OF PICKLE IN PARISH OF SPALDING]
[LCC 1532–34, fos. 182v–183r]

1 February 1532/3. I, Laurence Mylner of Pycall within the paryshe of Spaldyng, with hole mynde and good remembraunce havyng, or[d]en and make my testament and last will. In the fyrst I bequethe my soule to God allmyghtty, Our Lady St.

Mary and all saintes of heven. My body to be buryed in the churcheyerde of the privelege place of Cowbyt.[61] To the high altare of Cowbyt xij*d*. To Cowbyt churche iij*s* iiij*d*. To Our Lady's warke of Lincoln iiij*d*. To the pore chyldren of St. Catheryn's ij*d*. To the churche of St. Nicholes at Lutton Hyrne iij*s* iiij*d*. To Richerde Sander xl*s*. To Laurence Sander vj*s* viij*d*. Moreover I will Isabell my wyff have my place that I dwell in Pycall duryng her lyff, and aftyr her decesse I will the sayd place be solde by the churchewardens of Cowbyt, callyng to them ij or iij honest of Cowbyt that tyme beyng, and the sylver apon cumyng to be disposyd in Cowbyt churche with sum ornamentes and prestes syngyng, with oder dedes of charyte in Cowbyt and Pykall. I will Isabell my wyff have [fo. 183r] iiij acres pasture callyd Egges Medoy lying in Weston the terme of her lyff, and aftyr her decesse I will the sayd iiij acres remayn to Cowbyt churche for thys intent: for the mayntenance of the sepulture light in the sayd churche, and the sayd lande to remayn in the feoffers handes allway, and when any of them decesse the church-ewardens of Cowbyt to make new feoffers by the advice and nominacion of the chauntry preste that tyme beyng, yff the lawe will suffer it. And yff the lawe will not suffer it, then I wyll the sayd iiij acres remayn to Cowbyt churche the space of xx[ty] yeres, and when the xx[ty] yeres be expyryd, then I will the sayd iiij acres be solde by the churchewardens with iiij other honest men of Cowbyt, and the sylver therapon cumyng to be disposyd and bestowyd in bokes or oder thynges aftyr ther discrecion for the continuance and mayntenance of the sayd light lyke as they will make answer before allmyghtty God. The resydue of my goodes not bequethyd I gyff to the disposicion off Isabell my wyff, which I orden and make my faythfull executrix, with the discrete oversight of Sir Thomas Sheryff, thys my last will to be performyd, and that he have for hys labor vj*s* viij*d*. Thes beyng wytnes; William Jesoph, Robert Herrys and John Howde. Mayd and wryttyn the day and yere abovesayd.

Proved before P at Cowbit, 1 August 1533.

149.   JOHN BRASSE [OF SKEGNESS]
       [LCC 1532–34, fo. 105r]

6 February 1532/3. I, John Bras of Skegnes, seke of body and hole of mynde, makes thys my last will. Fyrste I bequeth my soule to allmyghtty God, to Our blessyd Lady and to all the saintes in heven, my body to be buryd in the churche of St. Clement in Skegnes with my mortuary as the lawe requirith. To the warkes of Our Lady of Lincoln xij*d*. To the high altare at Skegnes iiij*d*. To other of the syde altares iiij*d*. To Johanne my doughter all my housholde stuff, one cowe, one burlyng and a fole. To Sir John Bekkyngham one fole. The resydue of my goodes I gyff to the sayd Sir John and John Brasse of Wynthorpe, whome I make myn executors that they may dispose it for the helthe of my soule and all my good frende soules. These witnesses; John Waterlade and Alexander Cokson, with others.

Proved before P at Partney, 29 April 1533.

[61] Cowbit chapel had the right of burial, usually reserved for the parish church: Daniell, *Death and Burial*, 88–9.

150. THE TESTAMENT OF ROBERT ALAN [OF CROFT]
[LCC 1532–34, fo. 106r]

7 February 1532/3. I, Robert Alan of Crofte, with a hole mynde and good remembraunce beyng, make my last testament. Fyrst I bequeathe my soule to God allmyghty, to Our Lady St. Mary and to all the holle compeny of heven. My body to be buryed within the churcheyerde of Crofte. To Our Lady of Lincoln xij*d*. To Our Lady's warkes at Lincoln viij*d*. To the high altare within the churche of Crofte for tithys forgottyn xij*d*. To Our Lady altare iiij*d*. To St. Nicholas altare iiij*d*. To the reparacions of the churche of Crofte x*s*. To the church of Stallyngburgh xij*d*. I bequethe to be done of my buryall day iiij*l*. I bequeth to a preste x*s* to say one trentall for my soule and all my good frendes soulys. To William Alan my sun my wayn with the tyres that belonges to it uppon thys condicion, that hys mother shall occupy it when she shall nede it. To Isabell Alan my doughter one cowe, x yowes, x hogges, one potte of brasse, one panne with one bed that ys to say one materes, one coverlyd, one pare of schetes flaxyn with the bolster and vj pecys of puter. To Catheryne Alan my doughter one cowe, x yowes, x hogges, one potte of brasse, one panne, vj pecys of puter with one bed. To Margaret Alan my doughter one cowe, x yowes, x hogges, one potte of brasse, one panne, vj pecys of puter, and one bed. To Agnes Alan my doughter one cowe, x yowes, x hogges, one potte of brasse, one panne, vj pecys of puter with one bed, provydyd alway yff any of my forsayd chylder departe thys worlde or they cum at laufull age then I will that the partes thereof to be devydyd equally emonge them beyng alyve and so every one to be other heyr. To everychon of my godchylder vj*d*. To John West my servant one yowe. To Thomas Whytyng of Crofte iij*s* iiij*d* to be supervisor. The resydue of my goodes I gyff them hole to Alyson Alan my wyff whome I make my executrix, and she to dispose them for the helthe of my soule and all christen soulys as she shall thinke moste necessary. Thes wtnes; Sir Thomas Rysell my curat, John Crake, William Hobster, with other mo.

Proved before P at Partney, 29 April 1533.

151. ROBERT HALMOTTE [OF LONDONTHORPE]
[LCC 1532–34, fo. 197v]

7 February 1532/3. I, Robert Halmotte of Lunderthorpe, hole of mynde and good of remembraunce, makyth my will. Fyrste I bequethe my soule unto allmyghtty God, and to Hys mother St. Mary, and to all the fare cumpeny of heven, and my body to be buryd in the churche of St. John of Lunderthorpe. To the warkes of Our Lady of Lincoln xij*d*. To the high altare of St. John Baptiste of Lunderthorpe xx*d*. To the churche warkes of Lunderthorpe vj*s* viij*d*. To the churche warkes of Belton xij*d*. To John my servant one lamme. To William Huggon my kynsman one quarter barly. To Thomas Qwyncy one bullok. The resydue of my goodes here not bequethyd I gyff to Johanne my wyff and Thomas Qwyncy my sun, whome I make my executors that they dispose for the helthe of my soule as it shall be better seyn unto theym. Thes wytnes; Sir William Howyt, Adam Tayler, Thomas Fundans, Robert Funtans, and other mo.

Proved before P at Grantham, 20 October 1533.

152.   ROBERT SKAYRLAY [OF FENTON]
[LCC 1532–34, fo. 153v]

11 February 1532/3. I, Robert Skayrlay of Fenton, of hole mynde and good
remembraunce, makes my testament and last will. Fyrste I bequethe my soule to
God allmyghtty, to Our Lady St. Mary, and to all the saintes in heven, and my body
to be buryed in the churchyerde off All Halloys in Fenton. To the high altare of the
same churche for forgottyn tithys ij*d*. To the high altare of Our Lady of Lincoln
xij*d*. To the churche of Fenton ij*s*. To Our Lady gylde of Fenton halffe a seame of
barly. The resydue of all my goodes I gyff to Henry Godsalve and William
Sewherde the yonger, whome I constitute my executors, that they may fulfyll my
will to the pleasure of God and to the helthe of my soule. Thes wytnes; Robert
Baker, Phylip Hartyll, Robert Preston, Thomas Ryngcrosse and other mo.
    Proved before P at Leadenham, 8 May 1533.

153.   ALICE CLAMONDE [OF KIRTON IN HOLLAND]
[LCC 1532–34, fo. 167]

12 February 1532/3. I, Alice Clamonde of Kyrton in Holande, of hole and constant
mynde, makyth my testament concludyng with my last will. Fyrst I gyff and
bequethe my soule to God allmyghtty, Our Lady St. Mary, and to all the celestiall
cumpeny of heven, and my body to be buryed in the churche of saintes Peter and
Paule of Kyrton before sayd, and for my mortuary as the statutes of our soverayn
lorde the kyng. To the high altare of Kyrton for necligent tithys iiij*d*. To the iij
Marys' altare ij*d*.[62] To reparacions of the sayd churche of Kyrton ij*s* viij*d*. To Our
Lady of Lincoln ij*d*. To the orphans of St Catheryn's ij*d*. I will that myn executors
or ther assygnes have one acre of lande lying in Sutterton in a certen place callyd
Ledebeteres for the terme and space of xx^{ty} yeres immediatly foloyng aftyr my
decesse, under thys condicion; that the sayd myn executors or ther assygnes do truly
performe and kepe, or cause to be kepte, yerely duryng the sayd xx^{ty} yeres, dirige
and messe with note in the sayd churche of Kyrton, and ther disposyng every yere
ij*s* viij*d* duryng the sayd xx^{ty} yeres for my soule, my husband soule and for all my
frende soules. And at the ende and terme of the sayd xx^{ty} yeres I will that Robert
Marable, hys heyres executors or assygnes, have the sayd acre of lande for ever,
yeldyng and payng therfore iiij marke of sterlyn money of Ynglande to an honeste
preste for the space of halffe a yere to syng and pray for my soule, my husband soule
and for all my frendes soulys in the sayd churche of Kyrton. And yff it so fortune
that the sayd Robert Marable, hys heyres or assygners, will not gyff iiij marke for
the sayd acre of lande, that then I will yt be proclamyd in the sayd churche to be
solde and the money therof to be payd to bothe myn executors or ther assygnes to
the use before namyd. Moreover I will that the rent of my house that I have be
coppyholde, the owt rent and reparacions deducte, remayn to the performance of
the sayd dirige so long as the copy will extende. I will that myn executors delyver or
cause to be delyveryd to Thomas Gylberde one yong cowe, one bed and all thynges
therto belongyng, one lyttyll brasse potte and one panne of a gallon at the age of
xx^{ty} yeres. And I will the sayd cowe and stuffe before namyd be in the custody of

---

[62] The Three Marys were the Virgin, the Magdalene, and St. Mary of Egypt, whose feast fell on
2 April in most English monasteries. A fifth-century penitent, St. Mary was a hermit in Palestine.

Robert Marable to the sayd Thomas be of the age of xx^{ty} yeres. And yff the sayd Thomas Gylberde departe thys worlde before the sayd age of xx^{ty} yeres, that then I will the sayd cowe and stuff remayn to the disposicion off myn executors or ther assygnes evenly betwyxte them to be devydyd. To John Heylande [fo. 167v] one cowe and one blake gray mare. To Adlarde Thomson one branlyd[63] cowe. To Robert Marable one browne mare. I will that my executors sell one whyte gray mare and a colte to the performance of thys my laste will. To Dorothe my doughter one violet gowne, one violet kyrtyll, one basyn, one laver, the beste puter platter save one withe a cownter, one of my best flaxyn schetes, ij cortyns, one sylver spone and ij kushyns. To George Heylande one calve. To Anne my doughter my fether bed as it standes with an hynger, ij coverynges, ij kytylls, one blak gowne with all the resydue of my schetes, one cupborde, one long table, one brasse potte, one panne, ij chestes with the best gyrdyll, one pare of beades of whyte ambre, one cawdryn, one thrawne chare, one laver, one candylstyk, one chauffyng dyshe, one leade, iij platters, iij sawssers, one curtyng, one syftyng cheste, iij yerdes of wolne clothe, one saltyng trough with one syftyng arke, one crosse of sylver, one pillo, one towyll, one pare of sylver hookes, ij sylver spones with iij cushyns. To the sayd Robert Marable one browne cowe. To the sayd John Heylande one brasse potte and my best beades. The resydue of my goodes I gyff them to Robert Marable and John Heylande, whome I constitute my executors to dispose my goodes to the moste pleasure off God and helthe of my soule. Thes beyng wytnes; Syr Thomas Este, Sir George Lincoln, Syr Richerde Oxman, with other.

Proved before P at Donington, 28 May 1533.

154.   JOHN WADESLAY [OF SOUTH WILLINGHAM]
       [LCC 1532–34, fos. 97v–98r]

14 February 1532/3. I, John Wadesley of South Wyllyngham in the countie of Lincoln, husbandman, beyng hole of mynde and of good remembraunce, make and orden my last will and testament. Fyrst and principally I bequethe my soule unto allmyghtty God and to Hys blyssyd mother Our Lady St. Mary, and to all the holly cumpeny in heven. My body to be buryed in the churcheyerde of St. Martyn in South Wyllyngham and that the law will require for my mortuary. To the churche of the sayd St. Martyn for one light to be founde before the roode in the same churche vj$s$ viij$d$. To the high altare in the same churche for my tithys forgottyn xij$d$. To the buyldyng of the steple of the same churche thre quarters barly. [fo. 98r] To Our Lady of Lincoln xij$d$. To Jenet my doughtter one whyte qwye with a calve and ij quarters barly. To John my sun ij yereyng calves and a qwye, and a dun mayr and ij quarters of barly. To Abraham my sun ij qwyes and a balde colte stag, and ij quarters barly. To Agnes my doughter ij qwyes of ij yeres age apece and ij quarters barly. To Elizabethe my doughtter a red dowed cowe, one calve, a gray fole and ij quarters barly. To Robert my sun v markes. I will that all my rayment that longys to my body be equally devydyd emongeste all my sayd chyldren, and I will that, yff it happen eny one of my sayd chyldren to decesse afore they shall be of laufull age for to take and receyve theyr sayd legaces, then I will the legaces of every one of my sayd chyldren so decessyd do reste and remayn to those my chyldren then lyffyng,

---

[63] 'Brindled'.

evenly to be devydyd emongyste them. To Sir Henry Herne for to syng one trentall for me x*s*. To every godbarne that I have iiij*d*. The resydue of my goodes I gyff unto Agnes my wyff whome I make my executrix, she for to dispose theym for the helthe of my soule, all my good frende soulys and all Crysten soulys. Thes wytnessyng of thys my last will and testament; William Williamson, Abraham Agworthyngham, Robert Dowce, John Dowce and Henry Dowce off South Wyllyngham, husband-men, with other mo. I will that William my brother helpe my wyff in all her busynes, and he to have for hys labor vj*s* viij*d*.

Proved before P at Lincoln, 16 April 1533. Adm. granted to the executrix.

155.   JOHN TOWNESHENDE [OF HORBLING]
         [LCC 1532–34, fo. 170r]

17 February 1532/3. I, John Townesende of Horblyng, seke of body and hole of mynde, makes my testament and last will. Fyrst I bequethe and gyff my soule to God allmyghtty, Our Lady St. Mary, and to all the holy cumpeny in heven. My body to be buryed in the churcheyerde of St. Andro in Horblyng. To Our Lady of Lincoln iiij*d*. To the fatherles chyldern at St. Catheryn's ij*d*. To the high altare in Horblyng churche ij*d* for my tithys forgottyn. To the churche of Horblyng xij*d*. I will that my wyff cause a preste to syng v messys of the v woundes within the paryshe churche of Horblyng for me. I will that Catheryne my wyff have my house and lande in Swaton with the appurtenances therto belongyng to my sun John be at laufull age, and then to remayn to hym and to hys heyres of hys body laufully begottyn. And yff my sun John departe withowt suche issue, then I will that my wyff have it her lyve. And aftyr I will that house and lande with appurtenances to remayn to Catheryne my syster and to her heyres of her body laufully begottyn, savyng one acre of lande in the northe felde of Swaton, whiche lande I gyff to Swaton parsyhe churche, for my fader and moder George and Helene, and my selve. To John my sun ij qweys, one seame barly and iiij schepe that hys graunsser[64] gaff hys iij brether and hys syster. To reste my goodes bothe moveable and unmoveable not bequethyd nor gyffyn, I bequethe and gyff to Catheryne my wyff, whome I make my true, faythfull and sole executrix, to pay my dettes, fulfyll my legaces, and to dispose for the helthe of my soule as she thynkes best. Also I make Sir John Browne the supervisor of thys my last will. Thes beryng wytnes; Sir John Hyll, Richerde Bawdwyn, Roger Preston, Henry Twyll, with oder mo.

Proved before P at Lincoln, 16 June 1533, by the executrix.

156.   RICHARD KYRKE [OF HORNCASTLE]
         [LCC 1532–34, fo. 172]

18 February 1532/3. I, Richerde Kyrke off Horncastell, beyng of good and hole remembraunce to God, makes and declarys thys my last will and testament. Fyrst I bequethe my soule to allmyghtty God, Our Lady St. Mary, and to all the holly cumpeny of heven, and my body to be buryed in the paryshe churche off Horncastell. To the blessyd sacrament of the sayd churche for tithys forgottyn vj*s* viij*d*. To St. Catheryne gylde iij*s* iiij*d*. To Our Lady off Lincoln xij*d*. I will that all

[64] 'Grandsire'.

my landes and tenementes within the townes and feldes of Horncastell, Kele, Coottes, Bollyngbrok and Hareby (my wyffe's joynter excepte) remayn in the handes of my executors to all my dettes be payd and thys my last will and testament be fulfyllyd. Then I will that all my landes and tenementes with th'appurtenaunces holy remayn and retourne unto my right heyres. I will that all my coppyholde lande for my yeres be in the occupying and holdyng of Catheryne my wyff for the terme off her lyff, and aftyr her decesse then I will that Richerde Kyrke have them. The resydue of all my goodes not wyllyd nor bequethyd, I gyff them unto Catheryne my wyff, she to distrybute theym to my chylder aftyr her discrecion by the syght of my executors and supervisors. I make Catheryne my wyff, William Westfelde, Robert Dawson of Lincoln and Thomas Stevenson my executors, and every one of them to have for ther labors iijs iiijd, and my lorde abbot of Kyrkstede the supervisor, to se it be performyd, fulfyllyd and kepyd after the woord aforesayd, and he to have for hys payn xs. Thes wytnes; Sir Michell Whytehed, paryshe preste, Jamys Burton, Thomas Robynson, William Hudson, Thomas Dylson and William Moresby, with other mo. [fo. 172v]

> Proved before P at Baumber, 17 July 1533. Adm. granted to Catherine the relict and Thomas Stephynson, the executors, reserving power to grant to William Westfelde and Robert Dawson, also executors, when they shall come.

157.   JOHN MASON [OF METHERINGHAM]
       [LCC 1532–34, fo. 158r]

20 February 1532/3. I, John Mason of Medryngham, hole off mynde, with good advysement makethe my will and testament. Fyrste I bequethe my soule to allmyghtty God and to Our Lady St. Mary and all the saintes in heven, and my body to be buryd in Trinite chappell in St. Wylfryde churche in Medryngham. To the high altare of the forsayd churche of Medryngham for forgottyn tithes iijs iiijd. To the kyrke warke of Medryngham iijs iiijd. To Our Lady warke in Lincoln mynster xijd. To Our Lady light in the same churche of Medryngham xijd. To every house of frerys in Lincoln a stryke barly. To Robert Thomson a dun stag and to eche of hys chylder a schepe. To Thomas my sun a cople of yong bullokes, one red and a blake dowd, and a red mare. Also my house that Edwarde Dyxon dwellyth in with the appurtenances. To every chylde of my sun Thomas a schepe. To Martyn my sun a quarter of barly and my house where Thomas Thomson dwellyth, with all that longyth to it for ever, and to every chylde of hys a schepe. To Jenet my wyff my hole housholde and iiij oxen, with iij horses and vj kye, a mare, ij red fylles and a blake, and ij qwyes of ij yeres olde, ij bullokes of one yere olde and halffe my croppe and my house that Norysh wyffe dwellyth in, with the landes and the proffytes that longes to it duryng her lyff. And aftyr her decesse it to remayn to Richerde my sun, to hym and hys heyres for ever. To the sayd Richerde my sun a blak fylly, my houses in Born Broughtton with that longyth to them, and another house with the purtenances in Blankney, also a close at the walke mylne with all that longes to it. And also I will that Richerde my sun have Melton House with all that longyth to it for ever. To every chylde of hys a shepe. The resydue of my goodes not gyffyn nor bequethyd I gyff and bequethe to Jenet my wyff, to Richerd, Thomas and Martyn my suns, whome I make my executors to bryng me furthe to my buryall, and they to

dispose it for the helthe of my soule as they thynke best for the helthe of my soule. Wytnes heroff; John Enderby, Edwardus Rydot, John Rye, William Stele, with other mo.

Proved before P at Navenby, 17 May 1533.

158.   WILLIAM BALET [OF BOLINGBROKE]
       [LCC 1532–34, fo. 256]

25 February 1522/3. I, William Balet off Bollyngbroke, beyng hole of mynde and of good memory, make my last will and testament. In the fyrste I bequethe my soule to allmyghtty God and my body to be buryed in the churcheyerde of the churche of the holy appostellys Peter and Paule of Bollyngbroke, with that thyng that the law requirys in the name of my mortuary. [fo. 256v] To Our Lady's warke of Lincoln vj*d*. To the high altare of Bollyngbroke for forgottyn tithes vj*d*. To the light of All Halloys ther iiij*d*. To the light of the sepulcre ther iiij*d*. To the light of Our Lady of Grace ther iiij*d*. To the light of the Holy Trinitie ther iiij*d*. To the light of Our Lady of Pety ther ij*d*. To the helpe of payng for the feyrter vj*s* viij*d*. To the removeyng of the funte ther vj*s* viij*d*. To the parson of Bollynbroke, my curate, to pray for me iij*s* iiij*d*. To the high altare of Harby for forgottyn tithes xx*d*. To the churche warke ther vj*s* viij*d*. To Margaret Jakson my russyt gowne, my blak gowne and ij pare of hardyn schetes and xx*d* of money. To a preste to syng at Harby for the soulys of Richer Beg, Agnes and Beatrix his wiffes, by the space of a hole yere v*l*. To a preste to syng at Bollyngbroke for me, Agnes my wyff and Alice my doughter, by the space of a yere v*l*. To John Balet my sun, preste, a close callyd Dykhyll Close lying in the felde of Harby the terme of hys lyffe, and aftyr hys decesse to be solde by the executors of the sayd John Balett, preste, or hys assygnes, at the best price that may be, and vj*s* viij*d* of the money receyvyd for the sayd lande to be gyvyn to the churche warke of Harby, and every order of the frerys at Boston to have iij*s* iiij*d* owt of the sayd sum of money. And the resydue to be disposyd in charytabyll warkes for the helthe of the soule of the sayd Wylliam Balett and all Christen soulys, by the discrecion of the executors or the assygnes of the sayd John Balet, preste. The resydue of my goodes I gyff to John Balet my sun, preste, whome I make my executor. Thes men beyng wytnes; Sir Robert Cowper, parson of the churche of Bollyngbroke, Thomas Wytton of Harby, with other mo.

Proved before P at Horncastle, 4 May 1534.

159.   JOHN MANNE [OF GRANTHAM]
       [LCC 1532–34, fo. 197]

26 February 1532/3. I, John Manne of Grantham, hole of mynde and of good remembrance, make my testament and last will. Fyrste I bequethe my soule to allmyghtty God, Our Lady, and to all the holy cumpeny of heven. My body to be buryd in the churcheyerde of St. Vulfrane in Grantham. To Our Lady of Lincoln vj*d*. To Our Lady warke of Lincoln vj*d*. To the high altare in Grantham xij*d*. To the churche of Grantham iij*s* iiij*d*. I will my buryall day be kepyd vij day, xxx^{ty} day and yere day with all the hole qwere of Grantham. To John my son halffe my croppe, one cople of sterys, a cowe, one dun stag, one ballyd horse, x schepe and a fether bed. To Robert my sun xl*s*, one qwye, iiij schepe and ij quarters barley. To Alice my

doughter xl*s*, one qwye, iiij schepe [fo. 197v] and ij quarters barly. To John my sonne a shodde wane. The resydue of my goodes I gyff them to Agnes my wyff, whome I make my executrix, and Robert Horner supervisor, to the intent that he will se it performyd as he thynkes expedyent for the helthe of my soule. Thes beryng wytnes; Sir Thomas Newton, Stephyn Aman, with mo.

Proved before P at Grantham, 20 October 1533.

160.   JOHN COWPER [OF SIBSEY]
        [LCC 1532–34, fo. 104]

2 March 1532/3. I, John Cowper of Sybsay, makethe this my last wyle. In the furst I geve my sowle tyl allmytty God and the Blissyd Virgyn Mary, and tyll all the compane of hevyn. My body to be buryd in the chercheyarde of Sant Margaret of Sybsay, my paryche churche. To the sacarment of the sayd churche iiij*d*. To Sant Margaret lyght ij*d*. To Ouer Lady of Grayse ij*d*. To Sant Sythe ij*d*. To Ouer Lady of Pety ij*d*. To Sant Bryde ij*d*. To the olde rowde ij*d*. To Ouer Lady of Lincoln iiij*d*. To the pwerryf[65] of Sant Catryn in Lincoln ij*d*. To the belles xij*d.* To the ryngers xij*d*. To Isabell my wyff my howsse that I do dwell in the terme of hir lyfe on this condicion, that sche kepe ytt in deu repare. And after hyr dessese I wyll that John Couper my godson have itt to hyme and his ares of ys body laufully begottyn [remainder to] Henry Couper my broder and to his arres of his body [remainder to] Elesabeth Cowper my sester and to hyr assynars. To the sayd Esabell my wyffe iiij kyne and thare calves, and I quy byrlyng. I wyll the sayd Esabell my wyffe have of myne executores x*s* with all my hawsold stowffe and my crope. To Thomas my broder my best dublytt, j rowde and j halfe in Wolsted, to hown and his arres or assynarres, to gar ryng for my yerely and offer j mes paney[66] for evermore for me, also my gray amlyng mere. To Stevyn Busche ij steres of ij yere old of the best and my best coult. To Henry Couper my brother ij accarres and a halfe in the est of the reed to hym and his assynes, and iij gaddes in flays and on a cart att Warloe Hyrn, and iij stange in Howm and a halfe, j acarre of crabyll growend in the sowthe west feld to hyme and his assynerres. I wyll the sayd hares have xl*s*. To John Cowper my godson vj*s* viij*d* and William Couper his broder vj*s* viij*d*. I will that ather of them be uther aryss. To every on of Elsabethe my susteres chelder vj*s* viij*d,* and I wyll that every on of thame be others ares. To Esabell my suster iij*s* iiij*d*. To Janett Bawn my goddowther ij*s*. To Janet Smythe of Townton vj*s* viij*d*. I wyll myne executores sell iiij oxeyn and iiij steres for to pay the forsayd monny and to bery me withall. I wyll that myne executores bestowe on the [fo. 104v] iij prencipawle days for the wyle of my sowle xxvj*s* viij*d*.[67] I wyll that on abell prest do syng ij trentawlles in Sybsay cherche for my sowle, my father and my mother sawell, and all Crystyn sowllys. To every on of my godbarnes iiij*d,* and all other thynges nott sett nor beqwathed, my dettes payd and my last wyll fulfellyd, I putte to the dyscrestion of Thomas Cowper my brother and Stevyn Busche, whome I make myne executores for to dyspose my

---

[65] 'Poor orphans'.

[66] The mass penny was offered before receiving communion (in one kind), at Easter. Such a perpetual donation was, like the provision of obits, a form of commemorative intercession for the soul of the deceased.

[67] This may be an error for 'the iiij prencipawle days', which would be the traditional quarter days of Christmas, the Annunciation of the Virgin (25 March), the Nativity of St. John the Baptist (24 June) and Michaelmas (29 September).

gudes for the most profett of my sowle, father and mother sowle and all gud frendes sowlles and all Crystyn sowlles. Before thes wytnys; William Porter, John Clerke, Sir Adam Pottes with other dyvers. To Elazabeth my ferter on brasse pott and a cattell after the deces of my wyffe.

Proved before P at Partney, 29 April 1533. Adm. granted to Thomas Cowper an executor, reserving power to grant to Stephen Bushe.

161.   JOHN CADE [OF LUDBOROUGH]
        [LCC 1532–34, fos. 234v–235r]

4 March 1532/3. I, John Cade of the paryshe of Ludburgh, husbandman, of hole mynde and a good remembraunce, lovyd be God, makes thys to be my last will. Fyrste I bequethe my soule to God allmyghtty and to Our Lady St. Mary and to the holy cumpeny of heven, and my body to be buryd within my paryshe churche of Ludburgh, gyffyng for my buryall vjs viijd. To the sacrament of my paryshe churche iijs iiijd. To Our Lady of Lincoln ijd. To the warke of the mynster of Lincoln viijd. I will ther be a light fun[68] afore the crucifyx in my paryshe churche for the space of x yeres. To Alyson my wyffe a copyll of oxyn, ij ky, ij marys with all my housholde stuff aftyr me. To John Cowtte xxvjs viijd and it to be valuyd in penyworthe. To John Conne my wane, my plowe with all my plowe tyrys and my yrne harroy, a acre wheate, a acre barle and a acre beanys. To Robert Cayd my sun halffe a acre barly, halffe a acre beanys with all my warke rayment. To William Cade my sun halffe a acre barly, halffe a acre benys with my russyt cote. To Beatrix Cade my sun doughter a yeryng qwye. To Christian Coke a bushyll whete. To Isabell Lowe a bushyll wheate. I will that my body be brought honestly to the grounde the day of my buryall. I will that my xxx[ty] day be honestly kepte. The resydue of my goodes [fo. 235r] I gyff them to Alyson my wyffe and to John Conne whome I make executors, they to dispose them as they may answer to God and salvacion to my soule. Thes beryng wytnes; William Furlyngton, Richerde Barton, Sir Robert Fen with other mo.

Proved before P at Louth, 6 February 1533/4.

162.   THOMAS NORTHE [OF STAPLEFORD]
        [LCC 1532–34, fo. 145v]

4 March 1532/3. I, Thomas Northe of Stapleforthe in the countie of Lincoln, of hole mynde and good memory, makes my last will and testament. Fyrste I bequethe my soule to God allmyghtty, Our Lady St. Mary and to all the holy cumpeny in heven, and my body to be buryed in the churche of Stapleforthe beforesayd in the yle before the high crucifix. To the high altare of Stapleforthe for tithys forgottyn xijd. To Our Lady warke of Lincoln vjd. To the iiij orders of frerys in Lincoln, to every order iiijd. To the sayd churche of Stapleforthe ij yowes and iij hogges. To Jenet Kyrton ij qwyes with calve, ij bullokes, ij yowes and iij hogges. The resydue of my goodes not gyffyn nor bequethyd I gyff them to Margaret my wyff, whome I make my sole executrix that she may dispose them for the helthe of my soule as she thynkes best. I will that my master William Dysnay be supervisor, and he to have

---

[68] 'Found', i.e. 'funded'.

for hys labor vj*s* viij*d*. Thes beyng wytnes; Sir Robert Brygges, vicar off Stapleforth, Robert Flear the elder, William Andro, Robert Baxster of the same towne, with other mo.

Proved before P at Lincoln, 23 May 1533.

163.   JOHN TAYLLER [OF EAST KEAL]
        [LCC 1532–34, fos. 101v–103v]

9 March 1532/3. I, John Tayller of Ester Kele the elder, draper, beyng seke of body but hole of mynde and of good memory, makes my testament and last will. Fyrst and principally I gyff and bequethe my soule to allmyghtty God, Hys blessyd mother Our Lady St. Mary, and to all the saintes in heven, and my body to be buryd within the churche of the Invencion of the Holy Crosse off Ester Kele, and the churche to have for my buryall vj*s* viij*d*, and that to be my mortuary that [fo. 102v] the lawe requiryth. To the blessyd sacrament of Ester Kele aforesayd for tithys forgottyn x*s*. To the churche warkes of the same iij*s* iiij*d*. To every comun light within the sayd churche xij*d*. To Our Lady of Lincoln viij*d*. To Our Lady's warke of the same viij*d*. To the motherles chyldren of St. Catheryn's of the same xij*d*. To the iiij orders of frerys in Boston xiiij*s* iiij*d*, that is to wyt, to iche one of the housys iij*s* viij*d*. To the churche warkes of Wester Kele xij*d*. To the churche warkes of Enderby Malvis xij*d*. To the churche warkes of Raythby xij*d*. To the churche warkes of Hyndylby xij*d*. To the churche warkes of Spillesby ij*s*. To the churche warkes of Waynflet All Saints ij*s*. To the churche warkes of Toynton Peter's xij*d*. To the churche warkes of Toynton All Saints xij*d*. To the churche warkes of Stykeforthe ij*s*. To Robert Trewe my servant a yowe and a lamme. To Thomas Tayllor my servant a yowe and a lamme. To every chylde of John Tayller my nevy, a schepe. To Agnes Smyth my servant v*s* in money. To John Chapman my servant a yowe. To Agnes Gybbynson my servant a yowe and a lamme. To every godchylde that I have iiij*d* in money. I gyff towards the byeing of a newe antiphoner[69] to the north syde of the paryshe churche of Ester Kele iij*l* vj*s* viij*d*. I will that ther be a new crosse of copper and a crosse clothe bought to Ester Kele churche, price of xl*s*. To vj pore folkes, that is to say, William Barbur, John Hudson, Agnes Underwoode, Robert Archer, Esabell Breyrley and Richerde Shepperde, ich one of thes, a new cote. To Thomas Burton, parson of the churche of Ester Kele aforesayd, my gostly father, for hys panys ij*s* iiij*d*. To Sir Leonerd Swete of Spaldyng all the dettes that he awys me, and so off hys charite to pray for me. To Sir Richerd Tayller my nevy x*s* that he yght[70] me upon thys condicion, that he shall syng v messes for me in Ester Kele churche of the v principall woundes of our lorde. To Sir [fo. 102v] Thomas Maysyng ix*s* of the money that he dothe awe me, and he of hys charite and goodnes to pray for me. I will that Alice Tayller my wyff be honestly found and kepte of my goodes, by the syght and assygnement off my executors, the terme of her naturall lyff. I will that Sir Michel Gybson, my preste, do syng for me, my wyff, my father and mother, and for all Christen soulys in Ester Kele churche the space of iiij yeres, and hys stipende to be yerely vj*l* uppon thys condicion, that he shall informe and teche mennys chyldren frely. And yff that it fortune or chaunce that John Tayller,

---

[69] An antiphoner was a book of musical antiphons or responses, usually intended for choral singing.

[70] 'He owes me'.

sonne and heyre of John Taller the yonger, do decesse afore that he cum to the full age of xxj yeres, then I will that the aforenamyd Sir Michel Gybson my preste, or in defawte of hym another honeste preste, do syng for me in the place afore limited other vj yeres, and hys stipende to be as is afore ratyd, and he to teche mennys' chyldren in maner and forme afore wryttyn. Thys is the last will of me John Tayller aforesaid, draper, mayd and wryttyn the day and yere afore specifyed. I will that John Tayller, my nevy, have my house in the southe ende of Ester Kele with all the appurtenances therto belongyng, to hym, hys heyres and assygnes in fee symple for ever, and also my coppy of St. John's of Jerusalem in Yngland nexte therto adjoynyng with the appurtenances therto belongyng after the maner and custome of the lordeschip, duryng the terme of my yeres. I will that John Tayller, sonne and heyr of John Tayller aforesayd, have my house that I dwell in with all the appurtenances therto belongyng, to hym, hys heyres and assygnes in fe simple for ever, and all other of my copys of St. John of Jerusalem aforesayd after the maner and custome of the lordeschip, duryng the terme of my yeres. I will that my executors do by, or cause to be bought, as myche lande as shall admounte to the yerely valour of iij$s$ iiij$d$ over and above all charges, for an obbet to be kepte for me and my wyff in Ester Kele churche for evermore, and the sayd iij$s$ iiij$d$ to be distributyd in maner and forme foloyng, that is to say, to ether of the parsons for the tyme beyng, or to ther deputys, [fo. 103r] iiij$d$, to say dirige and messe of requiem. For my messe peny iiij$d$. To the clerke for the tyme beyng ij$d$. To the ryngers iiij$d$. To all Christen soulys' light iiij$d$, and xiij$d$ to be delte and gyffyn to xiij pore folkes of Ester Kele wheras moste nede is. And the reste of the sayd iij$s$ iiij$d$ to go to the use and proffet of the churche of Ester Kele. I will that a taper of waxe be founde for evermore upon the proffyttes cumyng or growyng of my house in the southe ende of the towne of Ester Kele, uppon the gret latten candylstyk standyng in the high qwere of the north syde of the sayd churche of Ester Kele before the sacrament, conteynyng therin iij or iiij^{li} waxe at the leste, and the sayd taper to burne mattyns tyme, messe and evensong with beyttynges in every syngle feste and dobble feste, and in every principall feste the stok to burne mattyns, messe and evensong, provydyd alway that yff my executors do delay or upon ther frowardnes will not truly observe, fulfyll and kepe the obbyt as is afore sayd, whiche evermore shalbe kepte in Ester Kele churche the Sunday nexte after the feste of St. Cedde the byshop and confessor,[71] and in lyke maner also the forsayd taper of wax be not well founde and kepte accordyng to thys my last will, then I will that the parsons of Ester Kele for the tyme beyng, and the churchwardens of the same, do distrayne and take a distresse, and the distresse so taken to be praysd to satisfaction be mayd for the premisses, or ellys the sayd house with the appurtenances and the sayd londe of iij$s$ iiij$d$ to be at the lettyng of the sayd ij parsons, or ther deputes, and the churchwardens, for the performance and instablyshyng of thys my last will. The resydue of my goodes I will that they be at the disposicion of John Tayllor my nevy and John Tayllor hys sun, whome I orden my executors, and Sir Michel Gybson my preste to be supervisor, and he to have for hys labor iij$s$ iiij$d$ [fo. 103v] notwyth-standyng, provydyd alway that the sayd John Tayller my nevy shall have, receyve, and take all my goodes bothe moveable and unmoveable, landes, rentes, revercions and dettes unto the use and proffyt of John Tayller hys sun, unto suche tyme that the aforsayd John Tayller hys sun be fully xxj yeres of age. And so sone as the sayd

[71] 2 March.

John Tayller cumyth to the sayd age, then I will that he have, receyve and take all my goodes aforesayd, bothe moveable and unmoveable, landes, rentes, revercions with all my dettes, the sayd house in the southe ende of the towne of Ester Kele with the coppy of St. John's nexte adjonyng therto, as is afore specifyed only excepte. And in the mean season I will that the sayd John Tayller hys sun be honestly founde and kepte, other at scole or at sum other honest occupacion as shall be for hys proffyt in tyme to cum. With thes wytnes; Thomas Burton, parson and my gostly father, Robert Trewe, and John Chapman of the same, with other mo.

Proved before P at Partney, 29 April 1533.

164.   JOHN APE [OF WRANGLE]
       [LCC 1532–34, fo. 159r]

10 March 1532/3. I, John Ape the elder off Wrangle, of hole mynde and remembraunce, make my last will and testament. Fyrst I bequethe my soule to allmyghtty God and to Our Lady St. Mary, and to all the holy compeny of heven, and my body to be buryed within the churcheyerde of Wrangle by my fader. I will that my executors cause ij dirigis to be sung for my soule one at the day of my buryall and one at my vijth day. To Our Lady's warkes of Lincoln viij*d.* To the fatherles chyldren at St. Catheryn's viij*d.* To the vicare of Wrangle for tithys forgottyn viij*d.* To the high altare within the churche of Wrangle vj*d.* To every other altare within the same churche iiij*d.* I will that my wyff have my house and all my lande duryng her lyff, and after her decesse I will that William Ape my sun have my house and all my lande to hym and to hys heyres of hys body lawfully begottyn. And he to gyff every one of my doughtters then beyng alyffe v*s* within the space of ij yeres after he enter to the sayd lande. And yff William my sun dy withowt heyres of hys body laufully begottyn, then I will that my house and lande be solde be my executors and every one of my doughtters then beyng alyve to have v*s* of the money, and the resydue to be disposyd in warkes of charite for my soule and my wyffe's, my father, and my mother and all Crysten soulys. To my wyff iij kye of the best, my yong amblyng mare and all my householde stuff. Also I will that my wyff have my farme that I have takyn for yeres duryng the yeres. To William Ape my sun a cowe and to Isbell my doughtter ij schepe. And my wyff to have the proffet of the cowe and ij schepe to William and Isbell be xij yere of age. To Agnes my doughtter a cowe and to Crystyn my doughtter a qwye burlyng for to be at the rule of my executors to Agnes and Cristine be xvj yere of age, and then I will they have them delyveryd with the proffyt that shall clerely growe to that tyme. To William Dodes a cowe and a calve and a yowe. To John Hatson and John Whetney all my fyshyng lepys.[72] I make my wyff and William Stevenson the yonger my executors and William Stevenson to have for hys labor iij*s* iiij*d.* The resydue of my goodes, my dettes and charges borne and payd, I bequeth them to my wyff. Thes beyng wytnes; John Hatson, John Whetney, Thomas Ape and John Ape the yonger, with other.

Proved before P at Boston, 26 May 1533.

---

[72] Sections of a river or stream, naturally or artificially made to fall precipitately. The most common usage of the term is in salmon leaps, where salmon leap over such waterfalls on their journey upstream to spawn.

165. ROBERT BELL [OF BRANSTON]
[LCC 1532–34, fo. 155r]

10 March 1532/3. I, Robert Bell, hole in mynde and of good remembraunce, make my last will. Fyrst I bequethe my soule to allmyghtty God, to Our Lady and to all the saintes in heven. My body to be buryed in the churcheyerde of All Saintes of Braunceton. To the high altare of All Saintes, Braunceton for forgottyn tithis iiij*d*. To Our Lady warke at Lincoln iiij*d*. I will iij messes be celebrate, one for my soule, another for my father soule and the thyrde for my mother soule. To John my sun a blak meyr, a quarter of malte and a schepe. To Thomas my sun a blak meyr with a fole, a quarter of malte and a schepe. To William my sun a browne qwye of ij yere age, a quarter of malte and a schepe. To Catheryne my doughter a calve of viij or ix wekes age, a quarter of malte and a schepe. To Alice my doughter a bullok of one yere age, a quarter of malte and a schepe. The resydue of my goodes not bequethyd I gyff to Jenet my wyff to dispose it for the helthe of my soule as she thynke it best. And the sayd Jenet my wyff I make my executrix. Thes wytnes; Sir William Hazarde, curat, Lyon Shorte, Hugh Hyll, John Humberstone, cum multis aliis.
Proved before P at Lincoln, 9 May 1533.

166. JOHN TUR [OF GAINSBOROUGH]
[Stow 1530–52, fo. 16v]

11 March 1532/3. I, John Tur of the town of Gaynsbrugh in the diocese of Lincoln, seke of bodi and hole of mynd, prasid be God, make and orden this my present testament and last will. First I bequeth my saul too God almyghti and to Owr Lady Sent Mari and too all the hole company in hevyn, and my body too be beryid in the haloye grownd att such place as it shall plese God to take me. To the hy alter of Gaynsbrugh iij*s* iiij*d*. To the hy alter of Gunecester xx*d*. To the mother church of Lincoln xij*d*. To the iiij orders of feres in Lincoln, to every off them, iiij*d*. I gyff frele to Thomas Tur, my eldest son, all such landes as ar myne or may be within the town and the hole bowndes of Haxsay within the Yle of Haxam. To Robert Tur my yongest son, and to his heires of his body, all my landes wich I have within the town and hole bowndes of Gaynsbrugh after the decesse of thar mother. I will that all such substance as it hath plesid God to leve me shal be devided in thre parttes, that is to say, on parte to my wyff, the seconde parte to my childer and the thurde parte to be devydid in ij parttes, the on parte of hit for the helth of my sol, and the odur parte for too be devydit emonges my childer and kynsfolke att the discrecion of my executrix Katerene Tur, my wyff. I make supervisor my father-in-law, Hew Thornell. Witnes; Hew Thornell, Robert Williamson, Richard Barmbe and Richard Billyngton, prest, with other mo.
Proved before L, 15 May 1533. Adm. granted to the executrix.

167. JOHN GREENWELL [OF CONINGSBY]
[LCC 1532–34, fo. 98v]

14 March 1532/3. I, John Grenewell of Conesby, beyng of hole mynde and good remembraunce, make my testament. The fyrste I gyff and bequethe my soule to allmyghtty God, to Our Lady St. Mary and to all the holy cumpeny of heven, and my body to be buryed within the churche of St. Michel of Conesby. To Our Lady's

worke of Lincoln iiij*d*. To the high altare of Conesby for tithys forgottyn iiij*d*. To Sir William Porter, the Ihesus preste of Conesby, to pray for me, vj*s* viij*d*. To Mr. Skypwyth 40*s* and to hys wyff x schepe, and to every chylde of the sayd Mr. and Masterys Skypwyth ij schepe. The resydue of my goodes I will that my to bretherne and Anthony Loblay of Tumby have, the whyche I make my executors to ministre and to dispose them for the helthe of my soule and all Crysten soulys, in the workes of mercy as they shall thynke moste necessary. And I will that Mr. Skypwyth be supervisor to se that my goodes be disposyd to the helthe of my soule and all Crysten soulys. Thes men wytnes; Sir William Porter, Thomas Kele.

Proved before P at Horncastle, 28 April 1533. Adm. granted to Anthony Loblay an executor, reserving power to grant to other executors.

168. THOMAS STORER [OF CAREBY]
[LCC 1532–34, fo. 199v]

15 March 1532/3. I, Thomas Storer of Careby, hole of mynde, make my testament and last will. Fyrste I bequethe my soule unto allmyghtty God, and to Our Lady St. Mary and to all the holy cumpeny in heven, and my body to be buryd in the churcheyerde of St. Stephyn of Careby, and my mortuary as the law requiryth. To the high altare of Careby for tithys forgottyn v*id*. To Our Lady of Lincoln vj*d*. To William Ymnay, my sun-in-lawe, a brandyd qwye. To John Storer my sun a flekyd qwye. To Thomas Storer my sun a flekkyd calve. To Margaret Storer my doughter a dowffet calve. To Elizabeth Saddler, my doughter-in-lawe, a red calve. To Henry Storer my sun the fyrste calve that God fortunyth me to have aftyr the date herof. And the sayd legacy to go to the commune profet of ther mother and theym so long as she is unmaryd. And yff it fortune her to mary, then I will that my chyldren have ther legacy delyveryd before the day of mariage, to go to ther own proffet. To William and John ij acres of barly to be partyd betwyxte them. To Thomas and Henry ij landes of barly in Welcrofte. To Margery my wyffe my house in Bitham duryng her lyffe, and aftyr her decesse to John Storer my sun and my heyr. To Margery my wyff the copy of my house in Careby, and to her assignes duryng the date of the copy yff she fortune to lyff so long, or ellys aftyr her decesse to my chyldren. The resydue of my goodes I bequethe to Margery my wyff, whome I make my full exectutrix, she to dispose them as she shall thynke beste for the helthe of my soule and to the bryngyng up of my poor chyldren. The beyng wytnes; Sir Nicholes Slater, parson, Thomas Walpole and Thomas Gyllam, and other mo of Careby aforesayd.

Proved before P at Bitchfield, 21 October 1533.

169. ROBERT BURWELL [OF WEST KEAL]
[LCC 1532–34, fo. 97]

16 March 1532/3. I, Robert Burwell of Wester Keill, husbandman, beynge in holl mynde and memorye, makes my laste will and testament. Furste I bequeithe my saule to God almyghtye and to Owr Ladye Sante Marye and to all the holye compenye in hevyn, and my bodye to be buryed within the churcheyarde of Wester Keill. To the hye auter of Wester Keill xij*d*. To the lyghte that standys before the sacrament in the hye qwer iiij*d*. To every lyghte within the churche at the same

Wester Keill ij*d*. To the bellys of the said churche xij*d*. To the hye auter in the cath[edral] churche of Lyncoln x*d*. To Owr Ladye's warkes of the same x*d*. To Johanne my wyffe vj kye, xl^tye yowys with ther lammys and ij steiris, a brandid and a goldynge iij yerris olde, and all the howshold stuffe that sche brought with hir, and all the howsholde stuffe that can bee provyd to bee myn owne. And I will the xl yowys aforsaid schall be deliverid after this maner: I will that all my yowys togyther schall be pute in holde and lette runne, and xx yowys with ther lammys that runne firste and other xx of the laste runnynge owte of the holde schall bee delyverid to Johanne my wyffe, and iff ther bee ij or iij of the yowys that sche lyke not I will that better yowis schall be delyverid to hir for them. Also I bequeithe to Johanne my wyffe xviij*s* viij*d*, the whiche Isabell his sister owith to me and halfe of all the dettes that bee hawynge to me. And if my said [fo. 97v] wyffe please to tarye with my mother and John my brother I will sche schall have meitte and drynke of free coste for hirselfe iij yerrys, and also schall have iij kye pasturid of free coste by the same iij yerris, and I will that sche schall have all the profyttes of the same kye by that space. To Alice and Elizabeth my doughters xx markes of sterling money to bee devydyt equallye betweyn them when they cum to the aige of xviij yerris. And if one of them dye befor sche cum to that age I will that the other schall have the holl moneye aforsaid, and if it fortune bothe to dye afor they cum to that age I will that Johanne my wyffe have xl*s* of the same money and the resydewe therof to bee devydid emonge my bretherne, they to gyve parte therof for my fathers saule and myn. The resydewe of all my goodes I gyve to Elizabeth my mother, and I will sche be good to my bretherne. I will that John my brother schall have this forsaid xx markes in his kepynge and he to delyver it to my said doughters when they cum to the forsaid aige withowte trobull. To Thomas Grene my father-in-lawe iij*s* iiij*d* to se that my wyffe have all suche goodes that I have bequeithid to hir. I give to John my brother my beste cotte to se that my chylderne have all ther righte, the whiche John my brother I make myne executor. Whitnesses herof; Sir Herrye Kaye, Willyam Todde, John Wesmels, with other.

Proved before P at Lincoln, 8 April 1533.

170.   THOMAS FELDE [OF LEAKE]
       [LCC 1532–34, fos. 180v–181r]

16 March 1532/3. I, Thomas Felde off Leeke in the countie of Lincoln, makes thys my will and testament. Fyrst I bequethe my soule to God allmyghtty, Our Lady St. Mary and to all the holly cumpeny of heven, and my body to be buryd in the churcheyerde of Leeke, and that the lawe requiryth to be my mortuary. To the blessyd sacrament iij*d*. To every altare besydes ij*d*, also for tithys forgottyn iiij*d*. To the buyldyng of the churche of Leeke vj*s* viij*d*, to be payde at iij paymentes within thre quarters of the yere aftyr my decesse. To Our Lady warkes at Lincoln vj*d*. To St. Catheryn's ij*d*. To every one off my chylder and to my wyffy's chylder, a yowe and a lamme. To Agnes my syster a yowe and a lamme. I will that fyve messys of the fyve woundes off Our Lorde be sung at Scala Celi by priviliges.[73] I bequethe for the syngyng of one trentall in the churche of Leeke for my soule, my frendes' soulys and all Crysten soulys x*s*. To my wyff my plough, ij sterys, ij marys, iij kye,

---

[73] It was common for masses to be arranged in numbers with theological significance. Here the masses correspond with the five wounds.

one qwye with calve, and one calve. I will Alice my wyff have all my landes and tenementes, to the kepyng and bryngyng up of my chylder in good order and rule unto suche tyme as my sun cum and be at the full age of xvij yeres, and for and in defawte sche not so doyng, I will my brother have the gydyng and rule of my sun duryng the sayd tyme, and the one halffe of my sayd landes and tenementes to the bryngyng up of hym wythe. And aftyr the xvij yere of the age off my sayd sun, I will my doughter have all the hole issuys and proffyttes of my sayd landes and tenementes the space and tyme of iij yeres towarde her mariage yff she lyff so long, and ten yowes the whiche are in the kepyng of my broder at thys day. And at suche tyme as my sayd sonne [fo. 181r] cumys to the full age of xxj yeres, I will Alice my wyff have the one halffe of my sayd landes and tenementes duryng her naturall lyff, and my sun the other halffe, to hym and hys assygnes. And aftyr the decesse of my sayd wyff, I will her halffe parte of my landes and tenementes aforesayd, remayn hole unto my sayd sun in fe symple. And yff yt fortune my sayd sun to decesse afore he cum to the full age aforesayd, I will the sayd landes and tenementes remayn unto my doughter in fe symple aftyr the maner and forme aforesayd, kepyng one obyt in the churche of Leeke of viijs to be waryd therof for my soule and all Crysten soulys. And yff it fortune bothe my sayd chylder decesse afore they cum to the age of xxj yeres aforesayd, I will Alice my wyff have all my hole landes and tenementes duryng her naturall lyff, kepyng one obyt yerely duryng the sayd tyme of vjs viijd within the churche of Leeke aforesayd, and also to pay yerely to my syster Elizabethe vs. And aftyr the decesse of the sayd Alice my wyff, I will all my sayd landes and tenementes remayn to my brother and my thre systers and ther chylder, so that my brother do kepe one obyt yerely in Sutterton churche of viijs by yere for my soule and all Crysten soulys. Also I will that my brother, with the consent of my wyff, have the fermyng and occupying of the sayd landes and tenementes for hys yerely rent, to be payd to the partes as aforesayd duryng the nonage of my sayd chylder, and makes my said brother and the sayd Alice my wyff juntly my executors, and he to have for hys labor vjs viijd. And the resydue of all my goodes not bequethyd nor gyffyn afore in thys my wyll, my dettes payd and my legaces performyd, I gyff and bequethe unto Alice my wyff. In wytnes wherof ther beyng present the day and tyme aforesayd; Sir Roger Pysche, chaplayn, John Mawnus, Walter Knyght, with other.

Proved before P at Skirbeck, 5 August 1533.

171.   WILLIAM JOWYTSON [OF STICKFORD]
        [LCC 1532–34, fos. 264v–265v]

16 March 1532/3. I, William Jowytson, of Stykforde, beyng hole of mynde and of good remembraunce, makes my laste testament. Fyrst and principally I gyff and bequethe my soule to allmyghtty God my maker, to Our Lady St. Mary, and to all the saintes of heven. My body to be buryd wheras it shall please allmyghtty God. To Our Lady warke of Lincoln xvjd. To the high altare of Lincoln xijd. To the motherles chylder of St. Catheryn's of Lincoln xijd. To the churche warke of Stykforde foresayd xxs. To bying of a vestment to Stykforde churche xxiijs iiijd. To the sayd churche of Stykforde a mes boke price iiijs. To a preste to pray for my soule the space of iiij yeres, and to pray for my wyff soule and all my good frendes, with all Christen soulys yerely, to have for hys stipende cs, yff he will teche the

chyldren of the sayd towne of Stykforde. And yff he will not teche none, then he is to have yerely for hys stipende but vij markes. To iiij orders of frerys of Boston xiij*s* iiij*d*, that is to wit ich one of the housys iij*s* iiij*d*. To Alice Jowitson, the doughter late of Thomas Jowitson my sun, x*l*, and it to be payd her at the day of her mariage. And yff she dye or she be maryd, that then I will that Beatrix my doughter may have the sayd x*l*, a sylver spone, a brasyn morter with a pestyll, a foldyn table, ij [fo. 265r] best candylstykes, a leade standyng in fornace and another leade besyde my best spyt and a medyll spyt, iiij cobberdes, ij yren wedgys, a gret panne and the nexte gret panne, ij brasse pottes, a spruce chyste, the beste chaffyr and a chaffyng dyshe, ij puter podyshers, a basyn and a laver, two tabyll clothys, ij pare of schetys, one pare of them flaxen, the other pare of harden. Also I will that all the foresayd bequest to the sayd Alice be heyrlomys to Larke house excepte onely the x*l*. To the sayd Alice a blake cowe, which cowe I will that she be in the kepyng and occupying of Beatrice Kyme, my doughter, to suche tyme that the sayd Alice be at laufull age. And then I will that Beatryx my doughter do delyver, at the syght of my executors, another cowe to the sayd Alice of lyke goodnes, valure and of age. To the sayd Alice my best brasse potte, to be her and her heyres of her body laufully begottyn. And yff she dye withowt issue then I will it remayn to Thomas Kyme, my doughter sun [remainder to] the nexte heyre of Beatrix my doughter, and so from heyr to heyr. I will that the sayd Alice Jewytson be founde of Larke's house with the appurtenances, at the sight and puttyng of my executors, and that Thomas Yong and Jane hys wyff, mother to the sayd Alice Jewytson, may not have or shall not have any interest or mellyng in Larke's house, or in Synner house, or in any stuff therto belongyng. To Beatrix Kyme my doughter my whyte ambelyng meyr. I will that my pykeryllys and other fyshes be at the will off Beatrix Kyme my doughter, and myn executors. To Dorothe Kyme, doughter of John Kyme, a fether bed, a pare schetes, a coverlyd and xl*s* of money, and it to be payd to her at the day of her mariage, and a sylver spone with a harte. To Margaret Kyme xl*s,* and it to be payd at the day of her mariage, and a sylver spone with a harte. To Johan Kyme xl*s*, to be payd her at the day of her mariage, and a sylver spone. To John Kyme my doughter sun xl*s*, to be payd what tyme he cumys to xxj^ty yeres of age, and a sylver spone. To Thomas Kyme xl*s*, to be payd hym at the sayd age of xxj^ty, and a sylver spone. To Austyn Kyme a sylver spone and a yong horse of a gray color. Provydyd alway that yff any of the sayd [fo. 265v] chyldren of John Kyme do decesse or they cum to xxj yeres of age, and the sayd doughters of John Kyme do decesse lykewyse or they be maryd, then I will that ich on of them be other heyres of my legaces aforesayd. To John Kyme, my sun-in-lawe, all my nettes, all my botys, all my trunkes and my copys of my fyshyng. And in case be that the sayd John Kyme will not be content, or that he do vexe or trobyll at any tyme or tymys my executors, than I will that the sayd nettes, botes, trunkes and copys of fyshyng be at the will of my executors. The reste of my napery ware or inwarde stuff unbequethyd I will that they may be devydyd in equall porcions to the chyldren of John Kyme by the handes of my executors. The resydue of all my goodes not afore gyvyn ne bequeste, all my dettes beyng payd, I gyff them to Mr. John Whytwell, preste, of Cambryge, Beatrix my doughter, of Stykforde foresayd, and John Kyrke of Wester Kele, whome I make my executors to dispose them accordyng to thys my last will, haveyng ich on for ther labors singlerly xiij*s* iiij*d*, and John Lyster of Boston to be supervisor, havyng for hys labor xiij*s* iiij*d*. Thes beyng wytnes; John Lownde, Hugh Lownde, William Gyllys,

William Fysher, and John Hopster of Stykforde foresayd, and Robert Wryght, prest of Kyrkeby ny Bollyngbroke, with many mo.

Proved before P at Partney, 6 May 1534. Adm. granted to John Whytwell the co-executor, reserving power to grant to Beatrix, daughter and co-executor.

172.   WILLIAM WRYGHT [OF PINCHBECK]
       [LCC 1532–34, fo. 161]

16 March 1532/3. I, William Wryght of Pynchbek, with good mynde and hole remembraunce, makes my last will and testament. Fyrst I bequethe my soule to God allmyghtty and to Hys mother, Our Lady St. Mary, and to all the saintes in heven. My body to be buryd in the churcheyerde of Our Lady in Pynchbek. To the high altare within the churche off Pynchbek viij*d*. To Our Lady of Lincoln for oblacion iiij*d*. To the pore chylder in St. Catheryn's ij*d*. To John my sun my best matterys, ij of my best coverlydes and vj pecys of my best puter, and iij candylstykes. To Agnes Tylson, the doughtter of William Tylson, a heder calve. I will that the sayd John and Agnes shall receyve ther calves at Ester nexte cumyng. To Margery [fo. 161v] my wyff my house that I dwell in the space and terme of xx^{ty} yeres with the purtenances longyng therto, she kepyng the sayd house with laufull reparacion. And aftyr the sayd xx^{ty} yeres be expyryd then I will that John my sun have the sayd house with the purtenances to hym and to hys heyres of hys body. Yff so be that Margery my wyff fortune to dy or the sayd xx^{ty} yeres be exspyred, then I wyll that William Tylsun have the governance of John my sun and of all suche stuff that I have bequethyd to hym. And also I will that the sayd John my sun shall enter apon the sayd house with the purtenances immediatly after her decease. Also I will that yff so be that John my sun dy withowt heyres of hys body, then I will that the sayd house with the purtenances be solde by the handes off William Tylson or hys assygners, and the money therefore takyn be disposyd for the helthe of my soule and my good frendes' soulys, in a preste syngyng or in other dedes off charyte as the sayd William Tylson thynkes best for the welthe of my soule. I will that one of my kye be solde for to bryng me furthe with the resydue off my goodes ungyffyn and unbequethyd I put them to the disposicion of Margery my wyff, whome I make my trewe executrix, and William Tylson to supervisor, and I will that he have for hys labor and payn a dowffyd calve. Thes beryng wytnes; William Bewyk, preste, John Yong, John Knottes, Thomas Sparro, with other mo.

Proved before P at Spalding, 27 May 1533.

173.   ROBERT HYNDE [OF DONINGTON IN HOLLAND]
       [LCC 1532–34, fo. 165v]

18 March 1532/3. I, Roberte Hynde of Donyngton in Holland within the countie of Lincoln, beyng of hole mynde and good remembraunce at thys tyme, lovyed be God, make my testament and last will. Fyrst I bequethe my soule to God allmyghtty, and to Our Blessyd Lady St. Mary, and to all the saintes in heven. My body to be buryd within the churcheyerde of Donyngton. To the high altare within the churche of Donyngton for tithys forgottyn iiij*d*. To every altare within the same churche ij*d*. To every light that standes abowt my herse at my buryall day

j*d*. To Our Lady of Lincoln ij*d*. To the fatherles chyldren at St. Catheryn's ij*d*. To the bellys iiij*d*. Thys is my will, that Robert Comfettes my sun-in-lawe and Catheryne hys wyff have my house that I dwell in with the purtenance therto belongyng lying in Donyngton, to them and to ther heyres of ther ij bodys after my decesse owt off thys worlde. And yff they dy withowt heyres of ther ij bodys then I will the same house with the purtenances therto belongyng remayn to John Dallys and to Jenet hys wyff, to them and ther heyres of ther ij bodys. And yff they dye all withowt heyres of ther ij bodys then I will it be solde be the churchewardens off Donyngton and the money theroff to be disposyd by them beyng in cauces within the same towne of Donyngton for my soule and all my frendes soulys. The resydue of all my goodes unbequethyd I gyff them to Robert Camfettes and to Catheryne my doughter, whome I make my executors that they to kepe me honestly and to pay my dettes and to bryng me furthe. Thes beyng wytnes of thys my last will; Thomas Raner, Jamys Byell, William Toplysh, with other mo.

Proved before P at Donington, 28 May 1533.

174.   MARGARET SMYTH [OF TETNEY]
        [LCC 1532–34, fo. 156r]

18 March 1532/3. I, Margaret Smyth, otherwyse callyd Clerke, vido, of hole mynde and good remembraunce makes my last will and testament. Fyrst I bequethe my soule to God allmyghtty, Our Lady St. Mary, and to all the saintes in heven. My body to be buryed in the churcheyerde of St. Peter and Paule in Tetney, with that that the lawe will. To the high altare of Tetney iiij*d*. To Our Lady of Lincoln, to the high altare iiij*d*. To Our Lady warke of Lincoln iiij*d*. To Our Lady gylde of Tetney ij*d*. To the high altare of Tetney ij*d*. To John Halyngton the yonger a yowe hog. To Alyson Clerke a russyt cote. To Alyson my doughtter a gret panne. To Thomas my sun a cople of oxyn, a horse and a meyr to the plowe and to the wane. To Nicholes my sun a yeryng calve. To Alison my doughter a bawstyn mare.[74] I have ij kye; I will that one of them be solde to bryng me to the grounde honestly. The resydue of my goodes not gyffyn I gyff to Thomas my sun and to Nicholes my sonne whome I make my true executors, that they may pay my dettes and dispose for the helthe of my soule as they thynke best to the plesure of God. Thes wytnes; Gy Jekyll, John Halyngton the yonger, Robert Blancherde, Richerde Bryan, with other many mo.

Proved before P at Grimsby, 13 May 1533.

175.   CHRISTOPHER BEE [OF BARROW UPON HUMBER]
        [LCC 1532–34, fos. 194v–195r]

20 March 1532/3 I, Christofer Bee of Barow, hole of mynde and full of memory, make thys my will and testament. Fyrste I gyff and bequethe my soule to allmyghtty God, to Our blessyd Lady St. Mary and to all the saintes in heven. My body to be buryd in the churche of Our Lady in Barow aforesayd. To the high altare in the sayd churche of Barowe for forgottyn tithys xx*d*. To Our Lady's warke of Lincoln vj*d*. To the high altare of the same churche of Lincoln vj*d*. The reste of my goodes not bequethyd I gyff to Dorothe my wyff, whome I make myne executrix to dispose

---

[74] A piebald mare.

for my soule and for the well of my chyldren as she [fo.195r] thynke necessary. Thes men wytnes; Thomas Hopkynson, preste, James Clerke, James Hudson, Stephyn Wryghte, with other mo.

Proved before P at Caistor, 14 October 1533.

176.   ROBERT JAKSON [OF HAMMERINGHAM]
       [LCC 1532–34, fo. 154]

23 March 1532/3. I, Robert Jakson of Hameryngham, seke of body and good of memory, makes my testament and last will. Fyrste I commyt my soule to allmyghtty God and to all the saintes in heven, and my body to be buryed in the churcheyerde of All Halloys at Hameryngham, and to my mortuary as the lawe will. To the holy sacrament in Hameryngham churche iijd. To Our Lady of Lincoln viijd, the one halff of it to her warke. I will that my gret oxen be solde to kepe a prest to syng for my soule and all Crysten soules in the churche of Hamerygnham. I will that myne executors have xiijs iiijd to by a crosse to Hameryngham churche, and oder xiijs iiijd to by a banner clothe to the sayd churche to be in the high qwere of the same. Also I will that ther be a light founde afore the sacrament for evermore, wherto I beqeth xs, and that the churchewardons have the rule of the same. And yff the churche-wardons will not fynd it, the parsone of Hameryngham for the tyme beyng to have the rule of the same and to fynde it hymselff. I will that my wyff have, in recompense of thyrd or oderwyse, iij kye, xx^{ty} schepe, iiij seame of barly to be payd thys nexte yere that commythe of the barly that God sendes nexte yere. Also I will that my wyff and my doughtter Alice have all my housholde stuff betwyxte them, excepte that my doughter Alice have one leyd, one pare of quernes, ij tabyll bordes, one gret arke, one chyste in my chamber. I will that my doughter and my wyff make devision betwyxt them off all my pullan and swyne, as gese and all other pullan whiche I bequethe them. Also I will that my doughtter Alice have iiij seame malte thys yere and the nexte yere v seame barly. To my doughter Alice ij kye and one of her owne, whiche I have in my custody, ij burlynges, one gray mare, a gray stagge, a fole, xx^{ty} schepe and x lammys, also one gret brasse potte withe a dyshe bynk standyng in my hall, and a flekkyd qwye. To John Jakson, my sun and my heyr, ij cople oxen, a cople sterys, iij kye, ij merys, the one amblyng, ij stagges, lx schepe, xxty lammys, [fo. 154v]ten seame barly nexte yere to be delyveryd and sex seame malte thys yere to be delyveryd. I will that the parsone of Wynceby have the rule of my sun John Jakson and all hys goodes to he cum to lawfull age. To John Kyme my sun-in-lawe bothe my wanys when my croppe is innyd aftyr harvest and my carte. To every one of my godchylder a lamme. To Isabell Kyme my doughtter a grette brasse potte with a lyppe owt. Also the resydue of my goodes not gyven nor bequethyd I gyff to my executors Sir William Hunter, parsone of Wynceby, Syr Christofer Stevenson, parson of Hameryngham, and Thomas Parys of Malteby in the Marshe, to dispose for the helthe of my soule and all Christen soulys, whome I make myn executors. And they to receyve ather xl off John Dunstroppe of Hemyngby for the take of my ferme in Hameryngham, or ellys to injoy my leys of hym accordyng to the effecte of a pare of indenturs mayd betwyxte the sayd Dunstroppe and me the sayd Jakson. Also yff it fortune my sun John Jakson to dy or he cum to laufull age, as God forbyd, that then John Kyme my sun-in-law shall have xls, and Alice my doughtter other xls. The resydue of hys parte to be bestowyd for the helthe of my

soule and all Christen soulys by myn executors. These wytnes of the sayd testament to be trewe; William Fetherstonhalgh of Hameryngham, William Pape of the same, Wylliam Fysher of the same, with other mo.

> Proved before P at Lincoln, 9 May 1533. Adm. granted to Sir Christopher Stevenson and Robert Parys, executors, reserving power to grant to William Hunter, also an executor, when he shall come.

177.   RICHARD STAPLEFORTHE [OF SOUTH ORMSBY]
           [LCC 1532–34, fo. 251v]

25 March 1533. I, Richerd Stapilforthe of South Ormesby, preste, hole of mynde and in good remembraunce, makyth my testament and last will. Fyrste I bequethe my soule to allmyghtty God and to Our Lady St. Mary and to all the hevenly cumpeny, and my body to be buryed within the churche of South Ormesby, gyveyng to the sayd churche for my sepulture there vjs viijd. And that admyttyd by the lawe to be my mortuary. To the monastery of Our Lady of Lincoln xijd. To the house of Observance in the towne of Newarke my chalys.[75] To the house of Our Lady Frerys in Lincoln iijs iiijd. To the monastery of Mary Magdalen in Nocton Parke all my bokes pryntyd, as my *Portas Vita Christi* of Loidoffe, *Annotacions of David*, *Salter of St. Augustyne*, *Tresdecem Sermones*, *Dieta Salutis*,[76] *Lauacrum Consciencie Virgill[i]* with the compundes of verbys doctrynall glosa monach[i] and wryttyn as 'pupill[i] repertorium q[ue] sic incipit "licet nonnulli",[77] and *stimulus amoris*.[78] To Thomas Stedeman and Margaret hys syster, equally to be devydyd betwene them, iijl xvs. To my syster my syde gowne, and to my brother Sir Thomas my best shorte gowne. To Thomas Braytofte my secunde shorte gowne. To John Sellie my cloke. To John Collyn my best hose. The resydue of all my goodes not bequethyd I do commyt to the distribucion of Sir John Cocke, parson off South Ormesby, whome I make myne executor to order and dispose for the helthe of my soule and all Christen soulys. Thes beyng wytnes; John Wodthorpe, John Colyn, with other.

> Proved before P at Lincoln, 20 April 1534.

---

[75] The Observant Fransiscans were an order particularly favoured by Henry VII. The newly established Newark house received £200 by his will in 1509. Henry's son, however, found the Observants staunch opponents of the royal supremacy, and he took strong action against them. Thomas Hayfield and Hugh Payn of the Newark Observants both fled after expressing their opposition, being apprehended in disguise at Cardiff while awaiting a ship to Brittany: C. Brown, *A History of Newark on Trent*, 3 vols. (Newark, 1904), I, 205–7; *L. & P. Henry VIII*, VIII, no. 939; G.R. Elton, *Policy and Police: the Enforcement of the Reformation in the Age of Thomas Cromwell* (Cambridge, 1972), 14.

[76] It has not been possible to identify all of these items. The following identifications are secure: Ludolphus of Saxony, *Vita Christi* (1474); St. Augustine, *Manuale de Aspiratione Animae ad Deum*; Michael of Hungary, *Sermones Tresdecem predicabiles per totum annum* (numerous editions before 1513); St. Bonaventura, *Dieta Salutis* (1497). Dates given are the earliest known editions, since the precise editions owned by Stapleforthe are unknown.

[77] '*The Bath of Virgil's Conscience*, with the compunds of verbs doctrinal glossed by a monk and wryttyn as the repertory of a pupil which begins thus "although some"'.

[78] St. Anselm, *Stimulus Amoris*.

178.   RICHARD CONY [OF SWINESHEAD]
       [LCC 1532–34, fo. 168]

26 March 1533. I, Richerde Cony of Swyneshed, of hole mynde and of good memory beyng, make my testament and laste will. Fyrste I bequethe my soule to God allmyghtty, to Our Lady and to all the saintes. My body to be buryed in the churcheyerde of Our Lady in Swyneshed. To the high altare there for tithys forgottyn viij*d*. To every altare in the sayd churche iiij*d*. To the churche warke ther iij*s* iiij*d*. I will that Robert my sun shall have aftyr my decesse the house lying in Draton and a acre of lande lying under it, be it more or lesse, and ij acre of arable lande lying in Draton felde, now beyng in the tenure of Richard Massyngberde, to hym and to hys heyres of hys body. And yff it happyn the sayd Robert to dye withowt heyres of hys body, then [remainder to] George Cony hys brother, to hym and to hys heyres of hys body. And yff it happyn the sayd George Cony to dy withowt heyres of hys body, then I will the sayd house with the acre of lande lying under it and the sayd ij acres of arable lande be solde be myn executors or ther executors, and the money theroff cumyng be devydyd to my yong chyldren, that is to say to Thomas Cony and Anthony Cony, or to any of them beyng alyve. To Robert my sun all my tollys of my occupacion within my shoppe and certen bordes in the garthe, excepte certen toyllys that I have gyffyn to my wyff, and one chyste beyng in hys chamber. To George my sun one house with the appurtenance lying under it, beyng and lying in Kyrton Ende nygh the stone bryg, to hym, to hys heyres and assygnes, [fo. 168v] and also I will that Robert Cony his brother shall gyff to the sayd George xx*s*. I will that Johanne my wyff have the house that I dwell in with the housys theruppon bulydyd with ther appurtenaunces duryng her lyff, to the kepyng up off my ij chyldren, and she to kepe it in laufull reparacion. And aftyr her decesse I will the sayd house with th'appurtenaunces be solde be my executors or theyr executor, and the money therof cumyng be devydyd betwene Thomas Cony and Anthony Cuny, or to them then beyng alyve. To Thomas my sun one cowe and xx*s*, and one chyste when he cumys to the age of xvj yeres. To Anthony my sun one cowe and xx*s*, and one chyste when he cumys to the age of xvj yeres. The resydue of all my goodes I gyff to Johanne my wyff whome I make my executrix. Also I will that Thomas Hawle shall be executor with her, gyffyng hym for hys labor vj*s* viij*d*. Wytnes herof Sir Thomas Garton, vicar, Simon Moyn, William Noppy and Edwarde Jugge.

       Proved at Donington, 28 May 1533, by the executors.

179.   WILLIAM COLLYN [OF ASGARBY]
       [LCC 1532–34, fo. 166v]

31 March 1533. I, William Collyn of Asgarby, hole in mynde and good of remembraunce, makes my testament and last will. Fyrste I bequeth my soule to allmyghtty God, to Our Lady St. Mary and to all the holy cumpeny of heven, and my body to be buryd in the churche of St. Andro of the sayd Asgarby. To the high altare ther for tithys forgottyn viij*d*. To Our Lady altare ther iiij*d*. To St. Margaret altare ther iiij*d*. To the reparacion off the bellys of the sayd churche iiij*d*. To the high altare of our mother churche of Lincoln iiij*d*. To the reparacions of our sayd mother churche of Lincoln iiij*d*. To the pore orphans of St. Catheryn's ij*d*. To every on of my godchyldren halff a stryke of barly. To the sayd churche off Asgarby one cowe

to kepe a continuall obbyt for my soule. To Robert Coollyn my sun ij bullokes, one cowe, iiij schepe, a acre of barly and a quarter of barly. To Jenet my doughtter one cowe, iiij schepe, a acre of barly and a quarter of barly. To Isabell my doughtter one cowe, iiij schepe, a acre of barly and a quarter of barly. To John Collyn, Henry Collyn and Alice my chyldren, to every one of them thre, a qwe calve, iiij schepe, a acre of barly and a quarter of barly. And yff it fortune at any tyme that allmyghtty God call any of my vj chyldren to hys mercy before that they cum to laufull age, that they that overlyffys shall have that distribute emong them. The resydue of my goodes not gyffyn nor bequethyd I bequeth it to Isabell my wyff whome I make the executrix. Also I make my brother John Collyn and Christofer Bente the supervisors. Thes beyng wytnes; Sir Charles Wellys, curate ther, William Garrotte, with other mo.

Proved before P at Heckington, 29 May 1533.

180.   THOMAS HAWE [VICAR OF GLENTHAM]
[D&C 1534–59, fos. 22v–24r]

31 March 1533. I, Sir Thomas Hawe, vicare of Glentham, beyng of hole mynde and good remembrance, loveyng be to allmyghtty God, makyth and ordenyth thys my laste will and testament. Firste I bequethe my soule to allmyghtty God, besechyng Our Blessyd Lady and all the holly cumpeny of heven to pray for me, and my body to be buryed where God pleasyth. I will my dettys be payd and restitucion be mayd for eny wronges by [fo. 23r] me done. I will my kynsman Roger Hawe have all my landes and tenementes, rentes, medoys, mores and pastures within the towne and feldes of Est Rasyn and Myddell Rasen with the appurtenances, to hym and to the heyres of hys body laufully begottyn for ever. And for lacke of suche issue to remayn to William Mounson and to hys heyres for ever, excepte that the same landys and tenementes and other the premisses shall be chargeyd, for the termes of twenty yeres nexte and immediatly foloyng aftyr my dethe, with the payment of ten shyllyng yerely for one obbyt in Myddyll Rasyn Tupholme, to be done yerely on Tenebre Weddynsday[79] for the soulys of the father and mother in forme foloyng: the vicare to have for messe and dirige sayng and also for fyndyng of wyne, brede and waxe, xijd. Also the vicare of Myddell Rasyn Drax if he do messe ther the day of the sayd obbyt, to have iiijd. To the bell ryngers for a peale iiijd. The resydue to be distrybute to the pore people most indigent in Myddyll Rasyn Tupholme and Est Rasyn aforesayd, by the discrecion of my executors. And in defaute of my sayd executors, to be distribute by the churche masters of the sayd towne yerely duryng the sayd yeres in forme above sayd. And also other ten shyllynges for an obbyt to be done at Glentham yerely the day of my dethe for the soulys of me, the sayd Sir Thomas, and all Crysten soulys in forme foloyng: the vicare to have for messe and dirige sayng, and also for fyndyng wyne, breade and wax, xijd. To the vicare of Norton, the parson of Caneby, the vicare of Normanby, the chauntry preste of the same, the chauntry preste of Glentham, the parson of Ownby, the vicare of Glentworthe, every one of them doyng messe at Glentham aforesayd the day of my obyt, iiijd. To the bell ryngers for a peale iiijd. And the resydue to be distrybute to the pore people of Glentham by the discrecion of myn executors, and for defaute

---

[79] Ash Wednesday.

of them, by the churche masters of the same towne. And also excepte a house off fyve shyllynges' rente, parcell of the premisses, that John Cobbyn shall have for terme of hys lyffe, and he to reparell the same in all maner of reparacions of hys owne propre costys and chargeys yerely. Also I will that Elizabeth Todkyll, my servaunt, shall have my farme callyd the [fo. 23v] Lounde, with all the landys, medoys and pasturys therto belongyng in Glentham aforesayd, whiche I have by lease of the deane and chapiture of Lincoln, duryng the yeres conteynyd in the same lease yf she kepe her unmaryed and lyve the same yeres [remainder to] the sayd Roger Hawe immediatly aftyr the dethe or maryage off the sayd Elizabeth, to hym and to hys heyres and assignes duryng the resydue of the yeres conteynyd in the same lease. I will that John Smithes shall have my farme callyd the Burnyd House with all the landes, medoys and pasturys therto belongyng in Glentham and Byshop Norton aforesayd, whiche I have by lease of the abbot and convent of Barlynges, for terme of hys lyff. And aftyr hys decesse to remayne to the sayd Roger Hawe, hys heyres and assignes duryng the yeres conteynyd in the same lease then not expyryd. To Our Lady warke at Lincoln ij*s*. To the high altare of Our Lady of Lincoln xx*d*. To the prior of the Blacke Frerys in Lincoln x*s*, a quarter wheate and a quarter malte. To every of the other thre orders of frerys a bushyll wheate and a bushyll malte. To the reparacions of Cadney churche, Glentworthe churche, Caneby churche and Myddyll Rasyn Tupholme churche, every of them, vj*s* viij*d*. To Glentham churche xiij*s* iiij*d* and a long ladder lying in the churche. To Norton churche iij*s* iiij*d*. To Est Rasyn churche xx*d*. To the mayntenaunce of Bysshope Brygges iij*l* vj*s* viij*d* to be at the order of myn executors. To the parson off West Rasyn my beste sylver spone. To Sir Thomas Foster, parsone of Normanby, my secunde sylver spone. To Elizabeth Todkyll ij kye, my beste matteres, a pare of lyn schetes, too pare of hardyn schetes, a pare of blankyttes, ij coverlyttes and ij pilloys. To Margaret Stevenson a cowe, a matteres, a pare of lyn schetes, a pare of hardyn schetes and ij coverlyttes. To Roger Hawe my corne growyng of my landes belongyng to the parsonage or otherwyse beyng in myne owne occupacion or tenure sowne or to be sowne for the nexte croppe aftyr my dethe. To my master John Mounson, esquyer, xx*l*, and to Master William Mounson hys sun other xx*l* to be takyn owt of my beste goodes. To Mrs. Elizabeth, wyff of the sayd William Mounson, my beste [fo. 24r] fether bedde with all that perteynyth therto, with my greate brasse potte and my greate panne. I will that a preste shall syng for me a hole yere in Glentham churche that will teche children, and he to have for hys stipende fyve poundes. The resydue of my goodes, I will that they be disposyd by the sayd John Mounson, William Mounson and Roger Hawe, whome I make myn executors of thys my present testament and laste will. I will that Robert Brokylby of Glentworthe shall be supervisor of thys my laste will, to se it performyd in forme abovesayd, and he to have for hys labor xx*s*. Thes beyng wyttenesses; Nicholes Downe of Glentham, William Twydale of the same, yoman, William Wright of the same, John Smythies off the same, husbandman, Sir John Neyler, Sir Thomas Browne, Sir Robert Tayllor, prystes, Alexander Tubbyng of the same and Gilbert Pattryke of Glentworth, with diverse others.

    Proved before Mr. George Henage, dean, and the chapter of the cathedral church of Lincoln, 7 January 1534/5, in the cathedral church. Adm. granted to William Mounson and Roger Hawe, executors, reserving power to grant to John Mounson when he comes.

181.   SIR JOHN WADE [OF RUCKLAND]
        [LCC 1532–34, fo. 151]

1 April 1533. I, John Wade, parson off Ruklande, seke of body, hole of remembraunce, makyth my testament. In primis I bequethe my soule to God allmyghtty,
to Our Lady St. Mary and to all the sayntes [fo. 151v] in heven, and my body to be
buryed in the chauncell off the paryshe churche of Ruklande. To the reparacions of
the churche before namyd xl*s*. To Our Lady warkes of Lincoln xij*d*. To St. Hugh
vj*d*. To the paryshe churche of Tetforthe xx*d*. To the churche of Burwell xij*d*. To the
churche of Farforthe xij*d*. To William Walgrave v yowes and v lammys, and to
Catheryne hys wyff a yowe and a lamme, and to every one of hys chylder a yowe
and a lamme. To John Wade a yowe and one lamme. To the churche off Gretham
xij*d*. To every one of my godchylder iiij*d*. To Walter Wade one stere and ij
weders. To Richerd Wryght ij weders. To William Wade one yowe and a lamme.
To Isabell Wade a wedder. To Jenet Lamme a matterys, ij pare of schettes, a
coverlyd, a cowe, x wedders, a brasse pot and a kettyll. To Sir William Wade a
ambre, my best gowne, a tepet, a bonet, a horsse and vj wedders. To William Burrell
iiij oxen, iiij mares, ij wanys, a plugh and all that belonges unto hit and all my
houshold stuff, and x yowes and x lammys and xx^ty wedders. I bequeth for iij
trentallys xxx*s*. I make William Burrell and Walter Wade myne executors, that they
dispose the resydue of all my goodes, my dettes payd and my wyl fulfyllyd, as they
thynke moste necessary for the helthe of my soule, my frendes' soulys and all the
soulys that be in purgatory. Thes wytnesses; Sir John Snarry, vicare of Burwell,
John Johnson and Edwarde Melton.
        Proved before P at Louth, 5 May 1533. Adm. granted to William Burwell an
        executor, Walter Wade renouncing.

182.   HENRY WESTE [OF GREAT COATES]
        [LCC 1532–34, fo. 156]

1 April 1533. I, Henry Weste, laborer of Gret Cotes, makyth my last will and
testament. Fyrst I bequethe my soule to God allmyghtty, to Our Lady St. Mary and
to all the saintes in heven, and my body to be buryed in the churcheyerde of St.
Nicholes of Gret Cotes. To the altare for tithys and offerynges negligent forgottyn
and done a yowe and a lamme. To Alan my sun an ox with thys condicion, that he
shall go pilgrimage for me till good Kyng Henry of Wynsore.[80] To Isabell my
doughtter a yowe. To John Weste a lamme. To Our Lady [fo. 156v] warke of
Lincoln ij*d*. To the forsayd Alan my plough and wane with all suche thynges as ther
is belongyng to husbandry. The resydue of my goodes not bequethyd I gyff them till
Helene my wyff, whome I make my sole executrix that she may dispose them in
suche good dedes as it may be pleasure to allmyghtty God and helthe of my soule.

---

[80] King Henry VI had become popularly reputed a saint since his second and final deposition by
Edward IV in 1471. Wholly unofficial, the cult never received papal approval, but was one of the
fastest growing foci for devotion in the later fifteenth and early sixteenth centuries. The early Tudor
monarchs, basing their claim to the throne through Henry VI's line, did not discourage the cult until
the general suppression of saint's shrines and gilds under Henry VIII and Edward VI. The
pilgrimage centre at Henry's tomb at Windsor was particularly successful in the fifty years of its
existence, basing its popularity on its reputation for miraculous healing. Chertsey Abbey was
another well attended healing shrine associated with Henry VI: Duffy, *Stripping of the Altars*, 195.

Thes wytnes; Mr. John Barnston, Peter Button, Sir Robert Cokhyde, with other mo.

Proved before P at Grimsby, 13 May 1533.

183.   ROBERT GREG [OF ROWSTON]
       [LCC 1532–34, fo. 143]

2 April 1533. I, Robert Greg of Rowston in the countie of Lincoln, dredyng the perell of dethe, make my testament. Fyrste I betake my soule to allmyghtty God, Our Lady St. Mary and to all the blessyd cumpeny in heven. My body to be buryed in the kyrkyerd of St. Clement off Rowston aforesayd. To the reparacions of the kyrke of Rouston a quarter wheate. I bequethe vj*s* viij*d* to fynde a light afore the ymage of Our Lady of the holy bred altare. To the high altare ij*s*. To the iij housys of frerys that I am broder,[81] to every house a stryke barly. To Elizabethe, my syster doughtter and my servant, ij kye, one callyd Moderlyke and anoder in the handes of Richerde Hellerton, and iiij*s* for the hyre of the cowe or ellys the sayd Richerde to have [fo. 143v] the cowe and to gyff to the sayd Eliazabethe xv*s*. To the sayd Elizabethe ij sterys oderwyse callyd ij yong bullokes, the one red and the oder brendyd. To Richerde Hall my servant a qwye that I bought of Hellerton. To Robert Morwyk, my broder-in-lawe, a bay fylly, half a quarter barly and my violet cote. To William Hadesworthe a browne cowe, half a quarter barly, ij strykes malte and a russyt jakket. To my broder William ij yong bullokes, half a quarter barly and a russyt cote. To John my servant a blak qwye. To Dygby Kyrke xij*d*. To Kyrkby Kyrke xij*d*. I will have halffe a trentall sayd in the kyrke of Rowston for my soule, my fader soule, my moder soule, and for all Crysten soulys. To my wyff the copy of my house aftyr my decesse. Also I make to be my executors Michel Beche of Rouston, William Greg of the same, my broder, and Johanne my wyff, and I gyff to Michel Beche for hys labor ij*s* iiij*d*, and also to William my broder for hys labor iiij*s*. The resydue of all my goodes not bequethyd, the tithes and all the dettes payd, I gyff to Johanne my wyff. Wytnes of the same; Godfrey Huddelstone of Rouston, Robert Byrt of the same, John Dause of the same, Robert Morwyk of the same, with diverse mo. Datum ut supra.

Proved before P at Navenby, 17 May 1533.

184.   NICHOLAS GRAY [OF BOSTON]
       [LCC 1532–34, fo. 181v]

3 April 1533. I, Nicholes Gray of Boston, myghtty of mynde, hole of wytte and understandyng, makes my testament. Fyrste I bequethe my soule to allmyghtty God and to Our Blessyd Lady and to all the saintes in heven, and my body to be buryed in the churche of St. Botulphe in Boston, and that to be my mortuary that the law will. To the high altare of St. Botulphe in Boston xij*d*. To Our Lady of Lincoln xij*d*. To her warkes iiij*d*, and to the orphans of St. Catheryn's viij*d*. To Agnes my wyff xxiij*l* vj*s* viij*d* and iij partes of my housholde stuff. To Sir Richerde Goodale my best gowne and a pare of hose clothe of Lichefelde carsay and lynyng to them. I will that

---

[81] Lay brotherhood of friaries was widespread among those who could afford it. Its purpose was primarily to secure post-mortem intercession on behalf of the dead.

Agnes my wyff [and] Steven Capper sell my keele for cvjs viijd, of the money that is taken for her to be delyveryd to Sir Richerd Goodale towarde the fyndyng off William Kytchyn, the sonne of Robert Kichyn. Yff the sayd William decesse before the money be spente, I will the reste be disposyd for the helthe of hys soule, my soule and my benefactors. The rest of the money taken for the kele I will it be devydyd equally betwyxte Emote and Isabell my doughters, yff they thryve and do well. I will that Agnes my wyff cause iiij trentallys to be done for the helthe of my soule, my father soule, my mother soule and all Christen soulys. To the churche warkes of Bollynbroke iijs iiijd. To Father Sampe xxs and my russyt gowne. I will that Agnes my wyff dispose in highwayes mendyng iijl, and ware it where she thynkes moste nede and necessary, if it may be sparyd my dettes payd and legacy afore rehersyd fulfyllyd. The resydue of my goodes not gyffyn nor bequethyd I put them to the disposicion of Agnes my wyff, whome I make my executrice of thys my last will. Yff Steven Capper will be good unto her and take payn for her, I will she gyff hym for hys labor xiijs iiijd. Wytnesses; William Annable, William Bollys, Peter Scotte, with other mo.

Proved at Boston, 5 August 1533.

185.   WILLIAM STYKNEY [OF FRAMPTON]
       [LCC 1532–34, fos. 163v–164r]

3 April 1533. I, William Stykney off Frampton, of hole mynde and good remembraunce, makyth my testament with my last will. Fyrst I bequeth my soule to God, Our Lady St. Mary, and to all the cumpeny of heven, and my body to be buryede in the churchyerde off Owr Lady of Frampton in Holland. To the high altare off Frampton for tithys forgottyn iiijd. To the gylde of Our Lady of Frampton one yowe. To the churche warke iiijd. To every altare in the sayd churche ijd. To the bellys iiijd. To Our Lady of Lincoln box viijd. To the orphans of St. Catheryn's withowt the wallys of the citie of Lincoln [fo. 164r] ijd. To Elizabeth my wyff my mansion that I wonne in with the purtenances beyng one acre and a half for the terme of her lyff, kepyng it in reparacion. And aftyr her decesse it to remayn to Thomas Styknay my sun, to hym, hys heyres and hys assygnes. To Thomas my sun one acre and a half of lande lying at the wyndemylne, to hym, hys heyres and hys assygnes. I will that Elizabeth my wyff, Thomas Stykney my sun and William Grafte the yonger have all my awn housholde stuff equally devydyd betwyxt them, excepte that I will my wyff have all my lardyr, my yarne, my grane that is in the house, ij kye, one burnyng, one meyr, j stag, x of my best schepe, iij stong of beyr and wheate, half one acre benes, all my pullan and all my swyne, excepte that I will that Thomas my sun have the best hog. Also I will that Isabell Romforthe my wyff doughter have one calve. To Robert Stykney one calve. To William Grafte my plough, my carte with the geres pertenyng therto, with iij mares, that is to say olde Darlyng, one gray balde mare and littyll Pryn, one cowe and one qwye. The resydue of all my goodes not bequethyd I put to the disposicion off Thomas Stykney my sun, whome I make my faythfull executor to pay my dettes and dispose for my soule as he thynkes best to please God, and most helthe to my soule. Thes beyng wytnes; Sir John Lee, paryshe preste, William Johnnyson, William Curtes, Robert Brygges, Thomas Rawlet and many mo.

Proved before P at Donington, 28 May 1533.

186.   THOMAS PHILIPSON [OF TETFORD]
[LCC 1532–34, fos. 100v–101r]

4 April 1533. I, Thomas Philipson of the paryshe of Tetforthe, beyng of an hole mynde and perfecte remembraunce, makyth my testament and last mynde. Fyrst I bequethe my soule to God allmyghtty, to Our Lady St. Mary and to all the holy cumpeny of heven, and my body to be buryed in the churcheyerde of Our blessyd Lady of Tetforthe. To Our Lady's warke of Lincoln viij*d*. To the high altare of Tetforthe for tithys forgottyn viij*d*. To the bellys of Tetforthe xij*d*. To the churches of Salmonby, Summersby, Oxham, Belcheforthe and Rukland, iiij*d* [each]. To William my sun one acre of rye, one acre of barly, threscore schepe, xx^ty lammys, ij steres, one calve, one quarter of malte and ij weders. To George my sun ten schepe, one acre of barly and one qwye. To Thomas my sun ten schepe and one sheder calve. To Robert my sun ten schepe. To Margaret my doughter ten schepe and one brasse pot. To Mawde my doughter ten schepe. To Alice my doughter iiij*l* [fo. 101r] and one schepe, and the sayd William my sun to pay the sayd iiij*l* to the sayd Alice at the xviij^th yere of her age, provydyd yff she dye before the sayd age off xviij yeres, then I wil the sayd foure poundes to be devydyd evenly emong my sayd fyve chyldren George, Thomas, Robert, Margaret and Mawde. To John my sun iiij schepe. To Robert Phylipson my brother ij schepe. To Helene my syster one schepe. To Agnes my syster one schepe. To Johanne my wyff, whome I make my hole executrix, all my hole goodes for to fynde John my sun unto that tyme he be xxiiij^ty yeres of age, and to fynde and bryng up my sayd vj chyldren unto suche tyme they shall be of sufficient age. Also I will that aftyr the decesse of the sayd Johanne my wyff, the hustylment^82 of my house be equally shyftyd and devydyd emonges my sayd sex chyldren, provisyd yff the sayd Johanne my wyff departe owt of thys worlde afore the sayd John my sun accomplyshe hys sayd age of xxiiij^ty yeres, then I will the sayd William my sun fynde the sayd John in all thynges to he be full the sayd age of xxiiij^ty. To All Halloys gylde of Tetforthe one weder. To Sir Robert Bradforthe one schepe. Thes to wytnes; Sir Robert Bradforthe, paryshe preste to Tetforthe aforesayd, Christofer Tayllor of the same and John Phylipson of the same, with other.

Proved before P at Horncastle, 28 April 1533.

187.   GILES SMYRTHWITH [OF EDLINGTON]
[LCC 1532–34, fos. 99r–100r]

4 April 1533. I, Gylys Smyrthwyth of Edlyngton, hole of mynde and goode remembraunce, makes my testament. Fyrst I bequethe my soule to God omnipotent, to Our Lady St. Mary and to all the holy cumpeny of heven, my body to be buryed in the churcheyerde of Edlyngton. To Our Lady's warke of Lincoln xij*d*. To the high altare of Edlyngton aforesayd viij*d*. To the buyldyng of the steple in Edlyngton iiij*l*, and my executors to make up the fourte pounde yff they may. To the churches of Bamburgh, Wyspyngton and Horsyngton xij*d* [each]. To Margery Smyrthwyth my doughter xx^ty yowe schepe and xx^ty lammys. I bequethe, and by thys my last will or testament to the foresayd Margery my doughter and to here heyres for ever, one mesuage set lying and beyng in the towne and feldes of

---

^82 Household goods, principally articles of furniture and moveable goods.

Edlyngton wyth all landes arable, medoys, pasturys, fedyng places and th'appurtenances therto belongyng (excepte fowre landys [fo. 99v] arable, as hereafter dothe foloy). To Grace Smyrthwyth one qwye, ij yowe shepe, ij lammys, one potte, one panne and one bed with all thinges necessary therto belongyng. To Robert Whytehode one yowe and one lamme. To Thomas Whytehode one yowe and one lamme. To Richerde Sele ij yowes, ij lammys and one blak fole. To John Elwyn iij yowes and iij lammys. To Sir William Smyrthwyth one bay fole. To Robert Margeson one ij yere olde fole. To Jenet Connam one yow lamme. To Margaret Kytson one yowe lamme. To the forsayd churche of Edlyngton ij*l* for to by too candylstykes. To Agnes my wyff all the reste of my goodes and ij landes arable for ever of the northe syde of the towne, lying of the hether syde of Kyrke lande, and other ij landes of the south syde agenst the clay pyttes. I will that Watkyn Amore and my doughter Margery, hys wyff, shall not cum to the foresayd mesuage or May Day cum twelvemonyth, and then they to have the croppe sawne of the grounde withowt costes or chargeys. And yff it happen that the sayd Watkyn and Margery not to come that yere, I will that my wyff have the house with all landes arable, medoys, pasturys, fedyng places and th'appurtenances therto belongyng, payng the rent yerely to Watkyn Amore and Margery hys wyff, and they to let the sayd mesuage with all thynges therto belongyng to no other. And the croppe this yere to be solde, my wyff to have one parte, Watkyn Amore and hys wyff another parte, the thurde parte to be solde and delte for my soule, father and mother soulys, and all Crysten soulys. Also I will that the sayd Watkyn Amore, hys wyff, or the heyres of her body shall cause one annuall obbyt for ever to be done at St. Ursula Day,[83] and the vicare for tyme beyng to have for beyd rolle for my father and me viij*d*, for ij dirigys [fo. 100r] viij*d*, and ij messe pennys to be offeryd by one off the foresayd, a bushyll of wheate to be takyn and a bushyll of malte to be bruyd and dolte the same day. I will that Agnes my wyff and Watkyn Amore, whome I make my executors, cause a trentall to be sayd for the helthe of my soule, father and mother soulys and all Crysten soulys. Wytnes heroff; Sir Leonerde Norsse, vicar, Sir Richerde Barker, William Dycson, with other.

Proved before P at Horncastle, 28 April 1533.

188.   THOMAS SWYNE [OF TATTERSHALL]
       [LCC 1532–34, fo. 100]

5 April 1533. I, Thomas Swyne of the paryshe of Tateshale, off good memory and hole mynde, makyth my last will and testament. Fyrst I bequethe my soule unto God allmyghtty, Our Lady St. Mary and to all the holy cumpeny of heven, and my body to be buryd within the holy churcheyerde of Tateshale paryshe. To the high altare of Tateshale for forgottyn tithys xij*d*. To the paryshe altare viij*d*. To the bellys xij*d*. To Our Lady of Lincoln iiij*d*. To the gylde of the gloriose Trinite viij*d*. To the gylde of St. Anne viij*d*. To Isabell my doughter a matteres bed and all thynges perteyning therto, too brasse pottes, one of the grettest sworte and another of the lesse, a gret panne and ij lattyn basyns. To Agnes my wyff one house in Tateshale Thorpe with one garthe belongyng therto duryng the terme of her lyff. And aftyr her decesse I gyff it unto Isabell my doughter and her issue. And yff she have none issue, I will it shall be gyffyn unto the reparacion of highways belongyng unto

---

[83] 21 October.

Tateshale paryshe. To Agnes my wyff one dale lying in Tymberland paryshe duryng the terme of her lyff. And aftyr her decesse I gyff it unto [100v] Isabell my doughter and her issue, and yff she have none issue I gyff it unto Thomas Swyne, sun to Henry Swyne. The resydue of my goodes I gyff unto Agnes my wyff, whome I orden my executrix to dispose the sayd resydue of my goodes for the helthe of my soule and all Crysten soulys. Thes wytnesses of the premisses; Syr Edward Flynt, Johanna Wylcokes, Margaret Wynter and Margaret Shawe, cum multis aliis.

Proved before P at Horncastle, 28 April 1533.

189.   ROBERT FELYNGHAM [OF BOSTON]
        [LCC 1532–34, fo. 87v]

6 April 1533. I, Robert Felyngham of Boston, hole of mynde and seke of body, make my wyll and last testament. Fyrst I bequethe my soule to God allmyghtty, to Our Lady St. Mary and to all the holly cumpeny of heven, and my body to be buryd in the churcheyerde of St. Botulphe of Boston. To my mortuary as the lawe will require. To the high altare of St. Botulphe of Boston xij*d*. To Our Lady of Lincoln iiij*d*. The resydue of all my goodes, fyrste my dettes payd and my will fulfyllyd, I gyff them unto Alice my wyff, whome I make my executrix, she to pay my dettes and fulfyll my will as my trust is in her, by the oversyght off Sir Thomas Cersy, whome I make supervisor. Thes beryng wytnes; Sir Thomas Cersy, Richerd Kitchyn, Robert Carnaby and William Knyght, with other mo.

Proved before P at Lincoln, 1 May 1533.

190.   CECILY BOUSTERDE [OF FISHTOFT]
        [LCC 1532–34, fo. 173]

7 April 1533. I, Cecily Bousterde of the paryshe of Tofte, beyng of hole mynde and good remembraunce, makes my last will and testament. Fyrst I bequethe my soule to allmyghtty God, to Our Lady St. Mary, and to all the cumpeny of heven. My body to be buryd in the churcheyerde of St. Guthlak of Tofte, with my best good to be my mortuary as the lawe of the cuntry requyrys. To the high altare in Tofte churche vj*d*. To Our Lady chapell in Tofte ij*d*. To the Trinite altare ij*d*. To St. George altare ij*d*. To Our Lady's warke of Lincoln vj*d*. To the fatherlesse chyldren at St. Catheryn's iiij*d*. To Agnes my doughter a house with one acre of lande under it, be it more or lesse. To the sayd Agnes ij acre lande, one of them arable and the other pastur grounde. Also ij kye, iiij marys, my plough with all the gerys belongyng therto, my best gowne, my best kyrtyll, my best beades, bothe my cappys, my best kyrchyff, iij brasse pottes, one gret panne, ij calves, one fether bed with the bolster, vij lynnyn schetes, vij hardyn schetes, ij towellys, my best table clothe, my best matteres, my best coverlyt, one chaffyng dyshe, one candylstyk, iij dyshys, iij platters, iiij pylloys with hyllynges and fyllynges, a hangyng of a bed and iij chystes. I will that Laurence Tayllor have the custody and gydyng of all the sayd landes and goodes bequethyd to Agnes my doughter, to she comme to the age of xviij yeres. And then I will the sayd Laurence delyver to my sayd doughter Agnes the sayd lande and goodes with all the issuys and proffyttes that shall comme of the sayd landes the meyn tyme (chargeys off reparacions and other necessarys laufully deductyd). And yff it fortune my sayd doughter Agnes to decesse or she comme to

the age of xviij yeres, then I will that Lawrence Tayllor, Phylip Scherpe and John Scherpe have the sayd goodes evenly devydyd emonges them. And yff it fortune the sayd Agnes to dy withowt heyres of her body laufully begottyn, I will that all the landes and tenementes to her bequethyd remayn to Laurence Tayllor, Phylip Scherpe and John Scherpe, evenly to be devydyd emonges them. [fo. 173v] To John my sun ij burlynges, ij schepe and a pare of sherys of the best, one gyrdyll, a pare of beades, one matteres, one coverlyd, ij pilloys with hyllynges and fyllynges, ij lynyn schetes, ij hardyn schetes, one brasse potte, one panne, one cote of violet, one puter dyshe, ij puter platters and one candylstyk. To Alice Robynson a pare off schetes and my best brasse potte. To Cecily Tayllor one puter platter and a blake yowe lamme. The resydue of my goodes not gyffyn nor bequethyd I gyff and bequethe to Agnes Westmellys my doughter, whome I ordain and make my true and lawfull executrix, to dispose for the helthe of my soule aftyr her discrecion. I will xs be gyffyn for a trentall, yff it may be borne. Thes beyng wytnesse; Richerd Romforthe, Phylip Scherpe, Thomas Rabdyn, with diverse other.

Proved before P at Lincoln, 19 July 1533. Adm. granted to the executrix.

191.   ISABEL ALYN [OF LONG BENNINGTON]
         [LCC 1532–34, fos. 145v–146v]

8 April 1533. I, Isabell Alyn, wydow, of Long Bennygton, makes my will and testament. In primis I bequeth my soule to God almyghtye and Our Lady St. Mary and to all the saintes in heven, and my body to be buried in the churchyerde of St. Swithyne of Long Benyngton. To Mr. Deane a cowe and a calf to the high awter. To Our Ladie's awter iiijd. To St. Thomas awter iiijd. To the reparacions of the churche of Benyngton a cow and calf. To the cawsey of Benyngton iijs iiijd. To Fen Brig vjd. [fo. 146r] To the reparacion of the chapell of Our Lady in Benyngton iijs iiijd and a lynyn shete. To every gild within the towne ijd. To Our Ladie's werke of Lincoln xijd. To the iiij ordres of freres in Lincoln and one at Grantham, every one of theym, a stryke barly at yere tyme. I will that a trentall be done at freres of Newerk for my husband and for me. To Richard Alyn my son xl schepe, som wethers and som ewes and lambes, at the delyveraunce of Thomas Robert the yonger and Richard Alynson the elder, and of my brother Robert. To Richard my son a wayne and my ij best oxen, ij kye and qwye, iij silver spones of the best, a webbe of cursey and a webbe of lynyn clothe and the best pan, iij brasse pottes, half a dosen peauter vessell, iij candilstikes, ij potyngers and a shaffer, the best basyn, ij materesses, ij payre of shetes, a coverlyt, a bolster. To Jenet my doughter xl shepe, a cowe and a calf, a qwye, a feder bed with the bolster, a coverlite, a payre of shetes, one heden and lynyn and all my yerne of this yere, the best brasse pot with another pote, a dowbler and ij dishes, ij potyngers, ij candilstikes, my best beades and all that is at theym, my best gowne, a basyn, a laver, a curtell, a towall, a qwyshyn, an arke, ij bakon flekes,[84] a swyne in the yerde, iij silver spones, a bee hyve. To Thomas Est my son iiij quarters of barlye. To Margare my doughter xl shep, a cow and ij sterys, a materesse, ij shetes, one lynyn and one herden, ij brasse pottes, the secund panne, a basyn, a laver, a shawfer, a charger, ij dishes, ij potyngers, iij sylver spones, my ambre beades, my violet gowne, iij yerdes of rousset, a chiste, a qwyshyn, ij

---

[84] Sides of bacon.

bacon flikes, a swyne in the yerde, a towell and a bee hyve. To my iij maydens, every one of theym, a coverlit and a payre of shetes, one harden, the other thre of hempe. To William Colson a bochell of whete. To Rauf Crawchey a bochell of whete. To Margaret Morley a bochell and a roset kyrtil. To George Margetson a bochell whete. To John Knyght a stryke whete. To every godchilde a ewe and a lambe. To eyther of Richard Alyn sonnes a ewe and a lambe, and a strike of whete. To Jenet his doughter a strike whete and my best hate. To Agnes a strike whete and my best cappe. To John Morley half a quarter malte. To my sheperd ij ewes and ij lambes. To John Bocher a ewe and a lambe. To John Cooke a ewe and a lambe. To Sybell Nyde a white cotte and rouset kyrtill. [fo. 146v] To John Kychyn a fylie. To Richard Kychyn a colte. To Agnes Kychyn and Jenet, either of theym, a lynyn shete, or elles as moche cloth to make theym. To Richard Alyn the elder a qwye. I will that half of my croppe in the grond be parted among my iij children and the other half to be done for my husband and for me. To Christofer Est a coultre and a share with all other yerne thynges that wil serve for iiij horses. To Agnes, Robert and Jenet, eyther of theym, a pewder dishe. To Alice and Margaret, either if theym, a new pewder sawcer. To Richard Faderys a fylie. For amendyng of the lane from the cawsey to the chapell ward iiij*s*. To Jenet Morley a shete or a shete cloth. To Thomas Stevenson son that is with me, a ewe and a lambe, and a brasse potte. The residue of all my goodes not bequethed I will that it be keped in handes of Richard Alyn my sonne, for to be done yerly somdelle[85] for my husband and for me as it will endure for evermore and as thies men thynk that may be don of the goodes that he shall have to do withall. I make Richard Alyn my son, Thomas Robert the yonger, Richard Alyn th'elder dowers for me, to se that my will be fullfilled, and the forsaid Richard Alyn the elder and Thomas Robert the yonger, either of theym, to have for ther labours vj*s* viij*d*. Robert Kychyn my broder to be oversyer, haveng for his labour vj*s* viij*d*. Witnes this; Sir John Atkynson, Richard Alyn th'elder, Thomas Robert, John Morley, John Gammull, with other mo.

Proved before P at Lincoln, 26 May 1533. Adm. granted to the executors.

192.   ELIZABETH CLERKE [OF KINGERBY]
       [LCC 1532–34, fo. 157r]

8 April 1533. I, Elizabethe Clerke of Kynynerby, beyng hole of mynde, makes my testament conteynyng my last will. Fyrst I wyt my soule to God allmyghtty and to Our Lady St. Mary, and to all the blessyd cumpeny of heven. My body to be buryed in the churcheyerde of St. Peter of Kynyerby and that the lawe will in the name of my mortuary. To Our Lady warke of Lincoln iiij*d*. To Our Lady Frerys of the same city of Lincoln iiij*d*. To the churche warke of West Rasyn viij*d*. To the churche warke of Kynyerby viij*d*. To the buyldyng of the churche porche in Tevelby xij*d*. To Robert Osnay vj*s* viij*d*. To every one of my doughtters' chyldren viij*d*. To Alice Tyler a yowe lamme. To Robert Coke one lamme. To Alice Clerke my doughtter a panne. To Margaret Clerke a brasse potte. To Isabell Clerk a cowe and iij yowes and iij lammys. To Thomas Clerke my sun for hys chylde parte iij*l*. To the sayd Thomas vj*s* viij*d*. The resydue of my goodes here not wyt, I gyff to John Osnay of Kynyerby whome I make my executor, he to dispose it for the welthe of my soule. I

---

[85] Probably 'some dole [of alms]'.

make Robert Barde off Tevelby the supervisor. Thes wytnes; Sir William Doughtty, vicar, Thomas Barde, Robert Cowper, with other mo.

Proved before P at Market Rasen, 14 May 1533.

193.   STEPHEN LORDO [OF WHITTON]
        [Stow 1530–52, fos. 14r–15v]

10 April 1533. I, Stevyne Lordo of Whittyn, tanner, hole of mynde and in gud memorie beyng, thankes be unto allmyghtie God, consyderyng and knowynge the mutabilite and unstabilnes of this transitory worlde, and that after manny's fraylnes of condicions deth to every creture ys certayne and the howre thereof most uncertayne, not willyng to die intestate, therefore in the helthe of my soule I provyde and ordayne thys my present testamente [fo. 14v] contaynyng my last will. First and principallye, above all thynges, I gyfe and recommende my soule unto almyghtye God my maker, savyour and redemer of all the worlde, to Owre Blissid Lady Sant Mari and to all the companye of heven. My body to be buryed in the churche of Sant John Baptyst of Whittyn. To the hygh alter of the same churche for my tithes and oblacions by me necligentli forgotyn and withholdyn, in the dyscharge of my soule, iijs iiijd. To reparacions of the same churche xxs. To the churche warkes of Lincoln iijs iiijd. I wil that all my goodes be devydid in thre partes, and Margaret my wiffe to have the thurde parte therof, and myne executor to have the othere tow partes to the behufe of my childer. I bequeth on of my best kye to be solde to fynde a perpetuall light afore Oure Lady of the porche, a ponde of wax yerelye in the light and every Gud Frydaye to gyffe ijd to tow powre folkes and jd to be offerde in the same churche to the high alter. I bequethe a redde foole to the commonus for a staland.[86] Also I will that the sayde commynaltey schall have halfe a quarter of malte to occupye and fynde the sayde folle withall, and yff the sayde foole dye, the sayde halfe quarter to bye another. I bequethe ijs to be gyfuyn to the poore folkes in the same towne. To Jenet Moote a yowe and to hir sone a lamme. To Jenet Barnarde a yowe and a lamme. To Thomas Hudsone a yowe and to Thomas his sone a lame. To vij poore folkes within the sayde towne vij yowe hogges. To Agnes Elsame a cowe of hir fyrste calfe at the will of myne executor. To Christofor Jenkynsone halfe a quarter of barle. To William Harsey halfe a quarter of barle. To Thomas Dynsdale a yowe and a lame. To the covent of Newsome a quarter of malte. To Christofer my sone my beste swerde, best bokeler, a salet and a bylle [fo. 15r] To Wylliam my sone a swerde and a bokeler. To Richarde Stevenson a toftested onely holdyne of the abbot and covent of Thorneton by copye for the space of vj yerrys, yeldyng and payynge to my executor xxd, and he to uppeholde sufficient-ley the sayde house with thake and walle.[87] And yff he wil not make reparacions, then myne executur to reonter, and hym to discharge. To tow woman servantes tow yowys and tow lamys. To every on of my menservantes xijd. I will that myne executor shall selle my house that I dwell in cauled Rayne's Thyng with a barkehouse byldid on the same, and all the implementes apon the same grounde to the sayde barkehouse belongyng, to the profete of my childer. To Margaret my wyfe all my fre landes and copyes that I have in the same towne and fyldes,

---

[86] A stallion for the use of the parish community.
[87] 'Thatch and walling'.

Reynes Thyng onlye excepte, as long as she doth not mary, to kyppe my childer withall. Ande yf the sayde Margaret my wyfe do marye, then yt shall be lefull for myne executure to enter and occupie all suche fre landes and copys as I have at this day within the sayde towne and fyldes, and the sayde Margaret to kyppe thaym with all reparacions sufficiently as yt shall be thoght by myne executur. To Richarde my eldest sone all my fre landes and copis within towne and fyldes aforesayde, and yff yt shall fortune the sayde Richard to be prest or to dye, than Christofor my sone to have all my fre landes and copis. And yff the sayde Christofer dye afore xxj yere, then the eldyst of my men childer beyng xxj yere olde to have tham. And yff all my male childer do dye afore these yeres (there mother maryd), then I will all the fre landes and copis to my doghters and the eyrys of thare bodes [remainder to] Nicholas my brother and to his childer of his body. To Sir William and Nicholas my bretherne the take and premisse that I have in the forte parte off the fyfthe [fo. 15v] garth of Wynterynggame and all that therto belonges of my parte to thare use and profette, whome I ordeyne myne executures. These wittnes; Sir Richard Maude, vicar of Whittyn, William Wilkynsone, Christofer Dynsdale, William Harsley and monye mo.

Proved before L in the cathedral church of Lincoln, 16 April 1533. Adm. granted to the executors.

194.   SIR STEPHIN CHAMBERLYNG [OF ASLACKBY]
       [LCC 1532–34, fo. 143r]

12 April 1533. I, Sir Stephyn Chamberlyng, hole of mynde and of good remembraunce, make thys my last will and testament. Fyrste I bequethe my soule to allmyghtty God and to Our Lady St. Mary, and to all the holy cumpeny of heven, and my body to be buryed in the churcheyerde off Aslakbe. I will at my buryng to be disposyd for the helthe of my soule vs. I will at my xxx^{ty} day vs. I will that a preste syng for my soule in the churche of Aslakby with the licence of Mr. Vicare, and he to have iiij$l$ xiij$s$ iiij$d$. I will that my mother have my best gowne and my syster Jenet my secunde gowne. I will that my mother have a pyllo and my syster Jenet another, and my brother John wyff, the elder, a pyllo, and John wyff the yonger, another. To Henry my brother a flok bed, a matteres, a bolster, a pare of schetes and a coveryng of red. To elder John my brother a fether bed, a bolster, a blankyt, and I will to yonger John a folden table and a coveryng of a bedde and a pillo. I will that John Chamberlyng the elder and John the yonger be my executors to fulfyll the thynges afore namyd. And all other thynges not gyffyn nor bequethyd I put unto theyr discrecions for to dispose for the helthe of my soule that way that they thynke be best, and as I shall speke of unto them, and they to have for ther labors, the elder John my best jaket and the yonger John xs. Thes wytnes; Sir Thomas Harmeston, John Porter, with many mo.

Proved before P at Lincoln, 2 May 1533, by the executors.

195.   JOHN BEFORTHE [OF GOXHILL]
       [LCC 1532–34, fo. 155]

15 April 1533. I, John Beforth, of hole mynde and memory, make my last will and testament. Fyrst I bequethe my soule to God, to Our Lady, and to all the cumpeny

in heven. My body to be buryed in the churcheyerde off Gouxill. To the high altare xij*d*. To the churche of Gouxill halffe an acre of every grayn, that is wheate, beanys and barly. To Our Lady of Lincoln iiij*d*. For my oblacion and iiij*d* to the reparacion of the churche of Lincoln. To William Beforthe my sun viij*s*, to by hym a wayn wyth when he begynnyth husbandry for hymselff, and a cople of stottes of ij yeres olde. And yff the lesser stotte will not matche the other, then I will my wyff take hym and by hym that will matche hym. Also a dunyd stag of iij yeres olde and the amblyng meyr I use to ryde of, [fo. 155v] a plowe and all thynges that belongyth to a plowe, halffe a skore of schepe, the one halff yowes, the other hogges such as my wyff hys mother will delyver to hym and a quarter of malte. To Henry my sun a cople of yeryng stottes, a blak fylly fole and red qwye of ij yeres olde. And when he cumys to xxij yeres I will my wyff gyff hym a wayn, a plowe and all thynges that longyth to a plowe, and halffe a skore of schepe as hys brother William hayth. I bequethe all the peasse lande and barly lande that I hyeryd of Christofer Cokke and ij acres and a half off Bryme Hill, the croppe to William and Henry my sunnys equaly to be devydyd betwyx them. To Mawde my doughter a qwye of ij yeres olde and a yeryng qwye, halffe a skore a schepe after the same maner that her brethern hathe, and a red chyste. To Johanne my doughtter and to Alice my doughter, to iche of them a qwye, and when they cum to mariage then I will myn executors make them as good as ther syster Mawde. To my curate Mr. John Paradise a yowe, and to my shepperde a yowe lamme, and to Helene my servant a yowe lamme. To Thomas my brother my russyt cote and pare of blak hose and my botes, provydyd that yff any off my chyldren do dye afore ther goodes ought to be delyveryd unto them, then I will that ther porcions remayn to my executors be equall divicion. I will have a trentall sung or sayd at St. Jamys altare for my father William Beforthe, Mawde my mother, and for myselffe. The resydue of my goodes I gyff to Agnes my wyff and to John my sun, whome I make my executors to fulfyll my will, pay my dettes, and to bryng me to the yerthe (whiche done) I will the resydue be equally devydyd betwyxte them, provydyd that suche utensyles or implementes of house as I fonde do remayn to John Beforth my sun yff they do last and endeuer, or ellys not. Wytnes herof; John Paradice, prest, Henry Wynchep, Thomas Penet, William Bullyson, William Clerk, Hamelet Ramsbotell, William Walker, Alexaunder Mody, with other.

Proved before P at Caistor, 12 May 1533. Adm. granted to Agnes the relict, the said John the co-executor being a minor.

196. MAUD PECHILL [OF NORMANTON]
[LCC 1532–34, fo. 153r]

15 April 1533. I, Mawde Pechyll of the paryshe of Normanton, of good remembraunce, make my testament. Fyrst I bequethe my soule to God allmyghtty and my body to be buryed within the churcheyerde of Normanton. I bequethe for my tithys forgottyn to the high altare of the churche aforesayd xij*d*. To Our Lady warkes off Lincoln xij*d*. To the churche of Normanton iij*s* iiij*d*. To my ij doughters unmaryed all my housholde stuff and iiij nete light, to be devydyd betwyxt the sayd ij doughters, and ij ewes, ij lammys to the sayd mades. To Denys my sun ij ewes, ij lammys. To the chyldren of my sun John ij hogges schepe. The resydue of my goodes I will be disposyd aftyr the mynde of my sunnys John Pechell and Denys

Pechell whome I make my executors. Wytnes of the premisses; the parsone of Normanton, William Dobleday, William Botheby, with other.

Proved before P at Ledenham, 8 May 1533.

197. ELIZABETH BROWNE [OF BURGH LE MARSH]
[LCC 1532–34, fo. 101v]

17 April 1533. I, Elizabeth Browne wydoy of Burgh, makes my will. Fyrste I bequethe my soule to God allmyghtty, to Our Lady St. Mary and to all the saintes in heven, and my body to be buryed in the churcheyerde of St. Peter in Burgh. To the high altare for tithys forgottyn iiij*d*. To the high altare a towell. To Our Lady of Lincoln ij*d*, and to her warke ij*d*. To Thomas my sun a mare, a cowe, vj schepe, the best brasse pot and the best brasse panne. To Robert Browne my sun a cowe, vj schepe, the secunde brasse potte and panne, a calve and the blake arke in the chamber. To Agnes my doughter a qwye, vj schepe and my best gowne and kyrtyll. To Christofer Orsby a lyttyll brasse potte. To every one of my doughtter's chylder a lamme. To my syster a lamme. To Thomas Baget a yowe and a lamme. To every one of my godchylder iiij*d*. My dettes payd, the resydue of all my goodes not gyffyn, I will that Thomas Browne my sun dispose it for the welthe of my soule and all Christen soulys, who I make my true executor, and Robert Browne my sun to be supervisor. Wytnes to the same; Sir John Peychell, Christofer Magnus, Robert Putter, John Barber, Robert Mathewe, with other mo.

Proved before P at Partney, 29 April 1533.

198. GEORGE GRETHAM [OF TETNEY]
[LCC 1532–34, fo. 229r]

17 April 1533. I, George Gretham, of my hole mynde and good remembraunce, makes my last will and testament. Fyrst I bequeth my soule to God allmyghtty, Our Lady St. Mary and to all the saintes in heven. My body to be buryd within the churche of St. Peter and Paule in Tetney with that the lawe will to my mortuary. To the high altare of Tetney iiij*d*. To the high altare of Our Lady of Lincoln iiij*d*. To Our Lady warke of Lincoln iiij*d*. To Our Lady gylde of Tetney iiij*d*. To Dorothe my doughter liij*s* iiij*d*. The resydue off my goodes not gyffyn I betake into the handes off John a Gretham my father and Elizabeth Gretham my wyff, whome I make my executors, they to pay my dettes of the hole and bryng me honestly to the grounde as they thynke best to the plesure of God. And that remanys over, I gyff Elizabeth my wyff, it with better [sic]. Thes wytnesses; Godfray Thomas, Richerde Horncastill, Richerd Bryan, Robert Blancherde, John Spryng, with other mo.

Proved before P at Lincoln, 23 June 1533. Adm. granted to the executors.

199. HENRY DARWYN [OF PANTON]
[LCC 1532–34, fo. 108]

18 April 1533. I, Henry Darwyn of the paryshe of Panton, hole of mynde and good remembraunce, dothe make my last will. The fyrste I bequethe my soule to God allmyghtty, to Our Lady St. Mary, and to all the holy cumpeny of heven. My body to be buryed in the churcheyerde of St. Andro in Panton. My mortuary as the order

of the churche requirethe. To Our Lady warke of Lincoln viij*d*. To the high altare of the paryshe churche of Panton vj*d*. To the churche of Panton iij*s* iiij*d*. I gyff x*s* to cause one trentall to be sayd for my soule. To the churche of Donham one yowe. To John Darwyn of Donham iiij schepe. To William [fo. 108v] Darwyn my brother one oxe. To John Baxster one oxe and ij schepe. To John Welcom off Lincoln, hys wyff and chyldren, viij schepe. To John Darwyn viij schepe. To Thomas Darwyn ij sterys with a cowe and fyve schepe. To Alice Darwyn ij oxen, a potte wyth a panne, a matteres and ij coverlyttes, a marke. To Henry Syblay x schepe. To Thomas Lee a cowe and v schepe. To Robert Syblay one schepe. Over that I gyff to Alice Syblay a schepe. The resydue of all my goodes I gyff to John Darwyn and Thomas Darwyn my sunnys, the whiche I constitute my executors, to dispose for my soule helthe and all Crysten soulys as it shall become them the best for to do. Wytnes heroff; Sir John Feldehouse, the paryshe preste, Richerde Ellerby the elder and William Darwyn, with other mo. Geven the day and yere above sayd.

Proved before P at Wragby, 30 April 1533. Adm. granted to the executors.

200.   WILLIAM STATER [OF SKEGNESS]
[LCC 1532–34, fos. 173v–174r]

18 April 1533. I, William Stater, hole of mynde and good of memory, makes my last will and testament. Fyrste I bequethe my soule to God allmyghtty and to Our Lady St. Mary and to all the saintes in heven, and my body to be buryed in the churcheyerde of St. Clement off Skegnes. To the sacrament iiij*d*. To ij altares in the sayd churche, other of them, ij*d*. To Our Lady's warke of Lincoln viij*d*. To Our Lady of Walsyngham iiij*d*. To Alice my wyff ij kye and viij ewes and ther lammys, and all my housholde stuff. To Agnes my doughter one burlyng qwe and vj yowes and ther lammys. To Jenet my doughter a burlyng qwe and vj yowes and ther lammys. To Robert my sun a burlyng qwye and vj schepe and one pot. To Helene my doughter one qwe, iiij schepe and a pan. I will that a cowe shall be solde to bye ij qwyes withall, one to [fo. 174r] Robert and another to Helene. I will that a mare and a fole shall be solde for my buryall. I will that a trentall shall be done for my soule and all Crysten soules in the churche of St. Clement aforesayd. The resydue of my goodes not bequethyd I will thay be devydyd emonges my chylder, to theym that hath moste neyd of it. I will that Alice my wyff and John my broder shall be my executors, to se that thys my last will shall be performyd. Thes beryng wytnes; Mr. Thomas Wymbyshe and Thomas Richerdson, with other mo.

Proved before P at Lincoln, 25 July 1533. Adm. granted to Alice the relict and executrix, John the co-executor being prevented by death.

201.   RICHARD WEBSTER [OF SWINESHEAD]
[LCC 1532–34, fo. 162v]

19 April 1533. I, Richerd Webster off Swynneshed, of hole mynde and good memory beyng, make my testament and last will. Fyrste I bequethe my soule to God allmyghtty and to Our Lady and to all saintes. My body to be buryed in the churcheyarde of Our Lady's in Swynneshed. To the high altare ther for tithys forgottyn viij*d*. To Our Lady's warke of Lincoln ij*d*. To the fatherles chylder of St. Catheryn's nygh Lincoln ij*d*. To John my sun one horsse mylne and ij horssys and

one cowe. To William my sun ij yong marys of iij yeres of age and one cowe. To Helene Colson one byrlyng. The resydue of all my goodes not bequethyd I gyff to Agnes my wyff whome I make my executrix, she to dispose to her chylder when they cum at laufull age as she thynkes best, with the supervision of Sir John Webster, my brother, gyffyng hym for hys labor one gray horsse. Thes beyng wytnes; Sir Thomas Garton, vicar, John Welche, Adam Browne.

Proved before P at Donington, 28 May 1533.

202.   THOMAS SMYTH [OF WIGTOFT]
        [LCC 1532–34, fos. 164v–165r]

21 April 1533. I, Thomas Smyth of Wygtofte, husbandman, in good mynde and hole memory, makes my testament and last will. Fyrst I bequeth my soule to allmyghtty God, to Our Lady St. Mary, and to all the holy cumpeny of heven. My body to [fo. 165r] be buryed in the churcheyerde of Saintes Peter and Paule in Wygtofte. To Our Lady of Lincoln iijd. To the fatherles chylderen of St. Catheryn's ijd. To the high altare of Wygtofte iiijd. And to my mortuary as the lawe inquirys. To Our Lady's altare ijd, and to St. Nicholes altare iijd. To the churche warke of Wygtofte xijd. To Our Lady of Pety one pounde wax. To Thomas Smyth my sun v yowes and v sheryng schepe, one yong meyr, blak gray. To John my sun x yowes, one bay fylly, one chyste. To Richerd my sun vj yowes, on the best that I have in Kesten, and one arke aftyr the decesse of hys mother and one brown burnyng. I will that all the goodes aforesayd gyffyn to my chyldren be delyveryd and put to ther proffyt at Mydsomer next to cum, by the 'vise of John Johnnyson off Frampton, my brother, and Alyson my wyff, and every one of them to be other heyres. And yff it be so that all my chyldren dy afore lefull age, I will that the forsayd goodes be disposyd for the helthe of my soule and all my good frende soulys by the 'vise of John Johnnyson, my brother, and my wyff. To Agnes Angell one blak dowyd cowe and iiij yowes when they ar clyppyd. To Agnes Alege one lamme. To Henry Alege one lamme. Also all my goodes not bequethyd, my will fulfyllyd and my dettes payd, I bequeth them to Alyson my wyff, whome I make my executrix. I will that John Johnnyson my brother be the supervisor, and to gyff my wyff good councell and he to have for hys labor one bay amblyng colte. Thes men beryng wytnes; John Felde, Lambert Lowes and John Cooke, with mo.

Proved before P at Donington, 28 May 1533.

203.   THOMAS WRIGHT [OF KINGERBY]
        [LCC 1532–34, fo. 156v]

21 April 1533. I, Thomas Wryght off Kynyerby, beyng in a hole mynde and good remembrance, makes my last will and testament. Fyrste I bequethe my soule to God allmyghtty, to Our Lady St. Mary and to all the blessyd cumpeny of heven, besechyng them to pray for me, and my body to be buryed in the churcheyerde off St. Peter in Kynyerby beforesayd. I bequethe for my mortuary as the lawe dothe require. To the high altare of St. Peter in Kynyerby beforesayd xxd. I will have x messys sayd for the well of my soule and all Christen soulys, and I will that fyve of them be sayd in the Augustyne Frerys within Grymmesby, and they to have xxd. To Robert my brother a yowe and a lamme. The resydue of my goodes before not

gyffyn nor bequethyd, I will that they shall be devydyd in iij partes, one parte to myselff, the secund parte to Jenet my wyff, and the thurde parte to my chyldren. Also I will and bequeth my said parte to Jenet my wyff, Thomas Wright and Bartilmewe Wryght my sunnys, evenly to be devydyd emonges them, whiche Jenet, Thomas and Bartylmewe I make my executors. Thes beyng wytnes; Sir William Doughtty, vicar of Kynyerby, John Osnay and John Robson of the same, with other mo.

> Proved before P at Market Rasen, 14 May 1533. Adm. granted to Joan the relict and executrix, Thomas Wright and Bartholomew Wryght, executors, being under age.

204.   THOMAS OVERTON [OF SWINESHEAD]
       [LCC 1532–34, fo. 112v]

22 April 1533. Ego, Thomas Overton nuper de Swyneshed in comitatu Lincolniensis, generosus, condo testamentum meum.[88] Fyrste and principally I bequethe my soule unto God allmyghtty and to Our Lady St. Mary, and to all the holy cumpeny of heven. My body to be buryd within the churche of that paryshe wherin it shall please God that the departor [of] my soule and body shall happe or falle. And for my buryall ther vjs viijd, and my mortuary to be aftyr the custome ther. To Our Lady's warke of Lincoln iijs iiijd. Towarde the sustentacion of the orphans and pupyllys in St. Catheryn's withowt Lincoln ijs. To the high altare in the churche of Swynneshed aforesayd for tithes forgottyn xijd. To every other altare in the same churche vjd. I bequethe towardes the reparacions of the cawsys in Swynneshed xiijs iiijd. I will that a trentall be sung for my soule in the churches of the iiij orders of the frerys nexte to that place where it shall please God to call me to hys mercy, as sone aftyr as it can be done aftyr my departure, and they therfore to have xiijs iiijd devydyd emonges them, that is to wyt, to every house of the frerys iijs iiijd. I will that the preste that synges at Lincoln for the soulys of William Wyllesforde and Alice hys wyffe, father and mother unto my wyffe, shall syng ther for the sayd soulys by the space of iij quarters of a yere, so that in all he shall syng a yere full complete in lyke maner and forme as he hathe done thys quarter of the yere laste paste. And he to have for hys wages in lyke maner as he hathe had thys quarter laste paste. I will, yff so be that my wyffe have no issue of her body, I will that then the greate pare of corall beades gawdyd with gawdys of sylver and gylte aftyr her decesse be gyven unto our Lady's warke of Lincoln accordyng aftyr the laste will of her sayd fader, William Willesforde. The resydue of all my goodes, fyrste my dettes therof payd, I gyff unto Jane Overton my wyff, whome I make executrix that she dispose for my soule as she shall answer before the high juge. Thes beyng wytnes; Sir Thomas Garton, vicare of Swynneshed, Sir John Webster, chauntry preste of the same, Sir Robert Smythe of the same, preste, Sir William Trewe of the same, preste, and Richerde of the same, notary, with other mo. Datyd the day and yere abovesayd.

> Proved before P at Lincoln, 23 January 1533/4. Adm. granted to the executrix.

[88] 'I, Thomas Overton, late of Swineshead in the county of Lincoln, gentleman, make my testament.'

205.   AGNES GUNNELL [OF SPALDING]
        [LCC 1532–34, fos. 160r–161r]

23 April 1533. I, Annys Gunnell off Spaldyng, beyng seke and deceasyd of my body and of hole and perfyte remembraunce, makes my testament and last will. Fyrst I gyff my soule to allmyghtty God, Our Lady St. Mary and to all the holly cumpeny of heven, and my body to be buryd within the churcheyerde off Our Lady and St. Nicholes in Spaldyng, on the sowthe syde. To the high altare for my forgottyn tithynges xij*d*. To the church warke of the paryshe churche of Our Lady and St. Nicholes xij*d*. To the Trinite gylde viij*d*. To Our Lady's gylde viij*d*. To every devocion within the parysh churche of Spaldyng iiij*d*. To Our Lady of Lincoln vj*d*. To St. Catheryn's for the fatherles chylder ij*d*. I will that my executors gyff to the holly goste gylde within the paryshe churche of Spaldyng iij platters, [fo. 160v] iij dyshes and a meate clothe. To Our Lady's gylde iij platters, iij dyshes. To St. Sythe's altare ij bell candylstykes. I will that my house that I dwell in be soulde immediatly aftyr my decesse by my executors, and the money takyn for it I will be gyffyn and bestowyd thus and aftyr thys maner: fyrst iiij markes off good and laufull money to one able preste, to syng for me [and] my husbandes Thomas, Robert and Robert, the space of halff a yere within the paryshe churche of Spaldyng. Also I will that Robert Beston have of that money xx*s*, Agnes Drewry, the doughter of John Drewry, xiij*s* iiij*d*, John Drewry vj*s* viij*d*. Also I will that xxvj*s* viij*d* be disposyd in highways within the paryshe of Spaldyng. The resydue of the money takyn for my house I put to the disposicion of my executors, and by ther good advyse to be orderyd and gyffyn. To Robert Beston iij platters, iij dyshes, ij candylstykes, one lattyn bason of the best, a laver, one fether bed, one matteres, one red coverlet, one pare of blankyttes, ij pare of schetes, one of flaxyn, another myngtow, one towell, ij pilloys, a whyte hangyng, ij curtens, one brasse potte with the long seet, the gret panne above the loft, my masse, iiij sylver spones, one pare of bedstokes that I ly in. To Agnes Drewry one fether bed, one matteres, a pare of blankyttes, one yelowe coveryng, one pare of flaxyn schetes, another of myngtow, a whyte hangyng, ij curtens, one towell, one brasse potte nexte the best, ij pannys, a lesser and a bygger, ij candylstykes, a pare of whyte amber beades with the gawdys of jesper, a browne cowe, my gret arke, one pare of bedstokes in the chamber that I ly in, ij sylver spones, one kercher. To Elizabeth Drewry one matteres, one pare of flaxyn schetes, ij pilloys. To Agnes Whyte, the doughtter of Simon Whyte, one matteres, one pare of harden schetes, ij pilloys, ij dyshys, ij platters. To Alice Gonnell iij platters, iij dyshes, iij sylver spones, my Lundon tawny round gowne, one panne of iij gallons. To Amy Drewry a new red kyrtyll, my Lundon tawny tranyd gowne. To Emme my syster all my warkeday clothys, a blak gowne, a violet cappe, ij kerches for the halyday off my owne clothe, one appron for the hallyday, one [fo. 161] brasse potte, one whyte coverlyd, one pare of hardyn schetes, one hardyn meteclothe. To John Williamson one matteres, a russet coverlyd, one pare of myngtow schettes, one brasse potte, one panne. To John Gonnell a fether bed of my owne spynnyng, one cowe, one pare of bedstokes. To Sir Leonerde Swete one coverlyd, one fether bed, viij plath of lyn cloth. To John Beston one red cowe. To Beatryx Bull one dyshe. To Elizabeth Ranerd my wynter gowne. The reste of my goodes not bequethyd, gyffyn, nor set by will, my executors shall sell, and they shall dispose the money theroff takyn for the helthe of my soule where moste nede shall require, whome I make Sir Leonerd Swete and John

Beston, to brynge me honestly to the grounde. And they to have for there panes, ether of them, iij*s* iiij*d*. I will that Nicholes Woorlege be the supervisor, and he to have for hys labor iij*s* iiij*d*. Wytnes Sir Thomas Smythe, Richerd Lynsay, John Drewry, William Payne, with other mo.

Proved before P at Spalding, 27 May 1533.

206.   HENRY PURLE [OF CROFT]
          [LCC 1532–34, fo. 210]

24 April 1533. I, Henry Purle of Crofte, with a hole mynde beyng, makes my testament and my last will. Fyrste I bequethe my soule to allmyghtty Ihesu, to Our Lady St. Mary and to all the holly cumpeny of heven, and my body to be buryd within the churcheyerde off All Halloys in Crofte. To Our Lady of Lincoln iiij*d*. To her warkes ij*d*. To the high altare in Crofte churche for tithys forgottyn iiij*d*. To ij altares in the same churche iiij*d*. To the bellys in the same churche viij*d*. To St. Margaret of Kettesby ij*d*. I bequethe to be spente of my buryall day xx*s*. [fo. 210v] To one preste x*s* to syng one trentall for my soule and the soulys of my father and mother with all my benfactors' soulys. I will have, aftyr ij yeres aftyr my decesse, my yere day kepyd, spente the same day ether yere v*s*. To William Saylbe, sonne of Robert Saleby the elder, v*l* vj*s* viij*d*, to syng one yere in Crofte churche for my soule, my father and mother, and all my good frendes' soulys when he is prest, or ellys to another preste yff he be no preste. The resydue of all my goodes not gyffyn nor bequethyd I put to the disposicion of Robert Saleby of Crofte, the elder, and John Bawdre of the same, whome I make my executors for to fulfyll my last will and to pay my dettes withall as they shall be bund be ther othes, and ether of theym to have for ther labors x*s*. Thes wytnes; Sir Thomas Rysyll, my curate, Edwarde Bursay, with other mo.

Proved before P at Partney, 10 November 1533.

207.   WILLIAM WRIGHT [OF BARTON UPON HUMBER]
          [LCC 1532–34, fo. 195r]

24 April 1533. I, William Wryght of Barton apon Humber, hole of mynde and full in memory, makyth thys my last will. I bequethe my soule to allmyghtty God, Our Lady St. Mary and to all the saintes in heven. My body to be buryd in the chapellyerde of Barton aforesayd. To the high altares in St. Peter churche and St. Mary chapell in Barton aforesayd for forgottyn tithys, ether of them, xij*d*. To the reparacion of St. Peter churche iij*s* iiij*d*. To the reparacion of St. Mary chapell in Barton iij*s* iiij*d*. To Our Lady of Lincoln viij*d*. To Our Lady warke of Lincoln viij*d*. To William my servant iiij*d*. To Margaret my wyff doughter x*s*. To John Founder ij*s*. To Thomas Strangman xij*d*. To Sir George Darneton, my gostly father, v*d*. To Sir John Browne, preste, viij*d*. To Anne my doughter vj*s* viij*d* of my parte when my funerall expenses, dettes and legaces is dischargeyd, and that that leyffes of my parte I gyff it to my ij sonnys John and Hugh. The reste of my goodes not bequethyd nor wyt I gyff to Alyson my wyff and to my iij chyldren, whome I make my full executors for to dispose for the helthe of my soule, my frendes' soulys and all Crysten soulys as they thynke best. Also I will that my brother John Skelton be the supervisor, and he to have for hys labor xiij*s* iiij*d*. Thes to wytnes; Sir George

Darneton, Sir John Browne, prestes, John Founder, Richerde Bewan, Leonerd Arnalde and Thomas Strangman, with other mo.

Proved before P at Caistor, 14 October 1533.

208.   THOMAS STEDEMAN [OF GOSBERTON]
         [LCC 1532–34, fo. 164]

25 April 1533. I, Thomas Stedeman of the paryshe of Gosbertun, beyng perfyte of mynde and in good remembraunce, makes my last will and testament. Fyrst I bequethe my soule to allmyghtty God, to Our Blessyd Lady St. Mary and to all the holy cumpeny of heven, and I will my body to be buryed in the churcheyerde of Saintes Peter and Paule in Gosbertun. To the fermer of the benefice iij schepe. To the high altare for my tithys forgottyn vj*d*. To the plough light ij*d*. To the torche light ij*d*. [fo. 164v] To the churche warke xij*d*. To all Crysten soulys' light iiij*d*. To the edificacion of our mother churche of Lincoln ij*d*. To the chylder of St. Catheryn's ij*d*. To William Atkynson xx^{ty} schepe of myne, to the use and proffyt of John Stedeman, William and Helene my chylder. And I will that the sayd schepe, with the proffyt theroff cumyng, be delyveryd to my sayd chyldren by equall porcions when every one of them cumys to the age of xx^{ty} yeres. And yff any of my sayd chyldren dy or they cum to the age of xx^{ty} yeres, then I will that those chyldren beyng alyve have the parte of them that be departed owt of thys presente lyff. And yff all my forsayd chyldren dy or they cum to the age of xx^{ty} yeres, as God defende, then I will it shall be lefull to the churche masters of Gosbertun then beyng to sell the forsayd xx^{ty} schepe with the proffyt therof cumyng to the best price. And I will that the money theroff cumyng be disposyd for the use of my soule to hyer one preste to syng and pray in the paryshe of Gosbertun for my soule and all my good frendes' soulys, as long as the sayd money will extende and indure. I will that Gylbert Blankney be oversear of thys my last will to helpe my wyff, and I gyff hym for hys labor iij*s* iiij*d*. The resydue of all my goodes ungyffyn and not bequethyd, I gyff them frely to Alice my wyff to performe thys my last will and to pay my dettes, the whiche Alice I make my sole executrix. Thes beryng wyttnes; Sir Henry Toplys, William Thaker, John Smyth off Surflet, with other mo.

Proved before P at Donington, 28 May 1533.

209.   SIR JOHN GRAY [OF BELCHFORD]
         [LCC 1532–34, fos. 258v–259r]

27 April 1533. I, Sir John Gray off Belcheforde, beyng hole of mynde and good remembraunce, makes thys my last will. In primis I bequethe my soule to God allmyghtty, to Our Lady St. Mary and to all the hole cumpeny of heven, and my body to be buryd in the high qwere of the holly appostellys Peter and Paule. To the high altare of the sayd churche xij*d*. To the churche warke ij*s*, one mes boke coveryd with ledder, and one manuell.[89] To one tabernacle to St. Peter vj*s* viij*d*. To Our Lady's gylde xvj*d*. To Our Lady of Lincoln viij*d*. To her warke ij*s*. To Legborne churche xx*d*. To John Pratte of Malteby vj*s* viij*d* that I lent hym. To Thomas Ingolmellys x*s* that he hawys to me. To John Gray of Hameryngham v*s* that he

---

[89] The manual was a book of the forms to be used by the priest in celebrating the sacraments.

hawys me, and xx*d* more. To John Haldyn xiij*s* iiij*d* that I lent hym. To Richerde Gray off Bamburgh ij*s* that I lent hym, and I will he have ij*s* more. To Elizabeth Brakyn, wedo, one matterys, one yellow coverlyd, a pare lyn schetes, ij yowes and lammys, a lyttyll chyste standyng in the churche and x*s* in money. To Jenet my syster ij*s*. To Alyson her doughter xij*d*. To Jenet, the wyff of Walter Malteby of Beysby, xij*d*. To Thomas Pratte xvj*d*. To Agnes Browne of Louthe one yowe. To Alyson Gray of Scamelesby one yowe. To Jane Gray of the same one yowe. To John Gray the sun of Robert Gray xx*d*. To Arthure Gray xx*d*. I will that Thomas Denys have iij*s* of the noble that he awys me. To Malde Ingolmelles ij yowes and ij lammys. The resydue of my goodes I will they be solde for to hyer one honest preste to syng for the helthe of my soule and for my fader and my moder, with all my good benefactors' soulys, assygned by Robert Gray of Scamelesby and Syr Robert Pratte of Lytyll Carleton whome I make my executors, and other of them to have for hys labors iij*s* iiij*d*. I will Syr [fo. 259r] Thomas Leffnynge of Scamelesby be the overseer, and he to have for hys labor iij*s* iiij*d*. In wytnes wherof I, the foresayd Sir John Gray, wrote thys present testament and my last will with my propre hande, allmyghtty God to wytnes.

Proved before P at Horncastle, 4 May 1534.

210.   JOHN HALGARTHE [OF HORNCASTLE]
        [LCC 1532–34, fos. 149v–150v]

30 April 1533. I, John Halgarthe of Horncastyll, beyng hole of mynde and seke of body, makes thys my last will and testament. Fyrst I bequethe my soule unto allmyghtty God and to Our Lady St. Mary and to all the saintes in heven, and my body to be buryed within the churcheyerde of Our Blessyd Lady off Horncastyll aforesayd. I bequethe in the name of my mortuary as the lawe requyryth. [fo. 150r] To the high altare in Horncastill churche xij*d*. To the bellys in the same xij*d*. To Agnes my wyff ij of the best oxen, a horsse, a cowe, a wayn with all maner of tyrement that shall remayn to it. To Thomas Halgarther my sun the yonger cople of oxen, a yowe, a lamme, a cownter, a sylver spone, a quarter of barly. To William my sun a yowe, a lamme, a sylver spone, a quarter of barly. To Jenet my doughter a yowe, a lamme, a sylver spone, a quarter of barly, a basyn, a Lundon dubler and v puter dyshes, a matteres, a coverlyd, a pare of schetes, a pillo with bedstockes hole. To Elizabeth my doughter a yowe, a lamme, a sylver spone, a quarter of barly, a basyn, a Lundon platter and v puter dyshes, a matteres, a coverlyd, a pare of schetes, a pillo with a pare of bedstockes hole. To other of them ij spyttes and other of them a brasse potte and a candylstyk. I will that the forsayd iiij quarters of barly be delyveryd unto John Barker, smyth, and he to have it to that my chylder comme to laufull age, from the tyme that my wyff go to mariage, excepte that she fynde sufficient suerty. To St. Trenyande light iiij*d*.[90] To Robert Dawson a dooblet. To Jenet Chambres, my wyff syster, halffe a quarter barly. To Jenet Harte a lamme. I will that ther shal be a thrugh stone[91] layd of my syster Jenet Halgarthe grave by my executors of my coste. To Sir Henry Nowell v*s* for halff a trentall for my syster and

[90] St. Trenyande appears to be a local saint, unrecognised by the Church generally and about whom very little is known.
[91] A horizontal grave slab, or a slab laid over a tomb. This dialect term is confined to the north of England.

me. To Agnes my wyff my copy of my convent sealys of the byshop of Carlyll the terme of her lyffe. And aftyr her decesse to remayn to William my sun and to hys heyres duryng the yeres accordyng to my brother Robert Halgarth will. To John Barker, smyth, a quarter of barly to be good unto my wyff and my chyldren, whome I make to be supervisor. And yff that my wyff do mary, then I will that John Barker, smyth, have full power and strenkyth [fo. 150v] to receyve all my chyldren goodes for ther savegarde yff they fynde not sufficient suerty. The resydue off all my goodes not gyffyn nor bequethyd, my will fulfyllyd and my dettes payd, I gyff it frely and holy to Agnes my wyffe to dispose it as she thynkes best for the helthe of my soule and all Crysten soulys, and I make my executors Agnes my wyff and Thomas Halgarthe my sun. In wytnes of the same; John Barker, smyth, Gilberd Wyberde, John Hynde, William Symson, John Tayllour, smyth, and John Madynwell, with other mo. Mayd the day and yere aforesayd.

Proved before P at Lincoln, 23 June 1533. Adm. granted to Agnes, the relict, Thomas Halgarthe, the co-executor, being then in his youth.

211. ROBERT SYLAM [OF BENINGTON IN HOLLAND]
[LCC 1532–34, fo. 159v]

30 April 1533. I, Robert Sylam of Benyngton, hole of mynde and good remembraunce, makes thys my last will and testament. Fyrste I bequethe my soule to allmyghtty God, to Our Lady St. Mary and to all the cumpeny in heven, and my body to be buryed in the churcheyerde of All Halloys in Benyngton. To Our Lady of Lincoln, to her warkes vjd. To St. Catherin's ijd. To the anornamentes of the high altare in Benyngton iiijd. To every altare in the churche iijd. To the churche warkes iiijd. For tithys forgottyn iiijd. To Elizabeth my doughter a cowe and a calve, ij yowes and ij lammes. To Thomas my sun a cowe, ij yowes and ther lammes and a yeryng fylly. To Simond my sun ij qwyes, a black qwy to be one, a yowe and a lamme. To John my sun one fylly ij yeres olde and more, and a qwye of iij yeres of age. To William my sun a fylly, one of the best, iij yowes, iij lammes and a qwy burlyng. I will that and[92] Margaret my wyff mary agane, I will that my plowe, my corte and my carte with all the geres and tyryng that longes to them to be devydyd betwyxte John and William my suns, and the one to be the oder hayr, and in lyke maner after her decesse yff she mary not. The rest of my goodes not gyffyn nor bequethyd I gyff to Margaret my wyff whome I make my executrix and John Berdertun, supervisor, he to have for hys labor and payn iijs iiijd. The wytnes; Sir John Lee, John Cokler, William Tattersall, with other mo.

Proved before P at Boston, 26 May 1533.

212. JOHN WILSON [OF GRAYINGHAM]
[Stow 1530–52, fo. 17r]

30 April 1533. I, John Wilson of Graingham, holl of mynde and gud remembrance, makes my testament. First I bequeth my saull to almyghty God, Our Lady Saynt [Mary], and to all the holy compeny of hevyn. My body to be buryed in the churche of Saynt Radigounde in Greingham. To the blissyd sacrament xxd. To Awer Lady

---

[92] Read 'if'.

warke of Lincoln xx*d*. To Awer Lady of Lincoln xx*d*. To the church of Graingham vij yows and vij lammes, and an acre of rye and barley in Metilclevys. To Saynt Hugh his hedd at Lincoln iiij*d*. To every order of freers in Lincoln iiij*d*. To Syr John Cressy half a trentall to pray for my saull and all the saulles that I have fared the better for in tymes past. To Master Parson of Graingham on acre of rye and barley. To Master Plankney of Graingham iij*s* iiij*d*. To Thomas Barnarde a yow and a lame and a rosytt gowne. To John his sonne, my godsonne, a yow lame. To his wiffe on quye calfe, and to Nicolas his sonne on yow lame. To John Lupton on yow and a lame. To Margaret Baynton on yow and a lame. To William Kilppinge a hogge, and to his wiffe a hogge. To Beatrice Wilson a grett panne and a litill panne. To Master Robert Sutton of Burton my best charger, a candilstike. To Robert Bell a slevelys jackytt, a dublytt, a payr of hose, a shert and ij yerde and iij quarters of murrey. To John Wilson, the sonne of Robert Wilson, on yow hogge and a litill brasse pott. To John Lion my best violett jackyd. To Beatrice Wilson a quye calff. To Robert Lion iij*s* iiij*d*. To Thomas Lion iij*s* iiij*d*, a weder hogge and a payr of hose. To every on of my godchilder within the towne iiij*d*. The residew of my guddes I giffe to Thomas Wilson and John Wilson my sonnes, whom I make myne executers. Thies beinge witnesse; John Plankney, John Lacy, Thomas Barnarde, Robert Eston, with other moo.

> Proved before L at Lincoln, 27 June 1533. Adm. granted to Thomas the son and an executor, reserving power to grant to John the other executor when he comes to lawful age.

213.   MAWDE ARTHROWE [OF LEAKE]
         [LCC 1532–34, fos. 159v–160r]

1 May 1533. I, Mawde Arthrowe, vydo of Leeke, in hole mynde and off good remembraunce, makes my testament. Fyrst I bequethe my soule to almyghtty God, to Hys mother St. Mary, and to all the saintes beyng in heven. My body to be buryed in the kyrkyerde of Leeke. In the name of my mortuary as the law requyryth. [fo. 160r] To the high altare in the Leeke kyrke iij*d*. To the anornament of Our Lady of Leeke viij*d*. To every altare in the same kyrke ij*d*. Also for forgottyn tithys xij*d*. To Our Lady of Lincoln iiij*d*. To the orphans at St. Catheryn's iiij*d*. To John Grescrofte my sun, my plowe, my wayn, ij cople oxen, iij horsse, iiij of the eldest kye and one of the yonger kye. To William Grescrofte my sun, ij beys, the one of them of the best with one burnyng, v yowes with ther lammes, and to the chylder of the same William v schepe hogges. To Margaret Grescrofte one browne qwe with one calve. To John Mell chylder ij schepe. To the buyldyng of the kyrk of Leek iij*s* iiij*d*. I will that my executors kepe my buryall day, my vij day and xxx^{ty} day of my goodes before bequethyd. The resydue of my goodes not gyffyn nor bequethyd I gyff to William and John my suns, whome I make my executers to dispose for my soule as they thynke shall be moste plesure to God. Thes wytnes; Frere Thomas Camok and Thomas Kewyng off Leeke, with oder mo.

> Proved before P at Boston, 26 May 1533.

214. RICHARD FROME [OF BARTON UPON HUMBER]
[LCC 1532–34, fo. 253]

2 May 1533. I, Richerde Frome off Barton apon Humber, hole of mynde and full of memory, mak[es] thys my will and testament. Fyrste I gyff and bequethe my soule to allmyghtty God, to Our Blyssyd Lady and all the saintes in heven. My body to be buryd in the churche of St. Peter in Barton. To the high altare for forgottyn tithes xij*d*. To the high altare of our mother churche of Lincoln viij*d*, and to our warkes of the sayd churche viij*d*. To St. Peter churche of Barton [fo. 253v] aforesayd fyve nobyls. To Sir John Berde xiij*s* iiij*d*. I bequethe to a preste to syng for my soule and all Christen soulys, v*l*. To Elenore my doughter xx*l*, ij sylver sponys to be delyveryd before her mother go to mariage, and that Sir Christofer Dobson receyve the sayd goodes and have the custody of it to suche tyme as the sayd Elenore come to lefull age, and I will that she be founde at the scole at a nonery of the hole goodes, and aftyr that to be founde of the bequest bequethyd be my will. Also I will that the sayd Elenore my doughter have all my copy lande and closyng within the towne and felde of Barton, also one toftested buyldyd in the sayd towne of Barton, with vij acres lande in the felde and a halffe aftyr the decesse of her moder. Yff it so fortune that Elenore my doughter dye withowt issue, then I will that bothe the landes, copys and goodes remayn to my wyffe, and aftyr her the landes and copys to remayn to Richerde Willoys. Also I will that Alyson Grasson have her indenture and lande agane when my wyffe hathe had ij croppys of it. To Our Lady's house of Thorneton xl weders as they run. To Robert Frome xl*s*. To Agnes Willose, my doughter, v markes. To every order of frerys whome I am a brother unto, a quarter malte. To iche of my godchylder a yowe. The resydue of my goodes not bequeth I gyff to Marion my wyffe, whome I make my executrix, to dispose for my soule and all Christen soulys as she thynkes expedyent. Thes men wytnes; Thomas Blithe, John Wrytte, Robert Hobson, John Garbot, with other mo. Master Thomas Portyngton to be supervisor, and he to have for hys labor xiij*s* iiij*d*, and hys costes borne in all busynes concernyng the same.

Proved before P at Caistor, 27 April 1534.

215. RICHARD MYDDYLTON [OF LUDBOROUGH]
[LCC 1532–34, fos. 151v–152r]

2 May 1533. I, Richerde Myddylton of Louthburgh, beyng of good remembraunce, lovyd be God, makes thys to be my last will. Fyrste I bequethe my soule to God allmyghtty, to Our Lady St. Mary Hys mother, and to [fo. 152r] all the holy cumpeny of heven, and my body to be buryd within the churche of my paryshe churche off Louthburghe, gyffyng for my buryall vj*s* viij*d*. To Mr. Parsone my curate v*s*. To the warke of my paryshe churche iij*s* iiij*d*, and iij*s* iiij*d* the which was lente to Sir Alan Smyth. To the warke off the mynster of Our Lady of Lincoln viij*d*. To Our Lady of Lincoln iiij*d*. To Thursby churche iiij*d*. To Fulstowe churche iiij*d*. To Utterby churche iiij*d*. To Wyham churche iiij*d*. I will that my body be honestly buryd. To Robert Myddylton my sone v*s*. The resydue of my goodes I do gyff them to Agnes Medylton my wyff and to John Burman of Louthburgh, whome I make to be my executors, and they to dispose my goodes for my soule as they thynke best to plese God. Thes beryng wytnes;

Robert Barton, Thomas Howys, William Frende, Valentyne Leche, with oder mo.

Proved before P at Louth, 5 May 1533.

216. JAMES HOLLYNGWORTH [OF OLD BULLINGTON IN PARISH OF GOLTHO]
[LCC 1532–34, fo. 268v]

3 May 1533. I, James Hollyngworthe of the paryshe of Olde Bullyngton within the countie of Lincoln, keper and servant to Sir George Taylboys, of an hole mynde and remembraunce, lovyd be Jhesu, makyth and ordinyth thys my present testament and last will. Fyrste and principally I gyff and bequethe my soule unto allmyghtty God my creature and redemer, to Our Lady St. Mary and to all the saintes in heven. My body to be buryd within the churche of St. Jamys in the aforsayd Bollyngton, for the whiche buryall and romyth I gyff to the aforesaid churche of St. Jamys vs. To the high altare of the same churche for all forgottyn tithys and oblacions, with all other dutys anense the churche xijd. To Our Lady of Lincoln ijs. To Catheryne Hollyngworthe my doughter xxs. To Anne Edryngton xijd. To Margaret Edryngton xijd. To John Hollyngworthe my sun, every one of hys chylder, xijd. To Elizabeth my doughter Clay xs. I make Thomas Blow supervisor. The resydue of all my goodes not wyt I gyff to John Hollyngworthe and Robert my sonnys, whiche I make my executores for to dispose accordyng to conscience and as they shall thynke moste nedefull for the helthe of my soule. Wytnes herof; my curate Sir Nicholes Jakson, John Wryght and Thomas Blow, with other.

Proved before P at Wragby, 9 May 1534. Adm. granted to John Hollyngworthe the executor, reserving power to grant administration to the other executor when he shall come.

217. ROBERT BRENTON [OF KIRTON IN HOLLAND]
[LCC 1532–34, fos. 167v–168r]

4 May 1533. I, Robert Brenton of Kyrton in Hollande, of hole and perfyte remembraunce, makyth my testament concludyng with my last will. In the fyrste I gyff and bequethe my soule to God allmyghtty, Our Lady St. Mary, and to all the celestiall cumpeny of heven, and my body to be buryed in the churcheyerde of the holy appostellys Peter and Paule of Kyrton before namyd, and for my mortuary aftyr the statutes of our soverayn lorde the kyng. To the high altare of Kyrton for negligent tithes iiijd. To the iij Mares' altare iiijd. To Our Lady altare jd. To the Trinite altare jd. To the reparacions of the sayd churche of Kyrton iiijd. To Our Lady altare of Horblyng iiijd. To Our Lady of Lincoln ijd. To the reparacions of the sayd our mother churche of Lincoln ijd. To the orphans of St. Catheryn's ijd. I will that myn executrix or hys assygnes do pay or cause to be payd to Mr. Thomas Cheny of Kyrton, preste, or, in hys absence, to one of the same chauntry, prest, by the feste of the Nativitie of Our Lady[93] nexte aftyr my departyng, xxvjs viijd to by one vestiment to the altare of the iij Mares in the sayd churche of Kyrton. [fo. 168r] The resydue of my goodes not gyffyn nor bequethyd I gyff them unto Jenet my wyff,

93 8 September.

whome I orden executrix to dispose my goodes to the moste pleasure off God and helthe of my soule. And I make Roger Marser supervisor, and to have for hys labor iijs iiijd. Thes beryng wytnes; Sir Thomas Este, Sir Thomas Ashlay, Sir George Lincoln, with other yff nede require.

Proved before P at Donington, 28 May 1533. Adm. granted to the executrix.

218.   JOHN PAGE [OF GREETHAM]
        [LCC 1532–34, fos. 203v–204v]

4 May 1533. I, John Page off [fo. 204r] Gretham in the countye of Lincoln, of good and hole mynde, makes my laste will. Fyrste I bequethe my soule to our Lorde Jhesu Cryste, Our Lady St. Mary and to all the saintes in heven, and my body to be buryd in the churcheyerde of All Halloys of Gretham. To the high altare of Gretham for forgottyn or withholdyn tithys xijd. To Our Lady of Lincoln warke iiijd, and to Our Lady other iiijd. To the churche of All Halloys of Gretham one seame malte, a yowe, a lamme. To Agnes my wyff a cople oxen, a cople sterys, ij kye, a yeryng qwye, xx yowes and ther lammes, ij horsse, a mere and a fole, a wayn, a corte and a ploye with the gerys belongyng to them and halffe the croppe of the grounde beryng halffe the charges. To Thomas Pagge my brother a blak stagge, a yow and a lamme. To Elizabeth hys wyff a yowe and a lamme. To Margaret my doughter a cowe, ij yowes and ij lammes, a brasse panne, ij puter dooblers, a podeger and a bed with the stokkes, and a blake arke. To Elizabeth my doughter a cowe, ij yowes and ij lammes, ij puter doblers and a podeger, a bed as it standes and a holde hutche. To Alice my doughter a cowe, ij yowes and ij lammes and a brasse potte, ij puter dooblers, a chare and a lyttyll borde. To Isabell my doughter a cowe, ij yowes and ij lammes, a brasse potte, ij puter dooblers, a blake borde and a b[l]ak stole. To Matylde my doughter a cowe, ij yowes and ij lammes, a brasse potte, ij puter dooblers and a dyshe borde. And yff any of them departe owt of thys worlde afore the cum to lefull age, ther partes to remane to them that lyffys longeste. To Alice Collynson a schepe. To Aves Pagge a schepe. All the housholde stuff that remanys I bequethe to Agnes my wyff. Also I will that Sir William Longcaster, preste, have one yere sowde to syng for my soule and all Crysten soulys. To every towne that buttes of the felde mere iiijd. I will that my house that I dwell in with all the appurtenances therto belongyng be solde to fynde a preste to syng for my soule and ther soulys that I am bounde to pray for, as far as the money will extende. To Richerde Pagge one quarter barly and a yowe and a lamme. And every one of Thomas Pagge chylder, my brother, to have one schepe, and William Pagge chylder, every one, a schepe. The resydue of my goodes I bequethe to Agnes my wyff and to John Pagge my cosyn, whome I make my lefull executors to dispose for the helthe of my soule as shall be moste nedefull, and they to have resonably for ther [fo. 204v] labors. And Thomas Pagge to be the supervisor. Thes wytnes; Sir William Longcaster, paryshe preste of Gretham at that tyme, Richerde Lathorpe, John Richerdson and William Wales of Gretham, with other moy.

Proved before P at Horncastle, 29 October 1533.

219.   ROBERT RUTTER [OF BURGH LE MARSH]
[LCC 1532–34, fo. 215]

4 May 1533. I, Robert Rutter of Burgh, makes my last will. Fyrste I bequethe my soule to God allmyghtty, to Our Lady St. Mary and to all the saintes in heven, and my body to buryd in the churcheyerde of Burgh of St. Peter. To the high altare for tithes forgottyn iiij*d*. To the churche warke iiij*d*. To Our Lady of Lincoln ij*d*, and to her warke ij*d*. To Our Lady of St. Mary chapell ij*d*. To Catheryne Magnus my syster xij*d*. To Margaret my syster xij*d*. To Agnes my syster xij*d*. To Crystyan my wyff ij kye, ij yowes, to be founde to Candelmes, and iij lode hay and all my housholde stuff, savyng that belonges to the shoppe, and halffe a quarter malte, a bushell wheate and a yowe [fo. 215v] when she shall be cherched of the chylde that she is with.[94] To William my sun ij calves, iij yowes and iij lammys of the beste, and a meyr and a foldyn table, and a brasse potte that was my mother's. To Jenet Rutter vj*s* viij*d* and a lamme. To Jenet her doughter a burlyng qwye and a yowe. To Catheryne Magnus a yowe. To Richerde Dandyson a lamme. To John Magnus my godsun a lamme. To the byyng of a long towyll to the churche xx*d*. To the challans of Bullyngton xx*d*. To the nonnys of the sayd place xx*d*. My will fulfyllyd and my dettes payd, the resydue of my goods I will that it be equally devydyd betwyxte Robert Magnus, John Canne and my wyff, that they may be good to my chylder. I make Robert Magnus, John Canne my executors, and Sir John Pechyll my supervisor, and he to have for hys labor iij*s* iiij*d*. Wytnes to the same Christofer Magnus, Thomas Browne, Robert Robynson, with other mo.
    Proved before P at Partney, 10 November 1533.

220.   JOHN PAPULWIK [OF THE CITY OF LINCOLN]
[LCC 1532–34, fos. 144r–145r]

5 May 1533. I, John Papulwyk of the citie of Lincoln, brasyer, hole of mynde and of good remembraunce, dothe orden and make thys my last will and testament. Fyrst I gyff and bequethe my soule to God allmyghtty, Our Lady St. Mary and to all the holy cumpeny of heven, and my body to be buryed in the churche of St. Laurence in the northe ile afore the ymage of Our Lady. To the sayd churche for the romthe of my buryall x*s*. To the warkes off Our Lady of Lincoln xx*d*. To the gret gylde xx*d*. To the clerke gylde xx*d*. To the shomaker gylde iij puter platters of iij*l* a pece. To the sustentacion of the house of the Gray Frerys in Lincoln xx*s*. To the sustentacion of the other iij housys of the orders of frerys in Lincoln, iche one of them to have xx*d*. To Sybbyll Vincent my trendyll bed that I do ly apon, with all that longes to it.[95] To the same Sybbyll halffe one garnyshe of puter vessell with brode borders, ij basyns with ij ewres, one of puter and the other of lattyn, ij brasse pottes to the valew of vij*s*, a pare of beades of corall remanyng in her handes with all other tokyns that she hathe of myne, excepte a hope of golde. Also one gyrdell harneste with sylver to the valew of xiij*s* iiij*d*, halffe a dosyn sylver spones with gyltyd knoppes, a lyttyll salte of sylver with a cover and ij kyrchyffes. To William Johnson and Robert Johnson all

---

[94] The practice of churching, condemned by Protestant reformers as 'superstitious' and pagan, was extremely widespread before the Reformation. Its purpose was the ritual purification of a woman who had just given birth, and was considered essential before she could rejoin the parish community in worship: Duffy, *Stripping of the Altars*, 583–4.
[95] A turned, or jointed, bed i.e. a substantial and expensive piece of solid furniture.

the mooldes and toolys that I have belongyng to my occupacion, and I will that the sayd William and Robert have my prentys, Martyn [fo. 144v] Newall duryng the yeres of hys indenture, and at the ende and terme of the sayd indenture to gyff the sayd Martyn one hundrethe wyght of new pottes of brasse, or ellys the sayd Martyn to be at hys liberty aftyr my decesse. To Humfray Hoghson one hundrethe wyght of new brasse pottes. To Humfray Furmary one hundrethe wyght of new brasse pottes and one gray horsse with a saddyll. To Agnes Furmary one feder bed with the bolster, one cover with ymages and byrdes, one pare of schetes and halffe a dosyn puter dyshes. To Agnes Womak one of my tawny gownes withowt furre. To Jenet Blande in money or money worthe, iiij*s*. To olde Margaret Wryght, every weke duryng the space of one yere, iiij*d* a weke. To Richerde Clerkson one gowne with blake furre. To mother Mortlay ij kyrchyffes. To olde Margaret one gowne. To Dorethe Furmary one feder bed and one pare of schetes. To Thomas Turnay xx*s*. To John Utturby xx*d*. I bequethe to be disposyd to pore and nedy people, to the somme of x*l*. I bequethe the sum of xx*l* to a preste to syng for my soule and all Crysten soulys the space of iiij yeres in the churche of St. Laurence in the northe yle at the altare of Our Lady, and he to have to hys wages yerely duryng the sayd yeres v*l* of money. I will that Sir Thomas Ellys, preste, have my house, the whiche I have be indenture in the paryshe of St. Laurence duryng the space of the yeres that the preste shall syng for my soule, and that he shall yerely, the space of the sayd yeres, cause one obbyt to be done in the sayd churche of St. Laurence at such tyme of the yere as is accordyng to my buryall. At the whiche obbyt the sayd Sir Thomas shall distribute, or cause to be distrybute, iiij*s* to prestes and in br[e]de and ale to the paryshe. And also that the sayd Sir Thomas Ellys shall pay, or cause to be payd, yerely to the commun chamber of Lincoln duryng the yeres for an owt rent goyng owt of the sayd house xij*d*. And aftyr the sayd yeres that the preste dothe syng be fully fynyshyd and endyd, then I will that the churchewardens for the tyme beyng of the sayd churche of St. Laurence have the sayd house to the churche behoyff, and they to kepe the yerely obbyt and to pay the owt rent as is above rehersyd as long as the yeres dothe extende as more playnly dothe appere in a pare of indentures therof mayd, and at the overplus of the yerely rent of the sayd house shall kepe reparacions sufficiently of the sayd house. And yff any parte of the sayd yerely rent, the chargys and reparacions done, be overplus, than I will that the tyme that Sir Thomas Ellys have the sayd house, he to have the overplus. And aftyr hys tyme, that then the churchewardens receyve the sayd overplus, yff any be, to the behoyff of the sayd churche of St. Laurence, and at the ende and terme of the sayd indenture to leve the sayd house sufficiently [fo. 145r] repareled accordyng to the indenture. The resydue of all my goodes, my dettes payd, my legacy fulfyllyd, I depute to the disposicion of Robert Dyghtton, gentylman, and Sir Thomas Ellys, preste, whome I make my full executors, they to order and dispose it as shal be thought moste plesure to God and the proffet for my soule, to whome I bequethe for there pane and labors, that is to say to the forsayd Robert Dyghtton one hoope of golde and to the sayd Sir Thomas Ellys in money xx*s*. Wytnes wherof thys my last will and mynde; Frere John Smyth, Doctor Thomas Gressyngton, Sir Robert Deuyas, Thomas Turney and John Otturby, with other mo.

Proved before P at Lincoln, 16 May 1533. Adm. granted to the executors.

221.   ROBERT WESTE [OF BARNOLDBY]
        [LCC 1532–34, fo. 196r]

5 May 1533. Ego, Robert Weste de Barnolby, compos mentis saneque memorie, condo testamentum meum. In primis, lego animam meam deo patri omnipotenti, Beatissime Marie omnibusque sanctis celi, corpusque meum sepeliendum in cimiterio Sancte Helene in Barnolby, et pro mortuario meo ut lex vult. Lego summo altari in ecclesia de Barnolby pro decimis oblitis xx*d*, et fabrice eiusdem ecclesie iij*s* iiij*d*. Lego summo altari matris ecclesie Lincolniensis viij*d*, et fabrice eiusdem viij*d*.[96] To Agnes my wyff my house with the appurtenances for the terme of her lyff yff she kepe the housys in laufull reparacion of wood, thak and wall. And for fawtte of reparacions to be seasyd to the proffyt of my sun Richerde, and for defawtte of hym, to remayn to my sun John be the mynde of my brother Richerde or hys executors. The resydue of my goodes not bequethyd, thys my will fulfyllyd, I will thay be devydyd emong my wyff and my chylder be the mynde of my brother Richerde and Agnes my wyff, who I make my executors. Thes beyng wytnes; Sir Robert Lodyngton, parson of Barnolby, George Butler, Alanne Theker, with other mo.

        Proved before P at Grimsby, 15 October 1533. Adm. granted to the executrix, Richard, the co-executor, having died in the meantime.

222.   ELIZABETH DYKES [OF THORNTON BY HORNCASTLE]
        [LCC 1532–34, fos. 171r–172r]

8 May 1533. I, Elizabeth Dykes of Thorneton nexte Horncastle, makes my last will. Fyrste I bequethe my soule to God allmyghtty, to Our Lady St. Mary, and to all the saintes in heven, and my body to be buryed within the paryshe churche of Saynt Wylfryde of Thorneton aforesaid. To Our Lady warke of Lincoln viij*d*. To the high altare of Our Lady of Lincoln iiij*d*. To the high altare off Thorneton xij*d*. To the churche of Thorneton xij*d*. To Robert Dykes my sun the coppyholde that William Sawstrope wonnys in and the coppyholde that John Wylson wonnys in, also iiij oxen. To John Lincoln my sun-in-lawe a cople oxen. I will that Robert Dykes my [fo. 171v] sun have the chose of the best cople. I will that John Lincoln have the nexte best cople of oxen. To Robert Dykes my sun my best mare. To Thomas Richerdson one mare. To William Richerdson one mare. To Agnes Dykes, my sonny's wyff, my beste harnest gyrdell. I will that aftyr the decesse of the forsayd Agnes, that John Dykes, her sonne, have the sayd gyrdell, and aftyr the decesse of John Dykes I will that Elizabeth Dykes, hys syster, have the forsayd gyrdell. To Thomas Warthe the yonger, one pare of beades off vevery[97] with one ryng of sylver that is at the same beades. And aftyr the decesse of the forsayd Thomas Warthe I will that Emote Lincoln have the same beades with the ryng. To Thomas Warthe my beste matteres, a pare of lyn schetes, a coverlyd and a pillo, xx*s* that hys fader owys me, a brasyn morter and a cownter. To Emote Lincoln a red chyste that

---

[96] 'I, Robert Weste of Barnoldby, whole of mind and of perfect memory, make my testament. First, I bequeath my soul to God the father almighty, to the most Blessed Mary and to all the saints of heaven, and my body to be buried in the churchyard of St. Helen in Barnoldby, and for my mortuary as the law requires. I bequeath to the high altar in the church of Barnoldby, for tithes forgotten, 20d, and to the fabric of the same church 3s 4d. I bequeath to the high altar of our mother church of Lincoln 8d, and to the fabric of the same 8d.'

[97] Ivory.

standes in the chamber, my fether bed, a brasen morter. I will that every servaunte that I have at the howre of my dethe have one schepe or xij*d* in money. To Allys Hall, the wyffe of Thomas Hall, one of my gownys and a kyrtylclothe as my executors thynke best. I will that my executors cause a trentall to be done for my soule and all Crysten soulys. To my syster Jenet Broddyng a quarter malte. To Stephyn Woodall halffe a quarter malte. To John Woodall halffe a seame malte. To Emote Lincoln a pare of beades of red corall. To Jamys Baxster ij yowes and ij lammys. To Agnes Wenter ij yowes and ij lammys. To Elizabeth Wenter one schepe. To Jane Parys an arke in the chamber, a chyste in the parler, one cowe, iiij yowes and iiij lammys, a brasse potte, one kettyll, vj puter platters and a hole bedde. I will that every godbarne that I have, shall have ij*d*. The resydue of all my goodes not gyffyn nor bequethyd, I will that they be devydyd betwene Robert Dykes my sun and the iiij chylder of Helene Lincoln my doughter, at the mynde of Robert Palfreyman and Sir Andro Wade, whome I make my executors, and they to have for ther labors, ether of them, vj*s* viij*d*. And I will that Master John Ryge [fo. 172r] be supervisor, and he to have for hys labor x*s*. Thes wytnesses; John Pape of Thorneton, William Coxson, John Somarby and other mo.

Proved before P at Baumber, 17 July 1533.

223. THOMAS ATKYNSON [OF BARROW UPON HUMBER]
[LCC 1532–34, fo. 195]

9 May 1533. I, Thomas Atkynson of Barrowe, of a hole mynde and full of memory, makes thys my will and testament. [fo. 195v] Fyrste I gyff and bequethe my soule to allmyghtty God, to Our Blessyd Lady St. Mary, and to all the cumpeny of heven. My body to be buryed in the churche of Our Lady in Barrowe aforesayd. To the high altare in the sayd churche of Barrowe for forgetfull tithys iij*s* iiij*d*. To Our Lady of Lincoln iij*s* iiij*d*. To Barrowe churche vj*s* viij*d*. To Thorneton churche iij*s* iiij*d*. To Feryby churche iij*s* iiij*d*. For a trentall x*s*. To Henry Atkinson my brother vj*l* xiij*s* iiij*d*, also all my apparyll belongyng to my backe. To John Greynehoyde iij*l* vj*s* viij*d*. To Thomas Towle vj*s* viij*d*. To Margaret Towlle vj*s* viij*d*. The resydue of my good not bequethyd, I gyff to Thomas Towlle, John Greynhode and Henry Atkynson my brother, to dispose as they thynke best for the welthe of my soule. Hiis testibus; Robert Halle, Robert Neyle, cum aliis.

Proved before P at Caistor, 14 October 1533.

224. ROGER ROBYNSON [OF SWINESHEAD]
[LCC 1532–34, fos. 334v–335r]

9 May 1533. I, Roger Robynson, otherwyse callyd Maltmaker, abydyng within the abbay of Swynneshed, of a hole mynd and good memory beyng, make my testament and last will. Fyrste I commytte and bequethe my soule to allmyghtty God, and my body to be buryd within the conventuall churche of the monastery of Our Blessyd Lady St. Mary of Swynneshed, ny to the grave of Agnes my wyff. To Our Lady warkes of Lincoln ij*s*. To the pupill and orphans in the house of [fo. 335r] St. Catheryn nygh Lincoln xij*d*. To the iiij prior[98] to ther conventes of the iiij orders of

---

[98] The page is damaged here.

frerys in Boston xxvj*s* v[99] equally betwene them to be devydyd by evyn porcions. I will that my lorde abbot of Swynneshed have iij*s* iiij*d* for to execute all the observances and services to be done by hym in my burying. I will that every monke in the sayd monastery shall have at my buryall day, at my vij[th] day and at my xxx[ty] day, for syngyng of placebo, dirige and messes, for every of the sayd iij dayes every monke to have iiij*d*. I will that my executors or ther assygnes shall pay wekely duryng the terme of one hole yere nexte aftyr my decesse vij*d* to on of the sayd convent, to syng messe of Jhesu dayly at that altare in the sayd churche where as it hathe bene usyd afore tyme, so that the sayd convent shall syng the sayd messe of Jhesu in order, one aftyr another, as they shall be furthe of ther table and not chargeyd to any other messys. I will that Jenet my wyff have my pasture whiche [I] holdyth of Master Bolles of Quadryng by the rent of iiij*d* yerely, to her, her heyres and assignes. Also I will that all my landes and tenementes in Quadryng Edyke, with ther appurtenances, whiche I holde by copy of the abbot and convent of Peterborow, be solde by myn executors to the fulfyllyng of thys my last will. And also halff an acre of lande lying in Quadryng Edyke, holdyn of Master Thomas Hollande, to be solde be myn executors to the fulfyllyng of thys my last will. And I will that my sayd wyff have my tenement in the north ende of Swynneshed wythe th'appurtenances to her, her heyres and assignes, duryng the hole terme specifyed in my evydences therof to be mayd. I will that my sayd wyff shall have the rentes of all copyholde landes and tenementes in Quadryng Edyke one hole yere nexte aftyr my decesse, to the fulfyllyng of thys my last will. The resydue of all my goodes I gyff to Jenet my wyff, whome, with John Hall of Swynneshed, I make my executors. And I will he shall have for hys labor vj*s* viij*d*, that they pay my dettes and dispose as to the honor of God and the helthe of my soule to theym shall be sene to theym expedyent. Thes wytnesses; Thomas Baxster, William Frerneyffe, Stephyn Robynson off Swynneshed, with other mo. Dated the day and yere afore wryttyn.

Proved before P at Lincoln, 24 October 1534.

225.   THOMAS BROWNE [OF BARTON UPON HUMBER]
       [LCC 1532–34, fo. 110]

11 May 1533. I, Thomas Browne of Barton upon Humber, yonger, hole of mynde and full in memory, makyth thys my last will. Firste I bequethe my soule to allmyghtty God, Our Blessyd Lady St. Mary, and to all the saintes in heven. My body to be buryed in St. Peter churche in Barton. To the high altare in the sayd churche for forgottyn tithes viij*d*. To Our Lady of Lincoln vj*d*. To Our Lady warkes off Lincoln vj*d*. To the reparacion of the sayd St. Peter churche vj*s* viij*d*. To the reparacion of St. Mary churche in Barton one quarter barly. To George Browne my brother, my gowne or my best cote. I will that my wyff and my chyldren have all my goodes under thys forme, that is to say, my wyff to have one parte and my chyldren another parte, and the thyrde parte, my funerall expenses, dettes and thys my will dischargeyd, I will that my wyff have it to bryng up my chyldren to they cum at laufull age. And yff eny of the sayd chylder departe wythin laufull age, then I will that that parte be devydyd to them that lyffyth and so from one to another. I orden my father Thomas Browne my trewe and full executor, to se thys my last will

[99] The page is damaged here.

fulfyllyd to the use of my wyff and my chyldren, and he to have for hys labor vj*s* viij*d*, and expenses. Thes to wytnes; John Wellys. John Browne [fo. 110v] of Barton, prestes, Henry Rocclyff, Thomas Bossall, Jamys Bawdwyn, Thomas Blithe and Richerd Webster of the same, with other mo.

Proved before P at Lincoln, 19 September 1533.

226.   RICHARD MURRE [OF KIRTON IN HOLLAND]
        [LCC 1532–34, fos. 185r–186v]

11 May 1533. I, Richerde Murre of Kyrton in Holande, of hole mynde and perfyte remembraunce, makes my testament concludyng with my last will. Fyrste I gyff and bequethe my soule to God allmyghtty, Our Lady St. Mary and to the celestiall cumpeny of heven, and my body to be buryed in the churcheyerde of the blessyd appostellys Peter and Paule of Kyrton. And for my mortuary aftyr the statutes of our soverayn lorde the kyng. To the high altare of Kyrton for negligent tithys vj*d*. To every altare in the sayd churche ij*d*. To the reparacion of the sayd churche x*s*. To Our Lady of Lincoln vj*d*, and to the orphans of St. Catheryn's ij*d*. To Elizabethe my wyff the mansion with iiij acres pastur therto annexyd and iiij acres pastur liyng insyde crofftes, the whiche mansion and pastur I purchesyd of John Parlebeyn, and iij acres pastur callyd Edyke Grene, that I bought of John Saunderson, and iij acres land arable lying in Hantofftes and iij acres land arable lying at Golde Hylles that was purchesyd of the sayd John Saunderson, duryng her naturall lyff yff the sayd my wyff kepe her sole and unmaryd. And yff so fortune that the sayd my wyff do mary, that then I will the above namyd mansion wyth the sayd landes remayn to [fo. 185v] Thomas Murre my sun in fee symple, so that the sayd Thomas my sun pay, or cause to be payd, to the sayd Elizabethe my wyff yerely duryng her naturall lyffe for an annuyte xxxvj*s* viij*d*. To Thomas my sun my house whiche I dwell in wyth ij acres grounde, by estimacion, therto annexyd, and ij acres and a half lande arable lying in Kyrton ynges that I bought of Richerde Cony, and one acre pastur lying in Kyrton that I purchesyd off Roger, lorde of Frampton, and one acre lande arable lying in a felde callyd Gosman home, and ij acres and a half pasture lying in a felde callyd Tathy's, and a mansyon with one acre grounde therto annexyd callyd Robynsun house in the Le Edyke, in fee symple, also one acre lande lying in Cramer Dale in the sowth fenlandes aftyr the decesse of my wyff in fe symple with all the forsayd landes and tenementes as before rehersyd. And over I will that yff the sayd Thomas my sun departe thys worlde before the age of xx^ty yeres, that then I will all the forsayd landes and tenementes remayn to Agnes my doughter and to her heyres of her body laufully begottyn, so that the sayd my doughter do pay, or cause to be payd, to the sayd Elizabethe my wyff yerely duryng her naturall lyff vj*s* viij*d* over and above the sayd annuite off xxxvj*s* viij*d*, yff the sayd my wyff do mary as is above specifyed. And yff the sayd my wyff kepe her sole and unmaryed, that then she to have all the sayd landes and tenementes as is above namyd duryng her naturall lyff. And yff so fortune that the sayd Agnes my doughter departe withowt heyres of her body laufully begottyn, that then I will all the sayd landes and tenementes, aftyr the decesse off Elizabethe my wyff, remayn to my foeffys, and the sayd my feoffys to fynde an honest preste in the churche off Kyrton for the terme of xx^ty yeres, to pray for my soule, my wyffe's soule, my father and my mother soulys, and all my frendes' soulys. And aftyr the sayd terme of xx^ty yeres, that then all the sayd landes and

tenementes to be solde by the sayd my feoffes, the churchwardens for the tyme beyng, and iiij honest men of the sayd towne of Kyrton, and the money therof so receyvyd to be disposyd in charytable usys in the churche of Kyrton. I will that my executors delyver, or cause to be delyveryd, immediatly aftyr my decesse, to Agnes my doughter, xx*l*, [fo. 186r] one fether bed, ij matteresses, one coveryng, the price vj*s* viij*d*, and iij coverlyds, the price every pece iij*s*, vj pare of flaxen schetes and ij pare of hardyn, one tester of whyte clothe of ix yerdes, iij bolsters and viij pilloys, iiij brasse pottes, one gret panne, the price vij*s*, another panne, the price iiij*s* iiij*d*, one kettyll, the price ij*s* iiij*d*, and a panne, the price ij*s*, too candylstykes, the price v*s*, and other ij, the price iij*s* iiij*d*, and the fyfte, the price xij*d*, halffe a garnyshe of puter of the best makyng and one basyn, and a laver that was my grandam's, iij salte sellers, vj towellys, iiij borde clothes and one maser, vj mylke kye, iiij too yere oldes at Michelmes nexte aftyr my decesse, ij yong gray mares, xx^ty ewes and ther lammys belongyng to the sayd xx^ty ewes, the which was wyth John Smith. I will that my feoffes delyver a laufull estate immediatly aftyr my decesse of and in a certen house standyng in Ryngall Gayte to Robert Hunnyngham of Kyrton, the which house I have solde to the sayd Robert Hunnyngham for the somme of xij*l*. I will that Dorothe Thomson have, at the day of her maryage, iij mylke kye, one yong blak mare with a sterre in her hede, one matteres, one pare of flaxen schetes and one pare of hardyn, ij pilloys, a bolster, one coverlyd, the price iiij*s* iiij*d*, and one of our own coverlydes, ij brasse pottes, one panne, the price iij*s* iiij*d*, halffe a dosyn pecys of puter, iij candylstykes and iij*l* money of the payment of an house, the whiche is solde to the above namyd Robert Hunnyngam, the whiche shall be the secunde payment. And yff the sayd Dorothe do mary before the secund payment, that then I will she have the fyrste payment. To Thomas my sun my shodde carte, my best furryd gowne and one sygnet of sylver. To my wyff my bare carte and my plough and ther geres therto longyng, vj sylver spones duryng her lyff. And yff she mary, that then I will the spones remayn to Thomas my sun, and I will the sayd Thomas my sun have the sayd vj spones of sylver yff the sayd my wyff kepe her sole, notwithstandyng, aftyr her decesse. I will that Elizabethe my wyff and Thomas my sun have viij mylke kye evenly betwyxte them to be devydyd, and vj horsse and mares, that is to say, Byarde,[100] Claymonde, Broke and the blake mare that was stolne, the amblyng mare that is at John Smythe's, the amblyng [fo. 186v] geldyng and the scolde geldyng, evenly betwyxte them to be devydyd at ther wyll and plesure. To Richerd Smyth my best cote, and to every one of my godchyldren iiij*d*. The resydue of my goodes not wyt nor bequethyd, my dettes payd and funerall expenses, I gyff them unto Elizabethe my wyff and Thomas my sun, whome I constitute to be my true executors to dispose my goodes to the moste plesure of God and helthe of my soule. I make Mr. Anthony Erby, Thomas Cony the elder, Richerde Smyth and William Man supervisors, and I will the sayd Mr. Anthony have for hys labor xvj*s*, and every one of the reste to have ij*s* iiij*d*. Thes beyng wytnes; Sir Thomas Este, Richerde Cony, Humfray Heylande, wyth other.

Proved before P at Kirton in Holland, 6 August 1533.

---

[100] A popular name for horses, associated with the cart-horse Byard whose feat of courage gave the name to Byard's Leap.

227. THOMAS BROWNE [OF BURGH LE MARSH]
[LCC 1532–34, fos. 196v–197r]

12 May 1533. I, Thomas Browne of Burgh, makes my will and testament. Fyrste I bequethe my soule to the mercy of allmyghtty God, Our Lady St. Mary and to all the saintes in heven, and my body to be buryed in the churcheyerde of St. Peter in Burgh. To the high altare for tithes forgottyn xij*d*. To the churche warke xvj*d*. To Our Lady of Lincoln ij*d*, and to her warke iiij*d*. To St. Anne ij*d*. To Our Lady of Walsyngham ij*d*. To the good roode of Boston ij*d*. To St. Roke ij*d*.[101] To Robert Browne my brother my red meyr and my house that I wonne in, of condicion that yff he gyff to Jenet Parenell xl*s*, and to Thomas Horsbe and hys wyff xx*s*, and John Coke of Orby vj*s* viij*d*, and to do for my soule at my buryall day xiij*s* iiij*d*. And yff it please God that Robert Browne my brother dy withowt heyres laufully begottyn of hys body, then I will my house go to Thomas Horsbe and hys wyff, and to hys chylder laufully begottyn of hys body, of thys condicion, that Thomas Horsbe gyff and cause to be gyffyn to Robert Browne executors or hys assigners iiij*l* or ellys not, it to be ellys at the will of the executors and assigners of Robert Browne. To Thomas Horsbe a cowe. To my syster Agnes Horsbe the bed that I ly in and all my mother rayment unbequeste and iiij yowes. To Christofer Horsbe ij yowes and a brasse panne. To William Horsbe ij yowes. To Thomas Horsbe ij yowes. To Nicholes Browne iij yowes. To Jenet Parenyll xxxiij*s* iiij*d*, and thys to be rasyd off my moveable goodes, and she to have in the hole valure iij*l* xiij*s* iiij*d*, my best brasse potte and the bed as [fo. 197r] it standes in the chamber. And I will that it be delyveryd to Betterys Clerke to the tyme she be maryed, and yff she dy before she mary, then I gyff of that same xx*s* to Beatrix Clerke, that she may dispose all the resydue for the helthe of all our soulys, be the councell of my executors or ellys ij other honest men. To Beatrix Clerke my gray meyr for that I awe to her. To Robert Browne the other bed. I will that all that longes to the shoppe be solde and done for my father and mother and me, with all our frendes, and a trentall to be done for us besyde. To Agnes Kytchyn ij yowes and ij lammys. To William Chapman a yowe. To Jenet Bukyt a yowe. To Maryan Bryg a yow and a lambe. To Thomas Mathe a yow and a lamme. To Sir John Pechyll a yowe and a lamme. To Christofer Mawnus a lamme. To Robert Robynson a yowe and a lamme. To Jenet Mathe a hog. To John Tewyn a yowe. To every one that berys me to the churche a lamme. The resydue of all my goodes not gyffyn I will that Robert Browne and Thomas Horsbe dispose it for the well of my soule and all Christen soulys, whome I make my trewe executors. Wytnes to the same; Sir John Pechell, Robert Robynson, Thomas Mathe, William Basse, John Barber, with other mo.

Proved before P at Lincoln, 17 October 1533.

---

[101] St. Roch (c.1350–c.1380): according to legend a hermit who was fed by a dog while suffering from plague, whereupon he performed several miraculous cures upon other plague-sufferers. Often depicted in England as a pilgrim with a sore on his leg, accompanied by a dog with a loaf of bread in its mouth: Duffy, *Stripping of the Altars*, 167, 171–2.

228.   WILLIAM WYLSON [OF LINCOLN, ST. BENEDICT'S]
         [LCC 1532–34, fos. 172v–173r]

12 May 1533. I, William Wylson, in hole and perfyte mynde and remembraunce, thankes be to allmyghtty Ihesus, gevys and makes my testament and last will. Fyrste I gyff and bequethe my soule to God allmyghtty and to Our Blessyd Lady St. Mary and to all the holly cumpeny in heven, and my body to be buryd within the churche of St. Bennette's. To the high altare of the same churche for tithes forgottyn vs. To Our Lady warke in the cathedrall churche of Our Blyssyd Lady of Lincoln xxd. To the churche off St. Bennytte's for my buryall vjs viijd. To the high altare of Fyskerton viijd. To the high altare of Chery Willyngham viijd. To the high altare of Whassyngburgh viijd. To the fysher gylde xijd. To the clerkes' gylde xijd. To Our Lady gylde of Sayntt Bennytte's xijd. To the gret gylde xijd. To my godsun William Sergeaunt xld. To Orman Hyll xld. To Robert Wylson my sun all my harnes. To hys sun William, my cowe. The resydue of my goodes not gyffyn nor bequethyd I gyff to Elizabethe my wyffe, thys my will performyd and my dettes payd, she to have them to fynde her duryng her lyffe. And aftyr her decesse the remanent therof to remayn to my ij sonnys Sir Thomas Wylson and Robert Wylson, the whiche ij sonnys I make my executors of thys my last will and testament. And they to dispose parte therof for my soule and my sayd wyffe's soule and all Christen soulys, at suche tyme as they shall thynke moste convenyent. Thes [fo. 173r] beyng wytnes; Syr John Shakylton, Sir Thomas Frere, William Burton, William Southe and many other.

         Proved before P at Lincoln, 18 July 1533. Adm. granted to the executor.

229.   NICHOLAS WYMBYSHE [OF BLANKNEY]
         [LCC 1532–34, fos. 174v–176v]

12 May 1533. I, Nicholes Wymbyshe of Blankeney, gentilman, seke in body and hole in mynde and of good and stedfaste remembraunce, doys mak and ordyn thys my laste testament and will. Fyrste I bequethe my soule to allmyghtty God and to Hys blessyd mother, Our Lady St. Mary and to all the holy cumpeny in heven, and my body to be buryed within the chapell of Our Blessyd Lady within the churche of Blankeney aforesaid. To the high altare of Blankeney churche for tithys and oblacions negligently forgottyn in dischargeyng of my conscience xijd. To Our Lady of Lincoln a ryng of golde with ij stonys in yt. And yff so that my executores or any of my chylder demande to have the forsayd ryng, then I will they to have it compoundyng reasonable therfore, and not then to remayn to the use of Our Lady. I bequethe my sygnet to Our Lady warke aftyr the same forme and maner. I bequethe for the fyndyng of a preste for to syng by the space of x yeres within the paryshe churche of Lyttyll St. Peter's in Lincoln, for [fo. 175r] the soulys of my frendes whiche I am bounde and stonde chargeable to fynde duryng the same terme of x yeres, for every yere iiijl xiiijs viijd, and the forsayd preste to stande wyth wyne, wax and all other charges at hys owne coste. Also my mynde and will is that the nombre of xl or iiij skore schepe of myne shal be put in a stok for to ryn and yerely for to growe, and the incresse of them for to bere and pay yerely the sayd somme of iiijl xiiijs viijd for the fyndyng of the sayd preste duryng all the sayd terme by the provicion of my executors. And yff the sayd stoke decay, then I will it be restoryd and incressyd of my hole goodes moveable and unmoveable. As towchyng the disposicion of my landes and tenementes beyng in feoffys handes, I will that

Margaret my wyff shall peassably have and injoy, for terme of her naturall lyff, my chefe place or messuage in Blankney with all the appurtenance therto apperteyning or belongyng, wyth all my other tenementes, cotages, toftes, croftes, landes, pastures, fen grounde with ther commens and all other appurtenance in Blankney aforesayd, accordyng to the effecte of the dede of feoffment theroff mayd for the performance of thys my last will, which dede of feoffement beres date at Blankeney the secunde day of the monyth of July, in the xiij yere of the reyng of our soverayn lorde, Kynge Henry the Eight. In whiche dede Sir Christofer Wylloughby, Sir Thomas Boroughe, Sir Robert Tyrwhyt, knyghtes, Gylbert Taylboys, esqwyer, with diverse other feoffes stande and be feoffyd of trust to the use aforesayd, as more playnly apperys by my sayd dede of feoffement remanyng in the kepyng of my sayd wyff. And my will performyd and accomplyshed, then I will that aftyr the decesse of my sayd wyffe, that my sun Ryse Wymbyshe shall have and injoy my sayd chefe place or mese with all the appurtenance, with all other tenementes, cotages, curtilages, landes, medoys, lees, pastures, fen grounde and commyns therto belongyng in Blankeney aforesayd, to have and to holde to hym and to hys heyres males of hys body laufully begottyn. And yff it happyn my sayd sonne Ryse for to decesse withowt heyres males of hys body laufully begottyn, then I will that my sun Nicholes Wymbyshe have and injoy the sayd chefe place or messe, with all the appurtenances and allso other premisses, to hym and hys heyres males in maner and forme afore rehersyd. And for lake of suche issue of hys body laufully [fo. 175v] begottyn, then I will that all the premisses shall remayn to Edwarde Wymbyshe my sonne and to hys heyres males laufully begottyn [remainder to] my sun Oswalde Wymbyshe and to hys heyres males of hys body laufully begottyn [remainder to] the use and behoyff of my sonne Anthony Wymbyshe and to hys heyres males of hys body laufully begottyn [remainder to] my sun Christofer Wymbyshe and to hys heyres males of hys body laufully begottyn. And for lacke of suche issue males, I will my sayd cheffe place or messuage and singler the appurtenances with all other the premisses shall remayn to my ij doughters, that is to say Margaret Wymbyshe and Anne Wymbyshe, to have and to holde to them and ther heyres or assygnes for evermore. Also yff so be that my sayd wyff Margaret aftyr my dethe beyng right wake and feble as she now is, be not myndyd for to occupy and dwell uppon my sayd cheffe messe and for to occupy it for herselffe, then yff she be myndyd for to let it to ferme, then my wyll is that she shall let it to my sonne Ryse Wymbyshe afore any other man, payng to her suche a rent yerely that our sayd sonne Ryse may have convenient proffyt and gaynes by takyng of the sayd mese in consyderyng hys diligence and payn that he shall take for the proffyt and plesure of hys mother, my welbeluffyd wyff. Also I will that my sonne Nicholes Wymbyshe shall have aftyr my decesse my place or tenement with the appurtenance in the cite of Lincoln set and standyng within the paryshe of Lyttyll St. Peter above the Stanbowe[102] in the sayd cite, sometyme in the holdyng of Richerde Bolton, merchaunt and vyntyner, to have and to holde to hym and to hys heyres or assygnes for evermore. And also I orden and make Margaret my wyff and Ryse my sonne my executors, and I will that they shall bryng me aftyr my dethe honestly to be buryed, done for and to be prayd for and songen for with trentallys and other thynges as

---

[102] The Stonebow in Lincoln in its present form dates from the fifteenth century, and consists of a large central archway surrounded by a three-storey building. The guildhall occupies the main chamber above the arch: N. Pevsner, *The Buildings of England: Lincolnshire* (London, 1964), 148–9.

conveniently may be borne of my moveable goodes, my dettes and also my chyldren bryngyng up, and for ther fyndyng to be consyderyd of the remayns of my sayd goodes that shall [fo. 176r] or may remayn aftyr the charges borne and necessarye to be had, that aftyr so done that then my sayd executors for to rewarde every of my sayd chyldren and to suche of them as shall have moste nede of mariage or to be schortely maryd fyrst to be rewardyd and holpen and comforthe by ther discrecion and conscience. In wytnes wheroff; Mr. Robert Whichcote, Mr. Thomas Dalalande and Ryse Wymbyshe, with other mo and diverse.

Proved before P at Lincoln, 29 July 1533. Adm. granted to the executor.

230.   MARION HUTCHYNSON [OF SWATON]
        [LCC 1532–34, fo. 278]

13 May 1533. I, Marion Hutchynson of the paryshe of Swaton, of good mynde and remembraunce, makes my last will. Fyrste I bequethe my soule to God allmyghtty and to the Gloriose Virgyn St. Mary Hys mother, and to all the holy cumpeny in heven, and my body to be buryd in the churcheyerde of St. Andro the appostyll in Swaton. To the high altare in Swaton xijd. Also towarde the manetenyng of the light afore Our Lady in the north qwere in Swaton churche, a blak cowe. To Our Lady warke in Lincoln xijd. To the pore chyldren of St. Catheryn's in Lincoln iiijd. To every one of my go[d]chyldren iiijd. To Richerde Bowthe my sun my secunde brasse potte and my lyttyll red arke and a matteres and ij pare of schetes, one pare of lyn and another of hardyn, and ij pilloys and iijs iiijd to by hym a coverlet with, and the greater blak cowe and the dunyd mare and ij seame of barly and a seame of pease. To William Bowthe my grettist kettyll and my grettyst coverlet and a pare of schetes, one lyn schete and one hardyn, and a yow and a lamme. To Helene Bowthe my grettyste brasse potte and my secunde coverlet, a yow and a lamme. [fo. 278v] To John Bowthe my thyrde brasse potte and my lyttyll coverlet and a yow and a lamme. To Grace Bowthe my leste brasse potte and the matteres whiche I ly on and a yow and a lamme. To William Tayllor halffe a seame of malte and a gret chyste. To Thomas Wylkynson my wyff [sic] my worste russyt kyrtyll. I will that Robert Bowthe my sun kepe my buryall day and my vij day and my xxxty day. Also I will that he shall kepe, as long as he lyffys, a yerely obbyt for my husbande and me. And the obbyt shall be to the vicare iiijd. Also I will that he shall cause a trentall of messys to be done for me and all Christen soulys in Swaton churche. The resydue of my goode not spokyn off before I gyff it to Robert Bowthe my sun whome I make my executor, that he may dispose it for the helthe of my soule and all Christen soulys as he thynkes best. I make Richerd Carter the supervisor, and I gyff hym for hys labore viijd. Thes men beryng wytnes; Sir Thomas Smalle, vicare, Richerde Carter, John Smyth, with other mo.

Proved before P at Lincoln, 25 May 1534.

231.   THOMAS BARKER [OF EAST KIRKBY]
        [LCC 1532–34, fo. 209r]

14 May 1533. I, Thomas Barker, of hole wyt and mynde, makes my last will. Fyrste I bequethe my soule to allmyghtty God and to Our Lady St. Mary and to all the saintes of heven, and my body to be buryed in the churcheyerde of St. Nicholes of

Est Kyrkbe. To the high altare of Our Lady of Lincoln xij*d*. To St. Nicholes altare of Est Kyrkbe xij*d*. To William Barker my sun, my house in Sybsay for terme of hys lyff and a mare and her fole, and half an acre of benys. To Thomas my sun my sayd house in Sybsay aftyr the dethe of the sayd William my sun, to hym and to hys heyres male. And yff so be that Thomas my sun dye withowt a sun of hys body laufully begottyn, I will that Jenet my doughter have it to her and to her sonne, and for fawte of a sun of her body laufully begottyn, I will that Agnes my doughter have it to her and to her heyres, and to her assygnes for evermore. To Jenet my dowghter a cowe and a calve, and a yowe and a lamme. To Agnes my dowghter a cowe and a calve. The resydue of my goodes not bequethyd, I gyff to Isabell my wyffe, whiche I make my executrix that she may bryng me furthe honestly, and dispose them for the helthe of my soule. Thes wytnes; Sir John Parker, the vicare of Est Kyrkbe and Thomas Cresse, and William Cresse.

Proved before P at Partney, 10 November 1533.

232.   WILLIAM DYCKYNSON [OF BARNOLDBY]
       [LCC 1532-34, fo. 196]

15 May 1533. Ego, William Dyckonson de Barnolby, compos mentis saneque memorie, condo testamentum meum. In primis lego animam meam deo patri omnipotenti, Beate Marie, omnibus sanctis celi, corpusque meum sepeliendum in cimiterio ecclesie Sancte Helene in Barnolby, et pro mortuario ut lex vult. Lego summo altari in ecclesia de Barnolby pro decimis oblitis, dimidium ovis, et alterum dimidium altari Beate Marie in eadem ecclesia. Lego ecclesie matri Lincolniensis my best jaket, halffe to the high altare and the oder halffe to the churche warke.[103] To every one of my systers iij schepe. To Agnes my syster my chyste. To my broder's sun a cople sterys. To Richerde Thomson ij schepe. To Margaret Thomson one yowe and a lamme, and my best ryng. To Elizabeth Cosyn one yowe and a lamme. To John Wanman one jaket and one dooblet of worstyd, that he may beyr iiij*d* to St. Savior at Newburgh for my oblacion. To my brother doughter my housholde stuff. To Peter Overton [fo. 196v] one schepe. To St. Margaret at Kettysby one sylver ryng and iiij*d*. To John Stevynson one schepe. The reste of my goodes I gyff to my broder Robert, whiche I make my executor that he may dispose it for the helthe of my soule and hys bothe, by the mynde of Sir Robert Lodyngton parson of Barnolby, whiche I make my supervisor, and he to have my best schepe for hys labor. Hiis testibus; Alan Thomson, John Clatam, John Banbryg, Thomas Dyxson, cum pluribus aliis.

Proved before P at Grimsby, 15 October 1533.

---

[103] 'I, William Dyckonson of Barnoldby, whole of mind and of perfect memory, make my testament. First I bequeath my soul to God the father almighty, to the Blessed Mary and to all the saints of heaven, and my body to be buried in the churchyard of the church of St. Helen in Barnoldby, and for my mortuary as the law requires. I bequeath to the high altar in the church of Barnoldby, for forgotten tithes, half a sheep, and the other half to the altar of the Blessed Mary in the same church. I bequeath to our mother church of Lincoln my best jaket . . . '.

233.   SIR WALTER GYLDYN [VICAR OF SWARBY]
        [LCC 1532–34, fo. 239]

16 May 1533. I, Syr Walter Gyldyn, vicare of Swareby, hole and stedfaste in mynde and of good remembraunce, makes my laste will. Fyrste I bequethe my soule to God allmyghtty and to Hys blessyd mother Our Lady St. Mary, and to all the saintes in heven, and my body to be buryd in the chauncell off All Halloys of Swareby. To Our Lady of Lincoln xxd. To Our Lady of Croston xijd. To the churche of Swareby vjs viijd. To the bellys ijs. To the paryshe churche of Ownesby xijd. To the high altare of Ownesby vjd. To one light before St. Catheryne in the paryshe churche of Swareby vjs. To Margaret Day and her mother one cowe. To Margaret Freman one cowe. I gyff ij yowes and ij lammys to fynde one lampe before the sacrament. To Beatrix Henryson xs. To Isabell Alen iijs iiijd. To one honest preste to syng for me a yere, seven markes. To Swareby churche [fo. 239v] ij torchys. I gyff too kye and xxs to kepe a yerely obbyt for me and for Agnes Porter, to be kepyd the same day that Sir Richerde Thorsby's is kepyd on, and the vicare to have for beade rolle xijd. To St. Dionyse kyrke at Kyrkby Lathorp xxvjs viijd, to kepe an obbyt for me and for my father and mother the nexte day aftyr St. John Day the Baptiste,[104] and the parsons to have for ther beade rolle xijd. To John Gyldyn my house and my lande, yff it may be sparyd, and yff it be solde I will that Mr. John Fayrfax have it for hys money afore any man. To Richerd Gyldyn ij sterys. To Margaret Gyldyn xx^{ty} hogges schepe, a cownter and a fether bed. The resydue of all my goodes unbequethyd I gyff to William Gyldyn, the whiche William Gyldyn, Sir John Gyldyn and Roger Coote I make my executors. And I will Sir John Gyldyn to have for hys labor vijs vjd, and Roger Coote vijs vjd. Thes beyng wytnessys; John Bonys, William Robynson and John Betson, with other mo.
        Proved before P at Lincoln, 13 February 1533/4.

234.   WILLIAM SMYTH [OF LINCOLN, ST. PAUL]
        [LCC 1532–34, fo. 222r]

16 May 1533. I, William Smyth, with hole mynde, makes my will. Fyrste I gyff my soule to God allmyghtty. My body to be buryd in the churche of St. Paule in the yle before Our Lady. To the reparacion of the sayd churche viijd. To the high altare in the sayd churche viijd. To Our Lady's warkes viijd. I will have a trentall off messes celebrate, the one halff done the day of my buryall and the other halffe to be done by one honest preste in St. Paule churche. To my curate iijs iiijd. To every house of frerys within Lincoln iiijd. To my sun Adryan a matteres, a coverlyd, a pare schetes and a sylver spone. The resydew of my goodes I put to the rule and discrescion of my wyff Jenet, to order all thyng to the moste plesure of God and my soule helthe, with oversyght and helpe of Mr. Thorpe, whome I make supervisor of thys small will, and I gyff hym for hys attendaunce a pare lyn schetes. Hiis testibus; rectore nostro Ricardo Jakson, Johanne Gray, cum ceteris.
        Proved before P at Lincoln, 9 December 1533.

[104] The Nativity of St. John the Baptist fell on 24 June, his decollation on 29 August.

235.   RICHARD RANDALL [OF TATTERSHALL]
[LCC 1532–34, fo. 203]

17 May 1533. I, Richerde Randall of the paryshe of Tateshale, of a hole and good memory, makes my last will and testament. Fyrste I bequethe my soule unto God allmyghtty, Our Lady St. Mary and unto all the hole cumpeny of heven, and my body to be buryed within the holly churcheyerde of Tateshale paryshe. To Our Lady of Lincoln viij*d.* To Our Lady's warke of Lincoln iiij*d.* To the high altare of Tateshale for forgottyn tithys xij*d.* To the paryshe altare iiij*d.* To the bellys viij*d.* To William Laburne and hys wyffe a cowe. To Elizabeth Randall ij kye, a fether bed, a coverlet, a pare schetes, a bolster and a lyttyll cownter. Also I will that the sayd Elizabeth Randall continue with Jenet my wyff so long tyme as it shall please the satd Jenet to have her. And yff so be the frendes of the sayd Elizabeth will not suffer her to continue with the sayd Jenet, she to have no parcellys of the thynges aforesayd, but aftyr the discrescion of my wyff yff she, off her good mynde, will gyff the sayd Elizabeth anythyng. To Jamys Dune and hys wyff a qwye of ij yeres olde. To Jenet my wyff a toftested in Thorpe with too landes goyng downe to Westcrofte of the same, boundyng of the northe parte of a house of the sayd Richerde Randally's, and of the sowthe parte of a house of the kynge's in the holdyng of Thomas Maysson, and of the weste parte boundyng of a close perteynyng unto the college of Tateshale,[105] and of the este parte boundyng of the hygh kynge's strete. And too landes at Thorpe Folde belongyng unto the same toftested, also a acre off medoy grounde of the sowthe syde of Ferre Close and a dale in Tymberlande Fen, bowndyng of the northe parte of a dale perteynyng unto the prior and convent of Thurgarton, of the sowthe parte of a dale of Robert Redeam, of the weste parte of the ende dige, and of the este parte of the Water of Wytham. I will that the sayd toftested in Thorpe with too landes goyng downe to Westcrofte, the care of medoy grounde and the dale in Tymberlande Fen be solde aftyr the decesse of my wyffe, and a preste to syng at St. Anne chapell in Thorpe one day in the weke on Fryday, for the helthe of my soule and all my good frendes' soulys, and he to have yerely for hys labor and panys vj*s* viij*d*, so long tyme as the money will continewe. I will that Sir John Rokray be the supervisor, to se all thynges aforesayd be performyd for the helthe off my soule, and he to have for hys panys vj*s* viij*d*. The resydue of my goodes not bequethyd [fo. 203v] I gyff unto Jenet my wyff, whome I make my executrix to dispose the sayd resydue of my goodes for the helthe of my soule. Thes wytnes of the premisses; Thomas Abee, William Culyer, John More, William Wodthorpe, Sir Edwarde Flynte, cum ceteris.

Proved before P at Horncastle, 29 October 1533.

236.   MATYLDE NEWMAN [OF KIRTON IN HOLLAND]
[LCC 1532–34, fos. 281r–282r]

20 May 1533. I, Matylde Newman of Kyrkton in Holande, of hole mynde and perfytt memorye, makythe mye testamentt concludynge with mye last wyll. Fyrst I bequethe mye soull to God almyghtye, Ower Ladye Seyntt Marye and to all the celestyall companye of heven, and mye bodye to be beryed in the churcheyerde of

---

[105] Founded in 1439 by Ralph, Lord Cromwell, treasurer of England, the college at Tattershall was dissolved on 4 February 1545: *VCH Lincolnshire*, II, 237.

the holye apostylles Peter and Paull of Kyrkton before sayde, and for mye mortuarye after the kynge's statuttes. To the hye awlter of Kyrkton for tythes neclygentt iiij*d*. To the iij Mares' aulter. To the reparacyon of the sayd churche iiij*d*. To Ower Ladye of Lyncoln ij*d*. To the orphanes of Seyntt Cateryn's ij*d*. To John Newman mye son x schepe. I wyll that myn executores do brynge me forthe to the grownde honestlye at mye beryall daye, the vijth date and the trygyntall daye at theyr own dyscrecyon. [fo. 281v] The resydew of all mye goodes to be devyded in iiij parttes, that is to saye on partt to John Newman mye yongest son, the other iij parttes evenly to be devyded emonges the resydew of all mye chyldern bye equall porcyons. And I wyll that Cecyll, Jenett and Margarett mye dowghters have delyvered theyr porcyons and parttes imme[di]atlye after the probacyon of thys mye last wyll, and over I wyll that Rycharde Henolde, Wylliam Henolde and Robertt Henolde mye sons have theyr parttes at the age of xviij yeres, so that I wyll that myn executores have the custodye and kepynge of the sayd theyr porcyons to the sayd age prenomynate. And yff onye of the sayde Rychard, John, Wylliam and Robertt mye sons departt thys worlde before the sayde age of xviijth yeres, that then the porcyon and partt of hym so departynge to remayn to the resydewe of all mye chyldern that survyves by equall porcyons. I wyll that the sayd executores have the sayd x schepe wythe the iiij partt of the sayde goodes to brynge up the sayde John Newman, and if the sayde John Newman departt before the porcyon and partt of the sayde x schepe and the iiij partt of the sayde goodes be expendyd, that then the rest remaynynge evenlye to be devyded emonges all mye chyldern beynge onlyve. I wyll that myne executores have mye howse that I dwell in to se mye chyldern orderyd, and the sayde howse with the apurtenance to be keptt in suffycyentt repayre unto the sayde Rychard, John, Wylliam and Robertt mye sons be of the age of xxj^{ti} yere, and everye on of theym commynge to the sayde age to entre to his porcyon of the sayde howse with the purtenance in fe symple and bere hys charge after hys porcyon, to the sayde hys bretherne be of the sayde age of xxj^{ti} yere [remainder to the survivors]. To Jenet my doughter. I make Sir Robert Thomson and Sir Richerde Oxman my executors, and ether of them to have xx*d* for ther labors. I make Sir Thomas Est supervisor, and to have for hys labor xx*d*. Thes beyng wytnes; Sir Thomas Est, Thomas Forman, John Tiff, John Laurence, with other.

Proved before P at Swineshead, 8 June 1534.

237.   JOHN PECHILL [OF WEST WILLOUGHBY IN PARISH OF ANCAS-TER]
[LCC 1532–34, fos. 201v–202r]

20 May 1533. I, John Pechyll of West Willobe in the parysche of Ancaster, husbandman, hole of mynde and of good remembraunce, makyth my testament. Fyrste I bequethe my soule to allmyghtty God, to Our Lady St. Mary and to all the saintes in heven, and my body to be buryed in the churcheyerde of St. Martyn of Ancaster. To the high altare of Ancaster viij*d*. To Our Lady's warke at Lincoln xij*d*. To the upholdyng of the churche of Ancaster v*s*. To the churche of Hunyngton xx*d*. To every one of my [fo. 202r] godchyldren a lamme the price of xij*d*. I will that Margaret Pechyll my wyff have my housholde stuff hole to herselffe. To John Pechyll my sonne my house and my lande when he cumys at xviij yere of age. And

yff he dye before the sayd age, then I will that Margaret Pechyll my wyff have hit for her lyffe, and she to upholde it and kepe it in reparacions. Yff she do not, then I will that Robert Pechill my brother have it to hym and hys assygnes. The resydue of my goodes I will and bequethe in thre partes, one parte to myselffe, another to my wyffe, the thurde to my sun. And yff that my sonne dy within the foresayd age, then I will that hys parte shall be done for hym and me and the frendes that it come of, and I make Margaret Pechyll my wyffe and Robert Pechyll my brother my full executors. I make William Pec[h]yll my father the supervisor, and he to have for hys labor a cople of schepe and Robert Pechyll my brother another cople for hys labor. Wytnesses theroff; Sir William Torry, Robert Wryght, Hugh Smyth, Robert Mores, John Sanderson, with other mo, and every one of them to have iiij*d* for ther labors.

Proved before P at Ancaster, 24 October 1533.

238.   JOHN BAWDRE [OF LEAKE]
       [LCC 1532–34, fos. 229v–230r]

22 May 1533. I, John Bawdre of Leeke, in hole mynde and of good remembraunce, makes my testament and last will. Fyrste I bequethe my soule to allmyghtty God, to Hys mother St. Mary, and to all the sainctes beyng in heven. My body to be buryd in the kyrke of Leeke. In the name of my mortuary, as custome requiryth. To the anournament of the high altare in Leeke kyrke iiij*d*. To every other altare in the same kyrk ij*d*. To the anournament of Our Lady ther iiij*d*. To St. Catheryn's withowt Lincoln ij*d*. To Jenet Gregby one qwy. To Thomas Gregby one qwy. To every one of Agnes Fell chylder one lamme. To Agnes Holmys one calve. To John my sun, when he cumys to laufull age, one wayn, one plowe with the geres belongyng to them, ij oxen, ij horsse or mares. To the same John when he cumys to xvj yeres of age ij kye. To Richerd my sun at xvj yeres of age ij oxen, ij kye. I will that Thomas and William my sunys be fun[106] at the scole of my landes be my executors to they cum to xxiiij yeres of age. To the sayd Thomas and William when they cum to xvj yeres of age, oder of them, one cowe. To every one of my chylder a bed, that is to say one matteres, one coverlyd, one pare schetes, one bolster, one pillo when they cum to laufull age. To John my sun iiij acres lande arable, late John Emonson, in fe symple when he cumys to xx^ty yeres of age of thys condicion, that he gyff to every one of hys brether when they cum to laufull age xx*s*. The resydue of my landes I will be devydyd emong my chylder accordyng to the last will of John Bawdre my father. The resydue of my goodes I gyff to Agnes my wyff and Sir Thomas Paynson, whome I make my executors to pay my dettes, my legaces, and to bryng up my chyldren [fo. 230r] and dispose for my soule as they thynke shall be moste plesure to God, with Mr. Thomas Gyldon supervisor, and he to have for hys labor x*s*. Thes wytnes; Sir John Stotte, frere, Thomas Cammok, John Monke.

Proved before P at Lincoln, 24 June 1533. Adm. granted to the executors.

[106] 'Found'.

239.   JOHN LANGTON [OF LANGTON]
       [LCC 1532–34, fos. 233v–234v]

23 May 1533. I, John Langton of Langton in the countie of Lincoln, esqwyer, makyth my laste will and testament. Fyrste I bequethe my soule to the holy trinite, to Our Lady St. Mary and to all the holy cumpeny of heven, and my body to be buryed in the churche of St. Peter in Langton in Our Lady quere by Elizabeth my wyff, gyffyng for my mortuary that the lawe requyryth. To Our Lady warke of Lincoln xiij*s* iiij*d*. To the high altare of Langton vj*s* viij*d*. To the churche of Langton xiij*s* iiij*d*. To the churches of Sawcethorp, Dabby, Sutterby, Aswardeby, to ych on of the sayd churches xij*d*. To iiij orders of frerys in Boston, to ich order ther, xij*d*. To Elizabeth my doughter one hundrythe markes. And yff my sun John Langton will make her sewer of landes and tenementes to the yerely valewe of x markes a yere for terme of her lyffe, then I will that she [fo. 234r] have the sayd hundryth markes. To John Langton my sun and heyr iiij leades, that is to say too boylyng leads, ij brewyng leades and the mashe fatte and the knedyng fattes, ij long spyttes and ij gret cobbardes, a gret brasse potte and a lesse brasse potte, on kyste and a gret bedde in the gret chamber as it standyth with a fether bed and the coveryng of ymagery, a pare of bedstokes with a matteres and a coverlyd, a bolster and a pilloy, also the hangyng of the greate chamber and the hangyng of the hall, with bordes and the formys in the hall. I do gyff to all my sunys' and doughters' chyldren, that is to say the chylder of Alexander Langton, William Langton, Cassander Staynton, Catheryne Packe, Alice Darby, and to iche of ther chylder, sonnys and doughters, vj*s* viij*d*. I will that my feoffes stande in strenkyth and feoffment to the use that they where infeoffyd in. And they to suffer my executors to receyve and take owt of my landes off Salflethavyn and Salfletby, to the performance of thys my last will, xij markys yerely unto fyvety markes be run. And aftyr the sayd fyvety markes be run, then I will that Adelarde Langton have fyve markes a yere owt of the sayd landes, terme of hys lyff. To John Langton a challys and a vestment and all that belonges therto and a altare clothe, and all other my goodes that I have not gyffyn I gyff to William Langton and Jamys Packe for to dispose for the well of my soule, whome I do make my executors, and my brother John Lytylbery, esquyer, I make my supervisor. And I gyff to ich of them for ther labors xx*s*. In wytnes that thys is my laste will I have subscribyd my owne hande to thys presentes.

  Codicillus dicto testamento annexus. Thys is a codycill annexyd to thys will, made at Langton the xiiij day of June in the yere 1533. I will my housholde be kepte as I have usyd it by the space of xxx[ty] yeres aftyr my decesse, and that my servantes be rewardyd aftyr ther [fo. 234v] continuaunce by the discrecion of my executors. Also I will, aftyr my dettes and legaces payd and done, that my preste or another preste syng for me by the space of one hole yere aftyr my decesse, yff my goodes therto will extende. The resydue of my goodes not bequethyd I gyff to William Langton my sun and Elizabeth my doughter over and above ther porcions assygnyd to them by thys my last will. Teste Johanne Lytilbery de Hagworthyngham et Cassand[ra] Arpress, et aliis.

  Proved before P at Alford, 5 February 1533/4.

240. **JOHN HILL [OF PINCHBECK]**
[LCC 1532–34, fos. 183v–184r]

28 May 1533. I, John Hill of Pynchbek the elder, of hole mynde and good remembraunce, make my testament and last will. In the fyrste I bequethe my soule to God allmyghtty, Our Lady St. Mary and all the holy cumpeny in heven, and my body to be buryd wythin the churche of Pynchbek aforesayd. To the high altare ther for tithys and oblacions forgottyn x*s*. To St. Jamys' altare ther ij. [fo. 184r] To every other altare in the sayd churche xij*d*. To the churche warke off Pynchbek xl*s*. To our mother churche of Lincoln ij*s*. To the pore chyldren of St. Catheryn's withowt the walles of Lincoln viij*d*. I will that one honest preste, immediatly aftyr my decesse, celebrate messe at St. Jamys' altare within the forsayd churche of Pynchbek by the space of iiij yeres for my soule, my frendes' soulys and all Christen soules. To Our Lady gylde ther xxvj*s* viij*d*. To every gylde and every light within the sayd churche one pounde wax. To every godchylde that I have within the towne off Pynchbek vj*d*. To Edwarde Tenante one olde noble.[107] To Nicholes Maynerde too burnynges. To Helene Rugewyn one blak ryggyd cowe, one spanyd[108] cowe calve and foure yerdes of blankyt. To John Hill my sun all my landes and tenementes, medoys, fedyng places, pastures and fre rentes, with all and singuler the appurtenances within the towne and feldes of Pynchbek aforesayd or other where, to have to hym and to hys heyres and assygnes for ever. The resydue of all my goodes moveable and dettes not gyffyn nor bequethyd I gyff to the sayd John Hill my sun, whome I orden and make my sole executor, to order and dispose for the helthe of my soule as he shall thynk most necessary and expedyent. Thes beyng wytnes; Syr Thomas Hill, one of the paryshe prestes of Pynchbek, John Chators, William Tydde, John Obrey, Robert Atkynson, Edwarde Tenant and John Wylkynson of the same. The day and yere abovesayd.

Proved before P at Cowbit, 7 August 1533.

241. **JOHN STATUR [OF SKEGNESS]**
[LCC 1532–34, fo. 216r]

30 May 1533. I, John Statur of Skegnes, seke of body and good remembraunce, makes my testament and last will. Fyrste I bequethe my soule to God allmyghty and to Our Lady St. Mary and to all the saintes in heven, and my body to be buryd in the churcheyerde of St. Clement of Skegnes. To the high altare iiij*d*. To Our Lady's warke in Lincoln viij*d*. To ij syde altares in Skegnes churche oder ij*d*. To Agnes Cobbe xx*s*. To my moder viij yowes and ther lammys and a yeryng calve. To Cerston Swanne my godsone a yowe and a lamme. To Agnes Swanne a yowe and a lamme. To Anthony Parron a hogge: and all to be delyveryd with the wolle on. I wolde have ij trentals sayd for my soule and my fader's and all Cristen soulys. To Hugh Statur a pare of hose clothe, and the rest of the clothe I gyff to Robert Swanne. I orden and sette that Nicholes Temper and Hugh Statur shall be my executors, and other of them to have for ther labors v*s*. The reste of my goode, my body honestly brought to the grounde, I gyff them to Robert Swanne chyldren and

---

[107] A gold coin first issued in 1351.
[108] 'Spanged': northern dialect for 'spangled', or 'variegated'. In this context, 'brindled'.

Hugh Statur chyldren. Thes wytnes; Simon Bruster, Henry Henryson and William Sleight, with other.

Proved before P at Partney, 10 November 1533.

242.   ROBERT LANGWITH [OF BRANT BROUGHTON]
       [LCC 1532–34, fo. 110v]

2 June 1533. I, Robert Langwithe of Brant Broughtton, hole of mynde and good of remembraunce, makes my last will and testament. Fyrste I bequethe my soule to God allmyghtty and to Our Lady St. Mary, and to all the holly cumpeny of heven, and my body to be buryed in my paryshe churche of St. Helene of Brant Broughton, and also for my mortuary as the lawe doythe require. To the hygh altare for my forgottyn tithes xxd. To Our Lady's warkes at Lincoln xxd. To Bekyngham churche iijs iiijd. To Thorpe chapell iijs iiijd. To Carleton churche iijs iiijd. To Robert Langwith one mare and one brasse potte. To Thomas Langwyth one mare and one brasse potte. To Jane Langwyth one brasse potte and all my puter vessell, one arke, one pare of jeate beades. To John Langwyth my sun ij mares and one cowe whiche Richerd Hoslyng hathe in kepyng, and one dosyn sylver sponys for terme of hys lyff. And aftyr, they to be devydyd to hys iij sonnys William, Robert and Thomas. And yff it fortune any of them to dy withowttyn issue, that parte to be devydyd to the other ij brether. I make my executor John Langwyth my sun, for to order and dispose all my goodes as he thynkes best to be done for my soule helthe, and all my good frendes. Wytnes heroff; Sir Thomas Hyrde, Sir Robert Lewty and William Yong, with other mo.

Proved before P at Lincoln, 26 September 1533.

243.   ROBERT UMFRAY [OF FULNEY IN PARISH OF SPALDING]
       [LCC 1532–34, fo. 182]

4 June 1533. The yere and reigne of Kyng Henry the viij[th], xxv[ty]. I, Robert Vumfray of Fulnay in the paryshe of Spaldyng, beyng of good and hole mynde and stedfastly belevyng in all the articles of the fayth, thus makyng my testament and last will. Fyrste I gyff my soule to God and my body to be buryd in the parysche kyrkeyerde of Our Lady and St. Nicholes in Spaldyng. To the high altare in the sayd kyrk for tithynges forgottyn vjd. To the Trinite gylde xijd. To Our Lady of Lincoln xvjd. To Our Lady warkes viijd. To Helene my doughter my best brasse potte and my best brasse panne. To Robert Umfray that [fo. 182v] was the sun of Richerd Umfray vjs viijd. To Elizabethe Umfray that was the doughter of the sayd Richerde vjs viijd. To John Dawson iijs iiijd. I will that Elizabeth my wyff have my house that I wone in duryng her lyff, and aftyr her decesse I will the sayd house remayn to Helene, my wyff doughter, to her heyres of her body laufully begottyn and brought furthe. And yff it so happen that the sayd Helene dye wythowt issue, then I will the sayd house with the purtenances be solde and the money therof cumyng to be disposyd in prestes syngyng in Spaldyng kyrke and in other charitable warkes, for me and my wyff, and for all my good frendes. The resydue of my goodes, my dettes payd, I put to the disposicion of Elizabethe my wyff whome I orden and make my true executrix with the good helpe of John Toche, and he to have for hys labor iijs iiijd. I will that John Jakes be supervisor of thys my testament and last will, and he to have for hys

labor iiij*s*. Thes wytnes; Sir Thomas Love, curat, Robert Paret, John Gannesby, William Harpelay, Thomas Howyt, with other mo.

Proved before P at Spalding, 7 August 1533.

244. JOHN BLANKE [OF MOULTON]
[LCC 1532–34, fos. 184r–185r]

8 June 1533. I, John Blanke of the parysche of Multon in Hollande, hole of mynde and seke of body, makes thys my testament and last will. Fyrst I bequethe my soule to God almyghtty, Our Lady St. Mary, and to all the cumpeny in heven. My body to be buryd in the churcheyerde of All Halloys in Multon, with my mortuary as the [fo. 184v] lawe will require. To the high altare of Multon for tithys and oblacions forgottyn vj*d*. To the light of Our Lady's gylde of Multon iij*d*. To the skouse light iiij*d*.[109] To the iij lighttes of Multon churche iij*d*. To the rode light of Multon churche for the terme of xx^ty yeres, every yere iiij*d*. To the makyng of the churche royff of Multon vj*s* viij*d*; iij*s* iiij*d* at the begynyng and iij*s* iiij*d* when it is mayd an ende of. To St. Jamys' chapell of Multon iij*s* iiij*d*. To Our Lady's warke of Lincoln iiij*d*. To the fatherles chylder of St. Catheryn's in Lincoln iiij*d*. Thys is the laste will of me John Blanke, mayd the day and yere above wryttyn. To Isabell Blanke my wyff iiij kye, ij horse, iij schepe and all my housholde stuff. And I will she have a chamber and the mylhouse to her behoyff for the terme of her lyff. I will that Richerd Blanke and Robert Blanke, my sunys, do fynde Isabell Blanke my wyff bred corne and ale corne, and her cattell wynter meat and somer meate for the terme of her lyff. To Richerde Blanke my sun iij meres and a amblyng yeryng, and hys wyff a cowe and hys doughter a burnyng. To Robert Blanke my sun a yong meyr, and hys wyff a cowe and hys doughter a burnyng. To Richerde Blanke, my sun, my hed house with x acres of lande and a halff that long to it, and iiij acres that was sometyme Roger's, to hym and hys heyres for ever. To Robert Blanke my sun my house over the way and xv acres of lande, and iij acres of lande that was sometyme Jhon's, and vj acres of arable lande that is yonde west dyke, to hym and hys heyres for ever. I will that Robert Blanke my sonne have hys gryndyng at my myl for the terme of hys lyff, so that he fynde hys owne horse to grynde withall. I will that the entre that gose to the lande behynde my hed house be fre to bothe my sonnys, and yff any of my sunys do sell ther house [fo. 185r] and lande, then I will that my t'other sonne have it better chepe be iiij nobylls in price then any other man. Also I, the forsayd John Blanke, have surrenderyd all my landes and tenementes holden by copy of courte rowlle into the handes of Robert Nicoll and Robert Gunby to the use and performance of thys my last will. The resydue of all my goodes not gyffyn nor bequethyd, my dettes payd and my legacy fulfyllyd, I will that Richerd Blanke and Robert Blank my sunys have them, whome I do orden and make myn executors, they for to dispose for the helthe of my soule and all Christen soulys as they thynke moste expedyent. I will that Robert Nicoll and Thomas Blanke be my supervisors. The beyng wytnes; Sir Gefferay Haynes, Robert Nicoll, Robert Gunby, with other mo.

Proved before P at Cowbit, 7 August 1533.

---

[109] The precise meaning is obscure, although it is possible that 'skouse' derives from 'scorse' (barter or exchange), in which case the light would represent an association with local trading or market activity.

245.   JOHN ROSE [OF STRUBBY]
        [D&C 1534–59, fo. 24]

9 June 1533. I, John Rose of Strubby, seke in body and hole in mynde, makes my laste will. Firste I bequethe my soule to God allmyghtty, to Our Lady Saynt Mary and to all the holy cumpeny of heven, with my body to be buryed in the churcheyerde of St. Oswolde of Strubby. To the high altare of Strubby xij*d*. To St. Erasmus within Strubby churche xij*d*. To the bellys of Strubby xij*d*. To Our Lady of Lincoln iiij*d*. To Our Lady's warke iiij*d*. To Our Lady of Strubby [fo. 24v] chapell iiij*d*. To Alice my syster a calve. To Richerde my brother and to Alice my syster a gret potte betwene them. Also to Richerde my brother my beste cote, my beste dooblet and a yowe. Also to Alice my syster a yowe. To Henry Watterton a wane body full of woode. To the ij orders of frerys of Grymmesby x*s* to syng a trentall for my brother William soule. To Sir William Clerke xx*d* to say v messys of the v woundes of our lorde for me. The resydue of my goodes I gyve to Alice my doughter, to Robert Merycoke and to Thomas Wryght of Alforde, whome I make myn executers. Also I bequethe to Robert Merycoke and to Thoms Wryght for ther labors, to ever other of theym, iij*s* iiij*d*. Thes beyng wytnes; Sir Charlys Thorneton, Richerde Cramer, Thomas Wylde, with other.

> Proved before Mr. George Henage, dean, and the chapter of the cathedral church of Lincoln, 19 June 1535, in the chapter house of the cathedral church of Lincoln. Adm. granted to Robert Merycoke the executor, reserving power to grant to Alice the daughter and Thomas Wryght the co-executors.

246.   JOAN WHASHYNGBURGH [OF WYBERTON]
        [LCC 1532–34, fo. 182r]

10 June 1533. I, Jenet Whassyngburgh of Wyberton, hole of mynde and good remembraunce beyng, makyth my testament and last will. Fyrste I bequethe my soule to God allmyghtty and to Our Lady Saynt Mary, and to all the holly cumpeny of heven. My body to be buryd in the churche of St. Leogerde of Wyberton with that thyng to my mortuary aftyr the custome of the lawe usyd. To the high altare in Wyberton churche iiij*d*. To Our Lady of Lincoln warkes iiij*d*. To the fatherles chylder withowt the barre at Lincoln iiij*d*. To the churche warkes of Wyberton vj*s* viij*d*. To the bying of an ornament to the churche of Wyberton x*s*. To iiij godchylder, every one of them, a flaxen schete. I will that ther be one trentall done for my soule, my husband soule, my frendes' soulys and all Christen soulys. All other thynges not gyffyn nor bequethyd I gyff and bequethe them to Jenet Whassyngburgh my doughter, whome I orden and make my executrix to dispose my goodes to the plesure of God for the helthe of my soule and my frendes' soulys and all Christen soulys. And Richerd Jolyson to be oversear of thys my last will, and he to have for hys panys and labor iij*s* iiij*d*. Thes beyng wytnesses; Syr Richerd Stevenson, Sir Robert Alger, John Dauson, with other mo.

> Proved before P at Kirton, 6 August 1533.

247. RICHARD TREWE [OF TEALBY]
      [LCC 1532–34, fos. 187v–188v]

15 June 1533. I, Richerde Trewe of Tevelby, hole of mynde and good of remembraunce, makes my last will or testament. Fyrst I bequethe my soule unto allmyghtty God, to Our Lady St. Mary and to all the blessyd cumpeny of heven, and my body to be buryed within the paryshe churche of All Halloys of Tevelby. To the high altare of Tevelby aforesayd for forgottyn tithys iijs iiijd. To Our Lady's warkes of Lincoln xijd. To the churche or bellys of Tevelby vjs viijd. To Clemens my wyffe vijl of money and lxxx schepe, she to have chose, also iiij kyen and all my housholde stuff, halffe of my croppe, bothe corne and hay, and halffe of my hyves and beys, my best horse. Besyde thys all suche dettes and dutys as her sun-in-law Thomas Catur doys owe unto me, that is to say xxvty quarters of barly and iiijl of money and xliijs iiijd that he awys me for v horssys, also vijs that I lent hym and vjs viijd that I payd for meltyng of xxty quarters of barly. Also the iiijs that he awys me for a pare of olde wheles that where yren bounde, also the ten schepe that he hathe of me to the halffe. Moreover I will that she have the house rente fre that I dwell in, unto the feste of Phylip and Jamys the appostellys nexte ensuyng.[110] Also I will that she have fewell and fyrewoode sufficient unto the sayd feste. And she servyd, I gyff unto William Bell all my tymber and sawn borde. To William Bell the other halffe of my croppe, bothe corne and hay, and the other halffe of my hyves and bees, [fo. 188r] xxty schepe and x lammys, my drought, that is to understande myne oxen, horsses, wane and plugh, with all suche instrumentes as to them pertenys, and he to let Clemens my wyff have the wayn and the draught so ofte as she shall have nede betwyxte thys and the feste of Pylip and Jamys the appostellys nexte insuyng. Also the instrumentes of my occupacion, and he for to receyve all these goodes bequethyd as laste parte of mariage goodes. To William Bell and to Margaret hys wyff and to the heyres of there bodys laufully begottyn all my herytage, that is to say, housyng and lande wyth all the appurtenances that therto pertenys and all my copyes clerely to hymselffe, save that Thomas Walshe, otherwyse callyd Thomas Ducheman, shall have ij days and ij nyghttes mylnyng at my walke mylne[111] every weke, and he for to pay for the sayd ij days and ij nyghttes xvs, and the sayd Thomas to stande with no coste nor chargys of reparacion, and he shall entre at the feste of Phelip and Jamys the appostellys nexte ensuyng and continue so long as the tenor of my coppy shall laste. Besyde thys I bequethe to every one of my brother Pape chyldren a lambe. To every one off my brother John True chyldren a lambe. To every one off William Bell chyldren a lambe. To every one of my godchyldren iiijd. To Agnes Walshe my servant vj schepe and vjs viijd of money. To John Suddeby my prentyse ij schepe. The resydue of goodes not bequethyd and gyffyn I betake to the disposicion of Clemens my wyff whome I make my executrix, and she to dispose it aftyr my dettes be payd for the helthe of my soule and all Crysten soulys. I will that my brother John True be the supervisor of thys my present will, and he to have for hys well doyng xxs. Moreover, yff any man to whome I have mayd any legacy or bequethyd eny parte of my goodes in thys my present will do take on hande to besy or troble Clemens my forsayd wyff and executrix for any suche goodes as I have bequethyd her, or demande any parcell more then afore is conteynyd and bequethyd to them, she beyng myndyd to fulfyll

---

[110] 1 May.
[111] A mill operated by a treadmill.

thys my present testament [fo. 188v] or will, I will that the sayd legacy or bequeste so bequethyd stande as voyd and be of none effecte to the vexant, or at the leste I will that it stande in her gentylnes as she will rewarde them. Thes beryng wytnes; Sir Jamys Wallys the vicare, Sir Edwarde Surflyt, Thomas Barde, Robert Barde, Thomas Frere, John Clerke, Wylliam Whasshe, with other mo.

Proved before P at Lincoln, 22 August 1533.

248.   JOHN WADYNGHAM [OF ASWARBY]
         [LCC 1532–34, fos. 204v–205r]

15 June 1533. I, John Wadyngham of Aswarby, makes thys my last will and testament. Fyrste I bequethe my soule to allmyghtty God and to Our Lady St. Mary and to all the gloriose cumpeny off heven, and my body to be buryd in the churcheyerde of St. Helene of Aswarby on the owttesyde of my wyff. I make Thomas my eldeste sonne, John my sun, John Thewe and Thomas Thewe my executors. I will that xxx^{ty} schepe and x lammes be solde on the best for the fulfyllyng of thys my last will. To Thomas my sonne x schepe, a cowe and a potte on the best. To John my sun x schepe and a potte on the worste. I will that Isabell, Mawde and Agnes my doughters have all my inwarde stuffe, and every one of theym to have a cowe, a potte and x schepe, and the eldest of my doughters to chose fyrste the potte. Also I will that every one of them have a burlyng. And yff any of my sayd doughters dye or they cum to the age of xv yeres, that then I will the sayd parte be devydyd to the survivors of them. To William and Robert my suns, ether of them, a cowe, a burlyng, a potte and x schepe, and William to have the best burlyng. To Our Lady of Lincoln viij*d*. To Aswarby churche viij*d*. To the Trinite gylde vj*d*. To the sacrament for forgottyn tithys viij*d*. To the churches of Harryngton viij*d*, Sotby viij*d*, Sawsthorpe iiij*d*, Langton iiij*d*. I will that thre trentallys be done for me and my wyff and all Crysten soulys. To Thomas my eldest sonne my house and land with all the purtenances therto belongyng, lying in Sotterby, the which house, lande and appurtenances I purchesyd of one John Carter, to hym and to hys heyres forever on thys condicion, that the sayd Thomas shall peassable suffer [fo. 205r] John my secunde sonne to injoy my house and lande with th'appurtenance in Soterby, whiche my father purchesyd of William Tayllor off Kele Cotes. I gyff the sayd house and lande with th'appurtenances in Soterby and Langton, that my father purchesyd of William Taylor, unto John my sun and to hys heyres forever. And yff it happen the forsayd Thomas or John my sonnys to dye withowt issue of ther bodyes laufully begottyn, then I will that all the forsayd landes and tenementes with the hole appurtenances remayn to the survivor of theym and to ther heyres for ever. I will that the resydue of my goodes not bequethyd to be devydyd emonges my chyldren by the syght of my executors, and, thys my will fulfyllyd, I will that Robert Crosse have one lamme. I wyll that Isabell my doughter have my wyff best gowne, best kyrtyll and best gyrdell. Thes wytnes; Syr John Howet, Sir Vincent Guy, John Adlarde, Adam Halden, William Halden and Robert Crosse, with other mo. To ether of my ij brethren vj*s* viij*d*.

Proved before P at Horncastle, 29 October 1533.

249.   GILBERT TYLSON [OF PINCHBECK]
        [LCC 1532–34, fos. 192r–193v]

16 June 1533. I, Gylberde Tylson of Pynchbek, with good mynde and hole
remembraunce makes my last will and testament. Fyrst I bequethe my soule to
God allmyghtty and to Hys mother, Our Lady St. Mary, and to all the saintes in
heven. My body to be buryd in the [fo. 192v] churcheyerde of Our Lady in
Pynchbek. To the high altare within the churche of Pynchbek xij*d*. To every altare
within the sayd churche iiij*d*. To the churche warkes of Pynchbek xx*d*. To Our
Lady of Lincoln for oblacion ij*d*. To the pore chyldren in St. Catheryn's at
Lincoln ij*d*. To Alyson my doughter my best chyste. To Elizabeth my doughter
my nexte beste chyste. I will that Alyson and Elizabeth my doughters do shyfte
equally betwyxte them the stuffe that is within the best chyste. To Alyson my
doughter my best matres. To Elizabethe my doughter my nexte beste matteres, ij
coverlydes, one of the best and another of the worste. To Alyson my doughter the
other ij colverlydes, one of my beste brasse pottes and another of the worste of the
iiij pottes. To Elizabethe my doughter the other ij pottes. To Alison my doughter
v pecys of puter and my best bulyone panne and ij candylstykes, and my payntyd
tester with the hangynges longyng to it, my best fether bed with the bolster
longyng to hit, a panne and a basyn and ij lavers and a yelowe table, and a forme
and a salte seller and my best chaffyng dyshe, and a bushyll of lynen sawyn, and
my presse and my gyrdell and a pare of beydes with the jewellys beyng by them,
and ij of my best kye that she will take standyng in a stalle. To Elizabethe my
doughter v pecys of puter and my nexte best bulyone panne and a lattyn panne
and a basyn, and ij lavers and ij candylstykes, and my whyte tester with the
hangynges longyng to it, and my secunde fether bed wythe the bolster longyng to
hit and a salte seller, and my secunde chaffyng dyshe and the secunde gyrdyll, and
a red rugyt cowe. To John my sonne the yonger v pecys of puter and ij pannys,
and my best laver and the grettyst basyn, and an arke that was hys mother's and a
brasse potte that was hys moder's, and a foldyn table and a thrawn chare, and a
forme and my lyttyll fyshyng bote which I will that he have immediatly aftyr my
decesse, also a yeryng fylly and a red amblyng mare. To the same John the house
that Edmund Tyngyll dwellys in, in fe symple, with the purtenances longyng to it,
a red dowyffyd cowe that shotte her calve. And I will that the sayd John my sonne
the yonger shalle receyve [fo. 193r] hys bequestes at the age of xviij yere, and I will
that Thomas my sonne shall have John my sonne the yonger in governaunce and
all hys bequestes, unto the sayd John my sonne cum to the age of xviij yeres. To
the sayd John my sonne ij candylstykes. To Agnes Tyngyll my doughter my
thurde materes and ij pannys. To Roger my sonne my grettest panne of brasse, my
carte with the gerys longyng to it and my plough with the geres longyng to hit
with iij marys, my for mare and my pyn mare, and a yong mare with a fether
snowte. To the sayd Roger my house in Fengate that was William Frauncys' with
the purtenances longyng to hit in fe symple. I will that Thomas my sonne and
Roger my sonne have togeder conjunctely the ferme that I toke off the abbot of
Burne by indenture. I will that Thomas my sonne have the one halffe of the sayd
ferme and Roger the other halffe of the sayd ferme. I will that Thomas my sonne
have the indenture in kepyng. I will that yff so be that Roger will not pay dewly
hys renttes for the sayd ferme, for lak of payment I will that Thomas my sonne
shall have the hole ferme to hymselffe. I will that Thomas my sonne shall have hys

entre and passage with hys water thoro Roger's parte unto Fengate. To Gylberte Tylson, sonne of Thomas Tylson, a sheder calve. To Rayff Tylson, sonne of John Tylson, a blak dowffyd heder calve. To Gylberde Tyngell a blak rugyt heder calve. The resydue of all my housholde stuff that is ungyffyn and unnamyd, I gyff them to be equally devydyd emonges my iiij chylder, that is to say Alyson, Elizabethe, Roger and John the yonger. I gyff my iij swyne to my iij chylder, that is to Alyson, Elizabethe and John the yonger. I will that my executors do cause ij trentallys to be sung for the soulys of my good frendys at the Whyte Frerys at Boston, and one trentall to be sung within the churche of Pynchbek for the helthe of my soule and my good frendes. I will have done for me, at my burying day, in messe and dirige and to pore fokes, xxs, and I will have a yong cowe kyllyd and ettyn emonges my nyghbors. The resydue of my goodes, as my croppe apon the erthe and my catell that is unbequethyd, I gyff them to my iij sonnys, John, Thomas and Roger, whome I make my [fo. 193v] trewe and faythfull executors, for to pay my dettes and to bryng me forthe and to fulfyll my will. And I will that every one of them have for ther labor and payn vjs viijd. And William Tylson my sonne be supervisor of thys my laste will. And I will that he have for hys labor and payn vjs viijd. I will that a pare of mustarde qwernys and a b[l]ak borde remayn styll with the house that I dwell in. Thes beryng wytnes; William Bewyk, preste, Thomas Laughton, Richard Robynson, William Brystyll.

Proved before P at Spalding, 10 October 1533.

250. JOHN SPENDLOWE [OF SALTFLEETBY ST. PETER]
    [LCC 1532–34, fo. 176]

20 June 1533. I, John Spendlowe off Salfletby Peter, hole of mynde, makes my last will. Fyrste I bequethe my soule to allmyghtty God, to Our Lady St. Mary and to all the saintes in heven, and my body to be buryed in the churcheyerde of Salfletby aforesayd, and that thyng for my mortuary as lawe and custome is. To Our Lady's warkes of Lincoln xijd. To the churche of Salfletby Peter aforesaid vjs viijd. To Margaret my doughter one cowe and x yowys. To Agnes my doughter one cowe that hase had one calve and x lammys. To Barnerde my sun too sterys, one blak fely and my plugh, wane, harroys and all that longes therto. To Richerd Rasyn one yereyng stere. To Jenet Rasyng one yereyng qwe. To Agnes Rasyng one yereyng qwye. To Margaret my yongest doughter one cowe. To Nicholes my sun v markes of money. To Catheryn my doughter v markes in money. Yff eny of thes my chyldren decesse or that they cum to laufull age, then I will that the parte of them so decessyd be devydyd emong the other. To Helyn my doughter x lammys. To Jenet my wyff vj kye, iiij merys and xx yowes, and xx lammys. I will that all my housholde stuff be devydyd betwyx my wyff and my chyldren that is unmaryd. I will that all my rayment of my body be devydyd emong my chyldren by the discrescion of my executors. I will Sir Thomas [fo. 167v] Hewytson syng ij trentallys in the churche of Salfletby Peter for my soule, my fader and moder soulys, Robert and Agnes Spendlowe. The reste of my goodes not giffyn nor bequethyd, my legacy fulfyllyd, my chargys borne, I will that they be devydyd emong my chyldren, bothe maryed and unmaryed, by the discrecion of my brother Thomas Spendlowe and Jenet my wyff, whome I make my faythfull executors. Thes to wytnes; Sir Christofer

Richerdson, parson of Salfletby Peter, John Parker, Thomas Goodnen of the same, with other mo.

Proved before P at Lincoln, 25 August 1533.

251. JOHN HARGYT [OF NORTH SOMERCOTES]
      [LCC 1532–34, fo. 218r]

22 June 1533. I, John Hargyt of Somercotes, in hole mynde and good memory beyng, makes thys my present will. Fyrste I bequethe my soule to God allmyghtty, to Hys mother St. Mary and to all saintes of heven. My body to be buryd in the kyrkeyerde of North Somercotes. To Our Lady warke of Lincoln iiijd. To Our Lady of Walsyngham iiijd. To St. John off Wyngall iiijd. To the high altare of North Somercotes for tithes forgotten iiijd. To the kyrke warke of North Somercotes vjd. I will Our Lady gylde of North Somercotes have for my wyffe ijs. To Jenet Porter ij hogges. To Richard Hargyt my sun a dyshe borde, a foldyn table, a forme, a chaffer of lattyn, iij of the best dooblers of puter, my best brasse potte, a panne of a gallon, and another panne of a pottyll, a chyste of wanyscotte. To Agnes Harde, late wyffe of John Harde of North Somercotes, xiijs and viijd in money, or ellys of my housholde stuff to the sayd Agnes a stotte calve. To Anne my syster a fether poke,[112] a pare of hardyn schetes, a blewe gowne that was my wyffe's and a jaket of tawny to her chylder. To Alice Manby a kyrtyll of rede. The resydue of all my goodes not wyt nor gyffyn, I gyff and wyt to Richerde my sun whome I make my executor, he to performe my wyll and to pay my dettes with counsell and helpe of John Gonnelde, yonger, of North Somercotes. Wytnes; Walter Rasyn, John Robertson, John Johnson, with other mo. Day and yere aforenamyd.

Proved before P at Muckton, 12 November 1533.

252. RICHARD WYLLE [OF BURGH LE MARSH]
      [LCC 1532–34, fos. 213v–214r]

25 June 1533. I, Richerde Wylle of Burgh makes thys my last will. Fyrste I bequethe my soule to the mercy of allmyghtty God, Our Lady St. Mary and to all the saintes off heven, and my body to be buryd in the churcheyerde of St. Peter in Burgh. To the high altare off the sayd churche for tithys forgottyn iijs iiijd. To the churche warke vjs viijd. To Our Lady's warke off Lincoln vjd. To the chyldren at St. Catheryn's vjd. To every one of my godchyldren a lamme. To every one of my chyldren vl. Yff any of them decesse before they be of laufull age or be maryd, then [fo. 214r] I will that xxs of ther partes be disposyd for ther soule, and the resydue to be equally devydyd emong them that lyffes. To Agnes my wyff all my housholde stuff and all my croppe to the fyndyng of my chyldren, xxty wedders, xxty lammys and xl yowes, iiij kye, ij marys with ther folys and ij calves. To Nicholes Wylson and hys wyff iij yowes. To Robert Wyll iij yowes. To Edmunde Will iiij yowes. To Robert Thomson one yow. To William Jude one yowe. To Johanne Thomson my servant one yow. To Margaret Barber my servant one lamme. To Catheryne Johnson ij yowes. I will, yff my wyff be maryd, that he that dothe mary her fynde suffycient suerty to fynde my chyldren honestly, and to delyver ther partes to

---

[112] A feather pillow.

them at the tyme of laufull age or mariage, or ellys my executor to take them and ther partes. To Thomas Gleyne my blake amblyng fole to be founde to Lammys cum twelvemonyth, whome I make my true executor. I will that my wyff have all the landes and the house that I dyd hyre of Thomas Gleyn so long as she is good to my chyldren. And yff she be maryed, yff ther be any varyaunce emonges them, I will then she have but xxx^{ty} acre of it. The resydue of all my goodes not gyffyn nor bequest, and the landes that I hyeryd of Richerde Pynchbek of Butterwyk, be disposyd for the helthe of my soule for the space of vj yeres by the mynde of Thomas Gleyn whome I make my true executor. I will that my wolle money go to paying of my rentes. Thes wytnes; Sir John Pechyll, Gylberde Rasyn, Richerde Symson, Christofer Magnus, with other moy.

Proved before P at Partney, 10 November 1533.

253. EDWARD CAMOK [OF BROTHERTOFT IN PARISH OF FRAMP-
     TON]
     [LCC 1532–34, fo. 180r]

29 June 1533. I, Edward Camok of Brothertofte and of the parysche of our Lady of Frampton, make my testament and last will. Fyrste I bequethe my soule to God allmyghtty, to Our Lady St. Mary, and to all the saintes in heven. My body to be buryed in the churche of Our Lady of Frampton before the rode. To the high altare in Frampton for tithys forgottyn xij*d*. To the orphans of St. Catheryn's withowt the barres at Lincoln iiij*d*. To the churche warke of Lincoln iiij*d*. To Adlarde Camok my sun too acres of arable lande lying in the paryshe of Wyberton, also one halff acre of arable lande lying in Frampton. I will that the sayd Adlarde shall sell the ij acres lying in Wyberton. To Helene Camok my wyff a red cowe. To the foresayd Adlarde Camok one cupborde. I will that Helene my wyff have all her housholde stuff that she brought unto me, as neyr as she can. I will that Adlarde my sun and Maryon my doughter, that they devyd equally betwyxte them all my housholde stuff. To Adlarde Camoke my sun one cowe. To Maryan Mole my doughter one cowe. To Richerde Camok one cowe and one calve. I will that my executors sell my ij botes and my carte. I will that Adlarde my sun have my mancion in Brothertofte as long as my yeres last. To Jenkyn Camok my best dooblet. The resydue of my goodes not geven nor bequethyd I gyff to Leonerde Mole and Adlarde Camok whome I make my executors, that they shall dispose it for the helthe of my soule as they shall thynk best. Thes beyng wytnes; Sir Christofer Smyrke, vicare, John Abraham, George Bowman, with other mo, the day and yere above wrytten.

Proved before P at Skirbeck, 5 August 1533.

254. THOMAS WEBSTER [OF ALFORD]
     [LCC 1532–34, fo. 217]

30 June 1533. I, Thomas Webster off Alforde, tanner, of hole mynde and good memory, ordens and makes my testament and last will. Fyrste I bequethe my soule to allmyghtty God, Our Lady St. Mary and to all the saintes in heven, and my body to be buryd in the churcheyerde aforesayd, yff it so please God. Also to the ornamentes of the blessyd sacrament in the same churche xij*d*. To the hygh altare ther for tithes forgotten xx*d*. To the ornamentes of our Lady altare in the same viij*d*.

To the ornamentes of St. Laurence altare in the same viij*d*. To Our Lady altare over the churche porche in the same vj*d*. To Kyng Henry light in the same xij*d*. To St. Anthony light in the same vj*d*. To the sepulcre light in the same vj*d*. To the warke of the cathedral churche of Lincoln ij*s*. To Malde my wyff my house that I do dwell in to the terme of her lyff. And aftyr her decesse I will it shall remayn to Robert my sun and to hys heyres of hys body laufully begottyn [remainder to] Thomas my sun and to Elizabeth my doughter, and to ther heyres and assygnes. I will that all my tenementes and landes that I have in the townys and feldes of Hoggesthorp and Orby shall be set furthe for the space of ij yeres next immediatly foloyng my decesse, for the payng of the fyne accordyng to the custome ther. And then aftyr I will the sayd tenementes and landes be devydyd into iij equall partes, Robert my sun to have ij partes, and to be delyveryd to hym at the age of xviij yeres, or at the day of hys maryage. And the thyrde parte of my sayd landes I will Malde my wyffe shall have. And aftyr, I will the sayd landes shall remayn to Robert my sun and to hys heyres of hys body laufully begottyn, accordyng to the custome off the lordeschyp ther. And in case it fortune the sayd Robert my sun to decesse afore the sayd xviij yeres, or the day off mariage, then I will that hys ij partes of the landes above namyd shall remayn to Thomas my sun and to Elizabeth my doughter, to be devydyd betwyxte them by even porcions at the yeres and day above specifyed. Also I will, my dettes payd and thys my will fulfyllyd, all my moveable goodes be devydyd into ij equall partes, Malde my wyff to have the one parte and my iij chyldren, that is to say Robert, Thomas and Elizabethe, to have the other parte, to be delyveryd to theym by iij equall porcions at the day and yeres above namyd. And yff it fortune that any of my sayd chyldren decesse [fo. 217v] afore the age of xviij yeres or the day of ther mariage, that then hys or ther parte or partes so decessyd, be devydyd emonges the other that lyff. And yff it fortune all my chyldren above namyd decesse afor the aforesayd day or age, then I will that the aforesayd legacy be at the disposicion of Malde my wyffe and Sir Robert Henryson. And also I will that the sayd Malde my wyffe have the custody and kepyng of all my sayd chyldren legaces to the yeres and day above sayd excepte that the sayd Malde do mary. And then I will the sayd Malde shall, afore her sayd mariage, delyver the sayd legaces and bequestes to Sir Robert Henryson, and to my supervisors sufficient suertys or obligacion to delyver the aforenamyd legaces to my sayd chyldren at the yeres and days above specyfyed. I make Malde my wyffe, Sir Robert Harryson and Robert my sun my true and faythfull executors, and the sayd Sir Robert Harryson to have for hys labor my best gowne. And Mr. Thomas Totheby and Gilbert Schawe to be supervisors, and other of them to have for ther labors iij*s* iiij*d*. Thes wytnes; Mr. William Johnson, vicar of Alforde, Sir John Browne, paryshe preste of Ryggesby, John Mason, William Walker of Alforde, and other mo.

Proved before P at Alford, 11 November 1533.

255.   GEORGE ATKYNSON [OF SKENDLEBY]
       [LCC 1532–34, fo. 210r]

1 July 1533. I, George Atkynson of Skendylby, hole in mynde and good of remembraunce, makes my testament. Fyrst I bequethe my soule to allmyghtty God, to Our Lady St. Mary, and to all the holly cumpeny of heven. My body to be buryd in the churcheyerde of St. Peter of Skendylby. To the high altares in the

churches of Skendylby and Scremby xx*d* each. To Our Lady warke of Lincoln xx*d*. To the churche warke of Skendylby xx*d*. To the churches of Bambur, Scamton and Carleton vj*d* each. To Alice my doughter a brown qwye. To Wylliam my sun a brown stere. To Catheryne my doughter a browne sternde qwye and a yow and a lamme. The resydue of my goodes not bequethyd, my dettes payd and my will fulfyllyd, I will they be at the disposicion of Elizabethe my wyffe and Richerde my sun, whome I make my executors to dispose for the helthe of my soule and all Christen soulys as they thynke beste. Thes wytnes; Sir Nicholes Fawn, vicar, Edmunde Michell, Simon Merell. I will that Isabell my wyffe have my copy duryng the yeres, and that Richerde my sun have for hys labor a yowe and a lamme.

Proved before P at Partney, 10 November 1533.

256. ROBERT AWGERE [OF SCOTTERTHORPE IN PARISH OF EDEN-HAM]
[LCC 1532–34, fo. 198v]

1 July 1533. I, Robert Awgere of Scotylthorp in the paryshe of Edenham, make my testament. Fyrste I commende my soule to God allmyghtty, and my body to be buryd in the churcheyerde of Edenham. To the high altare of the same for tithys forgottyn or not payd vj*d*. To Our Lady of Lincoln iiij*d*. To Our Lady of Edenham a stake barly. To Our Lady of Walsyngham ij*d*. I wolde have fyve messys done for my soule and my frendes soulys. The resydue of my goodes not bequethyd I gyff to the disposicion of Alice my wyff, whome I make myn executrix to dispose for the helthe of my soule as she thynkes best. Thes beyng wytnes; Sir Edwarde Thomas, preste, John Dawes, and other, the day and yere above wryttyn.

Proved before P at Bitchfield, 21 October 1533.

257. WILLIAM BURTON [OF LEAKE]
[LCC 1532–34, fo. 121r]

1 July 1533. I, William Burton of Leeke, in hole mynde and of good remembraunce, makes my testament and laste will. Fyrste I bequethe my soule to allmyghtty God, to Hys mother St. Mary, and to all the saintes beyng in heven. My body to be buryd in the churcheyerde of Leeke. To the high altare in Leeke churche ij*d*. To Our Lady of Lincoln viij*d*. To St. Catheryne withowt Lincoln ij*d*. I bequethe a trentall to be sung in Leeke churche for my soule by the advice of my curate. To Agnes my wyffe iij kye, x schepe, one whyte mare and fole, and all my houshold stuff as it standes within my dores. To William my sun ij yong oxen, ij mares, ij stages. To every one of my iiij doughters vj*s* viij*d*. To Elizabeth Jefferay one burnyng. To Jenet my doughter one cowe. To every one John Pekeryng chylder one lamme. Moreover I will that Agnes my wyff have all my landes to the terme of her lyffe, and aftyr her decesse to remayn to William my sun and to hys heyres and assygnes. The resydue of my goodes I gyff to Agnes my wyff and William my sun, whome I make my executors to dispose for my soule as they thynke shall be moste pleasure to God. Thes wytnes; Sir Edwarde Hamonde and Thomas Alenson, with other.

Proved before P at Boston, 3 March 1533/4.

258.   WILLIAM CARTEWRIGHT [OF CAYTHORPE]
[LCC 1532–34, fo. 201v]

3 July 1533. I, William Cartewryght of Cathorp, hole of mynde and of good memory, make and orden thys my testament and last will. Fyrste I bequethe my soule to allmyghtty God, Our Lady St. Mary and to all the holly cumpeny of heven, and my body to be buryed in the paryshe churche of St. Vincent in Cathorp. To the high altare of the same churche for my tithes withholden or forgotten iiij*d*. To Our Lady's warkes of Lincoln iiij*d*. To my paryshe churche of Cathorp one bushell of barly. To every one of my godchyldren iiij*d*. To every one of John Pykworthe chyldren iiij*d*. To Fulbek churche iiij*d*. To Welborne churche xvj*d*. To Richerde my sonne, besyde hys parte, one balde fylly, ij schepe and one quarter of barly. To John my sun one yowe with a lamme. The resydue of my goodes not bequethyd I bequethe to Jenet my wyff and Richerde my sonne whome I orden my executors, and they to dispose it for the helthe of my soule as they wyll answere to God. Geven at Cathorp the day and yere above wryttyn. Thes wytnesses; Sir John Stotte, John Kyng, John Thomson, Thomas Scotte, and other mo.

Proved before P at Ancaster, 24 October 1533.

259.   WILLIAM SMYTH [OF STAINTON BY LANGWORTH]
[LCC 1532–34, fo. 174]

3 July 1533. I, William Smyth of Stanton, in hole mynde and memory, make my last will and testament. Fyrste I bequethe my soule to allmyghtty God, to Hys blessyd moder and to all the holy saintes of heven. My body to be buryd in the churcheyerde of Stanton. To the vicare of Stanton for my mortuary iij*s* iiij*d*. To the high altare of Stanton viij*d*. To Our Lady warke at Lincoln mynster viij*d*. To Jenet my wyf all suche goodes as was her owne as well qwyk as ded. And yff she will kepe my ij chyldren namyd Jenet and Agnes well and honestly, with all necessary thynges to them belongyng, unto they be at the age of xiiij yeres, then I will she have off my goodes ij kye, x schepe hogges, ij swyne, one acre of wheate, one acre of barly, ij acres pees now growyng, one stone and ij flesys of woolle, halffe off my hempe and halffe of my lyne now growyng, halffe a quarter bredcorne, halffe a quarter malte. And yff she wyll not kepe my sayd chyldren well and honestly at the oversyght of my broder John Smythe, and to fynde hym suche suerty so to do, then I will that my brother John Smythe put them to kepyng with all the goodes before namyd as he shall thynke best. To Jenet my wyff the house namyd Jakson house with all the appurtenances duryng her lyff, payng the rente accustomyd therefore and beryng [fo. 174v] the charges theroff accordyngly to myn indenture. Also my bay meyr. To my brother John Smyth myne indentur with all the proffyttes therto belongyng duryng the yeres to me grauntyd by my lorde abbot of Barlynges and the convent of the same, beryng all charges therto belongyng. Also I will my sayd brother distribute all other my goodes when my dettes be all payd emonges my chyldren as he shall seme best [sic], and to order them as he shall thynke good and proffyt to them. I orden and make my sayd brother John Smyth my full and sole executor, to dispose my sayd goodes as he thynkes best for the helthe of my soule and proffyt of my sayd chyldren. Wytnes heroff; Sir John Benton, vicare of Stanton, Thomas Osgarby, John Langley and John Urry of Stanton, with many oder mo.

Proved before P at Lincoln, 28 July 1533.

260.   JOHN MULLET [OF SKIRBECK]
       [LCC 1532–34, fo. 223]

6 July 1533. I, John Mullet of Skyrbek, hole in mynde and perfyte in remembraunce, make my testament. Fyrste I bequethe my soule to allmyghtty God, to
Our Lady St. Mary and all the celestyall cumpeny in heven. My body to be
buryed within the churche or churcheyerde of St. Nicholes in Skyrbek. To my
mortuary as the lawe requyryth. To the high altare of Skyrbek for tithys forgottyn
ij*s*. To the churche warke of Skyrbek iij*s* iiij*d*. To Our Lady of Lincoln iiij*d*. To the
orphans at St. Catheryn's withowt the barres at Lincoln iiij*d*. To every one of the
iiij orders of freres in Boston, to accompany my body to the churche, xx*d*. Thys is
the last will of me, the sayd John Mullet, mayd and wryttyn the day and yere
abovesayd. I will that all my householde stuff be equally devydyd betwyxte
Margaret my wyff and Catheryn my doughter, and the sayd Catheryne to have
her parte owt of the best stuff. And the same to be in the custody of William
Laverok of Boston, unto suche tyme she be of the age of xviij yeres. I will that the
sayd Margaret my wyff have my iij house in Kyrton duryng her lyff naturall,
wythe all and singler ther appurtenances to them belongyng. And aftyr her decesse
I will that John Mullet my sun have the sayd houses with all and singler
th'appurtenances and ij pare of bellos, ij stedies with iiij gret hammers to hym
and hys heyres uppon thy condicion, that the sayd John shall pay, or cause to be
payd, unto the churchewardens of Matsall churche in the countie of Norfolk, ten
poundes sterlyng, to be payd and delyveryd unto my executors or ther assygnes
within too yeres nexte aftyr hys entryng therof. And yff he refuse thus to do, then
I will Catheryn my doughter have the sayd housys to her and her heyres, payng
the sayd x*l* in manner and forme as is aforesayd. Yff the sayd John Mullet my sun
decesse before Margaret my wyff, then I will the sayd housys remayn to the sayd
Catheryn and her heyres in manner and forme as is aforesayd, I will that
Margaret my wyff have my house that I dwell in duryng her lyffe naturall. And
aftyr her decesse I will it remayn to Catheryne my doughter and to her heyres. And
yff it fortune the sayd Catheryne to decesse before her mother withowt heyres,
then I will afftyr my wyff decesse the sayd house be solde be my executors [fo.
223v] or the executors of them, and the money therof receyvyd to be delyveryd
and payd to the churchwardens of Matsall, and there to be bestowyd of a crosse
and candylstyckes or other anornamentes as shall be thought necessary by the
sayd churchewardens. To Catheryne my doughter my house at Benyngton, to her
and her heyres at the age of xviij yeres, or soner yff she be maryd. And her mother
to have the proffyt of the same unto the sayd tyme yff she fortune to lyff. And yff
the sayd Catheryn decesse before the sayd age, or withowt heyres, then I will the
sayd house with th'appurtenances, be solde be my executors or the executors of
them, and the money therof receyvyd to be bestowyd uppon a vestiment or other
anornamentes in the churche of Skyrbek, so far as the money commys to. I will
that yff it fortune Kateryn my doughter decesse before she be of the age of xviij
yeres or before she be maryd, then I will that Margaret my wyff have all my sayd
householde stuff. The resydue of my goodes not gyffyn nor bequethyd I put them
to the disposicion of Margaret my wyff and William Laverok of Boston, whome I
make my executors, they to pay my dettes and bryng me forthe, and to dispose the
reste as they shall thynke best. And I will the sayd William have for hys labor
other my best dooblet, my best jaket, or my harnes at hys plesure, whiche he will.

These beyng wytnes; Sir Thomas Crawe, preste, Nicholes Blewet and Thomas Mobrey, with other mo.

Proved before P at Lincoln, 15 December 1533.

261. THOMAS OTBY [OF BEELSBY]
      [LCC 1532–34, fo. 195v]

6 July 1533. I, Thomas Otby of Billesby, beyng of hole mynde and good memory, have ordenyd and mayd thys my testament and last will. Fyrste I bequethe my soule to God allmyghtty, unto the Virgyn Mary and unto all the saintes of heven, and my body to be buryd in the churche of St. Andro the appostell of Billesby. To Our Lady warke of Lincoln viijd. To the high altare of the same iiijd. To the high altare of Billesby churche for forgottyn tithes viijd. To the iiij orders of frerys of Lincoln, every order, iiijd. The resydue of my goodes not wit I will that they be at the disposicion of Elizabeth my wyff and Jamys Otby my brother, whome I make my true executors that they may dispose for my soule and pay my dettes. Thys wytnessys; Sir Oliver Osgodby, John Gretham and William Otbe, with other mo.

Proved before P at Grimsby, 15 October 1533.

262. THOMAS BELE [OF KIRTON IN HOLLAND]
      [LCC 1532–34, fos. 191r–192r]

12 July 1533. I, Thomas Bele of Kyrton in Hollande, of hole mynde and perfyte remembraunce, makes my testament concludyng with my last will. In the firste I gyff and bequethe my soule to God allmyghtty, to Our Lady St. Mary, and to all the celestyall cumpeny of heven. My body to be buryed in the churcheyerde of the blessyd appostellys Peter and Paule. For my mortuary aftyr the statutes of our soverayn lorde the kyng. To the high altare of Kyrton for negligent tithys vjd, and every altare in the sayd churche ijd. To Our Lady of Lincoln ijd, and to the reparacion of the sayd our mother churche ijd. To the orphans of St. Catheryn's [fo. 191v] ijd. To the reparacion of the sayd churche of Kyrton iijs iiijd. To Agnes my wyffe, my landes and tenementes aftyr my decesse duryng her naturall lyff, excepte one pasture callyd Bele Yng, one house that I bought of Richerde Cony therto annexyd, and one acre lande that I bought of Robert Sheperde, the whiche I gyff and bequethe to Richerde Gryme immediatly aftyr my decesse in fe symple. To Robert Gelson, sonne of John Gelson, aftyr the decesse of Agnes my wyff, one house, the whiche I bought of the sayd John Gelson, in fe symple. And yff the sayd Robert Gelson departe thys worlde before the age of xvj yere, [remainder to] Jenet Gelson, the daughter of the sayd John Gelson, in fe symple. To Richerde Gelson one pasture that I bought of Michel Robynson aftyr the decesse of the sayd Agnes my wyff, in fe symple. And yff the sayd Richerde Gelson departe thys worlde before the age abovenamyd, that then I will the sayd pasture remayn to Humfryd Gelson and John Gelson in fe symple, evenly betwyxte them to be devydyd. To Phylip Turbek, sonne of Thomas Turbek, my hede mansyon that I dwell in and one pasture that I bought of Phylip Parsone aftyr the decesse of my wyff, in fe symple. And yff the sayd Phylip departe before the age of xvj yere, [remainder to] Agnes Albeyn in fe symple. To Thomas Turbek, sonne of John Turbok, one house with the purtenaunces that I bought of Richerde Johnson aftyr the decesse of my wyff, and

one pasture that I bought of Richerde Cony off Swyneshed, in fe symple. And yff the sayd Thomas Turbok departe before the age of xvj yere [remainder to] William Turbok, sonne of the sayd John Turboke, in fe symple. To Peter Turboke one pece of lande that I bought of Thomas Fowlle of the Meres, and a pece of grounde that I bought of Richerde Tonnarde of Frampton, aftyr the decesse of Agnes my wyff, in fe symple. And yff the sayd Peter Turbok departe thys worlde before the age of xvj yere [remainder to] Laurence hys brother, in fe symple. To the sayd Larence Turbok one house that I bought of [fo. 192r] Roger May, aftyr the decesse of my wyffe, in fe symple. And yff the sayd Laurence departe before the age of xvj [remainder to] Peter Turbok hys brother, in fe symple. To Christofer Turbok one house in Kyrton Home, aftyr the decesse of my wyff, in fe symple. To Richerde Alger, sonne of Robert Alger, one pasture conteynyng iiij acres and a acre that I bought of John Parlebayn, aftyr the decesse of my wyff, in fe symple. To John Gryme, the yonger sonne of John Gryme the elder, one acre and a halffe of lande lying in Kyrton Ynges, and halff an acre callyd Toope Walles, aftyr the decesse of my wyff, in fe symple. And yff the sayd John Gryme departe thys worlde before the age of xvj yere [remainder to] Agnes Albeyn, in fe symple. To the sayd Agnes Albeyn ij yong kye and ij burlynges. To Thomas Turbok one cowe and one lyttyll grysselde meyr. To Phylip Turbok one kowe and one yong browne mare with her fole. To Elizabeth Albeyn one burlyng. The resydue of my goodes not gyffyn nor bequethyd, my dettes payd and funerall expenses, I gyff theym to Agnes my wyff, whome I make, constitute and orden to be my trewe, trusty and faythfull executrix, to dispose my goodes to the moste pleasure of God and helthe of my soule. And I make Robert Alger supervisor, and to have for hys labor vj*s* viij*d*. Thes beyng wytnes; Sir Thomas Este, Humfryd Ordyng, John Donyngton. Moreover, I will that yff the withinnamyd Richerde Alger departe thys worlde before the sayd Agnes my wyff, that then the sayd pasture of iiij acres and one acre of lande as is above namyd, remayn to Robert Alger, hys father, in fe symple. Thes above namyd beyng wytnes with other.

Proved before P at Swineshead, 9 October 1533.

263.   THOMAS LAYNE [OF WELBOURN]
    [LCC 1532–34, fo. 205v]

12 July 1533. I, Thomas Layne of Welborne, hole of mynde and good of remembraunce, makes my will and testament. The fyrste I gyff and bequethe my soule to allmyghtty God, Our Lady St. Mary, and to all the celestiall cumpeny of heven. My body to be buryed in the churcheyerde of St. Ceade of Welborne. To Our Lady's warkes of our mother churche of Lincoln vj*d*. To the house of Our Lady Frerys of Lincoln vj*d*. To the house of the Blak Frerys of Lincoln vj*d*. To the high altare off Welborne churche for forgottyn tithys iiij*d*. To the reparacions of the churche of Welborne vj*d*. To prestes and clerkes in the day of my buryall, to be disposyd as my gostly father thynke the best, iij*s*. At the vij day ij*s* viij*d* to suche prestes and clerkes, and ij dosyn breade to be distrybute to the pore people of the towne of Welborne. To Sir Ranolde Wadyngton, my gostly father whome I make supervisor, xij*d*. To Jenet my wyff all and singuler goodes whiche she dyd bryng with her to me at the tyme off our mariage. And wher it is mynyshyd and wastyd I gyff to her halffe a quarter barly. To the sayd Jenet my wyff iij quarters barly and halffe a quarter wheate, and one cowe and one calve, the best she will chose in my

garthe. To Peter Cawnell halffe a quarter pease. To my sun John Layne one bushyll pease. To my sun Thomas my carte and the gerys therto belongyng, and one cowe and one stere. To my sun Robert one stere. To my sun Lenerde ij schepe. My dettes payd and the rente of my house and reparacions payd and mayd, the resydue of all my goodes not bequethyd I gyff to my iij sonnys, Thomas, Robert and Leonarde, to be devydyd by even porcions emonges them. I make my true executors my sun Thomas and my sun Robert, that they may dispose my goodes and fulfyll thys my forsayd will as they thynke the best and will answere afore the hye juge of heven. Thes wytnes; Sir Ranolde Wadyngton, Robert Tyngyll and Thomas Sparrowe, with many other.

Proved before P at Navenby, 4 November 1533.

264. JOHN TURPYN [OF FRIESTON]
[LCC 1532–34, fo. 179]

12 July 1533. I, John Turpyn of Freston, beyng of hole mynde and perfyte memory, do make my testament and last will. Fyrste I bequethe my soule to allmyghtty God and to Our Lady St. Mary, and my body to be buryed in the churcheyerde of St. Jamys in Freston. To the high altare for tithys forgottyn viijd. To Our Lady of Lincoln iiijd. To St. Jamys in the churche of Freston ijd. To Our Lady of Pety ijd. To St. Sythe ijd. To the churche warke of Freston ijs. To Richerd Turpyn my sun, a cowe. To William my sun, a cowe. To Wylliam Turpyn, the sun of Richerd Turpyn, a gray fole of a yere olde. To Robert Turpyn, the sun of Richerde Turpyn, a yowe and a lambe. To John Turpyn, the sun of Richerde Turpyn, a yowe and a lambe. To Cecill Turpyn, the doughter of Richerd Turpyn, a lambe. To John, the sun of William Turpyn, a yowe and a lambe. To Alice, the doughter of the sayd William, a lambe. To Alice, the wyff of William Wayd, a cowe and a yowe and a lambe. To Simon Turpyn, my sun, [fo. 179v] my house beyng in Halftofte Ende in Freston with the purtenaunces of the same, and one acre of land arable lying in Freston fen landes in fee symple. I will that the sayd Simon have the pasture of vij acres whiche I holde of Mr. Welby by copy. The reste of my goodes not bequethyd, my will performyd, I gyff unto Simon Turpyn my sun, whome I make my sole executor. Thes beryng wytnes and beyng testes; Sir John Thyrlande, Richerd Dowsse, John Baker, John Sybsay, with other mo.

Proved before P at Skirbeck, 5 August 1533.

265. ROBERT BROWKE [OF FULSTOW]
[LCC 1532–34, fos. 219v–220r]

13 July 1533. I, Robert Browke of Fulstowe, with a hole mynde settes and ordens my will. Fyrste I bequethe my soule to God allmyghtty, to Our Lady St. Mary, to all the saintes in heven. My body to be buryd in the churche of St. Laurence in Fulstowe, and the sayd churche to have vjs viijd for my bereley. To the high altare of Fulstowe iiijd. To Our Lady's warke of Lincoln viijd. To the churche of Marsh Chapell iiijd. To the churches of Cathorp, Utterby, Ludburgh, Thoresby, iiijd [each]. To the churche of Fulstowe a cowe, to remayn to the most proffet to the sayd churche. To Robert Browke my nevo a cowe, a qwye, ij lyne lowmys, a wollyn lowme with ther gerys and iiij schepe. To Isabell Grene a cowe, a qwye, a brasse

potte, ij puter dooblers and iiij schepe. [fo. 220r] To Helene my wyff a colte stage. To Robert Browke my nevo a colte stage. To Andro Grene a cowe, a qwe and iiij schepe. To Jenet Browne a qwy calve. To Jenet Bryand a yowe lamme. To Robert Richerdson a lyne gere and a hardyn to a lowme. I will have myn executors hyer a preste to syng for me halffe a yere, and mo may be. The resydue of my goodes not gyffyn nor wyt, I gyff to Helene my wyff and to Robert Browke my nevo, whome I make my executors to dispose for the helthe of well off my soule [sic], and Sir Richerde Raynolde to be supervisor, and he to have for hys labor a stall of beys and one wether. Thes wytnes; Sir Richerde Raynolde, vicar, Robert Richerdson, Amor Bryane, with other mo.

Proved before P at Louth, 12 November 1533.

266.   ROBERT PYTTES [OF STUBTON]
        [LCC 1532–34, fos. 177v–178r]

15 July 1533. I, Robert Pyttes of Stubton in the countie of Lincoln, husbandman, with hole mynde and memory, ordens and makes thys my last will and testament. Fyrst and principally I bequethe my soule unto allmyghtty God my creator, to Hys most blessyd mother, Our Lady St. Mary, and to all the holy cumpeny in heven. My body to be buryd in the churcheyerde of St. Martyn in Stubton beforesayd. To the high altare in the sayd churche for tithys forgottyn iiij_d._ To Our Lady of Lincoln one belte with sylver stubbys. To St. George in the foresayd churche of Stubton one halffe pounde of wax. One trentall of messys to be done for my soule, my frendes' soulys and all Crysten soulys. To my syx godchylder, iche of them, iiij_d._ To Thomas Lyster one ploughe and one mare. To Elizabethe Snathe one qwe calve. To the cawsey afore John Pateman dore iij_s_ iiij_d._ To Claypole commens ij_s._ To William Hussey x_s._ The resydue of my goodes unbequethyd, my dettes payd and thys my last will fulfyllyd, I gyff and bequethe unto Margaret my wyffe and William Hussey of Stubton, whome I orden and makes my last executors. Yff the foresayd Margaret marry, then I will that the forsayd [fo. 178r] William dispose my halffe for my soule and all Crsyten soulys. I will that William Banester of Clapole be supervisor, and he to have for hys labor one fole and iiij_d,_ for to se thys my last will performyd. Thes beyng wytnes; Thomas Lestere and Sir Nicholes Chapman.

Proved before P at Lincoln, 12 September 1533.

267.   WILLIAM BAXSTER [OF FLEET]
        [LCC 1532–34, fo. 183]

20 July 1533. I, William Baxster, hole, stedfast and perfyte in mynde, do make my last will and testament. The fyrst I bequethe my soule to God, to Our Lady, and to all the holy saintes in heven. Also I bequethe my body to be buryd within the churcheyerde of Mary Magdalen of Flete. To the high altare for forgottyn tithys iiij_d._ To the mother churche of Lincoln ij_d._ To the pore chyldren of St. Catheryn's ij_d._ To the rode light ij_d._ To Johanne my doughter a cowe, a bullok, x schepe, a fether bed, a coverlyd and v schetes, vj pecys of puter, a brasse potte, a panne, a candylstyk, a salte seller and ij sawssers and a meyr. To Catheryne [fo. 183v] my doughter a cowe, a bullok, x schepe and a meyr, a fether bed, a coverlyd, v schetes, vj pecys of puter, a brasse potte, a panne, a candylstyk, a salte seller and ij

sawssers. I will that my wyff have rule and custody of my sayd doughters with the goodes aforesayd to them bequethyd, unto they cum to xvj yere of age. And also I will that the sayd merys, ij kye, ij bullokes and xx^{ty} schepe be solde and put to the best use to incresse for the proffyt of my sayd doughters. Also I will iche one of them to be other heyres. Yff they dy bothe, I will there goodes be disposyd within the churche of Flete. To Elizabethe my wyff my house and vij acres of fre lande, and ij acres and a half, and a halff rode of copyholde lande for the terme of her lyff. And aftyr her decesse I will that Johanne and Catheryne, my doughters, have the sayd house with all the lande beforenamyd. And yff one of them dye, I will the other be her heyr. And yff they dye bothe withowt issue, I will the churche of Flete to have the sayd house with all the lande therto belongyng. To Elizabethe my wyff vj of my best kye, iij marys and a geldyng with all other goodes not bequethyd, I bequethe unto the sayd Elizabethe, and make her my executrix to dispose my goodes for the welthe and savacion of my soule and in performyng of my last will and testament. I make my father John Baxter supervisor, and he to have for hys payntakyng vjs viijd. In wytnes herof; Thomas Mody, clerke, John Baxster, Thomas Baxster, with diverse other.

Proved before P at Cowbit, 7 August 1533.

268.   JOHN HALDYN [OF BURGH LE MARSH]
[LCC 1532–34, fo. 215v]

23 July 1533. I, John Haldyn the elder of Burgh in the Marshe, makyth my last will and testament. Fyrst I bequethe my soule to the mercy of allmyghtty God, to Our Lady St. Mary and to all the saintes in heven, and my body to be buryd in the churcheyerde of St. Peter in Burgh. To the high altare in Burgh for forgottyn tithys xijd. To the churche warke ijs. To Our Lady of Lincoln vjd, and to her warke vjd. To mendyng the Stanebow ijs. To the warke of Skegnes churche iijs iiijd. To Margaret my wyff xx^{ty} olde schepe, one cowe and halffe my houholde stuff. To Isabell my doughter xxx^{ty} olde schepe, ij ky and the other halffe of my housholde stuff. I will that my wyff and my executors have my ferme for my yeres. To every place of the iij orders of frerys in Boston, to the porist men kepyng the place xijd. I will that a trentall be done for my soule in Boston at Scala Celi. To Wynthorp churche xxd. To the high altare in Crofte xijd. To Our Lady gylde in Crofte xs, with that that I awe them. To Nicholes Wellwek iijs iiijd, whome I make my true executor. The resydue of all my goodes I will that he dispose for the well of my soule and my frendes' soulys. Wytnes of the same; Sir John Pechel, Christofer Magnus, William Meltham, William Broune and Thomas Anderson, with other mo.

Proved before P at Partney, 10 November 1533.

269.   JOHN POLLERDE [OF BOSTON]
[LCC 1532–34, fo. 179r]

23 July 1533. I, John Pollarde of Boston, puterer, seke in body and good in remembraunce, makyth thys my testament and last will. Fyrste I bequethe my soule to God allmyghtty, to Our Lady St. Mary and to all the holly cumpeny of heven, and my body to be buryed in the churcheyerde of St. Botolphe of Boston. To the high altare xijd. To the offeryng of Our Lady of Lincoln xijd. To the vij martyrs

gylde vj*d*. And further I will have a trentall of messes done for me. The resydue of my goodes moveable and unmoveable not gyffyn nor bequethyd, I put theym into the handes of Agnes Murre and William Scammolby whome I make my executors, they to dipose my goodes, pay my dettes, fulfyll my will as my truste is in theym. Thes beyng wytnes; Sir Thomas Cersy, curate and paryshe preste, Peter Barber and Henry Tynber, the day and yere above rehersyd.

Proved before P at Skirbeck, 5 August 1533.

270.   WILLIAM JAKSON [OF HOLBEACH]
        [LCC 1532–34, fos. 134v–135r]

26 July 1533. I, Wylliam Jacson of Holbeche, of hole mynde and memorye, make my last wyll and testamentt. Fyrst I bequethe mye soule to almyghtye God, to Owr Ladye Sayntt Marye, and to all the holye companye of heven, and mye bodye to be beryed in the churcheyerde of All Halowe of Holbeche aforsayd, and mye morturye to be gyvyn as the law wyll requyer. To the hye alter ther for tythys forgoten xx*d*. To the sayd hye altare, to the reparacyons therof, vj*d*. To the rode lyghtt ther viij*d*. To every altare in the churche ther viij*d*. To the churche warkes ther v*s*. To the plowe lyghtt ther iiij*d*. To Ower Laydye warkes of Lyncoln iiij*d*. To the orphans or fatherlesse chyldern of Sayntt Kateryn's of Lyncolln ij*d*. To an able and a honest preist for to synge for mye soule and all mye good frenddes' [fo. 135r] soules for the space of halfe a yere in the churche of Holbeche iiij markes and xx*d*. I wyll that Agnes mye wyffe have my howse that I dwell in the terme of her lyfe, and after the decease of mye sayd wyffe I wyll that mye sayd hows remayn to John Jackson the yonger and the sayd John Jackson, to kepe an obite of v*s* bye yere for mye soull and all mye good frenddes' soules, for the space of fyve score yeres and one, iff the kynge's laws wyll suffer itt, provided allwaye that iff the sayd John Jacson do nott kepe mye sayde hows in sufficyentt repare, then I wyll that itt remayn to the churchewardyns of Holbeche for to kepe and maynteyn mye sayd obyte of v*s* bye the yere. To Wylliam Betson, son of Rycharde Betson, ij lammes. To Christofer Penytt on lambe. To Johan Scherman, dowghter of Wylliam Sherman, on lambe. The resydewe of mye guddes nott bequethed I gyve to Agnes my wyffe, whom I make myn executryx to dysspose for the helthe of mye soule. I wyll that John Neyle of Boston be supervisor, and to have for hys labor and paynestakynge iij*s* iiij*d*. Theys wyttnesses; John Lessey, Wylliam Sherman, Roger Dyker, John Ranson and Rycherde Shepherde, with other moo.

Proved before P at Boston, 3 March 1533/4.

271.   ANDREW BROWNE [OF WRANGLE]
        [LCC 1532–34, fo. 179v]

27 July 1533. I, Andro Browne of Wrangle, husbandman, beyng of hole mynde and good remembraunce, make my last will and testament. Fyrst I bequethe my soule to allmyghtty God, Our Lady St. Mary, and to all the cumpeny of heven, and my body to be buryed within the churcheyerde of Wrangle. To the high altare in Wrangle churche and to Our Lady altare, ether of them, iiij*d*, and to every altare in the same churche ij*d*. To Our Lady of Lincoln iiij*d*. To St. Catheryn's ij*d*. To the vicare or hys proctor for tithys forgottyn iiij*d*. To Isabell my doughter one cowe, one yowe and a

lamme, and a pare of flaxen schetes. To Agnes my doughter one cowe, one yowe and a lamme, a pare of flaxen schetes. To Anne my doughter one cowe, one yowe and a lamme, and a pare of flaxen schetes. I will that thes my bequestes unto my chyldren be delyveryd unto them be my wyff or by sum other that she will assygne when they come to the yeres of xvj. And yff ony of my chyldren dye within the sayd yeres, then I will ther bequestes be disposyd for ther soulys, my soule and all Crysten soulys. The resydue of my goodes I gyff them to Jenet my wyff, whome I make my executrix, she to bryng me to the grounde and to pay my dettes. Thes beyng wytnes; Sir Thomas Potter, John Schyrme.

Proved before P at Skirbeck, 5 August 1533.

272. WILLIAM FORMAN [OF SCOPWICK]
      [LCC 1532–34, fo. 206]

27 July 1533. I, William Forman of Scawpwyk, of hole mynde and good remembraunce, makes my testament. In primis I gyff my soule to God allmyghtty, to Our Lady St. Mary and to all the blessyd cumpeny of heven, and my body to be buryd within the paryshe churche of Scopwyk. To the sayd churche for my buryall therin vj*s* viij*d*. To the forsayd churche iij*s* iiij*d* towardes the reparacions therof. For forgottyn tithes iij*s* iiij*d*. To the cathedrall churche of Lincoln iij*s* iiij*d*. To every house of the iiij orders of frerys within Lincoln xij*d*. To the prior of Nocton Parke and the convente of the same iij*s* iiij*d*. To the nonnys of Catlay iij*s* iiij*d*. To the nonnys of Haverholme iij*s* iiij*d*. I will that one preste [fo. 206v] do syng for my soule and all Christen soulys in the forsayd churche of Scopwyk at Our Lady's altare, for the space of halffe one yere, and to have for hys stypende as my executors and he can agre. To Sir Robert Husey, knyght, to be good and favorable to my chyldren xiij*s* iiij*d*. I will that Johan my wyffe have all my housholde stuff holy to herselffe, savyng that she shall gyve to every one of my chyldren therof a materes, a pillo, a pare of schetes and a coverlyd. To Edwarde my sun for hys chylde's xiij*s* vj*s* viij*d*. To Agnes my doughter viij*l*. To Emote my doughter viij*l*. I will that Edwarde my sun, the yere nexte aftyr my dethe, shall have hys fyndyng at the scole of my hole stoke. I will that the copye of the landes of Catlay be devydyd betwyxt Robert and Richerde my sunys, and to be occupyed betwyxte them too, and not to be solde nor releasyd, but from one of them to the other. To Johan my wyff the house that I bought of John Cantrell for the terme of her lyff, yff she kepe her unmaryd, and aftyr her decesse, or yff she be maryd agayn, to retorne unto Robert my sun. I will that she have my lease of the house of Barlynges and the landes therto belongyng with the resydue of the yeres contenynyd therin. To Margaret Browne xiij*s* iiij*d*. To William Browne a yowe and a lambe. To Robert Browne one yowe. To William Hyddylston one yowe. To Henry Browne one yowe. To John Howgate one yowe. To Sebastyan Forman on yowe. To John Colson one yowe. I will that George Browne be the supervisor, and to have for hys labor xiij*s* iiij*d*. I will that my hole housholde be kepte, and no particion of my goodes be mayd for the space of one yere aftyr my dethe, so that my will may be fulfyllyd of the hole stocke, and than the resydue of my goodes not bequethyd, I will that they be equally devydyd betwene Johanne my wyff and my ij sonnys Roberte and Richerde, whome I make with my sayd wyff my laufull executors, that they may performe thys my will to the honor of God and profet of my soule. Thes beryng

wytnes; Sir John Sutton, vicar of Scopwyk, Godfrey Huddylston, Robert Hall, Robert Webster, with other mo.

Proved before P at Navenby, 4 November 1533.

273.   JOHN MARGESON [OF TETFORD]
         [LCC 1532–34, fo. 203v]

28 July 1533. I, John Margeson, beyng in hole mynde, makes my will. Fyrst I bequethe my soule to God allmyghtty and to Our Lady St. Mary and to all the saintes in heven, and my body to be buryd in the churche erthe of St. Mary's of Tetforthe. To the high alter of Tetforthe iiij*d*. To the bellys of Tetforthe xvj*d*. To Our Lady of Lincoln iiij*d*. To Our Lady's warke in Lincoln ij*d*. To Belcheforthe church iiij*d*. To Salmonby churche iiij*d*. To Edwarde my sun ij yeryng sterys and one qwye, and fyve schepe. To Agnes my doughter one cowe and one calve. To Jenet one cowe and iiij schepe. To Elizabethe one qwy and iiij schepe. To Alice one qwye and iiij schepe. To Mathew one yeryng calve and one calve of thys yere, and v schepe. To John Regmunde one schepe. To Thomas Wade wyffe one schepe. To Alice Regmunde one schepe. To Grace Musgrave one schepe. To Sir Robert Bradforthe one hog. To Thomas Regmunde one schepe. To Thomas Margeson a bushyll malte. To Thomas Pygot a bushyll malte. To Walter Regmunde a bushyll barly. To Elizabethe my wyff, whome I make my hole executrix of the resydue of my goodes [sic]. And yff ought cum to my wyff at thys tyme, the sayd resydue of my goodes for to be devydyd emong my syx chyldren, Edwarde, Mathewe, Agnes, Jenet, Elizabeth, Alice. And yff owtte come to any of my vj chyldren, ilk[113] one for to be oder heyres. Thes be the wytnes of my last will; Sir Robert Bradforte, John Chappell, Christofer Tayllor, John Carter, cum aliis.

Proved before P at Horncastle, 29 October 1533.

274.   JOHN PAKEY [OF SUTTERTON]
         [LCC 1532–34, fo. 190]

28 July 1533. I, John Pakey of Soterton, hole in mynde and good of remembraunce beyng, makes my testament concludyng therin my last will. Fyrste I bequethe my soule to God allmyghtty, to Hys blessyd mother Our Lady St. Mary, and to all the holly cumpeny in heven. And I will and bequethe my body to be buryd in the holly churcheyerde of Our Blessyd Lady of Sutterton. And my mortuary aftyr the statutes newly orderyd by the parliamente of our soverayne lorde, Kynge Henry the Eight in the xxj[ty] yere of hys reigne. To our mother churche of Lincoln iiij*d*. To the orphans of St. Catheryn's withowt the wallys of Lincoln iiij*d*. To the high altare of Our Blessyd Lady of Sutterton for tithes necligently forgottyn iiij*d*. To the onornament of every altare within the same churche ij*d*. To every light counttable within the same churche ij*d*. To the churche warke of the same churche ij*s*. I will that one annuall seculare preste do syng one trentall at Our Lady's altare, callyd Our Whyte Lady, within the churche of Sutterton for my soule, the soulys of my father and mother, my good benefactors' soulys and all Crysten soulys, and he to have for hys wagys x*s*. To John Pakey my sonne one cowe of color red and my best

---

[113] 'Each'.

bed with the tester and all that to it belongys. To Roger Pakey my sonne one qwy of color red. To Agnes Pakey my doughter one brendellyd dowyd cowe, ij schepe, one matteres, one coverlyd the nexte beste, ij pare schetes, one pare flaxyn and the other pare hardyn, one bolster with the coveryng, ij pillose with the coverynges, halff one dosyn pecys of puter, one bassyn potte the nexte beste and one bed tester, also my best beades and my harnest gyrdyll aftyr the decesse of Catheryne my wyff. To Catheryne my wyff my hede messuage with all the landes and tenementes lying in Sutterton, to bryng up my chyldren and kepe my houses in repare unto John Pakey my sonne cum to and be of the age of xviij yeres, provydyd alway that yff [it] fortune Catheryne my wyff to mary agayne and John my sonne cannot agre with her husbande and her, then I will that Catheryne my wyff have the sayd mansion with the sayd landes and tenementes but the space of viij yeres nexte foloyng the date heroff. And then I will that Thomas Tonnerde have the custody of the sayd John my sun and the sayd mansion with the sayd landes and tenementes unto the sayd John my sun cum to and be the foresayd age of xviij yeres. [fo. 190v] And at the ende and terme of the sayd xviij yeres I will that the aforesayd John Pakey my sonne have the aforesayd mansyon with the landes and tenementes lying in Sutterton under thys condicion, that he pay, or cause to be payd, to Agnes Pakey my doughtter at the day of her mariage, xls sterlyng. To Roger Pakey my sun all my landes and tenementes lying in Swynneshed and Byker aftyr the decesse of Catheryne my wyff, yff John my sonne will be contente. Yff he will not be contente, then I will he have as muche lande and pastur lying in Sutterton in lyke valewe and porcion. Also I will that whoseoever shall have the forsayd landes and tenementes in Swynneshed and Byker shall upholde and kepe the obbyte of my grandsers of one of the acres of the forsayd landes as it dothe specify in hys will. Also I will that all my moveable goodes and catell that I have bequethyd and gyffyn to my chyldren in thys my testament and last will, I will that Catheryne my wyff shall let and delyver for the proffet of them continently after my decesse. And yff it fortune any of all my forsayd chylder dy or departe owt of thys present lyff or they cum to or be the aforesayd age, or at suche tyme as I have bequethyd or gyffyn them other landes or moveable goodes, I will the sayd landes and goodes remayn from one to another. And yff it fortune Catheryne my wyff and all my foresayd chyldren dy or departe owt of thys present lyff withowt heyres of ther bodys laufully begottyn, then I will that my hed mansion with the grounde under hit lying in Sutterton, remayn to the nexte of my blode. Also I will that all my other landes and tenementes lying in Sutterton and Byker be solde be the handes of the churchewardens of the sayd townys at that tyme beyng, to fynde one seculer annuall preste to say messe one yere at Our Lady's altare, callyd Our Whyte Lady, within the churche of Sutterton, and he to have for hys salary vl vjs viijd. The resydue of the money to be gyffyn to pore people within the sayd townys. The resydue of all my goodes not bequethyd nor gyffyn, I gyff and put to the disposicion of Catheryne my wyffe, whome I orden and make to be my true and faythfull executrix to bryng me forthe, pay my dettes, bryng up my chyldren and dispose my goodes as she shall thynke best to plese God, for the moste helthe and proffyt for my soule and for all Christen soulys, by the oversyght and good discrecion of John Benacle, whome I make the supervisor, and he to have for hys labor and busynes ijs. Thes wytnes; Sir John Eschedale, prest of Sutterton, Richard Benacle of the same and John Ketell of the same, with other mo.

Proved before P at Swineshead, 9 October 1533.

275.   JOHN SERGYAUNT [OF THE CITY OF LINCOLN]
       [LCC 1532–34, fos. 176v–177v]

30 July 1533. I, John Sergyaunt of the Citie of Lincoln, fyshmonger, hole of mynde and good remembraunce, lovyd be God allmyghtty, makes my last will and testament. Fyrst I bequeth my soule to allmyghtty God and Our Lady St. Mary and all the hole compeny of heven, and my body to be buryed within the churche or churchyerde of St. Benedycte's as my executors shall thynke most convenyent. To the high altare of St. Benedicte's for my tithys forgottyn vjs viijd. I bequethe for my mortuary as the use is at thys tyme. To the high altare of Bultham iijs iiijd. To the high altare of St. Botulphe xxd. To the high altare of St. Margaret in Wykford xxd. To Our Lady warke xvjd. To the clerke gylde xijd. To Our Lady gylde in St. Benedicte's xijd. To the Trinite gylde in the same paryshe xijd. To St. Thomas gylde in St. Swythune paryshe viijd. To Our Lady gylde in St. Mary paryshe viijd. To the gret gylde off Our Lady xijd.[114] To every order of the frerys within Lincoln xxd, and every house to say a dirige and messe of requiem for my soule and all Crysten soulys. To everych on off my chyldren fyve poundes a pece, to be takyn off suche goodes and money as I have, and they to be ordred [fo. 177r] and rewlyd by myn executors. And yff eny of them fortune to departe owt of thys worlde afore they cum to the age off xviij yeres, then I will that xxs of every partes of theym that so departes be done for ther soulys. And the resydue to be devydyd emonges them that shall fortune to lyve, and to Margery my wyff yff she then be alyve. And yff they all departe afore the sayd age, then I will that all ther partes, excepte xxs apece to be done for every one of ther soulys, the resydue to remayn to my executors to be disposyd for my soule and all Crysten soulys. And yff my executors put eny of them furthe to service and pay eny money therfore, I will that it shall be alowyd and takyn of ther partes that so is put forthe unto they cum to the age of xviij yeres of age. Also I will that yff they be not put forthe, then my sayd wyff to bryng them up of the resydue of my goodes which I bequethe not. And they to be not barryd of no parte of bequest of the sayd fyve poundes for eny charge for ther bryngyng up with her. To Orman Hyll vjs viijd. To Elizabethe Kater vjs viijd. To Alice Lamberde iijs iiijd. To the churche of St. Benedicte's for my buryall vjs viijd. I gyff and will at the day of my buryall ther shall be gyffyn emonges prestes and clerkes, suche as shall be at messe and dirige xxs as my executors shall thynk best. Also, whereas my brother Wylson and I dyd occupy joyntly certen fyshynges, the whiche was Thomas Scharper's, I will that Margery my wyff and Thomas Grene occupy the sayd ferme conjunctly togyder duryng the terme of my yeres, payng and doyng in all causys as my broder Wylson dyd. And the sayd Thomas to pay at hys intrest to my wyff xxvjs viijd. To everychon of my godsuns and goddoughters iiijd. I make and orden my executors my wyff Margery and Robert my yongest sonne, to order and dispose my goodes accordyng to my wyll. Also I make Robert Wylson my kynsman supervisor of thys my sayd last will and testament, to se it performyd, [fo. 177v] and he to have for hys labor xiijs iiijd. Thes beyng wytnes; Sir John Shakylton, my gostly

---

[114] The Great Gild of Our Lady was located in St. Andrew's, in Wigford, Lincoln, and was one of two in the same church, St. Anne's being the other: Chantry Certificates (1923), 205–6.

father and curet, William Dyghtton, Sir William Smyth, Thomas Grene, Hugh Sergeant. The day and the yere abovesayd.

Proved before P at Lincoln, 27 August 1533. Adm. granted to Margery the relict and executrix, reserving power to grant to Robert the son and co-executor when he shall come to lawful age.

276. EDMOND MICHELL [OF SKENDLEBY]
[LCC 1532–34, fo. 209]

2 August 1533. I, Edmunde Michell of Skendylbe, hole of mynde and remembraunce, makes my testament. Fyrste I bequethe my soule to allmyghtty God, to Our Lady St. Mary and to all the saintes in heven. My body to be buryed in the churcheyerde of St. Peter in Skendylby. To the high altare for forgottyn tythys, yff ther be any be my negligence, iijs iiijd or halffe a quarter wheate. To iij altares in the churche of Skendylby, every one of them, xijd. To Our Lady warke of Lincoln xxd. To the iiij orders of frerys in Boston, every one of them, iiijd. To Alice my wyffe my best oxen, a blak geldyng and a gray mare, the plowe, the wane with the purtenances, iij kye and as many schepe as to make vjl xiijs iiijd. Also a cownter, a ambre, the best brasse potte and one lyttyll potte of a gallon, the best panne, a laver, a chaffer, a bed coveryng, the best coverlyd and a blew coverlyd, ij best [fo. 209v] matteres, iij pare of flaxen schetes and one pare of hardyn, a xl presse, ij bordyn beddes in the seller, a chyste, iiij pilloys, ij longer and ij shorter, the puter to be devydyd in ij partes, my wyffe to have the one halffe and my ij doughters to have the oder halffe and a forme, so that my wyff have to the valor of xl. I will that my wyff have her fyndyng to Michelmas cum twelvemonthe yff she mary not or that tyme. And yff she mary, then I will she have to her maryage one quarter malte and half a quarter wheate and my russyt gowne. To John my sun a gray mare and a bay stagge, my draught sterys, a pare of new whelys, a pare of yren gales, the longyst table, my best gowne and best dooblet and best jerkyn, a fustyan dooblet, a violet jerkyn, my best cote and a brasse potte. To William my sun a dowyd stag, a blak stere and as muche money to be takyn of my croppe as to by hym a felloy. To Richerde my sun ij yeryng calves and upwarde. To Ame and Beatrix my doughters the resydue of my puter, and ether of them to have iiij quarters malte and a quarter wheate, and other of them to have a bed in the chamber. I will ther be a trentall done for my soule and all Christen soulys. The resydue of my goodes, my will fulfyllyd, my dettes payd, I will they be at the disposicion of John my sonne and Alexander Browne, whome I make my executors to dispose for my soule and all Christen soulys. Thes wytnes; Sir Nicholes Fawne, vicar, William Bartylmew, Simon Merell, and other mo. I will that John and William my sonnys have my copy duryng the yeres, and that Alexander Browne have for hys labor iijs iiijd.

Proved before P at Partney, 10 November 1533.

277. AGNES GODFRAY [OF WAINFLEET ALL SAINTS]
[LCC 1532–34, fo. 212]

8 August 1533. I, Agnes Godfray of Waynflet All Halloys, wydo, of one good mynde and memory, makes thys my last will. [fo. 212v] Fyrste I bequethe my soule to God allmyghtty, to Our Lady St. Mary and to all the holy cumpeny of heven. My

body to be buryed in the churcheyerde of All Halloys. To Our Lady of Lincoln one sylver ryng and iiij*d* in money to her warke. To the high altare in the churche of All Halloys Waynflet for tenttes forgottyn xij*d*. To Our Lady altare iiij*d*. To St. Nicholes altare iiij*d*. To Agnes Foster one cowe, one cownter, my best chare, best fether bed, the best spytt with cobbardes, one pare bedstokes, one forme bust, one pare flaxen schetes, one bolster, one red coverlyd, v pecys puter, one brasse potte, one panne, one candylstyk, one chaffer, one kertyll, one kyrchyff, one pare sylver hookes, my best ryng. To Emmot Foster junior one cobarde, one fether bed, one chare, one pare flaxen schetes, one grene coverlyd, one candylstyk, one pare bedstokes, one forme, one brasse potte, one panne, one sylver ryng, v pecys puter, one kyrchyff, one spyt, one long bolster, one sydeborde. To Richerd Caudray ij puter dooblers, one potte, one panne, xx*d* in money. To Robert Caudra ij puter dooblers, one potte, one panne, xx*d* in money. To John Olyver on panne. To Crystyne Jonson ij pare schetes, one matterys, one coverlyd, one pare bedstokes, one brasse potte, one panne, one dyshelfe, one kyrtyll, one petycote, one kyrchyff, ij candylstykes, one lyttyll borde, vj treyn dyshes. To Margaret Hyll one kyrtyll, one petycote, one kyrchyff. The resydue of my goodes not gyffyn I will be at the discrecion of John Caudray, whome I make my executor that done to occupy that dothe remayn in warkes of charyte for the helthe of my soule, all my frendes' soulys, with all Christen soulys, dischargeyng hys conscience as he will make answer, and he thus doyng to have for hys labor iij*s* iiij*d*. Thes beryng wytnes; Sir Richerde Ransun, curate of the sayd churche, Sir John Dykynson, cum quibusdam aliis.

Proved before P at Partney, 10 November 1533.

278.   EDWARD WARDALE [OF KILLINGHOLME]
        [LCC 1532–34, fos. 254v–255r]

9 August 1533. I, Edwarde Wardale of Kyllyngham, seke in body and hole in mynde and memory, makyth my will and testament. Fyrste I bequethe my soule to God allmyghtty, Our Lady St. Mary and [fo. 255r] to all the celestiall cumpeny of heven, and my body to be buryed in the churcheyerde of St. Dionise in Kyllyngham, with my mortuary aftyr the decre of the statute. To the high altare for oblacions and tithys forgottyn xij*d*. To the churche warke of Kyllyngham one acre of wheate. To the gylde of the Holy Trinite xij*d*. To every one of my godchylder ij*d*. To the altare of the cathedrall churche of Lincoln iiij*d*. To Our Lady of Hull iiij*d*. To St. Margaret of Kettesby iiij*d*. I will that my wyff, or ellys some of my chyldren, have a cowe to fynde a light before the ymage of Our Lady in the churche aforesayd, standyng in a piller in the northe syde, so long as any of them be disposyd to occupy it. And when the wyffe or chylder be not disposyd to fynde the light no longer, that then it shall be lefull for my wyffe or William my sun, whome I do make my executors, to delyver or cause to be delyveryd to the churchewardens of the churche of Kyllyngham, a cowe or a qwye to the value of vj*s* viij*d*. To Richerde Wardale my sun xl*s* for hys childe parte, a cople of stottes[115] and a cowe. To Agnes Wardaile and Isabell Wardayle my doughters, ether of them, xl*s* and a cowe for ther chylde partes. The resydue of my goodes I gyff to Christyan my wyffe and William my sun, whome I make my executors to dispose theym moste meritorios and

[115] 'Stoats'.

helthefull for my soule and all Christen soulys. Thes wytnes; Sir John Harpham, vicar, Steven Melson and John Berdesall, with other mo presente.

Proved before P at Caistor, 27 October 1534.

279. HERMAN ISBRANDE [OF THE NETHERLANDS]
[LCC 1532–34, fo. 121v]

12 August 1533. I, Herman Isbrande, Hollender, hole of mynde and remembraunce, makes my will and testament. Fyrste and formest I bequethe my soule to the mercy of allmyghtty God and to Our Lady St. Mary, and to all the holly cumpeny of heven, and my body to be humate and buryd within the churche of the Blake Frerys. To our mother churche of Lincoln xij*d*. To the pore orphans at St. Catheryn's withowt the barres in Lincoln xij*d*. To John Swyllyngton my rydyng cloke, my frese goune furryd with lamm, and a sherte. To William Smyth a sherte. I will that ther be a preste founde to syng for me the space of a yere in the appostellys quere within the paryshe churche of Boston, at ix of the clocke the sayd messe to begynne. I will that the iiij orders of frerys bryng me to my sepulture, and they to syng dirige for me, and for ther labors xiij*s* iiij*d*. I make my executor Alice my wyffe, and John Goldesmyth to be her assystant in the sayd execucion, he to have for hys panys and labor my beste gowne and my best bonnet, best dooblet and my lyttyll hanger. The resydue of my goodes not bequethyd, I bequethe and gyff them holy to Alice my wyff, she to order them and dispose aftyr her discrecion. Wytnes of thys my last will; William Smyth, John Berman, John Swyllyngton, John a Towres, with other mo. Sic finivit vitam in Christo Jhesu.[116]

Proved before P at Boston, 3 March 1533/4.

280. AGNES MYDDYLTON [OF LUDBOROUGH]
[LCC 1532–34, fos. 218v–219r]

14 August 1533. I, Agnes Myddylton of Ludburgh, beyng of good and perfecte remembraunce, makes thys my last will. Fyrst I bequethe my soule to God, and my body to be beryd in the churche or churchyerde as it shall please John Burman, whome [fo. 219r] I make my executor. I bequethe to Mr. Parsone vj*s* viij*d*, desyeryng hym to be good frende to my executor, John Burman. To Catheryne my doughter vj*s* viij*d*, or ellys so muche croppe as is worthe so muche money. And I will that my doughter Catheryn Palmer shall have no more of my goodes excepte it will please John Burman to gyff to her any more of hys own good will. The resydue of my goodes and my dettes perteynyng or belongyng to me, I gyff them to John Burman. Thes beryng wytnes; Mr. George Gylys, John Cayd, William Cayd, Robert Burton, with other mo.

Proved before P at Louth, 12 November 1533.

---

[116] 'Thus he ended his life in Christ Jesus.'

281.   JOHN WAKEFELDE [OF EWERBY]
       [LCC 1532–34, fo. 119r]

16 August 1533. I, John Wakefelde of Iwardeby, hole of mynde and good remembraunce beyng, makes my last will. In the fyrste I bequethe my soule to God allmyghtty, Our Lady St. Mary and to all the blessyd cumpeny of heven. My body to be buryd in the churcheyerde of St. Andro of Iwardeby. To the high altare ther for tithes forgottyn xij*d*. To Our Lady warke of Lincoln viij*d*. To Margery my wyff and to her assygnes, my house that I dwell in with the appurtenances. To Margaret Ley my servant one acre wheate, one acre barly, one acre peys and one yong qwye, the color red. To Agnes Sherpe xx*ty* kyrffe turvys and one cupborde. To Robert Greg one jerkyn. To Alice, Robert Greg doughter, one holdyng swyne. To Agnes, Robert Greg doughter, ij new brewyng vessell. To Richard Glover one fole, the color browne. The resydue of all my goodes I gyff to Margery my wyff, the which I make my true executer that she may order and dispose them for the helthe of my soule and my good frendes' soulys, by the oversyght of John Bole of Iwardeby, and he to have for hys labor vj*s* viij*d*. Thes wytnes; Sir Richard Typler, vicar, Robert Dewe, Robert Garwyll, with other mo.

Proved before P at Sleaford, 2 March 1533/4.

282.   JOHN BLANCHERDE [OF SWINESHEAD]
       [LCC 1532–34, fo. 191r]

19 August 1533. I, John Blancharde of Swynneshed, of hole mynde and of good memory beyng, make my testament and laste will. Fyrste I bequethe my soule to God, to Our Lady, and to all saintes. My body to be buryd in the churcheyerde of Our Lady in Swynneshed. For my mortuary as the lawe requiryth. To Our Lady warke of Lincoln iiij*d*. To the high altare of Swynneshed xij*d*. To the fatherles chylder of Saynt Catheryn's iiij*d*. To the churche warke ther xx*d*. I will be receyvyd as a dede brother in Our Lady gylde of Swynneshed, payng for the same iij*s* iiij*d*.[117] To John Cadbe of Byllesby one matteres, one coverlyd, one bolster, one pare of flaxyn schettes and one pare of harden schetes, one pare of bedstokes, one potte of brasse. To John Stonnys of Hanney one potte of brasse, one pare of flaxyn schetes. To Thomas Hall of Swynneshed my best gowne furryd with blak lamme. I will William Maydenwell my servant and Robert Cony shall equally devyde betwene them all my workyng toollys belongyng to my occupacion. To the sayd William my violet cote. The resydue of all my goodes not bequethyd, my dettes payd and funerall expenses deductyd, I gyff to Johann Cony my wyff, whome I make my executrix, she to pay my dettes and to dispose for the welthe of my soule. Thes beyng wytnes; Sir Thomas Garton, vicar, Thomas Hall, William Bennet, John Welche, with other mo.

Proved before P at Swineshead, 9 October 1533.

---

[117] An explicit statement of the practice of enrolling the dead as members of gilds and fraternities in order to secure intercession on behalf of their souls.

283.   RICHARD HYCKES [OF BOSTON]
        [LCC 1532–34, fos. 139v–141v]

19 August 1533. I, Richerde Hyckes of Boston, marcer, syk in body and in remembraunce perfyte, make my testament therin concludyng my laste will. Fyrste I bequethe my soule to allmyghtty God, to Our Blessyd Lady and to all the celestyall cumpeny in hevyn, and my body to be buryd within the paryshe churche of Boston agenste the schorte stolys of Our Lady.[118] To my mortuary as the lawe requiryth. To the high altare in Boston for tithys and oblacions forgottyn xxd. To the gylde of corpus Christi in Boston xijd. To the gylde of Our Lady ther as moche as shall be due unto me at the feste of St. Michell the archaungell nexte commyng,[119] yff I fortune to decesse before that tyme. To the gylde of St. Peter xijd. To the gylde of St. Catheryne viijd. To the gylde of St. George viijd. To the Trinitie gylde viijd. To the gylde of St. Jamys iiijd. To the gylde of the holly roode iiijd. To the gylde of the Assumpsion of Our Lady iiijd. To the gylde of the Ascension of Our Lorde iiijd. To the gylde of St. Thomas iiijd. To the appostyllys gylde xijd. To the gylde of St. John Baptiste iiijd. To the gylde of the appostyllys Simon and Jude iiijd. To the gylde of All Halloys vjs viiijd. To the gylde of vij martyrs xijd. To Our Lady's warke at Lincoln xxd. To the orphans of Saynt Catheryn's withowt the barrys at Lincoln xijd. Thys is the laste will of me Richerde Hyckes, mayd the day and yere before wryttyn. To Jeneyt my wyff for terme of her lyff the copy of the house that I dwell in, and aftyr her decesse I will it remayn to Jasper my sun yff he will dwell within the towne and occupy the occupacion the terme of my sayd yeres. And yff he do not dwell within the towne and also occupy the occupacion, I will it remayn to Christofer my sun uppon lyke condicion. And yff the sayd [fo. 140r] Christofore do not lyff and dwell therin occupying the sayd occupacion, then I will it remayn to Melchior my sun of the same condicion. And yff it fortune the sayd Melchior to decesse or not to dwell therin aftyr the condicion aforesayd, I will it remayn to Alice the wyfe of John Renolde my sun-in-lawe, in maner and forme as is aforesayd duryng the terme in the sayd copy conteynyd. And yff it fortune the sayd Alice to decesse before the ende and terme of the yeres conteynyd in the sayd copy, I will it remayn to Fredyswyde my doughter and her assygners duryng my yeres. And yff ought cum at my sayd wyff or any of my sayd chyldren before the yeres be expressyd, and none of them be hable to occupy the sayd house, I will the sayd copy be solde by my executrice or the executors of her, and the money therof receyvyd to be equally devydyd emonges my chyldren that be lyffyng. And yff there be none of them lyffyng unto the ende and terme of the sayd yeres, then I will the alderman of Corpus Christi for the tyme beyng, or hys levetennaunte, sell my sayd copy to the beste avauntage and the money therof receyvyd I will the sayd gylde have xs, and the reste I will the sayd alderman and brether dispose in dedes of charyte wher it shall be thought by them moste nede for the helthe of my soule, my wyffe soule, my frendes' and all Christen soulys. To my sayd wyff duryng her lyffe my tenement at the Whyte Frerys' gate,[120] and aftyr her decesse I will it remayn to Jasper my sun

---

[118] A stole is either an item of female clothing or an embroidered strip of linen hanging down in front of an altar. Hence Hyckes is requesting burial either at the foot of a large image of St. Mary, or by the altar belonging to her gild in St. Botolph's Boston.

[119] I.e. Michaelmas, 29 September.

[120] The house of Carmelite friars in Boston was granted its licence in 1293, and acquired its main site on the west bank of the river in 1307. After the dissolution, the town purchased the whole five-acre site in 1544–45: *VCH Lincolnshire*, II, 216–17.

and to hys heyres of hys body laufully begottyn [remainder to] Christofer my sun and hys heyres of hys body [remainder to] Melchior my sun and hys heyres of hys body [remainder to] Alice Renolde my doughter and to her heyres of her body [remainder to] Fredeswyde my doughter and her heyres in fe symple. To the forsayd Jenet my wyffe my tenement in the Sowthe Ende which I purchesyd of Julyan Nethermyll duryng the terme of her lyffe, and aftyr her decesse I will it remayn to Alice Renolde my doughter and the hayres of her body. And for lacke of heyres of her body laufully brought I [fo. 140v] will it remayn to Jasper my sun and hys heyres of hys body [remainder to] Christofer and Melchior my sunnys in lyke maner [remainder to] Fredeswyde my doughter, her heyres and assygnes in fe symple. To Jenet my wyff my house in Bochar Laine duryng her lyffe, and aftyr her decesse I will it remayn to Fredeswyde my doughter and to the heyres of body [remainder to] Jasper, Christofore and Melchar my sonnys lynyally in lyke maner [remainder to] Alice Renolde my doughter and to her heyres and assygners in fe symple. I gyff [to my wife] my gardyn at the coy pyt[121] which I bought of Julyne Nethermyll duryng her lyff [remainder to] Christofore my sun and to the heyres of hys body [remainder to] Japser Melcher and Alice Renolde in maner and forme as is before sayd [remainder to] Fredeswyde my doughter and to her heyres and assygnes in fe symple. To Melcher my sonne a tenement, a mose grounde[122] with a fyshyng therto belongyng which I purchesyd of Bulloke lying in Waynflet immediatly aftyr my decesse, to hym and hys heyres of hys body. And I will that hys mother have the oversyght therof unto suche tyme as he come to laufull age [remainder to] Jasper my sun and hys heyres of hys body [remainder to] Christofore my sun and hys heyres of hys body [remainder to] the assygnes of the sayd Christofor. I will that all my goodes moveable and unmoveable be praysed, and aftyr that I will my dettes be payd of the same, and that remanys to be equally devydyd in thre partes, the one for myselffe, the secunde to my wyff and the thyrde to my chyldren, that is to wyt, to Jasper, Christofore and Melchar, iche of them, forty markes sterlyng, and to Fredeswyde forty poundes sterlyng. And yff ther remayn anythyng of the thyrde parte over and above ther sayd legaces, I will it remayn to Jenet my wyff, to the bryngyng of them up. Also I will that none of my sayd sonnys have ther sayd legaces unto suche tyme they be of foure and twenty excepte a gret cause that it be thought for ther exhibicion or high proffyt. And yff the thyrde parte, that is to say my chyldren parte, will not amownt [fo. 141r] unto ther sayd legaces, I will it be deducte owt of every one of ther partes, rate and rate lyke. And yff it fortune any of theym to departe before they have ther parte delyveryd unto theym, I will the halffe of the parte of theym which shall so fortune to decesse to remayn to theym that be alyve equally emonges them, and the other halffe parte to bryng them to the grounde. And for the reste I will a preste syng a hole yere for my soule, my wyfe's, my chyldren and all Christen soulys, and he to have for hys stipende v*l* vj*s* viij*d*. And that remanys I will be bestowyd in dedes of charyty as to pore people and mendyng of highways. And yff it fortune them all to decesse before they have there partes delyveryd at the sayd age, then I will the one halffe of all ther sayd partes be bestowyd in mendyng of the highways within vj mylys nexte abowt Boston wher it shall be thought moste nede, and the other halffe I will have a preste to syng for my soule, my wyfy's soule, my chyldren and all Crysten soulys, the space of syx yeres,

---

[121] This seems literally to mean 'cess-pit'.
[122] A 'mossground', or peatbog, with fishing rights.

and he to have yerely for hys stipende v*l* vj*s* viij*d*. And that remanys I will it be gyffyn yerely duryng the sayd vj yeres in the Lente to pore people within the towne of Boston by even porcions. I will that Fredeswyde my doughter have her parte delyveryd her at the age of xxiiij^{ty} or the day of her mariage. I will that my parte be bestowyd and done for me in maner and forme as shall be conteynyd in a bill whiche I do leve with my wyffe and my gostely father. To John Reenalde my sun-in-lawe, Alice hys wyffe, Jasper, Christofer, Melcher and Fredeswyde my chyldren, every one of them, a black gowne at my buryall day. To Agnes Doughtty the wyffe of William Doughty a blak gowne whiche is at Butlar's. To my brother Thomas Hyckes of Tetbury my gowne furryd with hole foxe. To Wylliam Hyckes off Crommell my gowne furryd with foxe pultes. To yong Thomas Hyckes my brother my Frenche tawny gowne, gardyd with velvet and furryd with blak lamme. I forgyff my yong brother Thomas of Crommoll all the money that he awyth me. To Bullok my servant iiij yerdes off medlay tawny of the price of iiij*s* viij*d* the yerde of suche as is within my schoppe, of that pece the lynyng and makyng of the same, iiij pare of my best hose, a dooblyt of myn of blak chamlet, ij bonnyttes off myn awne were, a dooblyt to be mayd unto hym of suche fustyan as he will chose within my schoppe, iij new schertes of xv*d* or xvj*d*, the scherte suche as I by at Lundon, a jakkyt of cottom fresyd and furryd of my awne were, and my jakkyt that I were of unwateryd chamlet and halffe my schoys. To Thomas my prentice [fo. 141v] and servauntt, yff he do owt hys apprentyshyp with my wyff and do her trew service, xx*s* and new rayment in all thynges at hys goyng owt. And yff so be my wyffe and he cannot agre, I will he have iij yerdes and a quartern of Northam clothe brode of the new color to make hym a cote,¹²³ Welshe lynyng to the same, and my wyffe to pay for the makyng a new dooblyt of Holmys fustyan mayd to hys backe, a bonnet of myn awn weryng, halffe my shoys, a cople of schertes siche as I by at Lundon of a xj*d* or xij*d* a scherte. To John Renolde my sun-in-lawe my Frenche tawny gowne lynyd with chamlet. To John Webster my violet gowne facyd with chamlet. I will that Jenet my wyff be my sole executrice. I will that Thomas Gyldon esquyer be supervisor, and he to have for hys labor for to helpe my wyffe and gyff her good councell xl*s*. To Sir Andro Hedlay and Sir John Rokeray, ether of them, x*s* for to helpe my wyffe. To Agnes Lownde iij yerdes of blake clothe to make her a gowne. I will that all suche money as shall fortune to come to due disposicion aftyr the maner and forme as is before wryttyn, I will it remayn within the revestiary¹²⁴ of Corpus Christi gylde, and the alderman and the bretherne of the same to dispose the same accordyng to the intent herof, and the gylde to have yerely owt of the same for ther labor, unto suche tyme it be disposyd, iij*s* iiij*d*. Thes beyng wytnes the day and yere above wryttyn; per me Andream Hedlay, per me Johannem Rokray, per me Nicholaum Blewyt.

Proved before P at Boston, 3 March 1533/4. Adm. granted to the executor.

---

¹²³ Northern broadcloths were among the poorest quality cloths produced in England, known for their offensive odour: E. Kerridge, *Textile Manufactures in Early Modern England* (Manchester, 1985), 19–22.
¹²⁴ A chest or cupboard used for storing valuables, including vestments and equipment for celebrating the mass.

284.   JOHN LANGTON [OF GOLTHO]
       [LCC 1532–34, fo. 178r]

20 August 1533. I, John Langton of Golthagh, makyth my testament and last will.
Fyrst I bequethe my soule to allmyghtty God and to Our Lady St. Mary, and to all
the holly cumpeny in heven. My body to be buryd in the chapell of St. Jamys in
Olde Bollyngton. And for my mortuary as the lawe shall require, and for my
sepulture as the custome is ther. To the reparacions of the chapell xij*d*. To Our
Lady of Lincoln iiij*d*. To Our Lady's warkes of Lincoln iiij*d*. To St. Hugh's hede
iiij*d*. To my lady Taylboys one ryall in golde.[125] To Master William Taylboys one
ryall in golde. To Masterys Vernon one ryall in golde. To Simon Butler my gret
coffer. The resydue of my goodes not gyffyn nor bequethyd I gyff unto Mr. William
Taylboys and Sir Walter Ireland, preste, whome I make my full executors, they to
minister my goodes and to dispose them for the well of my soule, my father and
mother soulys, and all Crysten soulys, as they shall thynke moste necessary. In
wytnes wherof thes personnes present; William Sawdun, John Waters, Wylliam
Fyn, with other.
       Proved before P at Lincoln, 12 September 1533.

285.   JOHN SMYTH [OF SURFLEET]
       [LCC 1532–34, fos. 193v–194r]

24 August 1533. I, John [fo. 194r] Smyth in the paryshe of Surflet, perfecte in
mynde and good remembraunce, makes my testament and last will. Fyrste I
bequethe my soule to God allmyghtty, to Our Lady St. Mary and to all the
saintes in heven, and my body to be buryd where it shall please God. To the high
altare in Surflet churche xij*d*. To the reparacions of Our Lady altare vj*d*. To the
reparacions of St. John altare vj*d*. To the churche warkes xx*d*. To the bellys xij*d*.
To every light in the churche of Surflet ij*d*. To Our Lady warke of Lincoln viij*d*.
To the fatherles chylder vj*d*. I will that my house that I wonne in be solde by the
handes of my executors, and the money that my executors shall receyve for the
sayd house, I will it shall be disposyd of a preste to syng for me, my father, my
mother and for all my good frendes soulys for so long tyme as the money will
extende. To Henry Allege one blak qwye. To Alice my syster the best gowne
whiche was my wyffe's and one russyt kyrtyll. To John Lorde my godfather my
grene cote and my best cappe. To Robert Wryght my violet cote. To Jenet
Herryson one red borlyng. To Margaret Abot one petycote. To every pore house
that hase no plough, one stryke of rye. To John Bracebryg xij*d*. To John Baret
xij*d*. The resydue of my goodes that is unbequethyd I will that my executors shall
sell suche goodes to do my funerall expenses and pay my dettes with, and the
money that remanys besyde my funerall expenses and my dettes payd, then I will
that my executors shall fynde a preste to syng for me and my frendes in the
churche of Surflet as long as the money will extende of, and for the disposicion of
my goodes accordyng to thys my last will. To Richerde Obrey xx*s*, and to John
Smyth xx*s*, whome I make my faythfull executors, to dispose my goodes
accordyng to my will to the honor of God and helthe to my soule. Wytnessyth;

---

[125] The ryal was a gold coin, slightly archaic by the early sixteenth century.

Sir Robert Thomson, William Nicolson, William Gyldyn, Robert Elethorpe, with other mo.

Proved before P at Spalding, 10 October 1533.

286.   CATHERINE STEVYN [OF ASWARDBY]
       [LCC 1532–34, fo. 131v]

24 August 1533. I, Kateryn Stevyn wedow, of gud and hole mynde, makythe my last wyll. Fyrst I bequethe my soule to allmyghtye God, Oure Ladye Seyntt Marye and all seynttes of heven. My bodye to be buryed nye my husbonde in churcheyerde of Seyntt Denys of Aswardbye. To the hye aulter of Seyntt Denys iiijd. To Ower Ladye warke of Lyncolln viijd. To the churche warkes of Aswardbye. To Ower Ladye of Crosten ijd. To Ower Ladye of Lankaster ijd. I bequeth mye fleckyd cow to the churche of Aswardbye for to kepe my husbande's obytt, and myn parsone, for bed reill, deryge and messe, to have xd bye yere. In brede and ayll to pore folke xd. To my dowghter Alyce a cowe. To my dowghter Annes a cowe with a whyte hede. To Jane Bakhouse a browne quye. To Alyce Bakhouse bullocke calffe. To Christofer my son a whyte meyre. To Helen Stevyn a que calffe. To Roberde my son a blacke meyre. To Helyn Newcome halffe a seame of berlye. To Roberde Bakhowse, mye sone-in-lawe, a cowe for helpynge of mye sone John Stevyn. The resydew of mye gudes nott bequethed I gyve to mye son Stevyn, whom I dow make my full executor for to dyspose my gudes for the helthe of mye soule and mye husbande's soule, and all Crysten soulles, as we wyll answer before the hye judge of heven. Thes wytnesses; Sir John Wylson, parson of Thimylbye, Mayster Wylliam Grantham, gentylman, with other moo.

Proved before P at Sleaford, 2 March 1533/4.

287.   WILLIAM SUERDE [OF FENTON]
       [LCC 1532–34, fos. 205v–206r]

28 August 1533. I, William Suerde of Fenton, of good mynde and remembraunce, bequethe my soule to God allmyghtty, to Our Lady St. Mary and to all the saintes in heven, [fo. 206r] and my body to be buryed in the churcheyerde of All Halloys of Fenton. To the high altare of Fenton ijs. To the high altare of Our Lady of Lincoln xijd. A trentall to be done for my soule xs. I bequeathe a lampe to be fun[126] in the churche of Fenton for ever vjs viijd. To the iiij orders of frerys, iche of them, one stryke of whete. To ich on of my godchylder one stryke of wheate. To my sun Henry Suerde one bownde carte with all that longes thertyll, and also one plowe with all that longes thertill. To my doughter Jenet Suerde iiij quarters barly, a cowe, a qwye and xiij schepe, and halffe the housholde stuff. To the gylde of St. Catheryne of Stubton one bushyll off barly. To Our Lady gylde of Fenton halffe a seame malte. The resydue of my goodes unbequethyd I gyff them to Alyson Suerde my wyff and to Thomas Suerde my sun, which I make my true executors to dispose the goodes for the helthe of my soule, and thes to be supervisors: Robert Preston the elder, William Rygures, William Suerde the elder, Henry Suerde, John Baker, iche of them to have ijs to se that my will be

---

[126] 'Found', i.e. 'funded'.

performyd. Wytnes; Sir William Bryan, John of Preston, Richerde Mapyltofte, with other mo.

Proved before P at Navenby, 4 November 1533.

288.   ROBERT KYMSON [OF MARTON]
        [Stow 1530–52, fo. 19r]

3 September 1533. I, Roberte Kymson of Marton, hole and perfytte of mynde, makys, ordenys and constitute my laste will. Fyrste I bequeth my saull unto almyghti God, to Owre Ladye Saynte Mare ande to all the holy company of heven, and my body and boyns to be berede in the parische churche of Saynt Margarete's in Marton. To Ouer Lady of Lincoln vj*d*. To Master Vicar on quarter of barly for all forgotten tythes. I bequeth on quarter barly to the churche of Marton for the mantenauns. To Richard Kymson my son fyve yois and v hogges, too oxen. To Thomas Kymson childerne iiij hogges. To Agnes Smyth a yonge pigge and on halffe quarter barly. To Ellen Kymson mi doughter ij queys and xij schepe. To Betris Kymson mi doughter j schepe hogge. To Elsabeth my wiffe all my gudes, moveable and unmeoveable, the whiche Elsabeth I make my executrix. Thes men berynge wittnes; Sir Richarde Nicson, prest, John Broune, Richarde Katskyn and Thomas Coplande, with many mo.

Proved before L, 15 November 1533. Adm. granted to the executrix.

289.   ROBERT WARE [OF WEST ASHBY]
        [LCC 1532–34, fos. 109v–110r]

3 September 1533. I, Robert Ware of Asby next Horncastell, the elder, hole of mynde and good remembraunce, makes thys my last will and testament. The fyrste I gyff and bequethe my soule to allmyghtty God and to Our Lady St. Mary and to all the celestiall cumpeny of heven, and my body to be buryed in the churcheyerde of All Halloys of Ashby. I gyff for my mortuary that at the lawe dothe require. To Our Lady of Lincoln xvj*d*. To the high altare of Ashby xij*d*. I will that a trentall of messes be celebrate in Ashby churche for me and all my benefactors. To the bellys of Ashby halffe a quarter of barly. To Agnes my wyff the howse that I dwell in with all that longes to it duryng her lyff naturall. And aftyr her decesse I will that William Ware my sun have the sayd house to hym and to hys heyres for ever. To Robert Ware my sun ij of my best oxen and a arke. To William and Robert, my sunnys, Wyllobe lande. To William my sun ij oxen. I will that William and Robert my sunnys plowe the lande that longes to my house of ther owne proper costes and chargeys, for the use of my wyff duryng her lyff. To Sir Henry Parker xvj*d*. To Johanne my doughter halffe a quarter barly, and to Elizabethe my doughter halffe a quarter barly. [fo. 110r] To John my brother halffe a quarter barly, and to Catheryne my syster halffe a quarter barly. To Margaret my syster halffe a quarter barly. The resydue of my goodes I gyff to Agnes my wyff and to William and Robert my sunnys, whome I make my executors that they dispose it for the helthe of my soule and all Christen soulys. Thes wytnes; Thomas Tupholme, Thomas Symkynson, William Smyth, John Ware, cum aliis de Ashby.

Proved before P at Lincoln, 18 September 1533.

290.   ROBERT PARKER [OF SPALDING]
       [LCC 1532–34, fo. 193v]

5 September 1533. I, Robert Parker of Spaldyng, of a hole mynde and good remembraunce, makes my last will and testament. Fyrste I bequethe my soule to God allmyghtty, to Our Lady and to all the hole cumpeny of heven, and my body to be buryd in the paryshe churcheyerde of Spaldyng. To the high altare in the forsayd churche iiij*d*. To Our Lady of Lincoln iiij*d*. To the orphans of St. Catheryn's ij*d*. To the Trinite gylde of Spaldyng xij*d*. To Helene my doughter my red flecte cowe, a bordyn bed, a fether bedde, a bolster, a coverlyd, ij pillose, ij pilloberes, ij pare of schetes, one pare of flaxyn and another of hardyn, a bordclothe, a towyll, iiij napkyns, ij platters, ij dyshes, ij sawssers, ij candylstykes, one salt seller, a standyng laver, a chyste, a bed hangyng, a chare, my grettyst brasse potte, ij pannys and a payntyd clothe. The resydue of my goodes unbequethyd, my dettes payd, I gyff them holy to Maryan my wyff whome I make my hole executrice, and Robert Bawmer my supervisor, and he to have for hys labor xij*d*. Whtynes thereof; Sir Thomas Love, preste, John Glesbryg, Emunnde Drawry, with other mo.

    Proved before P at Spalding, 10 October 1533.

291.   THOMAS GRAY [OF BOURNE]
       [LCC 1532–34, fo. 201r]

6 September 1533. I, Thomas Gray of Burne, hole of mynde and good remembraunce, make my testament and last will. Fyrste I bequethe my soule to allmyghtty God, to Our Lady St. Mary and to all the holly cumpeny of heven, and my body to be buryd in the paryshe churcheyerde of the holly appostyllys Peter and Paule within the towne of Burne. To the reparacions of the mother churche of Lincoln ij*d*. To Our Lady's offerynges ij*d*. To the high altare of Burne for offerynges and tithes forgottyn iiij*d*. To the reparacions of the paryshe churche of Burne iiij*d*. To the Trinite gylde in Burne iiij*d*. To Thomas my sonne a dooblet of fustyan. To the same Thomas and to John hys brother my best gowne betwyxte them. To William my sonne a violet cote. To Edmunde my sonne a jaket, a calve. To Robert my sonne a calve. To Thomas Wakelyng a calve. I will that my legaces, my dettes, the chargeys of my buryall day, seventh day and xxx^ty day, and the chargeys belongyng to the probacion of my will with all other chargeys that I am now chargeyd with, be levyed and takyn of my hole goodes and payd. And so thereoff dischargeyd and payd (thys truly done), I will that the resydue of my goodes be equally devydyd by the oversight and discrecion of William Smyth, William Scherpe, John Thomson and Robert Alen. And my wyff to have the one halffe parte to her awn use and proffyt, and the other halffe parte to be equally devydyd emonges my chyldren by the discrecion of the forsayd William Smyth, William Scherpe, John Thomson and Robert Alen, the whiche Johanne my wyff I make my full executrix to pay my dettes and to dispose off my goodes as is before rehersyd. Wytnes herof; Robert Haryson, preste, John Gyrlyng, Thomas Bryngley, with mo.

    Proved before P at Pickworth, 23 October 1533.

292.   THOMAS HORNESY [OF WELTON LE MARSH]
        [LCC 1532–34, fos. 214r–215r]

9 September 1533. I, Thomas Hornesy of Welton, beyng of hole mynde and good remembraunce, make and orden my testament and last will. Fyrste I bequethe my soule to allmyghtty God, to Our Blessyd Lady St. Mary and to all the saintes in heven, and my body to be buryd in the paryshe churche of St. Martyn in Welton aforesayd, in the myd ally. To the sayd churche of Welton iij*s* iiij*d*. To the high altare of the sayd churche vij*d*. [fo. 214v] To the bellys in the sayd churche xij*d*. To Our Lady of Lincoln vij*d*. To the bellys in Willughby churche vij*d*. To Agnes my wyffe vj*s* yerely duryng the terme of her lyff to be takyn owt of my landes in Slouthby, so that she bere her parte of the fyne of the sayd landes. Also iiij*s* yerely for the terme of her lyffe to be takyn of my landes callyd Kemp house. To the same Agnes my wyff in moveable goodes the value of x*l* and one plough, and one wane withowt beasse. To Alice my doughter vj*l* xiij*s* iiij*d* and one ambre. To Elizabethe my doughter vj*l*. To Sybbell my doughter vj*l*. To William Goodale one burlyng qwye and one yowe and one lambe. To Thomas Goodale one lambe. To every one of my godchyldren iiij*d*. I will that yff any of my sayd ij doughters decesse before they cum to laufull age every one of them to be other heyre. To William my sun all my landes in Botheby and Welton that was Hogeson and Mawer lande, to hym and to the heyres male of hys body laufully begottyn. And in defawte of suche issue of hys body laufully begottyn [remainder to] Godfrey and Thomas my sonnys. To Godfrey my sun all my landes in Slotheby to hym and to the heyres of hys body laufully begottyn for ever, aftyr the custome of the lordeschyp, and for defawte of issue of hys body laufully begottyn [remainder to] Thomas my sonne, and for defawte of issue of the sayd Thomas laufully begottyn [remainder to] the nexte of the stok, that is to say William Hornesy. And for defawte of issue of the same William, to remane to my sayd iij doughters. To Thomas my sun my landes in Habertofte callyd Kempte house, to hym and to the heyres of hys body laufully begottyn for ever [remainder to] Godfrey my sun and to he heyres of hys body laufully begottyn [remainder] [fo. 215r] as is before wryttyn, aftyr the custome of the lordeschyp. To Robert Johnson of Welton a bushyll of wheate. To Alice hys wyff a bushyll of malt. I will that my executors cause xviij messys to be done all of one day at Our Lady's Frerys in Boston, for my soule and all Christen soulys. I will that my executors dispose, the day of my buryall, halfepeny dole and at the vij^th day aftyr my buryall met and drynke within the towne of Welton. To Master Martyn Wymbyshe ij*s*. To Richerde Smalley ij*s*. To Robert Johnson of Claxby ij*s*, whome I put in truste to se everythyng orderyd accordyng to thys my testament and last will. The resydue of my goodes not beuqethyd I put them to the discrecion of Godfrey and Thomas my sonnys whome I orden myn executors, they to dispose theym as they shall thynke moste expedyent for the helthe of my soule and all Christen soulys. I desyre Mr. John Lytylbery, esquyer, to be supervisor, and I bequethe to hym for hys labor xiij*s* iiij*d*. Thes wytnes; Mr. Martyn Wymbyshe, Robert Johnson, John Wylliamson, Richerde Rosse, with other mo.

   Proved before P at Partney, 10 November 1533.

293. SIR JOHN BENTON [VICAR OF STAINTON BY LANGWORTH]
[LCC 1532–34, fo. 239v]

10 September 1533. I, Sir John Benton, vicar of Staynton, make and orden thys my laste will and testament. Fyrste I bequethe my soule to allmyghtty God, to Our Lady St. Mary, and all the saintes in heven, and my body to be buryd in the qwere of St. John Baptiste in Staynton. To St. John in the churche of Staynton vjs viijd. To the high altare in the same churche iijs iiijd. To a preste to syng a trentall of messys in the sayd churche, to pray for my soule and all Christen soulys xs. To Margaret Faldys my syster iij kye and xij schepe, and halffe of all my housholde goodes equally to be devydyd. To Catheryn Sanderson my servante ij kye and xij schepe. To Jenet Urry one cowe and vj schepe. To Luce Urry one cowe. To Catheryn [fo. 240] Betteson one cowe and vj schepe. To John Parker ij kye and x schepe. To William Urry x schepe. The resydue of my goodes I gyff them to Nicholes Sandreson and Sir George Storre, whome I make my executors to dispose for the helthe of my soule as they shall thynke beste. Wyttenes herof; Thomas Osgraby off Staynton, John Urry of the same, John Hopkynson, with diverse other.

Proved before P at Lincoln, 13 February 1533/4, by the executors.

294. WILLIAM STAFLAY [OF GAINSBOROUGH]
[Stow 1530–52, fo. 18r]

12 September 1533. I, William Staflay of Gaynsbrugh, sound of mynd and hole of memorie, makes my testament and last will. Fyrst I bequeth and gyffes my saull to almyghty Gode, besekyng Our Blessid Lady and all the sayntes in heven to pray for me, and my bodi to be buried in the churche of All Halowes in Gaynsbrugh. To the hie auter in Gaynsbrugh church iijs iiijd. To Owr Lady of Lincoln iiijd. To the iij gyldes light in Gaynsbrugh church xijd. To my wyffe the kechen as it standes, the parler, the hall chamber as they stande, to her and to hir ij doughters. To Margaret my wiffe this house that I whon in for the space of x yeres, sche payinge therfore to John Staveley my eldest sone yerely durynge the said x yeres vjs viijd, and sche to upholde the sayd house with thake and morter durynge the sayd x yeres. To Marget my wyffe and John Staveley the yonger and Rouland my sones, the house in the churche lane, and they to pay my dettes and my bequestes. I make myne executors Margat my wyffe, John Staveley the yonger and Rouland my sones. To John Staveley the yonger my son and Marget my wyffe one house in the market stede as apperith in a dede of gyft, the whiche sche hathe in her kepynge. To John Staveley the yonger one shope in the sayd house for ever. I will that Rouland my son shall occupy his stoke as he hathe done before for the space of iiij yeres in the barke house. Thes beynge wittnes; Thomas Toppclyffe, prest, Myles Staveley, Johannes Dobson, John Staveley the yelder, Galfridus Medley, with other mo.

Proved before L, 25 September 1533. Adm. granted to the executors.

295. WILLIAM STATHAM [OF GREAT PONTON]
[LCC 1532–34, fo. 198]

15 September 1533. I, William Statham of Panton the More, hole of mynde and good remembraunce, makes thys my last will and present testament. Fyrste I bequethe my soule to God, Our Lady and all Hys saintes, and my body to be buryd

in the churcheyerde of St. Guthlak in Panton. To Our Lady warke of Lincoln xij*d*. To the high altare of Lincoln viij*d*. To my curate to pray for me one seame barly. To the churche of Panton one seame barly. I will that my croppe, that is wheate, rye, barly, peays, oyttes, be devydyd in iiij partes, ij partes to Alice my wyff, the thyrde parte to Thomas Towers, the iiij parte to be disposyd for my soule and all Christen soulys. To Alice my wyff ij horssys and iiij marys with ij folys, plowgh, and all thyng that pertenys to the sayd plough, ij kye of the best, ij yerlyng calves of the best and all my housholde stuff in my house. To Thomas my sun ij qweys. To Agnes my doughter a cowe and a calve. To the sayd Thomas Towers ij of the best horssys. To Alice my wyff halff my arable landes to sawe thys yere, and [fo. 198v] Thomas Towers afore namyd, the other halff of the sayd arable landes to sawe thys yere. The resydue of all my goodes, aftyr my dettes and funerall expenses be payd and done, I put it to the discrescion of Sir Henry my brother, the whiche I make my executor, and to dispose it for my soule and all Christen soulys as he thynkes beste. Thes wytnesses; Sir Robert Horneby, parson of Panton the Lesse, Robert Butler, curate, Sir Henry Statham.

Proved before P at Grantham, 20 October 1533.

296. ROBERT BOWSER [OF GOSBERTON]
[LCC 1532–34, fo. 242]

16 September 1533. I, Robert Bowser of Gosberton, hole of mynde and of perfyte remembraunce, dothe make, orden and dispose thys my present testament and last will. Fyrste I bequethe my soule to allmyghtty God and to Our Blessyd Lady St. Mary and to all the holy cumpeny of heven, and my body to be buryd in the churcheyerde of the holy appostellys St. Peter and St. Paule in Gosberton. To the high altare of the same churche for my tithes forgottyn or negligently withholdyn iiij*d*. To every gylde in the same churche viij*d*. To the ij gret lighttes, to ether of them, viij*d* a pece. To the churche warke iiij*d*. To all Christen soulys light iiij*d*. To the reparacions of our mother churche of Lincoln iiij*d*. To the offeryng of Our Lady of Lincoln iiij*d*. To the fatherles chyldren of St. Catheryne withowt Lincoln walles viij*d*. To Simon Bowser my sun one cowe and xj*s* iiij*d*. To Alice Bowser my doughter one cowe, one stonyd horse and xx^ty stone chese. To Agnes Wymbytche one cowe. I will that [fo. 242v] myn executors underwryttyn do cause ij trentallys off messes to be celebrate and sayd in the churche off Gosberton aftyr my decesse, for my soule, my father and my mother soule and all my good frendes' soulys. All the resydue of my goodes I gyff unto Alice Bowser my doughter, and I will that Robert Saverye and the sayd Alice my doughter be my true executors. Thes beryng wytnes; Sir Henry Toplys, paryshe preste, Simon Smythe, Thomas Vassell and John Kyrke, with other.

Proved before P at Swineshead, 5 March 1533/4, by the executors.

297. WILLIAM HARYET [OF MUCKTON]
[LCC 1532–34, fo. 235r]

18 September 1533. I, William Haryet, of a hole mynde, makes my wyll. Fyrste I bequethe my soule to allmyghtty God, and my body to be buryed in the churcheyerde of the Holy Trinite in Muckton. To Our Lady of Lincoln iiij*d*. To

the high altare of Mukton vj*d*. The resydue of my goodes not gyffyn nor bequethyd I gyff to Margaret my wyffe, whome I make my sole executrix. Thes wytnes; Sir John Thorpe, John Pyse, Richerde Barbar, with other mo.

Proved before P at Muckton, 6 February 1533/4.

298.   SIR ROBERT WEST [VICAR OF LINCOLN CATHEDRAL]
        [D&C 1534–59, fo. 22]

18 September 1533. I, Sir Robert Weste, vicare of the cathedrall churche of Our Lady of Lincoln, hole of mynde and memory, fermly trustyng and belevyng in the fathe catholicke, makyth my last will and testament. Firste I bequethe my soule to allmyghtty God, Our Lady St. Mary and to all the holly cumpeny of heven, and my body to be buryed within the monastery above namyd. To the warkes of Our Lady for my buryall xx*s*. To the high altare and to Saynt Hugh heade iiij*d*. I bequethe for myn obytt: fyrste to my lorde deane xx*d*, also to every canon resydent xvj*d*, to the executor of myne obyt and for doyng of the messe xij*d*. To custos Petri xij*d*.[127] To the cacristone[128] for hys office vj*d*. To the subchaunter vj*d*. To the vi[ce] chauncellor vj*d*. To every vicare chorall viij*d*. To every chauntre preste vj*d*. To every pore clerke iij*d*. To every chorester ij*d*. To the clerke of the revestrare for hys office ij*d*. [fo. 22v] To the clerke of the chapiter vj*d*. To the clerke of the commune chamber vj*d*. To the constable of the churche vj*d*. To the under provoste clerke iij*d*. To the clerke of the warkes vj*d*. To ij messyngers of the churche, ether of them, iij*d*. To iiij virgers, every one of them, iiij*d*. To iiij bell ryngers, every one, iij*d*. To ij vigillys, either of them, iij*d*. To the porter iij*d*. To the rectors of the qwere iiij*d*. To the deacon and subdiacon, ether of them, ij*d*. To hym that settyth the hearse ij*d*. To the clerke of the chappell ij*d*. To iiij orders of frerys within Lincoln, every house, xij*d*. To the churche of Willyngham vj*s* viij*d*. To my mother vij*s* vj*d*. To my brother Richerde v*s*. To my syster Cecill v*s*. The resydue of my goodes I will that they be ordered and disposyd aftyr the discrescion of Sir Thomas Flowre, subchaunter, and John Weste my father, whiche I make my executors of thys my last will, and to receyve all my dettes and dewtyes and dispose them for the helthe of my soule. And I will that ether of the foresayd myne executors have for hys labor v*s*. Thes wytnesses; Syr William Bateman, Sir George Bewsher, Syr Raphe Balgwy and Sir James Syll.

Proved before George Heneage, dean, and the chapter of the cathedral church of Lincoln, 26 September 1534, in the chapter house of the said cathedral church. Adm. granted to the executors.

299.   ROBERT BENEWORTH [OF RIBY]
        [LCC 1532–34, fo. 194v]

21 September 1533. I, Robert Beneworthe of Ryby, of a hole mynde and memory, makes my testament and last will. Fyrste I bequethe my soule to God allmyghtty and to Our Lady St. Mary, and to all the saintes in heven, and my body to be buryed in the churcheyerde of St. Edmunde of Rybe, with that at be due to the churche at the lawe will requyre [sic]. To the high altare within the churche of Ryby

---

[127] Wardens of the gild of St. Peter.
[128] I.e. 'the sacristan'.

for forgottyn tithes xij*d*. To Our Lady's gylde in the same churche ij*s*. To St. John gylde in the same churche viij*d*. To our mother churche of Lincoln x*d*. To Our Lady warke in the same churche x*d*. I bequethe halffe a yere wages to a preste to syng for me and my good frendes, to be done aftyr the discrecion of my executors. To Thomas Beneworthe my brother x schepe, my best cote, my best dooblet, my best bonnet. To Margaret Beneworthe my syster x schepe, my best cote but one. To Isabell Kyng my awnte a cote, a schepe, and to her ij chylder ij schepe. To everich one of my awnt Stampe chylder, a schepe. The resydue off my goodes not wyt, I bequethe to Master Robert and to Richerde Stampe my unkyll, whome I make my executors that they my dispose it for the helthe of my soule. Wytnes heroff; Sir William Yeff, vicar, Thomas Parker, Robert Sqwere, with other mo.

Proved before P at Caistor, 14 October 1533.

300. ROBERT LEYMAN [OF SURFLEET]
      [LCC 1532–34, fo. 126]

22 September 1533. I, Roberde Leyman in the parysshe of Surflett, hole of mynde and good remembraunce, doo mye testamentt and last wyll. Fyrst I bequethe mye soull to allmyghtye God, Ower Ladye Sayntt Maryre, and to all the companye in heven, and mye bodye to be beryd wher it shall please God. For tytheys forgoten v*d*. To everye alter in the churche of Surflett ij*d*. To the sepulker lyghtt xij*d*. To Ower Laydy's lyghtt ij*d*. To the plowgh lyghtt ij*d*. To Ower Lady's werkes of Lincolln iiij*d*. To the fatherles chyldern ij*d*. To Leman mye son ij acre and a half called Clark land and halffe acre callyd Stolles, to hym and hys eyers of hys bodye lawfullye begoten, and if it fortun so that John mye sun dye before hys wyffe, then I wyll hys wyffe shall have it the terme of hyr lyffe, the forsayd ij acre and a half callyd Clarke lande and halffe acre callyd Stolles. And after her decease I wyll it remayn to the eyers of John mye son [remainder to] Roberde mye son, to hym and hys eyers of hys bodye [remainder to] Jenett mye dowghter, to hyr and hyr eyers of hyr bodye. And if itt fortun so that Jenett mye dowghter dye withoutt eyers of hyr bodye, then I wyll that the forsayd ij acre and a half callyd Clerke lande and half acre callyd Stolles shall be solde bye handes of the [fo. 126v] churche masters of Surflett, to dyspose the sylver therof in charitable warkes wheras the best in the parysshe thynkkes it is best to be disposyd. To Roberde mye son j acre and a half lyinge of the sowthe syde of the ey[129] ageynst mye howse in fe symple, and if it fortun so that Roberde mye son fall to poverte that he must sell thys acre and a half land, then I wyll that John mye son shall bye itt if he able to pay for itt. And bye thys mye last wyll I wyll that John mye son shall paye noo more but xxvj*s* viij*d*. And if itt fortun that John mye son be nott able to pay for itt xxvj*s* viij*d*, then I wyll that Roberde mye son shall make the best of the sayd lande that he maye bye the syght of hys frenddes. To John mye son mye plowghe and a cartt, and all that longes thertoo, iij mares and on horse, on olde redd cow. To Roberde mye son on cow, on calffe, ij follys, ij schepe. To Jenett mye dowghter all mye howsholde stuffe, on cowe, ij calffes, vj schepe to chose the best she can bye her frenddes. To John mye son ij schepe and ij boottes, on lam. I wyll that iff it fortun that Roberde mye son or Jenett mye dowghter fall in seknes, then I wyll they shall remayn with John my son to wynter be past, of mye costes and charges of syche croppes and whyt mettes as longes to the howes. The resydewe of

---

[129] 'Island', often referring to an a area of raised ground in marshy or Fenland areas.

mye goodes I wyll John mye son shall sell them, whom I make mye executor to dispose mye goodes to the pleasure of God. To Thomas Teryngton one yowe, whom I orden to be mye supervisor. The resydewe of mye guddes that leves, besyde mye deyttes payd and mye wyll fulfylled and fenerall expenses done, iff so mytche maye be spared, then I wyll have xxx^{ti} messes as a trentall song in the churche of Surflett. Wytnessethe; Sir Roberde Thomson, John Mortymer, John Leyman, John Fyssher, with other moo.

Proved before P at Spalding, 3 March 1533/4.

301.   WILLIAM COPELAND [OF RUSKINGTON]
       [LCC 1535–37, fos. 12v–13r]

24 September 1533. I, William Copelande, of hole mynde and good will, do make my last will. In primis I bequethe my soule to allmyghtty God and my body to be buryed in the holoyd churcheyerde of All Halloys in Ryskyngton. To Our Lady of Lincoln ij*d*. I bequethe for forgottyn tithys ij*d*. To John my eldest sun a bullok calve. To Agnes my doughter a redde calve of this yere. To William Henryson a yeryng stagge. To Dane Richard Robson a stryke of malte and my best sherte. To Helene my wyffe a blak dowyd cowe and a redde cowe cromple-hornyd, and all the housholde stuff not bequethyd, and the dwellyng in the house all her lyffe. And my sun John to fynde for her lyveyng all her lyffe. To William Plummer a schepe hogge. I make John my sun the yonger hole executor, he to have mine house and my lande that longyth therto [fo. 13r] with all the resydue of my goodes unbequethyd aftyr the dethe of Helene my wyffe (my dettes payd). To Jenet Copelande a bushyll of barly. Wytnes of thys; John Wryghtson, John Plummer the elder, John Mabyson, John Copelande and John Braye, vicar.

Proved before P at Sleaford, 21 April 1535.

302.   JOHN GRENE [OF HAGWORTHINGHAM]
       [LCC 1532–34, fo. 306r]

27 September 1533, 25 Henry VIII. I, John Grene, hole of mynde and seke in body, make my testament and last will. Fyrste I bequethe my soule to allmyghtty God, to Hys mother St. Mary and to all the saintes in heven. My body to be buryd in the paryshe churcheyerde of Hagworthyngham. To the paryshe churche of Hagworthyngham vj*s* viij*d*. To Our Lady warke of Lincoln vj*d*. To the paryshe churche of Tetforthe vj*s* viij*d*. Concernyng my landes and tenementes in Hagworthyngham, I will that Catheryne my wyffe have all my mesuage, landes, tenementes, medoys, pasturys and fedyng places set and lying in Hagworthyngham which I purchesyd, for the terme of hyr lyfe naturall upon condicion that my wyffe fynde yerely an obyt in Hagworthyngham churche the yere day of my buryall, and that she shall expende the same day ij*s* yerely, goyng owt of a lityll close the whiche I inclosyd lying under home in maner and forme folyng, that is to say: to the curate iiij*d*, to the clerke ij*d*, to ryngers iiij*d*, to the curate for the beade roll iiij*d* and to the offeryng at messe j*d*, the reste to be disposyd aftyr the discrescion of my sayd wyff and churchewardens for tyme beyng. And yff my sayd wyff will not fynde the sayd obyt as is before sayd, then I will that the churchewardens of Hagworthyngham and ther successors for the tyme beyng shall distrayne for the sayd ij*s* in the close lying in the home aforesayd

with the arrerages, and they to fynde the sayd obyt as is aforesayd, and they to have the reste of the ij*s* for ther labor. I will that aftyr the decease of the sayd Catheryne my wyff, that the moyte of all the sayd mesuages, landes, tenementes, medoys, pasturys and fedyng places remayn to Robert Robynson, my wyff sun, hys heyres and assygnes for ever. And I wyll that the other moyte of the sayd mesuages and all the other premisses remayn to Agnes Woodhall, wyff to Stephyn Woodhall, hyr heyres and assygnes for ever, upon condicion that the sayd Robert and Agnes, theyr heyres and assignes, do fynde the sayd obyt yerely in maner and forme as is aforesayd, or ellys the churchwardens to distreyne as is aforesayd. The resydue of my goodes I gyff to Catheryn my wyff, whome I make my executrix. Wytnes; Robert Sparlyng, William Wytyll, Richerde Alcokeson, John Lupton, William Phylypson, William Sharpe, Richard Tasker, with other mo. The day and yere abovesayd.

Proved before P at Lincoln, 5 September 1534.

303.   **GILBERT DALE [OF BOSTON]**
       [LCC 1532–34, fo. 123]

1 October 1533. I, Gylbert Dale of Boston, of a hole mynde and good remembraunce, do make my testament and laste will. Fyrste I bequethe my soule to God allmyghtty, to Our Lady St. Mary, and to all the celestyall cumpeny of heven. My body to be buryd in the churcheyerde of St. Botulph in Boston nere unto the crosse callyd Powle Horde, with my mortuary as it is inactyd by the kinge's lawes. To the high altare of St. Butolphe for tithys and oblacions negligently forgottyn or witholden xij*d*. To Our Lade's warke at Lincoln xij*d*. To the orphans at St. Catheryn's withowte the barres at Lincoln vj*d*. To Our Lady's gylde in Boston ij*s*. To the gylde of the vij martyrs in the same churche iiij*d*. I will that ther be disposyd at my buryall day, vij[th] day, xxx[ty] day and yere day unto pore people, every one of those days, vj*s* viij*d* in bred. I will that ther be sayd a trentall of messys a[t] Scala Celi in Our Lady's qwere for my soule and all Christen soulys. I wyll that an honeste preste do syng for me the space of halffe a yere, and he to have for hys wages foure markes sterlyng. To Our Lady's Frerys callyd Carmelettes, to the reparacion of ther house, xx*s*, and they to pray for my soule and all Christen soulys as a brother of ther chapiter house. To Robert my sun twenty markes sterlyng, a flatte pece, sex sylver sponys, a fether bed and all thynges therto belongyng, to be delyveryd to hym at the age of xx[ty] yeres and one. And yff the sayd Robert decesse before the sayd age, then I will that a preste syng for my soule, Robert my sun soule, and all Christen soulys one hole yere, and he to have for hys wages v*l* vj*s* viij*d*. And the resydue of the forsayd xx[ty] markes I gyff to Isabell my wyff. Also yff my wyffe be with chylde, I will it have vj*l* xiij*s* iiij*d* sterlyng at the yeres of xx[ty] and one. And yff so be she be not wyth chylde, I will the sayd vj*l* xiij*s* iiij*d* be equally devydyd betwyxte Isabell my wyffe and Robert my sun. To Isabell my wyffe all my landes and tenementes with all and synguler ther appurtenaunces whiche I have within the towne and feldes of Freston duryng her lyffe accordyng to a dede of feoffement to her use mayd. And aftyr her decesse I will all the sayd landes and tenementes remane to Robert my sun and to the heyres of hys body [remainder to] the chylde that my wyff is with, and to the heyres of the body of it, [fo. 123v] [remainder to] the right heyres of me, the foresayd Gylberte Dale for ever. To every on of my John my

brother chylder, ij*s*. To Thomas Chapman my prentyce x*s*. To Isabell Leer my servant xij*d*. The resydue of my goodes I gyff to Isabell my wyff, she to bryng up my chylder, whome I make my sole executrix. I will that John my brother be supervisor, and he to have for hys panys and labor my beste gowne and x*s* in money. Thes beyng wytnes; Sir Stephyn Hethenes, Sir William Wryght and Syr Thomas Hynde, prestes, with other mo. The day and yere above wryttyn.

Proved before P at Boston, 3 March 1533/4.

304.   THOMAS ROCLEY [OF INGHAM]
       [Stow 1530–52, fo. 18v]

1 October 1533. I, Thomas Rocley of Ingham, hole of mynde ande gud memori, makes this my last will and testamente. Fyrst I bequeth my soule to almyghty God ande to Owre lady Saynt Mary and to all the sayntes in heven, and my body to be beriede in the churche of Yngham fondide of All Halous. To the hye alter of Yngham xij*d*. To the body of the same church iij*s* iiij*d*. To Stowie churche iij*s* iiij*d*. To Corryngham churche xij*d*. To the hie alter of Lincoln xij*d*. To the iij orders of freers, every on of them, iiij*d*. To Willingham church xij*d*. To Fillyngham church xij*d*. To Upton churche xij*d*. To Yngham churche, for to by on canoper,[130] a quarter of barli. To Henynges nunre xx*d*. To Robert Rocley my son a grete pane, on grete brase potte, malte qwernes, and after his dethe to remayne to the name. To Elsabeth and Agnes my doughters all my housholde stufe. To Roberte Rocley my son my house in Willingham with purtenance. To my children William, Roberte, Agnes and Elsabeth ij partes of my gudes. To Christofer Slefurth on byrlynge calfe ande on quarter of barly. To Thomas Was iiij*d*. To Willingham churche on baner cloth. To Ingham church on baner clothe. To John Roclay my son v nobillis of golde, and yf his parte cum to any more to have as muche as William, Roberte, Agnes and Elsabeth shall have to there partes. To the parson of Brawnswell my white horse, and John my son the yonger. To John Rocley my brother, whome I make my supervisor, vj*s* viij*d*. The residue of my gudes I geve to Henri Rocley my brother and Henri Rocley my brother's son, whome I make my executors for to dispose for the helthe of my soule and all Cristen saulles, as they will answer afore God, ande they to have no more of my gudes but other of them vj*s* viij*d* for ther labor. Thes men wittenes; Robert Lery, John Besyde, Roberte Parke, with other moo.

Proved before L at Lincoln, 22 October 1533. Adm. granted to the executors.

305.   THOMAS MARSHALL [OF ASLACKBY]
       [LCC 1532–34, fo. 201]

2 October 1533. I, Thomas Marshall off Aslakby, hole of mynde and of good remembraunce, makes thys my last will and testament. Fyrste I bequethe my soule unto God allmyghtty, and to Our Lady Saynt Mary and to all the fare cumpeny of heven, and my body to be buryd in the churcheyerde of Aslakbe. To the high altare of Alsakbe viij*d*. To Our Lady of Lincoln x*d*. To Our Lady of Walsyngham iiij*d*. To St. Peter chapell of Aslakbe ij stryke wheatte and one stryke malte. Also the resydue

---

[130] 'Canopy'.

of my goodes not gyffyn I gyff unto Alyson my wyff and Richerde my sonne and John Whytehode, whome I make my [fo. 201v] full executers to dispose for the helthe of my soule that way that they thynke the beste. Thes wytnes hereof; William Lace, William Cales and Richerde Marshall, with other mo.

Proved before P at Pickworth, 23 October 1533.

306.   ROBERT GOTTSON [OF ASHBY IN PARISH OF BOTTESFORD]
        [Stow 1530–52, fo. 20r]

5 October 1533. I, Robert Gottson of Askby, hole of mynde and of gud memory, makys this my testament and last will. Fyrst I gyffe and bequeth my sall to almyghty God, to Owr Lady Saynt Mare and to all the holy company of hevyn. Mi body to be buryede in the churcheyarde of Peter and Paule of Bottysforth. To the hye alter of the same for tythes forgotten viij*d*. To Owr Ladi's warke of Lincoln vj*d*. To my brother Richarde Gottson a quarter barly. To my syister Alys Gottson xvj*d*. To William Jakson iij strik rye. To Thomas Dawson a busshyll rye. To my brother William Gottson on akar lande lyenge in Bramby feld and a busshel of rye. I will that myne executers dispose for the sowle of myne unkyll Richarde Gottson iij*s* iiij*d*. To Sir Thomas Gryme to pray for my sowl ij*s*. To Margaret my wyff ij toftes at the yest ende of Askby for the terme of xij yeres, the lande pertenynge to thame. To William mi son a cart with wheylles appon ytt with all other maner of stufe therto pertenynge, and a payer of new wheylles. To Margaret my wyffe the reversion of my howse that I dwell in, with all the lande pertenynge to yt durynge the nonage of William my sone, after the costome of the maner of succage of Kyrton. The rest of my gudes I gyffe to Margaret my wyffe, to William my son and to Elsabeth my dowghter, whome I orden my executores to dispose for the helthe of my sowll. Thys men beynge witnessis; Thomas Lyell, John Fowler and Richarde Mayson, with other moo.

Proved before L, 2 December 1533. Adm. granted to the executors.

307.   THOMAS PYNDER [OF ALTHORPE]
        [Stow 1530–52, fo. 20v]

6 October 1533. I, Thomas Pynder, of hole mynde and gud remembrance, makyth my will ande testament. First I gyffe my saull to almyghty God, his blissed mother Mary and to all the glorius company off heven, ande my body to be beried in the churcheyarde of Saynt Oswolde in Authorpe, ande to the ornamentes of the hygh auter in the sayd churche iiij*d*. To the chapel of Sent James ij*d*. To Owre lady werke of Lincoln ij*d*. The residewe off my gudes to be devydyt in thre partes, on parte to Margaret my wyffe, another to my chylderne. The thurde parte I will that it be devidith in ij partes, the one parte to my childer and the other parte to Margaret my wyffe, the howse, croftes, lande, medew, more with the apurtinans therto belongyng dewrynge hyr lyffe as I dide promis her at the day of ower mariege. I make Margaret my wyffe my executor by the consell of Sir John Pynder and Henry Belton, supervisors. Witnesse John Pynder, curat, Henri Belton, with other mo.

Proved before L, 2 December 1533. Adm. granted to the executrix.

308.   SIR THOMAS GYBSON [OF BOSTON]
        [LCC 1532–34, fos. 141v–142v]

7 October 1533. I, Thomas Gybson, preste, beyng of perfyte remembraunce, make thys my testament, therin conteynyng my last will. Fyrste I bequethe my soule to allmyghtty God and to all the cumpeny of heven, my body to be buryd within the rode's quere in the Blake Frerys in Boston, and they to have for my sepulture xs. To the high altere of St. Botulphe for Mr. Babyngton for offerynges forgottyn ijs. To our mother churche of Lincoln viijd. To the fatherles chyldren ther at St. Catheryn's viijd. To the mendyng of Our Lady's altare in Boston xs. To St. Peter gylde ther xxs. To St. Catheryn's gylde ther iijs iiijd. To the gylde of the vij martyrs ther iijs iiijd. To [fo. 142r] my lady ancorys every Fryday duryng the space of one yere jd. To iche of Our Lady's beadmen jd.[131] To John Gybson, my brother, my secunde fether bedde with the bolster and bedstockes, with my third coveryng off verder, and aftyr hys decesse it to remane holy to William Gybson hys sun, also my lether dooblet and one of my beste worstyd dooblettes, vjs viijd. To John Gybson hys brother xiijs iiijd. To Margaret Felde, doughter of Nicholes Felde, a tester, iiij curtanys, a pare of schetes, ij fustyan pilloys of downe with ij of my nexte beste pillowbers with semys, fyve puter dyshes, iiij sawssers, syx potegers, a pottyll puter potte, one of the beste candylstykes, a lattyn bason, a pare of flaxyn schetes, a puter bason, a pare of blake jette beades with my best bedstockes with the paces. To Jenet Knyght my nexte beste matteres with a pare of schetes, ij pilloyberys withowt semys. To Jenet Brownell, mother Leyk mayd, my beste matres, a pare of schetes, ij plane pilloberys, a coverlyt of whyte and grene, a lyttyll chyste of waynscotte that my shetes do ly in, and vs. To mother Leke my beste mantyll and xs. To Margaret Phyporte my cownter, a gret spruce chyste with one of my best cupborde carpettes with roses, and the nexte beste carpet for the counter. To John Phyporte xxvjs viijd. To Isabell Brygges my cupborde with my beste carpet of verder,[132] my cheiar table, my gret chyste off waynscotte, a pare of schetes, ij pilloys with the berys with semys, a yelowe coverlyd, a thrawn chare of eshe and xxs in money. To Mr. Markham my gowne of mustarde vylles facyd with blake lamme. To every order of frerys in Boston iijs iiijd. I will that ther be xls bestowyd where moste nede of reparacions is within the blak frerys in the towne of Boston uppon thys condicion, that my assygnes may have my gardyn one yere nexte aftyr my decesse payng the rente, or ellys not. To John Felde, sun of the forsayd Nicholes Felde, my close presse and j close chare of waynscotte, my nexte best tester of fullary, xxs in money and vj cushyns of verder with a birde in the myddes of them. To Richerde Phyporte my clothe jaket, a pare of hose and xxxiijs iiijd that I lent hym as my dette boke dothe appere. To iche of hys chyldren xijd. To Masteres Florance Robertson an image of [the] crownyng of Our Lady. To Masteres Thomlynson a ymage of St. Francys. To Mrs. Margery Robertson a ymage of God at my bedde's hed. To Masterys Alice Robertson a picture of the king of Castell.[133] To Mrs. Bylby a crowne of vs. To

---

[131] The bedemen were twelve poor persons of the borough maintained by the five incorporated gilds of St. Mary, Corpus Christi, St. Peter, Holy Trinity and St. George in St. Botolph's church, Boston: Chantry Certificates (1926), 255.

[132] 'My best green carpet'.

[133] This is probably Charles, King of Castile and Aragon and Holy Roman Emperor. The nephew of Queen Catherine of Aragon, he had strenuously opposed Henry VIII's divorce proceedings, and ownership of such an image could indicate a measure of support for the Queen, particularly in view

Nicholes Smyth a thrawn chare of lynde[134] and one of my handekerchevys with a seame. To Richerde hys sun xij*d*. To Our Lady's house in Boston a twile towyll, vij plane napkyns, ij fyne napkyns with sylke, a plane table clothe of iiij yerdes [and a] half. To Margaret Nele a pynte puter potte of Flawnders werke and a ymage of [Our] Lady sette in waynscotte. To the forenamyd John Gybson my brother my frese jakyt. To the foresayd Richerde Phyporte my shorte blew gowne. To John Cokson the fletcher iij*s* iiij*d*. To Nicholes Blewet a dooblet of St. Thomas worstyt, a jerkyn of chamlet, a yerde [and a] half of hose clothe beyng at Jefferay Wace, which is payd for, all savyng xj*d*. I will that my ij fyne coverlettes of Hollande warke, a pare of fustyan blankyttes, a pare of schetes of iij bredes, to be solde and [fo. 142v] the money therof commyng to be disposyd in almys where moste nede is. I will that ij goblyttes, a maser and a sylver potte be solde, and the money therof to go towardes the wages of a preste whiche I will have to syng for me and all my benefactors within the paryshe churche of Boston the space of one hole yere, and he to have for hys stypende viij markes sterlyng. I will have a preste to syng for me and benefactors within the churche aforesayd one other yere then nexte foloyng, havyng lyke stypende. I will that me executors bestowe of mendyng of highways abowtte Boston where moste nede is xx*s*. To the forsayd mother Leke my shorte blake gowne. To the forsayd Margaret Nele, wyfe of John Nele, marcer, an angell noble to make her a jemmowe.[135] To my brother John wyffe a pare of whyte beades of bone. To Jenet Knyght aforesayd a pare of beades gawdyd with awmor.[136] I will that every gylde preste and every syngyng man within the churche of Boston have a pare of beades of dogeyon[137] and a jemmowe of sylver for a remembraunce. I will that all my handkyrcheves and my pryk shaftes[138] be distrybutyd emonges good fellows where my executors shall thynke beste for tokyns of remembraunce. The resydue of all my goodes not gyven nor bequethyd I put them to the disposicion of John Nele of Boston, marcer, and William Gybson of Stepyng, my nevoy, whome I make my executors, they to bryng me forthe and dispose the reste as they shall thynke best for the helthe of my soule and all Christen soulys, and I will ether of them have for ther labor xx*s*. I will that Mr. Nicholes Robertson and John Copelay the elder be supervisors, and ether of them to have for ther labor an olde noble. I will that yff my nevoy do not be agreable with the sayd John Nele and also to do in all thynges as it shall be thought beste by the councell of my supervisors for the performance of thys my laste will, that he be expulsyd clerely and not to medyll herin. Thes beyng wytnes; Nicholes Smyth, Thomas Leke and Nicholes Blewet, with other mo. The day and yere above wryttyn.

Proved before P at Boston, 3 March 1533/4. Adm. granted to the executors.

of the fact that Henry had divorced her and married Anne Boleyn by January 1533: D. MacCulloch, *Thomas Cranmer: a Life* (New Haven and London, 1996), 637–8.

[134] A turned chair of lime or linden wood.
[135] A double ring.
[136] Amber.
[137] Boxwood.
[138] Arrows for shooting at the 'prick', or target.

309.   EDMUND ROBSON [OF HOGSTHORPE]
       [LCC 1532–34, fo. 216r]

11 October 1533. I, Edmunde Robsun of Hoggesthorpe, beyng of a hole mynde and good remembraunce, makes and ordens thys my laste will. Fyrste I bequethe my soule to allmyghtty Jhesu and to Our Lady St. Mary, and to all the saintes in heven, and my body to be buryd in the churcheyerde of Our Lady in Hoggesthorpe aforesayd. To Margaret Yong iiij schepe to be delyveryd at Michelmes nexte cumyng. To Agnes Yong a qwy calve. The resydue of my goodes I gyff to Emme my wyffe and Jenet Robson my doughter, whome I make my executrices with the supervision of John Beone for to dispose for the helthe of my soule. Thes wytnes; Sir Henry Drowry, preste, William Lepzate and Alyson Ranger, with other mo.
       Proved before P at Alford, 11 November 1533.

310.   WILLIAM BETSON [OF MOULTON]
       [LCC 1532–34, fos. 223v–224v]

12 October 1533. I, William Betson, of hole mynde and full remembraunce, do make my testament and last will. Fyrste I bequethe my soule to God allmyghtty and to Our Lady St. Mary and to all the cumpeny in heven, and my body to be buryed in the churcheyerde of All Halloys in Multon, and my mortuary to be payd as the law will. To the high altare for tithys forgottyn ixd, and to every one of the lighttes in the sayd churche ijd. [fo. 224r] To the skouse light ijd. To Our Lady of Lincoln vjd. To the chylder, orphans at St. Catheryn's, iijd. To my wyffe ij kye, ij swyne, ij seame of wheate and halffe a seame of barly, and a seame of beanys and v yowes, and v hogges, to be delyveryd immediatly aftyr my dethe, nether of the best nor of the worste but mediatly. And also she to have all her housholde stuff that she brought with her, a rymble of flaxe and v yerdes of whyte, and a yong amblyng mare. And my wyffe to have her dwellyng and her lyffyng in my house as she had before, to May Day, and she to have the new lynnyn clothe. And also my wyffe to have all the weryng rayment that she brought with her, and at she fonde bothe for the holy day and for the warkyng day, and she to have a chare and ij tubbes. To William Garlande a yong fely and iiij yowes to be delyveryd imediatly aftyr my dethe. To Robert Betson my sun x schepe and a cowe calve, and a posnet. To Margaret Betson my doughter a cowe calve and ij yowes, ij lammes and ij of the best candylstykes and ij platters, and a matteres and the beste coverlyd and ij brasse pottes and ij pannys, and the blake arke and a bedde hyngyng and my best beades. To Richerde Betson my sun a cowe bullok of ij yere olde. To Gylbarde Betson my sun a bullok of too yere olde. To Robert Betson ij acres of lande arable lying agayn Simonde Elwarde's dore, and Gylberde and John to have the sayd lande xvj yeres to the use of the sayd Robert. Also yff Gylberde and John will not have the sayd lande, I will that Richerde Betson have the sayd lande to the use of Robert Betson. And yff the sayd Robert dye withowt heyres of hys body laufully begottyn, I will that the sayd lande remayne to Margaret Betson my doughter and to the heyres of her body laufully begottyn. And also yff she dye withowt heyres of her body laufully begottyn, I wyll it remayne to Richerde Betson my sun, and the goodes of the sayd Robert do remayn to Richerde Betson. To Richerde Betson ij yowes and ij hogges. To other of my wyff chylder a yowe hogge. To Gylberde Betson my sun fyve acres and [fo. 224v] a halffe of arable lande, iiij of the acres lying

in Long Landes, and an acre lying of the weste parte agenste John Betson, and the other half acre lying under the grene. And also I, the sayd William Betson, have surrenderyd all my landes and tenementes holden by copy of courte rolle into the handes of Thomas Strowtyng, to the use and performance of thys my last will. The resydue of my goodes not gyffyn nor bequethyd, I gyff them to John Betson and Gylberde Betson my sonnys, whome I make myn executors, to dispose for the helthe of my soule, and Richerde Betson to be my supervisor. In wytnes herof; Sir Henry Ryngere, prest, Thomas Geere, Thomas Strowtyng, William Wollsey, with other mo.

> Proved before P at Lincoln, 16 December 1533. Adm. granted to John Betson the natural son, executor, Gilbert Betson, the son and co-executor, being prevented by death.

311.   THURSTAN BYRTTE [OF ROWSTON]
        [LCC 1532–34, fos. 221v–222r]

14 October 1533. I, Thurstan Byrtte of Rowston in the countie of Lincoln, of a hole mynde, consyderyng the perell of dethe, make my testament. Fyrste I betake my soule to allmyghtty God, to Our Lady St. Mary, and to all the cumpeny of heven. My body to be buryd in the kyrkeyerde of St. Clement of Rowston. To the high altare of Rowston xij*d*. To Our Lady of Lincoln viij*d*. I will have ij kye to kepe my obyt for my soule, my wyffe soule, my father soule, my mother soule and for all Crysten soulys. I will have yerely a dirige and messe, and to be prayed for in the beade rolle, and for that he shall yerely have vj*d*. To my wyffe Isabell all the goodes that I had with her at her maryage that is within my house. I gyff her a cowe, a mare and a calve, and halffe parte of the croppe bothe in the lathe and the felde when my legacy is fulfyllyd and my dettes payd. To Helene, my wyffe doughter, my grettyst brasse potte. To Isabell my wyffe an olde wane and iiij flesys wolle. To William Thurton, my syster sun, my best wane and all that longes therto and my plough and all that longes therto, a mare, a gret panne, a brasse potte, a matteres, a coverlyd, a pare of schetes, and parte of the woode with my wyffe that is in the yerde. To William Thorneton the other halffe parte of my corne, bothe in the lathe and in the felde, my wyffe and he equally to parte the sayd croppe [fo. 222r] betwyxte them. To John Benton a stryke barly and a stryke rye. To Gylbert Wylson a stryke rye and a stryke barly. To John Thorneton my best cote. To every doughter of Robert Byrte's a stryk barly. To Robert Byrte a stryke wheate and ij strykes barly. To William Thorneton a meate borde. To Emote Dance a stryke barly. To William Waturs of Amwyk a stryke barly and a stryke malte, and a dooblet. To Nicoll Morewyk a stryke barly. To John Rowe a stryke wheate. To Thomas hys sun a stryke barly. I will have done for my soule v messys of the v woundes. The resydue of my goodes not bequethyd I gyff to Isabell my wyffe and Robert Byrte, whome I make my executors that they may dispose it for the well of my soule. The supervisor of the same I make Sir William Borow, my curate. Wytnes of the same; John Dance, John Rowe, Edwarde Grene and John Hellerton, with mo. Datum ut supra.[139]

> Proved before P at Lincoln, 21 November 1533.

---

[139] 'Dated as above'.

312. WILLIAM HARLANDE [OF WRANGLE]
[LCC 1532–34, fo. 122v]

14 October 1533. I, William Harlande of Wrangle, of hole mynde and good remembraunce, make my last will and testament. Fyrste I bequethe my soule to allmyghtty God, to Our Lady St. Mary and to all the holy cumpeny of heven, and my body to be buryd within the churcheyerde of Wrangle. To the warkes of our mother churche of Lincoln iiijd. To the vicare of Wrangle for tithys forgottyn iiijd. To every altare within the churche of Wrangle ijd. To the holy rode gylde iiijd. To Our Lady gylde iiijd. To my wyff halffe my plough and halffe the gere, and halffe the drought that longes to it, and she to have the chose. To John my sun the other halffe of my ploughe and halffe the gere, and halffe the drought that longes to it, for to be delyveryd to hym when he cumys at xiiij yere of age or other as good they ar now. Also my redde arke for to be delyveryd when he is xiiij yere olde. To William my sun my counter, to be delyveryd to hym when he is xiiij yere olde. To Agnes my doughter a schepe for to be delyveryd to her when she is xiiij yere olde. To Margaret my doughter, aftyr the decesse of my wyffe, a blacke arke. I will that my wyff have the rule of all that I bequethe to my chyldren unto suche tyme as I have assygned it to be delyveryd to them. And yff any of them dye before that tyme I wyll that ther partes be devydyd emong them that lyff. And yff they dye all before that tyme, I will that all ther partes be solde and the money disposyd in warkes of charyte for the helthe of my soule, my father's and my mother's, and all Christen soulys. To William Leeke my godsun iiijd. To William Knyght my godsun ijd. To William Ballak my godsun ijd. To Helene Knyght vjd. The resydue of my goodes I bequethe to my wyffe to the bryngyng up of my chyldren. I make Isabell my wyffe and my brother Roger Julyan my executors, and he to have for hys labor ijs viijd. Thes beyng wytnes; Sir Robert Symson, John Whyetney, with other.

Proved before P at Boston, 3 March 1533/4.

313. WILLIAM BOWDE [OF GOSBERTON]
[LCC 1532–34, fo. 125]

15 October 1533. I, Wylliam Bowde, beyng hole of mynde and of perfyte remembraunce, dothe make, ordayn and dyspose thys mye presentt testamentt and last wyll. Fyrst I bequethe mye soule to almyghtye God and to Our Blyssyd Ladye Seyntt Marye and to all the holye companye of heven, and mye bodye to be beryed in the chercheyerde of the holye apostelles Seyntt Peter and Seyntt Pall in Gesberkyrke. To the hye aulter of the same churche for my tythys forgoten or neclygentlye withholden vjd. To Corpus Christi gylde iiijd. To the same gylde of Corpus Christi ijs ixd, the whyche that Gylbore Laukneye dothe owe me. To Seyntt Peter's gylde iiijd. To Seyntt Jamys' gylde iiijd. To all sowlles lyghtt ijd. To the plowe lyghtt jd. To the reparacyons of ower mother churche off Lyncolln iiijd. To the fatherles chyldren of Seyntt Kateryn's ijd. To the gylde hall of Gosberkyrke on pewter dysche. Thys is the last wyll of me Wylliam Bowde, made the daye and the yere aforesayd. I wyll that Rawfe Bowde, mye son, have on aker of londe arable after mye decease lyenge in Gosberkyrke, callyd Northorpe Felde, to hym, hys eyres and assygners. The resydew of mye goodes I gyve them to Rawfe Bowde my son and to Elyzabethe Bowde mye doughter, whom I make mye true executors. To Rycharde Bowde and to Roberde Perkyn, [fo. 125v] to ether of them, xs, wyllyng

that they be coadjutors to myn executors. And the resydue of my goodes to be equally devydyd betwyxte my ij chylder, the whiche I have mayd myn executors. Also yff the sayd Richerde Bowde and Robert Parkyn have any coste or charges concernyng thys my laste will, I will that they be borne of my goodes. Thes beryng wytnes; Sir William Michyll, paryshe preste, William Betche, Thomas Grene, with other mo.

Proved before P at Spalding, 4 March 1533/4.

314. WILLIAM DRYNKDALE [OF BRUMBY IN PARISH OF FRODING-HAM]
[Stow 1530–52, fo. 19v]

22 October 1533. I, William Drynkdale of Brumbe of the parichynge of Owr Lady of Frothyngham, hole of mynde, seke of body, makes my testament ande last will. In primis I bequeth my salle to almighti God, Owre Lady and to all the sayntes in heven. My body to be beried within the churche of Frothyngham. To the hye alter of Owr Lady of Frothyngham xijd. To Owr Lady warke of Lincoln xijd. To eny honest prest xs, and therfore to synge a trentall of messis. To Elizabeth my dowgter a cowe. Dettable to me of Thomas Perp xxs. Detable to me of Mr. Robert Howdebie vjs viijd. Hugh Drynkdale and Nicholas detable to me viijs. Datable to me of Peter Chaydwen iijs. To Henri Dryndale and Thomas vjs viijd, whome I make my supervisors. The residew of my gudes I bequeth unto Custans my wyffe, William Drynkdale, Henri Drynkdale my sons, Elizabeth Drynkdale, Agnes Drynkdale, Alis Drynkdale, whome I mayke myne executors. Thes beyng witnes; Mr. John Wislynge, Mr. Richard Bellyngham, William Lightfoot, with other moo.

Proved before L, 2 December 1533. Adm. granted to the executors.

315. JOAN JAY [OF HARMSTON]
[LCC 1532–34, fo. 205r]

22 October 1533. I, Jenet Jay, hole off mynde, makes my will. Fyrste I gyff my soule to God allmyghtty and to Hys mother Mary, and to all the cumpeny of heven, and my body to be buryd in the churche of All Halloys of Harmeston. To the high altare of the sayd churche viijd. To Our Lady warke of Lincoln iiijd. To my iiij doughtters all my beddyng and my rayment, and all my napery, and it to be devydyd by even porcions. To John Thorpe chylder iiij schepe. To Robert Roper chylder iiij schepe. To Robert Jay ij schepe. The resydue of all my goodes I gyff to Thomas Jay my sun, whome I make my executor to dispose it for my soule, my frendes' soulys and all Christen soulys. Thes wytnes; Sir Leonerde Dycson, Sir Robert Hammonde, Thomas Stanlay, John Rawsby, with other mo.

Proved before P at Navenby, 4 November 1533.

316. THOMAS MASON [OF POTTERHANWORTH]
[LCC 1532–34, fo. 216v]

25 October 1533. I, Thomas Mason of Potterhanworthe, makyth my laste will. Fyrste I bequethe my soule unto allmyghtty God and to Our Lady St. Mary, and to all the cumpeny in heven, and my body to be buryd in the churcheyerde of St.

Andro. To the same churche a altare clothe. To the churche of Dunston iijs iiijd. To the churche of Necton iijs iiijd. To the high altare of Lincoln xvjd. To Our Lady's warke of Lincoln xvjd. To the iiij orders of frerys in Lincoln, every house, xijd. To Nocton Abbay xxd. To Sir John Holforthe, paryshe preste, for to pray for me vs. I bequethe for a trentall to be sayd for me and my wyff xs. To Robert Thomas x schepe, a cowe, a vyolet gowne with a worstyd dooblet, and a gret chyste. To every chylde of William Mason of Dunston a schepe. To every chylde of Thomas Jonson off Tymberlande a schepe. To every chylde of Jenet Bell in Potterhanworthe a schepe. To Isabell Schorte ij ewes with ij lammys. To Alice Schorte a schepe. To Agnes Dyckon a schepe. To Thomas Johnson of Tymberlande a russyt jakyt with bukskyn dooblet. To William Mason of Dunston a russyt jakyt with fustyn dooblet. The resydue of my goodes unbequethyd, I gyff to Lyon Schorte, whome I make my executor for to dispose for the helthe of my soule. Thes wytnes; Sir John Holforthe, Henry Drewry, Robert Tyde, Richerde Awcoke, with other mo.

Proved before P at Lincoln, 2 January 1533/4.

317.   THOMAS WOODTHORPE [OF MAREHAM ON THE HILL]
        [LCC 1532–34, fos. 117v–118v]

26 October 1533. I, Thomas Wodthorpe off Maryng the Hyll, holle off mynd and gud in remembraunce, and seke off body, makes thys my last wyll. Fyrst I bequeythe my salle to God almyghty and to Our Lady Sent Mary and to all the sainttes in hevyn, and my body to be baryde within the churcheyard off All Santtes off Maryng. To the hye auter of Maryng for oblacions forgotton xxd. To Our Lady warke off Lincoln viijd. To Our Lady lyght in Maryng churche iiijd. To Sent Antony lyght iiijd. To Sent Savior lyght iiijd. To Sant Sonday lyght iiijd. To the churche wark off Maryng ij quartars off barly. To Sent James' gyld off Maryng halff a quartar barly. To a lyght in the rode loft off iij candylstykes vjd. To a trentall xs. To the churche warke off Scrayfeld xvjd. To the churches of Hameryngham vjd and Overyngton vjd. To Sant Caterne gyld off Horncastyll vjd. To Issabell Wodthorpe my wyffe ij oxon, iiij kye, iij horsys and fyfty shepe. To Wylliam Wodthorpe my son a cupull off yong oxon, a mare, a fole and a bald stag and v schepe, and ij quarters off barly and my gretyst brasse pott, and the next best grett panne. To Rychard Wodthorpe my son ij sters, a gray mare, a gray fele and a cow and a quye. To Wylliam my son a cow and a quye. To Rychard my son v scheype, a greyt panne and my next best brasse pott, ij quarters off barly and to other off them a wayne when that they schall go unto the world, suche as sche hais at that terme, and to other off them a yoke and a yorne teyme. To Rychard Rawlinson my best violett coytt. To Rychard Carter off Hawthorn a yong cowe and violett coytt. To Jenytt Madynwell a blake dawffyd cowe and yowe and iij hogges scheype. To every on off my godchelderne iiijd. To Francis my goddawghter xijd. To my wyffe Issabell all my hole howshold within my howse, the wyche that I have nott bequethyd, and all my corne in the lathe and sawne off the grund. To John Madynwell of Horncastyll a cowe, and he to be supervisor. I wyll that my wyffe and chelderne fynd a lyght afore the sacrament for the terme off ther lyeffes, and after ther desseysse for to delyver forthe iijs iiijd for the fyndyng off the same yerly for evermore. The resydew off all my gudes I geve them unto Issabell Wodthorpe my wyffe, and to Wylliam and Rycherd my chelderne, whom I ordane myne executors. Thyes wyttnes; Sir Richard

Talyyar, the paryche prest, Mr. John Compton, Rychard Peryn, John Tornar off same, John Madynwell off Horncastle, with other mo. [fo. 118r] Thys ys the last wyll and testament off Thomas Wodthorpe off Maryng. To Issabell my wyff all my howssys, landys and tenementtes with all the appurtynance within the towne and feldes off Maryng for the terme of her lyeff. And after her disseysse, I wyll that Rychard Wodthorpe my son have my howsse in Maryng that lyes in the kyrke thorpe with the garthe under ytt as it lyes, to hym and to hys aires off hys body. To the sayd Rychard my son sex landys in the west feld off Maryng lyeng off Stokwell forlong with their acreeddes all together, and a land callyd A Garyng lyeng in Norston with ij acreeddes longyng to the same, and a swaythe off medow lyeng in Cruton Haythes callyd Qwhythed Swaythe, and v gaddes off grysground in same feld in Norston and viijth gaddys in same more and ij gaddys and ij foott in same more, and a dayll off iiij gaddes in same and a dayll off ix gaddes in same more, and that is ix gaddes in the on end and sex in the other, and a land with a acred buttyng off same and a dayll in the same more by Horncastyll feld syde off iiij gaddes in the on end and v in the other. And in the est feld off Maryng I geyff unto the sayd Rychard iiij landes together buttyng agaynce John Gainnoll garthe end and a hed land by the garthe end, and one land next by the same ij landys that buttes agaynce John Ulyott wyll, and ij littyll landes that lyes together att Screvelby Maire and iiij landes off the eynde together toward Hameryngham, and a land att the greyn mayre in the same feld, and ij landys att Smythe Styght and ij landes by a balke att Kyrke Layn end, and ij landys buttyng agaynce Hameryngham Mayre next by the furre with the acredes and a brode land in same feld att Kokysbush, and a peyce off medow that lyes by foure daylles off the southe syde and a peyce off motton ground off sex gaddes lyeng in the lyttyll more. And the sayd Rychard to pay yerly for evermore unto the Byshope of Kerlyll xij*d*. To Wylliam Wodthorpe my sone my howsys that I won in with Cowyn Cloysse and the landys and tenementtes, pastures, medows and fedyng within the towne and feldys off Maryng that I have unbequethed, unto the sayd Wylliam Wodthorpe and to hys ayrs off hys body lawfully gotton for ever. And yff that yt plesysse God to tayk the sayd Wylliam Wodthorpe from this present world withowt any ayrs off hys body, than I wyll that all the landys and medows, with the appurtynaunce, remayn unto Rychard my sonne and to hys ayrs off hys body [remainder to] the sayd Wylliam and hys ayrs. And yff that at the sayd Wylliam and Rychard bothe dye withowt any ayrs off ther bodys, then I wyll that all the landes and tenementtes, with all the appurtenance, be sold by the syght off my supervisor and ther executors, and the money to be devydyd in thre partes, one parte to be geffen unto the churche off Maryng, the secund parte to be devydyd emong all my brether chyldren, and the thyrd parte to be doone and delyd for my father saull, [fo. 118v] my mother saull, my saull, my wyff saull and all Crysten saulles. Thyes wyttnes; Sir Rychard Talyor, pariche prest, Mr. John Compton off same, Rychard Pereyn off same, John Tornar off same, John Madynwell off Horncastyll, with other mo.

Proved before P at Horncastle, 3 February 1533/4.

318.   JOHN JAKSON [OF DRY DODDINGTON IN PARISH OF WEST-
        BOROUGH]
        [LCC 1532–34, fo. 117r]

27 October 1533. I, John Jakson of Dodyngton, hole off mynde and good of
remembraunce, make thys my last will. Fyrst I gyff and bequethe my soule unto
allmyghtty God and to Our Lady St. Mary, and to all the saintes of heven, and my
body to be buryd in the churcheyerde of Westeborow. To the high altare of
Westborow xvj*d*. To the bellys of Westborowe viij*d*. To Dodyngton chapell ij*s*. To
Elizabethe Hunte a calve. To Our Lady warke of Lincoln vj*d*. To William Hunt a
stryke of wheate and a stryke of barly. To Richerde Jacson ij stryke barly. To Sir
Stephyn Howlotte vicar xij*d*. To Sir Thomas Harmeston xij*d*. To a habyll preste for
a trentall x*s*. To Robert Hunt and Thomas Hunt and Margarete Hunt iij calves. To
Margery Hunt a calve. To Thomas Dykes xij*d*. To Alice Hunt a panne. To Agnes
Hunt a panne. To Jenet Hunt a potte. To my doughter Alice Jakson iij*l* vj*s* viij*d* and
ij kye, and thys to have at laufull age, also the gretyst panne save one and ij
pottes. To Dodyngton brygges iiij*d*. The resydue off my goodes I gyff to Catheryn
my wyffe, whome I make my executrix and the disposore for my soule as she
thynkes the best. I make Robert Paryshe the supervisor, and he to have for hys
labor iij*s* iiij*d*. Hiis testibus; Richerde Jackson, Robert Barniston, John Clyfton,
John Thomson and Richerde Bendebreche, cum multis aliis.
        Proved before P at Ancaster, 31 January 1533/4.

319.   ROBERT MORELL [OF SKENDLEBY]
        [LCC 1532–34, fos. 209v–210r]

28 October 1533. I, Robert Morell of Skendylby, of a hole mynde and good
remembraunce, makes my testament. Fyrste I bequethe my soule to allmyghtty
God, Our Lady St. Mary and to all the saintes in heven. My body to be buryd in the
churcheyerde of St. Peter of Skendylby. To the high altare for tithys and oblacions
by my negligence forgottyn xij*d*. To Our Lady warke of Lincoln xij*d*. To the churche
warke of Skendylby iij*s* iiij*d*. To Oswalde Morell a colte fole. I will ther be a trentall
done in the churche of Skendylby for my soule [fo. 210r] and the soulys of my father
and mother, and all Christen soulys. The resydue of my goodes not bequethyd, my
will fulfyllyd, they to be at the disposicion of Jenet my wyff and Simon my sonne,
whome I make my executors to dispose for the helthe of my soule and all Christen
soulys as they thynk best. Those wytnes; Sir Nicholes Fawn, vicar, William
Bartylmew, John Smyth. To Simon my sonne, for hys labor, a gray fylly.
        Proved before P at Partney, 10 November 1533.

320.   JOHN GRYMBALDE [OF BRANSTON]
        [LCC 1532–34, fo. 111r]

29 October 1533. I, John Grymbalde, hole in mynde and of good remembraunce,
makes my last wyll. Fyrst I bequethe my sowle to almyghtye God, to Owr Ladye
and to all the santes in hevyn. My body to be buryed in the chyrcheyerde of
Alhalow att Braunceton. To the hye auter of Alhalow off Braunceton for forgotton
tythys iiij*d*. To Owr Lady wark at Lincoln iiij*d*. To the reparacyons off Owr Lade
chapell att Braunceton vj*d*. To the Whytte Freerres att Lincoln iiij*d*. I wyll v messes

off the v wowyndys be celebratyd for my sowle and therfor to be payd xx*d*. To Helin my doghter a browne qwe off ij yere age. I wyll the valow off xij*s* be dysposyd for my sowle. To Helen my wyffe, my ferme and house to the tyme she be disposyd to go to maryage. And aftyr she be maryed to have the copy and ferme the whiche John Alen dwellys in, to the ende and terme of the yeres in the sayd copy. To Robert Grymbalde a bay fely of one yere age, and the resydue of the yeres of my ferme and house yff the sayd Helene my wyff go to maryage. To Isabell Gell a styke of barly. To Agnes Anthony a stryke of barly. To Margaret Eshton a stryke of barly. To Margery Eshton a stryke of barly. The resydue of my goodes I gyff to Helene my wyffe to pay my dettes and to dispose it as she thynkes best for the helthe of my soule and to fulfyll thys my last will by the counsell of my brother, Nicoll Grymbalde. And the sayd Helene my wyff I make my executryx. Thes wytnes; John Brynkyll, Hugh Pacy and John Humberston, cum multis aliis.

Proved before P, 7 January 1533/4.

321. AGNES WEBSTER [OF WELBOURN]
[LCC 1532–34, fo. 132v]

29 October 1533. I, Agnes Webster of Welburn, wedow woman, of hole mynde and remembraunce, makes mye testamentt and last wyll. The fyrst I gyve and bequethe mye soull unto almyghtye God, to Ower Ladye Seyntt Marye and to all the celestyall companye of heven. Mye bodye to be beryed in the churche of Seyntt Ceade of Welburn in the southe yle afore Ower Ladye chapell dore, with licens of allmyghtye God and mye gud neghtburs. To the parson of Welburn for mye morturye iij*s* iiij*d*. To the hye aulter of Welburn church xij*d*. To the churche of Welburn iij*s* iiij*d*. To the churche of Weltyngore vj*s* viij*d*. To Ower Ladye warkes at ower mother churche of Lyncolln xij*d*. To mye dowghter Alys, mye son Thomas wyfe, mye best gowne. To mye dowghter Alys Hemslaye mye worssed kyrtyll. To Roberde Webster, son and are of Thomas Webster, mye best pott, a hangynge laver and a basyn. To Agnes Webster, dowghter of Thomas Webster, mye best beydes, also a candylstycke and a basyn. To Jane Webster my best scheytt, one candylstycke and a basyn. To Agnes Welster my servande a basyn, a candylstycke and j pare scheyttes and a coverlett, and j lynne sheytt and the teystor and hangynges belongyng to my bedde. To the same Agnes j brasse pott, j posnytt, ij pannys, j speytt and a pare cobyerynes, one bordclothe and a towell, iiij pesys pewder vessell and all other mye howsholde stuff nott bequethed, also j cowe and xx*s*. To Jane, dowghter of John Welster j brasse pott, ij pesys pewder vessell and one cowe. To Alys, John Welster dowghter, j brasse pott, ij pesys pewder vessell and one yerynge calffe. To my dowghter Mergerye a gowne, a matterys, a pare sheyttes and one pelowe. To every one of mye godchyldern xij*d*. To the reparacyon of a crosse in the northe ende of Welburne iiij*s*. To the makynge of a cannabye over the hye aulter in Welburn churche xij*d*. The resedewe of mye goodes I gyve to mye son Thomas Webster, whome I make mye true executor that he maye trulye fulfyll thys mye foresaid wyll and dyspose for the helthe of mye soule as he thynke best, and wyll answer afore the hye judge of hevyn. Theys wytnesses; Sir Raynolde Wadyngton, Rychard Pell, Roberde More, with other moo.

Proved before P at Sleaford, 2 March 1533/4.

322.   THOMAS TALER [OF RUSKINGTON]
        [LCC 1532–34, fo. 220]

31 October 1533. I, Thomas Taler of Ryskyngton, beyng of goode remembraunce, make my laste will and testament. Fyrste I bequethe my soule to God allmyghtty, to Our Lady St. Mary and to all the saintes in heven. My body to be buryed wythin the churcheyerde of Ryskyngton. To the high altare there xvj*d*. To Elizabethe my wyffe ij kye, iiij seame malte and a seame of breade corne thys yere, and as muche I gyff unto her thys nexte yere, and all the stuff of my house. And yff thys be not sufficient, then I will that Mr. William Pellys, parson, and my brother shall mende it upon ther conscience. To Robert my servant ij merys, ij bullokes and x schepe. To my brother Percyvall x ewe schepe and my amblyng mare, my croppe in the felde and my falloys. I will ther be a trentall sung for me at my buryall day, vij day or xxx^{ty} day, and I will my executor gyff suche dole for me at thes iiij days as my good will extende. I gyff a cowe to the churche of Ryskyngton for one obbyt accordyng to the use and custome ther. I will that all my goodes not gyffyn nor bequethyd be solde at lasure for the moste proffet at ther syght of Mr. William Pellys my curate and my brother Persyvall. And the money therof cumyng to be done in charytable dedes within the churche and towne of Ryskyngton [fo. 220v] and other places where they thynke moste nede. I make Percyvall Tayllor my brother my sole executor. Thes beryng wytnes; John Tayllor, Sir Thomas Yates, William Pellys, curate there.
        Proved before P at Lincoln, 15 November 1533.

323.   RICHARD HOLDERNES [OF CORBY]
        [LCC 1532–34, fo. 113]

1 November 1533. I, Richerde Holdernes of Corby in the countie of Lincoln, husbandman, hole of mynde and of good remembraunce, make my last will. Fyrste I bequethe my soule to allmyghtty God, to Our Lady St. Mary and to all the holly cumpeny of heven, and my body to be buryed in the paryshe churche of St. John th'Evangeliste of Corby aforesayd, by my deske wher I was accustomyd to sytte. To the high altare of Corby for forgottyn tithys. To the sayd high altare a dyaper table clothe to make an altare clothe of. To Our Lady warke of Lincoln xij*d*. To the churche of Corby, to be buryd therin, iij*s* iiij*d*. To the reparacions of the sayd churche vj*s* viij*d*. To the reparacion of the bellys of Corby churche vj*d*. To Our Lady light in the churche of Corby ij*s* and an ewe and a lambe. To Sir Thomas Ganesburgh, to syng for my sowlle, x messys in the churche of Corby iij*s* iiij*d*. To Sir Robert Andro, to pray for my soule, viij*d*. I will that ij of the best oxen to be solde and disposyd for the well of my soule by the discrecion of myne executors and supervisor. I bequeth to by a ornament with to the churche of Corby x schepe. To Elizabeth my wyff iiij kye and xl schepe. To William my eldeste sone vj kye and qwyes, xl schepe. Also viij of my sylver sponys, Elizabeth my wyff to have the custody of them duryng her lyff naturall kepyng her unmaryed. To William my sun my shodde carte with all thynges that longes therto, also iiij oxen and iiij horse and marys to hys draught with plough and plough gere, and all my carte gere, also a dyaper table clothe. To John Thorpe an ewe and a lambe and a calve. To Hugh Epwall my servant, an ewe and a lambe. To Thomas Holdernes my yongest sonne ij sterys of iiij yeres olde and ij sterys of ij yeres olde, a cowe and a qwye, a horsse and a mare, and xl of my schepe. Also vj of my sylver sponys. Elizabeth my wyffe to

have the custody of them duryng her lyff naturall, kepyng her unmaryd. To John Stephyn my shepherde one ewe. To Agnes Sherman my maydservante one ewe. To Alice Roger my kynswoman one ewe. I will that all the resydue of my goodes be equally devydyd in ij partes, Elizabeth my wyffe and Thomas Holdernes my yongest sonne to have the one parte, and William Holdernes myn eldeste sonne to have the other parte. And I make my executors Elizabeth my wyff and William Holdernes my sun. And all the premises with the devision of the goodes to be done by the syght and avyse of Thomas [fo. 113v] Armestrong, whome I make the supervisor. Wytnes herof; Sir John Obyn, vicar of Corby aforesayd, Thomas Armestrong, Robert Nicoll, with diverse other.

Proved before P at Bitchfield, 27 January 1533/4.

324. WILLIAM FOSTER [OF THE CITY OF LINCOLN]
[LCC 1532–34, fo. 249r]

2 November 1533. I, William Foster of the citie of Lincoln, tyler, hole of mynde and of good remembraunce, dothe orden and make thys my last will and testament. Fyrste I gyff and bequethe my soule to God allmyghtty, Our Lady St. Mary and to all the holy cumpeny of heven, and my body to be buryd in the churcheyerde of St. Swythune in the sayd citie. To the sayd churche for forgottyn tithys viijd. To St. Stephyn's in Newlande ijs. To the churche of St. Botulphe xvjd. To the warkes of Our Lady of Lincoln xijd. To the clerke gylde xijd, and a hundrythe thake tyle[140] of thys condicion, that they shall say every yere at ther dynner, at the rehersyng of my name, one *Ave Maria*. I will that my mother have my violet gowne lynyd with blake lynyng. To the iiij orders of frerys, every one of them, iiijd. To William Bryg my jaket of coton russyt, and a pare of olde hose. To my prentyse Bartylmewe Draghtgates one thowsand and a halffe of thake tyle and halffe a thowsand breke. To William Tayller my dooblyt of calve skyn. To my brother John Foster my sworde, my bowe and my best cappe with a george of sylver. To Robert my sun a gray stag. To my sun Thomas a cupborde aftyr the decesse of my wyffe. To my doughter Alice one brasse potte. The resydue of my goodes I gyff to Elizabethe my wyffe, whome I make my executryx, and she to bryng up my chyldren. I will that the sayd Elizabeth my wyff have the take of bothe my tyle kylnys the terme of my indenturys, and yff she be so disposyd to lette them. I will that my brother John shall have the take before another as they ij can agre. Wytnes; John Foster, Thomas Henbery, William Dounell, with other mo.

Proved before P at Lincoln, 31 March 1534. Adm. granted to the executor.

325. PHILIP HERTYLL [OF FENTON]
[LCC 1532–34, fo. 240r]

3 November 1533. I, Phylip Hertyll of Fenton, in good mynde and memory, make my last will. Fyrste I bequethe my soule to God allmyghtty and to Our Lady St. Mary, and all the saintes in heven, and my body to be buryd in the churcheyerde of Fenton. To the high altare of the sayd Fenton ijs. To the high altare of Stubton iiijd. To Our Lady of Lincoln xijd. To the iiij orders of frerys, ich of them, iiijd. To

[140] Bundles of thatch.

every one of my godchylder iiij*d*. The resydue of my goodes I gyff to Jenet my wyff, whome I make my executrix. I will that John Snenton be supervisor. Thes testes; Sir William Bryan, Robert Preston, John Preston, Richerde Preston, and other mo.

Proved before P at Lincoln, Penultimate day [27] of February 1533/4.

326.   LAURENCE SOWTER [OF SUTTON ST. EDMUND]
        [LCC 1532–34, fo. 240v]

3 November 1533. I, Laurans Sowter of the pariche of Sanct Edmundy's in Sutton in Holland, hole mynd and of remembraunce, order and make my last wyll and testament. Fyrst I bequeyth my sowle to God omnipotent and to Hys mother Mare, and to all the celestyall company in hevyn. My body to be buryd in the churcheyard of Sancte Edmunde's in Sutton. Also I bequethe to my mortuary that thyng that the law wyll requyre. To the parson for oblatyons and tythes forgotton viij*d*. To the vycar of the same viij*d*. To the reparacyons of the mother churche of Lincoln iiij*d*. To the infans of Lincoln iiij*d*. To the lyght of Sanct Edmunde and Sanct Peter, ether of them, a pownde wax, and to every lyght within the churche of Sanct Edmunde ij*d*. To the churche of Sanct Edmunde xxvj*s* viij*d*. To the pariche prest that tyme beyng for to syng for me and myne benefactors, and for to be payd by the handys of myne executors. To Johanna my wyffe all my cropys to the fyndyng of my chyldren. Also I gyffe my wyffe all my howshold goodes. To Isbell my dowghtar a bed with all that long to it. Also I wyll my table and a chare for to rest with my howse. To Robard my son iiij acars copyhold land with a howse upon ytt in fee symple, a sex freholdys in fee symple at the age of xviij. And yf it fortune that Robert to dye before the age of xviij, then I wyll the forsaid land for to remayne to Wylliam my sone. To Wylliam my sone vj acars in fee symple att Wylliam Harkynsun's, and iiij acars copyhold land at Thomas Haresun's in fee symple at the age of xviij [remainder to] Robart my sone. And yff it fortune that both my sons for to dye before the age of xviij, then I wyll the sayd landes be sold by the handes of myne executors or the executors of them, and the money theroff reseyved for to be dysposed within the church of Sanct Edmundy's in that thyng that the paryche thynke best. Also I wyll that my wyffe hathe the profettes of the sayd landes to suche tyme as my chylderne shuld entre the sayd landes, of thys condycyon, that I wyll that my wyffe kepe the howsyng reparacyons to the profett of my chylderne. I wyll that my wyffe hathe my plowe and my cart to the tyme that my chylderne enter ther landys, and then sche so to delyver my plow and cart and barnes longyng to them to my chyldarne. To Isbell my dowghtar ij kye and a hecforthe[141] for to be delyveryd at May Day next folowyng. To Robart my sone a mare and a geldyng and a hecforthe of ij yere olde, to be delyveryd att May Day next folowyng. To William my son a hecforthe of ij yere olde and a mare of ij yere olde for to be delyveryd att May Day folowyng. The resydew of my guddes I do poot them to the disposycyon of myne executors, that they may dyspose for the helth off my sowle and my benefactors as thay thynk best, whome I mayke Johanna my wyffe, and Wylliam Pore ovrseyer, and he for to have for hys labore

---

[141] ' A heifer'.

vj*s* viij*d*. Thyes beyng wyttnes; Nycholas Thomson, Wylliam Baldwar senior, Wylliam Baldwar junior, John Hareson, with other mo.

Proved before P at Spalding, 4 March 1533/4.

327. WILLIAM GLEPPYS [OF LONG SUTTON]
[LCC 1532–34, fos. 297r–298r]

4 November 1533. I, William Glepps of Sutton in Holand, in the dyocese of Lincoln, of hole mynde and good remembrans, make my laste wylle and testament. Fyrst I bequethe my sawle to allmyghty God, to Owr Lady Saynt Mary and to all the company in hevyn, and my body to be buryed in the churcheyarde of Ower Lady in Sutton aforsayd. To the hye aulter for tythes forgotten xij*d*. To the prior of Castleacre vj*d*. To reparacion of the mother churche in Lincoln vj*d*. To the pore chyldryn of Saynt Kateryn's there ij*d*. To Ower Ladye's gylde in Sutton iiij*d*. To the Trynyte xl*d*. To Saynt Thomas gylde and to Saynt John's gylde, to yche of them, iiij*d*. To Ower Lady of Grace, to Saynt Jamys and to Saynt Kateryn's gylde, to yche of them ij*d*, and to every smalle lyght withyn the churche of Sutton j*d*. To Agnes my wyffe xij ewys and ij kye with a baye mayr, with all the howsholde stuffe that she brought to me with all the beddyng as we lye excepte the stockes, and also I wyll the lynen be egally devydyd betwyxe my wyffe and Jone my doghter. I wyll that my sayd wyffe Jone and Ysabell my doughters have the resedue of my houshold stuffe, egally devyded amo[n]g them thre. To Yzabell my doghter on qwe and ij ewys. To Jone my doghter on kowe with ij ewes with there lambes. To Mawde my syster on burnyng. To Nicolas my son on burnyng with a kowe. To Thomas Gaunte a ewe. To every on of my godchyldren a lambe. To Thomas Koke on ewe and a lambe. To Laurens Arlyng a ewe with a lambe. To my sayd wyffe ij seme barly with vj stryke whete with a seme benys. To Mawde my syster a stryke of barly and a stryke of whete. Also I wyll that my sayd wyffe have an acre of whete on the gronde on the forther syde the eye in the pars felde[142] clerely withote coste or charge. I wyll the [fo. 297v] resydew of my goodes remayne to Robert Glypps and John Glypps my sons, whome I ordene my executors to bryng me forthe and dyspose for the helthe of my sawle at the oversyghte of Wylliam Garne, whom I make supervisor, and he to have for hys labor iij*s* iiij*d*. Thys ys the laste wyll of me Wylliam Glypps of Sutton, made the day and yere abovesayd. To Agnes my wyffe ij acre of lande, be yt more or lesse, with the buyldyng of ther purtenances that we dwell yn for the terme of her lyffe, kepyng the houses thereupon in no wurse reparacon then the be, and aftyr her decesse I wyll they remane to John my son and hys assygnes. To my sayd wyffe iiij acres of land lying in Dyesgate the tyrme of fyve yeres nexte foloyng my decesse, and at the ende of the sayd v yeres, or yff my wyffe departe within the v yeres, I wyll the land remane to Nicolas my son in fe symple, provydyd alway that yff the sayd Nicolas departe within the sayd fyve yeres, that may gyff the sayd acrys by wyll to hys assygne or assygnes after that my sayd wyff have enjoyd the sayd acres the terme of v yeres. And so I wyll that John and Robert my sons have lyke autoryte to dyspoce the landes wheche they shall have after the decesse of Agnes my sayd wyffe, yff they or other of them departe before my wyll as they or other them sholde have had yf they had survivyd my sayd wyffe, alway provydyd that my wyffe enjoe all

---

[142] An area of raised ground.

soche landys [fo. 298r] as I do gyffe hyr all the tyme assygned to hyr by thys my laste wyll. To Robert my son iiij acres of land lying in Oldegate in fe symple. To John my son v acres of land lying in Wautoasgate to hym and hys assign. To Agnes my wyffe ij acres lying in Danyell's Gate the terme of hyr lyffe, the wheche ij acres after my wyffe decesse with other iij acres lying in the sayd fylde, I remene to my iij sons eqally to be devydyd emong them thre, and iche to be others herys. To Nicolas my son the cote yarde at Se Dyke in fe symple. The landes gyfven into the handes of Thomas Denyell and John Denyell for the performans of thys my last wyll. Thes wytnes; Henry Ogle, pryste, Robert Adam, Robert Arlyng, with other mo.

Proved before P at Spalding, 9 June 1534.

328.   RICHARD OSBORNE [OF KIRTON IN HOLLAND]
        [LCC 1532–34, fo. 243r]

6 November 1533. I, Richerde Osborne of Kyrton in Hollande, of hole mynde and perfecte remembraunce, makyth my testament concludyng with my laste will. In the fyrste I gyve and bequethe my soule to God allmyghtty, Our Lady St. Mary and to celestyall cumpeny of heven, and my body to be buryd in the churcheyerde of the blessyd appostellys Peter and Paule of Kyrton beforesayd, and for my mortuary aftyr the statutys of our soverayn lorde the kyng. To the high altare of Kyrton for negligent tithys vj$d$, and to every altare in the sayd churche of Kyrton ij$d$. To Our Lady of Lincoln ij$d$, and to the reparacion of the sayd our mother churche of Lincoln ij$d$. To the orphans of St. Catheryn's ij$d$. I will that myn executrix and my supervisor sell ij yong horsse of the beste immediatly aftyr my decesse, and they to by a vestiment with the money therof to the high altare of Kyrton for the helthe of my soule. And over, I will that myn executrix do pay unto the performance of the vestiment ij$s$. I will that the churchewardens alway for the tyme beyng shall cause my soule to be prayd for every Sunday in the beade rolle. I will that my house that I dwell in, with all my landes unto me perteynyng, remayn unto Richerde Osburne in fe symple aftyr the decesse of Marion my wyffe. And yff the sayd my wyffe departe thys worlde before the sayd Richerde Osburne be of the age of xxj^{ty} yeres, that then I will the sayd house and landes remayn to Robert Osburne my brother, unto the sayd Richerde hys sun be of the age of xxj yere. To Robert Osburne xx^{ty} ewes, one yong qwye of iij yere olde, one yong mare, my gaberdyne, my worstyd dooblet and xiij$s$ iiij$d$, the whiche is owyng of John Osburne of Ounesby. To Richerde Osburne x yowes, one calve, one browne mare and one bedde and all thynges therto perteynyng, also iij platters, iij dyshes, iij sawssers and one candylstyke. I will that my wyffe do leyff in the sayd house aftyr her decesse one cownter, one tabyll, one chare, one leade, one boltyng arke and one blake chyste, as heyrlomys to the use of the sayd Richard Osburne. To John Whyte my beste gowne. To Simon Grave my kendall cote. To John Danyell my blak cote. To Thomas Thorneton one yowe. To Robert Thorneton on yowe. To Maryon Donyngton one ewe. To Alice Donyngton one ewe and to Robert Richerdson one lamme. The resydue of my goodes, I gyff them to Marion my wyffe, whome I make my executrix to dispose my goodes to the moste plesure of God and consolacion of my soule. And I make Sir Richerde Oxman supervisor, and to have for hys labor vs. Thes beyng wytnes; Sir Thomas Este, Thomas Hubbarde and Simon Grave, with other.

Proved before P at Swineshead, 5 March 1533/4.

329. THOMAS BOROWGHE [OF BICKER]
[LCC 1532–34, fos. 207v–208v]

9 November 1533. I, Thomas Borowghe off Byker, with hole mynd and gud remembraunce, make my testament and last will. Fyrst I bequeythe my sole to God my maker, to Hys mother Sante Mare, and to all santes, and my body to be buryed in the chyrcheyerd off Sancte Swythune off Byker. To my mortuary as the statute theron lymyttes. To the hyght alter for tythes forgotton xx*d*. To Our Lady's alter ther vj*d*. To Sancte Nicholas alter ther iiij*d*. To Sancte Katerin's alter ther iiij*d*. To Sancte Leonard auter ther iiij*d*. To the reparacions off Byker chyrche vj*s* viij*d*. To Our Lady of Lincoln in offeryng xij*d*. To the fatherles chylderne att Sancte Kateryn's withoute the gattes off Lincoln iiij*d*. Thys is my last wyll, the day and yer aforsayd. I wyll that all my feffers stande feffed to the use and performance off thys my sayd last wyll as hereafter folowythe. I wyll thatt all my feffers in my howse thatt Wylliam Johnson dwellyth in and the landys under ytt, and the landys that I bowght off Mr. Garrarde, to the use of Alys my wyffe the terme off hyr naturall lyffe with the condistion that she repere ytt sufficiently, provysyd yff she dye, or Wylliam my sone comme to the age of xxj yerres, then I wyll that my sayd feffer stand feffed to the use of Mr. Massyngberd, chansyllar off the cathedrale chyrche off Lincoln, Roger Hulton off Donyngton, gent[leman], and Sir Robert Johnson, chantre prest off Byker,[143] and they to take the profyttes theron to [be] bestowd on the exebycyon off Wylliam, Robert and Christofer, my sonnys, unto the sayd Wylliam my sone cum to the age off xxj yers, and then ytt to remeyn to hym and to hys heres. I wyll that my feffers off my howse that Wylliam Jakson dwells in and in Nundall with an acre and halffe yng grownd that I bought off Nicholes Long, stand feoffyd to the use of the sayd Alys my wyffe, toward the exebycyon off the sayd Wylliam, Robert and Crystover, my sones, unto the sayd Robert com to the ful age off xxj yers, and then to remane to the sayd Robert and hys hers, provysyd that yff Thomas Ranson or John hys sone pay or cawse to be payd unto the sayd Robert my sone att hany tyme hereafter vij*l* viij*s* iiij*d* sterlyng, then he soo payyng to injoy and redeme the sayd Nundall by the sayd sowme. I wyll that my feffer in my howse that I bowght off Wylliam Benytt, with the landys under ytt and ij acre I bowght off Thomas Ranson with all other landys that I bowght off Wylliam Benytt, stande feffyd to the use of my sayd wyffe towarde the exebycyon off the sayd Wylliam, Robert and Crsytover, my sones, unto the tyme that the sayd Wylliam my sone come to the age off xxj, and then to remane unto hym and hys hers. I wyll that the feffer off the howse that [fo. 208r] I dwelle in, with the pastur that I bowght off Thomas Ranson aforesayd with Peter Howse, stand feffyd to the use off the sayd Alys my wyffe, to the exebycyon off the sayd Wylliam, Robert and Crystover, my sones, unto the sayd Crystover come to the age off xix yers, and then to remene unto Wylliam my sone and hys hers, kepyng the obbyt off Mabull Wederbe, and Wylliam hyr sone expendyng theron yerly xij*d* as ytt ys notyd in the parment mess boke in Byker chyrche, the space off xx^ti and after as the law wyll suffer, yff my sayd wyffe dye or my sayd sones com to the ful age off xxj^ti,

---

[143] The chantry of St. Mary at Bicker was founded by the ancestors of Humphrey Lyttilbury to support a chaplain to pray for the founder's soul in perpetuity. By the time of the dissolution in 1548 the incumbent was one Geoffrey Cottingham, but Robert Johnson is attested serving in 1526, with a salary of £5 6s. 8d., and in the *Valor Ecclesiasticus* of 1535, with a slightly reduced salary of £5 5s.: Chantry Certificates (1926), 33–4.

that then all my sayd feffer stand feoffyd to the use off the sayd Master Massyngberd, chancyllar, Roger Hulton, gent[leman], and Sir Robert Johnson, chantre prest off Byker, to the use as ys aforesayd. I wyll yff Robert my sone dye or he come to the full age of xxj^{ti}, that then the sayd howse and landes to hym afore assynyd remene unto Crystover my sone and hys hers. I wyll yff Wylliam my sone dye or he comme to the full age off xxj^{ti}, then I wyll that the sayd howses and landes before assynyd to hym remene to Robert my sone and hys hers. Yff bothe the sayd Robert and Wylliam dye within the sayd age, then I wyll that all the sayd howsys and landes remene to Crystover my sone att the sayd full age of xxj^{ti}, and to hys hers. Yff ytt so be that any man shall take Wylliam my sone ward, I will he shall have no mor off my landys but that that she shalbe takon for. Yff all my said sones dye within the sayd age of xxj^{ti}, then I wyll that the sayd Alys my wyffe have all the sayd howses and landes the terme off hyr naturall lyff. And after I wyll that the howse that I dwell in remene to John my brother, and to the hers off hys body lawfully browght furthe. I wyll that all my other howsys and landys be solde by the sayd Master Chancyllar, Roger Hulton, gent[leman], and Sir Robert Johnson, or by the survivor off them. And for defowte off them beyng none alyffe ytt to be solde by my feffers and the chyrchewardennys then beyng off Byker chyrche, and the money theroff resevyd to be dysposyd in dedys off charyte by the sayd sellers in the cherche and to the towne off Byker aforesayd. To Wylliam my sone a sylver salt. I wyll yff he dye or he come to the age off xxj^{ti} yers that ytt remene to Crystover, the remener over to Robert my sone in lyke case. To the sayd Alys my wyffe, Wylliam, Robert and Crystover my sones, every one of them vj sylver spones. [fo. 208v] I wyll that all my dettes be fully payd, the legaces off thys my last wyll to be performyd and fulfyllyd, and my funerall expences takon owte, and the resydew off all my moveable goodys to be evynly schyftyd in iij partes, bey trew and equall schyft, betwex the sayd Alys my wyffe, Wylliam, Robert and Crystover my sones, to every on off them a lyke parte, provysyd that yff any off the sayd my sones dye wythin the sayd age off xxj, then I wyll that the over lyffers of them schyft hys parte emong or betwene them ij, the remener over to the last off them iij in lyke case. I wyll that yff my sayd wyffe be maryed agane, then I wyll that the sayd Mr. Chancyllar, Roger Hulton and Sir Robert Johnson, prest, schall take sufficient seuerte by good and lawfull bondys for the performance and paymenttes off my sayd chylderne goodes, and also ther fyndyng off my sayd landys as ys aforesayd, wherto I gyff them full autoryte and power in my sayd goodys to cause theys premyssys to be done. I make Alys my sayd wyff the sole executrix. I make the supervysors hereoff to gyde and consyll my sayd wyff and chylderne, the sayd Master Chancyllar, vicar off Byker, to whome I geffe xs, Syr Robert Johnson, prest, off the same towne, I gyffe vj$s$ viij$d$, Roger Hulton off Donyngton, gentyl-man, to whome I wyll that my wyff shall reward as she wyll att hyr plesur. Theys wyttnessys; Robert Tod, John Browghe, Hew Alporthe, Thomas Tollar, Rychard Cowke, with other mo, the day and yere aforesayd.

Proved before P at Lincoln, 15 December 1533. Adm. granted to the executor.

330.   JOHN ROBYNSON [OF ASHBY IN PARISH OF BOTTESFORD]
        [Stow 1530–52, fos. 20v–21r]

9 November 1533. I, John Robynson of Askby, hoyle of mynde and of gude
memori, makyth this my testament and last will. Fyrst I gyff and bequeth my sawle
to almyghty Gode, to Owr Lady Sant Mary ande to all the holy company of heven.
Mi body to be beriede within the churcheyerde of Peter and Pawlle off Bottisforth.
To the use and behove of the same churche iijs iiijd. To the hye alter of the same for
tithes forgoten xijd. To Owre Ladi's warke of Lincoln xd. [fo. 21r] To Saynt Jyles'
chappell of Askby. To Robert Robynson, the son of Thomas Robynson, a wether
lane. To Herry Robit Hoppkynson vd that his mother owith me. The rest of my
gudes I gyffe to Elsabeth my wyfe, to Edwarde and William my sonnys, whome I
make my executors. Thes men beynge witnys; John Fowler, John Bernard and
Thomas Hil, with other mo.
        Proved before L, 2 December 1533. Adm. granted to the executors.

331.   AGNES SWETE [OF HUTTOFT]
        [LCC 1532–34, fo. 233r]

9 November 1533. I, Agnes Swete late of Hotofte, vidoy, with a hole mynde and
goode remembraunce, makes thys my last testament. Fyrste I bequethe my soule to
allmyghtty God, my body to be buryd within the churche of Hotofte. To the red
arke of Lincoln viijd. To Our Lady of Lincoln a pare of beades. To the high altare
of Hotofte churche xijd. To John Swete the yonger one cowe whiche is with hym, x
schepe and one burlyng. To Thomas Swete, sun of John Swete the yonger, one feder
bed and all that longes to it, one arke, one pare of qwernys aftyr the dethe of John
Swete the elder. To John Swete the elder one red arke. To Alice Swete, the doughter
of John Swete the elder, one feder bed and all that longes to it, one qwye. To
William Swete, sun of William Swete, one pare of qwernys, one brasse potte, one
spytte, one pare off rakyns whiche ar harelomys. To Hagneby bellys one brasse
panne, or ellys the price of the panne. To allmys bed one coverlyt, one pare of
schetes, one matteres. To Agnes Swete, doughter of William Swete, one matteres:
every one of those chylder other hayr. I will that the house that is William Swete,
sun of William Swete, that John Swete the elder shall have the same house in hys
handes to the sayd William cum at laufull age. The rest of my goodes I gyff to John
Swete the elder, whiche I make my executor. Wytnes; William Stele, senior, Alan
Melton, Sir John Hope, preste, with other.
        Proved before P at Alford, 5 February 1533/4.

332.   SIR ROBERT LONG [VICAR OF TOYNTON ALL SAINTS]
        [LCC 1532–34, fos. 250r–251r]

10 November 1533. I, Sir Robert Long, vicare of Toynton All Halloys, beyng of
hole mynde and of good remembraunce, makyth thys my laste will or testament.
Fyrste I bequethe my soule to God allmyghtty, Our blessyd Lady St. Mary, and to
all the blessyd cumpeny of heven, and my body to be buryd within the chancell of
the paryshe churche of Toynton All Halloys, before my stall where I dyd sytte. To
Our Lady's warke of Lincoln xxd. To iiij commune lighttes of Toynton All Halloys
iiijs. To Spillesby churche xxd. To Halton churche xxd. To the churche of Toynton

Peter xx*d*. To Ester Kerle churche xx*d*. To the paryshe of Toynton All Halloys, to the dressyng of the table over the high altare, iij*l* vj*s* viij*d*. To Alyson Jenkynson my servant vj*l* xiij*s* iiij*d* and ij sterys, [fo. 250v] vj schepe ewys, one gowne, ij quarters of malte, ij rygges of wheate that buttyth apon the becke, ij holdyng pygges galtes, iiij hennys, one cocke and all my newe clothe unshapyn, lynyn and wollen, and all my hempe and flaxe, ij tubbys, xij kettyll bollys, my bedde that I do ly in myselffe and a long chyste. To the sayd Alyson Jenkynson my house by the churcheyerde syde for the terme of her lyffe, and aftyr her decesse the sayd house shall go to Alice Malteby and to the heyres of her body laufully begottyn [remainder to] Robert Long my nevewe, to hym and hys heyres for ever. I will that the sayd Alyson Jenkynson have all suche stuff as is intytelyd in a byll sealyd with my seale, the whiche stuff is the sayd Alyson's, and dyd bryng it with her when she dyd cum to my service. To Alice Malteby iij*l* vj*s* viij*d*, ij qwyes, iiij schepe, a spruce coffer, one brasse potte and iij puter dooblers. To Thomas Long iiij schepe, a basyn morter, my beste candylstyke, a pare of jeate beades of x, a lace with ij sylver aglettes, a jaket and a dooblet of worstyd. To Robert Long xx*s*, one chalder of barly, one cople of oxen with my drought and that that belongyth therto, and one cowe. To Mr. Francys Stoner xl*s*. To Sir Thomas Smyth xiij*s* iiij*d* and my redde stagge, ij quarters of barly, ij bordyn beddes and one gret chyste, and one lyttyll chyste. To Jane Lyneley vj*s* viij*d*. To the master of the college off Spillesby iij*s* iiij*d*, and to every brother xx*d*.[144] To Richerde Lownde vj schepe. To Elizabeth Este one gowne and iiij schepe. To x pore folke to pray for my soule, x stryke malte. To Richard Thaker a schepe. To every one of my godchylder within the paryshys of Wester Kele, Ester Kele, Toynton All Halloys, Toynton Peter and Halton, one schepe or xvj*d*. To the college of Spillesby one fether bed with a bolster and a coverlyd. I will that my preste that I have hyred for one yere do contynue hys service thorough the yere, or ellys another accordyng to hys wagys yff that I do departe within the yere. To the Augustyne Frerys in Boston xij*d*. To the Gray Frerys xij*d*. To the Blak Frerys xij*d*. To the Whyte [fo. 251r] Frerys xij*d*. To Sir John Westemellys my beste russyt gowne. To Roger Longe one brasse potte and one puter doobler. To Thomas Cokyshed ij wether hogges. To the paryshe churche of Thorneton Curtes iij*s* iiij*d*. To the paryche churches off Wynton xx*d*, Kelyngham xx*d*, Haburne xx*d*. To fowre doughters of Edwarde Long iiij*l*, that is every of them xx*s*. The resydue of my goodes I gyff to the disposicion of Mr. Francys Stoner and to Robert Long, whome I make my executors to dispose for the helthe of my soule and all Crysten soulys. Thes wytnessyng; Sir Thomas Smyth, Sir John Westemellys, with other mo.

Proved before P at Lincoln, 7 April 1534.

333. JOAN MUMBY [OF IRBY ON HUMBER]
      [LCC 1532–34, fo. 111v]

13 November 1533. I, Jenet Mumbe of Irby nexte Gret Grymmesby within the countie of Lincoln, vido, sumtyme the wyffe of John Mumbe, hole of mynde and remembraunce, tha[n]kyd be allmyghtty God, orden and devyse thys my testament to stande for my last will. Fyrste I commende my soule unto allmyghtty God my maker and savyor, and to Hys blessyd mother Our Lady St. Mary, and to all Hys

---

[144] See n. 47, will no. 112.

blessyd cumpeny of heven. My body to be buryed in the churche of St. Androw of Irby. For my buryall in the churche vj*s* viij*d*. To the high altare xij*d*. To Our Lady churche of Lincoln xij*d*. To the churche of Laceby xij*d*. To the chappell of St. Margaret xij*d*. To the churche of Byllesby xij*d*. To the churche of Swallo xij*d*. To the chapell of Our Lady in Rasyn vj*d*. To Our Lady's altare in the churche of Irby, to by a table and to reparacion it, iij*l* vj*s* viij*d*. To ich on of my godchylder iiij*d*. To Nicholes Clerke my kynsman iiij horse and a plough as it goys, and a carte and all to it belonges, and a acre of wheate and a acre of barle, and a acre peys when it is sawn, and the malte qwernys and a grynstone. To Sir Robert Skerne xiiij nobyls to syng for me a yere. To John Clerke of Tetney half a quarter barly. To Thomas Clerke half a quarter barle. To Alice Clerke half a quarter barly. To Thomas Burwell iij quarters barly. To Beatrix Smyth my servant a qwye of ij yere olde. To Malde Frankys a cowe. To Henry Butler a calve. To William Burwell doughter a qwye and hys syster a qwye calve. To sqwerre of Ryby half a quarter barly. To every frere of Grymmysby iiij*d*, and to every nun iiij*d*. To Nicholes Clerke doughter a matteres. To Robert Carter a fether bed. The resydue of my goodes I will that thes my executors, William Ustwayt, John Hell and Robert Carter distrybute them aftyr ther myndes for the helthe of my soule and my husbande's, and all our good frendes. In wytnes heroff; Sir Allen Tharolde, curate, John Berre, John Stalenbrewe, John Botheby and Nicholes Clerke, with other mo.

Proved before P at Lincoln, 9 January 1533/4, by the executors.

334. WILLIAM SOWTHE [OF THE CITY OF LINCOLN]
[LCC 1532–34, fo. 222v]

13 November 1533. I, William Sowthe of the citie of Lincoln, fysher, beyng hole of mynde and good memory, make thys my testament and last will. Fyrste I bequethe my soule to God allmyghtty, Our Lady St. Mary and all the saintes in heven. My body to be buryed in the churcheyerde of St. Benedicte's. To the warkes of the sayd churche vj*s* viij*d*. To the high altare of the same for tithys forgottyn vj*s* viij*d*. To Our Lady gylde in the sayd churche viij*d*, and to the Trinite gylde of the same xij*d*. To the clerke gylde iij*s* iiij*d*, and to the great gylde of the same xij*d*. To the high altare of the cathedrall churche of Our Lady of Lincoln ij*s*, and to the warkes of the sayd churche xij*d*. I gyff unto the bying of one cope in the churche of St. Bennete's vj*s* viij*d*. To the churche warkes of Stykforthe xx*d*. To Simon Emlyn and hys wyff vj*s* viij*d*. To Thomas Sowthe vj*s* viij*d*. To John Thomas vj*s* viij*d*. To Robert Muche vj*s* viij*d*. To John Thomas the yonger xx*s*. To William Sowthe xx*s*. To Elizabeth Naler x*s*. To Catheryn my servant iij*s* iiij*d*. To Jenet Licens iij*s* iiij*d*. To Robert Muche my trounke. To Alice Ernolde iij*s* iiij*d*. To Agnes Fed iij*s* iiij*d*. The resydue of my goodes I gyff unto Isabell my wyff, whome I make my sole executrix that she may dispose for the helthe of my soule as she thynkyth moste expedient. Sir Thomas Frere and Bartylmew Wyllesforde to be co-adjutors unto the sayd Isabell, to help to ade her in all her busyness, and they to have for ther labors xiij*s* iiij*d*. And John Wryght of Stykforthe to be supervisor, and he to have for hys labor vj*s* viij*d*. Thes beyng wytnes; Sir John Schakylton, John Smyth, John Dyghtton, John Thomas, Thomas Sowthe, and other mo.

Proved before P at Lincoln, 10 December 1533. Adm. granted to the executor.

335.   ROBERT HOLE [OF LITTLE HALE IN PARISH OF GREAT HALE]
        [LCC 1532–34, fos. 120v–121r]

14 November 1533. I, Robert Hole of Lyttyll Hale, beyng in a hole mynde and of good remembraunce, makes my will. Fyrste I bequethe my soule to God allmyghtty and to Hys mother Our Lady St. Mary and to all the saintes in heven, and my body to be buryd in the churcheyerde of Gret Hale. To my curate my blake rydyng horse, to pray for me and to discharge me of all my tythes and offerynges that I have bene negligent in. To Sir John Johnson the chauntry preste a stag, to pray for me.[145] To the high altare vj*d*, and to ether of the altares in the same churche ij*d*, and to Our Lady of Lincoln iiij*d*. To St. Catheryn's of Lincoln ij*d*. To my wyffe iiij kye, ij horse, Dudman and Hobbe, and iiij marys, Brocke, Lacon, Moppe and Shorlocke, and xx^ty schepe and my beste carte, and the gerrys and plough and plough gerys, and all my housholde stuffe excepte my high table, and that I will shall stande styll and be a heyrlome, and I gyff to my wyffe all her swyne and pullyn, and my house that I dwell in to my heyr cum to xx^ty yere of age, so that she kepe it in good reparacions. To John my sun ij marys, Pen and Con, and a fylly, the byger ballyd and carte and carte gerys, and plough and plough gerys, and a dowyd cowe and a qwye that standes together, and a yowe and a hogge and my beste whelys. To my sun John the grounde that I bought of John Samer, to hym and to hys heyres of hys body with the horse mylne that standes of the same grounde. To my doughter Agnes a browne qwye and a yowe and a hogge. To Thomas my sun a cowe and a yowe hogge and a balde fylly, and to Leonerde my sun a cowe and a yowe and a hogge. To Christofer my sun a cowe and a yowe and a hogge. To Alson my doughter a flecte cowe and a yowe and a hog. To Elizabeth my doughter a redde cowe and a yowe and a hogge. I wyll that Alson my doughter and Elizabethe my doughters have so myche delyveryd owte of my goodes to by ether of them an hable bedde with, that is to say a matteres, a coverlyd and a pare of schetes and ij pilloys and a bolster to ether of them. I will that every one off my chyldren be other heyres of my bequeste, so long as they kepe theym unmaryd. To Robert Abothe a browne fylly and a redde mare fole. To Robert Hight halffe a seame of barly. To William [fo. 121r] Abothe a bushyll to pray for me, and I will have disposyd at my buryng a dirige, disposyng therat iiij*s*, and I will have another dirige at my vij^th day, ij*s*. And yff it please God that my goodes be incressyd, me beyng alyff, more then they ar nowe, then I will that my chyldren partes be amendyd aftyr the discrecion of William Typler, and yff it pare then I will that they be batyd, and I make my wyffe and Robert Abothe myne executors. I bequethe x*s* to one honeste preste to syng a trentall for my soule. The resydue of my goodes to be aftyr the mynde of William Typler, that he may dispose them to my wyffe and my chyldren as he thynkes best and moste nede is. Wytnes herof; Sir George Pynder, vicar, William Typler, John Abothe, William Kyrton, John Smyth, with other mo.
        Proved before P at Sleaford, 2 March 1533/4.

[145] Sir John Johnson was presented to the chantry of St. Mary in Hale by the abbot and convent of Bardney Abbey on 8 May 1526. The chantry of St. Mary in Hale had been united with the chantry of St. Catherine in the same church as early as 1472, and the post carried a salary of £4 in 1526, which had risen to £4 18s. by 1535. Johnson died by February 1536: Chantry Certificates (1926), 57, 64.

336.   ROBERT BELL [OF AUSTHORPE IN PARISH OF EWERBY]
       [LCC 1532–34, fos. 119v–120r]

15 November 1533. I, Robert Bell of Awsthorp in the paryshe of Iwardeby, hole of mynde and good remembraunce beyng, makes my last will. In the fyrste I bequethe my soule to God allmyghtty, Our Lady St. Mary and to all the blessyd cumpeny of heven. My body to be buryd in the paryshe churche of Iwardeby. To the high altare ther for tithes forgottyn ij*s*. For my lying in the churche vj*s* viij*d*. To the bellys of the same xvj*d*. To Our Lady warke of Lincoln xij*d*. To every place of frerys in Boston xij*d*. I will that Isabell my doughter have all that was gyffyn to her by the last wylls of William Bell and Jenet Bell, sumtyme the wyffe of Thomas Greve. To the same Isabell one blake meyr for the mare that Robert Bell, my father, gaff her. I gave Jenet my wyff x markes of the hole stocke of my goodes. I will that [fo. 120r] the same x markes be devydyd and delyveryd to my ij sonnys when they cum to xviij yeres of age, and the one to be the other heyr yff ether of them decesse and departe afore he cum to the age of the sayd yeres. To Henry Lawklande ij bullokes that Hugh Haryman hath in kepyng. To the same Henry one acre wheate, one acre barly, and one acre peys. To Jenet my servant one yong cowe of iij yeres olde, the color redde. To James Haryman and Christofer, my servantes, ij schepe hogges. To every one of my godchylder in the paryshys off Iwardeby and Howyll, one stryke of barly. I wyll have a yerely obbyt to be kepte of iiij yeres, date to be takyn of the landes of Thomas Dykes, for my soule and Alyson my wyff, and my good frendes. I will that Jenet my wyff have the same lande duryng the sayd iiij yeres, payng the yerely rentes to the church masters of Iwardeby, and they to kepe the same obbyt, and it to be so kepte by the space of the sayd iiij yeres as ther may remayn iiij*l* to kepe it by the selffe for evermore. And in kepyng of the same obbyt, to the vicare of the same, for syngyng or sayng of the dirige iiij*d*. In offeryng iiij*d*. To the paryshe clerke ij*d*. To the belman j*d*. And the resydue of the money to be orderyd and disposyd by the churche masters and the towneshyp of Iwardeby, as they thynke it moste expedyent. The sum of the yerely rente of the same lande for one yere, xxvj*s* viij*d*, wherof ij*s* viij*d* is to be payd to the cheyff lorde for the lande, and the resydue therof to be payd to the same obbyt. To Jenet my wyffe the copy of the hallgarthe and rydynges with all the lande and medo, by the space of viij yeres nexte foloyng. And then aftyrwardes I will that Isabell my doughter have the sayd coppy with all that perteynyth to it, duryng the resydue of all the yeres perteynyng to it. To William my sun the proffyt of Cowke house in Iwardeby by the space of vj yeres nexte cumyng, payng to Robert Dykynson every yere ij*s* iiij*d*. I will that all my goodes be devydyd in thre partes, that is one parte hole to be disposyd for the helthe of my soule and my good frendes, the secunde parte to my iij chylder, and the thyrde parte to Jenet my wyffe, the whiche I order to be my faythfull executrix, that she may order my goodes for the helthe of my soule and my good frendes, by the oversyght of Michyll Beche of Rowston, and he to have the rule and gydyng of Isabell my doughter and her goodes and landes to the tyme she be hable to be maryd, and he to have for hys labor vj*s* viij*d*. Thes wytnes; Sir Richard Typler, ther beyng vicar, Thomas Pell of the same, and John Steynyt of the same, with other mo. The dat the day and yere aforesayd.

Proved before P at Sleaford, 2 March 1533/4.

337.   JOAN TOLLYN [OF LEVERTON]
       [LCC 1532–34, fo. 133r]

15 November 1533. I, Jenett Tollyn of Leverton, wedow, in hole mynde and of gudd remembraunce, makes mye testamentt. Fyrst I bequethe mye soull to allmyghtye God, to Hys mother Seyntt Marye, and to all the seynttes beynge in heven, and mye bodye to be beryed in the churcheyerde of Leverton. To Sayntt Helene for reparacyon in Leverton iiij*d*. To the anowrmentt of the hye aulter in Leverton chyrche iiij*d*. To everye other aulter in the same chyrche ij*d*. To Ower Ladye flower ij*d*. To Ower Ladye [of] Grace ij*d*. To Ower Ladye werke of Lyncoln iiij*d*. To the same Ladye a rynge of sylver. To Sayntt Kateryn withowtt Lyncolln ij*d*. To the parson for forgoten tythys iiij*d*. To Issabell mye dowghter one brandylde cowe and on skylled cowe, one quey burnynge of the best, on great panne and all mye pewter schelffe as it standes, one cawfe, a gryselde meyr, v yows and v lammys of the best, a lytyll chyste os ytt standdes, iij brasse pottes of the best, on matrys and os mytche clothe os wyll make a newe matrys and mye best coverlytt, one spynnynge wheyll, j boull, one soo, one tubbe, one chare, one spytt, on pare coberddes, on churn with all my flax that grew in x acars and v yerddes rosett clothe, mye vyolett gown and mye rosett kyrtyll, and one redd kyrtyll to be made of mye blackyd. Also I wyll that the sayd Issabell have her fyndynge of mye guddes to Ma[y] Day next cumynge wyth her catall. To Wylliam mye son mye grey hamlynge geldynge and mye redd mare, mye blacke mare, one dowyd cowe, one quey burnynge, one whytt burnynge, iiij yowes, iiij lammys with mye cartt and all the geyres longynge too ytt. To Thomas mye son on blacke cowe, one redd quye burnynge. To Margarett Hudson hys dowghter one cawfe and one lame. To Rychard Pekerynge one yowe and one lame. To Margarett Pekerynge mye rosett gown. To Herre my son mye yonge geldynge and mye olde geldynge, one balde meyr and one folle, ij kye, one stere, one blacke burnyng, viij scepe, one matrys, one coverlett, one pare scheyttes. To Jenett, the dowghter of Wylliam Hudson, on cawfe and on yowe. To Issabell Hudson mye vyolett kyrtyll. To the iiij orders of frears in Boston halfe a quarter barlye to be devyded amonge theym. To Herre, mye son, mye plowe with all the garres longynge to ytt. I bequethe v scores of flax to makynge on surplys in the churche of Leverton. I gyve mye cartt to Wylliam and Herre mye sons. The resydewe of mye goodes nott gyven I gyve to Wylliam and Herrye my sons, whom I make mye executors to brynge me forthe, and payinge dettes and mye legacyes, and dyspose for mye soull as they thynke shall be most pelasure to God, with Thomas mye son supervyser, and he to have for hys labor ij quarters barlye. Theys wytnesses; Sir John Scott and Rychard Pekerynge, with other moo.
       Proved before P at Boston, 3 March 1533/4.

338.   RICHARD THOMSON [OF MOULTON]
       [LCC 1532–34, fo. 135]

15 November 1533. I, Rychard Tomson of Multon in Holland, beyng in good mynd and perfyte remembrans, makes thys my last wyll and testament. Fyrst I beqweyth my sawll to God almyghty and too Our Lady Sant Mary and to all the company of hevyne, and my body to be beryd in the chyrcheyard of Al Halloys in Multon, with my mortuary as the law wyll require. To the hy awter of Multon church for thythys forgotton viij*d*. To the iij lyghtes in the sayd chyrch iiij*d*. I wyll to the Stony's lyght

ij*d*. To the reparacyons of the sayd chyrche viij*d*. To the mother chyrche of Lyncolne ij*d*. To the fatherlese chylderne at Sent Katern's in Lyncolne ij*d*. Thys ys the last wyll of me Rychard Tomson of Molton, mayd the day and the yer abow wrytton. Also I wyll that Issabell Tomson my doghter haw ij ky, xx^ti schepe, ij materys, ij coverlettes, iij pare of flaxyn schettes and iij pare of harden schettes, ij towels, ij tabylclothys, on of flaxyn and another of harden, [fo. 135v] a bolstar and ij pelows, a gret payn, ij potes, iiij pewter platers, iiij pewter dyschys, iiij sawsers and ij of the best candelstykes. Also I wyll that Margett Tomson my wyfe haw Yssabell Tomson my doghter in her kepyng and all her goodes to the day of her maryage, and than my doghter to haw here good at the day of her maryagg so good as my resawyd there. And also yf Margytt my wyfe do mary after my dyssese, and yf her hwsband and sche cannott agrey well together, than I wyll that Margytt my wyfe do put Isbell my doghter wher sche lystes with anny frend that sche hays, and he for to haw the sayd goodes of my doghter hent to the tym of her maryag, and then he for to delyver the same goodes agane at the day of her maryag soo good as he recewyd them at the fyrst tyme of her cummyng. And also yf my doghter Issabell dy before the tyme that sche be maryde, than I wyll that Margyt Tomson my wyfe haw all the goodes that I dyd gywe to Issabell my doghter. The resydew of all my goodes nott gywne, I gywe them to Margyd Tomsone my wyff whom I do mak my executryx, sche for to dyspose for the helthe of my sawll. I order and constytute Robert Harby supervysor, and I wyll that he haw for hys labor ij stryk of whett. Theys beyng wytnes; Sir Jeffray Hauys, prest, Robert Harby, Wylliam Cok, with other moo.

Proved before P at Spalding, 4 March 1533/4.

339.   RALPH HOSBORNE [OF DONINGTON IN HOLLAND]
[LCC 1532–34, fos. 137v–138r]

16 November 1533. I, Rayff Hosborne of Donyngton in Hollande within the countie of Lincoln, beyng of hole mynde and godde remembraunce, make my testament and laste will. Fyrste I bequethe my soule to God allmyghtty and to Our Blessyd Lady St. Mary, and to all the holly cumpeny in heven. My body to be buryd in the churcheyerde of Donyngton. To the high altare in the same churche for tithys forgottyn iiij*d*. To every altare within the same churche ij*d*. To the bellys viij*d*. To every lyght that standes abowte my herce at my buryall day j*d*. To Our Lady of Lincoln ij*d*. To the fatherles chyldren at St. Catheryn's withowt the wallys of Lincoln ij*d*. To Margaret Hosborne my wyffe my house with iij roode lande longyng to it lying within the towne of Donyngton, the whiche that Thomas Hosborne my brother dwellys in immediatly aftyr my decesse, to do with it what she will and as she thynkes beste to be done with it. The [fo. 138r] resydue of all my goodes I gyff them to Margaret Osborne my wyff, whome I make my executrix. Thes beyng wytnes; Sir John Gybson, vicar of Donyngton, Robert Comfettes and John Cottes of the same towne.

Proved before P at Swineshead, 5 March 1533/4.

340. ROBERT WHETLEY [OF SPALDING]
[LCC 1532–34, fo. 125v]

17 November 1533. I, Robert Whetlay of Spaldyng, of hole mynde and good remembraunce, make my testament and last will. Fyrste I bequethe my soule to allmyghtty God, Our Lady St. Mary and to all the celestiall cumpeny of heven, and my body to be buryd in the paryshe churcheyerde of Spaldyng. To the high altare in the paryshe churche of Spaldyng viij*d*. To Our Lady's gylde xij*d*. To the Trinite gylde xij*d*. To the 'postyllys gylde viij*d*. To Our Lady of Lincoln iiij*d*. To Dane John Crowlande my sun v markes sterlyng, so that he make me and hys father bretherne, and hys mother syster, in the chapiture house in Ramsay, or ellys I will it be at the disposicion of my wyffe. The resydue of my goodes I gyff to Cecely Whetlay my wyff, whome I orden my sole executrix to dispose for the helthe of my soule as she thynkes best, and George Hage supervisor and he to have for hys labor iij*s* iiij*d*. Wytnes herof; Sir Thomas Love, curate, Simon Thekstone, John Palmer, with other mo.

Proved before P at Spalding, 4 March 1533/4.

341. JOHN FOSTER [OF WITHERN]
[LCC 1532–34, fo. 233]

18 November 1533. I, John Foster of Witherne, with a good remembraunce beyng in stedfaste and hole mynde, make thys my present testament conteynyng my last will. Fyrste I bequethe my soule to allmyghtty God, to Our Blessyd Lady St. Mary and to all the holy saintes in heven. My body to be buryd in the churcheyerde of St. Margarete in Witherne. To the blessyd sacrament ij*d*. To the churche warke of St. Margarete in Witherne iij*s* viij*d*. To Our Lady of Lincoln iiij*d*. To Jenet Foster a red whyte flekyd qwye of iij yere olde. [fo. 233v] To Agnes Foster a red qwye of iij yere olde with a whyte sterne in her forhed. To Elizabethe Foster a blak qwyke of iij yere olde. To Catheryn Henryson a red cowe of iiij yere olde. To Thomas Foster iij yeryng sterys and a violet gowne, and a yeryng fole. To Edwarde Foster a redde stere of ij yere olde and my russyt cote. To Margarete Foster ij blake yeryng calvys and a hogge schepe. The resdyue of my goodes not wyttyd, my dettes payd, I put to the discrescion of Margaret my wyffe and to Nicholes Mellesent, and he to have iij*s* iiij*d* for hys labor, whome I make my faythfull executors, that they orden and dispose as they seme best and moste expedyent unto the plesure of God and welfare and helthe of my soule. I will that Richerde Henryson be supervisor. Thes beryng wytnes; Sir William Cowper, Sir William Ebton, Thomas Foster, with other mo.

Proved before P at Alford, 5 February 1533/4.

342. ROBERT WRANGILL [OF DONINGTON IN HOLLAND]
[LCC 1532–34, fo. 138r]

18 November 1533. I, Robert Wrangyll of Donyngton in Hollande within the countie of Lincoln, make my testament and laste will. Fyrste I bequethe my soule to God allmyghtty and to Our Blessyd Lady St. Mary and to all the saintes in heven, and my body to be buryd within the churcheyerde of Donyngton. To the high altare within the churche of Donyngton xij*d*. To every altare within the same churche ij*d*. To every light that standes abowt my herce at my buryall day j*d*. To the bellys ij*s*.

To Our Lady of Lincoln ij*d*. To the fatherles chyldren at St. Catheryn's ij*d*. To the iiij orders of frerys in Boston iij*s* iiij*d*. To Robert Johnson my godsun xij*d*. To Robert Underwater my godson xij*d*. To John Grave a borlyng. To Thomas Grave one calve. Thys is my will, that John Robynson have my house that I dwell in, to hym and to hys heyres of hys body, with all other landes longyng to it with thys condicion, that he gyff to Robert Robynson hys brother xl*s* within the space of vj yeres [remainder to] Robert Robynson hys brother under the same maner. And yff they bothe dye withowt heyres of ther bodyes, then I will it be solde be my executors, and be the kerke gravys and iiij honest men of Donyngton, and the money therof to be bestowyd apon a cawsy from my house to the churche as farre as the money will extende. Also I will that Agnes my wyffe have iij stong of hemp lande that I bought of her the terme of her lyffe, and aftyr to remayn to the heyres of John Robynson. Also I will that Agnes my wyffe have all suche goodes as she brought with her to me. The reste of all my goodes I will it be devydyd betwyx Agnes my wyffe and John Robynson, whome I make my executors to bryng me forthe and to pay my dettes. Thes beyng wytnes; Robert Luff and Thomas Johnson.

Proved before P at Swineshead, 5 March 1533/4.

343.   ALICE ELSTON [OF FULBECK]
        [LCC 1532–34, fos. 116v–117r]

20 November 1533. I, Alice Elston, late wyffe of Robert Elston of Fulbeck, hole in mynde and good remembraunce, makyth my last will and testament. Fyrste I bequethe and gyff my soule to allmyghtty God, Our Lady St. Mary and to all the saintes in heven. My body to be buryd in the churche of St. Nicholes at Fulbecke. To the high altare at Fulbecke xvj*d*. To Our Lady stok ther a bushyll of barly, and to the reparacion of the bellys ther one halffe seame of barly. To St. John hys gylde ther, one bushyll of barly. To Our Lady warke at Lincoln iiij*d*. To every of the iiij orders of frerys ther iiij*d*. To Catheryne Elston one qwe and v shepe. To one honest preste x*s* to syng a trentall of messes within the churche of Fulbecke for my soule and all Crysten soulys. To Sir Bryan Warde iiij*d*. To Thomas Cok halffe a seame barly. To William Jakson a bushyll barly. To Hugh Jakson one schepe. To Margarete Whyte one brasse potte. To Catheryne Elston one schepe. To the paryshe clerke iiij*d*. To Simon Elston my sun one cowe, x schepe and one brasse potte. The resydue of my goodes I gyff to John [fo. 117r] Elston and William Elston my sonys, whome I make my executors, they to dispose it for the helthe of my soule as to them shall beseme moste expedyent. Thes beyng wytnes; Gylys Alyste, John Aliste, William Elston, Henry Cappe, John Farnesfelde, Thomas Cok, Sir Bryan Warde, and other.

Proved before P at Ancaster, 31 January 1533/4.

344.   WILLIAM BOSTON [OF ASWARDBY]
        [LCC 1532–34, fo. 132r]

28 November 1533. I, Wylliam Boston of the paryche of Aswardbye in the countie of Lyncolln, yoman, hole of mynde and good of remembraunce, doo ordeyn and make mye testament and last wyll. Fyrst I gyve and bequethe my soule unto almyghtye God, Oure Ladye Seyntt Marye, and all the sancttes in heven. Mye body

to be buryed in the churcheyerde of Seyntt Dyonyse in Aswardbye. To Ower Ladye of Lyncolln xij*d*. To the hye aulter of Aswardbye churche xij*d*. To the same churche workes xij*d*. To Asbye churche xij*d*. To the parysshe churche of Laynton xij*d*. To Roberde Boston my sonne ij steyrys of iij yeres old. To Thomas Boston mye sonne ij steyrys of iij yeres olde. To Alyce my dowghter one quey of iij yerys olde and a calfe of one yere olde. To Margaret Boston my dowghter one cowe of iiij yeres olde. To Jane Boston mye dowghter on quey of one yere olde. To Elizabethe Boston one oxe calfe of on yere olde. To vj chyldern xx^{ti} yowes and xx^{ti} lammes, and xx^{ti} hogg shepe to be devyded emonge them equallye. Also after the dyscease of mye wyfe I bequethe to Alyce Boston mye dowghter a greatt panne. To Margaret Boston mye dowter ij pannes. To Joohan Boston mye dowghter j brasse pott. I gyve unto a prest to synge for mye sole on quarter of a yere xx*s*. To Elizabethe Boston mye dowghter j kettle. To Roberde Boston mye sonne j brasse pott. To Wylliam Boston mye brother x*s* to helpe mye wyfe in her besynes. The resydewe of my goodes I gyve to Margaret Boston mye wyfe and Wylliam Boston mye brother, whome I doo make mye executors for to dyspose mye gudes as they shall thynke most necessarye for the helthe of my soule and all Crysten soulles. Wytnesse; Sir Stephane Scarburghe, parsonne of Aswardbye, Symon Booyth, Nycolys Porter, John Stevyn, and other mo.

Proved before P at Sleaford, 2 March 1533/4.

345.   JOHN HELCOTE [OF WAINFLEET ALL SAINTS]
        [LCC 1532–34, fo. 262]

28 November 1533. I, John Helcote of Waynflet All Halloys, of a good mynde and of an hole memory, makes my testament and last will. Fyrste I bequethe my soule unto allmyghtty God and Our Lady St. Mary, and to all the hole cumpeny of heven, and my body to be buryd as nygh as may be before Mary Magdalene standyng in St. Nicholes qwere. To the high altare in the same churche xij*d*, and to ether of the lawe altares iiij*d*. To the same high altare for tentes forgottyn viij*d*. To Our Lady's warke of Lincoln viij*d*, and to the faderles chyldren at St. Catheryn's ij*d*. To the churche of All Halloys for my buryall vj*s* viij*d*. To the bellys in the same churche viij*d*. To Margarete Helcote my doughter xv moder schepe, one cowe, one matres, one pare of schetes, one coverlyd, one bolster, one pilloy, one brasse potte, halffe a dosyn of puter, iiij flaxyn schetes. To Emote my doughter xv moder schepe, one cowe, one matres, one pare of schetes, one coverlyd, one bolster, one pillo, one brasse potte, halffe a dosyn puter and iiij flaxyn schetes. To Richerde Helcote my sonne my ij lyttyng leades, one mare. And I will that iche of thes my iiij chylder be iche other heyr in case any of them dye before the cum at xvij yeres of age for madins, and Richerd my sun at xv yeres. To William Thyrlande one bedde. To John Thomson ij*s* to by hym a dooblyt. I will also have immediatly aftyr my dethe, for the helthe of my soule, one trentall sung, price x*s*. The resydue of all my goodes I gyff to Beatrix my wyff, whome I make my executrix. I will that Raynolde Herryson be supervisor and have for hys labor v*s*. Thes beyng wytnesses; Richerde Ranson, parson of the same Waynflet, William Johnson, Robert Norton, John Pecoke, cum aliis. Thys is the laste will of me, John Helcote, day and yere before sayd. I will that Beatrix my wyff have my hed house and vij acres lande in St. Mary's felde calyd Petcheller Tofte, arrable lande for the terme of her lyffe. And aftyr her decesse I will

my sun Robert Helcote have it all to hym and hys heyres of hys body laufully begottyn, and yff ought cum at hym withowt heyres off [fo. 262v] hys body laufully begottyn, then I will that my sun Richerde Helcote have it all, to hym and hys heyres of hys body laufully begottyn [remainder to] ther systers Margaret and Emote Helcote as the lawe will, so that iche of them be other heyr. In case they all iiij dye withowt heyres of ther bodys laufully begottyn, then I will it to be solde and disposyd for my soule and my wyffe's, and for the soulys of my father and mother and for all Crysten soulys. Thes beyng wytnesses; Richerde Ranson, parson of the same towne, William Jonson, Robert Norton, John Pecoke, cum aliis.

Proved before P at Spilsby, 5 May 1534.

346. THOMAS BOSTON [OF HACEBY]
[LCC 1532–34, fo. 277v]

1 December 1533. I, Thomas Boston of Haseby, good of mynde and hole remembraunce, makes my last will and testament. Fyrst I gyff my soule unto allmyghtty God and to Our Lady St. Mary, and to all the saintes of heven, and my body to be buryd in the churche of Haseby. To Our Lady warke of Lincoln xijd. To the high altare of Haseby xijd. To the kyrke warke of Haseby xijd. To the commune bryg of Haseby xijd. To the churche of Haseby, a cowe to fynde a light before the rode. To the kyrke of Laventon xijd. To John my sun a horse. All the resydue of my good I gyff to my wyffe and to my sonne William, whome I make my executors.

Proved before P at Sleaford, 20 May 1534.

347. ROBERT ROWTON [OF BARROW UPON HUMBER]
[LCC 1532–34, fos. 253v–254r]

1 December 1533. I, Robert Rowton of Barowe, of a hole mynde and full of memory, makes thys my will and testament. Fyrste I bequethe my soule to allmyghtty God and to Our Lady St. Mary and to all the blessyd cumpeny of heven, and my body to be buryd in the churche erthe of Barowe. [fo. 254r] To Our Lady of Lincoln iiijd. To the high altare of Our Lady of Barowe viijd. To St. John of Beverlay iiijd.[146] To Brantyngham churche viijd. To Barowe churche viijd. To my brother William Henryson a pare of hose clothe of whyte carsay. To every one of my chylder a yowe schepe. Also the resydue of my goodes not bequethyd I will that Jenet my wyffe have theym, whome I make my executrix to dispose for my souly's helthe as she thynkythe best. Thes wytnes; Robert Tayllor and William Henryson, cum aliis.

Proved before P at Caistor, 27 April 1534.

---

[146] St. John of Beverley was a famous image, attracting bequests and donations from a wide geographical area: Duffy, *Stripping of the Altars*, 161.

348.	ROBERT LOCKYN [OF TETNEY]
	[LCC 1532–34, fos. 245v–246v]

2 December 1533. I, Robert Lokkyn, of my hole mynde and good memory, makes my last will and testament. Fyrste I bequethe my soule unto God allmyghtty, to Our Lady St. Mary and to all the holy cumpeny of heven, and my body to be buryd in the churche of St. Peter and Paule of Tetney with my mortuary as the lawe will. To the high altare of Tetney xij*d*. To the warke of Our Lady of Lincoln xij*d*, and to the high altare of Lincoln iiij*d*. To ether house of frerys of Grymmesby vj*d*. To the bellys of Tetney iij*s* iiij*d*. To the ij chyrches off Bynbroke, to ether of them, vj*d*. I will that my wyffe have the house that I am in with the nether garthe and Plome house, otherways callyd Emeson house, and the olde lathe with the garthe that longes to Plome house [fo. 246r] the terme of her lyffe. And aftyr her decesse the aforesayd Adamson house to retorne to Thomas Lokyn the elder and to hys heyres of hys body laufully begottyn. To Thomas Lokkyn the elder all the lande and medo excepte the lande of Godfray Thomas, it to be devydyd, payng the rente yerely, and the aforesayd Thomas Lokkyn for to gyff to Helene my wyffe a qwarter wheate, a quarter barly and a quarter benys yerely. I will that Adamson house shall fynde a lampe before our Lady of pety for evermore. Also I will that Plome house, otherways callyd Emeson house, shall fynde one obbyt yerely evermore to bred and drynke ij*s*, messe and dirige vj*d*, the beade rolle iiij*d*. To Thomas Lokyn the yonger Plome house, otherways called Emeson house, and he to gyff to John Lokyn, the sun of Richerde Lokyn, ij*s* [sic] vj*s* viij*d*. Also yff it happyn the foresayd Thomas Lokyn the yonger for to dy withowt heyr of hys body laufully begottyn, then I will that the aforesayd house fo remayn unto the aforesayd John Lokyn. Yff he dye withowt heyr of hys body, I will that the house do remayn unto the nexte of kyn. Also I will that my wyffe have iij kye, the whiche she will take with ij pasturys in the Northe Marche. To Alyson Tayllor a browne qwye, a bedde with all that longes to it, ij puter dooblers, a brasse potte, a kettyll, a yowe and a lamme. To Thomas Lokyn the yonger a brandyd qwye with calve, a redde fylly of ij yere olde, a cople sterys of iiij yere olde. To Guy Andro a qwye of iij yere olde. To Robert Lokyn, the sun of Thomas Lokyn the elder, a yowe and a hogge, and John and William, hys bretherne, ether of them, a yowe. To Thomas Lokyn the yonger, a yowe and a hogge. To Margarete Lokyn a hogge. To Margaret Andro a yowe, a stryke wheate, a stryke barly and a stryke of benys, and every one of her iij chyldren for to have a hogge. To John Kyrmonde a horse and iij*s* iiij*d*. To Guy Andro a yowe and one stere. To Margaret Recarde a yowe, and to her doughter a hogge. To Thomas Lokkyn the elder one cople of sterys, a plough and a new wayn, and one gray mare with all the implementes therto belongyng, excepte the bestes that belonges to it. Also one bull. [fo 246v] To Thomas Lokyn the yonger the t'other wayn. To Our Lady gylde of Tetney one yowe. I will that one preste syng for my one quarter and nother frere, chanon nor munke.[147] I will that my executors kyll too of the beste wethers that I have, and to gyff them for the helthe of my soule. To John Otlay a yowe, a hogge, a fryndyll wheate, and as muche malte. To every godbarne that I have iiij*d*. To Nicholes Kyrmonde a yowe. Also I will that my wyffe have all the parcellys of all the housholde the terme of her lyffe, and aftyr to be devydyd

---

[147] This is a highly ambiguous phrase. It might be interpreted as an attempt to provide employment for one of the many poorly paid, unbeneficed priests in the diocese, or it might represent a more focussed anxiety over the commitment of the religious to maintaining their intercessory obligations.

emonges hys kyn and hers at the syght of myn executors. I will that Thomas Lokyn th'elder and Helene my wyffe have the shepcote togeder the terme of her lyffe. To John Kyrmonde ij yowes and one hogge. To John Lokyn, the sun of Richerde Lokyn, ij yowes and ij hogges. To Helene my wyffe xxx^ty schepe. To Thomas lokyn the elder viij hogges. To Thomas the yonger xij hogges. I will that my wyffe have my furryd cote and Thomas the elder the russyt and my best dooblet, and Thomas the yonger my violet furryd jaket, and Thomas the elder my jerkyn. The resydue of my goodes I put it to orderyng of my executors, and they to pay my legacy and dispose it for the helthe of my soule. Also I make John Kyrmonde and Thomas Lokyn the elder myn executors, and Thomas Kyrmonde my supervisor. Thes to wytnes; Sir Robert Blancharde, Godfray Thomas, Saunder Shomaker, William Croftes, with other diverse mo.

Proved before P at Lincoln, 16 March 1533/4.

349. WILLIAM PHILIP [OF HECKINGTON]
[LCC 1532–34, fo. 119v]

3 December 1533. I, William Phylip of Hekyngton, husbandman, dothe make my last will and testament. Fyrste I bequethe my soule to allmyghtty God and to all the holy cumpeny of heven. My body to be buryed in the churchyerde of Hekyngton, and my mortuary accordyng to the right of holy Churche. To the high altare iiijd. To Our Lady altare ijd. To St. Nicholes altare ijd. To Our Lady of Lincoln iiijd. To the churche of Hekyngton vjs iiijd. To the bellys xijd. I will that my house in the weste ende of Hekyngton be solde and bere the charge of funerallys. I will that my house whiche I dwell in shall kepe my yere day with my fader's and moder's yerely, to the vallor of ijs viijd. In performyng herof I will that William Nicolson be supervisor, and for hys labor iijs iiijd. The resydue of my goodes not bequeste I gyff to Alyson my wyffe and Robert Nicholas, John, Thomas and William my chyldren, whome I make my executors, and they to dispose as they shall thynke beste to be done to the plesur of God and the helthe of my soule. Wrytten the yere and day above namyd. Wytnes herof; Sir George Metcalve, Hew Haryman, John Dobkynson, with other mo.

Proved before P at Sleaford, 2 March 1533/4. Adm. granted to Alice and Robert, executors, the other executors being under age.

350. THOMAS JELOWE [OF BICKER]
[LCC 1532–34, fo. 128r]

4 December 1533. I, Thomas Jelow of Byker, with hole mynde and good remembraunce, make mye testamentt and last wyll. Fyrst I bequethe mye sowle to God mye maker, to Hys mother Seyntt Marye, and to all seynttes, and mye bodye to be beryed in the churchyerde of Seyntt Swythune of Byker. To the hye alter ther viijd. To Ower Lady auter ther ijd. To the churche werke of Byker xijd. To ower mother churche of Lyncolln for oblacyon iiijd. To the fatherles chyldern at Seyntt Kateryn's withowt the gattes of Lyncoln ijd. To Thomas mye son mye cartt with the gerres belongynge thertoo, mye pyn mere and derlynge mere,[148] a cowe, iiij

---

[148] A 'pin' mare takes the middle place in a team of three, while 'darling' seems to suggest simply that this was a favourite or pet horse.

yowes besyddes on yowe of hys own. To Wylliam mye son mye yonge derlynge mere and mye blacke feley, a cowe and iiij yowes, iij yowes and ij hogges of hys owne. To Kateryn mye dowghter a cowe and iiij yowes. To Maryan mye dowghter a cowe and iiij yowes. To Alys Halywell mye servantt a yoo houge. The resydew of mye goodes nott bequethed I gyve to Agnes mye wyffe, whom I make mye sole executrix to paye my dettes, to performe thys mye last wyll, and to brynge me onestlye forthe. The remaner to remane to hyr withowtt scropull of concyons. I make Mr. John Lyttelberye supervysor, to whom I gyve mye bay coltt. Theys wytnes; Sir Roberde Johnson, Roberde Jacson, thacker, Thomas Scheparde, with other mo.

Proved before P at Swineshead, 5 March 1533/4.

351. ROGER JOHNSON, alias HOGEKYNSON [OF SKIRBECK]
[LCC 1532–34, fos. 320r–321r]

4 December 1533. I, Roger Johnson, alias Hogekynson, of the paryshe of Skyrbek, hole of mynde and of memory, makes my testament and my last will. Fyrste I gyff and bequethe my soule to God allmyghtty and to the Blessyd Virgyn Our Lady St. Mary and to all the saintes in heven, and my body to be buryd within the churche of the blessyd confessor Sir Nicholes of Skyrbek. To the mother churche off Lincoln viij*d*. To the fatherles chylder off [fo. 320v] Lincoln viij*d*. I bequethe for my forgottyn tithes xij*d*. To the churche of Skyrbek iij*s* iiij*d*. To Sir Robert Browne my curate iiij*s* iiij*d*. To Margery Browne one matteres and one coverlyt and one pare of schete, ij pilloys and ij yowes and one qwye calve. To William Suyll one qwye and a mare stage. To Thomas Suyll one qwye and a mare stage. To Henry Suyll one yowe and one lamme. To Robert Johnson one yowe and one lamme. To Richerde Johnson my sun iiij gayde hogges and ij yowes and inne marys. To Alyson Suyll ij yowes and one calve. To Jamys Coper one yowe and one lamme. To iche of my godchylder one yowe and one lamme. To Beatrix Reynes ij yowes and ij lammys. To William Johnson my sun all my rayment. To William Johnson my sun and to Richerde Johnson my sun my coatte. Also the resydue of all my goodes within my house I bequeth to Alyson Johnson my wyff, and vj of the best kye and iij of the best merys, and my best horse and xlj^{ty} yowes and iiij gayd wedders, and all my swyne and one plugh and one carte with all that belonges therto, and as muche wheate and barly and malte as will fynde her house to newe come of the grounde. To Alyson my wyff iij acres of wheate sawne of the grounde and iij acres of pasture, and she for to pay the rent. To William Johnson my sun one acre of wheate sawne of the grounde. To the same William one olde house callyd Christofer house and all the grounde that belonges unto it and halffe an acre of lande lying within the paryshe off Skyrbek, and also fyve acres of lande, the parcell of x acres of lande that I bought of George Schypesy, that is to say halffe of the sayd x acres of landes lying within the sayd paryshe of Skyrbek to hym and to hys heyres for evermore. To Alyson Johnson my wyff my house that I do dwell in and one acre of lande belongyng therto, and v acres of landes, the udder halff of the sayd x acres of landes that I bought of Master George Schypesy as it is aforesayd, as long as she kepe here vidoy. And so it fortune that Alyson Johnson my wyffe do mary or dye, then I will that my house that I do dwell in and one acre of lande and all the purtenances belongyng therto, and the v acres of landes as it is aforesayd, for to remayn to Richerde Johnson my sun, and to hys heyres of [fo. 321r] hys body laufully

begottyn. And so it fortune that Richerde Johnson dye withowt eny issue of hys body lawfully begottyn, then I will that my house and one acre of lande and all the purtenances belongyng therto, and the foresayd v acres of landes remayn to William Johnson my sun and to hys heyres of hys body laufully begottyn for evermore. Thys done, my dettes payd and my funerall expenses well and honestly brought furthe, and my will fulfyllyd, the resydue of all my goodes I put it unto the discrecion of William Johnson my sun and Roger Johnson, the whiche I make my executors aftyr thys maner, that they for to do or cause for to be done one obyt, iijs iiijd, every yere as long as the value of my goodes do laste in the paryshe churche of Skyrbek, and they for to have for ther labor, iche of theym, vjs viijd. And I will that Nicholes Coper and Richerde Jolyson to be the supervisors, and for to have for ther labor, iche of theym, iijs iiijd. Wytnes herof; Sir Robert Browne my curate, John Symson, Nicholes Coper, with other mo. In the yere and the day abovesayd.

Proved before P at Boston, 10 June 1534.

352. RICHARD GROVE [OF TATTERSHALL]
[LCC 1532–34, fo. 257]

6 December 1533. I, Richerde Grove of the paryshe of Tateshale, of a hole mynde and good memory, makes my last will and testament. Fyrste I bequethe my soule unto God allmyghtty, Our Lady St. Mary and unto all the [fo. 257v] holy cumpeny of heven, and my body to be buryed within the churche of Tateshale, and for that I gyff unto the sayd churche vjs viijd. To the high altare for forgottyn tithys iiijd. To the paryshe altare iiijd. To Our Lady of Lincoln iiijd. I will a trentall of messes be sayd within the churche of Tateshale for the helthe of my soule and for all my frendes' soulys. To Robert Grove my sun a qwye and ij schepe. To Jenet my wyff the copy of my dwellyng house with the appurtenance therto pertenyng duryng her lyffe, and aftyr her decesse I gyff the copy of the sayd house with the appurtenances unto Richerde Grove and John Grove my chyldren. To Thomas Grove my sun the copy of another house with the appurtenances therto belongyng. Also I will (my dettes payd) the resydue of my goodes be devydyd in thre partes, one parte unto Jenet my wyffe, the secunde parte unto my chyldren Richerde Grove, Jone, Thomas and Dorothe, and the thyrde porcion unto myselffe, the whiche I gyff unto Jenet my wyffe, whome I make my executrix to dispose the sayd porcion of my goodes for the helthe of my soule. Thes wytnesses of the premisses; Jone Thyrlbecke, Richerde Yerborow, Henry Wynter, Richerde Schawe, cum ceteris.

Proved before P at Horncastle, 4 May 1534.

353. JOHN ROLLE [OF WALCOT]
[LCC 1532–34, fo. 114v]

6 December 1533. I, John Rolle of Walcot, of hole mynde beyng and good remembraunce, make my testament. Fyrste I bequethe my soule to God allmyghtty, to Our Lady St. Mary and to all the company in heven. My body to be buryd in the churcheyerde of St. Andro in Walcot. To the high altare of St. Andro in Walcote, for tithynges forgottyn, xijd. To Our Lady of Lincoln xijd. To St. John gylde in Walcote ij schepe. To All Hallo light in the same towne one stryke barly. To Richerde Rolle my sun my beste cote and one horse, or ellys xs. To Edmunde

Sylkby ix schepe, one russyt cote, one russyt jaket, one russyt dooblet. I gyff to a preste, to syng half a trentall in the churche of Walcote for my soule, my father soule, my mother soule and all Christen soulys, vs. To Robert Wylkynson one lamme hogge. To John Spenser one lamme hogge. The resydue of my goodes I gyff them to Agnes Rolle my wyff, whome I do make myn executrix to dipose them for the well of my soule. Thes beryng wytnes; Sir Thomas Pell, William Fysher, Thomas Bennyt, John Spenser, with other mo.

Proved at Bourne, 30 January 1533/4.

354. RICHARD LODYSDALE [OF THURLBY BY BOURNE]
[LCC 1532–34, fos. 113v–114r]

11 December 1533. I, Richerde Lodysdale of the paryshe of Thurlby, of an hole mynde and good remembraunce, constitute and orden my laste will. Fyrste and principally I commende my soule unto God allmyghtty, unto Our Lady St. Mary and to all the holy cumpeny in heven. My body to be buryd within the churche of St. Firmyne within the paryshe of Thurlby, ny to my seatte. To the high altare in my paryshe churche xij*d*. To the redde [fo. 114r] arche in our mother churche of Lincoln iiij*d*. To the reparacion of the bellys of Thurlby xij*d*. To the abbot and convent of Burne vj*s* viij*d*. To Agnes Elred my syster vj*s* viij*d*. To Nicholes her sun one ewe and a lamme. To every one of my syster chyldren a lamme. To my mother Harby iiij yerdys of clothe. To Wylliam Harby my beste russyt cote. To Richerde Harby my godsun an ewe and a lamme. To every one of William Harby chyldren a lamme. To every one of my godchyldren a lamme. To my father John Lodysdale xxvj*s* viij*d* of dette that I do owe hym. To Thomas Elrede my brother-in-lawe one of my best garmentes or cote. I will that dirige and messe shall be sung for me the day of my buryall, the vij^th day and the xxx^ty day. Also I will and very strately charge my executors that they fynde a preste to say messe for me the space of an hole yere together, within the churche of Thurlby. To the churche of Edenham xij*d*. The resydue of my goodes I gyff to Alice Lodysdale my wyffe and to my father John Lodysdale, whome I make executors to dispose my goodes for the helthe of my soule as they shall thynke convenyent. Wytnes herof; Robert Weldon, Thomas Hayre, Robert Grante, Roberte Clerke and John Grante, with other.

Proved before P at Bourne, 30 January 1533/4. Adm. granted to the executor.

355. THOMAS AWVE [OF STUBTON]
[LCC 1532–34, fo. 202]

12 December 1533. I, Thomas Awve of Stubton in the countie of Lincoln, husbandman, with hole mynde and memory, orden and makes thys my last will and testament. Fyrste and principally I bequethe my soule unto allmyghtty God my creature, to Hys most blessyd mother, Our Lady St. Mary, and unto all the holy cumpeny in heven. My body to be buryed in the churcheyerde of St. Martyn in Stubton aforesayd. To the high altare in the sayd churche viij*d*. To Our Lady of Lincoln viij*d*. I will ther be a preste founde to syng in the same paryshe churche halffe one trentall of messys for my soule and all Crystyn soulys, and he to have for hys salary vs. To the bellys in the forsayd churche ij*s*. To Thomas Hoose iiij schepe,

ij quarters of barly and [fo. 202v] one qwye of a yere olde. To William my brother my best gowne. To Alice Aweve one gray mayr. To Robert my servant a schepe hogge. To John Arnalle one schepe hogge. To John Robynson of Claypole one cowe, ij yowes and ij hogges. To Robert Hoose one cowe. To Thomas Aweve of Claypole ij schepe hogges. To the pore people in Stubton, every one of them, one pek of wheate. To Sir Nicholes Chapman my goostly father xij*d*. The resydue of my goodes unbequethyd, my dettes payd and thys my last will fulfyllyd, I gyff unto Jenet my wyff whome I make my sole executrix. To Rayff Aweve xx*s* and one qwye, he to se that thys my last will be fulfyllyd. I will that Sir Richerde Aweve, vicar of Norwell in the countie of Nottyngham, be supervisor, he for to se it be well and truly performyd, to whome I gyff iij*s* iiij*d* for hys labor. Thes testes; Sir Nicholes Chapman, my gostly father, Robert Hoose, Rayff Aweve, Robert Morton of Stubton aforesayd, husbandman, with other mo.

Proved before P at Lincoln, 19 December 1533.

356.   JOHN BLABY [OF LANGTOFT]
        [LCC 1532–34, fo. 113v]

12 December 1533. I, John Blabe of Langtofte, of hole mynde and of goode remembraunce, makes my will. Fyrste I bequethe my soule unto allmyghtty God and to Our Lady St. Mary and to all the holy cumpeny, and my body to be buryed in the churcheyerde of St. Michel the Archaungell in Langtofte. To the high altare of the same churche, a bushyll of barly. To the bellys of the same churche a stryke of barly. To All Hallo lyght, a stryke of barly. To Our Lady of Lincoln xij*d*. To John Whetlay ij strykes of barly. To Agnes Pynder a stryke of barly. To Thomas Blabe my sonne, a yow. To Catheryne my doughter, a cowe and an ewe. To Agnes my doughter, a cowe and an ewe. And yff my wyffe, ther mother, do mary agayn, I will that she loke better on them then thys that I gyff them by the councell of Robert Laxson her brother. The resydue of my goodes I will that Elizabethe my wyffe and Robert Laxson her brother, whome I make my executors, do order them for the helthe of my soule and all Crysten soullys as they thynke beste, and the sayd Robert to have for hys labor iij*s* iiij*d*. Wytnesses; Syr Gefferay Bull, vicar, Thurstan Hall, Gregory Nunton, with other mo.

Proved before P at Stamford, 28 January 1533/4.

357.   ALICE HOODE [OF ALFORD]
        [LCC 1532–34, fos. 231v–232r]

12 December 1533. I, Alice Hoode of Alford, wydowe, withyn the countie of Lincoln, of hoole mynde and good memory, ordyne and make my testament and last wyll. Fyrst I bequeythe my sawle to almyghty God, Owr Lady Sent Mary and to all the sayntes in heyven, and my body to be buryed withyn the churcheyarde of Alford. To ornamentes of the hye awter in the same churche viij*d*. To every awter with the same ij*d*. To the sepulker lyght in the same iiij*d*. To Saynt Antony lyght in the same iiij*d*. To Kyng Henry lyght in the same iiij*d*. To Mr. William Johnson, vycar of the same, xx*d*. To the stepull of Alforde aforesayd v*s*. [fo. 232r] To Ower Lady warke of Lincoln iiij*d*. To the churche warke of Ryggesby iij*s* iiij*d*. To Ower Lady in the chapell at Market Reyson iiij*d*. To Claryll my servand a blacke kowe

with a whytt sterre in the hedd, a brasse potte next the best, a lyttyll pan, a coverlett of red, a peyre of shetes of herden, on matteresse and iiij puter dysshys. To Margaret Madyson a red kowe with a whyte hed, the beste brasse pott and iij puter dublers. To Julyan Byrkehed, the wyffe of Thomas Byrkehed, my grett pan. To Alyce Bordwyn vjs. To William Koke wyffe my best hatt and my best cappe and iijs iiijd. To Arthure Wassyngley chylde callyd Jone a kowe. I wyll that iij days, that ys to say the day of my buryall, the vij^th day and the xxx^ti day be solemply kepyd with a placebo and dirige, and also masse of requiem. I wyll that the rest of all my goodes nott bequethyd shal be devydyd amonges the chyldryn of Arthure Wasshyngley be equall porcyons. I orden Arthure Wasshynglye afore specyfyed and William Coke of Alford my trew executers, the[y] to pay my dettes and performe thys my last wyll accordyng to the lawe of holy Churche. Thes wytnes; Mr William Johnson, vicar of Alford aforesayd, and Sir John Davy of the same, pryst, and other mo.

Proved before P at Alford, 5 February 1533/4.

358.   JOHN JAKSON [OF NORTH WILLINGHAM]
       [LCC 1532–34, fo. 238]

12 December 1533. I, John Jakson of North Wyllyngham, husbandman, of a hole mynde savyng seke in body, makes my testament. Fyrste I bequethe my soule to God. allmyghtty, to Our Lady St. Mary and to all the gloriose cumpeny in heven. My body to be buryd in the kyrke of St. Thomas th'appostyll in North Wyllyngham aforesayd. To the foresayd kyrke for my buryall vjs viijd. To the high altare of the same for my tithys and oblacions forgottyn xijd. To the bellys of the same xxd, and a schete to make [fo. 238v] ij altare clothys upon. To Our Lady altare of Lincoln viijd. To Our Lady warke of the same viijd. To the iiij orders of frerys, to every house singulerly, iiijd. To Tevelby kyrke iiijd. To Syxhill kyrke iiijd. To bothe kyrkes off Ludfurthe, to oder of them, iiijd. To the chanons of Syxhill Abbay xijd. To the nonnes of the same place xijd. To John Oldeman my godsun a yowe and a lamme. To John Robynson my godsun a yowe and a lamme. To Walter Robynson ij yowes and ij lammys. To Helene Utterby a yowe and a lamme. To Jamys Jackeson a cowe and ij yowes. To John Jackson hys brother ij yowes and ij lammys. To George Jakson ij yowes and ij lammys. To Isabell Jakson my brasse and my puter wyth all implementes of housholde. The resydue of my goodes not bequethyd I bequethe to Willum Jakson my sun the wyche I make my executer, and he to fulfyll thys my wyll and to pay my dettes as he thynkes moste expedyent for the well of my soule. Thes beyng wytnes; Syr Thomas Wollerdby vicare, Henry Butteler of the same, fremason, and Walter Robynson of the same, husbandman, with other mo.

Proved before P at Market Rasen, 12 February 1533/4.

359.   JOHN HANSON [OF BIGBY]
       [LCC 1532–34, fo. 236v]

14 December 1533. I, John Hanson of Bekeby, in a hole and perfyte mynde, makes my will. Fyrste I bequethe my soule to my savior Jhesu Cryste and to hys mother, Our Lady St. Mary, and to all the saintes in heven, and my body to be buryed in the churche of All Halloys in Bekeby. To Our Lady's warke at Lincoln iiijd. I wyt a cowe to fynde a perpetuall light before the image of St. Savior in Bekeby churche.

To Jenet Trowlope my beste cowe. To Elizabeth Remer my servant my beste panne. The reste of my goodes not wyt, my dettes payd, I gyff and wyt unto Sir Robert Tyrwhyt, knyght, whome I orden and make my full executor, for to minister and dispose my goodes to the plesure of God and the helthe of my soule. The wytnessys of thys; Sir William Swallow, William Sergean, John Smyth, John Rusweke, with diverse other.

Proved before P at Caistor, 10 February 1533/4.

360.   JOHN GRENE [OF SUTTON ST. EDMUND]
       [LCC 1532–34, fos. 285v–286r]

16 December 1533. I, John Grene of the paryshe of St. Edmunde's in Sutton in Hollande, of hole mynde and good of remembraunce, make thys my last will. Fyrst I bequethe my soule to God omnipotent and to Hys blessyd mother Mary, and to all the celestyall cumpeny in heven. My body to be buryd within the churcheyerde of St. Edmunde's, and in the name of my mortuary that thyng that the law will require. To the vicar of Sutton and to the parson of the same, ether of them, xvj*d*. To the mother churche of Lincoln iiij*d*, and to the infantes of the same iiij*d*. To the light of Corpus Christi, St. Peter, Our Lady, St. Edmunde, every one of them, a pounde waxe and to every light besyde ij*d*. To Johanne my wyff my house in Hallgate with v acres of lande the terme of her lyff, aftyr her decesse I will it remane to Catheryn my doughter and to her heres laufully begottyn of her body. And yff it fortune that she dye withowt heyres, then I will the sayd howsse and the fyve acars of land then for to be devided betwyx John my sone and Alys and Agnes my douthers. To John my sone, Kateryng, Alice and Agnes my douthers, xx acars of copyholld land of the west syde of Hallgatte, and to their ayers lawfully begottyn of ther bodys. And yff John my sone dey without ayers, then hys part to be devided betwyxt my iij douthers. And yff one or ij of myne douters dey withowt eyers, then I wyll the sayd xx^ti acars of copyhold land for to remayn holl to the last of myne chylderne beyng of lyffe. To John my sone iiij acars land of the sowth syde of Robart Burton in fe symple, and he that hath my sone in kepyng, he for to have the profet of the iiij acars of land. To the chyrche of Send Edmunde's ij acars of land at Lawdys Lake. I gyff v acars of land to a obyd day for the space of xl yere, and then I wyll the sayd v acars of land for to be sold by the handes of the chyrchewardenars of Sent Edmunde's, and the money therof resavyd for to be wared within the chyrche of Sent Edmund of that thyng that they thynk best. To Robert my brother ij acres of lande of the southe parte of John Sergeant in fe symple. To Johanne my wyff all my barly and a seame wheate. To John my sun a cowe and a burlyng. To ylke of my doughters ij burlynges to be delyveryd at May Day nexte foloyng. To John Hamonde [fo. 286r] a fylly of ij yere olde. To Mary Hamonde, doughter of John Hamonde, a calve. To Thomas Grene Barber's house with iiij acres of lande to it in fe symple. The resydue of all my landes and goodes not gyffyn nor bequethyd, I will they be solde by the handes of myn executor for to pay my dettes and my legaces withall, excepte that John my sun have xxvj*s* viij*d*, yff it may be sparyd, besyde my dettes and legaces. And my executor Thomas Grene, and he for to have for hys labor xiij*s* iiij*d*. Thes beyng wytnes; Sir William Johnson, John Hopkynson, John Sergeaunt, John Hamonde, with other mo. The yere and the date before rehersyd.

Proved before P at Spalding, 9 June 1534.

361.   JOHN PAPE [OF BAUMBER]
        [LCC 1532–34, fo. 231r]

17 December 1533. I, John Pape of Bawmburghe, beyng of hole mynde and of good memory, makes my laste will and testament. In the fyrste I bequethe my soule to allmyghtty God and to Our Lady St. Mary and to all the cumpeny of heven, and my body to be buryd in the churcheyerde of the churche of St. Swythune off Bamburgh with that thyng that the lawe requyrys in the name of my mortuary. To Our Lady of Lincoln xij*d*. To the high altare of Bamburgh for forgottyn tythys xij*d*. To the light of All Saintes in the churche of Bamburgh viij*d*. To the gylde of Our Lady in Bamburgh iiij*d*. To the reparacions of the churche of Bamburgh a quarter of barly, to be delyveryd by the handes of Thomas Pappe. To the roode of Boston viij*d*. To the house of Bardeney, to be prayd for, a quarter of barly. To the house of Kyrksted, to be prayd for, a quarter of barly. To my doughter Catheryne Pape a cowe and a quarter of barly. To my doughter Elizabeth Pappe a qwy of ij yeres of age and a oxe calve of a yere of age, and a quarter barly, and the jurysdiction of the chylde and the goodes bothe, and put them bothe to my sun Walter Plummer, to be at hys disposicion. To my doughter Isabell Pappe ij qwyes, one of a yere of age and the other of ij yeres of age, and iiij quarters of barly and vj schepe. Also I will that yff one of my chyldren or more departe before they cum at laufull age, that ther partes shall indifferently be devydyd to the other. The resydue of my goodes I gyff to Elizabethe [my] wyffe, whome I make my full executrix that thys my last will and testament may be well orderyd and disposyd for the helthe of my soule and all Crysten soulys. Thes men wytnes; William Drake, preste, William Myddylton, Andro Richerdsun, with other mo. Wryttyn at Bamburgh the day and the yere abovesayd. I will that my sun Walter Plummer and John Trow of Teylby be the supervisors of thys will.

Proved before P at Horncastle, 3 February 1533/4.

362.   ROBERT TULYE [OF LANGTON]
        [LCC 1532–34, fos. 235r–236r]

20 December 1533. I, Robert Tulye of the paryshe of Langton, hole of mynde and good remembraunce, do make thys my last will and testament. The fyrste I bequethe my soule to God allmyghtty, to Our Lady St. Mary and to all the holy cumpeny of heven. My body to be buryed in the churche of St. Gylys afore Our Lady the northe syde of the churche. To the high altare of St. Gylys in Langton churche for tythes forgottyn ij*s*. To the reparacions of Our Lady's warke of Lincoln xx*d*. To the mother churche off Lincoln xij*d*. To the iiij orders of frerys of Lincoln xvj*d*. To the churche of Langton vj*s* viij*d*. To the paryshe churche of St. Benedicte of Wood Henderbye vj*s* viij*d*. To the churche of All Halloys in Wragby xx*d*. To the churche of Panton xij*d*. To [fo. 235v] the churche of Moreby xx*d*. To Helene my wyff one house in Wood Enderby with all the appurtenances therto belongyng, the whiche was Robert Tuly's, the wever. Also foure parte of Tuly's landes in the sayd towne. Also I will that the sayd Helene my wyff do pay yerely to Jeffray my sun, to hys exhibicion and lernyng xiij*s* iiij*d* duryng the naturall lyff of the sayd Helene. To Agnes my yongest doughter too housys with the appurtenances in Asbe. To Thomas my eldyst sun all my landes wheresoever they be with all ther appurtenances, excepte the housys and landes that I have bequethyd my wyff duryng her

lyff, and the housys that I gyff to Agnes my doughter duryng her lyffe. I will that Thomas my sun shall pay to Jeffray my sun, duryng vj yeres every yere, xxvjs viijd of my landes. To Jeffray my sun xxl in money and ij colte folys, the one blake and the other bay colore with a starne. To Isabell my doughter fowre of the best oxyn that I have in the cuntrythe and vj kye and one bay amblyng mare, and one gray trottyng mare with a fole, xx^{ty} weders and xx^{ty} hogges, with xx^{ty} yowes from the date herof, with the incresce of thaym cumyng. Also to the sayd Isabell one ambry with a chyste that is now in the chamber. To Isabell my doughter and Agnes halffe my housholde goodes. To the sayd Isabell one chalder wheate or xxvjs viijd in money. To Agnes my wyff doughter xli in housholde stuff or other that be necessary for her. To Catheryne Holteby iij kye and one qwye wit ij whyte heddyd sterys and xxs in money. To Richerde Waddeslay one cople yong oxyn at Rughtton. To Alice Waddeslay my goddoughter one red dowyd qwye in the barne close. To Thomas Waddeslay, sun of Richerde Waddeslay, one schepe and to hys mother ij schepe. To John Plater one cowe with a bay nagge. Also yff the goodes I have gyffyn to Isabell my doughter be not worthe xxli, she shall be mayd worthe xxli. Yff it happyn Thomas my sun to dye wythowt heyres, I gyff all my landes to Jeffray my yonger sun. To John Plate halffe a quarter wheate, halffe a quarter malte with one quarter beanys and one violet cote. To John Athure, otherways callyd Depyng, iij schepe and ij sterys. To Rayff [fo. 236r] Leggerde one quarter corne. To John Wryght one yowe. To John Tulye of Wood Henderby one russyt cote and one yere rente. To Thomas Tulye my brother one bukskyn dooblet. To William Tulye one bukskyn dooblet. To Thomas my sun one cople oxyn with one yong horse. To Thomas my eldeste sun the lease and yeres of my farmeholde I do dwell in, and the yeres and lease that I have takyn of my lorde abbot of Kyrkestede and the convent of the same. To Sir Christofer Webster, the vicare of Wragby, one trottyng blake fole with halffe a quarter wheate. To every pore man and hys wyffe of Langton one stryke corne. To Agnes my doughter one newe ambry. I will that iij trentallys be sayd for my soule, my father and mother soule and all Crysten soulys. I make Jeffray my sun supervisor. The resydue of all my goodes not bequethyd I gyff to Helene my wyff, Thomas my sun and to Agnes my doughter, the whiche I make my executors to dispose for my soule helthe and all Crysten soulys. Thes beyng wytnes; Sir Christofore Walker, the vicare, Thomas Dykynson, William Hall, William Wady-slay, with other mo. Geven the day and yere abovesayd.

Proved before P at Wragby, 7 February 1533/4. Adm. granted to Helen the relict and Thomas Tulye the natural son of the deceased, reserving power to grant to Agnes, the daughter of the deceased and co-executrix when she shall come to lauwful age.

363. JOHN DOMYSDAY [OF QUADRING]
[LCC 1532-34, fo. 115v]

22 December 1533. I, John Domysday of Quadryng paryshe in Hollande, beyng of good remembraunce, makyth my testament. In primis I bequethe my soule to allmyghtty God, Our Lady St. Mary, and to all the saintes in heven, and my body to be buryd within Quadryng churche. To the high altare for tithys forgottyn viijd. To vj pryncipall lighttes in Quadryng churche xijd. To Our Lady of Lincoln per modum oblacionis iiijd. To the fatherles chyldren at St. Catheryn's ijd. To my vij chyldren

unmaryed, everychon of them, a cowe and a calve. To Robert my sun ij schepe. It is my will that Alyson my wyff have my house in Kyrton Holme with all my landes in Kyrton duryng her lyffe naturall. And also I frely gyff to Alyson my wyff my cotage house in Quadryng, to sell or kepe at her plesure. The resydue of my goodes I referre to the order and disposicion of Alyson my wyffe, who I make my full executors. Wytnes therof; Robert Londe, vicar of Quadryng, Sir William Michyll, Robert Atwell and William Chele, cum aliis.

Proved before P at Ancaster, 31 January 1533/4.

364. MARGARET GARRAKE [OF WYBERTON]
[LCC 1532–34, fo. 122r]

25 December 1533. I, Margarete Garrake of Wyberton in Hollande, hole in mynde and of good remembraunce, make and orden thys my laste will and testament. Fyrste I bequethe my soule to God allmyghtty, to Our Lady St. Mary and to all the saintes of heven, and my body to be buryd in the churchyerde of St. Leodegarn of Wyberton. To the high altare in Wyberton churche for tithys forgottyn viijd. To every altare in the sayd churche iiijd. To the altare of Our Lady in the cath[edral] churche of Lincoln ijd. To the fatherles chyldren withowt St. Catheryn's iiijd. To George Garrake my beste gyrdyll sylver harnes. To William Garrake another gyrdyll nexte the beste. To Richerde Garrake a house callyd Bacon Grene House and the grene under it in fe symple. And yff the sayd Richerde have no nede to sell the sayd house and grene, then I will that the sayd house and grene do remane to William Garrake, and yff he dye withowt heyres of his body, then I will it remaine to Robert Garrake. To Dorothe Garrake a gown of sangwyn color and a gerdyll that was her mother's, and a pare of beades nexte the beste. The resydue of all my goodes not wit nor bequethyd, I gyff to Richerde Garrake my sun, whome I make my executor to dispose for the helthe of my soule. Thes beryng wytnes; George Wylkynson, Robert Mendus, Yan Groyff, William Chamberlayn, with other mo.

Proved before P at Boston, 3 March 1533/4.

365. SIMON MARCANDE [OF THEDDLETHORPE ST. HELEN]
[LCC 1532–34, fos. 266v–267r]

25 December 1533. I, Simonde Marcande off Thedilthorp in the paryshe of St. Helene, of hole mynde and good remembraunce, do make my last will and testament. Fyrste I bequethe my soule to allmyghtty God and to Our Lady St. Mary, and to all the saintes in heven, and my body to be buryd in the churcheyerde of St. Helene abovenamyd, and that thyng that the lawe and custome requiryth to be my mortuary. To the high altare in my paryshe churche xijd. To Our Lady's warke of Lincoln xijd. To the buyldyng of the steple in my [fo. 267r] paryshe vjs viijd. To Richerde my sun xls and a wane. To John my sun xls and a plowe and a harrowe. To my doughter Elizabeth xls and a qwy of a yere olde, and every one of them to other heyr. And yff they dye under age, I will that the foresayd somme of my iij chyldren remayn to the churche of St. Helene aforesayd. I will that v messys be done for my soule and for all my frende soulys. To Sir William Marshe my curate, for hys labor, xijd. The resydue of my goodes not gyffyn nor bequethyd I gyff them holy to Alice my wyff, the whiche Alicie and Thomas Wyet I make my

executors. Wytnes herof; Sir William Marshe, curate, and Thomas Shardyand, with many mo.

Proved before P at Alford, 7 May 1534.

366.   JOAN GYBSON [OF DONINGTON IN HOLLAND]
        [LCC 1532–34, fos. 128v–129r]

26 December 1533. I, Jone Gybson of Donyngton in Howlande within the countie of Lyncoln, beynge of holl mynde and in god remembraunce at thys tyme, loved be God, make mye testamentt and last wyll. Fyrst I bequethe mye soull to God almyghtye and to Ower Blessed Ladye Seyntt Marye, and to all the synttes in heven. Mye bodye to be beryed within the churcheyarde of Donyngton, nye to mye husband Roberde Gybson. To the hye aulter of Donyngton for tythys forgotten xijd. To everye auter within the same churche ijd. To everye lyghtt that standes abowtt mye heyres at mye beryall day jd. To Ower Lady's werke of Lyncoln iiijd. To Ower Ladye of Lyncoln iiijd. To the fatherles chyldern at Seyntt Kateryn's withoutt the walles of Lyncoln iiijd. I wyll that Lambertt Kyrke mye son have for the performacyon of the bequest of Roberd Kyrke, his father will, to the sum of vjl xiijs iiijd, for the whyche I wyll that he shall have xx wolle schepe that Roberde Fowler of Hempryngham hathe of myn. Also, of Rycharde Roberde of Donyngton, v nobulles, whyte cowe and a redde cowe with classe price of theym xxs, a hors fole that was of mye dowed mare price vjs viijd. I wyll that Roberde Kyrke, son of John Kyrke, late of Hempryngham, have mye best red arke, the whyche was his grandam's, at the age of xxij yeres, and so to remayn to the Kyrkes as an arelome. Also v schepe at cleppyng tyme withowtt their wolle. And if the same Roberde dye or he com to the age of xxijti yeres, then I wyll hytt remayn to Lambertt, hys unckyll, after the same maner of forme. I wyll that Lambertt Kyrke mye son have mye best tester, coverled, ij pare of scheyttes, a pare of blankettes, iij pyllowes, mye best bras pott savynge on, on bolster with a doce of itt, a cownter, a feder bed, a sprues chyst, a longe spytt, a pare of cobberttes. I wyll that Alyce Kyrke alias Wengod have a bras pott best of iij, a spett, my rownde blacke gowne, my rossed gown, mye blacke worsted kyrtell, a pare of corall beiddes sylver gawdyd, a corse of sylke with the bukkell and the penand of sylver, a rybon of crane color, a pare of tryangelles. And I wyll that Ane Gybson mye dowghter have mye best bras pott, mye best beyddes with the juelles that belonges to them and mye red velvett purs, mye best gurdell, mye best blacke gown, mye vyolett gown, mye worsted kyrtell, a matres, a coverlett flowred with blacke and whytt, vj pares of scheyttes, vj pelowes, iiij new platers, v pewter dysches, iij sawcres, ij wortt leyddes, mye secunde red arke. To Lambertt Kerke mye son a masser and a sylver spone after the decease of mye brodyr, vycar of Donyngton. To Roberde Wengod the yonger, and Anne Wengod and Jone Wengod and John Wengod, chyldern of Roberde Wengod of Hempryngham, eche of them, v schepe att clyppyng tyme with theyr wolle. And if enye of theym dye yche of them to be other eyeres in mye bequeste. [fo. 129r] To Thomas Gybson vjs viijd. To John Gybson vjs viijd. I wyll that if oder Lamber[t] Kyrke mye sone, or Anne Gybson mye dowghters, dye or they cum to laufull age, then I wyll that the oder bye are the same bequest, and if that they dye boothe, as God forbeitt, then I wyll that all schech theinges as I have lefte them be dysposyd for mye soull and all Crysten soulles as mye executor thynkes best for to be down for mye soull

helthe. The resydewe of all mye goodes I wyll that they be devydyd in iij parttes, on partt of the best to be dysposed for mye soull and to bryng me forthe and to paye, and the other partt to be devydyd betwys mye iij chyldern, Lambertt, Alyce and Anne, bye equall porschons bye the othersyghtt of Sir John Gybson, vicar of Donyngton. I wyll that Anne Gybson mye dowghter be mayde of mye goodes and father's wyll to the valow of vj*l* xiij*s* iiij*d*, provyded allway that mye brother vycar of Donyngton shall have the ruell of Lambertt Kyrkbye mye son, and of Anne Gybson, mye dowghter, and of theyres to that they cum to laufull age, whom I make mye executor. Theys beynge wytnesses; Rycharde Jentell, Roberde Mawer, with other mo.

Proved before P at Swineshead, 5 March 1533/4.

367.   JOHN CROSBY [OF HOUGHAM]
       [LCC 1532–34, fo. 250r]

27 December 1533. I, John Crosby of Hougham, of a good mynde and goode remembraunce, makes my testament and laste will. Fyrste I bequethe my soule to God allmyghtty and to Our Lady St. Mary, and to all the holy cumpeny of heven, and my body to be buryd in the churcheyerde of All Halloys of Hogham. To the high altare of Hougham for forgottyn tithys xij*d*. To Our Lady of Lincoln xij*d*. To Jenet Crosby a calve. To Jenet Howson halffe a quarter of barly. To Richerde Howson vj*d*. To William Howson vj*d*. To Sir John Wymarke, paryshe preste, xvj*d*. To William Harvy chylder halffe a quarter barly. To Thomas Crosby chylder my best cote. I will that all my goodes be devydyd in thre partes, fyrste parte to myselffe to pay me dettes with and to performe my wyll, and to bryng me honestly to the erth. The secunde parte to my wyffe, the thyrde parte to my chylder equally to be devydyd. The resydue of my parte I gyff to Wylliam Crosby my sun and William Wryght, whome I make my executors that they may dispose for the well of my soule as they thynke best. Thes wytnes; Sir John Wymarke, paryshe preste, William Howson, Richerde Howson, William Wryght, with other mo.

Proved before P at Lincoln, 7 April 1534.

368.   WILLIAM HASSYLL [OF BOSTON]
       [LCC 1532–34, fos. 129r–130r]

27 December 1533, 25 Henry VIII. I, Wylliam Hassyll off Boston, beyng in holl mynd and gud memory, mak my testament conteynyng in it my last wyll. Fyrst I bequethe my soule to almyghty God, to Our Lady Sanct Mary Hys moder, in whome under God I put my most trust, and to all the holy company of hevyn. My body to be buryed within the chappell off Our Blessyd Lady in the parishe churche off Boston, and the churchewardons to have for the same their dewtye. To the parson for tythes forgotten xx^{ti}*d*. Toward the buyldyng off the cathe[dral] churche off Lincoln iiij*d*. To the fatherles chyldren at Sancte Kateryn's withoute Lincoln iiij*d*. I wyll that xj masses be sayd in Our Lady's chappell off Scala Celi for my father soule, my mother and all Crysten souls, the saym day it may please God my soule shall departe from my body, or ells the nexte day of Scala Celi after. And every prest to have for hys labor, and to say as well dirige and commendation as masse, vj*d*. I wyll that my wyffe, whyche I mayk myne executrix, shall offer att Our Lady's stok

for every on of the masses j*d*. I wyll that the fyrst masse be sayd in the honour off the father of hevyn, the secund in the honour of my redemour Ihesu Crist, the iij in the honour off the holy goost, the other v masses in the honour off the v pryncypall wondys off our lord Jhesu Cryst, and the v [fo. 129v] princypall joies off Our Blessyd Lady hys mother, the ix masse in the honor off the blessyd Trinite, the x masse in the honour off the apostylles, the xj masse in the honour of all sanctes. Also I wyll that my executrix shall sell all the howsys with the appurtenances sett and lyyng off the water whyche I purchased off Thomas Bellow, late off Boston, and sche to have the profytt theroff or ells to byde and remayne in the same howsys duryng her lyffe. And after hyr lyffe, she to dissposse it as she wyll and as she thynkes best, and I wyll that my feoffees shall relesse therunto accordyng to thys my testament and last wyll. To John Haliday, late my prentis, my dublett off lether and myne old partlet off lether. To Thomas Fox my prentes my gowne furred with blayk lam, my best worsted dublett, my new partlet off lether, the wod knyve or revettes that he weres, a payre off almane kenettes, a pare of splentes, a salot and a byll. To Cassandra my mayd my syngle gowne. I wyll that myne executrix shall mak a composicion eyther with the alderman off Our Lady's gylde or els with the alderman off Corpus Cristi gyld, and fownd for me, hyrselffe, Robert Bawman late off London gentylman and sumtyme clark off the prevy seall, one obit or anniversary with the mortmeyn to be done yerly within thre days afore or after such day off the monethe as it shall pleysse God to tayk my soule from my body, and there to be expendyd yerly xx*s*, off the wyche I wyll that iij pennys shal be offerd by the alderman off the same gyld yff he be present, and he to have for hys labor vj*d*. Also I wyll have yerly a xj preistys at dirige and masse by the advysement off the alderman off the sayd gild and every prest to have iij*d*. Also he that shall set the herse j*d*. Also I wyll have ij of the gretest belles rong all the tyme off masse, and for ryngyng off the same I bequeyth xij*d*. I bequeyth for waste off wax and weryng off vestementes xij*d*. Also I wyll the resydew off the xx*s* remenyng be gevyn to the pore peple most nedyng within the towne by the handys off the sayd alderman for tyme beyng, or elles in hys absens to one off them that have bene alderman, and not for dystribute within the churche but to go home to ther howses where the most nedy peple dwell and there for to gyve them the charite. And the sayd alderman iff he be present, or elles one of them that have bene alderman doyng the same, to have for hys labor vj*d*, but in any wysse I wyll have it purchased with the mortmeyne or els to remane styll in my wyffe's hand and she to order it with other counsell as she thynkes beste. Also I gyve to the churche of Sanct Mychaell in Upton besyde Ganysborow one flatt pece of sylver pownsed to make them sum chalece or sum jewell for the same churche. To the churche of Sanct Peter in Ketellthorpe one pece or one goblet to make therewith sum jewell, for ther lyes the bodyes off my father and mother, and ther was I maried. Also I will that all the resydew of myne apparell, as gowns, furrs and jackettes, be sold at the best pryce and the money therfore taykyn to be [fo. 130r] distrybuted by the discretion off my wyff. To my sayd wyff xl*l* and my tow gold rynges. To Our Lady's chauntre in Boston my gret cobierns off irne. Also the resydew of all my gudys I put them to the discretion of Agnes my wyff, whome I orden myne executrix for to distribute and gyve, and every parcell therof takyn, imonges pore peple most nedyng, and that to be done wythin one hole yere next after my dissesse. Also I make John Coplay off Boston supervisor, and he to have for hys labor xx*s*. Also I wyll that the said John Caplay shall as ofte and as many tymes as he shall thynk convenient, eyther onys in xiiij dais, or onys in a moneth, call afore hym my said executrix to se haw she hathe bestowede the resydew off my guddys, and for to gyve hyr for ther consell wat ys best to be done wyth the resydew of the said guddys unbequethyd, and as well off them that be bequethed. Also yff it shall happen me to lyve unto suche tyme as my guddys shall not be sufficient nor able to fulfyll thys my testament and last wyll, then I wyll it shal be moderated by the discretion off my said executrix and supervisor, and yff it so be that my supervisor shall thynk that I have not gyvyn my wyff sufficiently accordyng to my substans then I wyll that he shall reforme it by hys discretion resonably. And yff it so be that thys my present testament and last wyll be nott after forme off the law, then I wyll by the discretion of some lernyd man that it shal be put in termes after the law, but I wyll that no sentence shal be changeg [sic]. In wytness wherof; Wylliam Hassyll, Mr. Nycholas Robertson, John Hardcastell, Lawrence Bellman, Wylliam Clay, Peter Emery.

Proved before P at Boston, 3 March 1533/4.

369.   HENRY TOOLL [OF HABROUGH]
        [LCC 1532–34, fo. 254r]

28 December 1533. I, Henry Tooll, seke of body and hole of mynde, makes thys present testament as concernyng my laste will. First I bequethe and gyff my soule to allmyghtty God, my body to be buryd in the churcheyerde of St. Margaret in Haburgh. To the high altare in Haburghe churche iiijd. To Our Lady of Lincoln iiijd. To the high altare in Halton churche iiijd. To my fyve doughters, every one of them, one yowe schepe. To George Elstone sonne one yowe schepe. To William Tooll my sun a browne stotte. To Sir Robert Beke my confessore a blake qwe of one yere olde to pray for me. To the Trinite gylde of Haburghe iiijd. The resydue of my goodes I gyff to William Tooll my sun and to Elizabeth my wyff, whome I make myn executors. Wytnessyth of thys; Sir Robert Beke, vicar, Walter Tooll, William Brone, William Cussyn, with other mo.

Proved before P at Caistor, 27 April 1534.

370.   ROBERT GRENE [OF CLAYPOLE]
        [LCC 1532–34, fo. 116r]

30 December 1533. I, Robert Grene of Claypole in Lincoln diocese, seke in body and of hole mynde, make my testament. Fyrst I bequethe my soule to allmyghtty God, to Our Blessyd Lady St. Peter [sic] and to all the saintes in heven, and my body to be buryd in the churcheyerde of Claypole. To my mother churche of Lincoln iiijd. To the high altare of Claypole iiijd. To Agnes my doughter my gret arke with all the stuff that was in it at the wrytyng herof, excepte one schete to wynde me in yff it fortune me to departe. Item a lyttyll chyste, my best potte and my best panne, all the puter vessell that I have, a lytyll potte besyde, one other panne of a gallan and one other lytyll panne, a chare, a brewyng tubbe, a gyle fatte, ij ale pottes, ij of my beste coverlydes, ij yong kye, one pyed and the other browne, my best borde and one long forme in the seller, ij of my best candylstykes, my payr tonges, pothookes and rekyntynes, ij ewes and a wedder hogge. Item the branderyes. To Isabell, William Bette doughter, a bull calve. To Elizabeth hys other doughter a ewe hogge. To my curate and iiij prestes more to say v dirigys and v messys the day of my buryall for me, every one of them iiijd, the iiij messys to be appoyntyd by the mynde of my

curate. I will that my barly, wheate and pease be threshyd uppe and solde, yff I dye, by William Bette and Richerde Grene my sun, and with the same to pay my funerallys and dettes. I make the sayd William Bette and Richerde Grene, my sunys, my executors, and for ther labors I gyff them ij kye agre as they will betwyxte themselvys. To Richerde Grene my sun my fole and mare. To William Bate a stagge. To George Warton a ewe. The resydue of my goodes unbequethyd I will they be at the disposicion of my ij sayd executors, they to dispose them accordyng to ther good consciences for my soule, my wyff soule, our frendes soulys and all Crysten soulys. Wytnes Robert Whytbe, John Dukdale, William Alcocke, with diverse other mo, towne dwellers of Clapole, in presence of Mr. John Wyngar, parson and curate ther.

Proved before P at Ancaster, 31 January 1533/4.

371.   RICHARD ANDALL [OF DONINGTON IN HOLLAND]
        [LCC 1532–34, fo. 281r]

[31 December 1533] St. Cuthbert's Day, 1533. I, Rycharde Andall of Donyngton in Howlande, within the cowntte of Lyncoln, beynge of hole mynde and good remembraunce at thys tyme, loved be God, make mye testament and last wyll. Fyrst I bequethe mye sowle to God almyghtye, and to Owre Blessed Ladye Seyntt Marye, and to all the seynttes in heven. Mye bodie to be beyred within the churcheyarde of Donyngton. To the hye aulter of Donyngton iiij*d*. To the belles iiij*d*. To Seyntt John's auter vj*d*. To Seyntt Sondaye's lyghtt ij*d*. To the yomans' lyght j*d*. To the churche warke j*d*. To Ower Laydye of Lyncoln ij*d*. To Wylliam Node a borlynde and mye best cowte. To Thomas Tubuc a burlyng. The resydue of all my goodes unbequethyd I gyff to Alice my wyffe, whome I make my executrix. Thes beyng wytnes; Thomas Tarre, Richard Dandy and Sir John Gybson, vicar of Donyngton.

Proved before P at Swineshead, 8 June 1534.

372.   ROBERT JOHNSON [OF BOSTON]
        [LCC 1532–34, fo. 134r]

1 January 1533/4. I, Roberde Johnson of Boston, fysshmonger, beynge perfyte of remembraunce, doo make thys mye testamentt therin concludynge mye last wyll. Fyrst I bequethe my sowle to God allmyghtye, to Ower Ladye Sayntt Marye and all the companye in heven. Mye bodye to be beryed in the churcheyarde of Sayntt Botulphe in Boston, in the processyon wey ageynst the tavarne.[149] To my mortuarye acordynge to the custom. To the hygh alter of Sayntt Botulphe for tythys and oblacyon forgoten viij*d*. To Ower Lady werke at Lyncoln viij*d*. To the orphans at Sayntt Kateryn's withowt the barres at Lyncolln vj*d*. To Jhesus alter next unto the sowthe churche dore within the parysshe churche of Boston iiij*d*. To Wylliam

---

[149] Burial location could be highly significant in terms of proximity to the sacred. While burial within churches was highly prized, particularly in locations near to the images and altars of saints, outside the church a number of areas were preferred, such as under the eavesdrip, near the churchyard cross or, as here, under the processional way, a route regularly followed by rogationtide processions and those in honour of gild saints and the parochial patron saint. In this way, contact was maintained between the communities of the dead and the living in the context of the religious observances of the parish: Daniell, *Death and Burial in Medieval England*, 87–115.

Paynter of Boston, draper, vjs viijd. To John Bocher iijs iiijd. To Sir Thomas Hynde mye gostlye father viijd. To Wylliam Kydde, fysshemonger, vjs viijd. To Rycharde Wodale vjs whyche he dothe owe me. To Margarett Haryson of Freiston vjs viijd. To Rycharde Tonarde, bere brewer, and to hys chyldern vjs viijd. I wyll that a prest synge for mye soull, mye frendes' sowles and all Crysten soules the space of on hole yere within the parysshe churche of Boston, and he to have for hys stypende fyve poundes vjs viijd sterlynge. To Nycolas Blewytt xxd. I wyll there be dyssposyd amonges pore people iijs iiijd. The resydew of mye goodes I gyve unto Margarett mye wyffe whome I make mye executrix, she to pay mye dettes, fullfyll thys mye testamentt and last wyll and brynge me forthe as she shall thynke best. I wyll that Sir George Haukes, preist, be supervyser and to helpe mye wyfe and geve her hys best councell, and I wyll he have for hys labor xxs. Thes beynge wyttnes; Wylliam Paynter, John Bocher, Nycolas Blewytt, Wylliam Kydde, Rycharde Tonarde and other moo.

Proved before P at Boston, 3 March 1533/4.

373.   ROBERT BORNYT [OF KEDDINGTON]
        [LCC 1532–34, fo. 248]

2 January 1533/4. I, Robert Bornyt of Kedyngton, of goode and hole mynde, makes thys my last will and testament. Fyrste I bequethe my soule to God allmyghtty and to Our Lady St. Mary, and to all the holy cumpeny of heven, and my body to be buryd within the churche or churcheyerde of St. Margarete of Kedyngton, and I bequethe for my buryall vjs viijd. To the high altare of my paryshe for tithys forgottyn iijs iiijd. To the reparacions of my paryshe churche xxd. To the churche warke of our mother kyrke of Lincoln viijd. To Our Lady offeryng vjd. I will at the day of my buryall have dirige done, and every preste ther beyng to have iiijd. To Stuton xxd, Grymmylby churche xijd. To the paryshe churche of Est Barkeworthe xijd. To the churche of Wythcall xijd. I will that Agnes my wyffe have all the goodes whiche I had with her at the day of our mariage, and I gyff her of my goodes ten poundes or the valor therof, also my fermeholde and house that I have taken by lease of the prior and convent of Alvyngham for the terme of iij yeres foloynge aftyr my dethe. And the sayd Agnes to beare all maner of chargeys accordyng to the indenture duryng the iij yeres. And aftyr the sayd iij yeres be completyd and endyd, then I will that Richerde Bornyt my sun shall enter the sayd farme and yeres accordyng to the forsayd indenture, and to possede the same to it be completyd and endyd. To Richerde my sun on close or pasture takyn of the sayd prior and convent by lease. Also I will that the sayd Richerde shall fynde a preste to syng for me and Margery my wyffe, one yere. To Robert Bornyt my sun one cople oxen that he hathe in hys handes at thys day, and another cople oxen of vj yeres olde, ij kye and xxty schepe and ij marys. To Beatrix, wyffe of Thomas Thomsun of Grymmolby, xs and one cople oxen and ij kye. To Isabell her doughter one qwye. To Robert Markeand one qwye. To Helene Gante my servant a matterys, a coverlyd, a pare of schetes with a pillo and a cowe. To Roger Gante one qwye. To William, sun of Robert Bornyt, fyve schepe. To Henry Bornyt one qwye. To Thomas Glover one qwye. To the prior of Alvyngham and hys convent xs. To every monke of Louth Parke iiijd. To the prior of Ormesby and hys convent vjs viijd. To Agnes my wyffe [fo. 248v] my house in Est Barkeworthe aftyr the decesse of my syster Margarete,

and aftyr the decesse of the sayd Agnes my wyffe, I gyff the sayd house to Richerde my sun and hys assygnes for ever. To Thomas Thomson of Grymmolby my lease and indenture that I have of the prior and convent of Ormesby in Grymmolby, whiche the sayd Thomas now occupyeth, excepte viij acres medo perteynyng to the same, whiche I will Agnes my wyffe and Richerde my sun shall have to ther ferme in Kedyngton duryng ther yeres. And aftyr ther sayd yeres be expiryd, then the sayd Thomas shall enter of the sayd viij acres medo duryng hys indenture and lease, which I had of the prior and convent of Ormesby, to hym and hys assygnes. To the vicare of Kedyngton. To every one of John Bornyt chylder. To thre chylder of Thomas Thomson. To ij chylder of Robert Johnson. To iij doughters of John Harchers of Louthe. All my goodes not bequethyd I gyff to Richerd my sun to hys exhibicion and proffyt. I make my executors Richerde Bornyt my sun, Agnes my wyffe, and Robert Bornyt my sun. And I make William Raythby my supervisor, and I gyff hym iijs iiijd for hys labor. Thes beyng wytnes; vicar of Kedyngton, Thomas Cooke, Thomas Thomson, Robert Bornyt and Henry Bornyt.

Proved before P at Lincoln, 26 March 1534. Adm. granted to the executors.

374. THOMAS BRETFELDE [OF BRACEBY]
      [LCC 1532–34, fo. 303r]

2 January 1533/4. I, Thomas Bretfelde of Braceby, beyng hole in mynde and seke in my body, makes thys my last will. Fyrste I bequethe my soule to allmyghtty God and Our Blessyd Lady and Vyrgyn Mary, Hys mother, and my body to be buryd in the church of St. Margarete of Braceby. To the high altare of the same churche xijd. To Our Lady of our mother churche of Lincoln xxd. Also to Sir Robert Boston for to syng halffe a trentall of messys vs. I bequeth a cowe namyd Chery to the handes and kepyng of the churchewardons of Braceby for the tyme beyng, so that that proffet of her yerely shall kepe an obet for the soulys of me and my wyffes. And the cowe not to be delyveryd to the sayd churchewardens but immediatly aftyr the decesse of my sayd wyff, and duryng her lyff she to kepe the sayd obet with proffyt of the sayd cowe. And aftyr her decesse so to be continuyd yerely for ever by the discrescion of the sayd churchewardens, and oversight of the curate ther with proffyt of the forenamyd cowe. To the chylder of John Pell, everiche on of them, a schepe. To the chylder of Thomas Pell a schepe emong them. To Thomas Pell and Agnes hys wyff a payr of wernes. To Margery Bretfelde a schepe. To Jenet Baker a schepe. To the frerys of Grantham xxd. To Roppeslay churche xijd. To St. John of Cawthorp viijd. The resydue of my goodes I gyff to Margaret my wyff, whome I make my executrix, and she to do therwith for the helthe of my soule and hyrs as she thynkes best. Wytnes herof; Sir Robert Boston, William Wright, John Pell, Richard Rolle, Thomas Pell and diverse other honest persons, the day and yere above wryttyn.

Proved before P at Lincoln, 19 June 1534.

375. JOHN CALLO [OF GREAT GRIMSBY]
      [LCC 1532–34, fo. 236v]

2 January 1533/4. I, John Callo of Gret Grymmesby, with a hole mynde and good memory makyth my testament. In the fyrste I bequethe my soule to God

allmyghtty, to Our Lady St. Mary and to all the saintes in heven. My body to be buryd in the churche of Wello. To Our Lady warke of Lincoln xij*d*. To the high altare of St. Jamys for all my tithys forgottyn xij*d*. I will that Margarete my wyff have the rule and custody off all my goodes and of my chylder so long as she be unmaryd. And yff she mary, then I will that my goodes be devydyd in thre partes, one parte unto pay my dettes and to be disposyd for my soule, and another parte to be devydyd to my chylder, and the thyrde parte to Margaret my wyffe, whome I make my executrix, and Thomas Channer and Thomas Northe to overse that thys my last will be fulfyllyd. Thes wytnessys; Sir Peter Munde, Jamys Hatclyff, John Buryll, with other mo.

Proved before P at Grimsby, 11 February 1533/4.

376.   WILLIAM WRYGHT [OF BENINGTON IN HOLLAND]
        [LCC 1532–34, fos. 311v–313v]

2 January 1533/4. I, William Wryght of Benyngton, hole of mynde and of good remembraunce, makyth thys my testament and therin concludyth my last will. Fyrste I bequethe my soule to God allmyghtty, to Our Lady St. Mary and to all the holy cumpeny in heven. My body [fo. 312r] to be buryd within the churche of All Hallowyn in Benyngton and my mortuary to be delyveryd accordyng to the kynge's lawes. To the anornament of the high altare viij*d*. To the curate ther for my tithes and oblacions forgottyn x*d*. To the altare of Our Blessyd Lady iiij*d*. To the altare of Corpus Christi iiij*d*. To the reparacion of the churche of Benyngton xx*s*. To our mother churche of Lincoln iiij*d*. To the fatherles chyldren of St. Catheryn's ij*d*. To every order of frerys in Boston ij stryke barly. I will that my executors immediatly aftyr my decesse do gyff wagys to a seculer preste to ministre and celebrate Gode's service in the paryshe churche of Benyngton by the space of on halff yere, to pray and maytene Gode's service for the soule of me, my wyffes, my parentes, benefactors and all Christen soulys. To John Wryght my sun iiij*l* to be levyd and takyn of my goodes, and to be delyveryd to my sayd sun when he shall be the age of xviij yeres. To Thomas Wryght my sun iij*l* to be alenyd and takyn of my goodes, and to be delyveryd when he shall be the age of xviij yeres. And yff eny of my foresayd chyldren chaunge thys mortall lyff, I will every one of them to be other heyre. And yff bothe my foresayd sunys change thys lyff mortall afore they be the foresayd age of xviij yeres, I will the forsayd legacys be disposyd be my executors or ther assygnes in the churche and paryshe of Benyngton. The resydue of my goodes I gyff them to the disposicion of Sir William Wryght, preste of Algarkyrk, and William Cokeler of Boston, marcer, whome I make my executors to dispose my goodes for the welthe of my soule and all Christen soulys. And I will that every one of them to have for hys labor and payns herin, takyn of my goodes, as good conscience shall require. And the overplus of my goodes I will be evenly devydyd betwene John Wryght and Thomas Wryght my sunys. Thyes wytnes; Sir Roger Pyschey, paryshe preste of Benyngton, John Cokeler, John Loydon, John Crawe, Thomas Coke and Henry Botheby of the same, with other mo. I will and gyff to the foresayd Sir William Wryght and Wylliam Cokeler my executors ther expenses and chargeys when and so ofte tymys as they shall be in besynes concernyng my testament or will. Thys is the laste will of me, William Wryght off Benyngton, mayd the day and the yere abovesayd. I will that John Wryght and Thomas Wryght my

sunnys be in the [fo. 312v] custody and puttyng furthe of my executors unto they cum to the age of xviij yeres. I will that all my mansions buyldynges, pasture landes, arable and yng grounde lying in Benyngton, Butterwyk, Leverton and Leeke, wherin all my feoffys stande and be seasyd in feoffment as hereaftyr more playnly doys folowe, be seasyd and in possession to the intente, use and purpose hereaftyr foloyng. That is to say, I will the yerely renttes and proffyttes of ij acres and a halff land arable lying in Benyngton in a felde callyd Poller be disposyd be my executors or ther assygnes in kepyng of my yere day in the churche of Benyngton the terme of x yeres nexte aftyr foloyng my departyng owt of thys worlde, ther to be prayed for the soulys of my wyffes, my parentes, benefactors and all Crysten soulys. And further I will ther be a obbyt kepte in Leverton churche with the rentes and proffyttes of ij acres and a halff lying in Leverton nygh the churche be my executors or ther assignes the terme of viij yeres nexte aftyr my departyng, ther to pray for my soule, my wyffes, my parentes, my benefactors and all Christen soulys. I will my executors receyve and take all the rentes of the foresayd mansions buyldyng and of all other pasture, landes arable and yng grounde to John Wryght and Thomas Wryght my sunnys cum to the age of xviij yeres. Then I gyff to John Wryght my sun my mesuage that I dwell in, vj acre pasture lying under it, ij acre [and] iij stong lying in Seldyke felde, one acre and iij stong lying in Butterwyk felde, ix acre lying at Jafray's, one acre and iij stong lying in Leverton at Thomas Gat ende, v stonge at Metwelle, v acre lying in Leeke, v stonge lying at the new mylne, one acre in Leeke ynges, one acre in Benyngton lying in Medeylgate, ij acre at Benyngton brygges, iij stong at Costyd Hill, v stong in Leverton ynges, all the landes, pasture and arable, betwene Thomas Westelande and me now discendyd wherof no particion is mayd at the day of the makyng therof, and vj acre lying at Jafray's, a bothe sydes the se dyke. And yff it fortune the forsayd John my sun to decesse owt of thys present lyve or he be the age of xviij yeres withowt heyres of hys body laufully begottyn, then I will that the aforesayd mesuage, with all the appurtenaunce, to Thomas Wryght my sun when he shall be the age of xviij yeres. To Thomas Wryght my sun, when he shall be the age of xviij yeres, a pasture cont[aining] iiij acre callyd Robynson Grene, ij acre and a halffe lying in a felde callyd Poller, one acre at Dallgrafte, on acre at Richerde Pynchbek grene ende a bothe sydes the se dyke, on acre and iij stong sumtyme feldes, iiij acre lying in [fo. 313r] Leverton, ij acre and a half lying nygh Leverton churche and ij acre lying in Leverton ynges. And yff it fortune Thomas Wryght my sun to decesse owt of this present lyve or he be at the age of xviij yeres withowt heyres of hys body laufully begottyn, then I gyff to the foresayd John Wryght my sun, yff he overlyff hys brother, all the foresayd landes with ther appurtenances, to hym so overlyveyng the other, and to the heyres of ther too bodyes laufully begottyn, and so every one of them to be other heyres in fe tayley. And yff bothe my chyldren decesse, as God defende it so sholde be, withowt heyres of ther bodyes laufully begottyn, then I will all my foresayd landes with ther appurtenaunces, beyng in fee tayley, remayn to the last willys and gyftes of my awncetors, and all my other landes with ther appurtenances beyng in fe symple remayn to my executors and to other of theym overlyvyng the other. And yff it fortune my executors to chaunge ther lyvys afore my chyldren or aftyr, and my chyldren in lyke maner afore they cum to the age of xviij yeres, then I will the churchwardens of Benyngton, with iiij substanciall persons of the moste honest of the same towne at that tyme beyng, with the assent of my feoffes, do sell all the foresayd landes, and they to dispose the money therfore takeyn in reparacion of the churche of Benyngton, anornamentes, prestes, song, allmys emong pore people, and other dedes of charyte to the plesure of God and proffyt to my soule and all Christen soulys. Also I will that my executors, every yere ons the space and terme they have my landes in governance, do make accompte betwene themselff of all rentes, proffyttes, commodyties of all my landes cumyng to ther handes, for I will the one of them have no more in hys handes and custody then the other, and the rent of assyse with all other chargeys belongyng to my landes, bordyng, clothyng and exhibicion of my ij chyldren deducte and dischargeyd, the overplus of the forsayd proffyttes to renewe to my forsayd chylderyn and to be delyveryd them when they shall be the age of xviij yeres. And yff eny of my forsayd chyldren do chaunge thys lyff mortall afore they be the age of xviij yeres, I will every one of them be heyr to the other. And yff bothe my chyldren do chaunge thys lyff mortall afore they be the age of xviij yeres, then I will all the forsayd rentes and proffyttes be disposyd be myn executors or ther assignes in the churche and paryshe of Benyngton in warkes of charyte, to the plesure of God, proffyttes to my soule and all Crysten [fo. 313v] soulys. And wheras I, the sayd William Wryght, at the makyng of thys my last will doys lacke councell lernyd, wherefore thys my last will is not mayd and pennyd accordyng to the kynge's lawe, I will my executors do take to them any councell lernyd be ther discrescion to reforme and make thys my last will accordyng to the kynge's lawe, not alteryng thys my purpose, mynde and will. Mayd and wryttyn the yere and day aforesayd. Wytnes; Sir Roger Pyshe, paryshe preste of Benyngton, John Cokeler, John Loydon, John Crawe, Thomas Cooke, Henry Botheby of Benyngton, with other mo.

Proved before P at Boston, 9 October 1534.

377. RICHARD FYPORTE [OF SKIRBECK]
[LCC 1532–34, fo. 134v]

3 January 1533/4. I, Rycharde Fyporte, hole of mynde and of memorye, makes mye testamentt and mye last wyll. Fyrst I gyve and bequeth my soll to God allmyghtye and to the Blessyd Virgyn, Owr Ladye Sayntt Marye, and to all the saynttes in heven, and mye bodye to be beryed within the churchyerde of the blessyd confessor, Sayntt Nycolas of Skyrebecke. To the mother churche of Lyncolln iiij*d*. I bequethe for mye forgoten tythys viij*d*. To Geferaye mye son on cawfe and on fole yow and a lame. To Tomas mye son on cawfe, on yowe and a lame. To Margarett mye dowghtter one yonge mere, and so it fortune enye of mye chyldern dye within age, theyng I wyll that theyr parttes schall remayn to theym that be oflyve. To Jamys Nycolson on yonge hors. Thys down, mye deyttes payd, mye wyll fullfyllyd and mye feu exspensses well and honestlye browghtt forthe, the resydewe of all mye goodes I bequeth to Margarett mye wyffe, the whyche I make my executryx, and I wyll that John Howytson shal be the supervisor and he for to have for hys labor iij*s* iiij*d*. Wyttnes; Sir Roberd Browne mye curett, Roberd Carnabye, Jamys Necholson wyth other moo.

Proved before P at Boston, 3 March 1533/4.

378. HAMOND PAY [OF ST. MARTIN'S, LINCOLN]
[LCC 1532–34, fo. 112r]

3 January 1533/4. I, Hamond Pey off the paryches off Sent Martyn's in Lincoln, brassyer, makes my last wyll and testament. First I bequeythe my sawle to God allmyghty and to Our Blessyd Lade Sent Mare and to all the santes that ys in hevyn, and my body to be buryed in the chercheyard off Sant Martyn's in Lincoln. To the cherche warkes off Sent Martyn's iijs iiijd. To the hye auter off Sent Martyne's for tythes forgotten vjs viijd. To Our Lady's warke off the cathedrale cherche off Lincoln xijd. To the iiij orders off [friars] in Lincoln, hevery order, xijd. To Bloxholme cherche where I was born xijd. To the fyssers' gylde off Lincoln xijd. To Nycholas Benson my syster sune xxs and a bras pott. To John Bensson my syster sune xxs and a bras pott. To Jenet Pay my kynsswoman xiijs iiijd and a bras pott. To John Daleland in Burne vjs viijd. I wyll att my day off buryalle and my vij^the day, a trentalle off messes to be sayd for my sawle and all Crystyn sowlles, and every paryche clarke off Lincoln to have ijd. All the resedew off my gudes I put to the dysposycion off myne executors, that ys to say, Nycholas Kyndalle, wycare off Sent Martyn's off Lincoln and Robert Skynnar off Lincoln, merser, wome I mayke myne executors, and other off theme to have for there labor xxs. I mayke my supervysur John Halyle, p[e]wtrer off the paryche off Sent Martyn's, and he to have for hys labore a lyttyll rownd gowblytt off sylver. Thyes beyng recorders; John Bek, Thomas Freman and Thomas Tomson, with other mo.

Proved before P at Lincoln, 17 January 1533/4.

379. WILLIAM PYNCHBEK [OF BOSTON]
[LCC 1532–34, fos. 124v–125r]

3 January 1533/4. I, William Pynchbek of Boston, of a holl mynd and gude remembrance, makeith my testament concludynge therin my last will. Firste I give and bequeth my sowll to allmighty God, to Our Ladie Saint Marye, and to all the celestiall company of hevyn. My bodie to be beureid within the chircheyard of the holly confessour Sainct Botulph. To my mortuary as the lawe requireth. To the highe awlter in Boston for tithes and oblacions forgetun iiijd. [fo. 125r] To the reparacions of my mother chirche of Lincoln iiijd. To the orphans of Sainct Kateryne ther iiijd. To Beatrice my wif my house the wiche I doo dwell in duryng hir lif naturall. And after her dicesse, I will it remayn unto my too doughters and ther heers. The residew of my gudes I give theym unto the forssaid Beatrice my wif, to bring up my doughters, whom I maike my executrix. Thies being witnes; Robert Cony, Richard Tonnard and John Smyth, withe other moo. The daie and yer aforewriten.

Proved before P at Boston, 3 March 1533/4.

380. JOHN FEN [OF CROFT]
[LCC 1532–34, fo. 232v]

6 January 1533/4. I, John Fen off Crofte, in the countie of Lincoln, husbandman, beyng hole of mynde and in good remembraunce, makes my testament and my last will. Fyrste I gyff my soule unto allmyghtty God, to Our Lady St. Mary and to all the cumpeny of heven, and my body to be buryed wythin the churcheyerde of

Crofte, as nygh wheras my mother lyith as can be devisyd, and for my mortuary as the lawe requiryth. To the high altare off Crofte for tithys forgottyn, iiij*d*. To Our Lady altare ij*d*. To St. Nicholes altare ij*d*. To the bellys iiij*d*. To Our Lady of Lincoln, to the high altare ther viij*d*. The resydue off all my goodes I gyff to Margaret my wyffe, whome I make my full executrix, to her awne use and to bryngyng up of her chylder. Richerde Kelsay I make my supervisore, and he to have for hys labor iij*s* iiij*d*. Thes men beyng wytnes; William Drope, yonger, Robert Dandeson, Sir Rayff Gray, curate, cum aliis.

Proved before P at Partney, 4 February 1533/4. Adm. granted to the executrix.

381. ALICE HEKYNGTON [OF BOURNE]
[LCC 1532–34, fo. 114]

7 January 1533/4. I, Alice Hekyngton of Burne, vowys, hole of mynde and good remembraunce, make my testament and last will. Fyrste I bequethe my soule to allmyghtty God, to Our Lady St. Mary and to all the holy cumpeny of heven, and my body to be buryd in the paryshe churche of Burne aforesayd, in Our Lady's chapell. To the mother churche of Lincoln xx*d*, that is to say x*d* to Our Lady's warkes and x*d* to Our Lady's offerynges. To the high altare of Burne for offerynges and tithys forgottyn xx*d*. To the Trinite gylde in Burne xx*d*. To St. John gylde xij*d*. To the bellys xij*d*. To the fyndyng of one light before the high altare in the churche of Burne iij*s* iiij*d*. [fo. 114v] To Our Lady's chapell at the tornyng gates in the paryshe churcheyerde of Burne, one shete to make an altare clothe. To the prior and convent of Burne x*s* to pray for me. I gyff towarde the makyng of one cawsy in the eygate of Burne vj*s* viij*d*. To Jane Cecyll my doughter one cowe. To Wenyfryde Dyccons ij kye and one calve. To Catheryne my woman a gowne, a kyrtyll, her bed as she lyethe with, one pare of shetys and one qwye. I will that Mr. Robert Haryngton have the oversyght and rewle of my husbande's preste in Burne churche, to se that he do hys dewty and pray for my husbande soule and myne duryng the yeres conteyned in my husband laste will. The resydue of my goodes I gyff to Mr. Robert Haryngton and to Alice hys wyffe, whome I make executors to dispose to the plesure of God and helthe of my soule. Wytnes; Robert Haryson, preste, Thomas Feryby, John Dalalonde, with other mo.

Proved before P at Bourne, 30 January 1533/4.

382. RICHARD CAPPE [OF NORMANTON]
[LCC 1532–34, fo. 116v]

10 January 1533/4. I, Richerde Cappe of the paryshe of Normanton, of a good remembraunce, do make my testament. Fyrste I bequethe my soule to allmyghtty God and my body to be buryd within the churcheyerde of Normanton. To the high altare of the sayd churche viij*d*. To the churche warkes of the sayd Normanton iij*s* iiij*d*. I will that my landes that comme to me by inherytaunce do remayn to Margarate my wyff and my sun Oswolde, whome I make my executors to dispose the resydue of my goodes for the welthe of my soule. Wytnes of the premises; Thomas Asche, William Dobleday, Robert Hesylldyen, with other mo.

Proved before P at Lincoln, 31 January 1533/4.

383.   JOAN ROTHER [OF FISHTOFT]
        [LCC 1532–34, fo. 133v]

10 January 1533/4, 25 Henry VIII. I, Jenett Rother of the parysshe of Sayntt Cutlarke of Fyschtoft, beynge of hole mynde and of good remembraunce, make thys mye last wyll and testamentt. First I bequethe mye sowle to allmyghtye God, Our Blessed Ladye Seyntt Marye, and to all the holye companye in heven. Mye body to be beryed within the churcheyerde of Seyntt Cutlerke of Toft aforsayd, and for mye morturye as the law now dothe requyre. To Ower Ladye of Lyncolln iiijd. To the fatherles chyldern of Sayntt Kateryn withowt Lyncoln ijd. To the hygh aulter in Tofte churche iiijd. To Owre Ladye gylde in the churche of Wester Kele vjs viijd. To the reparacyons of the belles in the same churche iijs iiijd. To the pore folkes in Wester Kele aforesayd iijs iiijd. To Ower Ladye in the same churche halfe a stone wax. To Sayntt Myghell chapell in the Fenn ende of Tofte a pownde wax. To Alyce Brygges, mye dowghter, a russet kyrtyll. To Elizabeth Dauson, mye dowghter, a russet gown. To Jenett Jugge, mye goddowghter, a kerchey and a sylver rynge. To Jenett Shareman, mye goddowghter, a kerchey and a sylver rynge. To Isabell Dodyke a kerchey and a sylver rynge. To the makynge of a sylver pyckes to the blessed sacramentt in remanynge in the chappell of Sayntt Myghell aforsayd iijs iiijd. The residew of mye goodes nott gyven I gyve to Ellyn Clegge, mye dowghter, whom I doo ordeyn and make mye executrix, she to pay my dettes, fulfyll thys mye last wyll, and to dispose for the helthe of my soule and my husbande soule as she shall thynke best, and Robert Benysun to be supervisor, and to have for hys labor vjs. Thes beyng wytnesses; Sir Richerde Parker, preste, Simon Temper, Robert Benyson, John Jugge, with other mo.

        Proved before P at Boston, 3 March 1533/4.

384.   MARION BROWNE [OF HORBLING]
        [LCC 1532–34, fo. 115]

11 January 1533/4. I, Maryon Browne off Horblyng, wydoy, beyng of hole mynde and reason, makes my testament and last will. Fyrste I commyt my soule to allmyghtty God, Our Lady St. Mary, and to all the cumpeny in heven. My body to be buryd in the churcheyerde of St. Andro of Horblyng besyde my husbande. To Our Lady of Lincoln xijd. To St. Catheryn's iiijd. To the house of Sempyngham xs. To Our Lady's Frerys of Boston viijd. To the high altare of Horblyng xijd. To the churche of Horblyng vjs viijd. To the lighttes, equally to be devydyd, xijd. I will that Christofore Browne my sun firste have all suche thynges as was hys father's legacy, that is to say v markes in lawfull money, ij kye and ther calves. And that fulfyllyd, I gyff hym more of my goode one fether bed, one pare of schetes, one coverlyt, ij pilloys, xxty schepe, my best hose, one candylstyk, iij sylver sponys. I will that my executors deliver to hym within halffe a yere aftyr vjl xiijs iiijd. To ether of my doughters Elizabeth and Jenet one qwye and one cowe. To Elizabethe one pare of hardyn schetes, on lyn schete, one coverlyd, a potte, [a] panne, my best violet kyrtyll, one tynker panne, the barbar bason, ij saltes, my redd cappe, one kerchyff, half a dosyn puter, that is to say iij platters, ij dyshes, one sawcer, my byggest tubbe, one candylstyk, my blew gyrdyll. To Jenet my doughter one pare of har[d]yn schetes, one lyn schete, one coverlyd, one potte, one panne, my violet gowne, one kettyll, one basyn, ij saltes, my blake cappe, one kerchyff, half a dosyn pewther, that

is to say, iij platters, ij dyshes and one sawcer, one candylstyk, my red gyrdyll. To every one of my doughters' chyldren one lamme. To Alice, my sonne John chylde, one lamme, one sylver spone. To William Adall one seame barly. To William Preston one lamme. To John Robyn one lamme. To every one of my housholde that had no legacy before iiij*d*. To every one of my goddoughters one platter and one dyshe. To Alice Atwyk her mother's gowne. I will that Alice Atwyk and Isabell have there mother's legacy, xxvj*s* viij*d*. To George Gawthorne wyffe one yowe. To Richerde Bawdwyn one yowe. To Richerde Crowne one yowe. To Alice Atwell one bushyll malte. To Margery Mawdwyn one stryke malte. To John Bruster one stryke malte. To Richerde Crowne hys platter layd to pledge. To Catheryn Stell a platter and a potte layd [fo. 115v] to pledge. To St. Catheryn's altare one tabyll clothe. I will that a hable preste syng one trentall in the paryshe churche of Horblyng immediatly aftyr my decesse. To John Browne my sun iij sylver sponys, whome I make my sole executor to have the resydue of my goodes, to dispose for the helthe of my soule as he thynkes best, with the councell of Mr. Vicare of Horblyng, whome I make supervisor, and he to have hys costes borne frely at all tymys when he shall go or ryde with the rewarde of my executor. Thes beryng wytnes; Henry Atwyk, Richerde Crowne, Richerde Bawdwyn, with other mo.

Proved before P at Bourne, 30 January 1533/4.

385. RICHARD GRONE [OF KIRTON IN HOLLAND]
      [LCC 1532–34, fos. 243v–244r]

11 January 1533/4. I, Richerde Grone of Kyrton in Hollande, of hole mynde and perfyte remembraunce, makyth my testament concludyng with my laste will. Fyrste I gyff and bequethe my soule to God allmyghtty, Our Lady St. Mary and to all the celestiall compeny of heven, and my body to be buryd in the churcheyerde of the blessyd appostellys Peter and Paule of Kyrton beforesayd. And for my mortuary aftyr the statutes of our soverayn lorde the kyng. To the high altare of Kyrton for negligent tithes vj*d*. To the iij Marys altare ij*d*. To St. Nicholes altare ij*d*. To Our Lady altare nexte the pulpyte ij*d*. To the Trinite altare ij*d*. To the reparacion of the sayd churche of Kyrton xvj*d*. To Our Lady of Lincoln ij*d*. To the orphans of St. Catheryn's ij*d*. I wyll that yff so fortune that William Grone my sun and Elizabethe my doughter departe thys worlde withowte laufull issue, accordyng to the effecte of ther mother joyntry, that then I will my capitall messuage with all the appurte-naunces therto perteynyng, remayn to Richerde Grone my sun and to hys heyres of hys body laufully begottyn [remainder to] William Grone sonne of William Grone the elder, and to hys heyres of hys body laufully begottyn. And for defawtte of suche laufull issue to remane to William Grone the elder at hys wyll and discrecion. To William Grone my sun one brasse potte, the which hys owne mother bought. And I will that John Donnyngton the elder have the custody and kepyng of the sayd William Grone my sun with the sayd messuage and the appurtenaunces therto pertynyng, and also the sayd goodes before namyd to the sayd William my sun be of the age of xviij yeres, to the use and proffytte of the sayd William Grone my sun. To Elizabeth my doughter one calve redde dowyd with a runner calve and the beste panne that was her mother's, one bryght brasse potte, iij platters and one dyshe, one belde candylstyk, ij sawssers, one matteres, one coverlyd, one bolster, ij pilloys, ij pare of flaxen schetes and one tester. To Richerde Grone my sun my wyffe's best

gerdyll aftyr her decesse. To Cecyll Dykynson one matteres, one coverlyd, one pare of schetes of lyn and one pare of hardyn, a bolster, [fo. 244r] ij pilloys, one brasse potte that was Emonde Dykynson, iij platters, ij dyshes and one bell candylstyk. To William Grone my brother one yong dunde horsse of ij yere olde. To John Laurence my beste cote. I will that all the sayd porcions and partes as before planely is expressyd to my chyldren be delyveryd by myn executrix at May Day nexte ensuyng, to the use and proffyt of the sayd my chyldren, at the discrecion and orderance of John Donyngton the elder or hys assynges. I will that myne executrix do by, or cause to be bought, William my sun and Elizabethe my doughter owte of theyr wardeschyp of my capitall messuage, and I will that the sayd myn executrix do cause hole my chyldren heddes of her owne coste and charge. And I will that the sayd myn executrix do leyff immediatly aftyr my decesse in the sayd house the bedstokes that I ly in, one table, one chare, one forme and one leade stondyng in fornace as heyrlomys. I will ther be disposyd at my buryall day vjs viijd, at my seventh day vjs viijd and at my trigintall day vjs viijd. To the sayd Elizabethe my doughter one pare of beades and one arke that was her owne mother's. To the sayd William Grone my sun one fether bedde, one coverlyd, one pare of schetes, one bolster and ij pilloys to be delyveryd to John Donyngton the elder in maner and forme beforesayd. I will that yff any of the sayd my chylder departe thys worlde before the age of xvj yeres, that then ther porcions of the sayd goodes and catallys as before repetyd of theym so departyng to be disposyd in charytable usys at the discrecion of my supervisors or ther assygnes. The resydue of my goodes not gyvyn I gyff them to Emote my wyff, whome I orden to be my true executrix to dispose my goodes to the plesure of God and helthe of my soule. And I make John Donyngton the elder and William Grone my brother supervisors, and ether of theym to have for ther labors vs. Thes beyng wytnes; Sir Thomas Est, John Thomson, John Heylande, Roger Tonnerde, John Longley and Phylip Blyssebery, with other yff nede require.

Proved before P at Swineshead, 5 March 1533/4.

386. JOAN HAUKE [OF KILLINGHOLME]
       [LCC 1532–34, fo. 254v]

11 January 1533/4. I, Jenet Hauke of Kelingholme, vidoy, seke of body and hole of mynde and of good remembraunce, makyth thys my last will. Firste I bequethe my soule to God allmyghtty, to Hys blessyd mother, Our Lady St. Mary, and to all the holy cumpeny in heven, and my body to be buryd in the churche garthe of Kelyngholme. To the holy sacrament iiijd. To the churche warke a stryke of barly. To Our Lady of Lincoln iiijd. To Alice Crabanne, goddoughter unto my husbande, and to Henry Holme hys godsun, ether of theym, a fryndell of wheate. The resydue of all my goodes I gyff to John Hauke, Henry Hauke, Robert Hauke and Alice Hauke, my iiij chylder, and to Alice Nele my mother, whome I make my executours. Thes wytnes; Sir John Herpham, vicar, Robert Marshall.

Proved before P at Caistor, 27 April 1534. Adm. granted to Alice Neyle, executrix, the other executors being under age.

387. EDMUND THAKWARE [OF ASLACKBY]
[LCC 1532–34, fo. 131r]

11 January 1533/4. I, Emond Thakware, hole of mynde and of good remembrauns, makes thys my last wyll and testamentt. Fyrst I bequethe my sowll unto almyghtye God and to Ower Ladye Sayntt Marye, and to all the seynttes in heven. Mye bodye to be buryed in the quere of Seyntt Jamys of Aslakbye. I gyve xxs to bye a curtyn to hynge before the hygh aulter. To Seyntt John stocke of Aslakbye xvjd. To Seyntt Peter gylde of Aslakbye vjs viijd. To Ower Ladye of Lyncoln xxd. To Sir Christofer Myddylton of Aslakbye vjs viijd. To the chalans of Sympryngham vjs viijd. To the nuns of the same hows of Sympryngham iijs iiijd. To the abbott and coventt of Vade for to saye a trentall xs. To Sir John Foster of Donyngton my best gowne. To everye godchylde that I have, a schepe. To my cosyn Ane Brown v yows and v lammys, and a kow, coller rede. To John Floteres a kow, coller blacke. To John Clyntt of Folkyngham the lesser of my brasse pannys. To Alys Brown a brasse pott. To Sir Rycharde Warde, parson of Pyckworth, my best serssynytt typpytt. The resedew of my goodes I gyve to Mylles Floteres and John Floteres hys brother, whom I make my executores to dyspose for my sowll, bye the syghtt of Thomas Loughton whom I make superwysure that theye vayrye not, and he to have for hys labor vjs viijd. Theys wytnes; John Mylnes, Wylliam Barbor, Wylliam Swan and many other.

Proved before P at Sleaford, 2 March 1533/4. Adm. granted to Miles the executor.

388. THOMAS BARNSWELL [OF HARMSTON]
[LCC 1532–34, fo. 256r]

12 January 1533/4. I, Thomas Barnswell off Harmeston, hole of mynde, lovyd be God, makes my will. Fyrste I will my soule unto God allmyghtty and to Our Blessyd Lady, and to all the celestyall cumpeny off heven. My body to be buryd in the churcheyerde of All Halloys in Harmeston. To the high altare iiijd, and to Our Lady of Lincoln iiijd. To the orphans of St. Catheryn's withowt Lincoln iiijd. To my fyve chyldren, every one of them, one yowe lamme. I wyt the copy of my house to my wyffe duryng her lyffe, and aftyr it to remayne unto my eldeste sun. Yff anythyng happyn hym that he dye, then it to remayn to my yonger sun. The resydue of my goodes I gyff to my wyffe, whome I make my executrix to pay my dettes and to dispose for the helthe of my soule, and to bryng up my chylder. Thes wytnesses; Sir Leonerde Dyxson, John Rawsbe, Thomas Lokyng and John Bowers, with other.

Proved before P at Branston, 30 April 1534.

389. ROBERT JEFFERAY [OF LITTLE HALE IN PARISH OF GREAT HALE]
[LCC 1532–34, fo. 277r]

12 January 1533/4. I, Robert Jefferay of Lyttyll Hale, beyng in a hole mynde and of good remembraunce, makes my last wyll. Fyrste I bequethe my soule to God allmyghtty and to Hys mother, Our Lady St. Mary, and to all the saintes in heven, and my body to be buryd in the churcheyerde of Gret Hale, and I gyff to my curate to pray for me a cowe, and to discharge me of all the tithys and offerynges that I have bene negligent in. To the high altare vjd. To Our Lady's altare and to St.

Catheryn's altare in the same churche, ether of them, ij*d*. To Our Lady of Lincoln vj*d*. To St. Catheryn's off Lincoln ij*d*. To Jhesus gylde xij*d*. To my wyffe the house that I dwell in the terme of her lyff, and aftyr her dethe I gyff it to Thomas my sun. And I will that he gyff to every one of hys bretherne and systers vj*s* viij*d*, excepte Richerde hys brother, and I will he shall have but that that is hys heritage. To the sayd Thomas my sun a cowe and a gray mare, a yowe and a hog. To John my sun a qwe and a fole, and halffe a seame barly. To Robert my sun a qwye. To Hugh my sun a flecte calve. To William my sun a qwye and a fole. To Elizabeth my doughter a cowe, a yowe and a hog, a bed. To Margaret my doughter a cowe, a yowe and a hog. To the thorpe[150] that I dwell in xij*d*. The resydue of my goodes I gyff to my wyffe and to William Smyth, whome I make my executers that they may dispose them as they thynke best for the better helthe of my soule. And I will that William Smyth have for hys labor iij*s* iiij*d*. Wytnes herof; Sir George Pynder, vicar, Hugh Tylton, Robert Thorpe, John Hole, Robert Kyrton, with other mo.

Proved before P at Sleaford, 20 May 1534.

390.   ROBERT CALYS [OF LITTLE HALE IN PARISH OF GREAT HALE] [LCC 1532–34, fo. 119r]

13 January 1533/4. I, Robert Cales of Lyttyll Hale, beyng in a hole mynde and of good remembraunce, makes my wyll. Fyrste I bequethe my soule to God allmyghtty and to Hys mother, Our Lady St. Mary and to all the saintes in heven, and my body to be buryd in the churcheyerde of Gret Hale. To the high altare iiij*d*, and to Our Lady's altare in the same churche iiij*d*. To Our Lady of Lincoln iiij*d*, and to St. Catheryn's of Lincoln iiij*d*. I will have a trentall done for me and my good frendes in Hale churche. To the pore frerys at Boston iij*s* iiij*d*. I will have done for me at my buryng day v*s*, and at my vij[th] day v*s*, and at my xxx[ty] day iij*s* iiij*d*. To my doughter Alyson iiij schepe. To my curate, to pray for me, iij*s*. The resydue of my goodes I gyff to Herry my sun and to Thomas my sun, whome I make myn executers that they may dispose them the better for the helthe of my soule. Wytnes herof; Sir George Pynder, vicar, Thomas Hole, Thomas Danbe, John Grene, with other.

Proved before P at Sleaford, 2 March 1533/4.

391.   JOHN AKEY [OF BOSTON] [LCC 1532–34, fo. 124]

14 January 1533/4. I, John Akey of Boston in the countie of Lincoln, wefar, makeith my last will and testament. Firste I bequeth my soull to allmighty God and to Our Blisseid Ladie Sainct Marye, and to all the holly company of hevyn. My bodie to be beureid in the chircheyard of Sainct Botulph of Boston. I bequethe in the name of my mortuarie as the kynge's lawe requireth. To the highe awter for my tithes forgetin. To Our Ladie of Lincoln iiij*d*. To Graice, my wif, my house that I dwell in for terme of her lif, and after hir dicesse I will the said house be sold by the discrescion of the alderman and chamberlane of Ouer Ladie's gild of Boston, and they to have the oversighte of the moneye to bestowe it in mending of highwas wheir the moste neid is. And they to have in ther remembrance the calcye in the Shod

---

[150] 'Village', or 'hamlet'.

Freer's Layn as far as my housynge goeith, and this to be doon for my soull and all Cristen soulles, and the said alderman and chamberlayne to have for ther payntakyng, and to see this performeid, vj*s* viij*d*. To Isabell Hochynson my doughter's doughter a bed, a chiste, a counter, a dosen peaces of peuter vessell, and iiij markes, and this to be delivereid to Isabell Hochynson at the aige of xx^ti yeres. To the said Isabell my house in the Schod Freere Lan jonyng next to the kychen the term of hir lif, and after hir dicease I will that it be sold by the discrestion of the foresaid alderman and chamberlane of Ouer Ladie's gild of Boston afore reherseid. And they in lyke maner to bestowe the moneye of the forssaid house in amendyng the highwaies at the discrestion of the forssaid aldermane and chamberlayne for the tyme being. All the rest of my howsold stuff to Graice my wif of this condicion, that sche gif unto my moder Alice Akey, duryng hir lif, ij*d* every weike toward hir fynding. I will that my tenauntrie next unto my dwelling house reman to the kepyng [fo. 124v] of a obite in the Blake Freers for the term of xx yeres, and the said freers to have for the same ij*s* in peny or penyworth, and iiij*s* viij*d* to be gifen to pore peopill at the discrestion of Grace my wif, and the residew of the rent of my said tenaunterye to reman to my said wif Grace. To Alice Akey my dowghter, my howse of the west side of the wauter, to hir and to hir heers foreever. Also I will that all my gudes not gyven, the residew of theym, I will that Graice my wif have, whom I maike my executrix by the advice and councell of Master Nicolas Robertson, whom I make my supervisor, and he to have for his labour ij*s* iiij*d*. In witnes herof; Master Nicolas Robertson, Merchaunt of the Estaple at Calie, Sir Thomas Bekytt, prior of the Blak Freers in Boston, Freare Aleyn Echard of the same, Sir William Almonson of Boston, preste, and William Rouce of the same, withe other moo.

Proved before P at Boston, 3 March 1533/4.

392. AGNES SHEPPARDE [OF BENINGTON IN HOLLAND]
      [LCC 1532–34, fos. 121v–122r]

14 January 1533/4. I, Agnes Shepparde of Benyngton, of good and hole mynde, makes my testament. Fyrste I bequethe my soule to allmyghtty God and to Our Lady St. Mary, and to all the saintes in heven. My body to be buryd in the kyrke of All Halloys in Benyngton, and as the custome of the cuntrith to be hadde. To the high altare in Benyngton viij*d*. To Our Lady's altare viij*d*. To the t'oder altare vj*d*. To the rode over the dore vj*d*. To Our Lady of Lincoln viij*d*. To Mr. Nicholes Lee one cowe. To Margaret Shepparde a stone woolle and a halffe stone woolle, a brasse potte. To Isabbell Schepparde and Margaret Schepparde all my flaxe and yerne to be equally devydyd. To Jenet Pedder one yowe and vj*s* viij*d*. To Jenet Felde on hogge. To Agnes Tayllor on hogge. To Simon Shepparde a qwye. All my other money to be devydyd equally to John [fo. 122r] Shepparde, Simon Shepparde and William Shepparde, Isabell Shepparde, Margaret Shepparde, Jenet Shepparde, Elizabeth Shepparde. To John Shepparde.[151] Yff any of thes vij chylder dy within agys, so the partes of them so departyd remane to them lyffyng, and so from one to another. The resydue of all my goodes I gyff them to Mastres Cecyll Lee whome I make my executor, she to orden and dispose as she thynkes the best for my soule.

---

[151] No bequest is specified.

Thes wytnes; Mr. Nicholes Lee, Sir William Stedman, Richerde Shepparde, with other mo.

Proved before P at Boston, 3 March 1533/4.

393.   ROBERT TAYLLOR [OF CUMBERWORTH]
        [LCC 1532–34, fos. 327v–328r]

15 January 1533/4. I, Robert Tayllor of Comberworthe, husbandman, hole of mynde and good remembraunce, makyth thys my last will and testament. [fo. 328r] Fyrste I bequethe my soule to God allmyghtty and to Our Lady St. Mary and all the saintes in heven, and my body to be buryd in the churcheyerde of St. Helene of Comberworthe. And it to be my mortuary that the lawe requyryth. To the high altare in the churche of St. Helene of Comberworthe xx*d*. To Our Lady tabernacle in the chaunsell aforesayd xij*d*. To Our Lady warkes of Lincoln vj*d*. To Our Lady of Lincoln iiij*d*. To Alice Maxsay ij kye, ij marys, iiij yowes, ij beddes and it that longes to them, that is to say, ij matteresses, ij pare of shetes, one pare of lyn and the other pare of hardyn, ij coverlydes, ij pilloys, a brasse potte, a panne, iiij puter dyshes, a tubbe and a boll. I will that the sayd Alice shall have no d[enomi]nacion of thes goodes afore she cum to the age of xx^ty yeres, excepte she may mary. And yff it pleas God that she dy or she cum to the age aforesayd, I will that Jenet my wyff have thes goodes and dispose them as to her shall thynk most nedefull. To Jenet my wyff v kye, a yoke of oxyn, iiij merys, x yowes and all the housholde stuff and all my croppe, plughe and wane, and that longes to them. I will that my lande remayn to Jenet my wyff the space of her lyff, yff she kepe her unmaryd. And yff she mary, then I will my lande be solde be the handes of my executors, yff it may be laufully solde, and a preste to syng and pray for my soule and my frendes' soulys and all Christen soulys whyles the value of the sayd landes will extende. To Jenet my wyff xxx*s*. To Helene Ledes a cowe. To Sir Thomas Mathew xx*d*. I will that Jenet my wyff and Christofer Hall be my executors, and other of them to have for ther labor xx*d*. I will that William Herdman the elder be supervisor, and to have for hys labor xx*d*. Wytnes herof Thomas Mathue, Thomas Lawson and John Penson.

Proved before P at Alford, 15 October 1534.

394.   CHRISTOPHER RAWLYNSON [OF NOCTON]
        [LCC 1532–34, fo. 269r]

18 January 1533/4. I, Christofor Rawlynson of the paryshe of Nocton, of hole mynde and good remembraunce, makes my testament and laste will. Fyrste I bequethe my soule to God allmyghtty and Hys blessyd mother, Our Lady St. Mary, and to all the holy cumpeny of heven, and my body to be buryd in the paryshe churche of Nocton before the roode, and to be payd in the steyd of my mortuary as the lawe requirys. To my paryshe churche xx*d*. To our mother churche of Lincoln iiij*d*. To the paryshe churche of Bardeney viij*d*, to be devydyd emonges the lighttes ther fun of the churche costes. To my brother John one yong meyr. To my syster Grace dwellyng in Lincoln one qwye of iiij yere olde. To William my servant ij yeryng calves. The resydue of my goodes I gyff to Alyson my wyff, whome I make my executrix that she may dispose it for the helthe of my soule and all my frendes' soulys, and John Hardy, my brother-in-lawe, to be supervisor. Thes wytnes;

Thomas Bale, vicar of Nocton, Sir Thomas Wyffyn, canon of Nocton Parke, Robert Fowler, John Fowller, John Mowbre of the paryshe of Nocton, with many other mo. The day and yere above rehersyd.

Proved before P at Lincoln, 15 May 1534.

395.   WILLIAM FYSHER [OF BILLINGHAY]
       [LCC 1532–34, fo. 276v]

20 January 1533/4. I, William Fysher of Depergarthe in the paryshe of Byllyngay, hole of mynde and remembraunce, makes my testament. Fyrste I gyff my soule to God allmyghtty, to Our Lady St. Mary and to all saintes of heven. My body to be buryd in the paryshe churcheyerde off Byllyngay. To the high altare in Byllyngay for tithes forgottyn iiij*d*. To the high altare of Our Lady of Lincoln iiij*d*. To the bellys at Byllyngay iiij*d*. I will have one trentall of messys sayd for my soule and all my good frendes' soulys in the paryshe churche of Byllyngay. To the reparacion of the churche of Byllyngay iiij*d*. To Alice my doughter ij qwyes of ij yeres olde and upwarde, the one is blake with a whyte backe, and the other browne with a whyte sterne in the heade, also one matteres, one bolster, one pare of schetes and one coverlet. To Elizabeth my doughter ij qwyes of the foresayd age that is red flecte, one matteres, one bolster, one pare of schetes with a coverlet. To Agnes my doughter ij qwyes that is browne flecket of the foresayd age, one matteres, one bolster, one pare of schetes with a coverlet. Also I will yff eny of these iij systers dye or they be maryd, that the goodes shall remayn to the other ij systers. I will that all my goodes not bequeth be disposyd in iij partes, that is one of the sayd partes to Marion my wyff, the other parte to my chyldren of our bodys laufully begottyn, and the thyrde parte be disposyd for helthe of my soule, by the syght of my wyff. I will that Marion my wyffe have ij housys uppon the Chapell Hill unto the tyme she have the money that I layd owt for the foresayd housys that was xl*s*, and then the foresayd housys to remayn to the ryght heyres. The resydue of all my goodes not bequethyd, I gyff them to Marion my wyff and William Fysher my sun, which I orden my executors that they dispose for the helthe of my soule. Thes beryng wytnes; Sir William Ludlam, preste, John Robynson, Edmunde Cowt, John Baker, William Fysher and John Rawcebye, with other.

Proved before P at Sleaford, 20 May 1534. Adm. granted to Marion, relict and executrix, William Fisher, son of the deceased and co-executor, being underage.

396.   JOHN SHARPE [OF FISHTOFT]
       [LCC 1532–34, fo. 130]

20 January 1533/4. I, John Sharpe of Toft, beyng of hole mynd and gud remembraunce, makes thys my last wyll and testament. Fyrst I bequeyth my soule to almyghty God, Owre Blyssed Lady Sanct Mary and to all the holy company off hevyn. My body to be beryede withine the churcheyard off Sanct Goodlace in Toft. To the hyght alter in the church aforesaid viij*d*. To the Trinite alter in the same churche ij*d*. To Sanct John alter in the same churche ij*d*. To Our Lady chapell in Toft churcheyard aforesaid iiij*d*. To Oure Lady of Lincoln iiij*d*. To Jenyt my doyghtar a quy, a blak ark, a gowne, a kertly, a matresse, a coveryng for a

bed, a pere off linnyn shetes, a paer off harden shetes, a sheyt with a sylkyne seme, iij pillois, a bolster with the fyllyng and pylloybeyrs, a tester and bedstokes. To the said Jenyt my doyghtar a bras pott, ij pewder platters, a pewder salt, ij candylstykes and a harnest gyrdyll. To Agnes my wyff my howsse with the grownde lyyng under it unto my doyghtar shall cum at the age of xvj yers, and then the said howse with the ground under it shall remayne to Jenyt my doyghtar and to the haers off hyr body lawfully begotton, and yff she decesse without haers off hyer body, then I wyll that [fo. 130v] the said howse with the ground under it shal be solde and the money therof to be resevyd shal be expendyd in warkes of charyte within the paryche churche of Toft aforesaid. The resydew of my goodys I gyve to Agnes my wif, whome I doy mayk myne executrix, she to dispose for the helth of my soule and all my gud fryndys' sowls as she shall thynke best. And Robert Thakkar of Toft to be supervisor, and the sayd Robert to have for hys labor and payne iijs iiijd. Theys beyng wytnes; Syr Nycholas Kytloke, pariche prest of Toft, Robert Brome of the same and Thomas Bayte of the same, with other mo.

Proved before P at Boston, 3 March 1533/4.

397. ROBERT HUTCHYNSON [OF SWATON]
[LCC 1532–34, fo. 139]

22 January 1533/4. I, Robert Hutchynson of the paryshe of Swaton in the countie of Lincoln, of good mynde and remembraunce, makes my laste will. Fyrste I bequethe my soule unto God allmyghtty and to the gloriose Virgyn St. Mary, Hys mother, and to all the holy cumpeny of heven, and my body to be buryd in the churcheyerde of the blessyd appostyll St. Andro in Swaton. To the high altare in Swaton viijd. To the paryshe churche in Swaton xiijs iiijd towarde the bying of banner clothys with, yff the churchewardens will by them, and yff they will not by them I will that my wyff have the forsayd xiijs iiijd agane. I gyff towarde the makyng of the light afore Our Lady in the north quere in the parysche churche of Swaton xxd. To Our Lady warke in Lincoln viijd and to the pore chyldren of St. Catheryn's in Lincoln iiijd. To every one of my godchyldren ijd. To the prior of Bryghende towarde the mendyng of the highways iijs iiijd. To William Tallour my brother a browne qwye of iij yeres olde and my secunde russyt cote, and to hys sun a brasse potte of halffe a gallon. To Richerde Bowthe my redde jaket and my lether dublyt. I will that ther shall be a trentall of messes sung in the [fo. 139v] paryshe churche of Swaton in Our Lady's qwere for me and all Crysten soulys. The resydue of my goodes not spokyn of before I gyff them to Maryon my wyff, and she to dispose it for the helthe of my soule as she thynkes best. And I make my wyffe my full executrix, and I make Richerde Carter the supervisor, and I will he have for hys labor xijd. Thes men beryng wytnes; Sir Thomas Smale, vicar, Richerde Carter, John Smyth, Robert Hosburnebye, with other mo.

Proved before P at Helpringham, 3 March 1533/4.

398. JOHN STALLYNGBORO [OF IRBY ON HUMBER]
[LCC 1532–34, fos. 237v–238r]

22 January 1533/4. I, John Stallyngboro of Irby, beyng in hole mynde and good remembraunce, makyth my laste will and testament. Fyrste I bequethe my soule to

God allmyghtty and to Our Lady St. Mary and to all the saintes in heven, and my body to be buryd in the churcheyerde of St. Andro in Irby. To the high altare of Irby for tithys and offerynges negligently forgottyn vj*d*. To the churche warke of Irby viij*d*. To Our Lady's warke of Lincoln iiij*d*. To the high altare of Lincoln iiij*d*. I will that ther be fyve messys of the fyve woundes of Our Lorde sayd for my soule and all Crysten soulys at my burynd day. [fo. 238r] I will that the people beyng in the churche that day have a dole of brede and drynke. I will that Sir William Asby syng halff a trentall for my soule and all Crysten soulys, and he to have therfore v*s*. I will that Thomas Stallyngburgh, my suny's chylde, have my murray jackyt made in a cote and halffe a quarter of barly when harveste the nexte cumyng is done. I will that Margaret hys syster have my blewe jacket made to her backe and halffe a quarter barly when harvest is done. To John Stallyngurgh, myn awne sun, my gret brasse potte and the thyrde parte of my goodes, and when hys mother dothe mary agane, he that dothe mary her shall fynde ij honeste sewertys to be bounde in obligacion to my supervisor and to the chylde, that he shall delyver the chylde hys parte when he cumyth to lawfull age be the syght of my supervisor. Yff he will not thus be bounde, then I will that my supervisor take my chylde parte and put it to the proffyt of my chylde, to hym that will be bounde to delyver it at lawfull age to the chylde. Yff ought cum at my chylde I wyll that it be disposyd for my soule as my wyff and my supervisor thynkyth best. I will that my wyffe be my sole executrix, and Sir Alen Tharade my supervisor, and specially to be good to my chylde, and he to have for hys labor vj*s* viij*d*. Thes wytnes; Sir Alan Tharolde, John Bery, Robert Hebray, Thomas Borwyll, and other mo.

Proved before P at Grimsby, 11 February 1533/4.

399. WILLIAM SOWLLE [OF PINCHBECK]
[LCC 1532–34, fos. 136r–137r]

25 January 1533/4. I, William Sowlle of Pynchbek, with good mynde and hole remembraunce, makes my last will and testament. Fyrst I bequethe my soule to God and to Our Lady St. Mary, and to all the saintes in heven. My body to be buryd in the churcheyerde of Our Lady in Pynchbek. To the high altare within the churche of Pynchbek viij*d*. To every altare within the sayd churche ij*d*. To Our Lady of Lincoln for oblacions iiij*d*. To the pore chyldren at St. Catheryn's at Lincoln ij*d*. To Robert my sun the house that I dwell in with the appurtenances longyng therto, with vj acres of pastur copyholde and ij acres of arable lande callyd Calve's Heyr, to hym and to hys heyres of hys body laufully begottyn [remainder to] John my sun, to hym and to hys heyres of hys body laufully begottyn [remainder to] Thomas my sun, to hym and to hys heyres of hys body laufully begottyn [fo. 136v] [remainder to] William my sun, to hym and hys heyres of hys body laufully begottyn [remainder to] Jenet my doughter, to her and to her heyres of her body laufully begottyn. And for lacke of suche issue, I will the sayd house and all the landes before namyd remane to the nexte of my kyn. To Robert my sun my ambry and my gret brasse potte and my gret arke and a leade, which as my wyff will delyver hym, and to the same Robert ij marys the price xvj*s*. To John my sun the house that I bought of Thomas Averton, to hym and to hys heyres or hys assygnes, and to the same John ij calves to be burnyd att nexte May Day, and ij burnynges that was burnyd at last May. To Jenet my wyff my copy of v acres the terme of her lyff, and aftyr her decesse I will that the

sayd copy of v acres remane to Thomas my sun, to hym and to hys assygnes. To Jenet my wyff the house that I dwell in with the appurtenances and vj acres of pastur and ij acres callyd Calve's Heyr, unto the tyme that Robert my sun cum to laufull age. To Jenet my wyff the house that I bought of Thomas Averton, unto the tyme that John cum to the age of xvj yeres, and I wyll, yff so be that my wyffe kepe my name styll and mary not, I will that she shall have the house that I bought of Thomas Averton the terme of her lyffe, and aftyr her decesse I will that the sayd house that was Thomas Averton remayn to John my sun, to hym and to hys heyres or hys assygnes. I will that Jenet my wyff shall kepe the house that I dwell in with laufull reparacion, wynde theght and water theght. And yff so be that my wyffe so mary agane and he that shall mary her make any waste opon my housys or of my grounde, then I will that Robert Menarde and William Tylson, supervisors, I gyff to them full powre and strenthe and auctorite clerely to expulse and put forthe my wyff and her husbande from the sayd house with the appurtenances, and the sayd Robert Menarde and William Tylson shall let to ferme the sayd house with the appurtenances to the moste proffyt and use of Robert my sun. To Thomas my sun a calve to be burnyd at nexte May, and a burnyng that was burnyd at the laste May. To William my sun a burnyng that was burnyd at the laste May and a calve to be burnyd at the nexte May. [fo. 137r] And I will that my iij sonnys John, Thomas and William shal receyve ther cattyll at the nexte May Day cumyng. To Jenet my doughter ij calves. And I will that my wyffe shall kepe the sayd ij calves at her coste to they be iij yeres olde, and then to delyver them to Jenet my doughter. Yff that my wyffe do mary agane, then I will that she, or her assignes, shall deliver to Robert my sun a carte worthe x*s*, or ellys x*s* in sylver. And to the same Robert my sun a plough worthe vj*s* viij*d* or ellys vj*s* viij*d* in money. And I will that the sayd plough and carte, and the ij marys before namyd, be delyveryd to Robert my sun at the day of hys mariage. And yff Robert my sun dye before he be maryed, then I will that the plough and the carte be delyveryd with the ij marys to John my sun at the day of hys mariage. Yff John my sun dye afore he be maryed, then I will that the sayd plough and carte, with the ij marys, be delyveryd to Thomas my sun at the day of hys mariage. Yff Thomas my sun dye, I will that the sayd ploughe and carte, with the ij marys, be delyveryd to William my sun at the day of hys mariage. Yf William mye son dye, then I wyll that the sayde plowgh and cartt, with the ij maryes, remayn styll with mye wyfe. I wyll that the chylde, the whytche mye wyfe is with, have ij mylke kye if itt please God itt come to the worlde. To John Tylsson, the son of Wylliam Tylsson, iiij*d*. To Agnes Tylsson, the dowghter of the sayd Wylliam Tylsson, iiij*d*. To Elizabethe Northe iiij*d*. To Elyn Gon xij*d*. To John Menarde, son of Robert Menarde, iiij*d*. To Elizabeth Menard, dowghter of the sayd Roberde Menarde, iiij*d*. The resydewe of all mye goodes ungyvyn, I putt them to the dysposycyon of Jenett mye wyffe, whom I make mye true executrix, to pay mye deyttes and to fulfyll mye wyll, and to brynge me forthe, and Roberde Menarde and Wylliam Tylson to be supervysores, and I wyll that ether of them have for theyr labor iij*s* iiij*d*. Thyes wytnesses; Wylliam Bewyk, preist, Rycharde Tylson, Crystover Northe, John Davys.

Proved before P at Spalding, 4 March 1533/4.

400. JOAN KETTYLL [OF SUTTERTON]
[LCC 1532–34, fo. 178v]

26 January 1533/4. I, Jenet Kettyll of Suttertun, in goode mynde and holle remembraunce, makyth my last will and testament. Fyrste I bequethe my soule to allmyghtty God, to Our Lady St. Mary and to all the holly cumpeny of heven. My body to be buryed in the churcheyerde of Sutterton. To the high altare ijd. To Our Whyte Lady jd. To Our Lady of Lincoln ijd. To the fatherlesse chyldren at St. Catheryn's ijd. To Agnes Fraunces one cowe and one brasse potte that was her fader's, and one gret panne. The resydue of my goodes not bequeste, my dettes payd, my body brought to the grounde, I gyff to Mr. Thomas Hylton and Catheryne my syster, whome I make my trewe executors for to dispose to the pleasure of God and the helthe of my soule as they shall thynke. Wryttyn the yere and day above namyd. Wytnes herof; Sir Jamys Mower, Thomas Gaxeson, William Clerke, with other mo.

Proved before P at Lincoln, 2 February 1533/4.

401. THOMAS BOURDLAY [OF QUADRING]
[LCC 1532–34, fo. 288]

27 January 1533/4. I, Thomas Bourdlay of Quadryng paryshe, beyng of good remembraunce, makyth my last testament. Fyrste I bequethe my soule to allmyghtty God, Our Lady St. Mary, and to all the celestiall cumpeny of heven, and my body to be buryd within the churche of Quadryng. To the high altare for tithes forgottyn viijd. To Our Lady altare ijd, and to St. John's altare ijd. To the plowe light one pounde of waxe dewe be promission. To the fyve principall lighttes in Qwadryng churche xd. To the fatherles chyldren at St. Catheryn's ijd. To the organs in Quadryng churche a yereyng calve. To Jenet Rud a yeryng fole and a yeryng calve, and a burlyng qwye. To Elizabeth Burdley ij kye, a burlyng, iij yong merys, ij brasse pottes, x pecys of pewder vessell, a matteres, a coverlyd, ij pare of schetys, [fo. 288v] a bolster and ij pilloys. To Richard Burdley a burlyng qwye, a dooblet and a blak jaket. Yff Elizabeth my diughter dye or she be maryd, then I will that Anne Burdlay have all her parte of goodes, and in lyke maner yff Anne dye or she be maryd. The resydue of my goodes unbequethyd I bequethe to Catheryne my wyff, who I make my full executrix. I will that William Chele be coadjutor to my wyff, and he to have for hys labor iijs iiijd. Wytnes of thys my last will; William Hodale, John Gyll and Thomas Shypwryght, cum aliis.

Proved before P at Swineshead, 8 June 1534.

402. WILLIAM SCARCROFTE [OF CADEBY IN PARISH OF CAL-CETHORPE]
[LCC 1532–34, fo. 267v]

28 January 1533/4. I, William Scarcrofte of Cadbe in the paryshe of Calesthorpe, off a hole mynde and good memory makes my last will. Fyrste I bequethe my soule to God allmyghtty and to Our Lady St. Mary and to all the cumpeny of heven, and my body to be buryed in the churcheyerde of St. Fathe in Calesthorp. To the high altare of Calesthorpe aforesayd for tithy forgottyn viijd. To Our Lady warke of Lincoln viijd. The resydue of my goodes I bequethe to Margaret my wyff

to dispose for the helthe off my soule as she thynkes beste, whome I make my executrix. Thes wytnesses; Sir John Barron, Thomas Chapman, William Weste, with many mo.

Proved before P at Louth, 8 May 1534.

403.   WILLIAM TONNERD [OF KIRTON IN HOLLAND]
        [LCC 1532-34, fo. 138v]

28 January 1533/4. I, William Tonnerde of Kyrton in Hollande, of hole mynde and good memory, makes my testament wherwith is concludyd my last will. Fyrste I commende my soule to God allmyghtty and to Our Lady St. Mary and to all the celestiall cumpeny of heven, and my body to be buryd in the churcheyerde of the holy appostellys Peter and Paule in the forsayd towne of Kyrton. To the sacrament of the high altare in the same churche for tithys forgottyn. To every altare in the same churche ijd. To Our Lady of Lincoln iiijd. To the fatherles chyldren of St. Catheryn's in Lincoln ijd. To Agnes my wyff one acre and an halffe of arable lande callyd Twyn Dalys the terme of her naturall lyffe, and aftyr her dececesse [sic] to remayn to John my sun in fe symple. I will that John my sun have one acre arable and a halffe of pasture callyd Fox Dalys immediatly aftyr my decesse in fe symple. I will that bothe my doughters Isabel and Jenet have, ether of them, a cowe and a qwye, a bedde with the perteynynges therto belongyng accordyng to ther mother mynde. To William Albyn a burlyng calve. To Agnes my wyffe all my housholde stuff hole as it standes to hyr owne use. To John my sun my bote, my carte, my plough with the gerys to them belongyng to hys own use. The resydue of my goodes I gyff to Agnes my wyffe and John my sun, whom I make my executors to pay my dettes and dispose the resydue to the honor of God, for the welthe and consolacion of my soule and all Christen soulys. Of the whiche thes be the testes; Syr John Cowper, Richerde Tonnerde, Humfrey Tonnerde, with other mo.

Proved before P at Swineshead, 5 March 1533/4.

404.   THOMAS WYLSON [OF HORNCASTLE]
        [LCC 1532-34, fos. 257v-258r]

29 January 1533/4. I, Thomas Wylson of Horncaster, glover, of hole mynde and off good remembruance, makyth thys my testament and last will. Fyrste I gyff and bequethe my soule to allmyghtty God and to Our Lady St. Mary and to all the holy cumpeny of heven, and my body to be buryd in the churcheyerde of the paryshe churche of Horncastle. To the high altare of Lincoln iiijd. To Our Lady warke of Lincoln iiijd. To the high altare of Horncastle xxd. To St. Catheryne gylde of Horncastle iijs iiijd. To Our Lady of [fo. 258r] Pety light in the same iiijd. To All Halloys light iiijd. To St. Michel light iiijd. To St. Christofer light ijs iiijd. To the torche light iijs iiijd. To iiij men that shall beare me to the churche iiijd. The resydue of my goodes not wyt I put to the discresion and conscience of Catheryne my wyff and Mathewe Sandes my brother-in-lawe whome I make my executors, and they to gyff unto my chylder ther porcion of my sayd goodes as they thynke beste, and to dispose for the helthe of my soule and all Christen soulys by the advyse of my good nyghbore Alexander Boys, whome I make supervisor, and he to

have for hys paynestakyng as my sayd executors thynkes reasonabyll. Thes beyng wytnesses; Sir Michel Whythed, paryshe preste, William Gray, Miles Stavelay, with other mo.

Proved before P at Horncastle, 4 May 1534.

405.   CHRISTOPHER RUSTE [OF INGOLDMELLS]
       [LCC 1532–34, fos. 263r–264v]

30 January 1533/4. I, Christofer Rust of Ingolmellys, beyng of hole mynde and good memory, ordens and makes my testament and last will. Fyrste I bequethe my soule to allmyghtty God, to Our Blessyd Lady St. Mary, and to all the holly cumpeny of heven, and my body to be buryd in the churcheyerde of St. Peter of Ingolmellys, and to my mortuary as the lawe requiryth. To the high altare of the churche of St. Peter of Ingolmellys for tithes forgottyn xxd. To the reparacion of the ornamentes of the same altare xijd. To Our Lady altare within the same churche of Ingolmellys vjd. To St. Nicholes altare in the same churche vjd. To every of the other iij altares in the sayd churche iiijd. To the bellys in the sayd churche xxs. To the churche warke of the same churche xxs. To the high altare of Our Lady of Lincoln xijd. To Our Lady's warke of Lincoln xijd. To the pore chyldren at St. Catheryn's without Lincoln viijd. To the high altare of St. Nicholes of Ardelthorpe for tithys forgottyn xijd. To the churche warke and to the bellys of the same churche vs. To the high altare of the parysche churche of Hoggesthorpe for tithys forgottyn viijd. To the churche warke of the same churche iijs iiijd. To the bying of a sylver pax[152] to the high altare of the churche of St. Peter of Ingolmellys aforesayd xiijs iiijd. To Our Lady's gylde of Ingolmellys aforesayd iiij schepe, to be delyveryd clyppyd, to the mantenance of the same gylde. To the sepulcre light in the same churche iiijd. To the yong mens' light in the same churche iiijd. [fo. 263v] To the maydens' light in the same churche iiijd. To every of my godchyl[d]er iiijd. To every of the iiij orders of frerys in Boston vjs viijd. To the ancorys in Boston xxd. To Sir Robert Hoge of Lynancer xxd. To Thomas Putterell and to Robert Putterell, my wyff chylden, either of them, vjs viijd. To Thomas Kay iij schepe and ij lambys aftyr the schepe be clyppyd. To Alice Kay his wyff vjs viijd. To every of the chyldren of the sayd Alice that now lyffys iiijd. To every of the chyldren of my wyffe's sonnys and doughters iiijd. To every of the chydren of John Wapuell iiijd. To John Burtwesell iijs iiijd. To Henry Burne iiijd. To Thomas Ingman iiijd. To Henry Bonner my servant one lambe. To Alice Gunthorpe my servant one lambe. To Thomas Burton ij yowes with ther lambys when the yowes be clyppyd. I bequethe to one preste for to celebrate the space of one hole yere in the paryshe churche of St. Peter of Ingolmellys, for my soule and all Christen soulys, vl vjs viijd. And I wyll that the sayd preste be at the election of Sir Nicholes Sarrott, the parson of the sayd Ingolmellys. I bequethe to Sir John Cokson, preste, for to celebrate ij trentallys for my soule and all Christen soulys, xxs. To Nicholes Rust my sun one

---

[152] The pax, or paxbred, was a consecrated host or a symbol of it, which was passed around the parish community in order of social precedence at the celebration of the Easter Mass. Kissing the pax symbolised communal harmony and was an important means of ensuring that those about to receive communion were 'in charity' with the community and one another. This silver pax was either intended as a container for the paxbred, or as a pax in its own right. See Duffy, *Stripping of the Altars*, 126–7.

cupborde which was hys mother's. To Sir William Skypwyth, knyght, xxs. To my lady Skypwyth hys wyff iijs iiijd. To Mr. William Skypwith, sun and hayr of the sayd Sir William Skypwyth, xiijs iiijd. To the other chylder of the sayd Sir William Skypwyth and my lady hys wyff, to be devydyd equally emong them, iijs iiijd. To John Walpoll xls. To Sybyll Burton xs, one quarter of barly and one quarter of beanys. To John Walker of Thyrlby one lambe. To Stephen Parone one lambe and my pety cote, one pare of hose and one sherte. To Thomas Gyrne my bukskyn dooblet, one olde violet jaket and one pare of hose. To John Baly my jaket furryd with lambe. To Helene Burton my servant all the proffyttes of one cowe for the space of iiij yeres from the feste of the Penthecost nexte foloyng aftyr my decesse. And at the ende of the sayd iiij yeres I will the sayd cowe remayn agane to myn executors to the performance of thys my laste [fo. 264r] will. I will that iij acres of pasture callyd Broddyng lande be to the performance of thys my last will for the space of ij yeres aftyr my decesse, aftyr the maner and custome of the lordeschyp of Ingolmellys aforesayd. And at the ende and terme of the sayd ij yeres, I will the sayd iij acres of pasture remayn to Nicholes Rust my sun. Also I will that vij acres of pasture which I bought of William Paycoke remayn in the handes of my feoffys to the performance of thys my last will, unto Nicholes my sun be xxj yere of age. And my executors to have the governance of the sayd vij acres of pasture, and they to gyff yerely accompt therof to Sir Nicholes Sarrot, parson of Ingolmellys. Also I will that iiij acres of pasture lying in Ardelthorp, immediatly aftyr the decesse of Johanne Goshoke, remayn in my feoffys' handes to the performance of thys my last will, unto Nicholes my sun be xxj yeres of age. And I will that my executors have the governance of the sayd iiij acres of pasture, they to gyff yerely accompte therof to the sayd Sir Nicholes Sarrot. Also I will that my executors cause to be done yerly duryng the terme of xx^{ty} yeres next immediatly foloyng aftyr my decesse one obyt with placebo and dirige overnyght, and messe of requiem in the mornyng, of one preste in the churche off Ingolmellys aforesayd for my soule and all Christen soulys, at the which obyt I will that they shall expende as hereafyter foloyth; that is to say, the sayd preste to have vjd, to the paryshe clerke ijd, for ryngyng of the bellys xijd, in bred, chese and drynke to the ryngers of the bellys xijd, for the messe penny jd, to be gyvyn in almys vijd. All the which money concernyng thys sayd obyt I will shall be takyn of my goodes duryng the lyffe naturall of the aforesayd Johanne Goshake. And aftyr her decesse I will that the same money concernyng the sayd obyt be takyn of the aforesayd iiij acres of pasture lying in Ardelthorpe unto th'ende and terme of the aforesayd xx^{ty} yeres to be fully complete and endyd. Also I will that yff Nicholes my sun decesse before he be xxj yeres of age, that then the aforesayd iij acres of pasture callyd Broddyng lande, vij acres of pasture lying in Wynthorp and iiij acres of pasture lying in Ardelthorp be solde be my executors, and the money therof receyved to be disposyd in warke off charite in the churche and in the towne of Ingolmellys. And yff John Walpull will by the aforesayd landes, I will that he have fyve marke bayt in the price that another man will gyff therfore. Also I will that the resydue of my goodes, my will fullfyllyd and my dettes payd, be devydyd in thre partes, one parte to Isabell my wiff and ij partes to Nicholes my sun, [fo. 264v] excepte that I will that the fourthe parte of the ij partes be disposyd in almys for my soule and all Christen soulys. I make Nicholes Rust my sun, Thomas Skegness and John Walpull my executors. I gyff to every of them for ther labors xxs. And I desyre Sir Nicholes Sarrot, parsone of Ingolmellys, to be supervisor, and I gyff to hym for hys labor xxs. Thes wytnes; Sir Richard Sherman,

Sir John Bokeson, prestes, William Thore, John Willerton and Thomas Flesher, with other mo.

Proved before P at Partney, 6 May 1534.

406. ROBERT DEYRSSE [OF PINCHBECK]
      [LCC 1532–34, fos. 126v–127r]

4 February 1533/4. I, Roberde Deyrsse of Prynchebek, with good mynde and hooll remembraunce, makes my last wyll and testamentt. Fyrst I bequethe mye soull to God and to Our Ladye Sayntt Marye, and to all the companye in hevyn. My bodye to be beryed in the churcheyarde of Ower Ladye [fo. 127r] in Prynchebeke. To the hye alter within the churche of Prynchebeke iiij*d*. To everye alter within the sayd churche ij*d*. To Ower Ladye of Lincolln for oblacyons ij*d*. To the pore chyldren it Sayntt Kateryn's att Lyncolln ij*d*. To Elyzabethe, mye wyffe, mye hows that I dwell [in] with the purtenans longyng thertoo unto the tyme that Gylbderde mye son cum to the age of xxj^ti yeres, and then I wyll that the sayde hows with the apurtenans remayn to Gylberde mye son, to hym and hys eyers of his bodye laufullye begotton [remainder to] Thomas and John, mye sons [remainder to] mye ij dowghteres Elyzabethe and Cysylye. To Elyzabethe mye wyfe iij kye and a que with calfe, and iiij mares and mye plowgh. To Gylberd mye son a yong mayr that is in the ferme and a que with calfe. To Thomas mye son a yong felye and a que with calfe. To John mye son a lytyll redd felye and to be burned at next May. To Elyzabethe mye dowghter a payr of flaxin scheyttes and a mattrys, a coverlet and a pyllow. To Cysylye mye dowghter a payr of flaxin scheyttes and a mattrys, a coverlet and a pyllow. To Elyzabethe mye dowghter a pann and a pewter plater, and a candylstycke. To Cysylye mye dowghter a pan, a pewter plater and a candylstycke. To Gylberd mye son a payr of scheyttes and a pyllow. To John mye son a payr of scheyttes and a pyllow. To Thomas mye son a payr of scheyttes and a pyllow. To Gylberd mye son my bylle and mye sadyll and mye brydell. The resydew of all mye goodes I putt them to the dyspocysyon of Elyzabethe mye wyffe, whom I make mye executryx, and Thomas Schepard to be supervisor. Thyes berynge wytnes; Wylliam Bewyk, preist, Wylliam Massaie.

Proved before P at Spalding, 4 March 1533/4.

407. THOMAS STAYNBORN [PARSON OF THORNTON]
      [LCC 1532–34, fos. 244v–245r]

4 February 1533/4. I, Thomas Staynborne, parson of the churche of All Halloys of Thorniton, seke of body and, Jhesu be lovyd, of good and hole remembraunce, makes thys my last will and testament. Fyrste I wyt my soule into the mercyfull handes of my savior Criste Jhesus, and into the handes of Hys blessyd mother Mary, and into the handes of all the angellys and archangellys, and to the holy patryaches and prophetes, appostelles, martyrs, confessors, virgyns, with all the celestyall congregacion of heven, and my body to be buryd in the qwere of All Halloys of Thorneton at the nethermest grese before the high altare, with that thyng that the constitucion determens. To Our Lady of Lincoln viij*d*. I wyt to Our Lady warke of Lincoln xij*d*. To Saynt Anne gylde iiij*d*. To St. Crystofore iiij*d*. I wyt to the churche warke of All Halloys of Thorneton xx*d*. To the churche warke of Owresby

viij*d*. To the high altare of the same iiij*d*. To Kyrkbe churche viij*d*. To Kynyerby churche viij*d*. To Ussylby churche iiij*d*, and to St. Margaret of the same iiij*d*. To the high altare of Claxby viij*d*, and to the churche warke of the same viij*d*. To the churche of Kelsay Marie xij*d*, and to the high altare of the same xij*d*. To the high altare of Kelsay Nicholes iiij*d*. To the churche warke of the same iiij*d*, and to Saynt Nicholes light of the same iiij*d*. To Our Lady light of north ile in Kelsay Marie iiij*d*. To Our Lady churche off Wadyngham iiij*d*. To the high altare of the same viij*d*. To Saynt Peter churche in the same towne iiij*d*. To the church warkes of Snetterby xx*d*, and to the church warkes of Byshop Norton iiij*d*. To John Watson ij yong oxyn, that is to say a blacke and a belde broune, and ij sterys of iij yere olde of my awne brede, ij mylke kye, that is to say a redde flekyd and a blake flecte, and a yereyng qwye calve with my gret dunde horse. Also I will that my executors fynde hym all maner of sede a[nd] beanys and barly to saw hys lande. Also I will that they fynde hym breade corne and [fo. 245r] malte corne to the laste sheyff be in. Moreover I will that they pay May Day rent nexte cumyng, that is to say, ix*s*. To the sayd John Watson ij plowe yokes tyryrd, ij teamys, a plough, a gret wane and lyttyll and gere for iij horse to drawe in, and a nepe yoke. To Elizabeth Doket my mayd x*l*. To John Smyth my servant a yowe and a lamme and a yereyng qwye calve. To Catheryne my mayd a yow lamme and to Jenet my mayd a yow lamme. To John Page and to every one of my godchylder a yow lamme. To Elizabeth Thomson my goddoughter my basyn and my ewer. I will that my executors delyver unto her assignes xx^{ty} gymers new clyppyd, one of her awn unclyppyd, a yowe and a lamme unclypyd. To my brother Christofer iij*s* iiij*d*, and to syster Catheryne and to her chyldren vj*s* viij*d*. To Thomas Westroppe a yeryng calve. I wyt to my lady of Cottom and her systers vj*s* viij*d* to pray for me. To my lady of Irforthe and her systers v*s*. To my lady of Goquell and her systers v*s* to pray for me. I wyt to the Austyn Frerys of Grymmesby xij*s* for doyng a trentall of messes at Scala Celi within themselffe for my soule and for my nexte frendes' soulys, and for all Crysten soulys. To the Gray Frerys of Grymmesby for a messe and a dirige ij*s*. To the prior of the Gresfote[153] in Lincoln and hys brether for doyng a obyt aftyr my dethe iij*s* iiij*d*. To Our Lady Frerys in Lincoln for a obbyt doyng iij*s* iiij*d*. The resydue of my goodes I gyff to Umfray Redde, John Wryght of Thorneton and Christofer Cater of Owresby, whom I make my executors. And I gyff to every one of them x*s* for ther pane and labor. I make Sir William Askugh, knyght, supervisor. I will that he take acownte bothe of proffyt and expenses. Thes persons beyng wytnes; Sir Robert Clerke, William Browne, Robert Page, with other. To the sayd Sir William Askugh, knyght, for hys labor, ij oxen. To my lady hys wyff a dunde horsse.

Proved before P, 13 March 1533/4. Adm. granted to the executors.

408.   THOMAS BOWTHE [OF MAVIS ENDERBY]
       [LCC 1532–34, fo. 261]

6 February 1533/4. I, Thomas Bowithe of Malvis Henderby, husbandman, of a hole mynde and good remembraunce, makes thys my laste will and testament. Fyrste I bequethe my soule to allmyghtty God, to Our Lady St. Mary, and to all the fare cumpeny of angellys in heven. My body to be buryed in the churcheyerde of the

---

[153] 'Grayfriars'.

blessyd archaungell St. Michel at Enderby. To the high altare in the same churche for tithes forgottyn xij*d*. To the sepulcre light iiij*d*. To the roode light viij*d*. To Our Lady light iiij*d*. To St. John light iiij*d*. To All Halloys' light and All Saulys' light iiij*d*. To Our Lady [fo. 261v] at our mother churche in Lincoln vj*d*. To Our Lady warke in the same churche vj*d*. To the churche warke of Enderby xiij*s* iiij*d*. To the bellys in the same xij*d*. To Ratheby churche iij*s* iiij*d*. To Wester Kele churche iiij*d*. To Bollyngbroke churche iiij*d*. To Lusby churche iiij*d*. To Hagworthyngham church iiij*d*. To the iiij orders of frerys at Boston, ich order of them, xij*d*. To my iij chyldren Richerde, Robert and Lion, ich one of them when they cum to the age of xx^ty yeres, a wane or ellys viij*s*, one cople of oxen of iiij yeres of age, one mare off iij or iiij yeres of age, one cowe and one qwye, xx^ty schepe, a potte and a panne, and to ichon of them a bed. Yff any of my forsayd chylder dye or they cum to that age, they that be lyffyng to have the parte or partes of hym or of them so departyng or dying, and so ich on of them to be other heyres. And yff so be that they all thre dye or they cum to the forsayd yeres, then I will that the moste parte of all the goodes and catall bequest unto my chyldren to be solde, and done in charytable warkes for me and them, and for all my good frendes ded or alyve. To Jenet Bowyth my kynswoman ij kye and a borlyng, xij schepe, her awne schepe to be rekenyd emonges thes xij, ij beddes, a potte and a panne, a lyttyll kettyll, a posnet, iiij pewter dooblers, a whyet chyste and a chare. To Margaret Bray my syster her May Day rent. To Agnes my syster iiij*s*. To Richerde Bowthe of Bollyngbroke a bushyll rye, a bushyll malte and a bushyll of barly, and ij schepe. To John Wathe ij schepe. To Margaret Wallys one qwye of iij yeres of age and iiij schepe. The resydue of my goodes I gyff to Helene my wyff and John Holteby, whome I make my executors. And the sayd John Holteby to have for hys labor x*s*. And also John Bowys to be the supervisor, and he to have for that x*s*. Thes wytnesses; Mr. George Lilborne, parsone of the same towne, Jamys Dodys, Thomas Tuln, Robert Holteby, Richerde Bowthe, with other mo.

Proved before P at Spilsby, 5 May 1534.

409. SIR THOMAS CLYFF [OF HACCONBY]
[LCC 1532–34, fos. 238v–239r]

7 February 1533/4. I, Sir Thomas Clyff, preste, makyth thys my last will and testament. Fyrste I bequethe my soule to allmyghtty God and to Our Blessyd Lady St. Mary, and to all the cumpeny of heven. My body to be buryed in the qwere of St. Andro in Hacconby churche. I gyff in oblacion to the blessyd sacrament in the same churche iij*s* iiij*d*. To Our Lady of Lincoln in oblacion iiij*d*, and to Our Lady warkes iiij*d*. To the fatherles chyldren xij*d*. To the light of the blessyd sepulcre xij*d*. To the light of St. Andro xij*d*. To the light of Our Lady a taper of waxe. To the plugh [fo. 239r] light iiij*d*. To All Saulys' light iiij*d*. To the light of St. Thomas vj*d*. To Our Lady of Stenwhet xx*d*. To the reparacion of the bellys iiij*s*. To the ladys off Sempyngham halffe a dosyn sylver sponys and a mazer. To Henry Boston vj*s* viij*d*. To Thomas Pell vj*s* viij*d*. To Mawde Aswayll a cowe with a calve and iiij schepe, a brasse potte, a coverlyd, a spytte and a pare of cobbardes. To Isabell Clapole a qwe of ij yere olde. To Elizabeth Carter a candylstycke. The resydue of my goodes unbequethyd I will it be vertuosly disposyd for the helthe of my soule at the discrescion of Henry Boston and

Thomas Pell, whome I make my executors. Thes wytnesses; Thomas Clapole, William Clerke, Richerde Auger, wyth other mo.

Proved before P at Lincoln, 13 February 1533/4, by the executors.

410.   AGNES TEMPESTE [OF GOSBERTON]
        [LCC 1532–34, fos. 127v–128r]

7 February 1533/4. I, Agnes Tempast, wyddowe, of the parysshe of Gosberkyrke, holl of mynde and in perfyte remembraunce, makes mye last will and testamentt. The fyrst I gyve mye soull to allmyghttye God and to Hys blessyd moder Sayntt Marye, and to all the holye companye of heven, and I wyll my bodye be buryed in the churche of the holye apostylles Peter and Pall in Gosberkyrke. To the hye alter for mye tythys forgotten iiijd. To the reparacion of the same alter ijd. To everye alter in the same churche ijd. To everye lyghtt in the same churche ijd. To the churche werke ijd. To everye gylde in the seyd churche ijd. To the gylde hall one pewter charger. To the offerynge of Ower Ladye of Lyncolln ijd, and one hye beddes of lambur with one rynge of sylver and gyltt. To the pore chyldern of Seyntt Cateryn's ijd. I wyll that mye executors aftyr mye bereall cawse ij trentalles of masses to be celebrated att ower Lady's aulter for mye husbande's soule, mye soule and all Crysten sowlles within the space of one yere after my decease. Thys is the last wyll of me the forsayd Agnes, mayd the yere and daye before namyd. Fyrst I wyll that Alys Humpe, the dowghter of Roberde Humpe, have my best gown reversyd with velvett and lyned with Seyntt Thomas worsted, mye blacke worstyd kyrtyll, mye beddes of whyte albur, one tache of syllver and gyltt manylet, mye triangyll with iiij pypys of sylver thereto perteynynge, also one feder bedd and ij coverchers, mye coverynge of tapstre worke, one blacke chyst, one spruce cofer, one redd chyst with iiij pare of flaxin scheyttes and ij pare of myngtow scheyttes, one greatt schete of iiij webes with a blacke seym, on whytt terstor, one dyaper towyll, one flaxin towyll, ij flaxin borde clothes, vj dyaper napkyns, vj lynnyn napkyns, ij velvett patlettes, one sersnett neckende, vj pillowes of the best with theyre coverynges, vj pweter platers, vj pewter dysscheys, iij bras candylstyckes of the best, vj pewter podyngers of the best, one chafyng dyssche and mye best brasse pott. I wyll that the forseyd Alys have all the forsayd goodes and reymentt delyvered hur at the day of hur maryage, or, if so fortune the seyd Alys be nott maryed, I will that sche have all the forseyd goodes and reymentt delyvered hur be Roberde mye sun or hys assygners when sche cumys to the age of xxti yeres. And if the seyd Alys dye or sche cum to the state of maryage or of the age of xxti yeres, then I wyll that the forseyd goodes remayn to Rose Humpe, syster to the seyd Alys at the forsayd age. And if so fortune Alys Humpe and Rose her syster decease bothe or they cum to the forseyd terme of xxti yeres, as God deffend, then I wyll that all the forseyd goodes remayn to Roberde Humpe mye sun, to dyspose theym for mye sowle as he shall best devyse. To Rose Humpe, dowghtter of Roberde Humpe, one feder bed, one pare scheyttes, ij pillowys, one coverlett and one dyaper towell, and I wyll that the seyd Rose have the forsayd stuffe when sche cumys to the state of maryage or of the age of xxti yeres. And iff the seyd Rose dye or sche cum to the forseyd state, then I wyll that the seyd goodes remayn to Roberde [fo. 128r] mye son, to dyspose theym for mye sowle as he schall best devyse. To Mr. Thomas Tempast esquyer, to be good

mayster to mye son, mye best feder bed butt one, exceptt with a bolster, one pare of flaxin scheyttes, one dyaper tabeyllclothe, one latyn candylstycke, the whytche hyngithe in the hall. To Mistrys Tempast hys wyffe mye best kerchyffe. The resydew of mye goodes, I gyve theym to Roberde mye son to dyspose for mye sowll and all Crysten sowlles, and I wyll that Mr. Thomas Tempast esquier and Roberde Humpe mye son be mye executores, for to se and to performe thys mye last wyll, to paye mye deyttes and to brynge mye bodye to the grownde. Theys berynge wytnes; Sir Henrye Topplys, preist, Wylliam Gayst, Wylliam Scottun, Gylys Foster, Thomas Longe, wythe other moo.

Proved before P at Swineshead, 5 March 1533/4.

411. HUGH WYLKYNSON [OF ST. PAUL IN THE BAILEY, LINCOLN]
[LCC 1534 &c., fo. 9r]

7 February 1533/4. I, Hugh Wylkynson, barber in the paryshe of St. Paule in the Bale of Lincoln, makes my testament and last will. Firste I gyff my soule to God allmyghtty and my body to be buryed in the churche of the sayd St. Pauly's. To the repare and upholdyng of the foresayd churche viijd. To the high altare of our mother churche in Lincoln iiijd. To our parson my curate to pray for me ijs. The resydue of my goodes not gyffyn I gyff to Jenet my wyff and my sonnys Robert and Anthony, whome I make my executors (my dettes payd) to dispose, rule and order them as shall be the most plesure to God allmyghtty and my soule helthe, with oversight and helpe of Sir John Lamme, and I gyff hym for hys attendance, helpe and forderaunce vs. Thes beryng wytnes; Sir John Hudson, my curate, Thomas Wyloon, John Dowse and other mo.

Proved before P at Lincoln, 25 February 1534. Adm. of the goods was committed to the executrix, reserving power to grant to the other two executors when they shall come.

412. JOAN BERNE [OF GOSBERTON]
[LCC 1532-34, fos. 138v-139r]

10 February 1533/4. I, Jenet Berne, vido of the paryshe of Gosberton, beyng in good mynde and of a perfecte remembraunce, makes my last will and testament. Fyrste I bequethe my soule to allmyghtty God and to Hys blessyd mother St. Mary, and to all the holly cumpeny of heven, and my body to be buryd in the churcheyerde of St. Peter and St. Paule within the paryshe of Gosberton. To the high altare for my tithys forgottyn vjd. To the reparacion of every altare in the same churche ijd. To every light in the same churche ijd. To every gylde ijd. To the [fo. 139r] gyldehalle, one pewter platter. To the churche warke xijd. To Our Lady offeryng of Lincoln iijd. To the chyldren of St. Catheryn's ijd. To the high altare of Gosberton my beste kerchyff to make a corporax of, and one towyll. To Anne Berne one yowe with her lamme, one coverlyd and all the goodes and stuff, the which I receyvyd with the sayd Anne. To Catheryne Remy, doughter of William Remy, ij brasse pottes, iij puter platters, one puter dyshe, one candylstyk, one pare schetes, one pillo, one coverlyd, one towyll, my beste gowne and my best kyrtyll. The resydue of all my goodes ungyven and not bequethyd, I gyff them frely to Simon Ganesburgh my sun, to be my true executor, to dispose for the helthe of my

soule as he shall thynk and devyse the best. Thes wytnes; Sir Henry Toplys, Robert Dethe, John Vassell, with other mo.

Proved before P at Swineshead, 5 March 1533/4.

413.   ROBERT SHAKYLTON [OF ST. PETER IN EASTGATE, LINCOLN]
        [LCC 1532–34, fo. 269r]

10 February 1533/4. I, Robert Shakylton of Lincoln, of the paryshe of St. Peter in Estgate, makyth my laste will. Fyrste I bequethe my soule to God allmyghtty, to Our Lady St. Mary and to all the saintes in heven, and my body to be buryd in the churche of St. Peter in Estgate. To the highe altare of our mother churche of Lincoln xij*d*. To Our Lady's warkes of the same xij*d*. To the high altare of St. Peter in Estgate for forgottyn tithys xij*d*. To the clerkes' gylde xij*d*. To every order of frerys within the citie of Lincoln xij*d*. The resydue of my goodes not bequethyd I gyff to Agnes my wyff and Edwarde Shakylton my brother, whome I make my executors to dispose for the helthe of my soule as they thynke best, gyffyng my brother Edwarde for hys labor xl*s*. Those beryng wytnes; William Mylner, Richerde Drowry, John Laurence and Raphe Kyrkby, with other mo. To Robert Kyrkby my godsun a yowe schepe.

Proved before P at Lincoln, 15 May 1534.

414.   ROBERT DAWSON [OF ROXHOLME IN PARISH OF LEASING-
        HAM]
        [LCC 1532–34, fo. 276r]

12 February 1533/4. I, Robert Dawson of Roxham in the paryshe of Lessyngham, hole in mynde and goode in remembraunce, makes my testament and laste will. Firste I bequethe my soule to allmyghtty God, to Our Blessyd Lady St. Mary, and to all the holy cumpeny in heven, and my body to be buryd in the churcheyerde of St. Andro of the sayd Lessyngham. To the high altare of the sayd Lessyngham iij*s* iiij*d*. To the reparacions of Our Lady warke in the cathedrall churche of Lincoln xij*d*. To the churche of the sayd Lessyngham one cowe to that intent that the churchewardons for tyme beyng gyff at the mariage of every mayd, the day of her mariages that she is maryd in the sayd churche of Lessyngham, iiij*d*. The resydue of my goodes not gyffen I gyff to Johanne Dawson my wyff, whome I make the executrix to that intent my sayd wyff Johanne Dawson kepe my chyldren of my goodes to they be of lawfull age. And yff it so fortune that my sayd wyffe Johan Dawson mary before all my chyldren be at laufull age, then I will that all suche goodes that she hathe at suche tyme that she makes contracte with eny man to be devydyd in ij partes, and that my sayd wyffe, Johanne Dawson, have the one halffe of my sayd goodes, and that the other halffe of my goodes be devydyd by equall porcions to every one of my sayd chyldren, John Dawson, Robert Dawson, Mathewe Dawson, Alice Dawson, Beatrice Dawson, Elizabetto Dawson, Emote Dawson and Isabell Dawson. I will that William Atwell of the sayd Lessyngham have the orderyng of the goodes of my sayd chyldren yff so be that my sayd wyff Johanne Dawson fortune to mary before my sayd chylder be of lawfull age. I make the sayd William Atwell the supervisor, and he to have for hys panystakyng xx*d*. Thes beyng wytnesses; Sir John Grene, the parsone of the northe parte of the sayd

Lessyngham, and Sir Christofer Hochynson, the parsone of the southe parte,[154] with other mo.

Proved before P at Sleaford, 20 May 1534.

415. **WALTER WYSTED [OF CARLTON LE MOORLAND]**
[LCC 1532–34, fo. 247v]

12 February 1533/4. I, Walter Wysted, of hole mynde and good remembraunce, makes my testament. Fyrste I bequethe my soule to God omnipotent and to Our Lady St. Mary and to all the saintes in heven, and my body to be buryd in the churcheyerde of Our Lady of Carleton in Morelande and for my mortuary as the lawe will give it. To the high altare of Carleton iiijd. To the same churche for [to] fynde a light before the rode iijs iiijd. To Our Lady of Lincoln warke iiijd. To every order of frerys in Lincoln iiijd. To Thurlby churche iiijd. To Stragylthorpe churche iiijd. To Bassyngham churche vjd. To Helene my doughter one yowe and a lamme. To Thomas Everyngham hys chylder a yowe and a lamme. To Agnes Coke a lamme. The resydue of my goodes I gyff to Agnes my wyff and Richerde my sun, whome I make my executors that they may dispose it for the helthe of my soule. Also I will my sun be supervisor. Thes beyng wytnes; Mr. John Dysney of Carleton aforesayd, gent[leman], Sir John Marshall, vicar of the towne, and Sir Rayff Lee, preste, with other mo.

Proved before P at Lincoln, 24 March 1533/4.

416. **JOHN WHITE [OF PINCHBECK]**
[LCC 1532–34, fos. 135v–136r]

15 February 1533/4. I, John Whyte of Pynchbek, goode of mynde and remembraunce, makes my last will. Fyrste I bequethe my soule to God allmyghtty, to Our Lady St. Mary and to all the saintes in heven, and my body to be buryd in the churcheyerde of Pynchbek. To the high altare ther for tithys and oblacions forgottyn xijd. To every altare in the sayd churche of Pynchbek vjd. To Our Lady gylde of Pynchbek iiijd. To the churche warke of Lincoln vjd. To the fatherles and motherles chyldren beyng at St. Catheryn's withowt the wallys of Lincoln vjd. I will ther be disposyd at my buryall day to prestes, clerkes and to pore people xs. I will ther be sung a trentall of messes for my soule and all Christen soulys, and the preste to have for hys labor xs. To every godchylde that I have a lamme. To my doughter Margaret [fo. 136r] xxiijs iiijd, a cowe, viij schepe, that is to say fyve yowes and iij hogges, and they to be delyveryd at May Day with all the proffytes, that is to say wolle and lamme, ij brasse pottes, a chyste beyng above the garret, a bras panne, a candylstyk, ij puter platters, fyve puter dishes, ij sawssers, a pare of schetes, a flaxyn and a hardyn. To Elizabeth my doughter a cow, sexe yowes and they to be delyveryd at May Day with the proffyttes off wolle and lamme, ij brasse pottes, a kettyll, a bras pan, a candylstyk, ij puter platters, fyve puter dyshes, ij sawssers, ij schetes, a flaxyn and a hardyn, and iijs iiijd. The resydue of all my goodes not gyffyn

---

[154] The division of parishes into two or more cures was not uncommon in the later medieval and early modern period, some parish churches maintaining separate portions for congregations from different parts of the same parish: G. Rosser, 'Parochial Conformity and Popular Religion in Late Medieval England', *TRHS*, 6th ser., 1 (1991), 173–89.

I gyff them to Helene my wyffe, whome I make my true executrix with the supervision of Andro Williamson, and he to have for hys labor vj*s* viij*d*. Thes beyng wytnes; Thomas Hyll, preste, William Toche, Robert Slator, Thomas Hall, Thomas Hode, William Frenton, with other mo.

Proved before P at Spalding, 4 March 1533/4.

417.   RICHARD BLAKYT [OF BARDNEY]
        [LCC 1532–34, fo. 268r]

16 February 1533/4. I, Richerde Blakyt off Bardeney, hole of mynde and good memory, makes thys my last will. Fyrste I bequethe my soule to God, Our Lady and to all saintes in heven, and my body to be buryed in the parysh churche garth of Bardeney. To the high altare of Our Blessyd Lady of Lincoln iiij*d*. To the Trinite gylde of Bardeney xij*d*. To Richerde Blaket my sun a cowe and a yowe and her lamme. To Jenet Blaket a cowe, one yowe and her lamme. To Margaret Blakct a cowe, one yowe and her lamme. To my lorde off Bardeney iij*s* iiij*d*. The resydue of my goodes I gyff to Isobell Blaket my wyff, to bryng up my chylder and to dispose for the helthe of my soule and all my good frendes soulys. Thes wytnes; Sir Edmunde Watson, vicar, Thomas Hochenson, George Brantyngham, with other.

Proved before P at Wragby, 9 May 1534.

418.   RICHARD FRESTON [OF ASHBY PUERORUM]
        [LCC 1532–34, fo. 257r]

16 February 1533/4. I, Richerde Freston of Ashby Puerorum, of hole mynde and memory, make my testament and laste will. Fyrste I bequethe my soule unto God allmyghtty and to Our Blessyd Lady St. Mary, and to all the holy cumpeny of heven, and my body to be buryd in the churcheyerde of St. Andro in Ashby Puerorum. To the high altare in the same churche iiij*d*. To the sepulcre light in the churche aforesayd viij*d*. To Our Blessyd Lady of Lincoln iiij*d*. To the red arke iiij*d*. To Salmonby churche iiij*d*. To my mother a schepe. To John Beke my brother a schepe. To Elizabethe Beke a schepe. My dettes payd and brought to the grounde, I bequethe unto Agnes my wyffe ij partes of my goodes, and my chyldren the thurde parte of my goodes truly departyd. I will that my wyffe have the kepyng of the thurde parte of my goodes unto the tyme that my chyldren cum unto the age off xiiij yeres, every one of them. And yff it so be that she go unto mariage, then I will that he that shall marry her and she shall fynde sufficient suerty unto John Thewe, Thomas Thewe and John Beke by obligacion that the goodes shall be forthecumyng unto the use of the sayd chyldren, or ellys to delyver the sayd goodes unto them. I make Agnes my wyffe my executrix, that she may dispose my goodes to the plesure of God as she thynkes best. Thes beryng wytnes; Sir Robert Glover, vicar of Ashby Puerorum, Thomas Thewe, John Beke, Steven Anker, with other mo.

Proved before P at Horncastle, 4 May 1534.

419. WILLIAM EDWARDE [OF ST. MARTIN'S, LINCOLN]
[LCC 1532–34, fo. 301]

17 February 1533/4. I, William Edwarde, barber and fishmonger of the paryshe of St. Martyn in the citie of Lincoln, ordens and makes thys my last will and testament. Fyrst I gyff and bequethe my soule to God allmyghtty, Our Lady St. Mary and to all the holy cumpeny of heven. My body to be buryd in my paryshe of St. Martyn within Lincoln. To my paryshe churche warke vj*s* viij*d.* Also I do compounde with my gostely father for my privy tithys thys yere past, and to pray for me I gyff hym vj*s* viij*d.* To Our Lady warke in Lincoln iiij*d.* To the clerke gylde in Lincoln a sylver spone. Also I will at my buryall, and at suche tyme as my assygners may convenyently, that they dispose for my soule in suffrage of the churche and in almys dedes to pore people of my goodes xl*s.* The resydue of my goodes I gyff to Isabell my wiff and to the helpe and bryngyng up of Anne my doughter, whiche Isabell I make my executrix, to dispose my goodes as she thynkes most expedyent for helthe of bothe our soulys. I make Richerde Wyndebanke, my wyff brother, supervisor, and I [fo. 301v] gyff hym for hys labor my best gowne. Wytnes heroff; Sir Nicholes Kendall, vicar and my gostely father, John Beke, Alan Walkeman, with many other mo.
Proved before P at Lincoln, 19 June 1534.

420. WILLIAM ALPHYN [OF PINCHBECK]
[LCC 1532–34, fo. 241]

18 February 1533/4, 25 Henry VIII. I, Wylliam Alphyn of Pynchebeke, beyng of hole mynd and in perfyte remembraunce, makes thys my last wyll and testament. Fyrst I bequeth my sowle to God allmyghtty, to Our Lady Sent Mary, and to all the company of heven, and my body to be be buryd in the churche off Pynchebek in the quere of Sent Peter in the same churche. To the hye alter in the same churche for tythes forgotton, iij*s* iiij*d.* To every other alter in the sayd churche iiij*d.* To Our Lady of Lincoln viij*d.* To the pore chyldarne of Sent Kateryn's withowt Lincoln iiij*d.* As concernyng the ordre and dysposycion off my landes and tenementes, fre and copyehold, I geve them as hereafter folowyth. To Jenyt my wyffe one acre and a half of fre land lyeng in Bullen with the appurtynances and one rode of ground called the Blechyng Plott with th'appurtenances, to hyr and to hyr assygns duryng hyr lyffe. Also my howse that I dwell in with th'appurtenances and nyne acres of land and pasture with th'appurtenances in Pynchebeke, wherof viij acres lyethe under my sayd howse, and on acre lyethe nye Crowstow, tow acres of medow lyeng in Lowgayt, sex acres of arrable land lyeng in hye feld, and halff a acre of wode ground called Lyffe's Pyngle with th'appurtenances lying ther and all other my copyehold land, medew and pasture in Pynchbek, holden of my lord prior of Spaldyng, to hyr and to hyr assigns duryng hyr lyffe, kepyng the seyd howse in lawfull reparacyon. And after the decesse of the sayd Jenyt my wyffe, I wyll that Rychard Harlwyn, my godson, shall have the sayd ij acres of medow with th'appurtenances in Lawgayt, to hym and to hys heires and assign after the custome of the maner of my seyd lord prior of Spaldyng. I wyll that after the decesse of the seid Jenet my wyffe, the seid acre and halff, and one rode of fre land shall remayn to Robert Alphyn my brother, to hys heyers and assignes forever. I wyll that also after hyr deceasse the seyd howse

that I dwell in, and all other the seyd copyehold land and pasture unbequethed, remayn to the said Robert my brother, to hys heyrs and assignes accordyng to the custome of the seid maner. I wyll that after the deceasse of the seid Jenet my wyffe, in consideracion of the seid gyft and bequest to Robert my brother made, as well of my copyehold as of my fre land, that he shall yerely kepe a obyt of fyve shyllynges by the yere for the terme of xx^{ti} yers within the seyd churche of Pynchbek for the helth of my soule, my fryndes and benefactors souls, and all Crysten souls. I wyll that a honest prest shall syng one yere in the seyd church of Pynchebek att the alter of Sent Peter, and pray for my soule, my fryndes and benefactors soules, and all Crysten souls, and he to have for hys stypend viij markes. To Jenet my wyffe all my howshold stuff and all my corne, and all my goodes and catellys that shalbe within my howse or ground the day of my decesse. [fo. 241v] The resydew of my goodes I put to the ordre of the seid Jenet my wyffe and of Wylliam Cole of Mylthorp, whome I mayk my executors with the ayde of Robert Alphyn, whome I mayk the supervisor, and the said Wylliam Cole and Robert Alphyn to have every of them for ther labor vj$s$ viij$d$. To the reparacions of the belles xx$d$. Thyes wyttnes; Sir Wylliam Bewyk, prest, John Claer and John Thomson, and other mo. I, the seid Wylliam Alphyn, surrender into the handes of John Claer, a tenant of my lord prior of Spaldyng, of hys lordshyp in Pynchebek, my howse that I dwell in and all other my copyehold land, medow and pasture holden of my seid lord prior, to surrender into the lorde's handes to the behove of my seyd wyffe duryng hyr lyffe, and after hyr deceasse to the behove of the seyd my last wyll and testament, in the presens of Rychard North and Wylliam Belle.

Proved before P at Spalding, 4 March 1533/4.

421.   GEORGE BROWNE [ALDERMAN OF THE CITY OF LINCOLN]
         [LCC 1532–34, fo. 249v]

21 February 1533/4. I, George Browne, alderman of the citie of Lincoln, seke of body and hole of mynde, thynkyng my laste howre in thys miserable worlde to drawe ny, makyth my testament and laste will. Fyrste I bequethe my soule to allmyghtty God, to Our Lady St. Mary, and all the holly cumpeny of heven, and my body to be buryd in the churche of St. Laurence in Lincoln. To Our Lady warkes in Lincoln mynster xij$d$. To every house of the iiij orders of frerys in Lincoln xx$d$. To a preste vl to syng one hole yere for my soule and all ther soulys whome I am bounde to pray for, and for all Crysten soulys. To the clerke gylde iij$s$ iiij$d$ to say every yere aftyr dynner one *Pater Noster* and *Ave* for my soule and all Crysten soulys. To the chyldren of Robert Howes my sun-in-lawe iij$l$, whiche the sayd Robert Howes awythe me, and besyde I bequethe to every chylde of the sayd Robert Howes xx$d$. The resydue of my goodes I will be devydyd into iij partes, of the whiche I bequethe one parte to Elizabeth my wyffe, and another parte of them to Edwarde my sun, and I will that the other iijrd parte of the same iij partes shall be bestowyd in payment of my dettes and legaces, or otherwyse disposyd for my souly's helthe as my sayd wyffe thynkyst best accordyng to good conscience, the whiche Elizabeth my wyffe and Edwarde my sun I make myn executors. And also I make Mr. Robert Alanson, alderman of the sayd Lincoln, supervisor. Thes beyng wytnes; the sayd Mr. Robert Alanson, Sir Jamys Gyll,

preste, the sayd Mr. Alanson wyffe, the wyffe of Jamys Goodknape of Lincoln aforesayd, with other mo.

Proved before P at Lincoln, 31 March 1534. Adm. granted to Elizabeth, the relict and executor, reserving power to grant to Edward Browne, the son and co-executor being now an infant.

422.   ROBERT GREVE [OF ROPSLEY]
        [LCC 1532–34, fo. 336r]

21 February 1533/4. I, Robert Greve of Roppeslay, hole of mynde and good of remembraunce, makyth my will and last testament. Fyrste I bequethe my soule unto allmyghtty God, Our Lady St. Mary and to all the saintes of heven, and my body to be buryd in the churche of Roppeslay. To the high altare of Roppeslay a wether. To the same churche ij ewes. To Our Lady's warke of Lincoln xijd. To every one off my foure chyldren v schepe. To my syster Elizabethe ij ewes. To the parson of Sapperton a wether. To Sir William Jarcoke a wether. To Richerde Rawlynson iij seme barly. I will that ther be v messes of Scala Celi, to be done for the helthe of my soule, and a trentall of messes. To Nicholes Hecoppe. The resydue of my goodes I gyff to Margarete Greve my wyff, whome I do make myn executrix, and my brother Master Richerde Greve to be supervisor, to se that thes thynges be disposyd for the helthe of my soule. Hiis testibus; Thoma Warde, Willielmo Spragyn et domino Willielmo Jarcoke.

Proved before P at Ancaster, 29 October 1534.

423.   WILLIAM WALTON [OF CUMBERWORTH]
        [LCC 1532–34, fo. 267r]

22 February 1533/4. I, William Walton of Comberworthe, hole of mynde and goode remembraunce, makes thys my last will and testament. Fyrste I bequethe my soule to God allmyghtty and to Our Lady St. Mary and to all the saintes in heven, and my body to be buryed in the churcheyerde of St. Helene in Comberworthe, and it to be my mortuary that the law requiryth. To Our Lady warke of Lincoln xvjd. To the churche of St. Helene in Comberworthe viijd. To the high altare in the churche of St. Helene in Comberworthe viijd. To Anthony my sun a too yere olde fely and a sheder calffe of thys yere, a jerkyn and my worsted dooblet. I will that Jane my wyff have my lande the terme of her lyffe. To Thomas Bower a gymer, a lamme and my kendall cote. To William Bower my bukskyn dooblet. To the abbot of Hawnby xijd, and every prest beyng brother in the house of Hawnby iiijd, and to every novys ijd. The resydue of my goodes not wyt and bequethyd, I bequethe them to Jane my wyffe to helpe my chylder withall. I will that Willum Herdman the elder and Jane my wyff be my trew executors, and the sayd William to have for hys labor ijs. Wytnesses; Thomas Herdman, Robert Grayff, William Penson.

Proved before P at Alford, 7 May 1534.

424.   HENRY HUDSON [OF LEVERTON]
       [LCC 1532–34, fo. 130v]

24 February 1533/4. I, Henry Hudson of Leverton, single man, hole myndyd and of gud memory, makes my testament concludyng therin my last wyll. Fyrst I bequeyth my saule to God almyghty, to Hys mother Sanct Mary and to all Hys sanctes in hevyn, and my body to be beryed in the churcheyard of Sanct Helene in Leverton. To the honowrmenttes of the holy sacrament and the hyght alter ij*d*. To the honowrmenttes of the other ij alterse in the sayd churche iiij*d*. To the honowrmenttes off Sanct Helene iiij*d*. Also for tythyng and oblacions forgotton iiij*d*. To the honowrmenttes of Oure Lady of the Flour[155] and Our Lady of Grace iiij*d*. To Our Lady of Pety j*d*. To Our Lady's warkes of Lincoln iiij*d*, and to the fatherlesse chyldryn att Sanct Katerin's without Lincoln ij*d*. To the churche warkes of Leverton xx*d*. To Mawid Belle iij yewis and iij lames, iij schepe hogges, on yong cow, on bald mare and iiij yardys and a halff of violet cloythe, also xx*s* to be payd to heyr or her assygners within on ycre after my decesse or soner yff she be maryed within this yer. To Wylliam Hudson on gamar. To Jenyt hys dowter on yowe lame. To Margaret Hudson on yowe. To Isabell my syster on yewe hogge. To Thomas Hudson myne old horsse and my plowght. The resydew of my gudys I gyff it to Thomas Hudson my broder whome I make myne executor, to dyspose it to the plesure of God as it is most nedeful for the helth of my sowle and all Crysten souls. Theis wyttnes; Sir John Fendyke the yonger, pariche prest, John Bell, John Bennett, John Lownd, Rychard Taylyar and Thomas Baxster, with other mo.
       Proved before P at Boston, 3 March 1533/4.

425.   THOMAS KENDALE [OF STENIGOT]
       [LCC 1532–34, fos. 259v–260r]

26 February 1533/4. I, Thomas Kendale of Stanygot, of good remembraunce and of a hole mynde, makyth my will and testament. Fyrste I bequethe my soule to God allmyghtty and to Our Blessyd Lady, and to all the holly cumpeny in heven, and my body to be buryed in the churche of Stanygot. To the high altare in the same churche for forgottyn tithes and oblacions viij*d*. To the same churche to the upholdyng therof and for my buryall iij*s* iiij*d* in money and one quarter of barly. To Our Lady warke in Lincoln viij*d*. To the high altare in the churche of Ashby nexte Horncastle viij*d*. To Wythcall churche iiij*d*. To the Gray Frerys in Grymmesby viij*d*. To the Blake Frerys in Lincoln viij*d*. I will that ther be a trentall of messes sayd within the churche of Stanygot for my soule, my wyff soule and all Christen soulys. To my sun Robert one cople sterys whiche is callyd Swanne and Blithe, also other ij sterys of ij yeres olde and upwarde, also one blake qwye with a whyte hede and a blake [fo. 260r] flekyd qwye, also xx^{ty} schepe, also halffe of all my croppe that is sawne or for to be sawne thys yere. Also my best wane and a plough with all thynges belongyng therto, also a meyr callyd Pen and a fylly and a gret brasse potte. I will that ther be halffe a trentall of messys sayd in Boston churche at the altare of Scala Celi for my soule, my wyffe soule, my father soule, my mother soule and all Christen soulys. To my doughters Jenet and Jane each ij kyne, xx^{ty}

---

[155] The cult of Our Lady of the Flowers was usually associated with fertility, the Spring and harvest.

schepe and iij quarters barly. To Alexander Kendyll one red qwye with a whyte hed. To Alice Quylzer a red qwye of one yere olde and upwarde. To William Adam iiij schepe. To William Marshall iiij schepe. To Edmunde Fresney one schepe. To every one of my godchylder beyng within Stanygot a hogge schepe. To Jenet Fresney a red calve with a whyte hed. To Robert Fresney and hys wyffe one acre of barly and halffe an acre of beens and pease. I will that my brother Robert Kendyll and my sun Robert be my executors, to whome I bequethe, ether of theym, xs for ther labors. I will that my brother Robert Kendyll have the tuicion and governance of my sun Robert and hys porcion to he cum at laufull age, and to order hym as she shall thynke beste for hys proffyt. The resydue of my goodes I will that my brother Robert Kendyll dispose them as he thynkes best for the helthe of my soule and the soulys of my wyffe, my father and mother, and all Christen soulys. Thes men beyng wytnes; Sir Anthony Bennet, curate of Stanygot, John Lokkyng, Edmunde Fresney, Laurence Wyggon, John Hawdon, William Marshall, George Tayllor, with other moy.

 Proved before P at Horncastle, 4 May 1534. Adm. granted to Robert Kendall the brother of the deceased, an executor, Robert Kendall the son and co-executor being under age.

426. ROBERT TURNEPENY [OF EAST ALLINGTON IN PARISH OF SEDGEBROOK]
  [LCC 1532–34, fo. 273v]

26 February 1533/4. I, Robert Turnepeny of Alyngton, beyng in hole mynde, make my testament and last will. Fyrste I bequethe my soule to allmyghtty God, to Our Lady St. Mary and to all the holy cumpeny of heven, and my body to be buryed in the churche of St. Jamys in Alyngton. To the high altare of the same churche iiijd and a stryke of barly. To the Trinite churche of Alyngton a stryke of barly. To Our Lady of Lincoln iiijd. To the frerys of Grantham a bushyll of barly. To Sir John Hollande iiijd. To Stawnton churche viijd. To Sygbroke churche iiijd. To Foston churche iiijd. To Nottyngham brygges iiijd. To Adam my sun too bullokes cally, a fely and a yowe. To John my sun a browne qwye and a yowe. To Agnes my doughter a blacke qwye and a yowe, a coverlyd, a pare of schetys, a brasse potte, a panne. To Jenet my doughter a brown qwye with a calve, a yowe, a hogge lamme, a coverlyt, a pare of schetes, a brasse potte, a panne. To Margaret my doughter a flekyd qwye calve, a yow, a coverlyt, a pare of schetys, a panne. The resydue of my goodes I will that they remane in the handes of my wyff, and she to make and dispose for me and for the helthe of my soule as she thynkes the best, and I make her my executrix, and Thomas Newcome of Gunwardeby to be supervisor. Thes bere wytnes; Sir John Hollande, William Richeman, Richerde Mason, and the foresayd William and Richerde to have xijd to be good to my wyff, and to se that my chyldren be orderyd by her.

 Proved before P at Ancaster, 18 May 1534. Adm. granted to the executrix.

427.   RICHARD GRYME [OF SOUTH FERRIBY]
        [LCC 1532–34, fos. 251v–252r]

1 March 1533/4. I, Richerde Gryme of Ferybe in the countie of Lincoln, hole of
mynde and good remembraunce, makyth thys my testament and last will. Fyrst I
gyff and bequethe my soule unto allmyghtty God, to Our Lady St. Mary and to
all the holly cumpeny in heven. My body to be buryd in the churcheyerde of St.
Nicholes of [fo. 252r] Feryby. To the high altare of the same for tithys forgottyn
viijd. To Our Lady's warke of Lincoln xijd. To the reparacions of the churche of
St. Nicholes aforsayd a quarter barly. To the upholdyng of the brydge over
Ancolm halffe a quarter barly. To Margarete my doughter vjl xiijs iiijd. To John
Maxa a quarter barly and a yowe lambe. To Richerde Maxa halffe a quarter barly
and a yowe lambe. To every godchylde of myne a pecke wheate, to be delyveryd
at Crystenmes nexte. To the chylder that John Gawdby and my doughter hath ij
yowe schepe callyd qymbers. To the chylder that Edwarde Pennyll and my
doughter hathe ij yowe schepe of the same age. To Thomas Fenby, sone of
Walter Fenby, a yowe. The reste of my goodes not bequethyd nor wyt I gyff to
Alson my wyff, to Thomas my sun, preste, and to John my sun, whome I make
my executors so that Alyson my wyffe shall have rule and governance of all
goodes that was myne for terme of her lyffe, as of the house that I dwell in, and of
a lytyll house with a close holdyn of St. Mary Abbay besyde Yorke. And the other
fermeholde that I dyd holde of the same abbay, I will that my sun John have it so
sun as it shall fortune hym to be maryd. And aftyr the decesse of my wyffe, the
foresayd John to have the indenturys of the yeres yff they be not expiryd of all the
housys with all my wanys and other stuff perteynyng to husbandry. Thes men
beyng wytnesses; Sir George Bayn, William Thorpe and Gefferay Atkynson. The
day and yere above wryttyn.

        Proved before P at Lincoln, 3 May 1534. Adm. granted to Thomas Gryme,
        the natural son of the deceased, one of the executors reserving power to
        grant administration to the two co-executors, when they shall come.

428.   ROBERT SOUTHE [OF FIRSBY]
        [LCC 1532–34, fo. 266]

1 March 1533/4. I, Robert Southe of Frysby, of hole mynde and good memory
beyng, makes my last will. Fyrst I bequethe my soule to allmyghtty God, Our Lady
St. Mary and to all the saintes in heven. My body to be buryd in the churchyerde of
the appostle St. Andro of Frysby aforesayd. To Our Lady of Lincoln xijd. To the
good roode in the Frere Austyns in Boston xijd. To the high altare in Frysby
churche for tithys forgottyn xijd. I bequethe xs to fynde a light for ever more in
Frysby churche [fo. 266v] to be light in tyme of service. To vj townes vjs for to be
delte unto the moste nedefull people in every towne, that is to say to Frysby xijd,
Gret Stepyng xijd, Candelesby xijd, Gunby xijd, Braytofte xijd, Irby xijd. To Willum
Southe my sun ij sterys of ij yere olde and a blake mare with a colte fole by her syde,
and a baye fylly of thre yere olde and sex schepe. To Julyan my doughter a cowe
and iiij schepe. To Isabell my doughter a cowe and iiij schepe. To Crystyn my
doughter a cowe and a qwye and vj schepe. To Willum Cowper a schepe, and to hys
wyff another. To the same Willum Cowper, my father-in-lawe, my best cote. To
Crystyn Yngson a schepe, and to George her sun a lamme. To Robert Southwell a

schepe and hys wyff another. To Julyan Pentryke a schepe. To Robert Watson a schepe. Every man and woman to marke ther owne parte within iiij days aftyr the burying of me, Robert Sowthe, and so to rest with the executor to the feste of St. Botulphe nexte aftyr foloyng.[156] And then every man and woman to have ther parte delyveryd. The resydue of all my goodes not gyffyn nor bequethyd, I put them to the disposicion of Jenet my wyff whome I make myne executrix. And also Sir Willum Prestman, parson of Frysby, to be the supervisor, and he to have for hys labor vjs viijd. In wytnes to thys my last will; Willum Cowper, Walter Ingson, John Harre and John Whyte.

Proved before P at Partney, 6 May 1534.

429. ROGER WILLYNGTON [OF TYDD ST. MARY]
[LCC 1532–34, fo. 296]

1 March 1533/4. I, Roger Wyllyngton off Tyd Saynt Mary, off hole mynd and memory, mayk my wyll and testament. Fyrst I bequeth my sowll unto almyghty God, Our Blessyd Lady and unto all the holy company off hevyn, and my body to be beryed within the church off Sanct Mary aforsayd. To the hye alter for my tithes forgottyn iijs iiijd. To every lyght off the saym church jd. To Our Lady off Lyncoln iiijd. To the fatherles chylder off the hows off Saynt Katerin's ther ijd. To Thomas Wyllyngton my eldyst son, on hows in whych I dwell in when he cumyth unto lawfull age. To Herre Wyllyngton my son, my hows nye the church with ij acres land pertanyng therunto. To Robert Wyllyngton my son, my hows agaynst the crosse in the way that goyth to the church, so that on be another heyr yff any off them dye withowt chylder off ther bodyes lawfully begotyn, so that yff it forton the aforsayd my childer mayll to dy withowt yssuy, than I wyll the sayd tenementes with ther appurtenauns unto Margret my doghter duryng hyr natrall lyeff. And affter hyr decesse, to be sowld by the handes of Christofer Gybson, prest, or elles by the handes off the wardenes off the church aforsayd and the mone theroff to be desposyd in charytabyll deydes within the sayd church and parysh off Tyd for the heylth off my sowl and all Crystyn sowlles: provydyd alway that Johan my wyff have the profett theroff untyll such tyme that my chylder cum at lawfull age yff that she do suffycient reparacion theroff within a yeir after she have lawfull warnyng by Christofer Gybson, prest, or, in hys absens, by the churchwardenes off Tyd aforsayd. Or elles, in the defaut that sche do nott hyr dewte in reparyng the saym tenementes, I wyll the aforsayd Christofer Gybson, or, in hys absens, the churchwardens aforsayd, retayn and seyse into their handes the sayd tenementes and profettes theroff for the only suffycient reparacion theroff, untyll succh tyme that my chylder cum unto lawfull age. To Johan my wyff. To every on off my chylder on bullok off the price off an nobyll, at succh tyme as cume unto lawfull age. And also unto every on off them v ews, so that after the decese off any off them that are onlyff. I wyll, after the decese off Johan my wyff, my chylder to have all my howshold stuff, or elles the price theroff as it is prasyd within myn inventory. [fo. 296v] The resydew off my goodes nott bequeth I gyff unto Johan my wyff, she to despoyse tham as she shall [th]ynk meyt for hyr neydfull supportacion and helth off my sowll. Thes wyttnes;

[156] 17 June.

John Hutiston, Rycherd Fyssher, prest, and Christofer Gybson, prest and parson therof. The yeer and day abowff sayd.

Christofer Gybson.

Proved before P at Spalding, 9 June 1534.

430. ROBERT TYLLYNG [OF GREAT GONERBY]
[LCC 1532–34, fo. 274r]

3 March 1533/4. I, Roberd Tyllyng off Gunnerbe within the dioces off Lyncolne, holl off memory, make thys my last testament. Fyrst I bequythe my sall to almygty God, to Owr Lady Sant Mary and to all the holy compeny off hevyn, and my body to be beryd at Our Lade's awter end in the sowthe syd off Gunnerbe cherche. To the hy awter off the same cherche xx*d*. To the vycar off Grantham to pray ffor my sall vj*s* viij*d*. To Owr Lady's warke off Lyncoln xij*d*. To on syngular pryst to syng and pray ffor my ffader sall and ffor my moder sall, and ffor my sall, for on yer servys, v*l*. To the ffrers off Grantham to pray ffor my sall x*s*. To the same place off ffrers ffor the spas off vij yers, every yer halffe a seme barly or els ij*s* off mony. To Wylliam Weslhede xx schepe. To Alyse hyse dowther ij seme off mawlt and on cowe. To the chylder off Roberd Tyllyng x schepe. To Wylliam Dobbulday xx schep. To Annas Clarke one seme off mawlt. I gyffe for on westment to Gunnerbe cherche x*l*. To Allyce Wamslay one seme off mawlt. To Wylliam Tyllyng ij oxun, on hors and on maer, also on bun wayn or els xvj*s*. To John Tyllyng my servand on seme malt and on calve. The resydew off my goodes I gyff to Margarett my wyffe, and sche to dysspoys ffor the welthe off my sall as sche dowthe thynke most best with the consell off hyr ffrendes, the wych Margarett I dowe make my executryx and Wylliam Wesselehede and Wylliam Dobbulday to be with hyr and to helpe hyr at all tymes off ned as my trust ys in them. Wyttnes off thys my last testament; Mathu Gybbonson, pryst off Gunnerby, Thomas Myller, John Roper and Rychard Scheperd, with oder mo.

Proved before P at Ancaster, 18 May 1534.

431. SIR ROBERT BARTYLMEW [PARSON OF ASHBY CUM FENBY]
[LCC 1532–34, fos. 246v–247v]

7 March 1533/4. I, Robert Bartylmew, parson of Ashby, hole of mynde and remembraunce, make my laste will. In primis I wyt and commyt my soule to allmyghtty God, the father, the sonne and the holy goste, and all the holly cumpeny in heven. My body to be buryd in the chauncell of the paryshe kyrke of Ashby aforesayd. To the high altare of Lincoln xx*d*. To the redde arke xx*d*. To Burgherse Chauntry vj*s* viij*d* [th]at they may pray for my soule and for the soule of Sir John [fo. 247r] Thomson, Sir John Shawe, Sir Henry Kyrkbe, Sir Roger Weldyng, Sir Robert Pacoke, Sir William Gaske and Sir William Flowre, sumtyme bretherne in the sayd chauntry and my good masters.[157] To the churche warke of Kyrton in

---

[157] The Burghershe chantry had been founded by Bartholomew, Henry and Robert Burghershe in 1340 to maintain five chaplains to pray for the souls of the founders and Edward III, as well as to support six poor boys at grammar school between the ages of seven and sixteen. By 1548, when the chantry certificates were compiled, the chaplains were paid £8 each. The altar of St. Catherine, providing the focus for the chantry, stood in the north-east corner of the choir in Lincoln Cathedral: Chantry Certificates (1923), 207.

Lyndesay vj*s* viij*d*. To the churche warke of Broughton iij*s* iiij*d*. To the churche warke of Reysby vj*s* viij*d*. To the convente of the house of Thorneholme vj*s* viij*d*. To the convent of the house of Gokewell vj*s* viij*d*. To Robert Bartylmew, sun of John Bartylmew and Anne, x*l* for suche goodes as I had of hys father and mother to hys bryngyng up. And yf it fortune the sayd Robert to dye before he comme to lawfull age, then that [th]at is lefte of the sayd x*l* to be waryd of a preste to celebrate messe and pray for the soulys of John and Anne, father and mother to the sayd Robert. To John Stokes xxvj*s* viij*d* under thys condicion, that infefte[158] and possesse Alice hys wyffe in and of hys tenement in Keydbe towne and felde for terme of her lyffe, ellys no peny he to have. To Agnes Walker a fether bed that I ly on with schetes, blankyttes, bolsters, pilloys, coverlyttes, with also a cownter that standes at my beddes seyt. To Robert Lanam a qwyl, a matteres and a dyaper towell. To Emme Popell, my syster-in-law and servant, a cowe, a quarter of wheate, a quarter of bredcorne and a quarter off malte, and ij bakon flyckes and a beyff flyke, and all the reste of my housholde stuff within dorys, as beddyng, coverlyttes, coverynges, mattereses, schetes, pilloys, bolsters, pottes, pannys, puter vessell, all maner stuffe, excepte vj sylver sponys and my rayment. I wyt iiij*l* to be waryd on a vestiment to Ashby kyrke. I will that Sir James Wylson have owt hys yere wagys aftyr vij markes and xl*d* to pray for the soulys of John and Alice, my father and mother. I will that the sayd Sir James have a draught of sermonde matters conteynyd in vj bokes called *sermones pomerii*.[159] To Stephyn Bartylmewe ij yong oxyn whiche William Panton hase in kepyng, also xx*s* dettes whiche Edwarde Cotes owyth to me. To Peter Dodylls my servant ij lyttyll sterys, one with a redde starre in the heade, another with a white heade, a gray horse and a sterne mare, a wayn and a ploughe with all thynges belongyng to them, with iryn harrowe, a colter, a quarter of wheate, a quarter of barly, a quarter off beanys and pease. To Robert Bette a yowe. To Robert Walker a yowe and a lamme. I will that Sir Christofer Askewgh and Dame Elizabeth hys wyff have all suche lande as belongyth to me of my parsonage, and whiche also I holde of the sayd Sir Christofer and Mr. Wymbushe, sawn with wheate, beanys [fo. 247v] and barly of my costes and chargeys, for that he shall be goode master and helper to my executors, whome I make Sir Thomas Blaxstone, parson of Cokewolde, and Sir Robert Lanam, chaplande, that they may dispose the resydue of my goodes as they thynke beste to the helthe of my soule. Thes beyng wytnes; Sir Jamys Wylson, Sir Robert Westerby, parson of Randall, parson of Howerby with Beysby, Sir Thomas Warde, parson of Hatclyff.

Proved before P at Lincoln, 17 March 1533/4, by the executors.

432.   JOHN HELLERBE [OF PANTON]
        [LCC 1532–34, fos. 267v–268r]

11 March 1533/4. I, John Hellerbe of Panton, off an hole mynde, makyth my last will and testament. Fyrste I bequethe my soule to allmyghtty God, Our Lady St. Mary, and to all the saintes of heven. My body to be buryd in the churcheyerde of St. Andro of Panton, my mortuary aftyr the custome of the province. To the high altare of Panton vj*d*. To Our Lady warke of Lincoln iiij*d*. To Jenet my doughter ij

---

[158] 'Enfeoffed'.
[159] Temesvari Pelbart, *Sermones Pomerii de Sanctis Hyemales et Estivales*. There were several editions between 1498 and 1507.

qwyes [fo. 268r] and x schepe. I will the chylde that is in the moder wombe have one of the qwyes and v of the x schepe yff so be that it lyff. And yff it dye then Johanne my doughter to injoy bothe the qwyes and the x schepe. The resydue of my goodes I gyff to Catheryne Hellerbe my wyff, whome I make my executrix to dispose for the helthe of my soule and all Christen soulys. Wytnessyth of the same; John Felde-house, preste, John Copper, Richer Ellerby, William Barkewyth.

Proved before P at Wragby, 9 May 1534.

433.   HUMPHREY ORDYNG [OF KIRTON IN HOLLAND]
         [LCC 1532–34, fos. 298v–299r]

12 March 1533/4. I, Humfride Ordyng of Kyrton in Holande, of hole mynde and goode remembraunce, makyth my testament concludyng with my last will. Fyrst I bequethe my soule to God allmyghtty, Our Lady St. Mary and all the celestiall cumpeny of heven, and my body to be buryd in the churche of the holly appostellys Peter [and] [fo. 299r] Paule of Kyrton before namyd. For my mortuary aftyr the kyng['s] statutes. To the high altare of Kyrton for tithes negligent viijd, and to the iij Mares' altare iiijd. To every altare in the sayd churche ijd. To Our Lady of Lincoln iiijd. To the orphans of St. Catheryn's ijd. To the reparacion of the sayd churche of Kyrton my yong bayd geldyng. I will ther be disposyd for the helthe of my soule at my buryall day vjs viijd, at my seventh day vs, and at my trigintall day vs. To Jenet my syster ij mylke kye with ther calvys and one browne mare with a yeryng at her fole. To John Hoberde one brandyll burlyng. To William Hobarde a browne burlyng. To Margaret Hoberde and Elizabeth, either of them one ewe. To William Ordyng ij of my nexte beste kye and one qwe of ij yere olde, fyve ewes and ther lammes. To Robert Ordyng iiij yong qwyes of iij yeres olde vj ewes and ther lammys. I will a tabyll, ij formys, a chare and shelffe remane in my hed mansion. The resydue of my housholde stuff I gyff to Jenet Hoberde, excepte that the sayd my syster doughters have ij brasse pottes, to the elder the lesser, to the yonger the byger. To William Donington my blake cote. To Jenet Hoberde one qwye. I will that one browne qwye be equally devydyd in iiij partes to the iiij orders of frerys at the tyme of Crystenmes nexte cumyng. I will that one marbyll stone be bought be my executor and my supervisor to ly one my father hys grave and myne, the price xiijs iiijd. I will that myn unkyll John Hoode have vjs viijd to helpe my executor to get my dettes. The resydue of my goodes not wyt nor bequethyd, I gyff them to Thomas Hoberde, whome I make my executor to dispose my goodes to the moste plesure of God and helthe of my soule. And I will that Simon Jakson be supervisor, and to have for hys labor vjs viijd. Of the whiche the ensewyng beryng wytnes; Sir John Cowper, John Hoode, yoman, Richard Gelson, Humfride Heylande, John Foxe and Simon Jakson, with other.

Proved before P at Boston, 10 June 1534, by the executor.

434.   JOHN RICHERDES [OF MORTON]
         [LCC 1532–34, fo. 275v]

13 March 1533/4. I, John Richerdes in Morton, hole of mynde and of perfyte memory, make and orden thys my testament and last will. Firste I bequethe my soule to allmyghtty God, to Our Lady St. Mary and to all the cumpeny of heven.

My body to be buryd in the churcheyerde of Morton. And to the high altare I bequethe for my tithys negligently forgottyn viij*d*. To Our Lady light in Morton viij*d*. To the Trinite gylde one bushyll of barly. To St. George gylde one stryke of barly. To the byng of a chalys in the churche of Morton xij*d*. To the churche of Lincoln xij*d*. To the orphans of St. Catheryn's viij*d*. To St. Laurence chapell in Hermethorpe iiij*d*. To Our Lady's chapell of Steintwhaite iiij*d*. To the bellys of Morton xij*d*. To the sepulcre light of Morton iiij*d*. I will my executor do kepe yerely an obbyt for me in the churche of Morton, and to bestowe therat iijs iiij*d*, wherof I will the vicare have iiij*d* for diriges, the clerke ij*d*, the bead rolle iiij*d*, and to offer for every soule of my frendes in the bead rolle namyd the same day j*d*. And the resydue of thes iijs iiij*d* to be bestowyd at the will of my executor whome I name Adam Richerdes, my sun, to whome I gyff the resydue of my goodes unbequethyd. And I make Henry Boston and William Beckyngham my supervisors. Thes beyng wytnes; John Townsende the elder and Sir Henry Anderson, vicare of Morton, with other mo. And to the sayd my supervisors I gyff iijs iiij*d* to ether of them.

Proved before P at Irnham, 19 May 1534.

435.   JOHN HYKSON [OF FRAMPTON]
        [LCC 1532–34, fos. 287v–288r]

15 March 1533/4. I, John Hykson of Frampton, of good mynde and remembraunce beyng, makyth my testament with my last will. First I bequethe my soule to God, Hys mother Our Lady St. Mary and all [the] cumpeny of heven, and my body to be buryd in the churcheyerde of Our Lady of Frampton. To the high altare of Frampton for tithys forgottyn xij*d*. To Our Lady gylde of Frampton one yowe and iiij*d*, when she is clyppyd. To every altare in the sayd churche ij*d*. To the bellys iiij*d*. To Our Lady box of Lincoln iiij*d*. To the orphans of St. Catheryn's withowt the wallys of Lincoln ij*d*. To Agnes my wyff fyve mylke kye and vj fen kye with ther calvys, iiij bullokes, vj burlynges, v merys of the best with plough and carte, x yowys and x lammys, and ther be so many at clyppyng tyme. I will that all my housholde stuff be equally devydyd betwyxte Agnes my wyff and Anne my doughter. To Anne my doughter x yowes and x lammys, and ther be so many and ij mylke kye and ther [fo. 288r] calves, iiij fen kye and ther calves, one gray meyr with a starre in her forhed and iiij*l* sterlyng in money. To John Cater, my wyffe sun, ij kye and ther calves, one bay stag and one lytyll blak nag, ij yowe hogges in wooll. I will that my mother have x*s* payd at iij tymes, that is to say at the feste of St. Michellmesse, Cristynmesse and May Day, and my russyt cote. To my godchyldren, every one of them, xij*d*. To Catheryne Ordyng, my syster doughter, xij*d*. I will have iij*l* to be waryd in iij days in the churche of Frampton, that is to say, at my burying, vij day and xxx^ty day. The resydue of all my goodes not bequethyd I put to the disposicion of Agnes my wyff whome I make my executrix, for to dispose for my soule as she thynkyth moste beste, to the plesure of God and the helthe of my soule. Thes beyng wytnes; Sir John Lee, preste, John Powlys, Thomas Browne and many mo. I make John Powlys supervisor.

Proved before P at Swineshead, 8 June 1534.

436.   JOAN WARNER [OF BOSTON]
[LCC 1532–34, fo. 245v]

15 March 1533/4. I, Jenet Warnar of Boston, of hole mynd and gud remem-brance, makes my testament and last will. Fyrst I bequeythe my soule to God and to Oure Ladye Saynct Ma[r]y and to all the celestyall company of hevyn, and my body to be buryed in the churchyerde of the holye confessore Saynt Botulphe, and for my mortuary as the law dothe require. To the high altare of Sent Botulphe for forgotton tyethes vj*d*. To the gyld of vij martars iiij*d*. To the reparacions of oure moder churche of Lincoln iiij*d*. To Sent Kateryn's wythowt the walles of Lincoln ij*d*. To Thomas Lemyng a blak hamblyng fylly and iiij yardes of flaxin clothe. To Hals my syster a cowe and a gowne and a kyrtyll, bothe blak. To Elisabeth Wylsall my best kyrcheffe and a ryng. To Margarett Beneson my goddowghter a flaxin shete and a hardyne kutt out of the webe. To Mawde my goddowghter a flaxin shete and a hardyne. To Alis Thorneton a whyt bakkyd cowe, the best brasse pott and the best bason, and a yowe and a feder bed with a bolster, and a hole bed as it standes, a rosset gowne and a red kyrtyll. To Agnes Waryner a whyt bakkid shedere calffe, a pott and a basene, a platere and a punedysche, a flaxyne shete and a hardyng. To Jenet Symson a yong cowe. To Agnes Rydere a bed as it standys, a pott next the best and a basyne. To Wylliam Huetson a flaxine sherte and a hardyne. To John Therlbeke wyffe my best gowne. The resydew of my goodys I gyve to Wylliam Halle, whome I make my executor. I wyll that John Ferman be my supervisor, and he to have for hys labor iij*s* iiij*d*. Thes wytnessyth; Wylliam Kellett, John Jugge, Wylliam Rottesey, John Wylly, with other mo.

Proved before P at Lincoln, 15 March 1533/4.

437.   STEPHEN CHAPMAN [OF SKILLINGTON]
[D&C 1534–59, fos. 21v–22r]

17 March 1533/4. I, Stephyn Chapman, hole of mynde, make and orden my last will. I bequethe my soule to allmyghtty God and to Our Blessyd Lady and to all the cumpeny in heven, and my body to be buryed in the churcheyerde of St. Andro in Skyllyngton. To the mother churche of Lincoln iiij*d*. To the high altare in Skyllyngton iiij*d*. To my gostly father xx*d*. To the paryshe churche in Skyllyngton vj*s* viij*d*, and the best schepe that I have. To the churche of Skyllyngton iij*s* iiij*d* to by a banner clothe. To the churche of Stoke a schepe. To the churche of Colsterworthe xij*d*. To the churche of Bukmynster xij*d*. To Raphe Typler and hys wyff and hys chylder xvj schepe. To Raphe Typler a wane bounde with yren. To John Typler junior a table and ij trestyllys and ij cupbordes, and the sayd John besyde to stande to the rewarde of my wyff. For the welthe of my soule to every person within the town of Skyllyngton, pore and riche, to every person a peny. To a preste to say halffe a trentall v*s*. To the cuntry, [fo. 22r] as many as commys, to every person [a halfpenny], love and drynke. I will that my wyffe kepe my yere day as long as she lyffys. Aftyr the decesse of my wyffe, I gyff to the churche of Skyllyngton a good cowe. The rest of my goodes I gyff to Margaret my wyff, whome I make my executor and William Geny with her. And the sayd William Geny to have well for hys labor. And the sayd Margaret my wyffe and William Geny to dispose my goodes for the welthe of my soule and my wyffe's as they shall answer

before God. In wytnes hereof my laste will; Master Vicare, John Geny, Robert Gage, Richard Hunton, wyth other mo.

Proved before the Dean and Chapter, 4 October 1534. Adm. granted to the executor.

438. EDWARD MAKWORTHE [PARSON OF ST. JOHN'S, STAMFORD] [LCC 1534 &c., fo. 4]

17 March 1533/4. I, Edwarde Makworthe, parson of St. John the Baptist paryshe in Stamforde, beyng off hole mynde and good remembraunce, make my testament and last will. Firste I bequethe my soule to allmyghtty God, to Our Lady St. Mary and to all the holy cumpeny of heven, and my body to be buryd in the chauncell there. To the sayd churche x*s*. To the chapiter yerly iij*s* iiij*d* to be payd yerely owt of the house in Peter paryshe in Stamforde, whiche house was myne and now is in the handes of Thomas Greneham of Ketton, gentylman. I wyll that the deane of Stamforde and hys bretherne shall kepe yerely myn obyt in St. John churche wher my body shall lye aftyr the laudable custome of the chapiter ther. And yff the sayd iij*s* iiij*d* be behynde in ony yere unpayd, then I will that the deane and hys bretherne shall enter into the foresayd [fo. 4v] house and distrayn, and the distress so takyn to be praysyd and solde and put to the sayd use of the chapiter. To Our Lady of Lincoln vj*d*, also to every curate off Stamforde, institute and inducte aftyr the custome usyd ther. I will that the prior of the Blak Frerys shall have aftyr the same maner. The resydue of my goodes not bequethyd I put to the disposicion of Mr. George Makworthe of Empyngham, esqwyer, and Mr. Thomas Greneham, gentylmam, whome I orden and make myn executors of thys my testament and last will, for to dispose them to the plesur of God and helthe of my soule. Thes beryng wytnes; Mr. Thomas Wytham, notary.

Proved before P at Stamford, 27 January 1534/5. Adm. granted to Thomas Greneham, an executor, reserving power to grant to George Makworthe, gentleman, the co-executor, when he shall come.

439. JOAN GOSSHOK [OF INGOLDMELLS] [LCC 1532–34, fo. 269v]

18 March 1533/4. I, Johanna Gosshok of Yngoldmels, with hole mynd and gud remembraunce, makes my testament and last wyll. Fyrst I bequeythe my sowlle to God, to Our Lady Saynt Mary, and to all the company in hevyn, and my body to be buryed in the churche of Sanct Peter and Pawle in Yngoldmells, and to my mortuary as the law has admyttyd. To Owr Lady of Lincoln to the hyght auter vj*d*. To Our Lady wark vj*d*. To the hyghe auter of Sanct Peter and Pawle in Yngoldmels viij*d*. To the ij syed auters, ether of them, vj*d*, and to the churche warkes xiij*s* iiij*d*. To the remenyng[160] of the organs xx*d*. To the churche one gret arke, and to the gylde of Our Lady one gret pott, on pan, on meteclothe of v yardes, iiij puter doblers. To Sanct Leonard chapell of Mumbe, to the reparyng of the same, xx*d*. To my syster Augnes Laysby one feder bed, one coverlyd, one pare of lynen shetes, my best aprone, my best bonyt, my best kyrcheff and my cloke. To Robert

---

[160] Read 'renewing'.

Reryng one feder bed, one coverlyd, one pare of lyne schetes, ij pelows, one bras pott, one pane, ij candylstykes, one towell, one meteclothe, the hede hangyng in the chaymber, a qwe, one yow, one hogg, one chayr, one chyst and halff on led. To John Heryng one materys, one coverlyd, one pare of lyne schetes, one pelow, one pott of bras and one qwe. To hys wyff on sangwyn kyrtyll. To Johan hys wyffe dowghtter one yow. To Water hys son one calff. To Margyt hys dowghtter on murry gown and one bras pott of one galawnde. To Jamys Skygnes on mettable with the trestylls that it standys on and vjs viijd. To Robert Skygnes one pare of malt qwarnys and one chyst. To Margaryt Srcryvener one sangwyn kyrtyll, and to Agnes Scryvener one sangwyn gowne. To Water Fendyll vjs viijd. To Agnes Glasanbe one blew gowne. To John Bally one materys, one coverlyd, one pare of schetes, one pelow, and to hys wyffe one smok. To Alyson Laverok one materys, one coverlyd, one pare of lyne schetes, one pelow, one puter dobblere, one basyng and one pane. To Margaryt Dalond one materys, one pare of schetes, one pelow, ij yowes. To John Gypson and to Rychard Gypson v yardes lyne clothe to mak ether of them one schete. To John Gypson wyffe one hoode and one aprone clothe, and to Alyson Gypson hys dowghter as myche cloth as to make her one pare schetes. To Rychard Gypson wyffe one kyrcheffe. To Mald Thore one pare of beddys and to John Thore one hogg. To Elizabeth Skygnes on sylkyn schet. To Sir John Barkworthe one pare of lyne schetes. To Mald Gatlay one yow, and to my goddowghter at Wylliam Olyvery's one puter dobbler. To Thomas Gye one schet clothe and one old bras pot. To Agnes Heryng one sangwyn gowne and one aprone clothe. To Yssabell Thore my harvest knyffe. To Alyson Trew one agnus dei. To Mald Laverok one aprone cloth. To Sybyll West one yard of clothe. To Betrex Flescher one vale. To every on of my godchylder vjd. To iiij power men for beryng me to the churche, every on of them, iiijd. The resydew of my guddys I put to the dyspocityon of Sir Nycholas Sarrotte, parson of Yngoldmels, and Wylliam Thore and John Laysbe, whome I mayk my executors, and mayster parson to have for hys labor viijs and Wylliam Thore and John Laysbe, ether of them, on sylver spone and vjs viijd. Wytnes; Sir John Barkworth. John Gypson, Wylliam Gatlay, with other moo.

Proved before P at Partney, 6 May 1534. Adm. granted to the executors.

440.   ROBERT MARSHALL [OF KIRTON IN HOLLAND]
       [LCC 1532-34, fo. 288v]

18 March 1533/4. I, Robert Marschall of Kyrton in Hollande, of hole mynde and good memory, makes my testament wherin is concludyd my last will. Fyrste I bequethe my soule to God allmyghtty and to Our Lady St. Mary and all the celestiall cumpeny of heven, and my body to be buryd in the churchyerde of the holy appostellys Peter and Paule in the sayd towne of Kyrton. To the sacrament of the high altare in the same churche for tithys forgottyn iiijd. To Our Lady of Lincoln ijd. To the fatherles chyldren of St. Catheryn's ijd. To Jenet Marshall my doughter a burlyng calve, a yowe and a lamme. To Agnes Fowlle my wyffe's doughter a hog schepe. The resydue of my goodes not gyffyn nor bequethyd I gyff to Cecyll Marshall my wyff, who I make my executrix to dispose to the honor of God and to pay my dettes to the welthe of my soule and all Christen soulys, of the whiche thes be testes; Sir John Cowper, Philip Clay, Nicholes Glost, with other mo.

Proved before P at Swineshead, 8 June 1534.

441. WILLIAM MORE [OF GRANTHAM]
[LCC 1532–34, fo. 303v]

18 March 1533/4. I, William More of Grantham, of hole mynde and good remembraunce, make my testament and last wyll. Fyrste I bequethe my soule to allmyghtty God, Our Lady St. Mary and to Hys saintes. My body to be buryd in the paryshe churche of St. Vulfram in Grantham. I bequethe to the churche and my lying ther, and to the churche warke, x schepe, of the whiche x I will fyve of them shall be weders and fyve ewes with fyve lammys. To the high altare for tythes forgottyn xijd. To Our Lady of Lincoln xijd. To St. Catheryn's in Lincoln iiijd. I will that all the resydue of my goodes shall be devydyd in ij partys. One parte I gyff to Margaret my wyff clerely. The secunde parte to my iiij chylder John More, Robert More, Jenet More, Thomas Cawthorpe, equally to be devydyd emong them. I will that the forsayd chylder, of all ther forsayd partes, do content and pay xiijs iiijd to George Thyrston. I make Margaret my wyff and John More my sun my executors, and William Skynner oversear. Thes beryng wytnes; Sir Richerd Sheperde, Thomas Alyn, alderman, Thomas Leys, with mo.

Proved before P at Lincoln, 19 June 1534.

442. WILLIAM FYLIPSON [OF WORLABY]
[LCC 1532–34, fo. 254]

20 March 1533/4. I, William Fylipson of Worleby nexte Ellesham, hole of mynde and of remembraunce, makes my last will. Fyrste I wyt my soule to allmyghtty God, to Our Lady St. Mary, and to all the sayntes [fo. 254v] in heven, and my body to be buryd in the kyrke garthe of St. Clement of Worletby. To the high altare of Worleby for oblivios tithys vjd. To Worleby kyrke one bushyll barly. To Our Lady of Lincoln iijd, and to Our Lady's warke iijd. The resydue of my goodes I wyt one parte to my wyffe, the secunde parte to my chylder equally, and the thyrde parte to Margaret my wyff and Robert my sun, whome I make my executors that they may dispose it to the plesure of allmyghtty God and helthe of our soulys. Thes wytnesses; Sir Robert Halton, vicar ibidem, Edwarde Grene, agnebamlus,[161] Thomas Tayllor, cum aliis.

Proved before P at Caistor, 27 April 1534.

443. THOMAS LUFFE [OF DONINGTON IN HOLLAND]
[LCC 1532–34, fo. 287]

[20 March 1533/4] St. Silvester's Day 1533. I, Thomas Luff of Donyngton in Holland, with hole mynde and good remembraunce, make my laste will and testament. Fyrste I bequethe my soule to God my maker, to Hys mother St. Mary and to all saintes, and my body to be buryd in the churcheyerde of Our Lady in Donyngton. I will for my mortuary as the statute limyttes. To the high altare in Donyngton churche for tithys forgottyn xijd. To every altare in the sayd churche iiijd. To every light in the sayd churche ijd. To the churche warke of Donyngton churche vjs viijd. To the reparacion of our mother churche of Lincoln viijd. To the fatherles chyldren at St. Catheryn's withowt the gatys of Lincoln ijd. Thys is my last

---

[161] Possibly 'shepherd'.

will, the day and yere beforesayd. To Robert my sun all my purchesyd landes in Donyngton, to hym, hys heyres and hys assignes. To John my sun all my landes in Pynchbek, to hym and the heyres of hys body laufully [sic] and for defawte of heyres of hys body laufully begottyn, I will that all suche landes os movyd by prestes remayn to Robert my sun and hys heyres of hys body. And all the resydue to remayn to Simon my sun and to hys [sic] of hys body. To Simon my sun all my landes in Spaldyng, Surflet and Gosberton, to hym, hys heyres of hys body laufully begottyn. And for defawte of suche heyres I will that my landes in Spaldyng remayn to John my sun and to hys heyres of hys body laufully begottyn, my landes in Surflete and Gosberton to remayn to Robert my sun and hys heyres of hys body laufully begottyn. To John my sun iij kye to v oolde hys owne, soo viij kye in all, and vj burnynges, vj calvys, fowre to ij on hys owne so vj in all, xx schepe, halff yowes, halff hogges. To Symon my sun iiij kye, vj burnynges and vj calvys, iiij marys to one of hys owne so v in all, xx^{ty} schepe halffe yowes, halff hogges. To John and Simon my sunnys, ether on them a pare schetes, a coverlyd, a bolster, ij pilloys, and ether of them ij brasse pottes, ij brasse pannys, iij puter platters, iij pewter dyshes. To Agnes my doughter a cowe, and to her thre chyldren, every one of them, a calve. To the sayd Agnes a brasse potte and a brasse panne. To Margaret my doughter a bed, a matteres, a pare schetes, a coverlyd, a bolster and ij pilloys, a brasse potte and [fo. 287v] a panne, iij puter platters, iij puter dyshes and xl*s* in money. To the iiij orders of frerys in Boston, to every house of them xij*d*. To Sir Robert Johnson of Byker, preste, vj*s* viij*d*. The resydue of all my goodes I gyff to Agnes my wyff and Robert Luff my sun, whome I make my executors to dispose for my soule and all Christen soules as they thynke best and plesynge to God. And all the remaner to be equally devydyd betwene the sayd Agnes my wyff and Robert my sun by equall porcion and shyfte, to remane to them withowt scropull off conscience. I make Sir Thomas Luff my sun the supervisor, to whome I gyff my best horse. Thes wytnes; Robert Luff, John Kercher, Jamys Blakely, John Felde, Thomas Mayson, Robert Rochester, William Perys, with other mo.

Proved before P at Swineshead, 8 June 1534.

444.   EDMUND MAXSAY [OF BLOXHOLM]
[LCC 1532–34, fos. 277v–278r]

20 March 1533/4. I, Edmunde Maxsay off Bloxham, beyng of good remembraunce, makes my testament. Fyrst I bequethe my soule to allmyghtty God, to Our Lady St. Mary and to all the saintes in heven, and my body to be buryd in the churcheyerde of Our Blessyd Lady of Bloxham beforesayd. To the sepulcre light in the same churche a quarter barly and a pounde waxe. To the same churche of Bloxham ij semys to remayn in the handes of the churchewardens to the best proffyt of the churche. To Robert Borowe a quarter barly. Item, iij semys barly to be mayd in malte, and the sayd malte to be solde and my executors to fynde a preste to syng a trentall of messys for my soule and for the soule of William [fo. 278r] Maxsay my father. To Avice Maxsay and to Agnes Maxsay my systers ij seamys barly. To William Bestrope, William Torner the yonger, George Whyte a halffe seame barly [each]. To Robert Pullay, Emote Pullay, William Torner, Jennet Bennet, John Torner, Richerde Torner, Thomas Torner a schepe [each]. I bequethe the fyve markes that my father bequethyd to me to Jenet Torner my mother and to Avice

Maxsay and to Agnes Maxsay, my systers, that is to say the one hallff to the sayd Jenet my mother and the other halff to the sayd Avice and Agnes my systers. I make William Torner my executor, and he to have for hys labor a halffe seame barly. Thes wytnes; Sir Milys Garnet, parson of the same, William Pullay, George Whyte, John Thorpe, with other moy.

Proved before P at Sleaford, 20 May 1534.

445.   JOHN PARKER [OF SWATON]
        [LCC 1532–34, fo. 275]

21 March 1533/4. I, John Parker, of good mynde and remembraunce, makes my last will. Fyrst I bequethe my soule to God allmyghtty and to the gloriose Virgyn St. Mary Hys mother, and to all the holly cumpeny of heven, and my body to be buryd in the churcheyerde of St. Andro the appostyll in Swaton. To Our Lady warkes in Lincoln xijd. To the pore chyldren of St. Catheryn's in Lincoln xijd. To the high altare in Swaton, for forgottyn tithys, a seame barly. To the paryshe churche of Swaton a seame barly. To the prior of Bryghende, towarde the makyng of the highway, a bushyll barly. To Thomas Salyerde a bushyll barly. To John my sun a blake cowe and a yowe and a lamme. To Stephyn my sun a red cowe and yow and a lamme. To Robert my sun a red qwye and a yowe and a lamme. To Richerde my sun a blake qwye and a yowe and a lamme. To Alice my doughter a qwy with her calve, and a yowe and a lamme. To Jenet my doughter a red qwye and a yowe and a lamme. [fo. 275v] I will that my executors shall cause a trentall of messys to be done for me and all Christen soulys in the paryshe churche in Swaton. The resydue of my goodes not spokyng of before, I gyff to Alice my wyff, and I make Alice my wyff and John my sun my executors that they may dispose my goodes for the helthe of my soule and all Christen soulys. I make Robert Parker my brother the supervisor, and I gyff hym for hys labor xxd.

Proved before P at Irnham, 19 May 1534. Adm. granted to Alice, the relict and executor, reserving power to grant to John the co-executor being an infant.

446.   RICHARD CLAY [OF FRIESTON]
        [LCC 1532–34, fo. 286r]

24 March 1533/4. I, Richerde Clay of Freston in Hollande, of hole mynde and good memory, makyth my testament. Fyrste I bequethe my soule to God allmyghtty, Our Lady St. Mary and all the holy cumpeny of heven, and my body to be buryd in the churche erthe of St. Jamys of Freston. I bequethe to the sacrament iiijd, and to Our Lady of Lincoln ijd. To Alice my wyff ij kye, vj yowes, vj lammys. To Richerd my sun my plough geres and a qwye. To Robert my sun my carte with gere therto belongyng. To John my sun my corte. To Agnes Knotte a burlyng and a horn hoge. To Jenet Rumfer my good doughter a calve. To Alice Clay a whyte calve. To Damme Peter my sun xs for to pray for me. To Thomas Clay a lamme. To Richerde Pedder a lamme. To Thomas Clay a calve. To Thomas Clay my brother iijs iiijd, that he may be supervisor. I will that Alice my wyff, Robert and Richard my sunnys, be my executors, and for to dispose the remanent of my good to the lawe of God and the helthe of my soule as they thynke best.

Thes wytnes; Sir Thomas Pykhall, Thomas Clay, John Wayd, Robert Rumfer, with other mo.

Proved before P at Boston, 10 June 1534.

447.   JOHN HARYSON [OF GOSBERTON]
       [LCC 1532–34, fo. 321]

26 March 1534. I, John Haryson of the paryshe of Gosberton, makes my last will and testament. The fyrste I bequethe my soule to allmyghtty God and my body to be buryd in the churcheyerde of St. Peter and St. Paule in Gosberton. To the high altare for my tithys forgottyn iiij*d*. To the reparacion of every altare in the same churche ij*d* apece. To every gylde ij*d*. To every light ij*d*. To the churche warke iiij*d*. To the reparacion of Our Lady of Lincoln iiij*d*. To the chylder of St. Catheryn's ij*d*. Item, v messys of Scala Celi for my soule and all Christen soulys. To John Haryson my sun my mesuage with eight acres of landc therto perteynyng, to hym, hys heyres, executors or assignes, my plughe and carte with the gerys therto perteynyng, my best brasse potte, my best arke, ij pare shettes, my best cowcher, ij puter dishys, one puter salser, my best brasse panne (one excepte), one flaxyn towell, one bordeclothe, ij kyne, on coverlyt, one bolster, ij pilloys [fo. 321v] one table, one forme, one chare, one pare bedstokes. To Jenet my doughter all the resydue of my housholde stuff, ij kyne, one lyttyll mare. I will that John my sun gyff or cause to be gyffyn to Jenet hys syster, at the day of her maryage, xx*s*. To Thomas Steber of Quadryng iij*s* iiij*d* to helpe John my sun and hys syster. The resydue of my goodes, I gyff them to John my sun to pay for my dettes, to bryng my body to the grounde and to se thys my last will performyd. I will that the foresayd John my sun and the sayd Thomas Stebert be my executors. Thes wytnes; William Thacker, Simon Smyth, Robert Saverye, Robert Fowlle, with other mo.

Proved before P at Swineshead, 8 June 1534. Adm. granted to John Haryson the executor, the said Thomas Stebert, the co-executor, having renounced.

448.   THOMAS WENSLAY [OF GRIMSBY]
       [LCC 1532–34, fos. 330v–331r]

26 March 1534. I, Thomas Wenslay of Grymmesby, beyng in good helthe and good remembraunce, lovyng be to allmyghtty God, makyth my laste will and testament. Fyrste I bequethe my soule to God allmyghtty and to Our Lady St. Mary and to all the cumpeny of heven, and my body to be buryd in Crysten manny's buryall where it shall please God. To the high altare for tithes and offerynges negligently forgottyn and done of St. Jamys' churche v*s*. To Sir Peter Mundy, vicare of St. Jamys' churche v*s* to pray for my soule. To Our Lady's churche in the same Grymmesby iij*s* iiij*d*. To the Augustyne Frerys iij*s* iiij*d*. To the Gray Frerys iij*s* iiij*d*. It is my will that where my body is buryed there shall be delte for my soule xl*s*. To Sir William Laceby whersoever he dwellyth iiij nobyls to pray for my soule the space of iiij yeres, and every yere to have vj*s* viij*d* for hys stipend. I will that all my goodes be prasyd by indifferent persons in thre partes, one parte of my good unto my wyff, the secunde parte geven unto my chyldren, the thyrde parte to be reservyd unto myselve therwith my will to be performyd. And the resydue of the sayd thyrde parte I will that it shall be devydyd in thre partes and so to be geven equally to my iij sonnys

Richerde, Leonerde and Robert. And it so distrybute and knaun, then I will that my wyff shall receyve all ther iij partes under thys condicion, that every chylde, when he goys to prentyschyp, shall receyve halff hys parte and the other parte to remayn with my wyffe ther mother's till they cum to laufull age. And yff it so be that my wyff be maryd agane, then I will that she shall delyver my iij chylder partes, or she be maryd, to William Wenslay my brother sun, and he to have for hys labor xl*s* to be good to my chylder, and he to delyver them ther partes when they cum to laufull age. To my syster Elizabeth v*s*. I will that my wyff shall injoy all my housys and medoys in the town and felde all the tyme of her lyff, and aftyr her decesse I will that it shall be solde and distrybute emong my iij chylder equally, excepte the new house at the haven syde, and that I gyff to Richerde Wenslay my sun and hys heyres. And yff he dye withowt issue, then I will it shall be solde by the mayr and hys xij bretherne, and they to have xl*d* for hys labor. And the sayd money yerely to [be] [fo. 331r] geven to a preste, vj*s* viij*d*, syngyng in St. Jamys' churche to pray for my soule, my frendes' and all Crysten soulys. Also I make my wyff my sole executryx to the performance of thys my last will. The day and yere above wryttyn. Thes wytnes; Sir Peter Munde, vicar of St. Jamys, Sir William Laceby, capellanus, Thomas Challander. Per me Thomam Wynslay.

Proved before P at Grimsby, 20 October 1534.

449.   WILLIAM CHAPELL [OF METHERINGHAM]
        [LCC 1532–34, fo. 294]

27 March 1534. I, William Chapell, hole of mynde and of good memory, make my testament. Fyrste I bequethe my soule to allmyghtty God, to Our Lady and to all the saintes of heven, and my body to be buryd in the churcheyerde of Medryngham. To the high altare for tithys forgottyn xij*d*. To the reparacions of the sayd churche xij*d*. To Our Lady warke of Lincoln xij*d*. To the chanons of Kyme Abbey x*s*, and the sayd chanons to say emonges them a trentall of messes for the helthe of my soule. To Welton churche xij*d*. To Braunceton churche vj*d*. To Richerde my sun vj schepe. To Edmunde my sun a cowe whiche he hays in possession. To Robert my sun a browne fleckyd cowe. To William Bruster, single man dwellyng with my sun Richerde, ij qwyes, one browne of ij yere olde and anoder blacke of one yere olde. To John Chapell, sun to Richerde Chapell, one bay stagge and one calve. To Agnes my mayd [fo. 294v] one yowe. To Thomas Brewster, servant to Richerde Chapell my sun, one yowe. The resydue of my goodes I gyff to Helene my wyff, and I make her my sole executrix. And she, aftyr her decesse, to dispose them aftyr her mynde as she thynkes best for the helthe of her soule and myne. Also I will that Richerde my sun be her ruler and gyder and no executor, but because she is impotent and may not se to do nothyng for herselve nor for me. Wytnes that thys is my last testament; Robert Swanne, Robert Barlynges, Thomas Jakson.

Proved before P at Lincoln, 19 June 1534.

450.   RICHARD BALDWAR [OF GEDNEY FEN]
        [LCC 1532–34, fo. 282v]

30 March 1534. I, Richard Baldwar of Gedney Fen, hole of mynd and of good remembrans beyng, makyth my testament. First I bequeth my solle to God

almyghtye, to Our Ladye Saynt Marie and to all the sayntes of heven. My bodie to be beried in the churcheyard of the Holie Trinyte in Gedney Fen. To the hight altar ther for tythynges and oblacions necligentlie forgotton iiij*d*. To our moder church of Lincoln iiij*d*. To the pore children of Saynt Kateryn's ij*d*. To Johan my wyff iij kyne and a bay fyllye and another blakke, starred, and vj*l* of money to be takyn of dettes, and all my howshold stuff, iiij scheippe and iij lambes and xx*s* of money when my cattell is sold. The residewe of all my cattell I will that myne executor selle them and bryng them to the best prisse betwixe this and Mighelmes, and the money to remayne in ther handes unto the tyme that my children com to the age of xx^{ti} yeres, and then to be devydyd among them by equale porcions. And if any of my children fortune to die before they com to the age of xx yeres, then ther parte that dieth schal be devydid among them that be livyng. And if all my children fortune to die before they com to th'aforsaid age of xx yeres, then I will that the said money schall remayn to the churche reves of Gedney Fen that tyme beyng, and they for to dispose it within the said church wher that thei schall se most neide. I make Johan my wiff and William Walsche senior myne executors with th'oversight of Sir James Here whome I make supervysor, and myn executor to have for ther labor, ich of them, x*s*. Theis beyng wytnesses; William Thyrkyll, Thomas Fischer, Thomas Parkyn, Robert Wilson and John Prevoste, with other moe.

Proved before P at Spalding, 9 June 1534.

### 451.	THOMAS TWELLE [OF WINTHORPE]
[LCC 1532–34, fo. 271r]

31 March 1534. I, Thomas Twelle of Wynthorp, hole of mynd and seke of body, maketh my last wyll and testament. Fyrst I beqweth my sall to the guidance of almyghte God my maker, and my body to be buryed in the churchyerd of Our Blessyd Lady the patronys of Wynthorp. To Our Lady's warke at Lincoln viij*d*. To the hyght auter at Wynthorpe xij*d*. To Sanct Jamys auter in the same churche vj*d*. To Sanct Kateryn auter vj*d*. To the belles viij*d*. To Thomas Pacoke and hys wyffe v*s*. To eche one of hys chyldren iiij*d*. To Elizabeth Twell my syster xl*s* yff it may be born of my guddes. To Betrex Synche of Ostrope iij*s* iiij*d*. To Robert Thore wyffe xx*d*. All other of my guddys I put to orderyng of Sir George Cooke the wycar of Wynthorp and Robert Thore, whome I make my executors to dyspose for my sall and the helth of all my frynddes' salles, other of them havyng for ther labore v*s*. Wytnes; Sir George Cooke, Wylliam Bownd, Robert Thore, John Olyver, Robert Soper, Thomas Pacoke.

Proved before P at Partney, 6 May 1534.

### 452.	ROBERT GAGE [OF SKILLINGTON]
[D&C 1534–59, fo. 21]

1 April 1534. I, Robert Gawge, hole of mynde and memory, make and orden thys my will. I bequethe my soule to allmyghtty God and to Our Blessyd Lady and to all the blesyd cumpeny in heven, and my body to be buryed in the churcheyerde of Skyllyngton dedicate in the honor of St. Andro. To the mother churche of Lincoln iiij*d*. To Our Lady warke in Lincoln ij*d*. To the high altare in Skyllyngton iiij*d*. To the churche of Skyllyngton a quarter of barly. To Our Lady in the southe yle a

quarter of barly. Apon my buryall day, for the helthe of my soule, iiij trentallys. I will that Frere Thomas Harryat have one of them, and Frere John Hussher of the sayd order have another of the sayd trentalles. And the ij trentallys that remayn, I will that they be at the disposicion of my wyffe and my executors. To my vij chylder, every one of them, Gode's blessyng and myne, and every chylde fyve schepe. A cope of the myddylmost bullokes and ij qwyes to be partyd emonges the vij chylder. To Margaret a coffer and a coverlyd and a pare of schetes, a matteres, vjs viijd of money and a new potte and a new panne. Item, ij pottes and a panne to be partyd emonges the vij chylder. The thyrde parte of the croppe thoroweowt to be partyd emonges the vij chylder. To Thomas and John, every of them, a stere. To Thomas a pare off musterde quernys, a hatte and a bagge. The reste of my goodes I gyff to Johanne my wyff, whome I make my executor, and Thomas my sun with her, and with them ij Richerd Mason. And the sayd Richerd to have for hys labor ijs. I make my gostly father and curate master vicare supervisor, to se in every condicion that my will be performyd as my specyall trust is in hym, and as he shall answer in tyme to cum, and the sayd Mr. Vicare to have for hys labor [fo. 21v] ijs. Wytnes; Stephyn a Manton, William Jeny, Richerde Hunton, William Mylner, John Mylnys, with mo.

Proved before Mr. Christopher Massingberde, chancellor, John Pryn, treasurer, and John Talbot, subdean in the choir of the cathedral church of Lincoln, 4 October 1534. Adm. granted to the executor.

453. JOAN LOWNDE [OF DEEPING ST. JAMES]
      [LCC 1532–34, fo. 301r]

1 April 1534. I, Johanne Lownde of Depyng Jamys, vido, make my last testament and will. Fyrste I bequethe my soule to God and to Our Lady St. Mary and to all the cumpeny and felloschip of heven, and my body to be buryed in the churche of the sayd Jamys Depyng and my mortuary aftyr the statute of Ynglande. To the high altare in the sayd Depyng xijd and to the bellys viijd. To the plough light iiijd. To the trelyse lights, iche of them, iiijd. To the churche warke iiijd and to Our Lady gylde vjd. To Our Lady of Lincoln vjd. To Agnes Jakson a browne bulloke and to John Jakson a flekyd bulloke and to iche of them a brasse potte and a panne, and ether of them a gowne and a kyrtyll and ij pare of schetys flaxyn and hardyn and a coverlyd. The resydue of my goodes I gyff them to my sun William Jakson, he to dispose them as he thynkes moste necessary to the plesure of God and welthe of my soule and all Chrsten soulys. Wytnes; Sir Richerde Bucke, vicar, John Pavy, William Coke, with other.

Proved before P at Stamford, 17 June 1534.

454. THOMAS OSSE [OF GOSBERTON]
      [LCC 1532–34, fo. 289]

2 April 1534. I, Thomas Osse of the paryshe of Goberkyrke, beyng hole of mynde and of perfyte remembraunce, dothe make, orden and dispose thys my present testament and last will. Fyrst I bequethe my soule to allmyghtty God and to Our Blessyd Lady St. Mary and to all the holy cumpeny of heven, and my body for to be buryd in the churcheyerde of the holy appostellys St. Peter and St. Paule in

Gosberkyrke. To the high altare of the same churche for my tithys forgottyn or negligently withholden viij*d*. To the reparacion of the same altare ij*d*. To the reparacion of every altare in the church besyde j*d* apece. To every gylde in the same churche ij*d* apece. To the ij gret lighttes, to ether of them j*d* apece. To all Crysten soulys light ij*d*. To the plowe light ij*d*. To the gilde hall one puter dyshe. To Our Lady offeryng of Lincoln ij*d*. To the fatherles chyldren of St. Catheryn's withowt Lincoln walles ij*d*. To Margaret Osse my doughter ij of my best mares, iiij of my beste mylke kye, iiij yowes, iiij lammys, ij hogges, ij arkes and a lytyll chyste. To my mother Agnes Osse one swyne, one yow and my fyrste wyffe's best gowne. To Agnes Osse my syster one cowe calve, one puter dyshe, one table that was Jenet my wiffe's and one olde materes. To Margaret my syster one hogge and one puter dyshe. To John Jarman one hogge. To Robert Jarman one braynelde burnyng qwye. To John Herryson one yowe lamme. To John Osse my elder brother one hogge. To John Parkyn my lether doblyt and my best jerkyn. To Agnes my servant one blake sleveles gowne. To my father-in-lawe Thomas Crabdam one yow hog, my gowne, my best dooblet and my best hose. To John Osse my yonger brother one olde gray horse, one yowe hogge with a lamme and my best cote. All the resydue of my goodes I gyff unto Thomas Crabdam to the behoyff of Margaret Osse my doughter. And I will that the sayd Thomas Crabdam and John Osse my yonger brother be my executors. And yff the sayd Margaret Osse my doughter dye or that she cum at the age of xviij yeres, as God defende, than I will that all the foresayd goodes remayn to the forsayd Thomas Crabdam and John Osse to dispose them in the churche of Gosberkyrk as they shall thynke beste for the helthe of my soule and Crysten soulys. [fo. 289v] And I make supervisors Thomas Wormslay and Simon Smyth, that they shall se that my executors do truly performe thys my last will. And I gyff to ether of them for ther labore iij*s* iiij*d*. Thys is the laste will of me Thomas Osse, mayd the day and the yere afore rehersyd. To Margaret Osse my doughter ij acre and iij stong of lande lying in More and the other acre and iij stong lying in Borylonde, to her and to her heyres and assygnes. And I will that Thomas Crabdam have the custody of the same lond toward the kepyng of the sayd Margaret my doughter to that she cum at the age of xviij yeres. And yff it happen that the sayd Margaret my doughter dye or she cum at the age of xviij yeres, I will that Thomas Crabdam and Margaret hys wyff, and the longer lyffers of them, have the forsayd ij acre and iij stong lande durynge ther naturall lyffe. And aftyr ther decesse I will that the londe be solde by iiij of the honest men of the towne of Gosberkyrk to the best value, and the money therof takyn for to be bestowyd in the churche of Gosberkyrk abowte suche thynges as the paryshe shall thynke most necessary for the helthe of my soule, my father and my mother soule and all Christen soulys. Thes beryng wytnes; John Vassell, Thomas Massyn, Thomas Vassell, John Kyrke and John Osse, the sun of Robert Osse, with other mo.

Proved before P at Swineshead, 8 June 1534.

455. RICHARD ROLLE [OF SAPPERTON]
[LCC 1532–34, fo. 274v]

2 April 1534. I, Rychard Rolle of Seperton, beyng holl of mynd and seke of bodye, make my last wyll and testament. Fyrst I beqweyth my sole to allmyghty God, to Our Lady Saynt Mary and to all the holy company of hevyn, and my body to be

beryyd in the churche of Saynt Nycolas of Saperton. To the holy awter of the sayyd churche xij*d*. To Our Lady of the sayd churche xij*d*. To Our Lady's workes of our mother churche off Lincoln xij*d*. To Ane Roll the yongar a ewe and iij shepe. To Richard Roll my sonne and to Anne Roll hys wyffe my howse in Seperton with all the appurtenance in the towne and fyldes of Seperton as it apperyt in a dede of fefftment of the same. To Henry Roll my sone my hows in Pykeworth with all the appurtenance in the towne and fyldes of Pykworthe. Also I wyll yf the sayd Henry hereafter be disposyd to sell the sayd howse, that then the sayd Richard shall have the sayd howse, gevyng to the sayd Herry therfore v*l* vj*s* viij*d*. The resydew of my goodes I geve to Annes Rolle my wyffe and to Richard Roll my son, to dyspose for the helthe of my sole. Thes beryng wytnes; Syr Raffe Irland, parson of Saperton, Thomas Crane, John Wryght and Richard Fostar of the same.

Proved before P at Ancaster, 18 May 1534.

456.　　SIR ANTHONY TODE [OF BOSTON]
　　　　[LCC 1532–34, fos. 262v–263r]

2 April 1534. I, Sir Anthony Tode, beyng of perfyte mynde and memory, do orden and make thys my laste will. Fyrste I bequethe my soule to God omnipotent, to Our Lady St. Mary and to all the celestiall cumpeny, and my body to be buryd in the churcheyerde of St. Botulphe of Boston. I bequethe my mortuary as the lawe requiryth. I will my body to be brought furthe with a generall dirige and messe with all the prestes and clerkes att my buryall day onely withowt any farther charge of vij day or xxx^(ty) day. To Our Lady of Lincoln in oblacion ij*d*. To the orphans of St. Catheryn's at Lincoln iiij*d*. Also in oblacion to sacrament in the churche of St. Botulphe ij*d*. To the vij martyrs iiij*d*. To St. Margaret of Kettesby in oblacion ij*d*. To ij chyldren of my brother-in-lawe, Robert and Jane, eche of them, vj*s* viij*d*. I bequethe the sayd Robert and Jane to be dischargeyd of xv*s* whiche he dothe awe me, also to one chylde of my brother Thomas Todde vj*s* viij*d*. And yff any of the sayd chyldren be departyd at the day of my departyng, I referre ther bequeste or bequestes to the discrecion of my executor. Also I will that an honest preste syng for me, my father and mother and all my benefactors, with all Christen soulys, the space of a quarter, and he to have for hys stipende xxvj*s* viij*d* yff it may be borne with thes premisses aforesayd and other costes and chargeys. To every one of my master Neyll chyldren viij*d*. To my [fo. 263r] dame Nele my tache[162] at my gowne. I will that the reste of my goodes be devydyd equally in ij partes, the one parte I bquethe to my brother Robert Jane [sic] and my syster hys wyff, and the other parte to Sir John Woodhouse, preste, he to do with it as it shall please hym for I frely gyff it to hym. I make Sir John Woodhouse myn executor, desyeryng hym, as I have put hym in trust, to se thes premisses performyd and he to have for so doyng a ryall in gold. Per me Thomam Austyn. Per me Johannem Waye. Per me Thomam Brygges.

Proved before P at Spilsby, 5 May 1534.

---

[162] A fibula, clasp or buckle.

457.　SIR THOMAS LYSTERE [VICAR OF BILLINGHAY]
　　　[LCC 1532–34, fo. 252v]

5 April 1534. I, Thomas Lystere, vicare of Billyngay, of hole mynde and good remembraunce, makes my testament and last will. In primis I bequethe my soule to God allmyghtty, to Our Lady St. Mary and to all the saintes of heven, and my body to be buryd in the qwere of St. Andro th'Appostle in the churche of Billyngay. To the bellys of Billyngay ij*s*. To the high altare of Our Lady of Lincoln iij*s* iiij*d*. To the nonnys of Catley iij*s* iiij*d*. To the chapell of St. Margarete of Walcote vj*s* iiij*d*. To Sir William Ludlam a tawny gowne. To Sir William Butler of Tateshale a velvytt typitt. To John Mason off Conesby a sarcenet typyt. To Catheryne Williamson a sarcenet typytte. To Robert Dykynson a blake jaket. To Walter Bate a blew jaket. To Alice Lincoln a blake gowne, a potte, a panne, ij candylstykes, a basyn of lattyn, vj pewter dyshes, a materes, a pare of schetes, an awmbrye and hogge schepe that is with Robert Dyconson. To Isabell my servant a matres and one pare of schetes. To Thomas Mathew my dooblet of bucke's leder, one pare of hose and a pare of shoyn. To every godchylde that I have within the parysh of Byllyngay iiij*d*. To every house of the iiij orders of frerys of Lincoln xij*d*. To the churche of All Halloys of Olde Sleforde iij*s* iiij*d*. To Sir Thomas Lystere frere of Lincoln ij*s*. To Agnes Dyconson a blake hatte. To Emote Spaldyng a kyrchyff. I will that iiij prestes bere my corps to the churche the day of my buryall, that is to say Sir William Butler, Sir William Borowe, vicar of Rowton, Sir Thomas Sarsynge of Kyrkby Grene and Sir William Ludlam and every one of them to have for ther labor a sylver spone. The resydue of my goodes I gyff to William Lystere of Blankney, whome I make my executor that he may order and dispose it for the helthe of my soule as he wolde that I dyd for hym yff he wer in lyke case as I am. The wytnesssys herof as thes; Sir William Ludlam, preste, Sir Thomas Lystere, preste, Robert Dyconson and Water Bate. Geven the day and yere above sayd.

　　　Proved before P at Lincoln, 15 May 1534.

458.　WILLIAM TROTTER [OF ST. STEPHEN'S, LINCOLN]
　　　[LCC 1532–34, fos. 277v–278r]

6 April 1534. I, William Trotter, fremason of the citie of Lincoln in the paryshe of St. Stephyn's, makes and ordens thys my laste will. Fyrste I bequethe my soule to God allmyghtty, Our Lady St. Mary and to all the saintes in heven. My body to be buryd in my paryshe churche aforesayd. To my paryshe churche warke of St. Stephyn's xij*d*. [fo. 278r] To Our Lady of the high altare in the cathedrall churche of Lincoln viij*d*. To the red arke iiij*d*. To St. Bennet churche warke viij*d*. To the clerke gylde iiij*d*. To William Trotter my sun my gowne with whyte fyrre. To William Trotter my prentys my marbyll jaket. Also to the sayd Wylliam I gyff of every tole one belongyng to my occupacion of that condicion that he shall geder togeder all my toolys and bryng them home to my wyffe. To Margarete hys syster my fustyan jaket. The resydue of my goodes I gyff to Matylde my wyff whome I make my executrix, she to pay my dettes and bryng up my pore chyldren. I make Sir Robert Torner supervisor. Wytnes herof [at *or* of] Normanby; Edmunde Byglyskyrke, William Trotter, with many mo.

　　　Proved before P at Lincoln, 22 May 1534.

459. WILLIAM PRESTE [OF PINCHBECK]
[LCC 1532–34, fo. 292]

9 April 1534. I, William Preste of Pynchbek, beyng of good mynde and hole remembraunce, makes my last testament and will. Fyrst I bequeth my soule to God allmyghtty, to Our Lady and to all the saintes of heven, and my body to be buryd in the churcheyerde of Pynchbek. To the high altare there for tithes and oblacions negligently forgotte viij*d*. To every altare in the sayd churche ij*d*. To the churche warke of Lincoln iiij*d*. To Margaret my doughter a pare of beades that was my wyffe moder's, also a qwy of iij yeres of age and she to have her delyveryd at the age of xx^{ty} yeres. To Anne my doughter another qwye of iij yeres of age, and she to have her delyveryd at the age of xx^{ty} yeres. [fo. 292v] And yff it fortune oder of mye dowghters to dye or they cum to the age of xx^{ti} yeres, than I wyll that mye dowghter than beynge alyve to have the partt of mye other dowghter than beinge deyd. And iff it fortune bothe mye dowghters to dye or they cum to the age of xx^{ti} yeres, than mye will is mye ij sons or other of theym as itt shall plese God to gyve theym lyffe, to have the gyftes of the other of my chyldern above wrytten. And iff fortune all mye chyldern to dye or they cum to the age of xx^{ti} yeres, than I wyll the ij quyes to be solde bye the hande of myn executores or bye the lenger lyver of theym bye the handes of the executores of the lenger of myne executores, and the money to be dysposed in the town of Pynschebek for mye soull and all Crysten soulles. The rest of all my goodes I gyve them to Agnes mye wyffe, whom I make mye executrix, and Rawfe Prest mye brother to be executor with mye wyffe, and he to have for hys labor xx*d*. I wyll have Wylliam Toche to be mye supervysor, and he to have for hys labor xx*d*. I make myn last wyll in the same day and date above named. Fyrst I surrender all mye copyeholde lande that I have in the handes of Wylliam Toche, to the use and performans of thys mye last wyll. I wyll that Agnes mye wyffe have all the copyeholde landes that I have, bey they more or lesse, the terme of hyr lyfe naturall, and after her decease I wyll that Thomas my sun have all mye copyeholde landes lyinge in the hye felde and Rycharde mye sun to [have] all the rest of mye landes lyinge in other places, to theym, theyr ayers and asyners for ever. I wyll that yff itt fortune one [of] mye sons [to] dye before mye wyffe, than I wyll that my son thon bey alyfe to have all mye landes more and lesse, and yf itt fortune bothe mye sons to dye before mye wyffe, than I wyll the next of mye blode to have all mye copyeholde landes more and lesse, to hym or hys [heirs] as itt shall please God, theyr ayers and asyners for ever. Theys beynge wytnesses; Sir Thomas Hyll, pryst, Harye Cust and Symonde Duen.

Proved before P at Spalding, 9 June 1534.

460. RICHARD PYNDE [OF HOLBEACH]
[LCC 1532–34, fo. 283v]

9 April 1534. I, Rycharde Pynd of Holbyche, hole in mynde and perfytt in remembraunce, do make thys mye last wyll and testamentt. In the fyrst I bequethe mye sowll to almyghttye God, to Our Ladye and to all the companye in heven, and mye bodye to be beryed within the churcheyerde of All Halowes in Holbyche. To the hye auter for tythes forgoten vj*d*. To the mother churche in Lyncoln v*d*. To the pore chyldern of Seyntt Kateryn's ij*d*. To Our Lady's auter in Holbyche iiij*d*. To the Trynite auter iiij*d*. To every auter in the seyd churche ij*d*.

To the rowde lyghtt ij*d*. To the churche werke iiij*d*. To Thomas my son a mayr. To Robertt mye son a mayr. To the seyd Thomas and Robertt mye baye mayr, mye cartt, mye plowgh with all manner thynges therto belonginge. To Thomas mye son a yerynge donne coltt to pay mye thythes unto mye curatt for hys est rolle v*s* iiij*d*. To Thomas mye son mye best gown, mye greatt bott and v aker londe lyinge in Spaldynge Drove. To Robertt mye son mye marbyll cote and mye chamlett dowblett. To John my son a kow, a burnynge and mye blunkytt chakett. To Rycharde Byller, son of John Byller, a burnynge burnyt at May Daye. To Alyce mye dowghter a hakfer. To John Byller a pyed calff. To Kateryn mye wyffe vj aker and a half lyinge in the fen end holdynge of the Lorde Barnysche. The resydewe of mye goodes not bequethed I bequethe to Kateryn mye wyffe and do make hyr mye sol executrix to dyspose mye goodes for the salvacyon of mye soull, and John Stow to be supervysor and he to have for hys payntakyng mye bull. In wytnesse herof; Rycharde Wykam, clarke and curatt, John Stowe, Wylliam Freman, John Ramis, with other mo.

Proved before P at Spalding, 9 June 1534.

461.   WILLIAM THORE [OF INGOLDMELLS]
        [LCC 1532–34, fos. 265v–266r]

9 April 1534. I, William Thore, the sun of Robert Thore of Ingoldmellys, with a hole mynde and good remembraunce, makes my last testament. Fyrste I bequethe my soule to God allmyghtty and to Hys mother St. Mary, and to all the cumpeny in heven. My body to be buryd in the churche of St. Peter in Ingoldmellys, in the name of my mortuary as the lawe dothe admit. To the high alter of Ingoldmellys for forgottyn tithys xij*d*. To every altare in the sayd churche iiij*d* and to the bellys xx*s*. To the churche of St. Nicholes of Ardelthorp xij*d*. To Our Lady of Lincoln unto the high altare vj*d* and to Our Lady warke vj*d*, and to the pore chyldren withowt Lincoln in St. Catheryn's xij*d*. To the iiij orders of frerys in Boston iiij*s* [fo. 266r] by even porcion. To Jenet Skegneys v marke to be payd at day off her mariage of hyr father which is in hys own hande. And yff she dye before she comme to mariage, I will that it remayn to the nexte doughter of Elizabeth Skegneys, and yff she have no doughters, then I will it remayn to the foresayd Elizabeth. To Richerde Gybson that was gyffyn me of a chylde v markes, the which v markes Thomas Thore shall pay to hym at the age of xxj yeres of the xx*l* which I have set owt of my landes. To Our Lady of Legborne xij*d* and every none in the sayd abbay iiij*d*. I bequethe Mawde my wyff all my stuff that be moveabyls within my house or housys or gardyns, iiij kye, xl^ty schepe and my amblyng horse. I will that my executors do for my soule [a] halfpenny apece to all that commys. Yff the foresayd Richerde Gybson dye before he cum to the age of xxj yeres, I will that the foresayd v markes remayn to John Thore my sun. To Robert Johnson ij schepe. To Olyff Skegneys ij schepe. To Thomas Skegneys iiij*l* which lyes in hys awn handes. The revarcyon of all my goodes, my dettes payd, my will performyd and my buryall performyd and one trentall for my soule and all Christen soulys, I gyff to John Thore my sun. Also I will that Thomas Thore and Thomas Skegneys be my executors and other of them to have vj*s* viij*d* for ther labor, and Sir Nicholes Serrot, the parson of Ingoldmellys, supervisor, and he to have vj*s* viij*d* for hys labor. Thes wytnes;

Mr. Anthony Byllesby and Thomas Thore, Thomas Cokson, John Gybson, Thomas Flecher and John Wapull.

Proved before P at Partney, 6 May 1534.

462. THOMAS WHITE [OF MOULTON]
[LCC 1532–34, fo. 295]

10 April 1534. I, Thomas White of Multon in Holand, hole off mynde and syke of body, makes thys my testament and last will. Fyrst I bequethe my soule to God almyghty and to Owr Lady Saynt Mary, and to all the compeny in heven. My body to be buried within the churchyarde of All Halows in Multon with my mortuary as the law will require. To the hyght aulter of Multon church for tythes and oblacions forgotten iiijd. To reparacion of the same churche xxd. To the stons lyght jd. To the iij lyghtes of the same churche ixd. To the hyght aulter of Weston church for tythes and oblacions forgotton iiijd. To the reparacion of the same churche xxd. To the iij lyghtes of the same church ixd. To ower mother church of Lynlcon iiijd. To the fatherles childer of St. Kateryn's in Lynlcon ijd. This his the last will of me Thomas White, mayde the day and yere above writyn. To John White my sonne my howse in Weston and xij acars of arrabull lande and pasture gronde in fe symple, my plowth and carte with the geyres there to belonyg, a blake fleykyd cow, a calfe and my best cote that ys mayde. To Thomas White my sonne a blake dowid cow, a calfe and cote cloth that ys unmayd. To Robert White my sonne a dunde cow, a cote clothe that hys unmayde and steyr burnyng. [fo. 295v] To Ales Bygott dawghter, a burnyng cow calfe. To Em Bygott my dawghter a burnyng cow calfe. To William Bygott my sonne a cow calfe. To Raffe Bygott my sonne a cow calfe. To Annes White my wyffe ij acars of pasture gronde lying at Tynkar's Crosse in fee symple. Also I, the seid Thomas White, have surrendered all my landes and tenementes holden by copye of court roll into the handis of Roger West, to the use and performance of this my last will. The ressedew of all my goodes I will that Annes White my wiffe have them, whome I make myne executryx, she for to dyspose yt for the helth of my soull and all my good frendes' soulles as she thynke most expedient. I will that John Carre be supervisor, and I will that he have for hys labur xs. Thies beyng wyttnes; Sir Jeffray Haynes, prest, Sir Robert Skare, prest, Thomas Irby, Robert Lyllay, with other moo.

Proved before P at Spalding, 9 June 1534.

463. RICHARD LAMBESON [OF SWINESHEAD]
[LCC 1532–34, fo. 322]

11 April 1534. I, Richerde Lambeson off Swynneshed, notary, beyng of hole and perfecte mynde and good remembraunce, makyth my testament and last will. Firste I bequethe my soule unto allmyghtty God, to Our Lady St. Mary and to all the holy cumpeny of heven, and my body to be buryed within the churcheyerde of Our Blessyd Lady in Swynneshed nigh unto the bodyes of my parentes. To my mortuary as use and custome is ther usyd. To Our Lady's warke of Lincoln iiijd. To the pupillys and orphans in the house of St. Catheryn's nygh Lincoln ijd. To the high altare of Swynneshed for tithes forgottyn viijd. To Our Lady's altare ther iiijd. To the thre altares in the same churche, to every one of them, ijd. To the churche

warke ther xij*d*. To Beatrix my wyff my mesuage and my tenement with all ther appurtenaunce duryng the hole terme of her lyff, to the intent to kepe up my chylder so that she kepe them in good reparacions duryng the sayd terme. And aftyr her decesse, the messuage with the appurtenaunce to remayn to Richerde my sun, to hym and to hys heyres and hys assignes, so that he yerely pay to Thomas and to William my sunnys, and to every of them, ij*s* unto the tyme they cum to the age of xxj^ty yeres. Also I will that the sayd tenement wyth the appurtenaunces shall, aftyr the decesse of my wyffe, remayn to Jane my doughter, and she to pay yerely to George my sun ij*s* to he cum to xxj yeres of age. And yff it fortune the sayd Richerde my sun to decesse afore the age of xxiiij^ty yeres, I will that then my sayd mesuage with the appurtenaunces shall remayn to the sayd Thomas, William and George my sunnes, to ther heyres and ther assignes equally to be devydyd betwene them, be the discrescions of iiij of the moste honest men then abydyng in Swynneshed, to the sayd iij sunys. And yff it fortune that all my sonnys and doughter decesse afore they cum to ther sayd age of xxiiij yeres, then I will that my sayd mesuage with the appurtenaunces shall be solde by the foeffes, ther heyres or assignes, and be Thomas Hollande esquyre or be hys heyres and be the church-ewardens of Swynneshed for the tyme beyng to the moste best price that then any persone will pay to the sayd sellers, so that then my sayd sellers, I will that then they immediatly repay the one halffe of the hole sum of money by them to be receyvyd for my sayd mesuage to the alderman and brether of Our Lady's gylde in Swynneshed, and they to put it to the most proffet of the sayd gylde of Our Lady in Swynneshed, and that then they shall pay yerely xx*d* to the alderman or to hys depute over and besyde the v*s* whiche they have usyd yerely to pay for the kepyng of the obyt of my parentes, so that then the sayd obyt may be kepyd yerely for my parentes and for me, and for my wyff, expendyng therat yerely vj*s* viij*d* in lyke maner as the other obyttes of vj*s* viij*d* [fo. 322v] be kepyd yerely be the sayd alderman or hys depute for ever. And also I will the other on halff to be receyvyd for my sayd mesuage shall be equally devydyd into ij partes and that they shall bestowe the one parte therof to the makyng of a cawsy from a corner of a certen house sumtyme callyd Hawdall house unto the stone bryg nexte ther beyng, and unto the reparyng off all the brygges and to the castyng up of a sufficient bancke from the sayd stone bryg unto the parke housys. And also I will that the other parte of the sayd money be bestowyd be my sayd sellers uppon the reparacion of the cawsey in the towne of Swynneshed, and also to the moste pore people then beyng in the sayd towne. And also I will that my sayd tenement with the appurtenances shall be solde be my sayd sellers of my sayd mesuage and be the advice of the abbot of Swynneshed then beyng. And then they to delyver all the money therfore to be receyvyd unto the sayd abbot to the moste proffet of hys house, so that he will gyff to hys convent parte of the money that they may syng a solempne dirige and messe with ryngyng for the soulys of my parentes, for my brother Sir William, for the soulys of me and my wyff and my chylder, and all Christian soulys as shall be sene. I will that Anthony my sun shall have one materes, one coverlyd, one pare of lynyn schetes, one bolster, my best gaberdyne, my best clavycordes and one cowe. The resydue of all my goodes I will it remayn to Beatrix my wyff, so that she delyver to every one of my sayd chylder, when they cum to laufull age, one hole bed with the appurtenaunces and brasse and puter, and a cowe to every one of them with other necessary thynges as she shall se moste profytable for them, as I put my full truste in her, whome I orden to be my executrix that she pay my dettes and orden and dispose as to the honor of God and the helthe of my soule to here better shall be sene. And I beseche Sir Thomas Garton, vicar of Swynneshed, he will be on of the coadjutors and helpers of my sayd wyff, and he to have for hys good help and councell iij yerdes of the lynnyn clothe that my wyffe hase mayd. And also I humely beseche and pray the right worschipfull Thomas Hollande esquyer to be coadjutor and helper of my sayd wyff in executyng of all the premisses. And also anenst my lord abbot of Swynneshed and all other haveyng eny cause agenst my sayd wyff, and he to have for hys good helpe iij*s* iiij*d*. Also I will and desyre Thomas Hulle of Swynneshed to be one of the coadjutors and helpers of my sayd wyff in the executyng of the presmisses, and he to have for hys good help and councell suche a rewarde as my sayd wyff shall content hym with. Thes beyng wytnes; Sir Thomas Garton, vicar, Sir John Webster, Sir Raphe Antrobus, preste, with other mo. Datyd the day and yere above wryttyn.

Proved before P at Swineshead, 8 June 1534. Adm. granted to the executor.

464. WILLIAM POTTERELL [OF FARLESTHORPE]
[LCC 1532–34, fo. 267]

11 April 1534. I, William Potterell of Fallesthorpe, beyng of hole mynde and good remembraunce, ordens and makyth my testament and last will. Fyrste I bequethe my soule to allmyghtty God and to Our Blessyd Lady St. Mary and unto all the holly cumpany of heven, and my body to be buryd within the churcheyerde of St. Andro of Fallesthorpe aforesayd. To Our Lady of Lincoln iiij*d*. To [fo. 267v] the churche warke of Our Lady of Lincoln iiij*d*. To the high altare in Falsthorp churche for my tithys forgottyn xij*d*. To Fallesthorpe churche xij*d*. To Isabell my doughter one cowe of iij yere olde and a calve, iij yowes and iij lammys, one kyste, one chare, one bed, one gret panne, a gret panotte and one possenet, one metborde, one gret tubbe, and ij puter dyshes. To Alice, my wyff doughter, a ij yere olde qwye. To Henry my sun iij hogges and iij lammys and a yren teym and one pare of hamyll treys. To William Dallyn a yowe and a lamme. To John Dallyne one lamme. To William Synson my godsun one lamme. I make Jenet my wyff my executor. I make Sir John Wollaye my supervisor, and he to have for hys laber iij*s* iiij*d*. Wytnes therof; William Pynder and John Symson and Thomas Lawson, with other mo.

Proved before P at Alford, 7 May 1534.

465. JOHN SCHERTE [OF GOSBERTON]
[LCC 1532–34, fo. 316v]

12 April 1534. I, John Scherte of the paryshe of Gosberton, makes my last will and testament. The fyrste I bequethe my soule to God allmyghtty and my body to be buryd in the churcheyerde of St. Peter and St. Paule in Gosberton. To the high altare for my tithes forgottyn iij*d*. To the reparacion of every altare in the same churche iij*d* apece. To every gylde in the same churche ij*d* apece. To the ij gret lighttes iij*d* apece. To the churche warke iiij*d*. To Our Lady's churche edificacion of Lincoln iiij*d*. To the chylder of St. Catheryn's ij*d*. To John my sun one cowe of the beste. To Agnes my doughter one qwye. The resydue of my goodes I gyff to Margaret my wyff, the which I make my executrix. I will that John Yomyn be the

oversear. Thes wytnes; Sir Henry Toplys, prest, John Stebert, John Breche, with mo.

Proved before P at Swineshead, 8 June 1534.

466.   JOHN WILLERTON [OF INGOLDMELLS]
        [LCC 1535–7, fo. 127]

12 April 1534. I, John Willerton of Ingolmellys, beyng hole of mynde and of good memory, makes my testament. Firste I bequethe my soule to God allmyghtty, Our Lady St. Mary and to all the saintes in heven, and my body to be buryd within the churcheyerde of St. Peter of Ingolmellys, with that that the lawe requiryth to be my mortuary. To the blessyd sacrament of Ingolmellys for tithes forgottyn xijd. To other of the ij altares in the sayd churche iiijd. To Our Lady's gylde within the same churche a yowe, and to St. John's gylde a yowe. To Our Lady's warke of Lincoln xijd. To Alice my wyff iij kye, xx^{ty} yowes shorne withowt lammys and halffe my housholde stuff. To Robert my sun xx^{ty} hogges, a wayn, a plough with all maner of tyre to them belongyng withowt oxen or horse. To the sayd Robert a pare of malte qwernys aftyr the decesse of Alice my wyffe, and a blak nagge. To Margaret my doughter a qwye and vj yowes clyppyd withowt lammes. I will that Richerde Willerton my sun have, aftyr my decesse, one horse and half oxgan of lande lying in the territoriis of Calkewell,[163] to hym and to hys heyres of hys body laufully begottyn. And yff that the sayd Richerde do dye withowt heyres of hys body laufully begottyn, then I will that the sayd house with the half oxgan of lande do remayn to Sir Willum Willerton my sun [remainder to] Robert my sun and to hys heyres of hys body laufully begottyn [remainder to] Margaret my doughter and to her heyres of her body laufully begottyn. And yff all my chyldren dye withowt heyres of ther bodys laufully begottyn, then I will that the foresayd house with the half oxgan of lande be solde be my feoffes, Mr. Anthony Smyth of Calkewell, Edwarde Alesby of the same, Robert Willerton off Yngolmellys my sun, and Thomas Richerdson of Toynton, and the money to be disposyd be my executors. The resydue of my goodes, my dettes payd and my legaces, and thys my last will fulfyllyd, I gyff them to my wyff and my iiij chyldren. And I constitute [fo. 127v] Robert Willerton my sun and John Gybson to be my executor, and John Gybson to have for hys labor vs. Wytnes; Sir Richard Sherman, Richard Gybson and Thomas Thore.

Proved before P at Partney, 17 May 1536.

467.   JOHN BARGE [OF HEIGHINGTON IN PARISH OF WASHINGBOR-
        OUGH]
        [LCC 1532–34, fos. 303v–304v]

13 April 1534. I, John Barge of Hekyngton in the paryshyng of St. John the Evangeliste of Whashyngburgh in the countie of Lincoln, husbandman, beyng of good and perfecte remembraunce, makyth and ordenyth thys my last testament and will. Fyrste I bequethe my soule to God allmyghtty, to Our Blessyd Lady St. Mary and to all the holy cumpeny of heven, and my body to be buryed in the paryshe churche of Whashyngburgh aforesayd in the myddyll [fo. 304r] space nygh unto the

---

[163] Within the *territorium* of Cawkwell Priory.

Holy Trynite. And for my mortuary as the lawe of Ynglande hathe admyttyd it at the convocacion. To the high altare of Whashyngburgh for tithes and oblacions negligently forgottyn. To the mayntenance of the light of St. John the Evangeliste viij*d*. To our Lady warke of Lincoln ij*s*. To the paryshe of Whashyngburgh x*s* for to bye a pare of sensurs. To Braunceton churche iiij*d*. To Hekyll churche iiij*d*. To the reparacion of the bellys of Whashyngburgh xij*d*. To the rode light of Whashyngburgh a quarter of barly. To the Trinite gylde halffe a quarter of barly. To the light of St. Andro of Hekyngton in the paryshyng off Whashyngburgh halffe a quarter barly. To the iiij orders of frerys of Lincoln iiij strykes barly, that is to say to every house one stryke. I bequethe at the day of my buryall, to every man, woman and chylde beyng ther precent, peny dole, and dirige to be done with messe of requiem. And also my seventh day and thyrty day to be kepyd with dirige and messe of requiem. I bequeth a trentall of messes to be done for me and all my benefactors in the churche of Whashyngburgh. To every godchylde that I have a stryke of barly. To Robert Borrell a yoke of bullokes or iiij nobylls in money. To John Borrell my godsun xx schepe, that is to say x ewes and x lammys. To Christofer Borrell x schepe, that is to say v ewes and v lammys. To Isabell my syster a calve. To Christofer Archer a qwye of a yere olde. To Alice Archer a schepe hog. To Isabell Archer a schepe hog. To Margaret my doughter a kowe and a calve. To Alice my doughter xl^ty marke in suche goodes as I have and vj sylver sponys. To the sayd Alice my doughter my house that I have in Hekyngton, that Thomas Clarke dothe dwell in, to her and her heyres of her body. And for lack of heyres of the sayd Alice, then I [fo. 304v] will that Margaret my doughter have the forsayd house, to her and to her heyres of her body for ever, aftyr the custome of the lordeschyp. To Jenet my wyff my house that I do dwell in for terme of her lyff, and aftyr the terme of her lyff naturall, I will that Alice my doughter have the sayd house to gyff and to sell at her awn pleasure. The resydue of my goodes I gyff to Jenet my wyff, whome I make my executrix. In wytness heroff; Sir Robert Becbayn, curate, John Gentyll, otherwyse callyd Brygton, and William Wallys, with other mo.

Proved before P at Lincoln, 19 June 1534, by the executor.

468.　SIMON EVE [OF HIGH TOYNTON]
　　　[LCC 1532–34, fo. 259]

13 April 1534. I, Simonde Eve of Over Toynton next Horncastle, beyng hole of mynde and good of remembraunce and seke of body, makes thys my last will and testament. Fyrst I bequethe my soule to God allmyghtty and to Our Lady St. Mary and to all the cumpeny of heven, and my body to be buryd within the churcheyerde of St. John Baptiste of Toynton aforesayd. To the sacrament in the churche of Toynton, for oblacions, iiij*d*. To Our Lady of Lincoln iiij*d*. To Our Lady warke of the same ij*d*. To Our Lady in Toynton churche iiij*d*. To Marget my wyffe ij of my beste oxyn, a cowe, ij mares and all my housholde within my house, my wayn, my plough, my carte with all my yokys and temys. To Thomas Eve my sun ij oxen, a cowe, a qwye and iij schepe, iij quarters of barly, a halberde. To every one of my iij doughters a cowe, a qwye, ij schepe and every one of them iij quarters of barly. To my sun Thomas Eve all my housyng, landes, tenementes, pasturys, medoys and fedyng groundes within the towne and feldes of Over Toynton, with all maner rentes and commens belongyng to the same, to hym and to the heyres of hys body

laufully begottyn for evermore. And yff that they sayd Thomas dye withowt any heyres of hys body laufully begottyn, then I will that my lande remayn unto my iij doughters evenly to be devydyd to them and to ther heyres of ther bodys for ever, so long as any of them or ther chyldren shall remayn, excepte that I will that Margarete my wyffe shall have a close callyd Howsson Close with the lande and medoy [fo. 259v] that lyes at the weste ende of the same close for the terme of her lyffe. And aftyr her decesse, to remayn unto Thomas my sun and my heyres that longest lyffys for evermore. I will that Rayff Chawner and John Madynwell of Horncastle have the custody of all my landes and the goodes that I have bequethyd to my sun Thomas, unto the tyme that he cum unto laufull age. The resydue of all my goodes I gyff it unto Margarete my wyffe, whome I make myn executor for to dispose it for the helthe of my soule and all Christen soulys. And thes to wytnes; Sir Martyn Roos, my curate, Alexander Stevenson of the same, John Hessyll of the same, Thomas Malynson of the same, with other.

Proved before P at Horncastle, 4 May 1534.

469.   JOHN GLASTON [OF LITTLE STURTON IN PARISH OF BAUM-BER]
        [LCC 1535–7, fos. 152v–153r]

13 April 1534. I, John Glaston of Lyttyll Styrton in the paryshe of Bamburgh, hole in mynde and in perfyte remembraunce, makyth thys my testament and last will. Firste I bequethe my soule to allmyghtty God, Our Lady St. Mary, and all the holy cumpeny of heven. My body to be buryed in St. Nicholes qwere within the paryshe churche of St. Swythune in Bamburgh. I bequethe in the name of my mortuary as the lawe requyryth. To Our Lady of Lincoln viijd. To the high altare for forgottyn tithes viijd. To the iiij orders of frerys within Lincoln, every house, iiijd. To Bamburgh churche xiijs iiijd. [fo. 153r] To every one of my godchyldren iijl vjs viijd. The resydue of my goodes unbequethyd I will and bequeth unto Agnes my wyffe, Willum Phylypotte and Willum Glaston my sun, whome I orden and make my executors. I will that Agnes my wyffe have the gydyng of my chylder partes for so long as she is unmaryed. And when that she dothe mary, I will that she delyver ther partes that be of laufull age, and for the orders of the partes of the reste of the chyldren, to be at the discretion of my executors. Also I orden and make my lorde Borowe that now is supervisor of my will, and he to have for hys labor and hys paynetakyng ij horses, one of yren blak which now is at brekyng at Bardeney, and the other a darke baye with one stone. Thes beryng wytnes; Richerde Salleman of Bamburgh, Thomas Lancaster of Hagworthyngham, James Goslyng, Willum Myddylton of Bamburgh, with other mo.

Proved before P at Lincoln, 26 July 1536. Adm. granted to Agnes the relict and executrix, reserving power to grant to William Philypotte and William Glaston, co-executors.

470.   SIR ROBERT WHYHAM [VICAR OF HELPRINGHAM]
        [LCC 1532–34, fos. 299v–300r]

14 April 1534. I, Sir Robert Whyham, vicare of Helpryngham, beyng of perfyte mynde and of good remembraunce, makes my testament and last will. Fyrste I

bequethe my soule to God allmyghtty and to Hys mother Our Lady St. Mary and to all the holy cumpeny of heven, and my body to be buryed within the high quere of Helpryngham. To the high altare of Helpryngham xij*d*. To the high altare of Lincoln iij*s* iiij*d*. To Our Lady's gylde of Helpryngham xiij*s* iiij*d*. To the iiij orders of frerys of Boston, to every one of them, halffe a seame malte. To the challons of Burne to syng a trentall for me x*s*. To the churche of Downsbe vj*s* viij*d*. To every godbarne that I have viij*d*. I bequethe to one honest preste to syng for my soule and my father's and mother's halffe a yere liij*s* iiij*d*. To Sir John Johnson, chauntry preste of Hole, my worstyd jakyt and my chamlet dooblet and my best fether bed and all my bookes.[164] To Margaret Rodys myn amblyng ffylly. To Robert Kyrke, William Rodys, Robert Rodys, Christofer Rodes and yong John Rodes, every one of them, one sylver spone. To Jennet Bounyng one gyrdyll with stothys of sylver. To Thomas Bounyng ij schepe. To Catheryne Bounyng ij puter platters, one doobler and one sawsser. To William Pyla v schepe. To Jenet Waryng one materes, one coverlyd, one pare of schetes, my secund worst gowne and halff my flax. To Christofer Waryng one yong colte. To Richerd Robertson my warste gowne and one stall of beys. To Agnes Robertson iij*s* iiij*d*. To Robert Robertson vj*s* viij*d*, my jaket, my dooblet, my house and one stall of beys. To Robert Gayton my lytyll yong horse, a materes, a coverlyd and one pare schetes. To Margaret Wayd my servand xxvj*s* viij*d* and one feder bedde and one coverlyd and one pare of schetes and my best schorte gowne, and halffe my flaxe. To Valerian Thomas iij*s* iiij*d*. To Renalde Hall iij*s* iiij*d*. To Bartholomew Thomas ij*s*. To Robert Lee ij*s*. To every one of William Bounyng chylder iij*s* iiij*d*. To the mendyng of the highway at Brygdyke a seame malte. To Gret Hale vj*s* viij*d*. To Burton v*s*. To Scredyngton iij*s* iiij*d*. To Swaton v*s*, thes to be delte emong pore people. To the churche of Helpryngham my prasse.[165] To John Rodes the elder my house at the est end of the towne [fo. 300r] and my house at the weste end of the towne with all the appurtenances to them belongyng, to hym and hys assygnes kepyng one yerely obbyt for my soule, my father's and mother's, for the space of xx^{ty} yeres, disposyng yerely iij*s* iiij*d*. And yff the sayd John departe afore he be xx^{ty} yere olde, then I will that William Rodes have it aftyr the same forme. And yff the sayd William departe afore the sayd xx^{ty} yeres, then I will it remayn unto Robert Rodes, and in lyke maner to Christofer Rodes and yong John Rodes. And yff all thes departe, as God forbyd it, afore any of them do cum to age of xx^{ty} yeres, then I will that my executors sell the sayd housys and dispose the money for the helthe of my soule. The resydue off my goodes I put to the disposicion of Henry Roodes and William Bounyng, whome I make my executors to dispose it for the helthe of my soule as they shall thynke the best, and other of them to have for ther labor vj*s* viij*d*, and Sir John Johnson to be the supervisor. The beyng wytnes; Richerde Roberdson, Hugh Parkyn, Christofer Waryng, Robert Jakson, Robert Getton, with other mo.

Proved before P at Sleaford, 11 June 1534.

---

[164] Sir John Johnson was chantry priest of Hale: see n. 144 above.
[165] 'Presse', i.e. 'cupboard'.

471.   EDWARD HUMBLE [OF ROUGHTON]
        [LCC 1532–34, fo. 258r]

15 April 1534. I, Edwarde Humble of Rughton, of hole mynde and perfyte helthe
and good memory, lovyd be God, make my will and testament. Fyrste I bequethe
my soule to God allmyghtty, Our Blessyd Lady St. Mary and all the holy cumpeny
of heven, and my body to be buryd in the churcheyerde of St. Margarete of
Roughton. To the high altare of Rughton. To William Humbyll my eldeste sun ij
yowes and ij lammes, and one cowe. To Nicholes Humble my yongest sun ij yows
and ij lammys and one cowe. To the altare of Lincoln ij*d*. To Our Lady's warke ij*d*. I
wyt the copy of my house to Jenet Humble my wyffe. The resydue of my goodes I
leyff to my executrix Jenet Humble my wyffe to dispose as she shall thynke the beste
for the helthe of my soule. Wytnes here; Sir Roger Chambers, parson, Robert
Morys, William Leghtte, Robert Holteby, with other mo.
        Proved before P at Horncastle, 4 May 1534.

472.   THOMAS LEEKE [OF GOSBERTON]
        [LCC 1532–34, fos. 289v–290r]

15 April 1534. I, Thomas Leeke of the paryshe of Gosberton, beyng perfyte in
mynde and of a good remembraunce, makes my last will and testament. The fyrste I
bequethe my soule to God allmyghtty and to hys blessyd mother St. Mary and to all
the holy cumpeny of heven, and my body to be buryd in the churcheyerde of St.
Peter and St. Paule in Gosberton. To the high altare therof for my tithys forgottyn
iiij*d*. To the reparacion of every light in the same churche iiij*d* apece. To the churche
warke iiij*d*. To the reparacion of our mother churche of Lincoln iiij*d*. [fo. 290r] To
the chylder of St. Catheryn's ij*d*. To Henry my sun iiij yong kyne with ther calvys,
one geldyng and one stonyd horse. To Richerde my sun iiij yong kyne with ther
calvys, fyve yowes with ther lammys, ij yong marys, one matrys, one coverlyd, one
bolster, ij pare of schetes. To Agnes my doughter ij yong burnynges, one hole bed
with all thynge therto perteynyng and xl*s* of laufull money of Ynglande. I will that
William Glover of Pynchbek be the overseer. The resydue of my goodes I gyff them
to Alice my wyff and to John Leyk my sun, the whiche I make my executors to pay
my dettes, to bryng my body honestly to the grounde and to dispose them for the
helthe of my soule as they shall best devyse. Wytnes herof; Sir Henry Toplys, prest,
Dane William Pygot, canon, John Vassell, Henry Marable, John Kyrkebe, with
other mo.
        Proved before P at Spalding, 9 June 1534.

473.   WILLIAM LANE [OF HOUGH ON THE HILL]
        [LCC 1532–34, fo. 274]

17 April 1534. I, Wylliam Lane of thes parysche of Howght, make my testament
and last wyll. Fyrst I bequeyth my sole to almyghty God and my body to be bereyd
in the churcheyarde of the parrysche of Howgh. To the hye awter in the churche of
Howgh vj*d*. To the mother churche in Lincoln iiij*d*. To the parrysche churche of
Howght on of my best kye, ij ewys and ij lamys. To Annes my [fo. 274v] doughter
one cowe and fyve schepe, one seame wheate and another of barly. To Walter my
sun one cowe, v schepe, one seame wheate and another of barly. To William my sun

one cowe, fyve schepe. To Barnerde my sun one cowe, v schepe. To Alice my doughter one cowe, fyve schepe, one seame barly. To Isabell my doughter one cowe, fyve schepe, one seame barly. To my iij sonnys afore namyd, iche of them, a bullok of ij yere olde. I will that yff any of my forsaid chylder dye afore the yeres of discrecion, the goodes to be devydyd emonges them that do lyff. To William my sun and Barnerde my sun, ether of them, a shodde wane or xxs in money, and to be delyveryd when they cum to laufull age. To the chyldren of my brother John, ich of them, a lamme. To the chylder of my brother Richerde, ich of them, a lamme. I will that Barnerde Yoile be my supervisor, and he to have for hys pane ij ewys and ij lammys. The resydue of my goodes I gyff to Isabell my wyff, whome I make my executor to occupy and dispose to the welthe of my soule and all Christen soulys, and to her awn welthe as she shall thynke moste necessary. Wytnes herof; Barnerd Yoile, Thomas Wetherhyll, Richerde Layne.

Proved before P at Ancaster, 18 May 1534.

474.   JOHN CLARE [OF PINCHBECK]
        [LCC 1532–34, fos. 291r–292r]

18 April 1534. I, John Clare off Pynchbek, beyng of good mynde and hole remembraunce, makes my last testament and will. Fyrst I bequethe my soule to God allmyghtty, to Our Lady and to all the saintes of heven, and my body to be buryd in the churcheyerde of Pynchbek. To the high altare ther for tithes and oblacions negligently [fo. 291v] forgottyn xijd. To the churche warke ther vs. To the churche warke of Lincoln vjd. To the fatherles childer of St. Catheryn's withowt the wallys of Lincoln iiijd. I gyff xxs to be disposyd of dirige and messe and to pore folkes of my buryall day. To Alice my doughter a chamber worthe xls and vl in money. To Thomas my sun xl, and he to have it payd as shall be thought nedefull be myne executors to hys lernyng. And yff it chaunce other the sayd Alice or Thomas to dy before the receyte of thys above wryttyn gyftes, then I will that the one of them that it shall please God to gyff lyffe to have the parte of the other that shall be deade. And yff [it] fortune them bothe to dye, then I will that bothe ther gyftes to theym above gyffyn shall remayn to William my sun. To Thomas my sun a fedder bed and all that belongyth therto. To William my sun a fedder bed and all that belongyth therto. To John Yong a mare fely now beyng at Pelle's. To William Yong a geldyng now beyng at Mr. Walpully's. To John Clare, my kynsman off Depyng, a dooblet. To Avice my mayd xxd. I will that Mr. Walpull and Mr. Hill be my executors and ever oder of them to have for hys labore vjs viijd. The reste of my goodes I gyff them to Anys my wyffe. Thes beyng wytnes; Sir Thomas Hyll, preste, Robert Halfen and John Yong. Also I make my last will in the same day and date above namyd. I surrender all my copyholde landes that I have into the handes of Robert Alphyn, beyng a tenant of the same, [to] holde to the use and performance of thys my last will. Also I will my house that I bought of William Russyll to be solde by the handes of my executors to the performance of thys my last testament and will. To Agnes my wyff one grene callyd Seyfule's Grene, to her, her heyres and assygnes for ever. Also all the rest of my landes, fre and bonde, in the towne of Pynchbek or ellyswher in the reame of Ynglande, the terme of her lyff naturall. And aftyr the decesse of the sayd Agnes my wyff, I will that all the sayd landes above wryttyn, save my house that I bought of William Russell and the above wryttyn

grene callyd [fo. 292r] Seyfulle's Grene, remeyn to William my sun, to hym, hys [heirs] and assygnes for ever. And yff it chaunce the sayd William my sun to dy before hys mother, or before he cum to the age of xviij yeres, then I will the sayd landes to remayn to Thomas my sun, to hym, hys heyres and assygnes for ever [remainder to] Alice my doughter and to the heyres of her body laufully begottyn. And yff it fortune the sayd Alice my doughter to dy withowt heyres of her body laufully begottyn, then I will al the sayd landes be solde be the handes of the churchewardons of the towne of Pynchbek then beyng, and the money therfore takyn to be disposyd for the helthe of my soule and all Christen soulys. And yff it chaunce my wyff to dy or William my sun cum to the age of xviij yeres, then I will the sayd William my sun to enter of all the sayd landes at the above wrytyn age of xviij yeres.

Proved before P at Spalding, 9 June 1534.

475.   RICHARD ELLERBY [OF PANTON]
        [LCC 1535-37, fos. 24v-25r]

18 April 1534. I, Richerde Ellerbye of the paryshe of Panton, hole of mynde and good remembraunce, do make thys my last will and testament. The fyrste I bequethe my soule to God allmyghtty, to Our Lady St. Mary, and to all the holy cumpeny of heven. My body to be buryd within the churche of St. Andro in Panton. My mortuary as the order and custome of the churche requiryth. To Our Lady's warke of our mother churche of Lincoln xviijd. To the iiij orders of the frerys at Lincoln xvjd. To the high altare of St. Andro in Panton vjs viijd. For my body to be buryd within the sayd churche. To the churche of St. Helene in Edlyngton xijd. To the churche of All Halloys in Wragby viijd. To Johan my wyff iiij of my best oxen, ij steres, ij yeres olde, with vj of my best kye and xx^{ty} of my beste schepe. I gyff all my housholde goodes and stuff to Johanne my wyffe, she to devyde emong my chyldren as she please, the moste convenyent to do. To Johanne my wyff all my corne and haye, to be devydyd as she please beste emonges my chyldren, and the sayd Johanne shall pay my rent and servauntes ther wagyes. To Robert my sun ij oxen myrked iij yeres olde and one yong cowe with a halff score schepe and one yeryng fole trottyng, with a whyte starne the color graye. To William my sun ij oxen iij yeres olde, one blake bellyd with a brown geldyng and a yong cowe, and halff score schepe, with a blake balde fylly iij yere olde. To Dorothe my doughter ij oxen iiij yeres olde, one whyte the other brown belyd, and one brown cowe with a whyte backe and a brandyd qwye and a whyte backe with viij ewes and viij lammys and one blake gray fylly ij yere olde. [fo. 25r] To Agnes my doughter ij browne geldyng steres ij yere olde with one qwye ij yere olde, a redde with a whyte backe and one redde calffe with a whyte backe, and a blak fylly a yere olde, with v yowes and v lammys. To Mathewe Chalyner my servaunt iij calves, ij oxe calves and one qwy calve. To Peter Ellerby my servaunt ij oxe calves and one qwy calve a yere olde. To Mathewe aforesayd iij ewes with iij lammys, and to Peter iij yewes and iij lammys. To the sayd Peter one whyte stag ij yere olde. To the sayd Mathewe one bay stagge with a whyte starre ij yere olde. To Margery my doughter one yowe, a lamme and a hogge. To Thomas Darwyn iij chyldren, iij yowe hogges. To Agnes Ellerbye yongest chylde one hogge and a lamme. To the chyldren of John Ellerby ij hogges and ij lammys. To every one of my godchyldren within the paryshe of Panton a lamme. To Agnes

Ellerby my goddoughter one qwye calve a yere olde. To Robert Smyth wyffe one lamme and to her sun Richerde another lamme. To Jenet Foster one lamme. To Richerde Whythode one hogge with a lamme. To Alice Wryght my syster one yowe with a lamme. To John Browne one yowe hogge. To William Browne one yowe hogge. I will that all the schepe that I have gyffyn and bequethyd to my wyffe or chyldren, or to eny other, all the wooll of the sayd schepe I do reserve in my handes to pay my dettes with. The resydue of all my goodes not bequethyd, my legacy fulfyllyd and my dettes payd, I gyff to Johanne my wyff, Robert my sun and William, the whiche I constitute and orden my executors to dispose as they thynke the moste convenyent to do for my soule helthe and all Christen soulys. Thes beyng wytnes; Sir John Feldehouse, the paryshe preste of Panton, John Johnson, John Darwyn, John Cooper and Richerde Ellerbye, with other mo, the day and yere abovesayd.

Proved before P at Wragby, 14 May 1535.

476.   CATHERINE HATCLYFF [OF GREAT GRIMSBY]
        [LCC 1532–34, fos. 255r–256r]

18 April 1534. I, Catheryne Hatclyff, wydoy, beyng seke in body and hole in mynde, makes thys my laste will and testament. Fyrste I bequethe my soule to allmyghtty God and to Our Lady St. Mary with all the saintes in heven, and my body to be buryd within the churche of St. Jamys in Grymmesby in the Assumpsion's Ile with my wel beluffyd husbande William Hatteclyff, with my mortuary aftyr the lawe. To Our Lady of [fo. 255v] Lincoln iiij*d*. To Our Lady warkes ij*d*. To the high altare of St. Jamys iiij*d*. I will ther be gyffyn, the day of my buryall, to xxx^ty prestes for one trentall of messes, x*s*. To every preste and clerke that is at my dirige ij*d*. I will ther be disposyd emong the poriste people in thys towne x*s*. To my sun Thomas Hatclyff my hyngyngs in the hall and parlure, my tester over my awn bed and vj cushens of grene verders. To my sun William Hatclyff my cownter, my secunde brasse potte, the lytyll pece of sylver, ij sylver sponys, one chyste in the chamber, vj cushyns, too platters of puter and one candylstyk. To my sun Richerde Hatclyff one sylver salte with a cover payng therfore xx*s*, one sylver spone, one gret potte of brasse with one posnet of brasse, iiij platters, iiij poddyngers of puter, iiij sawssers, the new chaffyng dyshe, ij candylstykes, one leade, one sperver, ij counterpoyntes, one of grene verders and the other that my sonne John Hatclyff levys, one Flaunders chyste standyng at my bedde's heade in the parler, one brasyn morter with the pestell, my beste tableclothe, one gret towell of lyn, iij harden towellys, ij coverlyddes, ij pare of blankyttes, ij pannys wherof one gret, one carpet lying in the chamber, the basyn and ewre of puter, and iiij pilloys with bearys. To my sun John Hatclyff my gret pece of sylver, ij sylver sponys, one counterpoynt, one cowe, and he to kepe her to she have a calve and the calve I gyff Jane Goodhande. Also to my sayd sun John ij platters and one candylstyk. To my doughter Anne Pavy my beste kyrtyll of worstyd. To my doughter Johanne Goodhande my lettes[166] bonnet, my sylver hookys, my best gyrdyll with pypys of sylver and gylte payng therfore xx*s*, and aftyr her decesse the sayd gyrdyll to remayn to Jane Goodhande her doughter. To Jane Goodhande one worstyd kyrtyll, one brasse potte, one pare of lyn schetys. To my

---

[166] 'Lettice' was a whitish-grey fur, possibly from the polecat.

sun Thomas Goodhande my blake mare. To my doughter Alice Hatclyff my beste gowne. To my doughter Dorothe Hatclyff ij kyrchyffes. To Mary Hatclyff my velvet pursse with a rebyn. To William Goodhande my cupborde in the buttery. To Elizabeth Goodhande my coffer at my beddesyde. To Elizabeth Mossay a kyrtyll off blake clothe. To Catheryne Butler my servant one matteres, one bolster, one pare of lyn schetes, one pare of hardyn schetes, one candylstyk, ij coverlydes, one lytyll brasse potte, one panne, iiij smale dyshes of puter, one tableclothe, one chaffyng dyshe, one lyn towell, one hardyn towell and ij gownes. [fo. 256r] The resydue of my goodes I gyve to my sonnys William Hatclyff, Richerde Hatclyff and John Hatclyff, whome I make my executors, and my wel beloveyd sun Thomas Hattclyff my supervisor. Thes beyng wytnesses; Sir Peter Mundy, vicar of St. Jamys, Thomas Goodhande, Andrewe Eschedale, with other mo.

Proved before P at Grimsby, 28 April 1534, by the executors.

477.   WILLIAM HOLME [OF ELSHAM]
        [LCC 1532–34, fo. 253r]

18 April 1534. I, William Holme of Ellesham, makes my testament. Fyrste I bequethe my soule to God allmyghtty and to Our Lady St. Mary, and to all the saintes in heven. My body to be buryd in the churcheyerde of All Halloys of Ellesham. To Our Lady warke of Lincoln xijd. To the high altare of Ellesham for tithys forgottyn xijd. To Our Lady gylde of Ellesham and St. Peter gylde iij bushylls malte. To William Holme my sun ij landes sawn with barly callyd Roper Landes, one lande callyd Muncell Ryges, one lande buttes of sande pyttes and half one acre of rye. To Helene Holme my doughter v marke of money or as moche goodes in value, one qwye and ij schepe. To Jenet Holme my doughter fyve marke of money or ellys goodes in value, one qwye and ij schepe. To Margaret Holme, my doughter, v marke of money or ellys goodes in value, one qwye and ij schepe, and also one calve of a yere olde. To William Sergeant my godsun xijd. To every godchylde x[d]. To the vicare of Ellesham one quarter malte and one halffe, and halffe a quarter rye. The resydue of my goodes I gyff to Catheryne my wyffe to dispose for the helthe of my soule, and I will the foresayd Catheryne be my executrix. Thes men wytnesses; Sir John Whaplode, vicare of Ellesham, John Parke, Richerde Sergeant and John Yolle, and other mo. To Richerde Sergeant xijd. To John Parke xijd. To John Yollo x[d].

Proved before P at Caistor, 27 April 1534.

478.   ROBERT GOODWYN [OF AUTHORPE]
        [LCC 1532–34, fos. 301v–302r]

20 April 1534. I, Robert Goodwyn of Awthorpe, with a hole mynde and good remembraunce, do make my last will or testament. Fyrste I bequethe my soule to allmyghtty God and to Our Lady St. Mary, and to all the saintes in heven. My body to be buryd in the churche of St. Margarete in Awthorpe. To the high altare in the same churche xijd. To Our Lady's warke of Lincoln xijd. To Margaret my wyff xx^ty marke, iiij oxen, one cople of iij yere olde steres, iiij geldynges, one amblyng mare, one ffylly, xx^ty yowes, xx^ty lammys, all the croppe in the chambers and the lathe and the felde owtake, ij acres wheate and ij acres beanys, nother the best nor the worste,

the best wayn, the corte and plugh and gere longyng to them, the best yren harrowe, and aftyr my dethe, to John Goodwyn, the same harrowe. To Henry my sun x*l*, my best gowne, my jaket, my dooblet, my hose and one fustyan dooblet the best of all thes. I will that my executors have thys money in ther handes for to gyff to me as I nede it. To John my sun vj*l* xiij*s* iiij*d*, ij marys, one cople of iij yere olde sterys, another cople of ij yere olde steres, ij colte stagges, x yowes, x lammys, a wane, a plough and all the gerys that long to them, one yren harrowe and, after decesse of hys mother-in-lawe, another yren harrowe, one bed, that is to say one materes, one coverlyt, a pare of schetes, one pillo, my best cote, ij doobletes, one pare of whyte hose and ij acres wheate, beanys ij acres, nother the best nor the worste. To Elizabeth my doughter vj*l* xiij*s* iiij*d*, iij beddes, that is to say iij matteres, iij coverlyttes, iij pare of schetes, iij pilloys, ij brasse pottes, iiij candylstykes, a dosyn of puter vessell, one cowe, one cupborde, x yowes, x lammys. To Thomas my sun xx*s* [fo. 302r] To Sir William Redde iij*s* iiij*d*. To John Hope one colte stagge. To Richerde my brother my russyt cote and every one of hys chylder one schepe. To Robert Skettyll wyff vj*s* viij*d*. To George Wyghtman wyff vj*s* viij*d*. To Robert Nicolsun wyff vj*s* viij*d*. To every one of my doughter chylder one schepe. To John Clay my servant ij schepe. To Agnes my servant ij schepe. I will that Sir John Hope, Richerde my brother, Robert Skettyll, George Wyghtman thes to be my executors, and Sir Henry Goodwyn to be my supervisor, and every one of them x*s*. The resydue of my goodes nother wyt nor gyffyn, I gyff to my executors for to dispose it for my soule and Christen soulys, as they thynk best. To Margaret my wyff one pasture which is is wedsett to me for xvj yere, she to have it her lyff. Aftyr her dethe, John Goodwyn to have it to the yeres be run above namyd.

Proved before P at Spilsby, 20 June 1534.

479.　ROBERT PRESTON [OF LITTLE STEEPING]
　　　[LCC 1532–34, fo. 261r]

20 April 1534. I, Robert Preston of Lytyll Stepyng, hole of mynde and seke of body, makes thys my laste will and testament. Fyrste I gyff my soule to God allmyghtty, Our Lady St. Mary and to all the saintes of heven. My body to be buryd in the churche of St. Andro in Lytyll Stepyng. To the sacrament of Lytyll Stepyng xij*d*. To Beatrix my wyffe fyve kye, iiij burlynges and ij calves, and xxv yowes and ther lammys. To Michel Preston my sun a mare with a fole of ij yere olde, all my rayment that belonges to my body reservyng my worste gowne, a gret brasse potte whiche was my fader's with a gret panne. To every one of my doughters a lamme. To Beatrix my wyffe my house at the fen syde with the appurtenance therto belongyng and a acre of medo lying in the este ynges savyng iiij*d* by yere. The resydue of my goodes I gyff them to Beatrix my wyff, whome I make my executrix. Thes beryng wytnes; Sir John Syce, William Saxton, William Stevenson, with other mo.

Proved before P at Spilsby, 5 May 1534.

480.　CATHERINE JAKSON [OF DRY DODDINGTON]
　　　[LCC 1532–34, fo. 275r]

22 April 1534. I, Catheryne Jakson off Dodyngton, of hole mynde and good remembraunce, makes my testament and my last will. Fyrst I bequethe my soule to

God allmyghtty and to Our Lady St. Mary, and to all the holy cumpeny of heven. My body to be buryd in the churcheyerde of All Halloys at Westeburgh. To the high altare of Westburgh vj*d*. To Our Lady's warke of Lincoln vj*d*. To Elizabeth Hunt ij pare of schetes, one pare of hardyn, another of lynyn, a bordeclothe, a towyll and a pilloy, vj yerdes of new clothe and vj*s* viij*d*. To William Hunt an olde tyre of yren. To Jenet Wryghte a bacon flycke. To Mr. Parsone of Westeburgh vj*d*. To Mr. Vicare viij*d*. To Sir Robert Alcoke iiij*d*. The resydue off my goodes to remayn to the behoyff of my chyldren. I make my executor John Loskawe of Sothewell, that he may dispose my good to the use of my chyldren, and he to have for hys labor vj*s* viij*d*. Thes wytnes; Sir Stephyn Howlat, vicar of Westburgh, Richerde Jakson, Robert Harmestrong, John Clyfton, with other mo.

Proved before P at Ancaster, 18 May 1534.

481.   ROBERT HOWTOFTE [OF RAITHBY]
       [LCC 1532 34, fo. 260v]

23 April 1534. I, Robert Howtofte of Ratheby, beyng of hole mynde and good remembraunce, makes thys my testament and laste will. Fyrste I bequethe my soule to allmyghtty God, Our Lady St. Mary and to all the holy cumpeny of heven. My body to be buryd in the churcheyerde of the Trinite of Ratheby and my mortuary as the lawe will. To the high altare of the churche of Ratheby for tithys forgottyn vj*d*. To Our Lady of Lincoln vj*d* and to Our Lady warke within the mynster of Lincoln ij*d*. To the faderlesse chyldren at St. Catheryn's of Lincoln ij*d*. To St. Hugh heade ij*d*. To the churche warke of Ratheby iij*s* iiij*d*. To the bellys within the sayd churche xij*d*. To every light within the churche of Ratheby ij*d*. To Jenet my wyffe ij kye and x schepe. To Richerde Rokelande the one cowe and fyve schepe in hys kepyng. To John Rokelande hys brother the other cowe and fyve schepe in hys kepyng, to the use [and] proffyt of the sayd Jenet my wyff, and the sayd Jenet to dispose the sayd kye and schepe at her laste ende as she please. To Thomas my sun at the age of xvj yeres xl*s*. Also, yff he dye within the sayd xvj yeres, then I gyff the sayd xl*s* to the churche of Ratheby to by a vestiment withall, to the honor and worschip of allmyghtty God. To Agnes Howtofte my kynswoman one cowe, ij yowes and ij lammys. To Jenet Rokelande, doughter of Richard Rokelande, one shedere burlyng. To Robert Rokelande, sun of John Rokelande, x*s*. To every one of ther chyldren of the sayd Richerde Rokelande and John one yowe and a lambe. I will have a trentall within the sayd churche off Ratheby for the helthe of my soule. The resydue of my goodes I gyff to Richerde Rokelande and John Rokelande, whome I make my executors for to dispose them for the helthe of my soule and to fynde and kepe Jenet my wyff duryng her lyffe, and to fulfyll thys my laste will and to pay my dettes. Thes wytnes; Sir William Gose, parson, Richerde Fysher and John Hotofte off Hyndylby, and other.

Proved before P at Spilsby, 5 May 1534.

482.   JOHN MARSHALL [OF FRIESTON IN PARISH OF CAYTHORPE]
       [LCC 1532–34, fo. 273r]

25 April 1534. I, John Marshall of Fryston in the parysche of Cathorpe, hole of mynd and of good remembrans, makes thys my last wyll and testament. Fyrst I

bequeyth my sole to allmyghty God and to Owr Lady Saynt Mary and to all the holy company of hevyn, and my body to be beryyd in the churcheyarde of Saynt Vincent of Cathorp. To Our Lady of Lincoln iij*s* iiij*d*. To the hye awter of my parysche churche of Cathorp xvj*d*. To Our Lade's awter of my parysche churche of Cathorp viij*d*. To the Trenyte awter of my parysche churche of Cathorp iiij*d*. To my parysche churche of Cathorp iij*s* iiij*d*. To the hygh churche on shepe. To every on of my godchylderne on ew and on lame. To Our Lade's Freyers of Lincoln halfe a quarter malte. To the Whyth Freyers of Lincoln halfe a quarter of malte. To the Awstyn Freyers of Lincoln halfe a quarter of malt. To the freyers of Grantan halfe a quarter of malte. To the fryers of Newyorke[167] halfe a quarter of malte. To John Hochynson on calve, on ewe, on lame. To Thomas Forman xx*s*. To Jane Forman xx*s*. To Allys Forman xx*s*. I wyll and ordyn John my son to be my executor for to dysspose the resydew of my goodes for the helthe of my sole as he thinkes the best. I wyll and ordyn Wylliam Hawdyn to be my supervysor, and to have for hys labur iij*s* iiij*d*. Wytnes; Syr John Skot, Wylliam Hawdyn, Rycharde Lane, John Kyrke, Raffe Elwarde.

Proved before P at Ancaster, 18 May 1534.

483.   WILLIAM BARKEWORTHE [OF BILSBY]
       [LCC 1532–34, fos. 324v–325r]

28 April 1534. I, William Barkeworthe of Billesby, off hole mynde and good memory, makes my last will and testament. Fyrste I bequethe my soule unto allmyghtty God, to Our Lady St. Mary and to all the holy cumpeny off heven, and my body to be buryd in the churcheyerde of the Holy Trynyty of Billesby aforesayd, or elleys where it shall please God. To the holy sacrament of the Holy Trynite off Billesby xij*d*. To the churche of the Trinite off Byllesby v*s*. To the churche of St. Margaret of Saleby xij*d*. To the churche of St. Oswalde of Strubby vj*s* viij*d*. To Our Lady of Lincoln x*d*. To Our Lady warke of Lincoln x*d*. To the Domynyk Frerys of Lincoln, to be devydyd emong them, xij*d*. I will ij trentallys to be sung in Strubby churche for my fader soule, my moder soule and all Christen soulys that God will have prayd for. I will one trentall to be sung for my soule and all Christen soulys in the churche of the Holy Trinite of Billesby aforesayd. To John my sun a wayn and a plugh with all the instrumentes to them belongyng, one cople steres and ij meres, the one is [fo. 325r] donyd the other is blake with a fole markyd in the forhed, one cowe, fyve schepe and sex lammys. To Thomas my sun c*s*, one cowe, iij olde schepe and ij lammys. To Agnes my doughter iij qwyes and one cowe, fyve yowes and vj lammys. To Elizabethe my doughter one cowe, ij of my best qweys, one mere, iiij yowes and iij lammys. I will that all my housholde stuff be equally devydyd emong my chyldren. Also I will that yff ony of them dye before they cum to lefull age, one to be another executor. All the resydue of my goodes I gyff to Richerde Thoresthorp and Alan Evan, to fulfyll my legacions and bequestes whiche I have commandyd and pay my dettes with. And that that remayns to be dysposyd by them aforesayd, whome I make myn executors, and ether of them to have v*s* for ther labors. And Sir Andro Billesby, whome I will be supervisor, to have for hys labor xx*s*. With thes wytnes; Sir Thomas Hopkynson,

the wryter of thys testament, William Mawnger, Thomas Walker, John Farmary and John Grondon, with other mo.

   Proved before P at Alford, 15 October 1534.

484. JOHN KYNGERBE [OF GRIMOLDBY]
    [LCC 1532–34, fo. 305r]

29 April 1534. I, John Kyngerbe of Grymmylby, husbandman, beyng in hole mynde and of good remembraunce, makes my will and last testament. Fyrste I bequethe my soule to God allmyghtty and to Our Lady St. Mary and to all the holy sayntes in heven, and my body to be buryed in the churcheyerde of St. Edithe of Grymmolby, to the whiche high altare I bequethe for tithys forgottyn and negligently payd xij*d*. To the reparacions of the sayd churche of Grymmylby one acre of wheate. To the sepulcre light of the churche xij*d*. To the high altare of Our Lady of Lincoln viij*d*. To the red arke iiij*d*. To the reparacions of the churche of Manby one acre of wheate lying on Crose Hile. To the churche of St. Leonerde of Cokryngton viij*d*. To the churche of Belcheforthe viij*d*. To Our Lady of Walsyngham iiij*d*. To the good roode of Boston iiij*d*. To St. Margaret of Kettesby iiij*d*. To the Augustyne frerys of Grymmesby to kepe one messe of Scala Celi for my soule xij*d*. To Agnes my wyff ij of my best oxen, ij kye, my best wayne and ij marys. To Elizabeth my doughter one cowe, one qwye with calve, the thyrde parte of all my puter, ij pottes of brasse, ij pannys, one kettyll, ij beddes with all ther apparell, one thrawn chare, on arke, one chyst, one cupborde, one tabyll, ij salttes, ij candylstyckes, on basyn, one chaffer, one acre of wheate lying on Godderde Hile and on acre of beanys. To Richerde my sun and to William my sun one pare of oxen, my oder wayn, one corte, ij marys, ij acres of wheate, ij acres of beanys. The resydue of my husbandry and housholde I will it shall be devydyd emong my wyff and my ij sonnys. To Margery Walker my goddoughter one lamme. I will that every godchylde shall have j*d*. The resydue of my goodes unbequethyd, my body buryd, I commit to the disposicion of my executors, whome I make Agnes my wyff and Richerde my sun to dispose them to the pleasure of God and for the helthe of my soule and all Crysten soulys, and Jamys Walker and William Kyngerby supervisors, and they to have for ther labor iij*s* iiij*d*. Thes wytnesses; Sir William Howtton, John Smyth, John Wyothe, with other mo.

   Proved before P at Lincoln, 28 August 1534.

485. ROBERT KELSAY [OF IMMINGHAM]
    [LCC 1532–34, fos. 293v–294r]

1 May 1534. I, Robert Kelsay of Imyngham in the countie of Lincoln, husbandman, with a full mynde and hole memory, makyth my testament and last will. Fyrste I bequethe my soule to allmyghtty God, to Our Lady St. Mary and to all the gloriose cumpeny of heven, and my body to be buryed within the churche of St. Andro of Ymyngham. To the high altare of Imyngham xx*d*. To Our Lady warke of Lincoln [fo. 294r] xij*d*. I will that iij trentallys be done for me, one at Imyngham, one at Caistor and one at Kyme Abbay. To Agnes my wyff a messe within Caistor callyd Newbalde Thyng with all the purtenaunce belongyng to it within the towne and felde of Caistor to the terme and ende of her lyffe. And aftyr she decesse, to remayn

to the right heyr of Robert Kelsay laufully begottyn of hys body. To Johanne Stevenson my doughter a cowe. To Alice Rocleff my doughter a cowe. The resydue of my goodes not wyt I bequethe to Agnes my wyffe and George my sun, whome I make my full executors that they may dispose it for the helthe of my soule. Thes men beryng wytnes; Sir Thomas Angell, vicare of Imyngham, Christofer Nottall, preste, John Stevenson, John Wylson, Robert Rocleff, with other mo.

> Proved before P at Lincoln, 19 June 1534. Adm. granted to Agnes the executrix, reserving power to grant to George the co-executor when he shall come.

486. WILLIAM COLSON [OF STROXTON]
[LCC 1532–34, fo. 307v]

2 May 1534. I, William Colson of Strouxton, of hole mynde and good remembraunce, make my last will. Fyrste I bequethe my soule to allmyghtty God, Our Blessyd Lady and saintes. My body to be buryd in the churcheyerde of Strouxton. To Our Lady of Lincoln ij*d*. To the parson of Strouxton to pray for my soule, a bushell of malte. To the churche of Strouxton a bushell barly. To my wyff a potte, a panne, a redde cowe. To Robert Marshall chylder of Harlaxton a barly lande. The resydue of my goodes I gyff them to Johanne my wyff and John my sun, whome I make my executors, and Sir John Nerde, parson, supervisor to the intent that he may se it performyd for the helthe of my soule.

> Proved before P at Lincoln, 24 September 1534.

487. THOMAS FEN [OF EDENHAM]
[LCC 1532–34, fo. 307r]

3 May 1534. I, Thomas Fen, seke of body and off a hole mynde and good remembraunce, makes my last will or testament. Fyrst I gyff and bequethe my soule to God allmyghtty, to Our Lady St. Mary and to all the saintes in heven, and my body to be buryd in the churcheyerde of Edenham. For my mortuary as the lawe doys admyt. To the high altare in Edenham churche halffe a seame barly. To our mother churche of Lincoln iiij*d*. To our Lady's gylde in Edenham one schepe. To the bellys in the same churche a bushyll of barly. I bequethe too bee hyves, bees' waxe and hony to kepe and mayntene a light before St. Sunday in the foresayd church of Edenham. Also it is my will that ther be vj lode of stonys layd in the strete of Grymsthorp of my coste and chargys. Also I gyff x*s* for a trentall of messes to be done in the churche of Edenham for me and my wyff, and all my good frendes. To every one of my godchylder a stryke of barly. The resydue of my good I gyff to Thomas Fen and John Fen, my sunys, whome I make my executors to dispose for the helthe of my soule, my wyff soule and all my good frendes' soulys. Wytnes therof; Sir Thomas Habur, Edwarde Thomas, John Nelson, with other mo.

> Proved before P at Lincoln, 18 September 1534. Adm. granted to John Fen the executor, reserving power to grant to Thomas Fen the co-executor, when he shall come.

488.   JOHN PYNDER [OF LEAKE]
        [LCC 1535–37, fo. 121]

3 May 1534. I, John Pynder of Leeke, hole of mynde and good remembraunce, makes my testament and last will. Firste I bequethe my soule to allmyghtty God, to Hys mother St. Mary and to all the saintes in heven, and my body to be buryed in the churcheyerde of Leeke. To the high altare of Leeke ij*d*. To every other altare there ij*d*. For forgottyn tithes iiij*d*. To Our Lady of Lincoln iiij*d*. To St. Catheryn's withowte Lincoln ij*d*. To Thomas my sun ij sterres of ij yeres age and ij yong mares of one yere age, and also one wane when he cumys to xxiiij yeres. To Richerde [fo. 121v] my sun a qwye and a dun mare. To ether of my doughters, that is to say Isabell and Margaret, a qwye of ij yeres of age, ij puter dooblers, a matteres, one coverlyd, a pare of shetes, a bolster and a pilloy, a brasse potte and one panne. Moreover I will that Agnes my wyffe have all my landes the terme of her lyff, and aftyr the decesse of the sayd Agnes, I will that Thomas my sun have one acre and one halffe lande lying on the toftes and to hys heyres of hys body laufully brought furthe. I will that Richerde my sun have one acre arable lande whiche I bought, lying on the toftes, and v roode of pasture lying in Leverton ynges, to hys heyres of hys body laufully brought furthe. Yff other of my sunnys dye withowt heyres laufully brought furthe, then I will that he that lyffes have the parte of hym that dyes. Yff bothe my sunnys dye withowt heyres laufully brought furthe, then I will that my foresayd landes be devydyd betwyxte my ij doughters and to ther heyres of ther bodys laufully brought furthe. Yff my sayd ij doughters dye withowt heyres of ther bodys laufully brought furthe, then I will that all my foresayd landes be solde be my sayd executors and feoffes, and the money therfore receyved be spente in warkes of charite aftyr ther discrescion. The resydue of my goodes not gyven nor bequethyd I gyff to Agnes my wyff and John Paynson, whome I make my executors to dispose for my soule as they thynke shal be most plesure to God, with Willum Larkes supervisor. I gyff to John Paynson and Willum Larkes, for ther labor, other of them xij*d*. Thes wytnes; Sir Richerde Woodroyff and Willum Hodgeson, with other moy.

        Proved before P at Sutterton, 17 July 1536. Adm. granted to Agnes the relict and executrix, John Paynson the co-executor renouncing.

489.   RICHARD SHEPPERDE [OF BENINGTON IN HOLLAND]
        [LCC 1532–34, fo. 286v]

3 May 1534. I, Richerd Scheperde, the sun of William Sheperde of Bennyngton, of goode and hole mynde beyng, makes my testament concludyng thys my last will. Fyrste I bequethe my soule to allmyghtty God and to all the saints in heven. My body to be buryd in the kyrke of All Halloys in Bennyngton. To the high altare viij*d*. To oder ij altares xij*d*. To Our Lady of Lincoln xiiij*d*. To the reparacion of the kyrke in Bennyngton vj*s* viij*d*. To my curate iiij*d*. To the madyns' light and the yong men light viij*d*. To one prest to syng for my soule, my fader and my moder one hole yere in the kyrk of Bennyngton, he to have to hys wages viij markes vj*s* viij*d*. Yf it please John Sheperde to be a prest, he to have the sayd servys, yff not anoder preste to have it. To all my godchylder one lamme. To John Clerke one stak. To Margaret Pynchbek one yowe. To Elizabeth Clerke one yow. To Margaret Shepperde one yowe. To Elizabeth Sheperde one yow. To Isabell Sheperde one yowe. To Jenyt Sheperde one yowe. To William Shepperde and Simon Sheperde ij sheryng schepe.

To the iiij orders of frerys in Boston xxs to pray for me and my good frendes. To William my brother my capitall messe with the grounde under it, with iij acres owr the gate accordyng to my fader will, as apperys in hys will. I will that Mr. John Frysney have the sayd lande that I bought of John Pekyll for the sayd sum of money that he and I was agreyd of. To John Sheperde iij stonge lande in Pollar in fe simple, with the barly apon it. To William my brother one acre in Seldyke in fe symple, so that he performe thys my last will, also iij acres of pastures in Leverton in fe symple of thys condicion, that he pay or cause to be payd to Elizabeth Clarke and Margaret Pynchbek xls. The resydue of all my goodes not gyff nor bequest, I gyff them to William my brother whome I make my executor, he to dispose for my soule as he will make answer, and Mr. John Frysnay, gent[leman] supervisor, and to have xiijs iiijd. Thes wytnes; Sir William Stedeman, John Fox, Richerd Pynchbek, John Sheperde, John Godsun, John Pekyl, and other mo.

Proved before P at Boston, 10 June 1534.

490.   THOMAS RABDYN [OF GOSBERTON]
       [LCC 1532–34, fo. 321v]

4 May 1534. I, Thomas Rabdyn of the paryshe of Gosberton, beyng perfecte of mynde and of a good remembraunce, makes my last will and testament. The firste I bequethe my soule to allmyghtty God and to Hys blessyd mother St. Mary and to all the holy cumpeny of heven, and my body to be buryd in the churcheyerde of St. Peter and St. Paule within the paryshe off Gosberton. To the high altare therof for my tithys forgottyn iiijd. To All Saule light ijd. To Our Lady's light ijd. To the plowe light jd. To the churche warke ijd. To the reparacion of the gyldehall ijd. To the offeryng off Our Lady of Lincoln ijd. To the chylder of Saynt Catheryn's ijd. To Margaret my wyff my house in Wyberton with iij acres lande therto perteynyng, to gyff and to sell at her pleasure of thys condicion, that she gyff or cause to be gyffyn aftyr her naturall lyff to Margaret Osse, doughter of Thomas Osse, xls when she cumys to laufull age. And yff she dye or she cum to laufull age, then I will my wyff or her assignes dispose the sayd xls in good warkes for the helthe of my soule and all Christen soules. To every order of frerys in Boston one stryke barly. The resydue of my goodes I gyff them to Margaret my wyff, the whiche I make my true executrix to performe thys my last will, to pay my dettes and to bryng my body to the grounde. Thes wytnes; Sir Henry Topplys, Thomas Whytemay, John Osse, Robert Thorpe of Quadryng, with other mo Thomas Masun.

Proved before P at Swineshead, 8 June 1534.

491.   THOMAS LEVYS [OF PINCHBECK]
       [LCC 1532–34, fos. 290v–291r]

10 May 1534. I, Thomas Levys off Pynchbek, beyng of good mynde and hole remembraunce, makes my last will and testament. Fyrste I bequethe my soule to God allmyghtty, to Our Lady and to all the saintes of heven, and my body to be buryd in the churcheyerde of Pynchbek. To the high altare ther for tithes and oblacions forgottyn iiijd, and to every altare in the sayd churche ijd. To the churche warke of Lincoln ijd and to the fatherles chyldren of St. Catheryn's withowt the wallys off Lincoln ijd. I will have a trentall sayd for my soule and all Crysten

soulys. To Thomas my sun fyve schepe with ther lammys and a bayd mare, and they to be delyveryd immediatly aftyr my decesse. To Richerde my sun v yowys and v lammys and a yong gray mare. To Robert my sun v yowes and x lammys and a yeryng mare fole. To Saunder my sun v yowes and v lammys and my yong ambelyng geldyng. To Elizabeth my doughter v yowes and v lammys and a yong browne cowe with her proffyttes. To the chylde that my wyffe is withall, yff it please God to gyff it lyff at the tyme of the birthe, v yowys and fyve lammys and my elder browne cowe. All thes above wryttyn gyftes to my chyldren to be delyveryd to them immediatly aftyr my decesse. Also yff one, ij or iij, or so many of my chyldren as I have to dye before the age of xviij yeres, then I will that the gyftes to them gyven that ar dead to remayn and evenly to be devydyd betwyxte that that it shall please God to gyff lyffe to. And yff it chaunce all my chyldren to dy or they cum to the age of xviij yeres and ther mother then be alyve, I will [fo. 291r] that all suche gyftes as was to them gyffyn returne agane to ther mother. And yff it chaunce my wyffe then to be deade, then I will that all suche gyftes as to my chyldren were gyffyn, to be disposyd in the churche of Pinchbek by the handes of the churchewardens then beyng, for the helthe of my soule, ther soulys and all Crysten soulys. The reste of my good I gyff to Alyson my wyff, whome I make my sole executrix. Thes beyng wytnes; Sir Thomas Hill, preste, Robert Slator, Andro Williamson, Thomas Hall. Also I make my last will in the same day and date above namyd. I surrender all suche copyholde landes that I have into the handes of Robert Slator, to the use of thys my last will. To Alyson my wyff my house and all my landes, fre and bonde, be they more or lesse the terme of her lyff, and she to kepe it in reparacion and to wede and shrede or to fell one, ij or iij treys to repare the sayd house withall, or ellys to make no waste. And aftyr the decesse of my wyff I will that Thomas my sun have all my landes, fre and bownde, to hym and to the heyres of hys body laufully begottyn, and he to gyff to the rest of my chyldern xl*s*, evenly to be devydyd emonges them that shall be alyve. And yff it fortune Thomas my sun to dy before hys moder, or to dy withowt heyres of hys body laufully begottyn, then my will is that my eldest sun shulde have all my landes more and lesse, provydyd alway that he that hathe my lande shall gyff to the rest of hys bretherne and systers xl*s*.

Proved before P at Spalding, 9 June 1534.

492.   JOHN GAWDBY [OF SOUTH FERRIBY]
        [LCC 1532–34, fo. 279]

12 May 1534. I, John Gawdby of Ferybe in the county of Lincoln, husbandman, hole of mynde and good remembraunce, makyth thys my testament and last will. Fyrst I gyff and bequethe my soule unto God allmyghtty, to Our Lady St. Mary and to all the holy cumpeny in heven. My body to be buryd in the churcheyerde of St. Nicholes of South Ferybe. To the high altare of the same, to the parson fee for tithys forgottyn, xij*d*. To the prior fee viij*d*. To the reparac[ion] of the cathedrall churche of Lincoln vj*d*. To the high altare of the same vj*d*. To the ymage of our Lady of the Whyte Frerys of Hull, iiij*d*. To St. John of Beverlay iiij*d*. To the reparacions of the churche of St. Nicholes of Ferybe [fo. 279v] a quarter barly. To the reparacions of the brige over Ancolm, half a quarter barly. To every one of my iij sonnys, for ther chylde's parte, iiij*l* in money. To Helene my doughter v*l*, provydyd so that yff it fortune any of my chylder to dye before they be of laufull age

and have ther parte, that then ther porcion of thys my legacy shall be devydyd emonges them that be lyveyng. To William Gawdby my brother a quarter barly. To Thomas my brother a quarter barly. To a preste for to sing a trentall of messys for my soule and Christen soulys x*s*. I will that a pounde waxe shall be burnyd in honor of the blyssyd sacrament of the altare. To Sir Roger[168] to pray for me xij*d*. To Alice Coke a yowe. To every one of my godchylder a pecke wheate. To Sir Thomas Gryme iij*s* iiij*d*. I will that Agnes my wyff shall have, to the bryngyng up of my chylder, the house that I dwell in with all the landes and medoys therto belongyng, with all the appurtenaunces, with all other housys, tenementes, landes and medoys, rentes or fredoms, with all ther appurtenaunces within the towne and feldes of Ferybe. Also all the landes and tenementes of myne within the towne and feldes of Barton with all ther appurtenaunce, unto suche tyme as my heyr be of the age of xxj yeres so that she shall cause my housys and lande to be upholdyn as it ought to be in all causys duryng the terme aforesayd, and suffer myne heyr to enter unto them when he shall be of the age aforesayd, aftyr the usage and custome of the lawe. Provydyd alway that yff it fortune Agnes my wyff to dye (whiche allmyghtty God defende) before my heyr of the age of xxj yeres, that then all my landes and tenementes above wryttyn with all ther commodytes and profyttes within the towne and feldes abovesayd shall be takyn unto the bryngyng up of my chylder, to whome the foresayd Agnes my wyff shall assigne them unto the tyme be that myne heyr be of the age of xxj yeres. The resydue of my goodes I gyff unto Agnes my wyff, whome I make myne executrix. Thes men beyng wytnes; Sir Roger Crosse, curate, John Doobler, Robert Fenby, William Wylkynson and John Wylson, with other mo. The day and yere above wryttyn.

Proved before P at Lincoln, 5 June 1534.

493.   ROBERT CHAMBERS [OF DODDINGTON]
       [LCC 1532–34, fo. 306v]

14 May 1534. I, Robert Chambers of Dodyngton in the countie of Lincoln, hole of mynde and perfyte of remembraunce, makyth and ordenyth thys my testament and last will. Fyrste I bequethe my soule to allmyghtty God, to hys mother Our Lady St. Mary and to all the holy cumpeny of heven. My body to be buryd in the churcheyerde of St. Peter in Dodyngton. To the sacrament of the high altare viij*d*. I will that ther be a trentall of messes done in the sayd churche of Saynt Peter for the helthe of my soule. I bequeth to my mortuary as the lawe and custome admyt. To Alexander my eldest sun a blak cowe with a sterne in the forheade, and a yowe and a lamme. To Jenet my doughter a browne qwye with a sterne in the forhed, and a yowe and a lamme. To John my secunde sun a brown bullok and a yowe and a lamme. To Robert my thyrde sun a whyte heddyd qwye and a yowe and a lamme. To Michel my sun a browne flekyd qwye and a yowe and a lamme. To William my fyfte sun a blake qwye with a taggyd tale and a yowe and a lamme. To Eleoner my yongest doughter a bullok whyte flekyd, and a yowe and a lamme. To Richard Peyrson my servant a blak flekyd cowe and a yowe and a lamme. To every one of my godchylder ij*d*. To the roode lofte, yff it be mayd, iij*s* iiij*d*. The resydue of my goodes I gyff to Beatrix my wyff and John Wylson whome I make

---

[168] Sir Roger Crosse, curate of the parish.

myn executors, and the supervisor of my will John Knyght. Wytnes herof; John Colson, John Palmer, Gregory Wyte and Thomas Walcar of the same towne of Dodyngton, with many mo.

Proved before P at Lincoln, 18 September 1534. Adm. granted to Beatrix the relict and executor, reserving power to grant to John Wylson the co-executor, when he shall come.

494.   WILLIAM BROKYLBY [OF BARKSTON]
[LCC 1532–34, fo. 335v]

16 May 1534. I, William Brockylby of Barston, of hole mynde and good memory, do order and constitute thys my last will and testament. Fyrste I bequethe my soule to allmyghtty God, to Our Lady St. Mary and to all the hole saintes in heven, and my body to be buryd in the paryshe churche of Barston in the myddyll yle. To Our Lady warkes in Lincoln viijd. To the pore chylder at St. Catheryn's iiijd. To the high altare in Barston one ewe schepe for tithes forgottyn. I gyff x ewe schepe and x lammys to fynde a light in Barston churche before the sacrament to burne all divyne servyce tyme as other lyghttes do and to kepe my obbyt with yerely, and thys to be orderyd as the townschyp semys best to contynewe for evermore. To the frerys of Grantham a bushyll barly. To Brandon chapell a bushyll barly. To the Trynite gylde in Hough a bushyll malte. To Hugh Brockylbe my sun halff my croppe in Hougham felde, bothe corne and hay, and vj schepe. To Agnes Upton ij ewes and ij lammys. To Isabell Beyll ij ewes and ij lammys. To Johan Brockylbe my doughter x schepe. To Alice my doughter x schepe. To Marie my doughter vj schepe. To Elizabeth my doughter vj schepe. To Margaret my doughter, the elder, vj schepe. To Margaret my doughter, the yonger, vij schepe. To William my sun x schepe and vj quarter barly and a bounde carte. The resydue of all my goodes I gyff to Catheryne Brackylbe my wyff, whome I make my executrix to dispose for the helthe of my soule as semys best. Thes wytnes; Robert Welbe, Robert Mapiltofte, Edwarde Beyn, with other mo. I make Sir William Seell supervisor.

Proved before P at Ancaster, 29 October 1534.

495.   ELIZABETH GOODWYN [OF AUTHORPE]
[LCC 1532–34, fo. 302]

16 May 1534. I, Elizabeth Goodwyn, of a hole mynde and of good remembraunce, makes my testament. Fyrste I wyt my soule to God allmyghtty and to Our Lady St. Mary and to all the saintes in heven, and my body to be buryd in the kyrkeyerde of St. Margaret in Awthorpe. To Our Lady of Lincoln warke viijd. To the high altare in Awthorpe kyrke xijd. To Our Lady light viijd. To Robert Nicolson wyff, my syster, vjs viijd. To Henry my brother one cowe. To John my brother one cowe. To Agnes my syster v schepe. To Robert Skyttyll wyff, my syster, one cowe. To Henry Goodwyn my broder v lammes. To John my brother v lammys. To my mother-in-lawe v schepe. I wyt Sir William Redde xxd to pray for me. To John Smyth wyff my beste gowne. To Jenet Hollande my best kyrtyll. [fo. 302v] To Agnes Watson my redde kyrtyll. To Jenet Chatterton my olde gowne. To the crosse a kyrchyff. To John Clay xijd. To Henry my brother and to John my broder ij brasse pottes and my candylstykes. To Henry my brother my ambre. To my mother-in-lawe ij of my best

dooblers. To John my brother v dooblers. To Henry my brother iiij dooblers. To Jenet Lowtton one doobler. To Henry my brother one bed and to John my brother one bedd. To Margaret Smyth one bed. To John my brother on brasse potte. To Agnes my syster my best cappe. To Robert Skyttyll wyff one other cappe. To Jenet Hollande my best rale. To Robert Skyttyll wyff my best beades. I will that a preste syng messys for me a quarter of the yere. The reste of my goodes I gyff to Robert Skyttyll and George Wythman, my brother-in-law. And I wyll that Henry and John my brothers be my executors, and other of them to have for ther labors vj*s* viij*d*. Thes wytnes; Sir William Rede, William Hope, George Wythman, cum aliis.

Proved before P at Greenfield, 20 June 1534.

496.   SIR RICHARD TYPLER [OF EWERBY]
         [LCC 1532–34, fo. 293]

16 May 1534. I, Sir Richard Typler, the vicare of Iwardeby, hole in mynde and goode of remembraunce, makes my testament and last will. Fyrste I bequethe my soule to allmyghtty God, to Our Lady St. Mary and to all the holy compeny of heven, and my body to be buryd in the qwere of the sayd Iwerby. To our mother churche of Lincoln xij*d*. To every preste that commys to the sayd Iwerby apon the day of my buryall, the vij[th] day and the xxx[ty] day vj*d*. I bequeth that ther to be disposyd to the pore people of the sayd Iwarby at every one of the foresayd days vj*s* viij*d*. To the reparacion of the bellys ther vj*s* viij*d*. To the reparacions of the seates in the churche ther vj*s* viij*d*. To Our Lady light vj*s* viij*d*. To the sayd churche of Iwarby xl*s* to that intente that the churchewardons for tyme beyng kepe a yerely obbyt for my soule and all Christen soulys in the sayd churche, and that ther be distribute at the sayd obbyt to the vicare for tyme beyng or to hys depute iiij*d* to be offeryd j*d*, to the paryshe clerke j*d*, to the bellman j*d*, to the ryngers of the bellys iiij*d* and to xiiij of the poreste people within the sayd Iwerby xiiij*d*. To Mr. Prior and to the convente of Kyme as to registre me as a brother of ther house. To the sayd Mr. Prior and to the sayd convent of the sayd Kyme to say for my soule and all Christen soulys a trentall x*s*. To Our Lady light of Hale vj*s* viij*d*. To a lighte before the Trinite of Burne Broughton one cowe beyng in the handes of Thomas Mylner of the same towne. To Agnes Nelson the house that is callyd Whyteloke house with the appurtenaunces for the terme of her naturall lyff, and after the terme of her lyff to remayn to Richerde Typler, also ij kye, xxvj*s* viij*d*, the bedde that she lyethe in as it standes, iij pare of schetes, halff of all maner of grane that is in my house, one chare, ij stolys, ij tabyllys, one chyste, one payntyd clothe, iiij puter platters, one olde charegeer, ij kettyls, one brasse potte, all my jewyll, halff my hemp, flax and yerne, ij pease landes with a barly lande lying within the feldes of Kyrkby, my secund gowne for her lyveray, my beste holdyng swyne, iiij ale pottes, a pare bed stockes, a hekyll and a ambry. To Agnes Fowlle ij yowys with ther lammys. To Richerde Typler my cownter, my ambry and a brasen morter. [fo. 293v] To Leonerde Markham one sylver spone and to hys wyff one sylver spone. To John Markham one sylver spone. To John Thomson of Kyrkby one quarter of barly that is in hys kepyng, halffe a quarter of wheate, one ewe and a lamme. To hys wyffe one ewe and a lamme. To John Thomson the yonger one ewe and a lamme. I will that the resydue of my schepe in the kepyng of the sayd John Thomson, that William Typler the yonger and John Markham have them. To William Neleson ij yowes and ij lammys. The

resydue of my schepe at Howell to Richerde Typler and Agnes Typler hys syster. To Robert Hole vj*s* viij*d*, my best jaket. To Mastres Fayrfax of Swareby a bee hyve. To my goddoughter, Mr. Grantham doughter, a be hyve. I will that the resydue of my bees and hyves be devydyd betwyxte Richerde Typler, Jane Typler hys syster and Agnes Neleson by equall porcions. To Sir Edmunde Hutchynson preste iij*s* iiij*d*. To Agnes Neleson a leade. The resydue of my goodes I gyff to my brother William Typler of Hole and to my nevoy Richard Typler hys sun, to that intente that they dispose it for my soule and all Christen soulys. I orden Leonerde Markham of the sayd Hole the supervisor, and he for to have for hys panetakyng vj*s* viij*d*. Thes beyng wytnesses; Syr Edmunde Hutchynson, preste, John Bowlle, George Browne, Thomas Dykes and John Collyng, with other mo.

Proved before P at Sleaford, 11 June 1534.

497.   ALEXANDER HOWDALE [OF SKIRBECK]
        [LCC 1532–34, fo. 316]

20 May 1534. I, Alexander Hawdaylle of Skyrbek, husbandman, of a good and hole memory, makyth thys my last will and testament. Fyrste I bequethe my soule to God allmyghtty and to Hys blessyd mother St. Mary and to all the hole cumpeny in heven, and my body to be buryed in the churcheyerde of St. Nycholes off Skyrbek. To Our Lady's warke at Lincoln vj*d*. To the ymage of Our Lady of Lincoln vj*d*. To the churche warke of Skyrbek of St. Nicholes iij*s* iiij*d*. To the high altare in Skyrbek iiij*d*. I will that a trentall of xxx^{ty} messys be sayd for the soule of me, Elizabeth my wyff soule, our frendys' soulys and all Christen soulys in the churche of Skyrbek. To Alexander Pynchbek a shodde carte and all the gerys for fyve horsys, one blake mare, another blak mare wyth a whyte foote, a gray balde mare, another gray bakde mare of ij yere olde and a redde ambelyng mare, ij of my beste kyne, ij qwyes, the one is blake flekyd and another is redde with a whyte sterre in the heade, x of my beste ewes and ther lammys when they be clyppyd, a plugh with all the gerys that longyth therto and the one halfe of my housholde stuff. To Agnes Alforde ij kyen, ij ewes and ther lammys when they be clyppyd, a quarter malte, halffe a quarter barly. To Alexander Pynchbek a counter and a spruce chyst besydes the halff of the housholde stuff. And the other halff I will it shall be devydyd betwyxt Elizabeth Pynchbek my doughter and Agnes Alforde by even porcions. To Elizabeth Rumforthe my goddoughter a ewe and a lamme when she is clyppyd. To Elizabeth [fo. 316v] Hobson ij ewes and ij lammys. I will that myn executors have the rule and order of all the legaces of Alexaunder Pynchbek withowt any waste at the syght of ther neyghbours to the sayd Alexander cum to the age of xx^{ty} yeres. The resydue of all my goodes I gyff them to Thomas Willes of Boston and Thomas Hawdayll of Kyrton, whome I make my executors to dispose them to the pleasure of God and the helthe of my soule and all Christen soulys. Thies beyng wytnes; Sir Richerde Salter, curate of Skyrbek, Sir Edwarde Ferroner, Sir John Markeby, prestes, Richerde Turpyn, William Rumforthe, with other mo, the day and yere above sayd.

Proved before P at Boston, 10 June 1534.

498.   ROBERT HOUDE [OF WESTON]
       [LCC 1532–34, fo. 290]

21 May 1534. I, Robert Houde, beyng hole of mynde and of good memory, makes my testament. Fyrst I gyff and bequethe my soule to God allmyghtty, to Our Lady St. Mary and to all the saintes in heven. My body to be buryd in the churcheyerde of Weston. To the holly sacrament for tithes forgottyn vj*d*. To the sepulchre light within the same churche iij pounde waxe. To the iij lightes within the same churche ix*d*. To the churche warke of Weston xx*d*. To Our Lady's altare of Lincoln vj*d*. To the pore chyldren at St. Catheryn's withowt Lincoln iij*d*. To Thomas Hoode one ij yere olde bullok with calve, one blake fely and a balde yeryng, one yowe and a lamme and my violet cote. To Richerde my wyff sun my browne cowe for x*s*. To Robert Browne on yowe. To Richerde Edreyng one yowe clyppyd. To Thomas Williamson one yowe and a lamme. To William Buze one lamme. To Isabell Buze one yowe lamme. To Robert Callowe one lamme. To John Preste sun one lamme. To Agnes Buze one lamme. The resydue [fo. 290v] of my goodes I gyff to Margaret my wyff whome I make my executrix and Richerde Edreige to be my supervisor, they to dispose my goodes as they thynk moste plesyng to God and helthe of my soule and all Christen soulys. In wytnes heroff; Sir John Poynttone, John Waryn, John Davyson, John Marchande, the day and yere abovesayd.

Proved before P at Spalding, 9 June 1534.

499.   RICHARD HUNTER [OF HOGSTHORPE]
       [LCC 1532–34, fo. 327]

21 May 1534. I, Richerde Hunter of Hoggesthorp, beyng off hole mynde and good memory, ordens and makes my testament and last will. Fyrste I bequethe my soule to allmyghtty God, to Our Blessyd Lady St. Mary and to all the holy cumpeny of heven, and my body to be buryd within the churcheyerde of Hoggesthorp. To the high altare of the same churche for my tithys forgottyn xij*d*. To the churche warke of Our Lady of Lincoln viij*d*. To the churche warke of Hoggesthorp xij*d*. To the chapell of St. Leonerde within the paryshe of Momby viij*d*. To the light of St. Leonerde within the same chapell one pounde of waxe. To Helene my wyff ij kye, xxx^{ty} schepe and all my housholde stuff. To Richerde my sun one wane, one plough and ij schepe. To Robert my sun ij schepe. To Anthony my sun ij schepe. To John my sun ij schepe and one calve. To Isabell my doughter one cowe and ij schepe. To Beatrix my doughter iiij schepe and one calve. To Margarete Ledegat one yowe. To Robert Ledegat one lambe. The resydue of my goodes I will that they be equally devydyd emonges my chyldren when they shall cum to laufull age. And yff any of them decesse before they cum to laufull age, I will the goodes to them before bequethyd that so decessys remayn to be equally devydyd emong them that then be of lyff. And yff it happen that all myn aforesayd chyldren decesse before they cum to laufull age, then I will that the goodes to them before bequethyd be disposyd for my soule and all Christen soulys. I make Thomas Borddall of Ardelthorp and William Russyll off Ingollmellys my executors, they to pay my dettes and fulfyll thys my last will accordyng to the lawe of holy churche. To ether of them for ther [fo. 327v] labors iij*s* iiij*d*. Thes wytnesses; Sir Thomas Weall, preste, Simon Halden, John Heryng and William Place, with other mo.

Proved before P at Alford, 15 October 1534.

500.   WILLIAM BAWDRYK OF SALTFLEETBY ST. CLEMENT]
        [LCC 1535–37, fo. 13r]

23 May 1534. I, William Bawdryk off Saltfletby Clement, hole of mynde and good of remembraunce, make my last will. Firste I bequethe my soule to allmyghtty God, to Our Lady St. Mary and to all the saintes in heven, and my body to be buryed in the churchyerde of St. Clement of Saltfletby, and for my mortuary as lawe and custome requiryth. To the high altare of St. Clement of Saltfletby aforesayd ij*s*. To the sayd churche of St. Clement ij*s*. To Our Lady of Lincoln warkes viij*d*. I will that Beatrix my wyff shall have my house in Saltfletby and the husse crofte, and the crofte that lyes at the northe ende of the same crofte with the wong lying at the northe ende of the husse crofte the space of xvj yeres, to bryng up my sun Richerde with. I will that any crofte of the south syde Mardyke be letyn the space off xvj yeres for the performance of my will and, one acre and one halffe acre lying in Fygarlandes, and I will that my wyff have xx*s* be yere as long as she lyvys aftyr . . . [169]

501.   JOHN BRAKE [OF GREAT COATES]
        [LCC 1532–34, fos. 331v–332r]

24 May 1534. I, John Brake th'elder of Gret Cotes, hole of mynde and seke in body, makes my last will and testament. Firste I bequethe my soule unto allmyghtty God and to Hys mother Mary and all the holly cumpeny in heven. My body to be buryed in the churcheyerde of St. Nicholes of Cotys. To Our Lady of Lincoln iiij*d*. To the high altare of Cotes aforesayd one shepe. To Alan Brake my sun a cople of sterys and one mayr. To John Brake my sun a cople of sterys and a mayr. To Margaret my doughter one schepe. To Sybell my doughter one schepe. To Robert Drowry one schepe. To Sir Robert Cokhed, paryshe prest of Cotes aforesayd, a bushell of barly. The resydue of all my goodes not bequethyd I gyff unto Isabell my wyff and Alan Brake my sun, whome I make my executors to order and dispose the sayd good for the helthe of my soule and all [fo. 332r] Crysten soulys as by ther discrescion shall be thought most mete and necessary. Wrytte the day and yere abovesayd. Thes beryng wytnes; the sayd Sir Robert Cokehed, paryshe preste, and Peter Button and other mo.
        Proved before P at Grimsby, 20 October 1534.

502.   ROBERT SWATON [OF MINTING]
        [LCC 1532–34, fos. 302v–303r]

29 May 1534. I, Robert Swaton off Myntyng, of good mynde and full memory, makes my testament. Fyrste I bequethe my soule to allmyghtty God and to Our Lady St. Mary and to all the saintes in heven, and my body to be buryd in the churcheyerde off St. Andro at Myntyng. To the high altare of Myntyng xx*d*. To the reparacion of Myntyng churche vj*d*. To Our Lady warke of Lincoln xij*d*. I will that halffe one trentall be sayd for my soule and all Christen soulys. To Alice my doughter one red flekyt cowe and ij yowes and ij lammes. To Richerde my sun one red flekyt qwye and one yowe and one lamme, and my gretest brasse potte aftyr the

---

[169] The will is unfinished, and has been cancelled in the register.

dethe of hys mother. To my doughter Catheryne one lamme. To Isabell my doughter one yowe and one lamme. To Bartylmew my sun one red cowe. [fo. 303r] To Elizabeth Wheatlay one yowe lamme. To John Swaby one weder. The resydue of all my goodes I gyff to Isabell my wyff, whome I make my executrix. I make John Swaby supervisor. Thes beyng wytnes; Hugh Dennys, Steven Twydale and Thurstan Lykkes.

Proved before P at Horncastle, 19 June 1534.

503.   THOMAS WHYTE [OF PINCHBECK]
        [LCC 1532–34, fo. 298]

31 May 1534. I, Thomas Whyte of Pynchbacke, beyng of good mynde and hole remembrance, makes my laste testament and wyll. Fyrst I bequethe my sawle to God almyghty, to Owr Lady and to all the sayntes of hevyn, and my body to be buryed in the churcheyarde of Pynchbek. To the hye awlter there for tythes and oblacyons forgoten xijd. To every aulter in the sayd churche ijd. To the churche warke of Lincoln viijd, and to the pupylls or orphans of Saynt Kateryn withoute the walles [of] Lincoln iiijd. I wyll have dysposyd of my beryall day, vijth and xxxti day of masse and deryge and to pore folkes xvs, that [is] to say every on of thos iij days vs. To Margarett my wyff halfe the howsehold stuffe that she broght to me, ij kye and vs in money, a seme of barly and a seme of wheyt, a burlyng, the soyng of a busshell flax, a cheste standyng at my beddy's hed and my best bras pan. To Richard my son my beste brasse pott and my leyd, also all my horsys, marys and all manar of horse kynke that I have, my carte and all my carte garyes that longothe thereto, [fo. 298v] my ploght, harowys, all my plowhe gayrs with al manar of thynges that longys to hosbandry, ij kye. To Gylberd Glover my kynysman a kowe calfe and Richard my son shall kepe yt on yere or so long as the [said] Gylbert taryes with hym. To Elyn my servand a payre of shetes. To Agnes Kydby a calfe. To sony's wyffe a burlyng. The reste of all my goodes I gyffe them to Margarett my wyffe and Richard my son whom I make my executors, and Sir Thomas Hyll to be my supervysor, and he to have for hys labor vs. Thes beyng wytnys; Robert Slatur, Thomas Hall, Thomas Thacker, Henry Keaby and Wylliam Day. Also I make my last wyll in the same day and date above namyd. I surrender all my copyholde landys that I have into the handes of Thomas Hall, to the use and performance of thys my laste wyll. To Rychard my son my howse that I dwell in with the appurtenances longyng there to be yt more or lese to hym, hys herys and assygnes for ever, and my wyll ys that Margaret my wyffe shall have hyr wonnyng in the sayd howse so long as she kepys hyr unmaryd, yff she wyll tary in the same with Richard my sun. And [if] she wyll nott abyde in the sayd howse with Richard my son, then my wyll ys the sayd Rychard my son to have the sayd house as above ys wrytten, and he to gyffe to the sayd Margaret my wyff yerely to hyr howse rent iijs iiijd so long as she kepythe name. To Rychard my son a gardenstyd that I boght of Thomas Hall and all my bonde land to hym, hys herys and assygnes for ever. Also my wyll ys that on pece of land abuttyng of clay pyttes be solde by my executors, and the money therfor taken to be dysposyd for my sawle and all Crysten sawlys.

Proved before P at Spalding, 9 June 1534.

504.   ROBERT HARE [OF SWINESHEAD]
       [LCC 1532–34, fo. 311v]

10 June 1534. I, Robert Hare of Swynneshed, of hole mynde and good memory beyng, make my testament and last will. Fyrst I bequethe my soule to God allmyghtty and to Our Lady, and to all the saintes in heven. My body to be buryd in the churcheyerde of Our Lady in Swynneshed. To my mortuary as the lawe requyryth. To the high altare ther iiij*d*. To every altare in the sayd churche ij*d*. To the churche warke ther ij*d*. To Our Lady's warke of Lincoln iiij*d*. To the fatherles chylder of St. Catheryn's nygh Lincoln iiij*d*. To William my sun one cowe, one brasse potte. To John my sun one cowe and one brasse potte. I will that Catheryn my wyff shall cause one trentall to be sung in the churche of Swynneshed for my soule and for the soulys of my wyffes and all Christen soulys. The resydue of my goodes I gyff to Catheryne my wyff, whome I makes to be my executrix, she to dispose for the welthe of my soule as she thynkes best. Thes beyng wytnes; Sir Thomas Garton, vicar, Sir William Trewe, Robert Henryson, William Pretty cum ceteris.

    Proved before P at Swineshead, 8 October 1534.

505.   THOMAS FLAWTER [OF GOSBERTON]
       [LCC 1535–37, fos. 53v–54r]

12 June 1534. I, Thomas Flawter of the paryshe of Gosberton, beyng perfyte off remembraunce and of good mynde, makes my last will and testament. The firste I bequethe my soule to allmyghtty God and to Hys blessyd mother St. Mary and to all the holy cumpeny of heven, and my body to be buryed in the churcheyerde of St. Peter and St. Paule in Gosberton. To the high altare thereof for my tithes forgottyn vj*d*. To the reparacion of every altare in the same churche ij*d*. To St. Peter gylde ij*d*. To Corpus Christi gylde ij*d*. To the offeryng of Our Lady of Lincoln ij*d*. To the chylder of St. Catheryn's ij*d*. To every one order off frerys in Boston xx*d*. I will that my executrix cause one trentall of messys to be celebratyd and sayd within the paryshe churche of Gosberton aftyr my decesse for my soule and all my good frendes' soulys. I will that John and Jenet my childer have halff of all my qwyk catell delyveryd to theym be equall porcions, when they cum to the age of xvj yeres, be the handes of my executrix or her assyngnes. And yff other of the sayd chylder dye or they cum to the age of xvj yeres, then I will that childe beyng alyve have the parte of the childe departyd owt of thys present lyffe. To the sayd John and Jenet, my chylder, halff of all my housholde stuff, and I will that yff [fo. 54r] my wyff mary or my childer cum to xvj yeres of age, that it shall be lefull be thys my will that Thomas Teryngton or hys assygnes to have the kepyng of the sayd housholde stuff to the use of my sayd chylder. Yff bothe my sayd chylder dy or the cum to xvj yeres of age (as God defende), then I will that all the foresayd catell and housholde stuff remayn to Lawrence Flawter my brother and Grace Flawter my syster, to be devydyd betwyxte them be equall porcions. To Laurence Flawter one yong mare, my best cote. To Grace Flawter my syster one burnyng. To Richerde Flawter one calve and one oringe cote. To Simon Nutkyn one ledder dooblet. To Margaret Bakhouse one calve. I gyff to Thomas Teryngton v*s* to be the oversear of thys my last will. The resydue off my goodes ungyffyn and not bequethyd I gyff them to Agnes my wyff, the whiche I make my true and fathefull executrix to performe thys my will, to pay

my dettes, to bryng my body honestly to the grounde and to dispose them for the helthe of my soule, as she shall beste lyke and devyse. Thes beryng wytnes; John Humpe, Simon Nutkyn, John Potte, John Dusyng, Willum Fylepotte, with other mo.

Proved before P at Swineshead, 14 July 1535.

506. THOMAS NOBLE [OF WOOLSTHORPE]
[LCC 1532–34, fos. 335v–336r]

12 June 1534. I, Thomas Noble, husbandman, seke in body and in good mynde, perceyvyng that ther is nothyng more certen than dethe and nothyng more uncerten then is the hower of dethe, makes my last will. Fyrste I bequethe my soule to allmyghtty God, to Our Lady St. Mary and to all the fare cumpeny of heven, and my body to be buryd in the churchyerde of St. Andro of Wolstrop. For tithes forgotten a yow and a lamme and a weder hog. To the high altare of St. Andro of Wollesthorp iiijd. To Our Lady of Lincoln iiijd. To Dennis Naubill too yowes and ther lammys. I will that Elizabeth Ryabe have her owne, that is xxviij schepe, a cowe and ij bullockes. I will [fo. 336r] that v messys be done for me. The resydue of all my goodes aftyr I be brought furth, I put to Elizabeth Naubill, my wyff, whome I make my executrix, she to dispose as she thynkes best for the welthe of my soule. Thomas Nawbyll supervisor. Thes beyng wytnes; Sir Robert Skotte, John Breges, John Mantyll, John Hornygwood.

Proved before P at Ancaster, 29 October 1534.

507. THOMAS OSLYN [OF FRIESTON IN PARISH OF CAYTHORPE]
[LCC 1532–34, fo. 336v]

12 June 1534. I, Thomas Oslyn off Fryston in the parysche of Cathorp, hole of mynde and good off remembraunce, makes thys my testament and last will. Fyrste I bequethe my soule to allmyghtty God and to Our Lady St. Mary and to all the hole cumpeny off heven, and my body to be buryd in the churcheyerde of St. Vincent of Cathorp. To Our Lady of Lincoln xijd. To the high altare of my paryshe churche of Cathorp xijd. To the Trinite gylde of Cathorp one bushell of barly. To William Hawden iijs iiijd. To Jane Wynlowe xxd. To the Whyte Frerys of Lincoln iiijd. To the Blak Frerys off Lincoln iiij. To the Austyn Frerys of Lincoln iiijd. To the Gray Frerys of Grantham iiijd. To William Hawdyn my coppyholde that I dwell in to the use of John my sun. I orden William Hawden to be my executor for to dispose the resydue of my goodes for the helthe of my soule. Wytnes; Sir John Stotte, Thomas Newcom.

Proved before P at Ancaster, 29 October 1534.

508. ELIZABETH OTBYE [OF TETNEY]
[LCC 1532–34, fo. 332]

16 June 1534. I, Elizabeth Otbye, wydoy, of my hole mynde and good remembraunce, makes my last will. Fyrst [fo. 332v] I bequethe my soule to God allmyghtty, Our Lady St. Mary and to all the saintes in heven. My body to be buryd in the churcheyerde of Peter and Paule in Tetney with that is due to be had as

my frendes thynkes best. To the high altare of Tetney vj*d*. To Our Lady warke of Lincoln iiij*d*. To the high altare of Our Lady of Lincoln iiij*d*. To the high altare of Bellesby vj*d*. To Richerde Otby my sun all my corne and cattyll excepte ij of the best ky, and thes I gyff Mary Otby my doughter, and all my houshold stuff with implement therto belongyng. The resydue of my goodes I gyff to John Gretham my fader and Edward Gretham my brother, whome I make my true executors and supervisors of the same, they to dispose for the helthe of my soule as they thynk best. Thes wytnes; John Wrynche, Thomas Smyth, Robert Mutsay, John Spryng, Robert Blancher, with other mo.

Proved before P at Grimsby, 20 October 1534.

509. ALAN ALANSON [OF GRIMOLDBY]
[LCC 1532–34, fo. 305v]

24 June 1534. I, Alan Alanson of Grymmylbe, husbandman, beyng of hole and perfyte remembraunce, makes my will and laste testament. Fyrste I bequethe my soule to God allmyghtty, to Our Blessyd Lady St. Mary and to all the sayntes in heven, and my body to be buryd within the churche of St. Edithe of Grymmylbe, to the whiche high altare I bequethe for my tithes forgottyn and ngligently payd iij*s* iiij*d*. To our Lady of Lincoln xij*d*. To the churche of Grymmylbe one quarter of wheate. To the sepulcre light within the sayd churche of Grymmylbe a bushyll of wheate. To the churche of St. Leonerde of Cokryngham xij*d*. To the churche of Manby a bushyll of wheate. To the churche of Stuton xij*d*. To the churches of North Reston xij*d*, West Saltfletby xij*d*, Belcheforthe xij*d*. To Isabell my wyff all my housholde with pullan, geys and swyne with plow and wayn and all therto belongyng, a cople of my best oxen, ij of the best marys, ij kye, ij qwyes, xx^{ty} yowes and xx^{ty} lammys. To Alyson my doughter a qwye of one yere age and ij yowes and ij lammys. To every godchylde a lam. I will have a trentall to be sung within the churche of Grymmylbe for my soule and all my good frendes' soulys. To Agnes Adderwyk a qwye, a yowe and a lamme. To William Clarkeson a yowe and a lamme. To Francys Jenson a yowe and a lamme. To Alice Clyld a yowe and a lamme. The resydue of my goodes unbequethyd and my body buryd I gyff to Isabell my wyff whome I make my executrix, she to dispose them to the pleasure and comforthe of my soule and all my good frendes' soulys and all good Crysten soulys, and John Smyth supervisor. Thes wytnesses; Sir William Pynder, clarke, John Wyeth, Thomas Mawe, William Smyth, with other mo.

Proved before P at Lincoln, 28 August 1534.

510. SIR JOHN COCKE [PARSON OF KETSBY IN PARISH OF LITTLE GRIMSBY]
[LCC 1532–34, fos. 271r–272v]

26 June 1534. I, John Cocke parson of Ketesby, in hole mynde and good remembraunce, make my testament and last will. Firste I bequethe my soule to God allmyghtty with the intercession of Hys blessyd mother Our Lady St. Mary and of all the saintes in heven, and my body to be buryd in the chauncell of Ketesby beforesayd, before the image of St. Margaret. To Our Lady's altare in the cathedral churche of Lincoln iij*s* iiij*d*. To the warkes of the sayd churche vj*s* viij*d*. To the

churche warke off Kettesby vj*s* viij*d*. To the churche warke off Ormesby vj*s* viij*d*. To the churche warkes off Willughby x*s*, and my jorenall that the preste of the chapell may have easment therwith, and so remayn in the churche for ever. To the upholdyng of Slouythby chapell xx*s*. To the churche warkes of Hoggesthorp xx*s*, and my boke callyd *Pupilla Occuli* and one boke callyd *Januences*.[170] To the churche warkes of Calceby ij*s*. To either of the churche warkes of Swaby ij*s*. To the churche warkes of Burwell ij*s*. To the churche warkes of Tetforde ij*s*. [fo. 271v] To every one of my prestys beyng with me in servys at my departyng a full quarter wagys, to that intente that they be at the commandementes of my executors all that tyme. To Dame Anne Gooderyk, priorisse of Grenefelde, vj*s* viij*d*, and to every nonne and preste ther beyng xij*d*, and to the syster ther viij*d*.[171] To the sacristone ther, for waxe, viij*d*. To the prior of Markeby iij*s* iiij*d*, and to every chanon ther beyng preste xvj*d*, and to every novys xij*d*, and to the sacristone for waxe xij*d*. To the priorisse of Brodholme iij*s* iiij*d*, and to every nonne ther xx*d*, to every preste and novys ther xij*d*, and to the sacristone for waxe xij*d*. To the priorisse of Irforthe vj*s* viij*d*, to every nonne, novys and preste ther xij*d*, and to the sacristone for waxe xij*d*. To the priorisse of Legborne vj*s* viij*d*, to every nonne ther xij*d*, to the novys and prestes ther, every of them, viij*d*, and to the sacristone for waxe viij*d*. To my master, Sir William Skypwyth, knyght, xl*s*, and to my lady hys wyffe xx*s*, and to my yong master William Skypwyth xxvj*s* viij*d* and one fether bedde with a bolster and ij coverlyddes, a tester, a syler with iij curtens as they are on the bedde in my parlure. To John Skypwithe my godsun one goblet with the cover or iiij markes. To my yong master William Skypwith, hys wyff, x*s*. To Master Bollys one yong horse and to Mastres Jane, hys wyffe, my awndyrens and halffe a garnyshe of my best best puter vessell. To Mastres Anne Skypwyth, doughter of my sayd olde master Sir William Skypwyth, the other halffe garnyshe of my beste puter vessell and xiij*s* iiij*d*. To Master George Fythwilliam the yonger xx*s*. To Mastres Margarete, Brydgitte, Elizabeth, Dorothe, George and Henry, chylder of the sayd Sir William Skypwyth, to every one of them singlerly, xiij*s* iiij*d*. To iiij gentyllwomen that wates on my lady, on my yong mastres, on Mastres Jane Bollys and one Mastres Mary, to every one of theym, xij*d*. To every woman servant in that house iiij*d*. To every officer and yoman in that place xij*d*, and to every other manservant ther beyng iiij*d*. I will that John Cocke, my kynsman and servant, have my wayn and my plough with all the gerys to them belongyng, and one cople of oxen, one sorrell geldyng and one soryd nagge, and also my yeres and lease in Cooke ferme, accordyng to the surrender that I mayd to hym, redy sowne excepte ij acres that Henry Scawflete shall have for thys one yere. [fo. 272r] To Avyse my servant xl*s*, my blake gowne and my warre schorte gowne, one fether bed, one pare of schetes, ij blankyttes, one coveryng and all her owne stuffe. To John Woodthorpe, my master['s] servant, vj quarters of malte. To John Kyrkman a chalder of malte. To Peter Pynder x*s*. I will that my feoffys of my house and landes in Grymmolby stande and be seassyd to the use of the sayd John Cocke and hys heyres of hys body laufully begottyn. And for lacke of suche issue, to the use of Randall Smyth and Elizabeth hys wyff and to the heyres of ther bodyes

[170] *Pupilla Occuli* has not been traced. *Januences* is probably Johannes Balbus de Janua, *Summa que Catholicon appellatur* (1503).
[171] Anne Gooderyk was the last prioress of Greenfield, elected in 1530. At the dissolution before Michaelmas 1536 the priory was worth £63 annually, and Anne was provided with a pension of £10 per annum: *VCH Lincolnshire*, II, 155–6.

laufully begottyn, so that the foresayd John Cocke or hys heyres, yff any suche be, and the sayd Randall and Elizabeth or ther heyres of ther bodyes laufully begottyn, do pay or cause to be payd furthe of the sayd house and landes yerely xs at tyme and place assygned by me or myn executors, provydyd alway that yff the foresayd John Cocke or hys heyres do not pay or cause to be payd the foresayd summ of xs yerely as is aforesayd, then I will the foresayd Randall and Elizabeth or ther heyres enter into the sayd house and landes, payng yerely the sayd summ of xs. And yff they or theyr heyres do not pay or cause to be payd the foresayd summ of xs yerely as is aforesayd, then I will that John Selly the elder and Agnes hys wyff and ther heyres of ther bodyes laufully begottyn, enter into the sayd house and landes, payng yerely the foresayd summ of xs as is aforesayd. To the whiche John Selly I bequethe one worstyt dooblet, one jaket, one corte and xxs. To John Selly the yonger my horse callyd Conscience. To Jenet Kelstone, wydowe, one chalder of malte and a lityll brasen morter. To Margarete Bleke, the wyffe off Thomas Bleke, iijs iiijd. To John Goodale, skolemaster of Louthe, xls on thys condicion, that he suffer Robert Lowys quyetly and at liberty to use and injoy my lease of hys ferme in Wynthorpe. To Thomas Bleke, John Selly the elder and to John Norton, to every one of them xxd on the condicion that they shal devyde the landes of the sayd Cooke house from the landes off the parsonage of Kettesby. I will that the resydue off my goodes be disposyd at the discrescion of Master John Pryn, doctor and commissary of the archidiaconry of Lincoln, Sir Nicholes Sarrot, parsone of Ingoldmellys, Sir John Snary, vicare of Burwell, and Sir Roger Barry, my preste, whome I make my executors, [fo. 272v] and every one of theym to have for ther labors xxxs and one gowne, and ther expenses when they have any busynes for me. And I will that it shall be laufull for one or ij of my sayd executors to call the other of theym to accompte before my lorde of Lincoln['s] officers, or ellyswhere, to se whether they have disposyd my goodes accordyng to my will and discharge of ther conscience. Thes beyng wytnesses; Syr John Cooke [and] Sir Thomas Tenende, chaplans, and William Snawdun, notary.

Proved before John Rayne, L.L.D., vicar general in spirituals, official principal of John [Longland], bishop of Lincoln. Adm. granted at Lincoln, 5 August 1534, to the executors.

511.   AGNES CLARE [OF PINCHBECK]
[LCC 1532–34, fos. 309v–311v]

27 June 1534, and in the yere of the reigne of our most dred and redowted soverayn lorde Henry the Eight, by the grace of God, of Yngland and France, Kyng, Defender of the Fayth and Lorde of Irelande, xxvj^ty. I, Agnes [fo. 310r] Clare of Pynchbek in the countie of Lincoln, wydo, late wyff of John Clare of the same, decessyd, beyng seke and febyll of body and of good remembraunce, makyth thys my last will and testament. Fyrste I bequethe my soule to allmyghtty God, Our Lady St. Mary and to all the holy cumpeny of heven, and my body to be buryd in the paryshe churcheyerde of Pynchbek so nere my husband as my be convenyently, yff it so please God. To the high altare of Pynchbek for tithys forgottyn viijd, and to every altare within the same churche iiijd. Towardes the church warke of Pynchbek xxd. I will that myn executors bestowe uppon my buryall day for messe, dirige and to pore folkes, xxs, at my vij day in lyke case for messe, dirige and to pore folkes,

xv*s*, at my xxx^{ty} day for messe, dirige and to pore folkes, xv*s*. I will that one honest preste, so schortely aftyr my decesse as he may, be gottyn say messe within the churche off Pynchbek one halffe yere for the soule of my sayd husbande, and for my soule, our fathers' and mothers' and all our frendes' soulys and all Christen soulys, and he to have for the same halffe yere, for hys salary and wagys, liij*s* iiij*d*. To my sun Thomas x*l*, to be payd within xx^{ty} days aftyr my decesse unto Thomas Poterell, preste, for the custody to the sayd Thomas Clare under whose governyng my sayd sun shall be, a dosyn of my best puter platters, halff a dosyn of my best puter dyshes of the newe facion, ij basyns lattyn and my basyn and ewer of puter, ij puter pottes, ij candylstkes of the beste, ij brasse pottes, one bygge and another lesser, a chaffer to stande in the fyer. Where afore thys tyme one John Yong off Pynchbek, decessyd, dyd will that one house in Hygate shulde be solde by hys executors and iiij markes therof to be gyven, as in the will of the same John Yong more playnly dothe appere, and the resydewe to be equally devydyd betwyxte John Clare my sayd husband and John Yong, brother of the sayd John Yong, decessyd, beyng hys executors, I therfore gyff all suche parte and porcion of money as shall fortune heraftyr to be takyn for the same house, and the whiche was or ought to be dewe unto my sayd husbande, unto my sayd sun Thomas. I will that my executors shall have the custody of the sayd goodes and catallys [fo. 310v] before to the sayd Thomas my sun bequethyd, unto he cum and be of age of xix yeres. To William my sun a foldyn table, a chare, a clothe payntyd over the desse, halff a dosyn of cushyns, a cupborde with eight off my gret platers, halff a dosyn dyshes puter, iij sawcers, vj candylstykes and ij lattyn basyns, one basyn puter, a prasse and my best arke, a standyng bedd, ij matteres, ij fether beddes, ij blankytes, ij pare of schetes, that is to say one pare of flaxyn and the other of myngtow, one coveryng beyng plane warke, ij bedde's hangynges whyte, a mazer and iij sylver sponys and ij brasse pottes, one of the beste sorte and another lesser, a panne and a kettyll, my leste chaffyng dyshe, a gret iren to stand in fyer, a pare of tonges, viij plate of flaxyn clothe, my brasyn morter with the pestell, a standyng laver, a spyt, one pare of cobyrns, too small towells and all the parsellys before wryttyn, to be delyveryd at the age of xix yeres. To Alice my doughter a fether bedde tyke, ij matteres, a pare of blankyttes, iiij pare of schetes wheroff ij pare flaxyn and one pare hardyn and a red hatte, my coverlyddes of the best not gyven, ij twylttes, a hundreth whyte yerne and a hundrethe of gray, x plate of clothe flaxyn, xx^{ty} plate of hardyn, ij dosyn of puter platters and ij dosyn of puter dyshes and halff a dosyn of puter podyshers, an arke above the lofte, halff a dosyn of sylver sponys, viij brasse pottes, iij kettyls, my best gyrdyll, my best hookes of sylver, my best pare of beades with x joellys at them, my best rebyn and my best pyn case, a pare of knyves, my ij best gowyns and my violet kyrtyll, my blak gowne and my red blankyt, iiij kyrchyffes, iij rales, my blake bonnet, iiij towellys and iij tableclothys, a table in the further parler, a new carpet, my new blankyt, my best spyt, a pare of cobyrnes, my best gose panne, my best bed hangyng, iiij candyl-styckes, iij pottes off pewter and ij saltsallers, and these parcelsse affore wryttyn and to the sayd Alyce my doughter be me gevyn. Y wyll that myne executors have the custode off the same unto suche tyme as she shal be come and be off the age of xix yeres, savyng only to geve her toward hur fydynd as shal be thowght necessary by mynde executors. To Elysabeth Alfyn [fo. 311r] my goddowghter a laten basyn and a pewter platter. To the chelderne off Robert Yone, to be devyded equaly amongst them vj*s* viij*d*. To every chyld of Jhon Yone a pewter plater. To Jhon my brother a jerkyn that was my husbande's, in lyke wyse the best hoose. To Wylliam Yong my brother a seme off maltte, my husbande's sanguen cotte. To hysse wyffe my sangwen kyrtyll. To every one off hys dowghter a pewter dysshe, and to hys sone a lame, to be delyveryd hym at clyppyng tyme. To my mother vj*s* viij*d* and a blankyt. To the wyffe of John Yong my brother my violet gown with the velvyt covys. To my gossyp Jane Menerde my blake hatte and a kyrchyff. To William my sun my beades with ix juellys. To every godsun and goddoughter iiij*d*. To Johan Robynson my doughter beades, one puter platter. To Agnes Clare my laver of lattyn that hangyth at the yerde dore. To my gossyp old Mastres Walpole my kyrchyff pyrlyd with whyte sylke. To my gossyp, Jefferay's wyff, my red rebyn. To Margaret Bollys my olde blake gowne. To Alyson Yong my olde kyrtyll of violet. To Helene Pore halff a seame of malte and a bushyll of wheate and rye. To Master Walpole my husband['s] jamlet dooblet. To John Yong my brother, my husband hys best cote. My will is that my grene callyd Stedeman Grene be solde for the performance of thys my testament, provydyd alway that my iij chylder, or every one of them as it shall please God to gyff them grace to lyve to they cum to the age of xvj yeres, that then to make ther testamentes of the goodes that I have to them. Also, iff eny of them dy before the age of xvj yeres, then my will ys that hys goodes shall be devydyd betwyxte the other ij then lyffyng. And yff ij of them dye before the age of xvj yeres, then the thyrde then lyveyng shall have all the goodes before bequest. And yff all dye before the age of xvj yeres, then the sayd goodes to be solde and the money therof takyn shall be gyffyn to one honest preste to syng for my soule, my husband souls and all Christen soulys within the churche of Pynchebek. My will is that Agnes my doughter shall have the gowne that was Sir Thomas Potterell's, preste. The reste of all my goodes, I put them to the disposicion of Mr. Walpole and John Yong, whome I make my executors, and ether of them to have for hys labor [fo. 311v] x*s*. To Master Foster vj*s* viij*d*, and to Sir Thomas Hyll as myche. Thes beyng wytnessys; Thomas Poterell [and] Thomas Walpole, clerkes, Robert Alphyn, with other mo.

Proved before P at Swineshead, 8 October 1534.

512.　　WILLIAM IBRE [OF BINBROOK ST. MARY]
　　　　[LCC 1532–34, fo. 323r]

1 July 1534. I, William Ibre, beyng hole of mynde, wyt and remembrance, makes my last will and testament. In the fyrste I bequethe my soule to God allmyghtty, to Our Lady St. Mary and to all the saintes in heven. My body to be buryd in the churcheyerde of Our Lady in Bynbroke. To the high altare in the same churche iiij*d*. To the same churche xij*d*. To Our Lady of Lincoln iiij*d*. To Our Lady warke ij*d*. To St. Gabryell churche in Bynbroke iiij*d*. To the high altare in the same ij*d*. I will that ther be a trentall of messys done in my paryshe churche for the helthe of my soule, and the preste to have x*s*. Also all my goodes unbequethyd I gyff to William Ibre my father and to John Ibre my brother whome I make executors, and they to dispose parte of it to my brother and systers and in other dedys of charyte as they thynke moste necessary for the helthe of my soule. Thes wytnes; Sir Mylys Gregory, John Coke, Thomas Ibre, with other mo.

Proved before P at Binbrook, 21 October 1534.

513.   WILLIAM HELVYS [OF SOUTH ORMSBY]
        [LCC 1532–34, fo. 329r]

4 July 1534. I, William Helvys of South Ormesby, of a hole mynde, makyth my will.
Fyrste I bequethe my soule to allmyghtty God, Our Lady St. Mary and to all the
cumpeny in heven, and my body to be buryd in the churcheyerde of the foresayd
Ormesby. To the high altare for tithes forgottyn iiij*d*. To the church warke iiij*d*. To
Our Lady of Lincoln iiij*d*. To her warke iiij*d*. To the churche in Somerby vj*d*, and to
the churches in Bag Enderby, Brynkhill, Calceby, St. Margaret in Swaby and
Ketesby iiij*d* [each]. I will that one trentall off messys with placebo, dirige and
commendacion be done for my soule and my ij wyffes Margery and Agnes, with all
other that God will have prayd for within the churche of St. Leonerde in Ormesby.
To Richerde Helvys my sun one tabyll, a cowe and ij schepe. To William Helvys my
sun a cowe and a horse. To Jenet my doughter a qwy and ij schepe. To William
Helvys the yonger a yowe and a lam. The resydue of my goodes I put it to the
disposicion of Agnes my wyff and Richerde my sun, whome I make my trewe
executors. Wytnes to the same; Sir John Pechyll, William Herland, Jamys Dawson,
Richard Burdall, with other mo.
        Proved before P at Horncastle, 16 October 1534.

514.   NICHOLAS LORDE [OF NEWSHAM]
        [LCC 1532–34, fo. 280v]

8 July 1534. I, Nicholes Lorde of Newsham, hole of mynde neverthelesse seke in
body, make my last will. Fyrste I bequethe my soule to allmyghtty God, and my
body to be buryed within the churche of St. Marcill off Newsham. To the house of
Newsham xiij*s*. To Our Lady of Lincoln vj*d*. To the churche of Brokelsby xiij*s* iiij*d*.
To the churche of Ulceby xx*d*. To Sir John Woode, subprior of Newsham, iij*s* iiij*d*.
To the convent of Newsham iiij quarters barly. To Thomas Watteres and Christofer
Watteres one quarter barly. To Robert Bonde of Ulceby iiij*d*. The resydue of my
goodes I put them to the discrescion of Sir William Lorde, parson of Brokelesby,
whome I make my executor to dispose them to the behove of my chyldren and for
the helthe of my soule. Thes beyng wytnes; Richerde Allot of Lymber Magna,
William Stanton of Brokelesby, Thomas Johnson of the same, John Welles of
Ulceby, with other mo.
        Proved before P at Lincoln, 23 August 1534.

515.   WILLIAM SWABY [OF MARSH CHAPEL]
        [LCC 1532–34, fo. 307]

9 July 1534. I, William Swaby of Marsh Chapell, of a hole mynde and good
remembraunce, makes thys my last will. Fyrst I bequethe my soule to allmyghtty
God, to Our Lady St. Mary and to all the cumpeny in heven. My body to be buryd
in the churcheyerde of Our Lady of Marsh Chapell. To Our Lady of Lincoln iiij*d*.
To Our Lady of Marsh Chapell [fo. 307v] iiij*d*. To Robert Swaby my sun a cowe, a
syde cote, a jakyt, ij hoggys to be delyveryd nexte May Day. To Charly Swaby my
sun ij ky, vj yowes and vj lammys, a pare of malte qwernys, a [blank] creddell. To
Agnes Swaby my doughter ij kye, iiij yowes and iiij lammys, a matteres and a
coverlyd, ij lyn schetes, ij hardyn schetes, a brons potte, ij pannys, iiij dooblers, a

meyt borde, a blak chyst. To John Person a yeryng qwe when he is at lawfull age. The resydue of my goodes I gyff to Charlys Swaby my sun, whome I make my sole executor that he may order and dispose it as he thynkes moste convenyent for the helthe of my soule, and Walter Storre to be supervisor, and he to have for hys labor xx*d*. Wytnes wherof thes beyng present; Sir Jamys Wryght, the paryshe prest𝘦, John Dawson the elder, Emote Doughty, with other mo.

Proved before P at Lincoln, 20 September 1534.

516.　　RICHARD EMERSON [OF SWABY]
　　　　[LCC 1532–34, fo. 329v]

12 July 1534. I, Richerde Emarson of Swaby in the countie of Lincoln, husband-man, hole of mynde and good of remembraunce, makes my testament. Fyrste I bequethe my soule to God allmyghtty, to Hys mother Our Lady St. Mary and to all the holy cumpeny of heven, and my body to be buryd in the churcheyerde of St. Nicholes in the sayd Swaby. To the same churche of St. Nicholes xij*d*. To St. Margaret churche of the sayd Swaby viij*d*. To Our Lady's churche in Lincoln iiij*d*. To Robert Batter of Alforde my blew cote, a leder dooblet, a pare of slyvyng hose. To John Brantyng my servant my ore[n]ge cote, a dooblet, a pare of hose and a lamme. To Edward Tayllor, sun of William Tayllor of Tetforth, iij*s* iiij*d*. To everych on of my godbarnes iiij*d*. To Rose Hereman a stoke of bees. To Elizabeth my doughter my wyff beste gowne, her best cappe, her best kyrchyff, her best beades. To Agnes my doughter a cappe, a kyrchyff and the best ryng at the best beades and my wyff tawny gowne. To Jenet my doughter my wyff russyt gowne and the nexte best ryng at the best beades. To Robert my sun my fustyan dooblet, a sleveles jaket, a coteclothe of russyt. I will that my chylder have all my goodes shyftyd emong them, everych on ther parte aftyr my dettes and my legacy be payd. And yff anny of them dy or they cum at xviij yere of age, I will that everych on of them be other executors. I will that Walter Long and William Tayllor, whome I make my executors, have, other of them for ther labors, vj*s* viij*d*, and ther costes borne when they go in anny busynes of myn for my chylder proffyt. I will that ther be done a trentall of messys for me and my wyff, and that they be sung in St. Nicholes churche qwere. I purpose to ly in the churchyerde. I will that Sir William Clerke be my supervisor, and to have for hys laber x*s*. These beyng wytnes; William Clerke, parson ther, Thomas Dente, Christofor Tode, with other mo.

Proved before P at Horncastle, 16 October 1534.

517.　　ROBERT BRANSTON [OF SWAFIELD]
　　　　[LCC 1534 &c., fo. 7]

14 July 1534. I, Robert Branston of Swafelde, of hole mynde and good remem-braunce, makyth my last hole will. First I gyff my soule to God allmyghtty, to Our Lady St. Mary and to all the blessyd cumpeny of heven, and my body to be buryd in the churche of St. Peter and Paule of Swafelde, and therefore I gyff iij*s* iiij*d*. To the high altare a bushyll of barly for tithes and offerynges forgottyn. To the mother churche of Lincoln xij*d*. To the bellys in Swafelde vj*s* viij*d*. To Burton churche halffe a seame of barly. To the churche of Corby halffe a seame of barly. To Swynstede churche halffe a seame of barly. To Couthorpe chapell halffe a seame barly. To all

my chyldren the croppe of the ij housys wher Haywerde and John Turner dwellyd in for the space of ix yeres, so to remayne to the proffyt of all my chyldren, and my wyffe to beare all the charge of plowyng and sawyng on her awn proper coste excepte the sede to saw it. And she to have chaffe, strawe and haye cumyng of the ij housys, and she to repare them at her costes and charge. To Robert my sun iiij bullokes and my rydyng mare and a colte and ij blak sterys that I bought, and White Horn and hys felloy; thes be the iiij bullokes that he shall have. I gyff to hym xx shepe and my beste gowne and my beste jaket and my best dooblet and my worstyd [fo. 7v] jaket, and my blak hose and my gret potte and the cupborde and the beste rekons, and my house I dwell in when he cumys to laufull age to occupy it. I gyff to all my chylder x seame of malte and halffe a seame of wheate that I bought, and to every one of my doughters x schepe. To every one of my childer a cowe. To William Weste a wenyng calve and a ewe and a lamme, and to every godchylde that I have iiij*d*. To all my chyldren vj*l* xiij*s* iiij*d* to be equally devydyd emonges theym. To my mother a ewe and a lamme. To Johanne my servaunt a lamme. To Thomas Tyde my servaunt a ewe. To John Warde's chylder a ewe and a lamme. To the chylde of Thomas Hoges a ewe. To the chylde off Oxman a ewe. To Joyce my syster doughter a ewe. To Helene Lawhtone a lamme and to Thomas Lawhtone a lamme. And all the resydue of my goodes not gyffyn, I gyff to Joyse my wyff, and I make her and Robert my sun my full executors to fulfyll my will accordyng to my mynde as they will answer afore God for it. And I make Henry Lawhtone, John Ayde, William Jelyan and Thomas Straysone supervisors of my wyffe and my sun, to se that they fulfyll my will, and every of theym to have xx*d* for ther labor and ther charges borne.

Proved before P at Lincoln, 19 February 1534/5. Adm. granted to executrix, Robert, son and co-executor, being an infant.

518. THOMAS LOCKYNG [OF TETNEY]
[LCC 1532–34, fos. 332v–333r]

15 July 1534. I, Thomas Lockyng of Tetney, hole of mynde and good remembraunce, makes my last will. In primis I bequethe my soule to God allmyghtty, Our Lady St. Mary and to all the saintes in heven, and my body to be buryd in the churcheyerde of St. Peter and Paule of Tetney with that that the lawe of the churche requiryth of right. To the high altare of Tetney iiij*d*. To our mother churche of Lincoln high altare iiij*d*. To Our Lady warke of Lincoln iiij*d*. To John my sun one meyr, one fole and one lamme. To William my sun one mere, one yeryng stag and one lamme. To Robert my sun one meyr, one stayke calfe and one lamme. And yff any of the sayd chyldren fortune to dye, I will that hys parte remayn emong them that longer dothe lyff. And yff fortune they all decesse, I will ther partes all be disposyd for ther soulys. I will that my wyffe and John Wrenche have my house callyd Adamson house to the behove of my chyldren from [fo. 333r] one to another as long as any of theym do lyff, from the yongest to the eldeste. The resydue of my goodes not gyffyn nor bequethyd I gyff to Cecill Lockyng my wyff and John Wrenche whome I make my executors, they to dispose for the helthe of my soule as they thynke best. Wytnes William Tharolde, John Kyrmond, John Tharolde, Robert Jolyff, Richerde Rasyn, John Tagge, with other mo.

Proved before P at Grimsby, 20 October 1534.

519.   JOHN UPTON [OF NORTHOLME WAINFLEET]
        [LCC 1534 &c., fos. 9v–10r]

17 July 26 Henry VIII [1534]. This is the laste will of me, John Upton, esquyer, mayd at Northolme besyde Waynflete. Firste I will that all my landes and tenementes in Northolme Waynflete, All Halloys Waynflete, St. Mary's Fryskeney, Crofte, Thorpe and Ingolmellys go to Elizabeth my wyff for term of her lyffe, in full recompence of her firste joynter and dower, and the sayd Elizabeth my wyffe to fynde a preste for xx^{ty} yeres accordyng to the laste will of my fader. And yff she will have her firste joynter or dower, she to have it. And that all the foresayd landes and tenementes in Northolme Waynflete, All Halloys Waynflete, St. Mary's Fryskeney, Crofte, Thorpe and Ingolmellys shall go then to the performance of my laste will and testament. Also I will that Nicholes my sun have to hys exhibicion to he cum to the age of xxj yeres x*l* yerely, the proffyttes theroff yerely to be takyn by myn executrix and feoffes of my landes lying in Legborne, Carleton, Reston, Gayton and Thedilthorpe, and they to make accompte to my heyre at hys full age, and the overplus to remayne to my sayd heyre. I will that my executrix and feoffes take and perceyve of the isshewes, proffyttes and revenuys of my landes to the sum of ccc markes be run, and that to be takyn immediatly aftyr my decesse for the payment of my dettes, funerallys, legaces and restitucions. I will my father['s] will be performyd as well for bequestes and legaces as other ways. I will that my hunkyll Adryan Upton have yerely, terme of hys lyffe, xxvj*s* viij*d* over and besydes xl*s* of my father bequeste, and the sayd xxvj*s* viij*d* to be payd be my wyffe owt of the landes to her assygned in Waynflete, anythyng in thys my will notwithstandyng, and the sayd xl*s* to be payd to my sayd hunkyll owt of my landes in Hollande accordyng to my father will. To my cosyn John Lytylbery and to my cosyn Thomas Moygne, ether of them xl*s* yerely duryng ther lyffes, and that to be takyn of my landes beyng in my feoffys handes, and they to be a councell with my wyffe and my heyr in the forderaunce of thys my will. The testament of the same John Upton. I, John Upton of Northolme besyde Waynflete in the countie of Lincoln, esqwyer, mayd the xvij day of July in the xxvj yere of the reyne of our soverayn lorde Kyng Henry the eight, and the yere of our lorde God m^l fyve hundrethe xxxxiiij,^{172} beyng of hole mynde and good remembraunce, makyth my testament. Firste I bequethe my soule [fo. 10r] to allmyghtty God, to Our Lady St. Mary and to all the holy cumpeny of heven, and my body to be buryd where it shall please God. To Our Lady of Lincoln v*s*. To the iiij orders of frerys of Boston, every one of theym, iij*s* iiij*d*. To the ancorys of Boston iij*s* iiij*d*. To St. Thomas churche of Northolme vj*s* viij*d*. I make Elizabethe my wyff my sole executrix. I will for my funerallys and other days xl*l* to be takyn of my landes beyng in my feoffys handes. I will to Elizabeth my wyff all my goodes, moveable and unmoveable, as well chatell ryall as persynall. To Dorothe Hatclyff my syster xx^{ty} markes over and besydes xxx*l* appoyntyd to her chyldren by the laste will of my fader, yff she be good to my wyffe. And all thys to be takyn owte of my landes beyng in my feoffys handes. Thes beyng wytnes; Sir John Copuldyke, knyght, John Lytylbery, esquyer, David Edwardes, doctor in medicens, Thomas Lytilbery, gentylman, Sir Robert Smyth, preste, Richerde Hartypole and William Johnson, withe many other. Per me Johannem Copuldyke. Per me Johannem Lytylbury.
        Proved before P at Lincoln, 3 March 1534/5. Adm. granted to executrix.

---

^{172} An error for xxxiiij.

520. THOMAS BROWNE [OF ST. PETER LE WIGFORD]
[LCC 1532–34, fo. 280]

18 July 1534. I, Thomas Browne, glover, dwellyng in Saynt Peter's paryshe within Wykforthe in the citie of Lincoln, hole in mynde and of good remembraunce, makes this my last will. Fyrste I bequethe my soule unto allmyghtty God and to Our Blessyd Lady St. Mary and to all the holy cumpeny of heven, and my body to be buryd in the churche aforenamyd, and the churchewardens of the same churche to receyve for my rowme vjs viijd for the well of the churche. I will that a preste shall syng a trentall of messes for my soule and all Crysten soulys in the same churche. To the same churche ij torchys. To Our Lady light one yowe and a lamme. To St. Brandon light one yowe. To the gret gylde vjd. To the high altare in our mother churche of Lincoln vjd. To the clerke gylde xijd. I will that my brother Richerde Newcum, William Broune and Thomas Broune my sonnys, be my hole executors, and my brother Richerde Newcum to have for hys payne xxs, and a pece of russyt or ellys a violet gowne furryd with blak lamme. I will that William Gefferay be my supervisor, and he to have for hys labor vjs viijd. To William Broune my sun the house that I dwell in for the terme of my yeres, and all my takes that I have incloseyng in Lincoln. To William my sun my blak geldyng and iiij sylver sponys, a fether bedde, a coveryng, a pare of blankyttes, a pare of schetes and all hyngynges that longes to it. To Thomas Broune my sun my ambelyng mare and v sylver sponys, another fether bed, a coveryng, a pare of blankyttes, a pare of schetes and all thynges that longes to it. To Thomas Newcum my brother my russyt jakyt. I will that all my goodes not bequethyd I gyff unto William Broune and Thomas Broune my sunys, for to be equally devydyd betwyxte them at the syght of [fo. 280v] ther frendys and myne bothe. Wytnes; Sir John Harryson, Robert Codder, Thomas Dymlyngton, wyth other mony mo.

Proved before P at Lincoln, 18 August 1534. Adm. granted to Richard Newcum and William Broune, executors, reserving power to grant to Thomas Broune, co-executor, when he shall come of age.

521. WILLIAM LYON [OF NORMANTON]
[LCC 1532–34, fo. 336]

20 July 1534. I, William Lyon of Normanton, hole of mynde and off good memory, make and orden thys my testament and last will. Fyrste I bequethe my soule to allmyghtty God, Our Lady St. Mary and all the hole cumpeny of heven, and my body to be buryd in the parysche churcheyerde of St. Nicholes in Normanton. To Our Blessyd Lady of Lincoln xxd. To the churche of Normanton xvjd. To Our Lady's lyght of Normanton xijd. To Henry Smyth off Fulbecke viijd. The resydue of my goodes [fo. 336v] I bequethe holy to Margaret my syster and Oswolde her sun, whome I make myn executors to dispose it for the helthe of my soule as they will answere to allmyghtty God. Geven at Normanton, the day and yere above wryttyn. Thes wytnesses; Sir Raphe Parker, Thomas Ashe, Robert Hesyldyne, Oswolde Dayppe and other mo.

Proved before P at Ancaster, 29 October 1534.

522. RICHARD SMYTH [VICAR OF LONG BENNINGTON]
[LCC 1535–37, fo. 70]

23 July 1534. I, Rychard Smythe, vicar of Long Benyngton, of goode and holle mynd, makys my testament and last will. Fyrste I bequeth my sowlle to God allmyghty, to Owre Lady Saynt Mary and to all the sayntes in hevyn, and my body to be bured in the hye chauncell of Saynt Swythune of Benyngton. To Our Lady of Lincoln xijd. To Dorythyn chapell a baner clothe to the crosse or ellys xs in mony. To the howse of Mounte Grace xxs.[173] To Sir Rychard Wodland all my pryntyd bookes and my best gown. To the vicar of Westebrurghe a sylver spone with a knobbe and my secunde gown. To Elizabeth Gen xls, a cowe, ij pare of schettes, one payre of hardyn and another of lynnyn, a mattris, ij coverlettes, ij pyllows, a boulster, a blanket, a chyste, a pott and a pan. I wyll that the sayde Elezabeth schall have xxxjs viijd in mony. To Edythe Gen her doughter a payre of schetes. To Wylliam Scharpullys xxti schepe yf thay stond, and yf thay dye to have none. The sayde Wylliam shall have the beste wayn, the wytte-faced bullokkes, a hors and a mare with geyrys for them, a wytte tester with iij curtens therto belongyng and a swyne. To Thomas Hart my lytyll feder bede with all that belonges therto, and in mony xls. To Wylliam Hert my gray horse or elles xxvjs viijd. To the iiij orders of freres in Lincoln, to every howse, a buschell of barly. To the freres of Grantham a quarter of barly. To John Porter my godson a dunne stagge. To Sir Robert Barnysley iijs iiijd. To every one of my gochyldren iiijd. To Sir Thomas Makante xijd. To Sir Robert Redde xxd. To the chapell of Benyngton iijs iiijd. I wyll that Sir Robert Barnysley schall synge a holle yere for me, havyng to hys wages vli. To Cottom church, Clapoll, Westebrughe, Alynton, Staynton, every one of tham, iiijd. To Sir Robert Walhyll, parson of Westebrugh, my brayzyn morter and the pestell, and my lytyll swarer borde. The resydew of my goodes not bequethede I wyll that Sir Stephan Howlott, the vicar of Westebrughe, Thomas Hert and Thomas Robert the elder dyspose theym for the profett of my sowle, whome I make my executors. I constitute Master Wylliam Thorolde supervisor of this my last will and testament, havyng for hys labor xls. Theys beyng wytnessis; Sir Robert Barnysley, Sir Robert Walhyll, parson of Westebrugh, Thomas Herper, Richard Smyth, Henre Walker, John Gambull, Wylliam Crosse, John Rawlynson, Wylliam Pynder, Wylliam Scharpullis, and others.

> Proved before P at Lincoln, 8 November 1535. Adm. granted to Thomas Hart, executor, Sir Stephen Howlet and Thomas Robert the elder renouncing.

523. HELEN KYNG [OF TYDD ST. MARY]
[LCC 1532–34, fo. 308]

26 July 1534. I, Helene Kyng of Tyd St. Mary, hole and perfyte in mynde with good remembraunce, do make thys my last will and testament. Fyrste I bequethe my soule to allmyghtty God, to Our Lady and to all the holy cumpeny in heven. My

---

[173] Mount Grace Priory in Yorkshire was a Carthusian house, which produced some significant works of spiritual mysticism in the later fifteenth century, and retained its reputation as a centre for devout piety long after its dissolution in 1539. As late as the reign of James I it remained the object of illicit night-time pilgrimages by 'superstitious persons' and Catholics: Dickens, *The English Reformation*, 40–2.

body to be buryd within the churcheyerde aforesaid. To the mother churche in Lincoln viij*d*. To the pore chyldren in St. Catheryn's withowt the wallys iij*d*. To the high altare for tithys forgottyn xij*d*. To the churche warke xij*d*. To Our Lady light iiij*d*. To St. John Baptiste iiij*d*. To the roode light iiij*d*. To St. Thomas light iij*d*. To the Trinite light iij*d*. To every smale light in the sayd churche ij*d*. To Helene Warde a cowe, vj yowes, vj lammys, a gret brasse potte, a pare of schetes, a new coverlyd, ij pewter platters. To Isabell Warde vj yowes, vj lammes, a gret brasse panne, my secunde brasse pot, a new coverlyd, a pare of shetes and my best matteres, iij pecys of pewter. To John Warde xx*s* at the age of xxj yere, a pare of schetes, a yowe lamme and a burnyng. To Em Warde xx*s* at the sayd age, a pare of shetes, a new potte of brasse. To Mawde Warde xx*s*, a pare of shetes, a brasse potte and a panne. To Margaret Warde xiij*s* iiij*d*, a pare of shetes, ij new puter dyshes. To Edward Symson a yowe and a lamme. To Edwarde Symson my godsun a yowe and a lamme. To John Smyth a yowe and a lamme. To William Alyn a come of wheate and a cowe calffe, and to hys chylde a kettell and ij puter dyshes. I will that a honest preste to have liij*s* iiij*d* for the space of halff a yere to syng or say messe for my soule, my husband soule and all my frendes' soulys, payd off the house the whiche my husbande dyd make a sale by hys lyffe. I will that Emme Warde have xx*s* of the foresayd house. Also I will that John Warde have xx*s* of the sayd house. Also I will that Mawde Warde have xx*s* of the foresayd house. I will that William Alyn have xx*s* of the forsayd house. The resydue of my goodes I bequethe unto Johanne my doughter and make her sole [fo. 308v] executrix for to dispose my goodes for the salvacion of my soule. I make Thomas Symson and John Ferrer supervisors, and they to be recompensyd for ther payntakyng as conscience shall requyre. In wytnes heroff; Sir Richerde Wykham, Robert Tofte, John Sowter, William Angell, with other mo.

Proved before P at Swineshead, 8 October 1534.

524. **HENRY BOSTON [OF STENWIGHT]**
[LCC 1534 &c., fo. 5v]

29 July 1534. I, Henry Boston of Stenwhyet, with a hole mynde, do make thys my last will and testament. Firste I bequethe my soule to God allmyghtty and to Our Lady St. Mary, and to all the cumpeny off heven. My body to be buryd in the churcheyerde of St. Andro in Hacconby. To the high altare in the same churche iij*s* iiij*d*. To the light of St. Sithe xij*d*. To the sepulcre light xij*d*. To Our Lady chapell of Stenwyth iij*s* iiij*d*. To Our Lady of Lincoln xx*d*. To the fatherles chylder ij*d*. To the light of St. Andro xx*d*. To the churche of St. John in Lunderthorpe vj*s* viij*d*. To Agnes my wyff a house lying in Stenwhyte duryng her lyffe. And aftyr her lyffe to remayne to Thomas Boston my sun and to hys heyres of hys body laufully begottyn. And yff the sayd Thomas do dye withowt heyres of hys body laufully begottyn, then the sayd house to remayn to Crystyne my doughter and to her heyres of her body laufully begottyn. And yff the sayd Crystyn do dye withowt heyres of her body, then to remayn to the nexte of the blode. To Thomas Boston my sun a cople of oxen. The resydue of my goodes unbequethyd I gyff to Agnes my wyff, whome I make my sole executrix for to dispose for the helthe of my soule as she shall thynke best. And Henry Boston the elder to be the supervisor of thys my last will, and he to have for hys labor ij*s*. Thyes wytnes; Robert Clay, John Foster and John Townsende, with other mo.

Proved before P at Bourne, 28 January 1534/5.

525.   ADAM STANWELL [OF COWBIT IN PARISH OF SPALDING]
       [LCC 1532–34, fo. 308v]

2 August 1534. I, Adam Stanwell of Cowbyt within the paryshe of Spaldyng, with hole mynde and good remembraunce haveyng, make my testament. In the fyrst I bequethe my soule to allmyghtty God, Our Lady St. Mary and all saintes of heven. My body to be buryd in the churcheyerde of the privilege place of Cowbyt. To the high altare of Cowbyt ij*d*. To Cowbyt churche ij*d*. To Our Lady's warke of Lincoln iiij*d*. To the pore chyldren at St. Catheryn's ij*d*. To William my sun one calve, one pare of schetes, one pyloy, ij puter platters. To Thomas my sun one calve, one pare of schetes, one pilloy, ij puter platters. To Robert my sun one calve, j pare of schetes, one pilloy, ij pewter platters. I will thes thynges be in the governaunce of John Stanwell, my brother, and iche one to be oders' heyres. To Elizabeth my wyff iiij kye, ij calvys and the resydue of all my housholde sstuff. The resydue of my goodes I gyff to the disposicion of John Stanwell my broder, which I make my executer. I will he have for hys labor vj*s* viij*d*. The resydue of my goodes I will be evenly devydyd betwene my chylder yf ony decesse, iche one to be odyr heyres. Thes beyng wytnes; Sir Thomas Sheryff, William Stanwell, Richerde Stanwell and Robert Taysche. Mayd and wryttyn the day and yere abovesayd.

       Proved before P at Swineshead, 8 October 1534.

526.   JOHN BRADER [OF KIRMOND]
       [LCC 1532–34, fo. 333r]

3 August 1534. I, John Brader of the paryshe of Kyrmonde, beyng of hole mynde and good remembraunce, makes and ordens thys my present testament contenyng my last will. Fyrst I bequethe and commende my soule to God allmyghtty and to Our Blessyd Lady St. Mary, and to all the holy cumpeny of heven. My body to be buryd in the churcheyerde of St. Martyn in Kyrmonde. To the chirch warke of Kyrmonde a quarter of barly. To the high altare of the foresayd churche vj*d*. To the cathedral churche of Lincoln iiij*d*. To the high altare of the sayd churche iiij*d*. To Catheryn Brader my wyff the take that I have of the prior of Thyxyll in my mylne and to my chyldren. And yff it fortune my sayd wyff to mary agane, and so be that her husbande wyl not be contente to have my chylder but put them away from her, then I will that the yeres that I have in the foresayd mylne remayn hole to my chylder to the brynyng up of them. The resydue of my goodes her not bequethyd, my dettes payd, I bequethe to Catheryne Brader my wyff and my iiij chylder whome I make my executers, them for to have it and dispose it for the helthe of my soule as it shall be best sene to them in tyme for to cum. Also I make Robert Brader supervisor. Thes wytnesses; Sir Richerd Calverlay, Robert Yarburgh, Thomas Fresan, with other mo. At Kyrmonde the day and yere aforesayd.

       Proved before P at Binbrook, 21 October 1534. Adm. granted to the executer, the said four children being infants.

527.   WILLIAM RYSYLL [OF MUMBY]
       [LCC 1532–34, fo. 327v]

9 August 1534. I, William Rysyll of Mumby, with my hole mynde and with good remembraunce, make my testament with my last will. Fyrste I bequethe my soule

unto allmyghtty God, to the Blessyd Virgyn Our Lady and to all the holy cumpeny in heven, and my body to be buryd in the churcheyerde of Mumby. To Our Lady of Lincoln ij*d*. To the churche warke of Lincoln ij*d*. To the high altare in Mumby iiij*d*. To Our Lady's altare ij*d*. To the Trinite altare ij*d*. To Our Lady of Pety ij*d*. To the bellys vj*d*. To Edmunde Rysyll a burlyng stere of a yere olde and vj schepe. To Christofer Rysyll a burlyng stere and vj schepe. To my iij doughters, every one of them, a yong qwye and vj schepe. To Agnes Adam iiij ewes and the wyffe's rewarde. The resydue of all my goodes I gyff unto Johanne Rysyll my wyff, whome I make my executrix. I make George Watson supervisor, to help my wyff and succurre my chylder, and I will that he have for hys pane and labor iij*s* iiij*d*. Thes men to wytnes; Richard Cartewryght, vicar, Hugh Schauffurth, Christofer Chellys and other mo. Wryttyn at Mumby the day and yere aforesayd. I will that my wyff have my ferme duryng my yeres specyfyd in my copy with the licence of my master. Also I will that ether of my sunnys be other heyr. Also I will that my doughters be ever ych on other heyr. And yff they all departe afore the age of xiiij yeres, then I will that ther partes be solde and disposyd for ther soulys and for all Christen soulys.

Proved before P at Alford, 15 October 1534.

528. JOHN DANDYSON [OF WAINFLEET ST. MARY]
[LCC 1532–34, fo. 318r–319r]

12 August 1534. I, John Dandyson of the pariche of Saynt Mary in Waynflete, of hole mynd and gud memary, makyth my testament and last wyll. Fyrst I bequyth my soull to almyghty God, to Our Lady Saynt Mary and to all the company of heven, and my body to be buryed in the church of Saynt Mary in Waynflet. To the sacrament there iiij*d*. To the reparacyons of the hye alter vj*d*. To every alter within the sayd church iiij*d*. To the belles xx*d*. To the reparacyons of the sayd church vj*s* viij*d*. To the parson of the sayme church for tythes forgotton iij*s* iiij*d*. To our Lady of Lyncoln xx*d*. To Jenyt my dowghter iij*l* vj*s* viij*d* in money, and as mych in valow in moveables at the age of xxiij yers. To Margaret my dowghter and Jane my dowghter, ether of them, as mych at the saym age of xxiij yers. To Martyn my son my wayne and my ploughe, ij mares of the worst and a yong gray mare that cannot bere, xx^{ti} schepe and an gret brasse pott. To Sir Thomas Dandyson my son xxvj*s* viij*d* in money, to be delyveryd within the yer I decess, in after that yerly to have delyveryd vj*s* viij*d* in money duryng the space of sex yers next insuyng. I wyll have iiij trentalles done for me immedyatly after my decesse yff my executors may convenyently. I wyll my doughters be mendyd of the rest of my guddes yf ther do remayn any over, my will performyd. I wyll that the rest of my moveables be sold after the dyscresyon of my executours. All other guddes not bequythyd I gyffe to Jon Atwell and Martyn Dandyson whome I make my executors, and thay to dyspose theym for my soull helth. To Wylliam Dandyson a gret chyst. To John Atwell for hys payntakyng in ocupyeng for me vj*s* viij*d*. I wyll that my sayd executors dystrybut yerly xiij*d* of Gud Fryeday to xiij pore peple duryng the space of xx yers. Theis men beyng wyttnes; Sir John Danyell, prest, T[homas] Tygges, Symon Loydon, Robert Coyll and Wylliam Dandyson my son, with other. [fo. 318v] Thys is the last wyll of me Jhon Dandyson, mayd the day and yere above sayd, of all my landes and tenementes beyng within the townes and feldes of Waynflet, Fryskeney, Bratoft and Toft next Boston, as herafter doth apere. To Martyn my son the meswage of Peper

Thorpe with the gardyns therto belongyng with ij acres arrable land callyd Hobtoft, to hym and to hys heirs of hys body lawfully begotton. Also a mesuege beyng in Fryskeney with iiij acres landes and halff to hym and to hys heirs of hys body lawfully begotton. Also ij acres land callyd Twyffylltes, to hym and to hys hers of hys body lawfully begotton. Also ij acres callyd Cokson Toft, to hym and to hys heirs and assygners, also a peas of ground callyd Lady Garth, to hym, hys heirs and assygnes. Also viij acres lyeng in Fryskeney callyd Bee Ynges, with a leege theron from the sayd pasture to acre goyt, to hym and hys heirs and assygnes. For the wych viij acres I wyll the sayd Martyne doye gyff yerly to the sepulture lyght in Saynt Mary church iiij*d* in wax or els iiij*d* in money. To the sayd Martyn iij parcelles of land, on callyd Holl Pasture, another callyd Wye Pyngle and the therd Muson Land, to hym, hys heirs and assygners, so that he cause yerly a trentall to be song to the performans of hys granser wyll, contenewyng unto the lx yers be fully complet and endyd. To Wylliam Dandyson my son my meswege lyeng at the ae syde with the ground therto belongyng and v acres land lyeng of both sydes the churche wey, to hym, to hys heirs and assigners. Also a meyse lyeng in North Moyssc, to hym, hys heirs and assygners. Also ij acres land callyd Gray Toft, to hym, hys heirs and assygners. Also ij acres callyd Short Ryges lyeng in Fryskeney, to hym, hys heirs and assygners. Also halff Cowis land, to hym and to hys heirs of hys body lawfully begotton. Also half the land callyd Busher Land, to hym and to hys heirs of hys body, and iij acres land bought of Mr. Wolner, and iiij acres and half lyeng in Fyshtoft, to hym and to hys hers and assigners. Also I wyll that the sayd Wylliam have after the deth of Margit Dygges other iiij acres lyeng in the sayd toft callyd Lokmayn, [fo. 319r] to hym, hys heirs and assigners. To the sayd Wylliam an acre and a half of land arrable callyd Schypyn Toft, to hym, hys heirs and assigners. I wyll that vij acres land lyeng in the parich of Al Halois, callyd Key Landes, be set furth by lees for the performans my wyll for the space of xx yers by the dyscresyon of my executors. I wyll that iiij acres land and half callyd Gress Merffe in the parich of Saynt Mary be set forth as long by the dyscresyon of my executor to performans of my sayd wyll. Also I wyll that after the sayd xx yers be fully complet and expyryd, then the forsayd vij acres and iiij acres do retorn to Martyn my son, and to hys heirs and assigners. Theis beyng wytnessis; Thomas Dygges, Symon Loydon, Robert Coyl, Wylliam Dandyson my sun, with other mo.

Proved before P at Spilsby, 14 October 1534.

529.   PETER POODE [OF FARLESTHORPE]
       [LCC 1532–34, fos. 326v–327r]

15 August 1534. I, Peter Poode off Fallesthorp, beyng of hole mynde and good remembraunce, makes my testament and last will. Fyrst I bequethe my soule to allmyghtty God, to Our Blessyd Lady St. Mary and to all the holy cumpeny of heven, and my body to be buryed within the churcheyerde off Fallesthorpe. To Our Lady of Lincoln x*d*. To the churche warke of Our Lady of Lincoln x*d*. To the high altare in Fallesthorpe churche for my tithes forgottyn xij*d*. To the churche warke of Fallesthorp xij*d*. To the light of Our Lady of Grace in the same churche iiij*d*. To the light of Our Lady of Pety in the same churche vj*d*. To the sepulcre light in the same churche iiij*d*. To the Trinite light in the same churche iiij*d*. To St. Catheryne light in the same churche iiij*d*. I will that one messe be celebrate at Scala Celi for my soule

and all Christen soulys, and I bequethe to the preste that celebrate the same messe vj*d*. I will that one trentall be celebrate in the churche of Fallesthorp for my soule and all Christen soulys. To the preste that shall celebrate the same trentall x*s*. To Johanne my wyff ij beddes, one of the best and the other warse, one gret panne, one gret potte, vj puter dyshes, x dooblers, one cowe of the color callyd dowyd, one schepe, one lytyll rige of barly, iij stong of benys, one spynnyng whele and one pare of wolle cardes. To Robert my sun one mare and fole, ij schepe and all my plowe geres. To Margaret my doughter one cowe of iiij yeres olde, one chyste and one posnet. To Alice my doughter one schepe and one lytyll kettyll. To Agnes my doughter one schepe, one chyste and one lytyll panne. To Elizabeth my doughter oone schepe and one lytyll panne. The resydue of my goodes I will they be equally devydyd emong my chyldren. I make John Poode and William Webster my executors, they to pay my dettes and fulfyll thys my last will accordyng to the lawe of holy Churche. And [fo. 327r] I bequethe to ether of them for ther labors iij*s* iiij*d*. I desyre Sir John Wollay, vicare of Fallesthorp, to be supervisor, and I bequethe to hym for hys labor xx*d*. Thes wytnesses; Robert Leeke, William Mawer and Thomas Wylson of Fallesthorp aforesayd, with other mo.

Proved before P at Alford, 15 October 1534.

530. WILLIAM SENE [OF BOSTON]
[LCC 1532–34, fos. 313v–314r]

18 August 1534. I, William Sene of the paryshe of St. Botulphe of Boston makyth my last will and testament. Fyrste I bequethe my soule to God allmyghtty, Our Lady St. Mary and to all the celestyall cumpeny of heven. My body to be buryd within the Gray Frerys of Boston, with my mortuary accordyng unto the actys of the kyng. To the high altare of St. Botulphe for tythys or oblacions negligently wythholdyn or forgottyn iiij*d*. To the house of the Gray Frerys in Boston for my buryall vj*s* viij*d*. To the high altare of the same house iiij*d*. To Our Lady of Lincoln ij*d*. To the warkes of the same ij*d*. To the orphans of St. Catheryn's ij*d* and to the gylde of the vij martyrs within the paryshe churche of Boston ij*d*. I wyll that at the day of buryall vj chyldren have vj*d* for bearyng and holdyng vj tapars to my body be buryd. I [will] that xx^c*d* be disposyd at the day of my buryall to xl^ty pore people to pray for me. I will that ther be sayd v messys of the v woundes for my soule and all Christen soulys. To my mother a ryng of golde. To John Hykson a jerkyn of frece and a sherte. The resydue of my goodes I gyff to Elizabeth my wyff, whome I make my sole executrix, she to pay my dettes and fulfyll my will for the helthe of [fo. 314r] my soule and all Christen soulys, and John Roge to be supervisor, and he to have for hys payns xvj*d*. Whytnes herof; Thomas Hynde, curate, Thomas Hare and William Grafte, with other mo.

Proved before P at Boston, 9 October 1534.

531. RICHARD WESTE [OF MARKET STAINTON]
[LCC 1532–34, fo. 329r]

23 August 1534. I, Richerde Weste of Market Staynton, make thys my testament conteynyng my last will. Fyrste I bequethe my soule unto allmyghtty God and to the Blessyd Virgyn St. Mare and to all the holy cumpeny of heven, and my body to

be buryd in the churcheyerde of St. Michel of Staynton. To the high altare aforesayd iiij*d*. To Our Lady's warke of Lincoln iiij*d*. To John Weste my sun iiij ewes and iiij lammys and a fole. To William Weste one ewe and one lamme. To Michel my sun one ewe and one lamme. To Michel Weste one ewe and one lamme. To Sacs West a lamme. To Robert Weste my kynsman iij seame barly and my best jaket, ij dooblettes and my jerkyn, and my best sherte. The resydue of my goodes I gyff unto Agnes West my wyff, whome I make my sole executrix. Thes wytnes; Sir William Jerman, my gostly father, John Dawson of Staynton, John Burryth of the same towne, Thomas Scausbe, William Dowis, with many mo.

Proved before P at Horncastle, 16 October 1534.

532.   SIMON PUTTRELL [OF TRUSTHORPE]
[LCC 1535–37, fos. 29r–30r]

26 August 1534. I, Simon Puttrell of Thursthorp within the countie of Lincoln, husbandman, beyng of a perfyte mynde and good memory, ordens and makes my testament and last will. Firste I bequethe my soule to allmyghtty God, Our Lady St. Mary and to all the sayntes in heven to pray for me, and my body to be buryed in the churcheyerde of Trusthorp aforesayd be at the order of my executors. To Our Blessyd Lady of the cath[edral] churche of Lincoln xx*d*, that is to say x*d* to the high altare ther and x*d* to Our Lady warke. To the high altare of Trusthorp xx*d*. To the churche warke of the same xiij*s* iiij*d*. To the performance of the rye holde of Our Lady of Trusthorp, one schepe with the stocke. To the plowe light of the same one schepe with the stocke. To the buyldyng of the est churche of Thedylthorp ix*s* vj*d*. To the weste churche of Thedylthorp xx*d*. To vij ryngers of the the bellys in the same churche ij*s* iiij*d*. To the churche warke of Thoresby xx*d*. To the churche warke of Aby xij*d*. To the churche warke of Saleby xij*d*. Also I will have iiij trentalles of messys for my soule and all Crysten soulys, that is to say ij of them at Grymesby, one Hagneby Abbey and the other in the churche of Trusthorp. To Margaret my wyff xl^{ty} schepe, iiij kye at her awn election. Also one cople of oxen and Rown my horse, and xiij*s* iiij*d* towarde another horse. To the sayd Margaret all the housholde stuff that she brought with her to have to her and to her chyldren begottyn betwyxt her and me. Also to the same Margaret my wyff ij yeryng beystes with ther calves and xl^{ty} shyllynges in money. To my sayd wyff a wane, a plowe and ij harroys so long as she remanyth vido, and when she mareith, then I will they remayn to my chyldren, that is to say, to John my sun a wane a plowe and a harrowe, and to Edwarde my sun a harrowe. Also I [fo. 29v] will that my sayd wyffe have my hole ferme that I dwell in be the same take and rente as I have it by duryng her wydohode, savyng one pasture of xx^{ty} acres for that rent aftyr the porcion. And yff that my sayd wyff do marry, then I will that my sayd ferme with the pertinens remane to all my children duryng my yeres that I have in it, and by the same rent that I have it by, and to be devydyd equally emonge all my sayd children. To Thomas my sun a cowe and xxx^{ty} schepe. To John my sun a cowe and xxx^{ty} schepe. To Robert my sun a cowe and xxx^{ty} schepe. To Edwarde my sun a cowe and xxx^{ty} schepe. To my doughter Helene a cowe and xxx^{ty} schepe. To Thomas my sun a yong horse and one cople of the best of my oxen. To John my sun a cople of oxen of the best and my best horse. To Edwarde my sun a cople of sterys of ij yeres of age. To Robert my sun a cople of sterys of ij yeres of age and a yong horse. To Edwarde my

sun aforenamyd a horse of ij yeres of age. I will that all the housholde stuff that I had with my other wyff be devydyd emonges all my sayd children, the whiche I hadde with my other wyff. And every one of theym to be other heyres in all the sayd goodes and in all other thynges as is afore bequethyd to them. I will that every childe that I have, have one sylver spone. I will that the ij jewellys the whiche is at my beades, remane to the use of John my sun. And yff that he dye to the other brother nexte, and every one of them to be other heyres in that. To Master Hiltofte vjs viijd. To Mastres Hylton vjs viijd. Also to Jone Marcham a yong qwye, iiij yowes and iiij lammys, and they to be kepyd and noryshyd a yere upon my grounde. To my own father xxvjs viijd. To my mother xs. To my wyffe's father xxs. To John Kovell a russyt jaket. To my unkyll Willum Puttrell of Willughby a dooblet off lether, a lether jerkyn. To Robert Puttrell of Alforde a dooblet of fustyann and one yowe schepe. Off thys present testament and last will I make Thomas Puttrell my fader and Thomas Spillesby of Thorseby my true and faythfull executors, they to pay my dettes and fulfyll thys my testament and last will after the lawes off God and holy Churche. And the resydue of my goodes to dispose for the helthe off my soule and all Crysten soulys as they shall thynk best. [fo. 30r] Thes beyng wytnes; John Covell, Willum Puttrell of Willughby, John Messynger, Willum Messynger, John Clerke of Mabilthorp and Mr. Robert Hansarde, parson of Thurthorp, with other. Also to every one of my sayd children xls in money.

Proved before P at Belchford, 3 June 1535. Adm. granted to the executors.

533.   SIR JOHN GRAY [PARSON OF CALCETHORPE]
       [LCC 1532–34, fo. 337v]

1 September 1534. I, Sir John Gray, parson of Callesthorp in the countie of Lincoln, makes my testament and last will. Firste I bequethe my soule to allmyghtty God, Our Lady St. Mary and to all the cumpeny of heven. My body to be buryd in the quere of the paryshe churche of St. Fathe in Callesthorp. To Our Lady of Lincoln iiijd. To Our Lady warkes iiijd. To Gregory Gray all the resydue of my goodes, and he to delyver unto Thomas and Henry, hys bretherne, and also to Jenet and Johanne, hys systers, to every one of them at ther mariage or at ther age of xv yeres, xls. I make the sayd Gregory Gray my executor, and Sir Henry Gray my brother supervisor. Thes wytnes; Thomas Chapman of Callesthorp, Roger Hulton and Sir John Kerrham, preste.

Proved before P at Lincoln, 3 November 1534.

534.   WILLIAM MAWER [OF FARLESTHORPE]
       [LCC 1532–34, fo. 326]

1 September 1534. I, William Mawer off Fallesthorp, of hole mynde and good memory, ordens and makes my testament and last will. Firste I bequethe my soule to allmyghtty God, to Our Blessyd Lady St. Mary and to all the holy cumpeny of heven, and my body to be buryd within the churche porche of St. Andro of Fallesthorp. To Our Lady of Lincoln viijd. To the churche warke of Our Lady of Lincoln iiijd. To the high altare in Fallesthorpe churche for my tithys forgottyn xijd. To the churche warke of the same churche xijd. To the light of Our Lady of Pety in the same churche iiijd. To the light of Our Lady of Grace in the same churche iiijd.

To the church warke of Alford xij*d*. To the high altare within the same churche for my tithys forgottyn xij*d*. To the churche of Wytherne viij*d*. To the high altare in the same churche iiij*d*. To the churche of Ryggesby viij*d*. I will that one trentall be celebrate in the churche of Fallesthorpe aforesayd for my soule and all Crysten soulys, and I bequethe to the preste that shall celebrate the same trentall x*s*. To Margaret Mawer my doughter vj*l*. To Margaret Skytell ij yowes and ij lammes. To John Blakyn ij yowes and ij lammes. To Elizabeth Baston one yowe and one lamme. To Humfray Walker ij yowes and one stere. To Elizabeth my doughter one cowe. To Thomas, my doughter's Elizabethe sun, one yeryng calffe. The resydue off my goodes not bequethyd I bequethe them to Alice my wyff, and I make the sayd Alice my wyff and Robert Hopster of Candelesby my executors, and I bequethe to the sayd Robert for hys labor vj*s* viij*d*, my best cote and my best doblet. I desyre Sir John Wollay, the vicare of Fallesthorp, be supervisor [fo. 326v] and I bequethe to hym for hys labor iij*s* iiij*d*. Thes wytnesses; Thomas Oresby and William Mawer, with other mo.

Proved before P at Alford, 15 October 1534.

535.   JOHN BAYTHLAY [OF ASTERBY]
        [LCC 1532–34, fo. 328v]

2 September 1534. I, John Baythlay of Asterby, good and hole off mynde, dothe make thys my last will. Fyrste I bequethe my soule to allmyghtty God, to Our Lady St. Mary and to all the saintes in heven. My body to be buryd within the churchyerde of St. Peter of Asterby. To Our Lady of Lincoln vj*d*. To Our Lady warke vj*d*. To the high altare in Asterby churche vj*d*. To Asterby churche vj*s* viij*d*. To Golceby churche xij*d*. To Helene my wyff my house in Styrton of v*s* rent duryng her lyff, and aftyr her dethe to remayn to Jenet my doughter and to her heyres. Also my copy of Mr. Lytylbery graunt in Asterby and Golceby, and aftyr her dethe to remayn to Thomas my sun. To Robert Baythlay the indentur of my mylne aftyr the dethe of Helene my wyff. To Helene my wyff my copy of the house in Golceby and aftyr her dethe to remayn to Agnes my doughter. To Agnes my doughter one cowe. To Robert Clarke one cople steres and x yowes. To John Robynson v yowes and v lammys. To Jane Schammulsby one flecte qwe, and to every one of her systers ij schepe. To Jenet Waterton ij schepe. The resdyue of my goodes I gyff to Helene my wyff and I do make my executors Helene my wyff and Richerd Rysse, and I will that the sayd Richerd have for hys labor vj*s* viij*d*. I will that the parson be supervisor, and to have for hys labor vj*s* viij*d*. Wytnes; Sir Robert Hewys, the parson, Richard Risse, John Corbryge and Robert Clerke.

Proved before P at Horncastle, 16 October 1534.

536.   CHRISTOPHER CHELYS [OF MUMBY]
        [LCC 1535–37, fos. 16v–17v]

3 September 1534. I, Christofor Chelys off Mumby, with my hole mynde and good remembraunce, make my testament with my last will. Firste I bequethe my soule to allmyghtty God, to Our Blessyd Lady and to all the holy cumpeny in heven, and my body to be buryed in the churche off [fo. 17r] Mumby. To Our Lady of Lincoln viij*d*, and to Our Lady's warke iiij*d*. To the high altare in Mumby churche xij*d*, and the

other ij altares iiij*d*, and to Our Lady of Pety ij*d*. To the bellys iij*s* iiij*d*. I will that a trentall be sayd at Boston for my soule and my wyffe's and all Christen soulys. To Maryon my doughter a new panne, a lytyll panne, x pecys puder, ij beddes, ij kye, xx^{ty} schepe, a brasse potte, a new tubbe, xx*s* in money, a shedere calve, a forme and a candylstyke. To Agnes my doughter a gret panne and a lesse panne, and panne of Agnes Chelys Wytworde, x pecys puter, ij beddes, a brasen potte, xx schepe, ij kye, a tubbe, in money xx*s*, a shedere calve, a forme and a candylstyk. To Johanne my doughter the thyrde panne and a lyttyll panne, a candylstyk, x pecys puter, ij beddes, a brasse potte and a gret potte of Agnes Chelys Wytworde, ij kye, xx^{ty} schepe, a tubbe and in money xx*s*, a shedere calve and a forme. And I will, yff ought cum at ether of my ij yong doughters afore the age of xviij yeres, that one of them shall be other heyre. And yff they bothe fortune to dye afore the age of xviij yeres, then I will that bothe ther Wytwordes remayn to Andro and Mary, evenly to be schyftyd. To Andro my sun the best cople oxen, the best wane, my best cote and iij yerdes and a halff of new clothe with lynnyng. And all other goodes, bothe lande and goodes, I gyff unto Andro that may be sparyd to remayn in the handes of Robert Betyson to he cum at laufull age. To Robert Marshall a mare and a fole, the secunde wane, a yong blak mare, my best russyt cote, a worstyd dooblet and my ferme for the space of iij yeres, and to enter of the hole croppe and housholde of thys yere, as swyne, butter and chese, geys, dukkes and hennys, to the fyndyng of my chylde, and to leave at hys departyng to Andro xx^{ty} quarters beanys and barly, ij quarters wheate, iiij swyne, butter and chese, geys, dukkes and hennys aftyr good maner as sum of everythyng. And I will that he pay no more to Andro for scutt lande for the space of iij yeres but x*s* by yere. Also I will that Maryon have her moder's best beades with ij lyttyll jewellys and Margaret and Agnes and Johanne, every one of them, a sylver ryng. To Thomas Marshall iij ewys and iij lammys and a burlyng qwye, and Johanne Chelys her mother beste apparell and Marion for her gowen. To Thomas Scherpe v yowes and v lammys. To Thomas Yong a lamme of hys wages and another lamme. To John Whyt a yowe. To John Watson a dooblet, a petycote and an olde russyt cote. To John Gammulbe my secunde russyt cote. To every ich on of my godchylder ij*d*. I will that all the clothe uncutte, bothe lyn and hardyn, in savyd to fulfyll my will and to reparell my chylder, ever as they have nede. To Henry Mawer [fo. 17v] iij*s* iiij*d* to be good kyndman to Andro Chelys. And yff it fortune Andro my sun to departe thys worlde afore he cum at laufull age, then I will that my lande shall be shyftyd betwene my ij yong doughters, Agnes and Johanne. And the remayn of all my goodes lefte unto Andro shall then be shyftyd emong my iij doughters, Margaret, Agnes and Johanne, and every one of them to be other heryre. Yff they dye withowt issue, and yff all my iiij chylder departe withowt issue, then I will that my lande and all other goode of thers remayn to Maryon and to her chylder. And yff they all fortune to departe and Maryon and her chylder, then I will that my lande be solde and all other goodes of mynde, and disposyd in Mumby churche for my soule, my wyffe's and all Christen soules. The resydue of my goodes I gyff unto my sun Andro Chelys, to remayn as is aforesayd in the handes of Robert Betyson, to hys behove till he cum at laufull age, and I make Robert Betyson and Robert Marshall my fathefull executors, and I will thay they have for ther pane and labors Robert Betyson xx*s*, and Robert Marshall an amblyng colte stag. Also I will that Master Richarde Cartewryght my curate be supervisor of thys my last will, to se that my dettes be truly payd and my will fulfyllyd, and to helpe to succurre my chylder with hys good councell, and I will that he have x*s*. Thes men beyng wytnes; William More, Robert

Schauforthe, Robert Grysse, George Watson and other mo. Wryttyn at Mumby the day and the yere abovesayd.

Proved before P at Alford, 11 May 1535.

537.   SIR WILLIAM HUNTER [PARSON OF WINCEBY]
        [LCC 1535–37, fos. 23v–24r]

3 September 1534. I, William Hunter, parson of Wynceby in the countye of Lincoln, of good and hole mynde, makes my last will. Firste I bequethe my soule to allmyghtty God, Hys mother Our Lady [fo. 24r] and to all the saintes in heven, and my body to be buryd within the churche of St. Margaret of Wynceby aforesayd. I will that Our Lady off Lincoln have xij*l*, the halffe to herselffe and the other to her warke. Also I will have v messys of the v principall woundes of Our Lorde done in Our Lady's qwere at Boston for the helthe of my soule. Also I will that the iiij orders of freres of Boston have, iche on of my them, viij*d* to pray for my soule. I will that my syster Agnes Hunter shall have all the goodes of myne as long as she lyffys and she kepe her unmaryed. And yff she be maryed, then I will that my cosyn Robert Hunter, her sun, to have to the one halffe of my goodes. I will that John Hunter, Robert sun, shall have, when he comys to xxj yeres of age, yff he lyff, one good wane with all that longes to it, xx^ty schepe, the thyrde parte of my housholde stuff, ij horssys or marys. The resydue of my goodes not bequethyd, my dettes payd, I bequethe to Agnes Hunter my syster, whome I make my sole executrix to dispose for the helthe of my soule as shall be most nedefull, and Robert Hunter, her sun, to be the supervisor of thys my last will. Thes wytnes; John Colen off Wynceby, Robert Alman of the same, Robert Wellys of the same, Rumbalde Peryn of the same, Sir Christofer Steffan, parson of Hameryngham, with other mo.

Proved before P at Horncastle, 13 May 1535.

538.   JOHN HARTBURN [OF BRADLEY]
        [LCC 1532–34, fo. 331]

6 September 1534. I, John Hartburne off Bradlay, with a hole mynde and good memory, makyth my testament. In the fyrst I bequethe my soule to God allmyghtty, to Our Lady St. Mary and to all the saintes in heven, [fo. 331v] and my body to be buryd in the churcheyerde of St. George in Bradlay. To the high altare of Bradlay for all my tithes xij*d*. To Our Lady of Lincoln vj*d* and to her warke vj*d*. To Laceby churche xij*d*. To Lyttyll Cotes churche xij*d*. To Scartho churche xij*d*. To Sir Peter Munde xij*d*. To Masteres Hylyarde vj yowes and for every one of her sunnys ij schepe. To William Theker of Cotes a weder hogge. To Thomas Barnabe of Laceby ij weder hogges, and to hys wyff a yowe. To Alan Este a schepe, to hys wyff a schepe, and to hys sun John j schepe. To Elizabeth Grayngham a schepe. To every one of my godchylderen a schepe. To my brother Robert a weder. To Helyn my wyff xx^ty schepe and ij of the best bestes besyde the plugh. To every one of my sunys Edwarde, Phylip, Martyn and William xx^ty schepe and ij bestes. To Alyson my doughter xx^ty schepe and ij bestes. The resydue of my goodes I bequethe them to Helene my wyff and to my iij eldest sonnys whome I make my executors, and my most trysty Mr. Martyn Hylyarde oversear, and he to have for hys labor vj*s* viij*d*.

Thes wytnes; Sir Peter Munde, Thomas Barnabe, Robert Hartburne, with other mo.

Proved before P at Grimsby, 20 October 1534.

539.   ALICE SYMSON [OF THORGANBY]
         [LCC 1532–34, fo. 323v]

6 September 1534. I, Alice Symson of the paryshe of Thurganby, beyng of a hole mynde and of good remembraunce, makes and ordens thys my present testament contenyng my last will. Fyrst I bequethe and commende my soule to God allmyghtty and to Our Blessyd Lady St. Mary, and to all the holy cumpeny of heven. My body to be buryd in the churcheyerde of All Saintes in Thurganby. To the high altare of the sayd churche xij*d*. To the cathedrall churche of Lincoln iiij*d*. To Elizabeth Tatam one qwy, a chyst and a pare of hardyn schetes. To Thomas Stevenson my sun ij swyne. To Margaret Stevynson my best gyrdyll, a pare of beades. The resydue of my goodes here not bequethyd, I bequethe to Richerde Bally whome I make my executor, he for to have it and dispose it for the helthe of my soule as it shall be best seyn in tyme to comme. Thes wytnes; Sir Robert Gyll, parson, Thomas Stevenson, wyth other mo. At Thurganby the day and yere above sayd.

Proved before P at Market Rasen, 21 October 1534. Adm. granted to the executor.

540.   HELEN BROOKE [OF FULSTOW]
         [LCC 1532–34, fo. 334]

11 September 1534. I, Helyn Brooke of Fulstowe within the diocese of Lincoln, wydoy, hole of mynde and in good [and] perfyte remembraunce beyng, make thys my testament and last will. Fyrst I bequethe my soule to God allmyghtty my savyor, to Our Blessyd Lady St. Mary and to all the holy cumpeny of heven. My body to be buryd within the churcheyerde of Fulstowe. To the cathedrall churche of Our Blessed Lady off Lincoln iiij*d*. To a preste for doyng off fyve messys for my soule and all Christen soulys xx*d*. To Isabell, the wyff of William Donham, the goyng and pasturyng of vj bestes and halff a beste gate in a certyn pasture callyd Esten Holme duryng terme of xj yeres. To Andro Grene a yowe and a lambe. I will that the foresayd William Donham have the custody of the foresayd Andro Grene with all and singler suche goodes as ar bequethen to hym by Robert Brooke my husband, and also by me the foresayd Elyner, to be delyveryd to the foresayd Andro when he comyth to the full age of xxj yeres. [fo. 334v] To Dane John Grene vj*s* viij*d*. To Peter Gray a lambe. The resydue of all my goodes I will that Walter Redman shall dispose them as he shall thynk best to the plesure of God, performance of thys my last will and payng of my dettes, whome I orden and make myn executor. And I gyff to hym for hys labor and payntakyng a stere of the age of ij yeres. Thes wytnesses; Thomas Donham, Amor Bryan and William Donham, with other.

Proved before P at Lincoln, 23 October 1534. Adm. granted to the executor.

541.   JOHN STAWPER [OF NETTLETON]
[LCC 1532–34, fos. 329v–330r]

13 September 1534. I, John Stawper off Nettylton in the countie of Lincoln, of a good and hole mynde, doys make my will. In primis I do wyt my soule to God allmyghtty, to Our Lady St. Mary and to all the compeny in heven. My body to be buryd within the churche of St. John Bapti[s]te of the towne of Nettylton. To the high [fo. 330r] altare of the same towne xij*d*. To the churche one schepe. To St. John's gylde one schepe. To Our Lady's warkes at Lincoln iiij*d*. To the high altare at Lincoln iiij*d*. To North Kelesye churche viij*d*. To every churche aboundyng on the towne of Nettylton iiij*d*. To John Carre one schepe. I do wyt x*s* to a good and a honeste preste to syng one trentall of messys for me within the churche of Nettylton. I will that Margarete Stawper my wyff and George my sun be my executors to dispose the reste of my goodes not bequeste, to them and to other of my chylder as right doys require. I do orden John Howdon and Thomas Franckys supervisors for to se that thys my last will to be fulfylled for the helthe of my soule and the proffyt of my chylder. Wytnes wherof; Robert Good, preste, Henry Benneworthe, Robert Cotys, cum multis aliis.

Proved before P at Caistor, 19 October 1534.

542.   JOHN ADDESON [OF WEST BARKWORTH]
[LCC 1535–37, fo. 24]

17 September 1534. I, John Addeson of West Barkworthe, hole of mynde and good remembraunce, do make thys my last will and testament. The firste I bequethe my soule to God allmyghtty, to Our Lady St. Mary, and to all the holy cumpeny of heven. My body to be buryd in the churcheyerde of All Halloys of Weste Barkworthe, my mortuary as the order and custome of the churche requiryth. To Our Lady's warke of Lincoln xij*d*. To the high altare vj*d*. To the churche of Sotteby xx*d*. To my father a whete lande, the whiche dothe lye on Rygges. To John my sun xxvj*s* viij*d*. To Johanne my doughter xxvj*s* viij*d*, besyde that I gyff to Elizabeth my doughter xxvj*s* viij*d*. To Catheryne my wyffe with chylde, yff it please God the chylde lyve, I gyff to the sayd chylde xxvj*s* viij*d*, and it happyn to dye, I bequethe to the foresayd Catheryne vj*s* viij*d*. And the reste of the money to be devydyd to John, Jenet and Elizabeth, my chyldren aforesayd. To everich on of my godchyldren [fo. 24v] a lamme, and I gyff to ether of my servauntes a lamme. The resydue of all my goodes not bequethyd, my legacy fulfyllyd and my dettes payd, I gyff to Catheryne my wyff and John Melton, the whiche I constitute and orden my executors. To John Melton, for hys labor, iiij*s*, the sayd Catheryne and John to dispose the premisses aforesayd as they may the moste convenyently do for my soule and all Christen soulys. Thes beyng wytnes; Sir John Chigh the parson, Edmund Swanne, Thomas Stampe, John Hall, with other mo.

Proved before P at Wragby, 14 May 1535.

543.   WILLIAM PYNCRAKE [OF BURGH LE MARSH]
[LCC 1532–34, fos. 319v–320r]

17 September 1534. I, Wylliam Pyncrake of Burgh in the Marsh in the county of Lincoln, hole in mynd, maketh my last wyll and testament. Fyrst I bequeth my

soull to God almyghty, to Our Lady Sant Mary and to all the holy company of hevyn, and my body to [be] buryed within the new quere at Burgh church. To Our Lady wark at Lincoln xij*d*. To the fatherles chyldre at Sant Katheryn's iiij*d*. To the chanons at Byllyngton xij*d*. To ych on of the iiij orders of freres in Boston iij*s* iiij*d*. To ych on of my godchyldre a lame. To Agnes my dowghter a red chyst, iij of the best bras pottes, iij of the best kettylles, x pannes, xij peses of puther, a led, a spyt and cobhyrnes, a medyltable, and an aymbery, a feder bed with that longyth therto, iij of the best materis with coverlydes, x pylowes, viij pare of playne shetes and iiij pare of arden shetes, also xx^{ti} yoywys, x hogge and x kye, also xx poundes of money to be taken of the det that Thomas Glen howyth to me and [fo. 320r] to be payd by my executor to the sayd Agnes my dowghter or to hyr use. I wyll that John Pyncrake my son and heire and hys succeders, shall fynd a prest to syng and pray for the saull of Wylliam Pyncrak and for hys fryndes' soulles within the church of Burgh wher hys body lyes, and to help to maynteyn Gode's servys ther the space and terme of xx yers next after my decesse, and the pryst wage to be taken of thos landes that I bought of Husay lyeng in Croft and Burgh, and of ix acres of my proper landes. And after the xx^{ti} yers be done, I wyll that John my son have the forsayd landes to hym and to hys heirs for ever, and all my other landes I wyll remayn to John my son and to hys heirs accordyng to my fader wyll for evermore, and I wyll that the sayd John my son have all the takyn landes and howsys that I have takyn within the lordschep of Burght or elswher terme of the indenters. The resydew of my guddes not gyfyn I put them to the dysposyng of John Pyncrake, Rychard Ward and Christofer Wytyng, whome I make my executors to performe my wyll and testament, and fynysh the new quere and dyspose for the helth of my saull and my fryndes' saulles. Wyttnes herto; Thomas Jordan, vycar, Thomas Glen, Robert Pelson and Peter Stevenson, wythe other mo.

Proved before P at Spilsby, 14 October 1534.

544.   JOHN POTTE [OF GOSBERTON]
[LCC 1532–34, fo. 309v]

18 September 1534. I, John Pott of the paryshe of Gosberton, beyng perfyte in mynde and of good remembraunce, makes my last will and testament. The fyrste I bequethe my soule to allmyghtty God and to Hys blessyd mother St. Mary and to all the holy cumpeny of heven, and my body to be buryed in the churcheyerde of St. Peter and St. Paule within the paryshe of Gosberton, and I gyff to the high altare therof for my tithys forgottyn iiij*d*. To the reparacion of every altare in the same churche ij*d*. To every gylde ij*d*. To every light ij*d*. To the churche warke iiij*d*. To the reparacion of the gylde hall iiij*d*. To the iiij orders of frerys in Boston, every order, vj*s* viij*d*. To our mother churche reparacion in Lincoln iiij*d*. To the chyldren of St. Catheryn's ij*d*. I will that my executore cause one trentall of messys to be sayd within the paryshe churche of Gosberton aftyr my decesse, for my soule and for all my good frendes' soulys. To Margaret my wyff iij of my best kyne, x yowys and x lammys and all my housholde stuff. To Thomas Lylle, sun of Robert Lille, one cowe, one yowe and one lamme. To Robert Lille one cowe. To Anne Lylle one cowe. To Simon Dawsyng one cowe. To every chylde of Simon Dawsyng one lamme. To Richerde Bawde one lamme. To every chylde of

John Dawsyng one lamme. To John Lille, Margarete Lille and Anne Lylle, every one of them, one lamme. To John Nutkyn, sun of Simon Nutkyn, one lamme. The resydue of my goodes I gyff them to John Dawsyng to be my executore, to se thys my last will truly performyd, to pay my dettes and to bryng my body honestely to the grounde, and to dispose my goodes for the helthe of my soule. Thes wytnes; Sir Henry Topplys, Richerde Bowde, Simon Nutkyn, John Vassell, with other mo.

Proved before P at Swineshead, 8 October 1534.

545.   JOHN HORNCLYFF [OF WELLOW]
       [LCC 1535–37, fos. 3v–4v]

20 September 1534. I, John Hornclyffe of the paryshe of Welhowe, beyng of hole mynde and good memory, makes my last will and testament. Firste I bequethe my soule unto allmyghtty God and to Our Lady St. Mary and to all the holly cumpeny of heven, and my body to be buryed within the churche of St. Jamys of Grymesby before the fygure of St. Erasmus. To my lorde abbot my beste horse apon a condicion, he be to my sun as he was to me. For my mortuary so muche money as is assignyd by the kynge's statute. To my brother Myffyn my velvet dooblet. To Thomas Hornclyff my sun x*l* and [a] blewe jaket, and it to be payd within a yere my will to be provyd. I will that ther shall be done for my soule, before Our Lady of Market Rasyn, on trentall aftyr thys forme foloying: I will have at every messe iiij pore men, and every man to have in hys hande a waxe candell burnyng duryng the messe tyme, and whenever messe is done, the preste to have iiij*d*, and he that helpys the messe to have ij*d*, and every pore man to have j*d*, and so to contynewe to the sayd trentall be fully at an ende. To St. Jamys kyrke of Grymseby vj*s* viij*d* for lying in it. To the vicar of the sayd kyrke iij*s* iiij*d*. To the gyltyng [of the] roud, Mary and John of the chapell of St. Austyn of Hedon xx*s*, and it to be payd when warkemen is in hande with the warke. To Sir John Deyn of Holdunes xxvj*s* viij*d*. To John Hornclyff my sun my corall beades with sylver gawdes. And where before the makyng herof I have mayd clere delyvery and gyft to Robert my sun of the iiij parte of a shyppe callyd Christoffe of Grymesby, with all suche goodes that before thys tyme was meyn, the whiche that shall cum with her to [fo. 4r] thys porte or eny other in Englande whersoever it be or shall happe the sayd shyppe to arryffe, I will that gyft never be denyd by my executor no[r] no other. Also where before thys makyng and date I have delyveryd all my leissys and the interest of the moveable goodes that remanys in any of my farmeholdes and other my tenementes and groundes in Holdernes to Robert my sun, and solde all suche leysses and goodes to the same Robert my sun apon condicion that he do not relese, mynyshe nor take away any goodes remanyng in or apon any suche groundes of suche leesses or tenementes from the tyme that yt shall please God to call me to hys mercy to the full ende of viij yeres then nexte foloyng be endyd, appon condicion that the sayd Robert my sun, by the advice of Sir John Clerke and hys assignes, suffer yerely duryng the sayd viij yeres withowt any contrary v*l* sturlyng of the remennys and proffyttes of the same my tenementes, leysses and other goodes in Holdernes be takyn to the fyndyng of John my sun, nowe canon in Welhowe, to be at universyte of Cambryge or Oxforde for the space of the sayd viij yeres, be suche licence as hys master, the abbot of the sayd Welhou hathe grauntyd to me to suffer the sayd John my sun ther to be for

lernyng, or ellys the sayd bargyn with my sun Robert to be voyd of none effecte.[174] And further, I will that accordyng to the sayd bargan I mayd with Robert my sayd sun, when I solde hym my sayd leysses and tenementes and moveable goodes, condicionally that he shulde of the yerely proffyttes the sayd v*l* suffer to be take to fyndyng of John my sun at universyte, it is my will the sayd bargan stande in full effecte and never to be denyed. And I will, yff my sun Robert do not fulfyll the sayd bargan of hys partie, but denye or refuse any parte therof, that then all my gyftes and bargan to hym shall be voyd, and then by thys my will I gyff and wyt to the foresayd Sir John Clerke all my foresayd leysses, tenementes, moveable goodes, payng duly and truly every yere duryng the sayd viij yeres v*l* stirlyng to my sayd sun John, towarde hys exhibicion at on universyte as is before sayd. And then the sayd Sir John or hys assignes, for dewly seyng executyng of thys my will, I will he have vj*s* viij*d* every yere of the proffyttes of the premisses. And suche costes borne of the sayd proffyttes and revenuys afforesayd as shall susteyn in optenyng thys my will to be truly performyd. And aftyr my will truly be performyd as is abovesayd, I will that the sayde viij yeres that the sayd John my sun shall receyve v*l*, and yff the sayd John be not [fo. 4v] trobelyd nor let be the sayd Robert my sun nor hys assignes, so truly to be payd as is aforesayd, that then all the proffyttes above v*l* shall be truly delyveryd to the sayd Robert or hys assygnes, and to Beatrix hys mother so long as she shall be wydo and no longer. For yff she mary, then I will she shall have so lyttyll of my goodes as reasonably may be kepyd from her. The resydue of my goodes I gyff to Beatrix my wyff and Robert Hornclyff my sun, whome I make my executors that they may lovyngly and kyndely occupy the same as they shall seme in ther conscience the best to the pleasure of God. In wytnes herof I set to my seale the day and yere abovesayd, thes wytness. Also I bequethe to Sir Robert Wryght vj*s* viij*d*, and to the subpriorysse vj*s* viij*d*.

> Proved before P at Grimsby, 13 April 1535. Adm. granted to Robert Hornclyff the son and executor, Beatrice the relict and co-executor being prevented by death.

546. ROBERT FOWLLER [OF HELPRINGHAM]
[LCC 1532–34, fo. 314r]

23 September 1534. I, Robert Fowller of the paryshe of Helpryngham in the diocese of Lincoln, hole in mynde and perfyte in remembraunce, make thys my last will and testament. Fyrste I bequethe my soule to allmyghtty God, Our Lady St. Mary and to all holy saintes in heven. My body to be buryed in the churcheyerde of Helpryngham. To the high altare of Helpryngham for tithes negligently forgottyn xij*d*. To the churche of Lincoln xij*d*. To the motherles chyldren at St. Catheryn's withowt Lincoln iiij*d*. To the reparacions of the bellys of Helpryngham xij*d*. To the bying of a notyd antiphoner for the churche off Helpryngham xij*d*.[175] I will that a trentall of messes be done in the churche of Helpryngham, for my soule and all Christen soulys betwyxte my buryall day and Wytsonday nexte foloyng. To Johanne my doughter thre quarters barly, thre ewe schepe and thre hog schepe, a yong cowe of a yere age. To Thomas Bayte, my sun-in-lawe, my ferme, and he to enter at the nexte falloys. To Robert my sun a bay mere and the fole, ij yowes and ij

---

[174] There is no record of a John Hornclyff at either Oxford or Cambridge University.
[175] An antiphoner with musical notation.

lammys, halffe a quarter wheate. To Agnes Bate sex schepe at the will of my executrix, a quarter barly. To Robert Bray my godchylde a stryke of barly. To Adlarde Cowke a stryke of barly. To Agnes Gybson a stryke of barly. The resydue of my goodes I gyff to Agnes my wyff whome I make my sole executrix, she to dispose them for the helthe of my soule and all Christen soulys as she shall thynke moste expedyent and necessary. Wytnes; Henry Rodes, Robert Bryan, Robert Sygrave, John Atwell, Richerde Goldyng, with other mo.

Proved before P at Sleaford, 10 October 1534. Adm. granted to the executrix.

547. HENRY THORNETON [OF SOUTH RESTON]
[LCC 1535–37, fo. 16v]

24 September 1534. I, Henry Thorneton, seke of body and hole of mynde, makes thys my laste will. Fyrste I bequethe my soule to God and to Our Lady St. Mary, and my body to be buryd in the churcheyerde of St. Edithe of Southe Reston. To the high altare of Southe Reston for forgottyn tythes iiijd. To the high altare of Lincoln iiijd, and to Our Lady's warke iiijd. To Sir Thomas the paryshe preste viijd. Also, may dettes payd, my will fulfyllyd and my body brought to the grounde, of the hole goodes the reste of my goodes to be devydyd betwyxte my wyff and my chylder. And yff enythyng berchaunce eny of my chylder, ther parte to be devydyd emong the other chylder. I bequethe a yow schepe to South Reston churche, a schepe to Robert Pratte and a amblyng fylly to John my brother, whome I make my executor with Agnes my wyffe, of thys my last will. Thes wytnesses; Sir Thomas Thorneton, Sir William Preston and William Chapman, with other mo.

Proved before P at Muckton, 10 May 1535.

548. ROBERT CHAWNER [OF HORNCASTLE]
[LCC 1532–34, fo. 334v]

28 September 1534. I, Robert Chawner of Horncastle, sadler, with hole mynde and good remembraunce, makyth my testament and last will. Fyrst I gyff and bequethe my soule to allmyghtty God and to Hys moste blessyd mother Our Lady St. Mary and to all the hole cumpeny of heven, and my body to be buryd in the churcheyerde of Our Lady of Horncastle. To Our Lady warke of Lincoln iiijd. To the high altare of Lincoln iiijd. To the high altare off Horncastle xd. To St. Catheryne gylde of Horncastle iiijd. The resydue of all my goodes I gyff them to Agnes my wyff, whome I make my hole executrix to dispose for the helthe off my soule and Christen soulys as she thynkyth best. Thes byng wytnes; Sir Michaell Whytehed, prest, with other mo.

Proved before P at Lincoln, 24 October 1534.

549. ROBERT HERDE [OF BILLINGHAY]
[LCC 1532–34, fos. 333v–334r]

29 September 1534. I, Robert Herde of Billyngay, hole of mynde and good remembrance, makyth my last will and testament. Fyrste I bequethe my soule to allmyghtty God, to Our Lady St. Mary and to all the gloriose cumpeny in heven,

and my body to be buryd in the churcheyerde of St. Andro in Billynghay. To the high altare in Billyngay churche xij*d*. To the bellys of the same churche vj*d*. To the same churche of Billyngay xij*d*. To Our Lady of Lincoln xij*d*. To my mother Beatrix Herde xx*s* that I awe to her. I will that my father Thomas Cocke have th'indenture whiche my father John Herde gave me that he had of Mr. William Compton, and the copy whiche I have of my lorde Taylboys, and the copy whiche I have of the prior of Cattelay. And the resydue of my goodes unbequethyd to be occupyed and manuryd by hym unto suche tyme as my chyldren cum to ther laufull age, to the [fo. 334r] bryngyng up of the same chyldren, and otherwyse for the proffyt and use of the same chyldren. And when my sayd chyldren, that is to say when every one of them, cumys to hys laufull age, then I will that my sayd father Cocke shall gyff and bestowe as myche of my sayd goodes to hym so cumyng and beyng at hys laufull age as my sayd father Cocke thynketh best, so that all my sayd indenture, copyes and goodes shall be fully gyven and bestowed emong those my chyldren that lyvys and cumys to ther laufull age at suche tyme as they cum to ther laufull age aftyr my sayd father Cockes will so order advyse and disposicion. The whiche Thomas Cocke my father I make myn executor. These beyng wytnes; Syr William Ludlame, preste, Robert Bate, Robert Johnson, Richerde Coke of Billyngay aforesayd, with other mo.

Proved before P at Lincoln, 22 October 1534. Adm. granted to the executor.

550. RICHARD BURTON [OF HUTTOFT]
[LCC 1532–34, fos. 325r–326r]

1 October 1534. I, Richerde Burton of Hotofte within the countie of Lincoln, yoman, of a hole mynde and good memory, ordens and makes my testament and last will. Fyrst I bequethe my soule to allmyghtty God, Our Lady St. Mary and to the saintes in heven, and my body to be buryd in the churche of Markeby. To the reparacions of the churche of Hotofte aforesayd iij schepe. To the vicar of the same one schepe. To Our Lady warke of the cathedral churche of Lincoln one schepe. To the priory churche of Markeby vj schepe, to be disposyd aftyr the discrescion of my lorde prior ther. Also to my sayd lorde prior and hys brether, ther to be mayd brother in ther chapiter house, x*s*. I bequethe for a trentall of messys to be done in the sayd churche of Markeby x*s*. I will that ther be gyffyn, at the day of my buryall and distributyd emonges the pore people of Markeby, aftyr the discrescion and mynde of my lorde prior ther and of my uncle John Randall, xx*s*. To Henry Blakmore vj schepe and to hys wyff ij schepe. To hys ij chylder, other of them, ij schepe [fo. 325v] To Elizabeth, servant to the sayd Henry Blakmore, ij schepe. To Sir Thomas Sharpneyff my nagge, my bowe and my shafftes. To my brother John Burton a cowe that is at William Bruester's and all my weryng gere excepte my blew cote, the whiche I gyff to Richerde Lecke, also my best cappe, the whiche I gyff to Henry Blakmore. To every yoman of my sayd lorde of Markeby a lamme.[176] To every one of my uncle John Randall chyldren one schepe. To every on of my godchyldren a lamme. To Thomas Cade a lamme. To Barnerde Tutbury, Thomas Woode and Thomas Ferley of Alforde a lamme [each]. I will that all my goodes not gyffyn shall go to my wyff Johanne Burton and to Clement Burton my sun, to be

---

[176] Probably tenants on lands belonging to Markby Priory.

devydyd betwyxt them bothe by even porcions. I will that my lorde prior off Markeby shall have my sayd sun Clement and hys parts off goodes to suche tyme as he com to age of xviij yeres and longer yff they can agre. And in the meantyme my sayd lorde for to fynde hym meate, drynke and lernyng. And as concernyng hys clothyng, my sayd lorde shall fynde it hym the tyme of hys beyng with my lorde, and my sayd lorde shall be alowyd therfore of hys sayd goodes. And at the ende of the sayd xviij yeres, I will that my sayd lorde prior shall delyver to my sayd sun Clement all hys sayd parte of goodes or legacy withowt further delay. And yff my sayd lorde prior and John Randall my uncle shall thynke it more profytable afore the tyme above expressyd, then I will that the sayd legacy and goodes be delyveryd to my sayd sun that tyme that they shall thynke best, provydyd allway that yff my sayd sun Clement do decesse afore the sayd xviij yeres or afore hys sayd legacy or goodes be delyveryd to hym, then I will that Johanne my wyff shall have the one halff of hys sayd legacy and goodes, and the other halffe to be disposyd aftyr the mynde and discrescion of my sayd lorde and off my sayd uncle John Randall. I make Johanne Burton my wyff, and Clement Burton my sun my executors, they to pay my dettes accordyng to the lawes of holy Churche, and my lorde prior of Markeby to be on supervisor and he to have for hys labor vj*s* viij*d*. And John Randall my uncle to be another supervisor, and he to have for hys labor a cowe that is with William Bruster. Thes beyng wytnes; Thomas Cade of Markeby aforesayd, Barnerde Tutbury of the same, John Randall of Hotofte, Thomas Barber off Markeby, Henry [fo. 326r] Blakmor of the same, and other moy.

Proved before P at Alford, 15 October 1534, Clement Burton being under age.

551.   JOHN PEDDER [OF BROWNTHORPE IN PARISH OF FRIESTON]
         [LCC 1532–34, fo. 315]

3 October 1534. I, John Pedder of Brounthorpe in the paryche off Freston, holl off myned and perfyt memory, makyth my testyment concludyng therin my last wyll. Furste I bequyth my solle to God almyghty, Owre Lady Sant Mary and the holy company off heven. My body to be beryed [in the] chyrchy[a]rde of Sant Jams off Freston, and allso I bequyth to the sacrament there vj*d*, and to Sent Jams there xij*d*. To Owre Lady off Pety iiij*d*. To Sant Syth iiij*d*. To the chyrch warke vj*s* viij*d*. To Our Lady off Lyncoln xij*d*. I surrender my copy off my hows with the appurtenauncys into the handys off Thomas Pedder to the use off Annes my doghter, my house that I dwell in to her and to her heyers and assignes [fo. 315v] after the custome, and more [to] her and her heyres and assynes affter the costom and manere. To the sayd Annes a copey off Styknay crofte duryng the heres therin contenyd. To the sayd Annes ij kye. To Margrete my hows in Kyrkraw and ij acres and a half off land duryng the tyme off hyr naturall lyffe, and after hyr dysseys I wyll that hows and a acar and a halffe off land remayne to Jenet my doghter and one acar off that land to Annes my doghter. And allso I bequyth to Annes and Jenet my doghters, ethar off thaym, on acar off yng grond. To Jenet Whytthed a kow and a calfe, a bede and a pott, a pan. To Jeffray Pedder a cart and iiij geyres, a grey felye and a calfe. To Thomas Pedder and Rafe Pedder, every one, a lame. To Mr. Dant iij*s* iiij*d*. To every on off my godchyldryn iiij*d*. The rest off my godes I gyve unto Margeret my wyfe and Annes my doghter, whome I make my exequitores to dyspose my goodes to the laude of

God and helth off my sall and all Crysten sall. Thes wynessys heroff; John Kyrke, Thomas Pedder, Sur Thomas Pykhall, with other moo.

Proved before P at Boston, 9 October 1534.

552. SIMON HOWSON [OF WALTHAM]
[LCC 1532–34, fo. 332r]

7 October 1534. I, Simon Howson of Waltham, hole of mynde and of good remembraunce, makes my testament and last will. Fyrste I bequethe my soule unto allmyghtty God and to Our Lady and to all the saintes in heven, and my body to be buryd in the churche of All Halloys of Waltham, and that at the lawe will to be for my mortuary. To the high altare of Our Lady of Lincoln vj*d*. To Our Lady warke iiij*d*. To the high altare of my paryshe churche of Waltham x*d*. To the iij gret bellys of my paryshe churche, every one of them, iiij*d*. To the churche warke of Fulstowe vj*d*. To the churche warke of Thoresby iiij*d*. To Asflyn Asby my doughter a cowe. To Margarete Tatam my doughter a cowe. To Elizabeth Asby ij schepe. To Christopher Tharolde my doughter sun ij schepe. To Robert Asby, sun to Richard Asby, a cowe and iiij schepe of the beste that I have. To Anne Vincent a schepe. I wyll that the foresayd Robert Asby shall have my house with all the landes, pasturys, medoys and fedynges within the towne and felde of Waltham, to hym, hys heyres and assignes. And yff it shall fortune the foresayd Robert to dye withowt heyres of hys body laufully begottyn, then I will that the sayd house with all the landes, pasture, medoys and fedyng groundes, with all the purt[enances] therto belongyng, shall mowe and go to Richard Asby, father unto the sayd Robert Asby, to hys heyres and hys assygnes for ever. The resydue of my goodes not wyt I gyff and I wyt to Richerde Asby and John Tatam, whome I make my executors for to dispose and devyde equally betwyxte them, and parte to do for the helthe of my soule as they thynke best. Before thes wytnesses; Sir Robert Lanam, curate, Sir Thomas Stonys, chauntry prest,[177] Robert Drowry, Richerde Vincent, with other mo.

Proved before P at Grimsby, 20 October 1534.

553. JOHN WHASHE [OF KIRMOND]
[LCC 1532–34, fo. 333v]

7 October 1534. I, John Whashe of the paryshe of Kyrmonde, beyng of a hole mynde and good remembraunce, makes and ordens thys my present testament conteynyng my last will. Fyrste I bequethe and commende my soule to God allmyghtty and to Our Blessyd Lady St. Mary, and to all the holy cumpeny of heven. My body to be buryd in the churcheyerde of St. Martyn in Kyrmonde. To the churche warke of Kyrmonde a quarter of barly. To the high altare of the sayd churche iiij*d*. To the cathedral churche of Lincoln iiij*d*. To the high altare of the foresayd churche iiij*d*. To Elizabeth Dyxson half a quarter of barly. The resydue of

---

[177] The chantry at Waltham was founded in 1329–30 to support one chaplain. In 1526 there was no chantry priest, but Thomas Stonys is recorded as a stipendiary priest, on a salary of £5, together with John Clerk, on £4 3s. 8d. By 1535 Stonys had become the chantry priest in his own right, on a salary of £4 3s. 5d. He died in 1540, eight years before the final dissolution of the chantry: Chantry Certificates (1923), 269–73.

my goodes I bequethe to William Whashe, John Whashe, Thomas Whashe and Peter Whashe my chyldren, whome I make my executors, them for to have it and dispose it for the helthe of my soule as it shall be beste sene to them in tyme to cum. Thes wytnes; John Woode, Thomas Hall, Raphe Bargh, Robert Yerburgh, with other mo. At Kyrmonde the day and yere afore sayd.

Proved before P at Market Rasen, 21 October 1534.

554.   THOMAS BEKYNGHAM [OF MORTON]
        [LCC 1534 &c., fo. 5r]

8 October 1534. I, Thomas Bekyngham of Morton, beyng in hole and perfecte memory, make my testament and last will. In primis I bequethe my soule to allmyghtty God and to Our Lady St. Mary and to all the holy cumpeny off heven, and my body to be buryd in the churcheyerde of St. Helene in Morton. To the high altare in Morton churche for tithes forgottyn iiij*d*. To the roode lofte ij strykes barly. To the bellys ij strykes barly. To the gyltyng of St. George ij strykes barly. To our mother churche of Lincoln iiij*d*. To St. Cithe in Hackonby churche, to the gilde, ij stryke barly. To the Trinite gylde and to St. George gylde in Morton one brasse potte. I bequethe one coverlyd to the high altare in Morton churche. To every one of my godchylder one stryke barly. To John Jakson one possenet with a starte and to the same John one stryke barly. To Alice Norys an arke and one coffer. To the high altare in Hacconby iiij*d*. I bequethe one acre of arable lande which lyethe in Hacconby felde, and also ij kye, to kepe one obyt yerely in Morton churche for the welthe of my soule and my ij wyffes' soulys, my father and my mother soulys and my good frendes' soulys, and for all Christen soulys. And so I will that my mynysters shall distribute or cause to be distrybute for the foresayd acre lande and ij kye iiij*s* yerely for evermore. To the vicare for messe and dirige iiij*d*. To other clerkes as my mynisters thynkes beste. The resydue of thys iiij*s* to be gyffyn emong pore people whereas moste nede is. I will that John Norys shall have xj acre lande and medoy whiche lyethe in Hacconby felde for one yere. And aftyr that yere I will that it returne unto John Francy and Robert Francy. The resydue of my goodes not bequethyd I gyff and bequethe to Thomas Norys and make hym my executor, and John Browne the yonger with hym, and the sayd John to have for hys labor ij strykes barly. And my funerall days, that is to say my buryall day, my vij day and my xxx^ty day at the disposicion of my ministers. Thes beryng wytnes; John Bothe, John Carter of Stenfeyt, Robert Allot the elder, with other mo.

Proved before P at Bourne, 28 January 1534/5.

555.   WILLIAM HEWTON [OF WALTHAM]
        [LCC 1532–34, fo. 331r]

12 October 1534. I, William Hewton of Waltham, hole of mynde and off good remembraunce, makes my testament and last will. Fyrste I bequethe my soule unto allmyghtty God and to Our Lady and to all the saintes in heven, and my body to be buryd in the churcheyerde of All Halloys of Waltham, and that at the lawe will to be for my mortuary. To Our Lady warke of Lincoln a ryng. To the high altare of Our Lady of Lincoln vj*d*. To the high altare of my paryshe churche of Waltham for tithys forgottyn xij*d*. To the bellys of my paryshe churche of Waltham iiij*d*. To Our

Lady of Waltham and to her gylde viij*d*. To Margaret my wyff syster a shepe. To Margery my servant a shepe. To John my manservant a shepe. To Jenet Wower iiij*d*. To ether of the orders of frerys of Grimsby, that is to say the Whyte Frerys and the Gray Frerys, ether of them, iiij*d*, and my brother Heade besyde. To Elizabethe Hewton my doughter xl*s* to be takyn furthe of my goodes, and my wyff her mother to have the order and occupyng of her and the foresayd summ to she be at laufull age. The resydue of my goodes not wyt I gyff and I wyt to Margaret Hewton my wyff, whome I make my full executor for to dispose for the helthe of my soule as she thynkes best. Before thes wytnes; Sir Robert Lanam, curate, Richard Stonys, husbandman, John Pootes, with other mo.

Proved before P at Grimsby, 20 October 1534.

556. RICHARD WILLOUGHBIE [OF INGOLDSBY]
[LCC 1534 &c., fo. 3]

13 October 1534. I, Richerde Willobie, seke of body hole of mynde and memory, makes thys my last will and testament. Firste I bequethe my soule unto allmyghtty God, hys blessyd mother and virgyn Our Lady St. Mary, and my body to be buryed in the churcheyerde of St. Andro of Indoldesby. I bequethe my sun Henry my ferme and tenement with the appurtenaunces therto belongyng for the space of xxix yeres as more playnly [fo. 3v] dothe appere in a pare of indenturs of the same. And yf it so fortune that my sun Henry departe within the terme of the forsayd yeres, I will that my sun William shall occupy the foresayd ferme and tenement for the yeres afore namyd. And yf that my forsayd sun William departe or the sayd yeres be expyred, I will that my sun Robert shall have the foresayd ferme and tenement for the resydue of the yeres afore namyd. To my doughter Jenet the house callyd Everodes Thyng with the appurtenaunce therto belongyng for the terme of fyve yeres, whiche yerely is to the valure of xiiij*s*. And aftyr the terme of the foresayd v yeres, I will that my wyff shall have the sayd house and tenement for the terme of her lyff yff that she do not mary. And yff that she do mary, I will that my sun Robert enter unto the sayd house and tenement, and to have for hym, hys heyres and hys assygnes for evermore. To my sun Thomas vj*s* viij*d*, x yowes, a qwye of ij yere olde. To my sun William a cowe, a mare, a fole, ij wethers, a matteres and a pare of shetes and half a seame of wheate. To Thomas Blayk my sun-in-lawe ij wethers. To my sun Robert x schepe. To my sun Herry iiij oxen, iiij horsse and the halff of the croppe when that he ys of a laufull age to be maryed. I will that he shall be in house with hys mother, and for to occupy the husbandry for them bothe yff so be they can agre. I bequethe for a trentall of messys x*s*. To Our Lady of Lincoln iiij*d*. To the high altare of St. Andro of Ingoldesby iiij*d*. The resydue of my goodes not bequestyd I will that Alyson my wyff and Thomas Blake my sun-in-lawe, whome I make my executors, shall have theym for to dispose for my soule helthe. I will that Herry Phyllip shall be supervisor off my will, and for to have for hys labor ij*s*. Thes beryng wytnes; Sir Hugh Cokshotte, Christofer Foster, Hugh Rawlynson, with many other.

Proved before P at Bitchfield, 26 January 1534/5.

557.   JOHN BURRE [OF BINBROOK]
        [LCC 1535–37, fo. 5v]

15 October 1534. I, John Burre off Bynbroke, beyng hole of mynde, wytte and remembraunce, make my last will and testament. In the fyrst I bequethe my soule to God, to Our Lady St. Mary and to all the saintes in heven. My body to be buryed in the churcheyerde of Our Lady in Bynbrook. To the high altare in the same viij*d*. To the same churche a quarter of barly, and to St. Gabryell churche halff a quarter of barly. To Our Lady of Lincoln iiij*d*. To Our Lady warkes iiij*d*. I will that ther be a light fun before the sacrament allway, a serge to burne on the holyday in servyce tyme, and they to have viij*s* to kepe it with. And also a light before Our Lady of Pety, iiij*s*. Also I will that all my goodes unbequethyd be devydyd to my wyff and to my chyldren. I make myn executors of thys my last will Alison my wyffe and Thomas my sun. Thes wytnes; Sir Mylys Gregory, John Marshall, Richerde Lowtham, William Morecrofte, with other mo.
        Proved before P at Market Rasen, 14 April 1535.

558.   THOMAS TOOLY [OF MOORBY]
        [LCC 1535–37, fos. 56r–57r]

16 October 1534. I, Thomas Tooly of Moreby, of a hole mynde and of good remembraunce beyng, makyth my testament and last will. Firste I bequethe my soule to allmyghtty God and to Our Lady St. Mary and to all the holy cumpeny in heven, and my body to be buryed in the churche of All Halloys in Moreby aforesayd. And for my mortuary that the lawe requiryth. To Our Lady of Lincoln xx*d*. To the high altare in Moreby xx*d*. For my lying in Moreby churche vj*s* viij*d*.[178] To Moreby [fo. 56v] churche to by a altare clothe. To Enderby churche vj*s* viij*d*. To Wylkesby churche xx*d*. To Claxby churche xij*d*. To Moreby churche xij*s*. To Swevylby churche xij*d*. To the iiij orders of frerys in Boston xiij*s* iiij*d*. To every one of my godchildren iiij*d*. To Cecill my wyff ij oxen, iij kye, a horsse, ij merys and the thirde parte of all my housholde stuff. And the oder partes to be devydyd to my doughter children. More to my wyff a wayn, a plough and all thynges that belonges unto theym. To my wyff Scherpe Thyng duryng her wydowed. To my wyff ij swyne, ij pygges and the thirde parte of my hennys and geys. To John Gray a cople yong oxen and to hys wyff and chyldren iiij yowes. And to the sayd John the house that he dwellyth in for the terme of hys lyff, kepyng yerely a obbyt of vj*s* viij*d* in Moreby churche. And yff he do not kepe the sayd obbyt yerely and repare not the housses, then I will that my godsun John Hogeson shall make a re-rentre into the sayd grounde and put the sayd John Gray furthe for ever thys presente gyffte notwith-standyng, the sayd John Hogeson kepeyng the sayd obbyt for ever. To Cecill my wyff ij seame barly, halffe a seame wheate and halffe a seame peays and x schepe. I gyff emong my doughter childern viij*l*. To Robert Spillesby a horse of iij yeres of age, and to hys wyffe a schepe and hym another schepe. To Robert Wright a yereyng fole, a cowe and ij schepe. I gyff to John Hogeson my godsun the arke at my bedde's fete. To Thomas Hogeson the arke in hawill. To Sibill Hogeson the rede arke. To John Hogeson my godsun a gret potte and a baysyn. The reste of my

---

[178] This may refer to the practice of laying the corpse in a hearse overnight for the performance of the Office of the Dead prior to the burial, as well as to payment for the intramural burial itself.

goodes remaynyng, my legacies performyd and gyffyn. My dettes payd, I gyff to Jenet Hogeson my doughter and to her issue. To Jenet Hogeson my doughter my houses by the churche with all the lande and medoy and pasture thereunto belongyng and Lyon Thyng with all the medoy, pasture and lande arable thereunto belongyng for terme of her lyffe. And aftyr her decesse, I gyff and bequethe the sayd houses and Lyon Thyng with all the lande arrable, medoy and pasture thereunto belongyng, to John Hogeson my godsun and to hys heyres of hys body laufully begottyn. And yff the sayd John Hogeson my godsun dye withowt heyres of hys body laufully begottyn, then I will that the sayd housys and other the premisses with the appurtenaunces to remayn to Willum Hogeson, sun of the sayd John Hogeson and Jenet, and to the heyres of hys body laufully begottyn. I will that the sayd John Hogeson my godsun [fo. 57r] take and receyve the thirde parte of all the proffyttes of the premisses with th'appurtenaunces with the sayd Jenet hys mother and my doughter, aftyr he cum to the age of xxj^{ty} yeres, duryng her lyff. And aftyr her decesse to remayn to hym in tayll as is aforesayd. I will that yff the sayd Jenet my doughter fortune to decesse afore the sayd John Hogeson my godsun cum to the age of xxj^{ty} yeres, that then the sayd John Hogeson her husbande to take the ij partes of the proffyttes of the sayd houses and other the premisses with th'appurtenaunces, yerely unto the sayd John Hogeson my godsun cum to the age of xxj yeres. I gyff to Willum Hogeson, sun of the sayd John and Jenet, Scharpe Thyng lying in Moreby, to hym and to hys heyres of hys body laufully begottyn. And for defaulte of heyres of the sayd Willum, to remayn to Thomas Hogeson and to hys heyres of hys body laufully begottyn [remainder to] John Hogeson, hys brother, and to hys heyres of hys body laufully begottyn. I will that John Tooly of Wood Enderby have to hym and to hys heyres my parte of the houses and landes lying in the towne and feldes of Wood Enderby aforesayd. The resydue of my goodes not gyffyn nor bequethyd, I gyff to John Hogeson of Est Kyrkby to performe my will, whome I orden and make my executor of thys my last will and testament, and Robert Palfreyman of Edlyngton supervisor of the same. And ether of them to have xx*s* for ther labor and payntakyng. Thyes men beyng wytnes; Sir Alexander Ebden, parson of Moreby, Richard Kell of the same, Robert Lewytson of the same, John Thomson and John Gray, with other mo.

Proved before P at Lincoln, 6 August 1535. Adm. granted to the executor.

559.   MARGARET QUYKRELL [OF BOSTON]
       [LCC 1532–34, fos. 337v–338v]

18 October 1534. I, Margaret Quykrell of Boston, vido, of hole mynde and good remembraunce, makyth thys my testament and in the same conclude my last will. Firste I bequethe my soule to allmyghtty God, to Our Lady St. Mary, the mother of marcy, and to all the celestyall cumpeny of heven, and my body to be buryd in the churcheyerde of the holly confessor St. Botulphe of Boston. To the high altare for my tithes forgottyn iiij*d* and a lynnyn towell. To Corpus Christi altare a towell. To Our Lady's warke in Lincoln iiij*d*. To the pupillys and orphans of St. Catheryn withowt the barres of Lincoln iiij*d*. To Jenet Lightton iij pare of schetes, one coverlyd red and yelowe, a blankyt and a crymsyn kyrtyll. To Jenet Clerke a gowne and a kyrtyll. To William Stubbys' wyff a gowne of musterdevillys purffelyd with blak. To John Parston in money vj*s* viij*d*. To Jenet Athlard one pare off schetes, a

pare of blak beydes of geate, the gawdys of sylver. To the goodwyff Brown a kyrchyff. To the goodwyff Hawthorne a kyrchyff. To Isabell Kychen my servant a brasse potte withowt [fo. 338r] fete and vj pecys of puter. To Masteres Browne a elne off sarsenet. To Jane her doughter a pyncase of golde. To Jenet Paipe a gown purffelyd with otter, my secund best gyrdyll, the beste hookes, the best pyn of sylver, my best corall beades gaudyd with sylver and gylte. To Elizabeth Harre a gowne purffelyd with velvet, the best gyrdyll, the secund best hookes, a pyn of sylver and gylte, the secund best beades of currall gaud[ed] with sylver and gylte. To Margaret Hawnby a pare of blak beades gawdyd with jaspers. To Margaret Carre a blak kyrtyll. To Elizabeth Harre my red kyrtyll. To Thomas Lightten in money vjs viijd. To Sir John Woodhouse a pare of schetes. To Sir Thomas Ashlay a pare of schetes. To Beatrice Woodhouse a say kyrtyll. To Cristyan Redde a brasse potte. To Atkynson wyff a kyrchyff. To John Pape the yonger the beste chyste. To George and Athelarde, sonnes of Mastres Brown, ether of theym, a chyste. To John Paype and Thomas Harre, myn executors, to other of theym, one of the best fether beddes. I will that my mansion, the house that I dwell in and a acre and one stong of lande lying in Leeke, be solde be myn executors and the money therof takyn to be gyffyn to a preste for hys wages to the sum of vl vjs viijd, to pray and syng by the space of a hole yere for my soule, my father's and mother's soulys, my husband souly's, our parentes and all Christen soulys. To Sir William Gefferay my brother my psalter boke and a bokyll of golde. I will that all suche goodes as Percyvell Quykerell gave to Richerd Quykrell hys father and to other persons that is conteynyd and specifyed in hys last will, the one halffe of the foresayd some of money to be gyffyn to Master John Carleton for the gettyng and obteynyng of the bequeste and legacy of the foresayd Percyvell Quykrell, it so beyng obteynyd, he to injoy it or ellys myn executors not to be chargeyd with payment therof, anythyng in thys will notwithstandyng to the contrary. And the other halff to myn executors to the performance and fullfyllyng of thys my testament and last will. To Ane Kelleit, wyff of William Kelleit, my weddyng gowne. To every godchylde that I have, to pray for my soule, every one of theym, vjs viijd. The resdyue of my goodes I gyff theym to John Paipe and Thomas Harre, whome I make my executors to dispose the overplus of my goodes emong the pore [fo. 338v] people to the high pleasure of God and proffyt of my soule, and they to have for ther payn and labors, ether of theym, a blak gowne and xxs. Thies beryng wytnes; Sir Thomas Ashelay, paryshe preste, Sir John Markeby, preste and notary, Sir John Woodhouse, preste, William Hawthorne, Thomas Atkynson, Thoms Lyghtton, William Browne, with other mo. Dated the day and yere above sayd.

Proved before P at Lincoln, 4 November 1534.

560. LAWRENCE MYLFORDE [OF BARDNEY]
[LCC 1535–37, fos. 43r–44r]

20 October 1534. I, Laurence Mylforde of Bardeney, with a hole mynde makes my testament and will. Firste I bequethe my soule to God and to Our Lady and to all the saintes in heven, and my body to be buryed within the monastery of Bardeney Abbay, bynethe the grece afore the roode, and my mortuary to be accordyng aftyr the lawe. I will that my lorde of Bardeney, at the day of my buryall, have iijs iiijd, and Mr. Doctor xxd, and every one of the convent xijd to syng a solempne dirige

and messe of requiem for me, and the bell ryngers to have at the same tyme to ther rewarde ij*s*. I will the same day ther be delte peny dole to pore people and seculer prestes to have vj*d* apece. I will that every gentylman and yoman of my lorde's have iiij*d* and every other servaunt of hys to have ij*d*. I will that ther be, at my vij^th day done at my paryshe churche a solempne dirige and messe of requiem, and ther to be gyven to the prestes, clerkes, bell ryngers and in almes xiij*s* iiij*d*. And yff the sayd some be not sufficient, more to be gyffyn at the discrecion of my executors. I will to the upholdyng of the same churche vj*s* viij*d*. To the Trinite gylde of the same xij*d*. I witte to Our Lady gylde xij*d*. To every light in the sayd churche ij*d*. I will, at my xxx^ty day at the abbay aforesayd, a solempne dirige and messe of requiem, they havyng to ther rewarde vj*s* viij*d*, and the bell ryngers ij*s*, and to be at the same tyme geven in almes at the discrecion of my executors. I will that Our Lady of Lincoln have xij*d* and to Our Lady warke of the same xij*d*. I will that ther be done at Staynfelde Abbey a solempne dirige and messe of requiem for my soule, they haveyng to ther rewarde vj*s* viij*d*. I will that ther be done at Tupholme Abbey a solempne dirige and messe of requiem for my soule, they haveyng to ther rewarde vj*s* viij*d*. I will that Master Doctor of Bardeney have vj*s* viij*d*. I will that Thomas Mylforde my sun have my beste gray amblyng stagge and I will that his wyff have my best gowne, and every one of ther childer ij yowes, and they to be delyveryd at Lammas[179] nexte aftyr my decesse, and all the other yowes that I have gyffyn here foloyng to be delyveryd in lyke wyse as is afore reheresyd. I will that Robert Cipryan have ij yowes and hys wyffe my secunde [fo. 43v] gowne, and every one of hys children ij yowes. I will that Richerde Charles, my sun-in-lawe, have my yonger gray stagge, and every one of hys childer ij yowes. I will that Elizabeth Marton, a nonne of Legborne Abbay, have yerely of my stokke, as long as it will indure, ij*s*. I will that Edmunde Michel my brother and every one of hys childer have ij yowes. I will that every one of my godchilder have xij*d*. I will that my maydyn have one yowe and also I will that Master vicare of Bardeney have ij yowes. I will that Willum Fyshe and hys wyffe have, ether of them, one yowe, and Robert Wryght and his wyff, ether of them, one yowe, and Thomas Robynson and his wyffe, ether of them, one yowe, and Richerde Erbe and his wyff, ether of them, one yowe. I will that Jenet my wyff have my corydye[180] in Bardeney Abbey with ij kye gate by reason of the same, and xx^ty kye besyde, and lx yowes and my bay ambelyng mare with halff my housholde stuff in a full contentacion that she nor no other in her name make no further clame, but utterly to be excludyd of all the thurdes that shulde happyn and come to the sayd Jenet as it more evidently apperys in a pare of indenturys therof mayd and a obligacion off the same in the payn of forfetyng of xl*li*. I will that Willum my sun have the other halff of my housholde stuff and all my harnes and a fether bedde, and ij sylver sponys that his grandam gave hym and a standyng goblet that hys aunte gave hym aftyr the decesse of hys mother, the whiche is in her kepyng. I will that Willum my sun have halff my stokke of neate and schepe and my executors to have the orderyng and gydyng of hym and hys stokke with the incresse, and to put hym to lerynyng unto he be xx^ty yeres of age, and then I will that the foresayd stokke of neatte and schepe be devydyd and he to have his parte delyveryd with halff my farmys and indentors takyn with a stokke

---

[179] 1 August.
[180] A pension or allowance of goods or land granted by a monastic house to a specified individual. Corrodies could be, and often were, dealt with as heritable possessions.

yff he be habble to gyde it. Yff he be not habble, then I will that my executors have the gydyng and orderyng of the sayd Willum, hys stokke of neatte and schepe with the incresce unto he be habble. And yff it so fortune that my executors decesse, I will that ther executors have the orderyng and gydyng of hym as is afore rehersyd. I will that all my goodes unbequethyd be disposyd on thys wyse. I will [fo. 44r] that a preste say messe for me at my paryshe churche of Bardeney, and he to have yerely to hys wages v*li*, and he to fynde brede, wyne and waxe. I will ther be a obbyt sang for me yerely in the abbay of Bardeney afore rehersyd, they haveyng to the rewarde yerely vj*s* viij*d* and the bell ryngers to have the same day for there labor xx*d*. I will that there be geven to pore folke the same day xx*d*, and to be geven yerely sumthyng in almys and in other good dedes and warkes by the discrescion of my executors. And when the yeres of my aforesayd farmys be expyryd or ellys put from them, I will that my executors gett other fermys for them to upholde my aforesayd stokke. I will that the premissys do contynew so long as the sayd stokke or eny parcell therof may indure by the polytyke ways, provision and councell of my sayd executors. And moreover I orden, constitute and make my executors of thys my last testament and will, Thomas Mylforthe my sun and Richerde Charlys my sun-in-lawe and Jenet my wyffe, and every one of them haveyng to ther rewarde at the begynyng vj*s* viij*d* and yerely aftyr as long as the sayd stokke contynewys, every one of them to have iij*s* iiij*d*. And I will that my lorde off Bardeney be my supervisor, he haveyng to hys rewarde xx*d*. Wytnesses therof; Mr. Edmunde Watson, vicare of Bardeney, John Bones of the same, Michell Byllyngay, Thomas Cypryan, Thomas Pery, Willum Loveday, Richerde Golke, John Godsawffe, Willum Cunne, with other mo.

Proved before P at Wragby, 2 July 1535. Adm. granted to executors.

561. SIMON PAWLLYN [OF WYBERTON]
[LCC 1535–37, fo. 46]

20 October 1534. I, Symon Pawllyn off Wyberton, hole of mynde and good remembraunce, makyth thys my testament and last will. Firste I bequethe my soule to God allmyghtty, Our Lady and to all the saintes in heven, and my body to be buryed in the churcheyerde of St. Leogerd of Wyberton. To the high altare of Wyberton xvj*d*. To Our Lady's altare in the same churche xij*d*. To St. Catheryn's altare viij*d*. To St. Anne altare iiij*d*. To Our Lady of Lincoln viij*d*. To the yong orphans at St. Catheryn's withowt Lincoln iiij*d*. Also I will be honestly brought to the erthe, that is to say my buryeng day, vij day and xxx^{ty} day, bred and drynke in the churche aftyr the custome of the towne. I gyff to my mother iiij kye. To Helene my syster a yong cowe. I gyff John Pawllyn, my brother, vj bestes to be kepte togeder to May Day apon my ferme. I will that John my sun have my parte of the house that my mother dothe dwell in. And yff John my sun decesse or that he cum to laufull age [remainder to] Willum my sun. And yff bothe happe to dye or that they [fo. 46v] cum to laufull age, then it to remayn to my father's will. All other thynges not gyffyn nor bequethyd I gyff to Willum my sun and John my sun. And yff the one decesse or that he cum to laufull age, I will that parte remayn to the oder, and yff bother dye it to be at the disposicion off John my brother, whome I orden and make my executor, and with hym Willum my sun. And I will that Richerde Garroke be supervisor of thys my last will, and he to have for hys labor iij*s* iiij*d*.

Wytnes of this; Sir Robert Alger, George Wylkynson, Richerde Garroke, with other mo, the yere and day above scribyd.

Proved before P at Swineshead, 14 July 1535. Adm. granted to John an executor, William, the son and co-executor, being under age.

562. THOMAS JEVETSON [OF SIBSEY]
[LCC 1535–37, fo. 110]

23 October 1534. I, Thomas Jevetson of the paryshe of Sybsay, beyng of hole mynde and good memory, makes thys my testament concludyng therin my last will. Firste I bequethe my soule to God allmyghtty, to Our Lady St. Mary and to all the cumpeny of heven, and my body to be buryed in the paryshe churcheyerde of Sybsay. To the sacrament iijd. To St. Margaret ijd. To Our Lady of Lincoln ijd. To Our Lady of Pety ijd. To Our Lady of Grace ijd. To Agnes Sharpe my doughter my house with appurtenaunces and all my landes and tenamentes that I have in the towne and felde of Sybsay and Boston duryng the terme of her lyffe naturall. And aftyr her decesse, I wil that Alexander Scharp, her sun, have the sayd house with grounde under it, halffe one acre lande in High Fery, halffe one acre lande in the weste felde, a stong of lande in the north-este felde, halffe on acre myddo at St. Helene chapyll aftyr the decesse of hys mother, to hym and hys heyres and assignes. To Andro Sharp iiij acre of lande lying in Boston felde, iij goodes of yng in the dayles, iij goodes in mosse and a stong by Mose Dyke aftyr the decesse of sayd mother, to hym, hys heyres and assygnes. To Hugh Scherp one acre lande in Northerest, v stong in Southfell landes, one roode and a halffe in west felde, and vij stong of mydoy lying in the Grope aftyr the decesse of Agnes hys mother, to hym, hys heyres and assignes, provydyd alway that yff the foresayd Hugh Scharp dye afore he cum to laufull age, than I will that hys landes afore bequethyd be equally devydyd betwyxte Alexander and Andro my doughter sonnes. I will that my executryx sell one stong of lande that lyeth in Willum Baryn crofte. To Alice Sharp a cowe. To Agnes a mayr. To Dorothe Sharp a mayr. To Andor Sharp all my fyshyng gere. The resydue of all my other goodes not gyffyn nor bequethyd, I gyff and bequethe them to Agnes [fo. 110v] my doughter, whome I make my executrix to dispose my goodes to the honor of God and the helthe of my soule, my frendys' soulys and all Christen soulys. And I will that Robert Sharp of Skyrbek be the surveour of thys my testament and laste will. The beyng wytnes; Sir Jamys Foster, paryshe preste and curate, Alan Jevettson and Richerde Benyworthe, with other mo. The day and yere abovesayd.

Proved before P at Lincoln, 12 July 1536.

563. ROBERT OBREY [OF SURFLEET]
[LCC 1532–34, fos. 336v–337r]

24 October 1534. I, Robert Obrey of Surflete in the countie of Lincoln, husband-man, constitute, orden and make my testament and last will. Fyrste I bequethe my soule to allmyghtty God, Our Lady St. Mary and to all the celestyall cumpeny of heven, and my body to be buryd within the churcheyerde of St. Laurence of Surflete. [fo. 337r] To the high altare of Surflete for tithes forgottyn xld. To the Trinite light within the churche of Surflete xijd. To every other smale light within the sayd churche of Surflete iiijd. To the churche warke of the cathedrall churche of

Lincoln xij*d*. To Emme my wyff viij off my best mylk kyne and all my croppe and grane as well that in the lathe and garners as that now growyng, also a hundrethe of my best schepe, my plugh and carte with the gereys belongyng to the same and my carte horssys and merys whiche drawe the same. To William my sun xxx^{ty} schepe to be indifferently takyn emonges the resydue of my schepe. To Thomas my servant vj schepe. To Agnes my mayd vj schepe. The resydue of all my goodes I put them to the disposicion of Emme my wyff and Robert my sun by the councell off Gilbert Ottes whome I make supervisor, and he to have for hys payn x*s*. Thies wytnes; Gilbert Ottes, Sir Robert Thomson and Richerde Burton. Thys is the laste will of me Robert Obrey mayd the day and yere above sayd. I will that all my feoffes shall stande and be seasyd of and in all my landes and tenementes in Surflete to the use of thys my last will. I will that Emme my wyff have all my sayd landes and tenementes duryng her lyff naturall. And aftyr her decesse I will that Robert Obrey my sun have my house that I dwell in to hym, hys heyres and assignes for ever. I will that aftyr the decesse of my wyff, that Robert Clerke, the sun of John Clerke of Holbeche, have my house whiche I bought of Richerde Bowde, to hym, hys heyres and assygnes for ever.

Proved before P at Lincoln, 3 November 1534. Adm. granted to Robert Obrey, the son, reserving power to grant to the relict. Adm. granted to the relict, 30 March 1536, by P at Pinchbeck.

564.   ROBERT WESTROP [OF STAINTON LE VALE]
        [LCC 1535–37, fo. 8r]

27 October 1534. I, Robert Westrop of Staynton, makes my testament. Firste I bequethe my soule to God allmyghtty and to Our Lady St. Mary and to all the saintes in heven, and my body to be buryd in the churche of St. Andrewe, to the whiche churche I bequeth for my sepulture a nobyll. To the hygh altare of the same xij*d*. To the hygh altare of Lincoln mynster iiij*d*. To the redde arke of the same iiij*d*. To Sir William Parker for syngyng of a trentall of messys x*s*. To the priorysse of Irforthe viij*d*. To every nonne singler iiij*d*. To Sir John, ther preste, iiij*d*. To Anthony Westrop my sun a amry, and to hys ij chylder, ether of them, one schepe. To the chylder of Robert Preston, to iche one of them, one schepe. To the ij chylder of Mathewe Westrop, to the elder iiij schepe, to the yonger ij schepe. To he chylder of John Hall, to iche one of them, one schepe. To Thomas Taylle one schepe. To the churche of St. Andro aforesayd a arke. The resydue of my goodes unbequethyd, I bequethe to John and William my sunys, whome I make my executors to dispose for the helthe of my soule as they thynke best. Testes; Thomas Westrop, Thomas Talyor, Andro Westrop, John Mangnoll, parson.

Proved before P at Market Rasen, 14 April 1535.

565.   THOMAS BUXSTONS [OF NAVENBY]
        [LCC 1535–37, fo. 52r]

31 October 1534. I, Thomas Buxstons of Naveneby, hole of mynde and memory and seke in body, makes my laste will and testamente. Firste I bequethe my soule to God allmyghtty and to Our Lady St. Mary and to all the holy cumpeny of heven, and my body to be buryed within the churche of St. Peter in Navenby. To the high

altare of Navenby for tithes forgottyn xij*d*. To the same churche for my buryall v*s*. To the upholdyng off our mother churche of Lincoln vj*d*. To the iiij orders of frerys iiij stryke of barly. The resydue of my goodes and acttyll not bequethyd, my dettes payd, I gyff to Elizabeth my wyff, whome I orden and make my true executrix. Wytnes; John Bukstone the elder, George Fullalove, with many other.

Proved before P at Navenby, 17 July 1535.

APPENDIX

UNDATED AND INCOMPLETELY DATED WILLS

566. MARGARET COLUMBEL [OF BLYTON]
      [Stow 1530–52, fo. 19]

[Undated] I, Margaret Columbel, of gude and hole mynde, lawde be unto almyghty God, make and orden this my present testament and last will therin contenyd. Fyrst I beqeueth my sawle unto allmyghty God my maker and redemer, to Owr Lady Saynte Mary, ande to all the hole company of hevyn. My body to be beried in Oure Lady queer within the parische church of Blyton, yff almyghty God it wil suffer. I wil that a prest do selebret mese in the sayde qweer the spase of one hole yere and pray for the salles of Henry Columbell my husbande and me, and all ther sawlles we ar specially bounden to pray for, ande his salarye or wage to be payde hyme of my goodes. To William Crane xx*s* for recompence of losses of sheype which he lost by a doge of [fo. 19v] Sir Robert Sheffelde, knyght. To every chylde of my sone George Columbel and Elezabet my dawghter some parte of my goodes or cattelles. To every one of my householde sarvandes parte of my goodes or catelles. The resydew I gyfe to John Sheffeld and George Columbell, whome I make myne executors. Thez persons beynge present; Sir Richarde Foster, chaplayn, John Fryston, gent[leman], John Clarke, Thomas Crode, Thomas Sattemane and George Corbrige.

Proved before Master Henry Litherlande, commissary, 2 December 1533.
Adm. granted to George Columbel an executor, reserving power to grant to John Sheffeld, the other executor, when he shall come.

567. ROBERT PARKYNSON [OF THIMBLEBY]
      [LCC 1532–34, fo. 328]

[Undated] I, Robert Parkynson of Thymmolby do make my last will. In primis I bequethe my soule to allmyghtty God and to Our Lady St. Mary and all the saintes in heven. For my forgottyn tithes xx*d*. To Our Lady's warke of Lincoln iiij*d*. To my doughter Elizabeth xx*s*. To Helene Barton a russyt gowne. To Jenet Bekwyth a yowe and a lamme. To Jenet [fo. 328v] Barton a schepe. To John Noddayll iiij*d*. To John Scutte iiij*d*. I will that ther be done for my soule and all Christen soulys a trentall of messys. To every one of my godchylder iiij*d*. To every order of frerys of Lincoln iiij*d*. To every one of the iiij lighttes within the churche of Thymmylbe one bushyll of malt. To the wessall light one stryke of malte. To the bellys xij*d*. The resydue of my goodes not bequethyd I gyff to Alice my wyff, whome I make my executor. I will that Alice my wyff have my house with all the purtenances therto belongyng in her disposicion, to bequethe to whiche of her chylder she will aftyr her decesse, or ellys to sell it for the helthe of my soule and hers and all Christen soulys. In wytnes therof; Sir Henry Wellys, William Williamson, Edwarde Wylkynson, Thomas Smyth, John Johnson, John Brumton, Robert Buknall, with other mo.

Proved before P at Horncastle, 16 October 1534.

568.   MARGARET APPULBE [OF HORBLING]
        [LCC 1532–34, fo. 90r]

1532. I, Margaret Appulbe, seke of body, hole of mynde, makes my last will. Fyrst I bequeth my soule to allmyghtty God and to Our Lady St. Mary and to all the saintes in heven, and my body to be buryed in the churchyerde of St Andro in Horblyng. To the high altare xij*d*. To the churche of Horblyng a kyst and a bullok. To Elizabeth Clypsam my best gyrdyll. To Sir John Hill a cowe and iiij yerdes of violet. To Richerde Smyth a gret arke. To Laurence Gylson a yowe and a lambe. To Richerde Smyth a bun carte. To Mr. Prior of Sempyngham a cowe. To Margaret Palmer my best gowne and a brasse pot and my best kyrchyff. To Elizabeth Clypsam my russyt gowne and a kyrchyff. To Richerde Palmer a calve. I make John Bell my full executor and Richerde Palmer my supervisor with the counsell of Mr. Prior of Sempyngham. Recordes; Sir John Hill, Richerd Palmer and Thomas Clypsham. To Our Lady of Lincoln warke vj*d*.

Proved before P at [Great] Hale, 17 February 1532/3.

569.   WILLIAM BURTON [OF HAGNABY]
        [LCC 1532–34, fo. 27r]

1532. I, William Burton of Hagnaby, makes my last will and testament. Fyrst I bequethe my soule to allmyghtty God and Hys blessyd mother Our Lady St. Mary, and to all the saintes in heven. My body to be buryed in the churche of Hagneby. To the high altare for tithes iiij*d*. To Our Lady off Lincoln iiij*d*. To the bellys viij*d*. To St. George iiij*d*. To the sepulcre light iiij*d*. To St. Andro light iiij*d*. To Our Lady of Pety in Dunesby a cowe. To St. John Baptist in Dunesbye churche a pounde wax. To every chylde my godchylder a yowe lamme. To every chylde of Thomas Pell a lamme. To ij chylder of John Burton the yonger a cote, the oder a cappe. To Elizabethe Sandall a yowe. To Jenet Sandall a yowe. To the pore peopyll of Hagneby xx*d*. To the pore people of Dunesby xx*d*. To pore people off Morton xx*d*. To the pore people of Repyngale xx*d*. I will that ther syng one honest preste iij yere, s[cilicet] one yere in Dunesby, ij yere in Hagneby. To the churche of Repyngale viij*d*. I gyff the resydue of my goodes to Helene my wyff whome I make executrix. I will that Thomas Pell and Edmund Sendall helpe and se my will be fulfyllyd and to have for ther labor x*s*. Thes beyng wytnes; Herry Boston, Robert Clayk, Thomas Watson, Sir Thomas Clyff, vicar of Hagneby, with other mo.

Proved before P at Bourne, 15 January 1532/3.

570. THOMAS FLYER [OF STAPLEFORD]
      [LCC 1532–34, fo. 146v–147r]

1532. I, Thomas Flier, in hole mynde and good memory makys my will. Fyrst I bequeth my soule to almyghtie God and to Our Lady Saynt Mary, and to all the sayntes in heven. My body to be buried in the churche of Stapulforth, of the southe syde of my broder William before St. Mary awter. To Our Ladye's warke of Lincoln vjd. To the high awter for tithes forgoten vjd. To the iiij religious of freres, every order, iiijd. [fo. 147r] To the reparacions of Barell Brig vjd. To my son Thomas my jaket and my best doublet, iij ewes and iij lambes, and a hyve of bees. To Margaret my daughter-in-law a hyve of bees. To Thomas Diconson my best hosses and my best jerkyn. To every godchild that I have jd. To my gostly fader xijd. The residue of my goodes not bequeathed I gyve to Jenet my wif and Richard my son whom I make my executours, and Robert myn eldest sonne supervisor, he to have for his labour the howse that Mathew Lyntham dwelle in within the towne of Stapulforth. To my son Robert children among theym all a ewe and a lambe. To John Flier, Oliver son, a yeryng calf a qwye kynnes. To John my son a hive of bees. To Margaret Wallys a ewe kynnes lambe. I will that Jenet my wif have a qwye and iij ewes, to dispose every yere for the helth of my soule iiijs, and that my children to se that it be done. I will that my wif and Richard my sonne have my ferme wyelle they be able to kepe it, and then it to remayne to Robert my sonne and his assignes. Thies beyng wytnes; Sir Robert Briges, vicar, Richard Knysesmyth, Alane Hodgeson, John Law, with other mo.

Proved before P at Lincoln, 26 May 1533. Adm. granted to the executors.

571. THOMAS GUDDERSON [OF LISSINGTON]
      [LCC 1532–34, fo. 78r]

1532. I, Thomas Gudderson of Lyssyngton, seke in body but hole of mynde and good remembraunce, makes my testament and last will. Fyrst I bequeth my soule unto God allmyghtty and to Hys mother Mary and all the cumpeny of heven, and my body to be buryed within the churcheyerde of St. John Baptist, and that thyng that the law will admyt to be my mortuary. To the high altare of Lyssyngton for tithys forgottyn iiijd. To Our Lady of Lincoln ijd, and to Our Lady warkes ijd. To the iiij orders of frerys a bushyll of whette and a bushyll barly. To the church of Lyssyngton a bushyll whete. To William my sonne a cople of oxen. To Robert my sun a cople sterys. To Thomas my Sonne a stere. To John my Sonne a yeryng calffe. To Oliver my sonne a yeryng calffe and to ether of my doughters a cowe. The resydue of my goodes not gyffyn nor bequethyd unto Agnes my wyff, William my sonne and to Robert my sonne, whome I make my executors they to dispose therof parte for the helthe of my soule as it shall be thought to ther credence. Thes beyng wytnes; William Gudderson, William Towynton, Henry Toynton, with other mo.

Proved before P at Wragby, 17 October 1532.

572. JOHN HOYGES [OF ADDLETHORPE]
      [LCC 1532–34, fo. 105]

1532. I, John Hoyges of Adylthorpe Yngoldmels, of good mynde and hole remembraunce, makes thys my last testament. Fyrst I bequethe my soule to God allmyghtty, to Our Lady St. Mary and to all the saintes in heven, and my body to be buryd in the paryshe churche off Adylthorpe with my mortuary as the lawe requiryth. To the high altare in Adylthorpe xij*d*. To the geltyng of the high altare vj*s* viij*d*. To every altare in the same churche iiij*d*. To the belles xij*d*. To the est churche iijs iiij*d*.[181] To Our Lady's warkes of Lincoln xij*d*. To my wyff iij kye, xxx yowes and xxx hogges, and x wedders. To my wyff my best horsse and the thurde parte of my housholde stuff. To Agnes my syster x hogges. To John my sun v*l* vj*s* viij*d*. To Anthony Hoyges v*l* vj*s* viij*d*. To Alice my doughter v*l* vj*s* viij*d*. [fo. 105v] To Agnes my doughter v*l* vj*s* viij*d*. To Isabell my doughter v*l* vj*s* viij*d*. To Helene my doughter v*l* vj*s* viij*d*. To Elizabeth my doughter v*l* vj*s* viij*d*. To Margaret my doughter v*l* vj*s* viij*d*. And yff any of thes my chyldren dy afore they cum to laufull age, then I will that halff ther porcion, that is to say iiij marke, to be disposyd at ther buryall, and the other iiij marke to be equally devydyd to my chyldren that lyffys, and every one to be other heres aftyr this manner aforesayd. And yff they all dye before they cum to laufull age then I will that all ther partes be disposyd to a preste by the handes and myndes of the iiij churche graves of Adelthorp and Yngolmells, to pray for my soule and for my wyffes soules and for my chyldren soules, for my fader and my moder, and all my good frendes soules. To Sir John Kyrgatte vj*s* viij*d*. To Robert Curtes vj*s* viij*d* for occupying for me, whome I make my executors. To Mr John Lytylbery x*s*, whome I make supervisor. The resydue of my goodes I will it remayn to the bryngyng up of my chyldren and to ther maryages. These witnesses; Nicholas Sarott, rector of Ingolmells, William Williamson, chaplain, William Thory, John Willerton, Thomas Flessher, with many others.

Proved before P at Partney, 29 April 1533. Adm. granted to Sir John Kyrkgate, an executor, reserving power to grant to Robert Curtes, co-executor.

573.   ROBERT KYME [OF BROTHERTOFT AND SWINESHEAD]
        [LCC 1532–34, fo. 69r]

1532. I, Robert Kyme of Brothertofte and of the parysh off Swynneshed, with a hole mynde unto allmyghtty God and to Our Lady St. Mary, and to all the cumpeny of heven, I make my last will. Fyrst I bequeth my soule to allmyghtty God, and my body to be buryed in Swyneshed churcheyerde. To our holy mother churche of Lincoln iiij*d* and to the fatherles chyldren of St. Catheryn's ij*d*. To the high altare of Swyneshed iiij*d*. To Agnes my doughter ij kye and ij meyres. To Nicholes Rankyn a calve. All the resydue of my goodes to my wyff. Wytnes heroff; Hugh Mablesone and Nicholes Blysbery.

Proved before P at Boston, 9 October 1532.

574.   WILLIAM REDE [OF SOUTH WITHAM]
        [LCC 1532–34, fo. 79v–80r]

1532. I, William Rede of Sowth Wytham make my testament. Fyrste I bequethe my soule to allmyghtty God and to Our Lady St. Mary, and to all the holy cumpeny in heven, and my body to be buryed in the churche of St. John in Sowth Wytham

---

[181] This probably refers to a chapel within the parish of Addlethorpe.

before Our Lady. To the high altare xij*d*. I bequeth for my mortuary accordyng as the law is ordenyd. To Our Lady of Lincoln viij*d*. To Richerde my brother my blak horsse and my best gowne and my best cappe, a reddowffe stere and bukskyn dooblet. To Richerd my brother halffe my wyrkyng toolys. To Helene my doughter ij kye, viij schepe, ij calvys, the new ambre, the whyte ark and all that longys to a hole bed, a chaffyng dyshe, a brasse pott with a panne and ij pewter platters. To Thomas Frace my shodde carte. To Robert Frace my sonne a browne qwy. To the churche of South Wytham vj*s* viij*d*. I bequethe ij schepe of the best in my folde to helpe to kepe a light before our Lady, the stok never to go to other use but to the sayd light. To the churche of Burton vj*s* viij*d* to the gyltyng of the roode lofte. To Agnes Red my syster a yow schepe. To my father a seame whet, a seame barly and a seame pease. To Wytham gylde [fo. 80r] xij*d*. I bequethe halffe a trentall to be sung in Sowth Witham churche at our Lady altare. I make Agnes Red my wyff my executrix, and Richerde Red my brother to performe thys my wyll and to pay my dettes. Whytnese heroff; William Nyx, John Doffe, Jefferey Todde, Robert Redde, William Doffe, with other mo.

Proved before P at Laughton, 5 November 1532.

575. WILLIAM THECKER [OF HUTTOFT]
[LCC 1532–34, fo. 152]

1532. I, William Thecker of [sic] not constreynyd nor counselde of no man, but of myn awn fre will, makes thys my last testament and will. Fyrst I bequethe my soule to allmyghtty God, besechyng hym to be mercyfull to yt. My body to be buryd in the churcheyerde of St. Margaret of Hotofte. To Our Lady of Lincoln xij*d*. To the high altare of Hotofte churche xij*d*. To the paryshe churche of Suttun xij*d*. To Anderby churche viij*d*. To Thurlby churche viij*d*. To Tallesthorp churche viij*d*. To St. Michel gylde in Hanney viij*d*. To John my sun my wayn, my plough, my harroys and all that longes to them, also my best gowne and my hat, and ij pare of quernys. To Isabell my doughtter one red kyrtyll, one cowe, one pare off lynnen schetes, a twyldyd coverlyd, also a stone of blak wooll. To Richerde my sun my best jaket. To every one of my barnes chyldren one schepe, and to be delyveryd betwyxte thys and Lammes. To Alice Johnson her mother best beades with the rynges and all the geyr at them. And to the same Alice, my last wyff best gowne. To Helene Rutter the nexte best gowne. To the wyves of Richerde and John my sonnys, other of them, one aprone, one kyrchyff. To Hugh Rutter doughter a russyt cote. To the same [fo. 152v] man sonne a jaket. I will that one preste syng for me halffe a yere in Hotofte churche. I bequethe vj*s* viij*d* to a clothe to hyng afore the sacrament in Hotofte churche. To Richerde and John my sunnys, and Helene and Alice my doughtters, all thes iiij to have all my housholde stuff as it standes, and to be devydyd in iiij partes be the syght of the vicare and other men, and thay that is not contentyd with ther parte when it is devydyd, they to have but halffe the parte. I make my executors Richerde my sun and John my sun. Wytnes; the vicare John Jaxson, with other mo.

Proved before P at Alford, 6 May 1533.

576.   JOHN CLERKE [OF TOFT IN PARISH OF WITHAM ON THE HILL]
       [LCC 1532–34, fo. 200r]

1533. I, John Clerke of Tofte within the paryshe of Witham, makes thys my last will
and testament. Fyrste I bequethe my soule to God allmyghtty and to Our Blessyd
Lady St. Mary, and to all the holly cumpeny of heven, and my body to be buryed in
the churcheyerde of Witham; and as for my mortuary as the lawe dothe require. To
the altare of Witham for tithynges and offerynges negligently forgottyn vj*d*. To the
reparacions of Our Lady churche off Lincoln iiij*d*. To the gylde of Witham halffe a
seame barly. To Manthorpe bryg a stryke barly. To Tofte bryg a stryke barly. To
Jefferay Clerke my sonne a cowe, a stere, a colte horse, a schepe and halffe a seame
barly. To Robert Clerke my sonne a cowe, a stere, a colte horse and halffe a seame
barly and a schepe. To John Clerke my sun a cowe, a schepe and halffe a seame
barly. To Richerd Clerke my sun a cowe and halffe a seame barly. To Helene Clerke
my doughter a cowe and kettyll. I wyll yff eny of my sayd chylder do departe owt of
thys worlde, that then the sayd chylder that dothe lyff shall have the dethe partes
devydyd emong them. And yff all departe owt of thys worlde, then ther partes shall
be devydyd to Agnes Clerke my wyff, to Robert Clerke my father and to Robert
Clerke my brother. I will that the sayd Jefferay Clerke, Robert Clerke and John
Clerke gyff, every one of them, a lamme to Richerde Clerke my yongest sonne. To
Robert Clerke my father, halffe a seame barly. To Agnes Clerke my mother a yowe.
To Robert Clerke my brother ij sterys and halffe a seame barly. To Agnes Knyght a
calffe. To Agnes Clerke a qwye. To Thomas Baker a colte horse. To John Mawer
halffe a seame barly. The resydue of my goodes not bequethyd, my dettes beyng
payd, I gyff to Agnes my wyffe whome I make my executrix, she to dispose my
goodes to the helthe and salvacion of my soule. Thes beryng wytnes; Sir John
Jameson the vicar, John Maltes, John Sander, with other mo.
       Proved before P at Bitchfield, 21 October 1533.

577.   HENRY MANBY [OF GREAT CARLTON]
       [LCC 1532–34, fo. 219]

1533. I, Henry Manby of Carleton, seke in body and hole in mynde, makes my last
will. Fyrst I bequethe my soule to God allmyghtty, to Our Lady St. Mary and to all
the saintes of heven, with my body to be buryd in the churche of St. Peter of
Carleton. To the churche of Gret Carleton iij*s* iiij*d*. I will that a pownde of waxe be
mayd in a serge and set up before the sacrament at Our Lady in Gret Carleton
qwere, and the value of the pownde of waxe yerely to be takyn owt of the lande
callyd Smyth Tofte. To Our Lady's warke of Lincoln vij*d*. To the fatherles chylder
of St. Catheryn of Lincoln vij*d*. To Lytyll Carleton churche vij*d* and a torche. To
Gaton, Tottyll, South Reston and to Castill Carleton churche, to every one of them,
vj*d*. To Robert Thorneton a wane and wane gere, plowe and plowe gere and ij acres
of barly and one acre benys at Steynton. To George Thornton ij schepe, one acre of
barly and one acre of benys. To Cassander ij schepe. To Jenet Thornton ij schepe.
To Anne Manby my doughter iij kye and ther calves, ij oxen, ij horse, xx^ty schepe, ij
fether beddes and the best cownterpoynt, a matterys and a coveryng, iiij of my best
brasse pottes, xiiij of the best puter platters, ij fyer chawffers, ij basyns, iiij
candylstykes and ij pare of the best schetes. To John Dyxson one acre barly and
to Robert Ely one acre barly. To George Manby a gray mare of iij yere olde and

halffe a qwarter wheate. To John Manby halffe a [fo. 219v] quarter barly. To Agnes my wyffe my house and my lande in Gret Carleton duryng her lyff, that is to say iiij leys lyeng of the sowthe parte of the house buttyng of the este parte of the highway, of the weste off the felde of the sowthe of John Shadworthe. And aftyr her I will Anne my doughter have it, and yff ought cum at Anne my doughter withowt heyres of her body laufully begottyn, then I will that Thomas Manby have it to hym and to hys heyres. The resydue of my goodes not gyffyn nor bequethyd I gyff to Agnes my wyff, whome I make my sole executrix with the supervisor to be John Lupton, and he to have for hys labor xs. Thes beryng wytnes; Sir Charles Thornton, John Lupton, Thomas Crosse, Robert Willerton, Richerde Rayner, with other mo. To Anne my doughter a harnest gyrdell, a maser with a bande of sylver parcell gylte, viij sylver sponys aftyr the decesse of her mother, and a brasyn morter with the pestell, ij long tables and ij chares.

Proved before P at Louth, 12 November 1533.

578. BARNERD PYKERYNG [OF TUPHOLME]
[LCC 1532–34, fo. 251r]

1533. I, Barnerde Pykeryng of Tupholme in the countie of Lincoln, tanner, beyng of hole and perftye mynde, dothe dispose and make my testament and laste will. Fyrste I bequethe my soule to God allmyghtty and unto Our Lady St. Mary, and unto all the holy and blessyd cumpeny of heven. My body to be buryed in the churcheyerde of Tupholm. To the lorde of Tupholm vjs viijd. To the subprior of Tupholm iijs iiijd. To the convent of Tupholm iijs iiijd. To Our Blessyd Lady of Lincoln iiijd. To my brother Richerde Pykeryng halffe a skore of yowes and my cloke and my bowe and my shaftes. To thre of my brother Richerde chyldern iiij schepe. To Margaret my brother doughter a qwye. To Robert Blande my swerd and my bukler. To Robert Ledes a fylly fole. To John Haldysworthe a dooblet and a schepe. To Alice Blande my beste jaket. To every one of my godchylder a grotte.[182] I bequethe for a trentall to be sung for me xs. The resydue of my goodes I gyff unto Margaret my wyffe, the whiche I make my full executrix, and Nicholes Westowe and John Ingram to be my supervisors. In wytnes wheroff; Sir Robert Boston, John Foster, Robert Blynckesoppe, with diverse mo.

Proved before P at Lincoln, 13 April 1534.

579. ROBERT BROMBE [OF MIDDLE RASEN TUPHOLME]
[LCC 1532–34, fo. 323r]

[1534]. I, Robert Brombe of Myddyl Rasyn Tupholm, beyng in a good mynde, makes my will. Fyrste I wyt my soule to God allmyghtty and to Our Lady Saint Mary, and to all the blessyd cumpeny of heven. My body to be buryd in the kyrkegarth of Rasyn Tupholme. I will to the high altare of Rasyn aforesayd xijd. To the kyrke of Rasyn Drax viijd. To Our Lady warke of Lincoln viijd. To the iiij orders of frerys, to every order, iiijd. The resydue of my goodes not wyt, I gyff to Alice my wyff, whiche I will be my executrix, and John Brombe I will be supervisor.

---

[182] Fourpence.

The yere of our lord God 1534. Wytnes; Sir Peter Thomson, John Brombe, John Gybbon, William Saynton.

Proved before P at Market Rasen, 21 October 1534.

580.   JOHN FOWNDER [OF BARTON ON HUMBER]
        [LCC 1532–34, fo. 330r]

1534. I, John Fownder of Barton upon Humbre, hole of mynde and full of memory, makes thys my last will. Fyrste I bequethe my soule to God allmyghtty, to Our Lady St. Mary and to all the saintes in heven. My body to be buryd in the chapell yerde of Our Lady in Barton. To the sacrament in the foresayd chapell xij*d*. To Our Lady of Lincoln viij*d*. I will that my wyff have xx nobyls and the thyrde off all the housholde stuff, and to mell with no maner of thyng ellys. To Elizabeth Fownder my eldeste doughter my best brasse potte. To my doughter Alice nexte brasse potte. To Jenet my doughter the Flaunders chyste. To the chylde that my wyffe hathe in her body a gowne that was my fyrste wyffy's when it please God to sende it into the worlde. To Robert my sun my best gown. To Edwarde my sun my best jakyt. The resydue of all my goodes I will that my chylder before namyd have it, my dettes and funerallys dischargeyd, the whiche chylder I make my executors to dispose for my soule, my frendes' soulys and all Christen soulys, as they shall thynk necessary and goode. And bycause my chylder be at under age, I will that Richerde Chantre, John Skelton, John Wylson be the executors and occupyers of thys my last will unto the behove and proffyt of my chylder, unto they cum to laufull age. And yff so be that any of thes my forsayd chylder dy before they cum to laufull age, then the parte of that chylde or chylder to be equally devydyd emonges the other that be onlyve. In wytnes heroff; George Darnton, prest, Thomas Emondson, Thomas Strangman, Roger Skelton, with other mo. I will that the executors have, every one of them, iij*s* iiij*d* for ther labor.

Proved before P at Caistor, 19 October 1534.

581.   JOHN LESSE [OF HOLBEACH]
        [LCC 1532–34, fos. 314v–315r]

1534. I, John Lesse off Holbeche in Holland, off hole mynde and perfytt remembrans, make my wyll and testament. I gyfe my sowll unto allmyghti God and my body to be beryd within the chorcheyard off All Halowes in Holbyche. To the hye awter ffor my tythes fforgotton xij*d*. To the infantes of the hous off Sant Katerine's at Lyncoln vj*d*. To Ower Ladye off Lyncoln xij*d*. To the alter of Sant Stevyn viij*d*. To every alter within the churche off Holbyche iiij*d*. To the reparaciones off the sayd churche vj*s* viij*d*. To the rode afore Ower Lady on pond wax yerly so longe as my wyffe kepes her beys. I wyll that ther be dyssposyd for my ssole opon my beryall day, vij[th] day and xxx day x*l* as myne executores sshall thynke beste. I will vj acres land that lyeth in Wegnill Gat to be solde to the beste pryse after it be iiij tymes proclamyd in the church ther, and x powndes off the pryce therof I wyll to be bestowyd by myne executores to by a blewe cope of velvet cotynely after, and to be gyffine unto the churche off Holbyche afforsad, and my name to be sowyd therin that I may be rememberyd in the yere afterwarde. To evary on off my brother Robart chylldar xx*s*. To my godson hys chylld xxvj*s* viij*d* at sutche tyme as they cume at xiiij yere of age, prowydyd allway yff any of them dy afore xiiij yers, that than I wyll hys or ther partes remane unto us that ar onlyfe. And yff that you all dy afore that age, than the sayd mony remayne to the performans off my laste wyll, so that yff John Thorpe off Holbych wyll by the fforsad vj acres land, than I wyll that he shall have it beter chepe than any man by vj*s* viij*d*. To Johan my wyffe the house that she dwellyth in with x acres landes that is in her joynter duryng her naturall lyffe, wyth iiij acres lande wheroff ij acres lyethe in Flete and ij acres in Algate, to kepe a yerely obbyt wyth all off vj*s* viij*d*. And after her dysses, I wyll the yerlly profyttes and renttes of the sayd iiij acres land clyrly unto an obbett ffolyng as the lawe wyll suffar yet. And affter I wyll the sayd iiij acris land to be solld for the perfformans of my last wyll by the handys off myne executores yff thay be onlyfe at that tyme, or elles by the churchwardyns at that tyme beyng for my ssolle, Mawd ssoll, Betrys [and] Jenit ssolles, and to pay iij mas pens and unto evary pryst iiij*d* and evary clarke ij*d*, the belman ij*d* and to glase viij*d*. I wyll my wyfe have all her owne howshold stuffe that she broght with her and catell and xl*s* of mony, and a kow that ys at Heppe's with a mare and a fole, and my best fether bed, a bolster, a coverlet and all the wod in the yeard with all red and straw and benes in the felde, so that she gyffe on c ryddys or to pore folkes the nexte Chrystenmas after my decesse. Allso I wyll after the dysesse of my wyfe that viij acres land and the howse that she dwellythe in be sold at the most wallure that be proclemyd iij tymes in the church by the handys of my executores yff thay be onlyffe at that tyme, or be my superwysor, [fo. 315r] or in the defaut by the churchwardyns at that tyme lyvyng, and viij markes off the mone therof and vj*s* viij*d* to be delte to an abull pryste quartarly as he nedyth hyt ffor the space off on yere next foloyng the sayll thereoff, to pray for my solle, Mawd, Beatryx and John sowlles, and the ressydw thereoff to be dyssposyd and gyffyn unto the pore pepull evary Fryday v*d* so longe as the mony last by the handes off myne executores or the curat there for that tyme beynge, and they to have ffor there payns yerly xij*d*. To Jenit my wyffe a brase pott that liethe in the kytchyn with long ffayte and my best gyrdyll of red with all my pewter in the hawle, bassons, candellstykes, lavors and hangynges. To Robart my brother my best cape and my blake gowne. To my brother Nycolas my best gowne and vij*s* vj*d* off mony. I wyll to be delyvaryd by the handes off my executores unto an abull pryst to pray ffor my ssolle and all Chrysten sollyes viij markyes vj*s* viij*d* for the space off a yeare quarterly as he dyssarvyd it, off the hows and land that I sowld unto Rychard Jasson. Allso I wyll that the ij acres land that lythe at Asgardyke in Whoployd, aftar the dyssesse off my wyffe, unto Sent Johne's chapell in Whaplode Droyffe yff the law wyll suffar yt. Allso I wyll that John Thorpe have ij acres land that lyeth at Crampes beter chepe than any man. To Augnes my dowther, at the day of her maryge, xl*s* and a matteres, ij pare of schetes, the on flaxyn and the other of myng tow, a towell, a coverlyd and a wyndo clothe, ij blanketes and hawff a dossyn pewter platars and dysshys, a pot, a pan and ij small candellstykes. And yff she dye afore she be maryd, I wyll that on parte off it bryng her fforthe, and the ressydew unto the performans off my last wyll. I wyll that Jenyt Sybsay have a lyttyll chest and a pylow, a covarlet and a pewter dyssh. To Elsabet Thorpe ij peuter dysshys, a plater and xij*d* off mony at her maryage. The ressydew off my gowdyes not bequeth, I gyffe unto myne executores, thay to dysspos for the helthe off my ssolle as them shall thynke beste, whom I ordyn unto thys my laste wyll, Robart Lesse, Rychard Howell and allso my supervysor John Thorpe, and he to have xx*s* and evary on off myn executores vj*s* viij*d*. In wytnes whereoff; Rychard Wycham, prest, John Thorpe, Thomas Pye, John Ranson and John Whype.

Proved before P at Swineshead, 8 October 1534.

582.   RICHARD MULSON [OF FLEET]
        [LCC 1532–34, fo. 309r]

1534. I, Rycharde Mulson of Flett, in hole myende and goode of remembrans, make my laste wylle and testament. Fyrst I beqweth my sowlle to allmyghthy God, Owr Lady Saynte Mary and to all the company in heven, and my body to be beryed within the chyrcheyerde of Mary Mawdelyne in Flett, to the wyche he awlter I gyffe ij*d*. To owre mother chyrche in Lyncoln ij*d*. To the poore chyldren of Saynt Katerne ij*d*. To Owre Lady's lygthe iij*s* iiij*d*, and to the makyng of the crosse in the chyrcheyerde of Flett so myche monye to paye for ytt.[183] To Saynt Crystofere's lygthe ij powndes of waxe redy made to sette uppe. I wylle that bothe my howssys with all the londe to them belongyng be sowllde be the handes of my executores to performe all maner of thynges beqwethede and to brynge me honestlye forthe with dyryge and messe of requyem, and the resydewe of the sayde money to stowyede within the chyrche of Flette were mooste nede ys by the dyscrecyon of the chyrchewarndynes that beynge. To Yssabelle my wyffe xx*s* and all my howsse-howllde stuffe complette. I wylle that ij meyers and on yeryng, ij kyn and ij burnynges to be sollde by the handes of my executors, and my grette botte and lytylle botte be sollde in lyke forme. The resydewe of my goodes I gyffe theyme to Nycholas Sowetter, wome I make myn executor to dyspose for the helthe of my sowlle and all my goode frendes, and he to have for hys payntakyng iiij*s*, ande I make John Wyett supervysor, and he to have for hys labor ij*s*. Wyttnesse; Thomas Pryste, Jhon Sadlam, John Heppys, with other moo.

Proved before P at Swineshead, 8 October 1534.

583.   THOMAS REDHED [OF BILLINGHAY]
        [LCC 1535–37, fo. 50v]

1534. I, Thomas Redhed of Billingay, of perfyte mynde and good remembraunce, make thys my last will and testament. Firste I bequethe my soule to allmyghtty God and Our Lady St. Mary and to all the cumpeny of heven, and my body to be buryd in the churcheyerde of St. Andro in Byllyngay. To the high altare of Billyngay iiij*d*. To Our Lady of Lincoln iiij*d*. To the churche of Billyngay iiij*d*. I will that x messys be done for the helthe of my soule within the churche of Billyngay. I will that my goodes be devydyd in iij partes, one parte to be done for the helthe of my soule, the secunde parte to my wyffe, the thurde parte to my chyldren. Also, yff they dye, all the thurde parte to be done for the helthe of ther soules and myn, and all Christen soulys. Also I do make Agnes my wyffe my executrix, to dispose my goodes for the helthe of my soule and as she thynkes beste. Wytnes herof; Robert Johnson, Walter Bate, Sir William Ludnam, preste.

Proved before P at Navenby, 17 July 1535.

---

[183] Medieval and early sixteenth-century parochial cemeteries usually had a cross at each corner and a larger one in the centre. These were frequently the subject of Protestant iconoclastic attacks during the Reformation and in the seventeenth century.

584.   JOHN WATERS [OF APLEY]
        [LCC 1532–34, fo. 268]

1534. I, John Waters of the paryshe of Applay in the diocese of Lincoln, servant to Sir George Taylboys, knyght, of hole mynde and perfyte remembraunce, do orden and make my testament and laste will. Fyrste I gyff and bequethe my soule unto allmyghtty God, to Our Lady St. Mary and to all the blessyd cumpeny of heven. My body to be buryd in the churcheyerde of St. Andro in Aplay. To the high altare of the sayd churche for tithes negligently forgottyn viij*d*. To Our Lady warke of Lincoln vj*d*. To Robert Waters my sun a yowe and a lamme. To William Waters my sun a yowe and a lamme. To my sun Arnolde Waters a yowe and a lamme. To George Waters my sun a yowe and a lamme. To William Waters my sun the yonger a yowe and a lamme. To Elizabeth Waters my doughter a yowe and a lamme. The resydue of my goodes not gyffyn and bequethyd I gyff [fo. 268v] unto Elizabeth Waters my wyff, whome I make my executrix to bryng up my chyldren and to dispose as she shall thynke moste necessary for the helthe of my soule. I will that Richerde Talbot be supervisor and to se that it be truly fulfyllyd, and I gyff hym for hys paynes and labor in thus doyng a matteres and a pilloy. Those beyng wytnes; Sir Richerde Wroose, preste, Richerde Talbot, and other mo.

        Proved before P at Wragby, 9 May 1534.

585.   JOHN WESTON [OF CARLTON LE MOORLAND]
        [LCC 1535–37, fo. 35r]

1534. I, John Weston late of Carleton, in a hole mynde and good remembraunce, makyth my will. Firste I bequethe my soule to God allmyghtty and to Hys blessyd mother St. Mary and to all the holy cumpeny of heven, and my body to be buryed within the churche of Our Lady of Carleton. Also for my mortuary aftyr the forme and custome of the lawe. To the high altare of Carleton xx*d*. To Our Lady warke of Lincoln xx*d*. To the iiij orders of frerys within Lincoln iiij*d* apece. To the churche off Bassyngham xij*d*. To the churche of Broughton xij*d*. To Nicholas Andro my servaunt a cowe yff he tary with hys dame another yere. To Robert Harbarde ij yowes. To Margaret Shepperde a yowe. To John Weston my sun all my schepe that is at Collyngham and ij sterys. Also of the same schepe, every one of hys chylder to have a yowe and a lamme. To John my sun a yooke and a gret teame, a wayn with a pare of bun wheles aftyr that hys mother have gyffyn up here husbandry. To John my sun ij sylver sponys. To William my sun ij sylver sponys, and to every one of William chylder ij yowes. To Thomas Harbarde a bushyll rye and a bushyll barly. To every one of my godchylder within the town a hogge. To Master John Dysnay, whome I make my supervisor, x*s*. To the churche of Carleton vj*s* viij*d*. The resydue of my goodes unbequethyd I gyff to Jenet my wyff, whome I make my executor to dispose at her mynde for the helthe of my soule. Thes beyng wytnes; Sir John Marshall, vicar, Mr. John Dysnay, William Weston, John Weston, John Preion, with other mo.

        Proved before P at Hykeham, 5 July 1535.

INDEX OF PERSONS AND PLACES

Arabic numbers refer to the number of the individual document, Roman to the page number in the introduction. Testators' names are indicated by bold print, as are the numbers of their own wills. Surnames have been indexed according to contemporary orthography, although in the case of common surnames these have been normalised according to the most frequently occurring form. Christian names have usually been modernised in the index, with the exception of universally occurring forms such as 'Jenet', or 'Johanne', which have been retained. Place names have, wherever possible, been listed in their modern forms, although in the case of field names particularly this has not always been practicable. In such instances the name has been indexed according to the form it takes in the register copy will.

Esterby, Simon, first husband of **Amee Swagge** 36; Simon, son of **Amee Swagge** 30, 36

Eston, Robert 88, 212

Eteson *see* Eston

Evan, Alan 483

Eve, Margaret, wife of **Simon** 468; **Simon**, of High Toynton 63, **468**; Thomas, son of **Simon** 468

Evedon 39

Church, St. Mary the Virgin:
Churchwardens 39, 44; Churchyard 39, 44; High altar 39, 44; High choir 44; Lights: – Our Lady, Assumption of, light before 44, – Our Lady of Grace, light before 39, – Our Lady's light 496; Seats, repairs 496; Sepulchre cloth 44

Curate *see* Sir Bartholomew Ingoldesby

Everyngham, Thomas 14, 415

Ewerby 281, 336, 496

Austhorpe 336; Bellman 336, 496; Chief lord of Ewerby 336; Church, St. Andrew 336, 496:
Bells 336, – Repairs 496, – Ringers 496; Choir, burial in 496; Churchwardens 336, 496; Churchyard 281; High altar 281, 336

Parish clerk 336, 496; Properties:
– Cowke House 336, – Whyteloke house 496

Vicar *see* **Typler, Sir Richard**

Faderys, Richard 191

Faldys, Margaret, sister of **Sir John Benton** 293

Farforth Church 181

Fargwat, Isabell 140

Farlesthorpe 464, 529, 534

Church, St. Andrew 464:
Churchyard 464, 529; High altar 464, 529, 534; Lights: – Holy Trinity light 529, – Our Lady of Grace's light 529, 534, – Our Lady of Pity's light 529, 534, – Sepulchre light 529, – St. Catherine's light 529; Porch, burial within 534; Works 529, 534

Vicar *see* Wollay, Sir John

Farmary, John 483

Farnesfelde, John 343

Fawn, Sir Nicholas, vicar of Skendleby 255, 276, 319

Fax, Richard, servant of **Thomas Herte** 66

Fayrfax, Mrs. —, of Swarby 496; Mr. John 233

Fed, Agnes 334

Felde, Agnes, sister of **Thomas** 170; Alice, wife of **Thomas** 170; Elizabeth, sister of **Thomas** 170; Jenet 392; John, of Wigtoft, son of Nicholas 25, 202, 308, 443; Margaret, daughter of Nicholas 308; Nicholas 308; Thomas, of Fosdyke 8; **Thomas**, of Leake **170**

Feldehouse, Sir John, parish priest of Panton 199, 432, 475

Fell, Agnes 238

Felyngham, Alice, wife of **Robert** 189; **Robert**, of Boston **189**

Felypson *see* Philipson

Fen, — (deceased), mother of **John** 380; **John**, of Croft, husbandman **380**; John, son of **Thomas** 487; Margaret, wife of **John** 380; Sir Robert 161; **Thomas**, of Edenham **487**; Thomas, son of **Thomas** 487

Fenby, Robert 492; Thomas, son of Walter 427; Walter 427

Fendyke, Sir John junior, parish priest of Leverton 68, 424; Sir John senior, chantry priest of Leverton 68

Fendyll, Walter 439

Fenhouse *see* Wigtoft

Fenton 152, 287, 325

Church, All Saints 152:
Churchyard 152, 287, 325; High altar 152, 287, 325; Lamp 287; Our Lady's gild 152, 287

Fenton, Margaret, wife of **Richard** 29; **Richard**, of Bassingham **29**

Ferley, Thomas, of Alford 550

Ferman, John 436

Ferrer, John 523

Ferroner, Sir Edward, priest 497

Feryby, Thomas, of Bourne 381

Fetherstonehalgh, William, of Hammeringham 176

Fewe, Jenet, wife of **Richard** 54; **Richard**, of Asterby **54**

Feyldhouse, Sir Thomas 74

Fillingham, Church, St. Andrew 304

Firsby 428

Church, St. Andrew:
Churchyard 428; High altar 428; Light, perpetual 428

Parson *see* Prestman, Sir William

Fisher, Agnes, daughter of **William** 395; Alice, daughter of **William** 395; Beatrix, wife of **Thomas** 107; Elizabeth 107; Elizabeth, daughter of **William** 395; Henry, son of **Thomas** 107; Jenet 107; John 136; John, of Surfleet 300; John, son of Richard 107; Lucy 73; Marion, wife of **William** 395; Michael, son of **Thomas** 107; Richard 107, 481; Richard, priest 429; Thomas, of Gedney Fen 450; **Thomas**, of Leake **107**; Thomas, son of **Thomas** 107; **William**, of Deepergarth, Billinghay parish **395**; William, of Hammeringham 176; William, of Stickford 171; William, of Walcot 104, 353; William, son of **William** 395

Fishtoft 86, 190, 383, 396

Church, St. Guthlac:
Altars: – High altar 86, 190, 383, 396, – Holy Trinity altar 86, 190, 396, – St. George's altar 190, – St. John's altar 86, 396;

Frace, Robert, son of **William Reede** 574; Thomas 574

Frampton xx, 32, 113, 139, 185, 262, 435; Brothertoft 253

Church, St. Mary the Virgin 253:
Altars 113, 185, 435; Bells 185, 435; Churchyard 113, 185, 435; High altar 113, 185, 253, 435; Our Lady's gild 113, 185, 435; Rood, burial before 253; Works 113, 185

Parish priest *see* Lee, Sir John; Roger, lord of Frampton 226; Vicar *see* Smyrke, Sir Christopher; Windmill 185

Frances, goddaughter of **Thomas Wodthorpe** 317

Franckys *see* Frankes

Francy, John 554; Robert 554

Frankes, Jenet 49; Maud 333; Thomas 541

Fraunce, Agnes 400

Fraunces, John 49; William, of Fengate, Spalding parish 249

Freman, John 69; Margaret 233; Thomas, of Lincoln 378; William 17, 460

Frende, Robert 138; William 215

Frenton, William 416

Frere, Thomas 247; Sir Thomas 228, 334; William, of West Rasen 81, 100

Frerneyffe, William 224

Fresan, Thomas 526

Fresmore, Sir John, vicar of Huttoft **82**

Fresney, —, wife of Robert 425; Edmund 425; Jenet 425; Robert 425

Freston, —, mother of **Richard** 418; Agnes, wife of **Richard** 418; Alice, maid of **Thomas Tedde** 58; **Richard**, of Ashby Puerorum **418**; William, of Coningsby 58

Frieston 28, 264, 303, 372, 446, 551
Church, St. James:
Churchyard 264, 446, 551; High altar 264; Sacrament 446, 551; Saints: – Our Lady of Pity 264, 551, – St. James 264, 551, – St. Sithe 264, 551; Works 264, 551
Land:
– Bastyngcroft, meadow 28, – Bowleryge, ing land 28, – Frieston Fens 264, – Haltofte End 264
Places:
– Brownthorpe 551, – Kyrkraw 551, – Swangape 264;
Priest *see* Pykhall, Sir Thomas

Frieston, Caythorpe parish *see* Caythorpe

Friskney 30, 36, 519, 528
Church, All Saints:
Altars 30: – High altar 30, Ornaments of 36; Bells 36; Churchyard 30, 36; Gilds 30, 36: – Rood gild 36; Porch 30; Repairs 30; Works 36
Land:
– Bee Ings 528, – Busher Land 528, –

Cokson Toft 528, – Cowe's Land 528, – Lady Garth 528, – Short Ryges 528, – Twyffyltes 528
Priest *see* Westmellys, Sir Robert 36; Smallney 30

Frodingham 75, 314
Brumby 75, 306, 314; Church, St. Mary the Virgin 75, 314:
Chantry (temporary) 75; High altar 75, 314; St. Catherine, light before 75; Works 75

Frome, Eleanor, daughter of **Richard** 214; Marion, wife of **Richard** 214; **Richard**, of Barton upon Humber **214**; Robert 214

Frysnay, Mr. John, of Benington in Holland, gent. 489; William 61

Fryston, John, gent. 566

Fulbeck 343, 521
Church, St. Nicholas 258, 343:
Bells 343; High altar 343; Our Lady's stock 343; St. John's gild 343
Parish clerk 343

Fullalove, George 565

Fulney, Spalding parish *see* Spalding

Fulstow 265, 540
Church, St. Laurence 215, 265:
Chantry (temporary) 265; Churchyard 540; High altar 265; Works 138, 552
Esten Holme, pasture 540; Vicar *see* Raynolde, Sir Richard

Fundans *see* Funtans

Funtans, Robert 151; Thomas 151

Furlyngton, William161

Furmary, Agnes 220; Dorothy 220; Humphrey 220

Fylepotte, William, of Gosberton 505

Fylipson *see* Philipson

Fyn, William 284

Fyporte *see* Phyporte

Fyshe, —, wife of William 560; William 560

Fysher, Fyssher *see* Fisher

Fythwilliam *see* Fitzwilliam

Gage, Margaret, daughter of **Robert** 452; Johanne, wife of **Robert** 452; John, son of **Robert** 452; **Robert**, of Skillington 437, **452**; Thomas, son of **Robert** 452

Gainnoll, John, of Mareham on the Hill 317

Gainsborough xx, 166, 294
Church, All Saints 294:
High altar 166, 294; Three gilds' light 294
Church Lane 294; Market place 294; Priest *see* Toppclyffe, Thomas

Gambull, John 522

Gammulbe, John 536

Gammyll, Alice, daughter of **Robert** 45; Elizabeth, wife of **Robert** 45; Helen, daughter of **Robert** 45; Johanne, daughter of **Robert** 45; John 191; **Robert**, of Swaton

Hertyll, Jenet, wife of Philip 325; Philip, of
    Fenton 325
Heryng, —, daughter of John 439;—, wife of
    John 439; Agnes 439; John 439, 499;
    Margaret, daughter of John 439; Walter,
    son of John 439
Herys, Herrys see Harys
Hessyll see Hassyll
Hesylldyen, Robert, of Normanton 382, 521
Hethenes, Sir Stephen, priest 303
Hetton, Thomas 126
Heveryngham, Thomas 93
Hewys, Sir Robert, parson of Asterby 535
Hewton, Elizabeth, daughter of William 555;
    Margaret, wife of William 555; William, of
    Waltham 555
Hewytson, Sir Thomas, priest of Saltfleetby St.
    Peter 250
Heylande see Haylande
Heynings Nunnery 304
Hight, Robert 335
High Toynton 63, 91, 468
    Church, St. John the Baptist 317:
        Churchyard 63, 468; High altar 63; Our
        Lady 468; Sacrament 468; Works 63
    Curate, see Rose, Sir Martin; Howsson Close
        468
Hill, Mr. —, of Pinchbeck 474; Hugh 165; John,
    of Irby on Humber 333; John, of
    Pinchbeck 240; John, son of John 240; Sir
    John, parson of Thoresby 69; Sir John,
    priest of Horbling 3, 155, 568; Margaret
    277; Orman 228, 275; Thomas, of
    Bottesford 330; Sir Thomas, parish priest
    of Pinchbeck 89, 240, 416, 459, 474, 491,
    503, 511; William 38
Hiltofte, Mr. 532
Hoberde, Elizabeth, niece of Humphrey Ordyng
    433; Jenet 433; John 433; Margaret, niece
    of Humphrey Ordyng 433; Thomas 433;
    William 433
Hobson, Elizabeth 497; Robert 214
Hobster see Hopster
Hochynson see Hutchynson
Hodale, William 401
Hode see Hoode
Hodgeson see Hogeson
Hoge, Sir Robert, of Lynancer 405
Hogekynson, Christopher 136
Hogekynson alias Johnson see Johnson
Hoges, Thomas 517
Hogeson, — 292; Alan 570; Jenet, daughter of
    Thomas Tooly, wife of John II 558; John I,
    of East Kirkby 558; John II, of Wood
    Enderby, godson & son-in-law of Thomas
    Tooly 15, 558; Sibyll 558; Thomas, son of
    John II 558; William, of Leake 488;
    William, son of John II 558
Hoghson see Hogson

Hogson, Humphrey 220; William I 12; William
    II 82
Hogsthorpe 254, 309, 499
    Church, St. Mary the Virgin 52:
        Altars: – Cloths 24, – High altar 24, 405,
        499, – Our Lady's altar 24; Churchyard
        309, 499; Works 405, 499, 510
Hoke, Robert 65
Holand, John 27
Holbeach xx, 7, 270, 460, 581
    Church, All Saints 581:
        Altars 7, 270, 460, 581: – High altar 7, 270,
        460, 581, – Holy Trinity altar 460, – Our
        Lady's altar 7, 460, – St. Stephen's altar 7,
        581; Bellman 581; Chantries (temporary)
        270, 581; Churchwardens 270, 581;
        Churchyard 7, 270, 460, 581; Cope 581;
        Easter sepulchre 7; Lights: – Plough light
        270, – Rood light 7, 270, 460; Our Lady,
        rood before 581; Repairs 581; Works 270,
        460
    Curate see Browne, Sir Robert; Wykam,
        Richard; Places: –
    Algate 581, – Fen End 460, – Holbeach
        Drove 65, – Wegnill Gate 581
Holdernes 545
Holdernes, Elizabeth, wife of Richard 323;
    Richard, of Corby, husbandman 323;
    Thomas, son of Richard 323; William, son
    of Richard323
Hole, —, wife of Robert 335; Agnes, daughter of
    Robert 335; Alison, daughter of Robert
    335; Christopher, son of Robert 335;
    Elizabeth, daughter of Robert 335; John,
    son of Robert 335, 389; Leonard, son of
    Robert 335; Robert 496; Robert, of Little
    Hale, Great Hale parish 335; Thomas, son
    of Robert 335, 390
Holforthe, Sir John, parish priest of
    Potterhanworth 316; Thomas 105
Holgate, Robert, Prior of St. Catherine's
    Priory, Lincoln 3n
Holland, Lincs.139, 519
Hollande, Jenet 495; Sir John 426; Mr. Thomas,
    esq. master of Sir Robert Leedes 57, 224,
    463
Hollyngworth, Catherine, daughter of James
    216; James, of Old Bullington, Goltho
    parish, servant & keeper to Sir George
    Taylboys, knight 216; John, son of James
    216; Robert, son of James 216
Holme, Catherine, wife of William 477; Helen,
    daughter of William 477; Henry, godson
    to Joan Hauke's husband 386; Jenet,
    daughter of William 477; Margaret,
    daughter of William 477; William 119;
    William, of Elsham 477; William, son of
    William 477; Dane William, godson of
    John Stotte 51

Howet (*cont.*):
50; Sir John 248; Margaret, daughter of
Helen 50; Robert, husband (?) of **Helen** 50;
Thomas 50; Thomas, of Spalding 243; Sir
William 151

Howgate, John 272

Howlotte, Sir Stephen, vicar of Westborough
51, 318, 480, 522

Howse, Peter 329

Howson, Jenet 367; John, of Wigtoft 25;
Richard 367; **Simon**, of Waltham **552**;
William 367

Howtofte, Agnes, kinswoman of **Robert** 481;
Jenet, wife of **Robert** 481; John, of
Hundleby 481; **Robert**, of Raithby **481**;
Thomas, son of **Robert** 481

Howtton, Sir William 484

Howys *see* Howes

Howyt *see* Howet

Howytson, John 377

Hoyges, —, wife of **John** 572; Agnes, daughter
of **John** 572; Agnes, sister of **John** 572;
Alice, daughter of **John** 572; Anthony 572;
Elizabeth, daughter of **John** 572; Helen,
daughter of **John** 572; Isabell, daughter of
John 572; **John**, of Addlethorpe **572**; John,
son of **John** 572; Margaret, daughter of
John 572

Hubbarde, Hubberde *see* Hubbert

Hubbert, —, wife of Thomas 123; Addelard,
brother of Clement 20; Alice, sister of
Addelard 20; Anne, daughter of **William**
20; Cassandra, daughter of Anne 20;
Margaret, daughter of Anne 20; Clement,
brother of Addelard 20; Elizabeth, sister
of Addelard 20; George, of Calais, brother
of **William** 20; John, of London, brother
of **William** 20; John, son of **William** 20;
Margaret, daughter of **William** 20;
Margaret, wife of **William** 20; Thomas, of
Kirton in Holland 123, 328; **William**, of
Wainfleet All Saints **20**; William, kinsman
of **William** 20

Huchenson *see* Hutchynson

Huddelstone, Godfrey, of Rowston 183, 272

Huddilston, Sir Miles, parson of Normanton
27, 196

Huddylston, William 272

Hudson, Anne, daughter of James 77; Sir
Edward, son of **Thomas II** 38; **Henry**, of
Leverton, single man **424**; Isabell 337;
James, brother of **Stephen** 77, 175; Jenet,
daughter of William II 337, 424; Johanne,
wife of **Stephen** 77; Johanne, wife of
Thomas II 38; John, of Appleby 38; John,
poor man of East Keal 163; John, servant
of **William Ashton** 27; John, son of **Stephen**
77; Sir John, curate of St. Paul's in the
Bailey, Lincoln 234, 411; Margaret,

daughter of Thomas Tollyn 337, 424;
Nicholas 127; Robert, son of **Stephen** 77;
Robert, son of **Thomas II** 38; **Stephen**, of
Barrow upon Humber **77**; Thomas I 193;
Thomas II, of Appleby **38**; Thomas III,
brother of **Henry** 424; Thomas IV, son of
Thomas I 193; William 156; William I, son
of James 77; William II, son of **Joan
Tollyn** 337, 424

Huetson *see* Hughetson

Huggon, William, kinsman of **Robert Halmotte**
151

Hughetson, Mr. Thomas 58; William 436

Hulton, Roger, of Donington in Holland, gent.
329, 533

Hull, Yorks, Our Lady 278; White Friars:
Image of Our Lady 492

Hulle, Thomas, of Swineshead 463

Humberstone, John, of Branston 165, 320

Humble, **Edward**, of Roughton **471**; Jenet, wife
of **Edward** 471; Nicholas, son of **Edward**
471; William, son of **Edward** 471

Humbyll *see* Humble

Humpe, Alice, daughter of Robert 410; John
505; Robert, son of **Agnes Tempeste** 410;
Rose, daughter of Robert 410

Humphrey, Elizabeth, daughter of Richard 243;
Elizabeth, wife of **Robert** 243; Helen,
daughter of **Robert** 243; Richard 243;
Robert, of Fulney, Spalding parish **243**;
Robert, son of Richard 243; —, wife of
Thomas 63; Thomas 63

Hundleby 2, 91, 112, 481
Church 2, 58:
Chantry (temporary) 58; Churchyard 112;
High altar 2; Lights: – five 2, – All Saints'
light 2, – Maidens' light 112, – Young
mens' light 112; Our Lady in high choir 2,
112; Works 163; Vicar, *see* Dawson, Sir
Robert

Hunington, Church 237

Hunne, Thomas, of Wigtoft 122

Hunnyngham, Robert, of Kirton in Holland
226

Hunt, Adam, of Walpole 8; Agnes 318; Agnes,
daughter of **Roger** 98; Agnes, wife of
Roger 98; Alice 318; Edward, son of **Roger**
98; Elizabeth 318, 480; Elizabeth,
daughter of **Roger** 98; James, son of **Roger**
98; Jenet 318; Jenet, servant of **William
Skalflete** 132; Margaret 318; Margery 318;
Robert 318; Roger 9; **Roger**, of Kirton in
Holland **98**; Thomas 318; Thomas, son of
Roger 98; William 318, 480; Sir William
52, 140

Hunte, Huntte *see* Hunt

Hunter, Agnes, sister of **Sir William** 537;
Anthony, son of **Richard** 499; Beatrix,
daughter of **Richard** 499; Helen, wife of

Kyrmonde, John 348, 518; Nicholas 348;
    Thomas 348
Kyrslay, Sir John, curate of Horbling 97, 110
Kyrton, Jenet 162; Robert, of Great Hale 389;
    Thomas 53; William, of Great Hale 4, 53,
    335
Kytchyn see Kechyn
Kytlok, Mr. Nicholas, parish priest of Fishtoft
    86, 396
Kytson, Margaret 187

Laburne, —, wife of William 235; William 235
Lace, William 305
Laceby 538; Church, St. Margaret 333, 538: St.
    Margaret's chapel 333
Laceby, Sir William, of Grimsby, chaplain 448
Lacy, John 212
Lafelde, John 111
Lamberd, Alan 32
Lamberde, Alice 275
Lambeson, Anthony, son of Richard 463;
    Beatrix, wife of Richard 463; Jane,
    daughter of Richard 463; George, son of
    Richard 463; Richard, of Swineshead,
    notary xviii, 463; Richard, son of Richard
    463; Thomas, son of Richard 463; William,
    son of Richard 463; Sir William, brother of
    Richard 463
Lamme, Jenet 181; Sir John 411
Lammyng, John 100
Lanam, Sir Robert, curate of Clee 146, 431,
    552, 555
Lancaster, Lancs., Friars Minor 70; Our Lady
    286
Lancaster, Thomas, of Hagworthingham 469
Lane see Layne
Langlay, John, of Stainton by Langworth 259;
    Sir Robert, parson of Toft by Newton 35
Langley see Langlay
Langtoft 356
  Church, St. Michael:
    All Saints' light 356; Bells 356; Churchyard
        356; High altar 356
  Vicar see Bulle, Sir Geoffrey
Langton by Partney 239
  Church, St. Peter 144, 239, 248, 344:
    High altar 239; Our Lady's choir, burial in
        239
    Plummer's Thyng 144
Langton by Wragby 362
  Church, St. Giles 362:
    High altar 362; Our Lady, north side, burial
        before 362
  Vicar see Walker, Sir Christopher
Langton, Addelard 239; Alexander, son of John
    II 239; Elizabeth, daughter of John II 239;
    Elizabeth (deceased), wife of John II 239;
    John I, of Goltho 284; John II, of Langton
    by Partney, esq. 239; John, son of John II

239; Thomas 48; William, son of John II
    239
Langwith, Jane 242; John, son of Robert 242;
    Robert, of Brant Broughton 242; Robert,
    son of John 242; Thomas, son of John 242;
    William, son of John 242
Lanrake, Isabell 123
Larkes, William 488
Lathorpe, Richard, of Greetham 218
Laughton 45, 574
Laughton, Alice, sister of Christopher Haghus
    91; Helen 517; Henry 517; Thomas 249;
    Thomas 517
Laukneye, Gilbor 313
Laurence, servant of Thomas Routon 110
Laurence, John 236, 385, 413
Laurenson, Jenkin 62; Steven 122
Laventon, Church 346
Laverok, Alison 439; Maud 439; William, of
    Boston 260
Law, John 570
Lawhtone see Laughton 517
Lawklande, Henry 336
Lawson, Thomas, of Cumberworth 393;
    Thomas, of Farlesthorpe 464
Laxson, Robert, brother-in-law of John Blaby
    356
Layne, Agnes, daughter of William 473; Alice,
    daughter of William 473; Barnard, son of
    William 473; Isabell, daughter of William
    473; Isabell, wife of William 473; Jenet,
    wife of Thomas 263; John, of Dunston
    101; John, brother of William 473; John,
    son of Thomas 263; Leonard, son of
    Thomas 263; Richard, brother of William
    473, 482; Robert, son of Thomas 263;
    Thomas, of Welbourn 263; Thomas, son of
    Thomas 263; Walter, son of William 473;
    William, of Hough on the Hill 473;
    William, son of William 473
Laysby, Agnes, sister of Johanne Goshoke 439;
    John 439
Leacye, Robert 88
Leadenham xiii, xiv, 41, 152, 196
Leake xx, 107, 170, 213, 238, 257, 376, 488, 559
  Church, St. Mary 238:
    Altars 107, 170, 213, 238, 488: – High altar
        213, 257, 488, Adornment of 238;
    Churchyard 107, 170, 213, 257, 488; Our
        Lady, adornment of 107, 213, 238; Repairs
        127; Sacrament 170; Works 170, 213
  Clergy:
    Curate 257; Parson 107
  Highgate 127; Leake Ings 376; Mill, new 376
Leasingham 414
  Church, St. Andrew:
    Churchwardens 414; Churchyard 414; High
        altar 414
  Roxholme 414; Parson, north part of parish

Turnepeny (cont.):
    Margaret, daughter of **Robert** 426; **Robert**,
    of East Allington, Sedgebrook parish **426**
Turner, Edmund, son of **Robert** 21; Elizabeth
    21; Jenet, mother of **Edmund Maxsay** 444;
    Johanne, wife of **Robert** 21; John 444;
    John, of Mareham on the Hill 317; John,
    of Swafield 517; John junior, son of **Robert**
    21; John senior, son of **Robert** 21; Richard
    444; **Robert**, of Dowsby **21**; Robert, son of
    Robert 21; Sir Robert 458; Thomas 444;
    Thomas, of Boston 73; William junior 444;
    William senior 444; Sir William 99
Turnstall, Church 140
Turpyn, Alice, daughter of William I 264;
    Cecily, daughter of Richard 264; **John**, of
    Frieston **264**; John, son of Richard 264;
    John, son of William I 264 ; Richard, son
    of **John** 264, 497; Robert, son of Richard
    264; Simon, son of **John** 264; William I,
    son of **John** 264; William II, son of
    Richard 264
Tutbury, Barnard, of Markby 550
Twede, Isabell 73
Twelle, Elizabeth, sister of **Thomas** 451;
    Thomas, of Winthorpe **451**
Twydale, Steven 502; William, of Glentham,
    yeoman 180
Twyll, Henry 155
Tyde, Robert 316; Thomas, servant of **Robert
    Branston** 517
Tydd St. Mary 429, 523
    Church, St. Mary 429:
        Chantry (temporary) 523; Churchwardens
        429; Churchyard 523; Cross, in way
        leading to church 429; High altar 429, 523;
        Lights 429, 523: – Holy Trinity light 523, –
        Our Lady's light 523, – Rood light 523, –
        St. Thomas' light 523; St. John the Baptist
        523; Works 523
    Parson see Gybson, Christopher
Tydde, William 240
Tygges, Thomas 528
Tyler, Alice 192
Tyllot, Edmund 110
Tyllyng, John, servant of **Robert Tyllyng** 430;
    Margaret, wife of **Robert** 430; **Robert**, of
    Great Gonerby **430**; Robert, son (?) of
    Robert 430; William 430
Tylson, Agnes, daughter of William, of
    Pinchbeck 172, 399; Alison, daughter of
    Gilbert 249; Elizabeth, daughter of
    Gilbert 249; **Gilbert**, of Pinchbeck xxii,
    249; Gilbert, son of Thomas 249; John
    junior, son of **Gilbert** 249; John senior,
    son of **Gilbert** 249; John, son of William
    399; Ralph, son of John senior 249;
    Richard, of Pinchbeck 399; Roger, son of
    Gilbert 249; Thomas, son of **Gilbert** 249;

William, of Pinchbeck, son of **Gilbert** 6,
    172, 249, 399
Tylton, Hugh 389
Tynber, Henry 269
Tyngyll, Agnes, daughter of **Gilbert Tylson** 249;
    Edmund, son-in-law of **Gilbert Tylson** 249;
    Gilbert, son (?) of Agnes & Edmund 249;
    Robert 263; Sir William 94
Tyngyll see Tyngell
Typler, —, wife of Ralph 437; Agnes, sister of
    Richard 496; Jane, sister of Richard 496;
    Jenet, daughter of **Cecily Pedder** 32; John
    junior 437; Ralph 437; Richard, son of
    William of Great Hale 496; **Sir Richard**,
    vicar of Ewerby 281, 336, **496**; Robert, son
    of Roger 32; Roger 32; William, of Great
    Hale, brother of **Sir Richard** 335; William
    junior 496
Tyrwhyt, Sir Robert, knight 229, 359

Ulceby 514; Church 15, 514
Ulyot, John 317
Umfray, see Humphrey
Underwater, Robert, godson of **Robert
    Wrangill** 342
Underwoode, Agnes, poor woman of East Keal
    163
Upton, Church, St. Michael 304, 368: Silver
    plate 368
Upton, Adrian, brother of **Nicholas**, uncle of
    John 139, 519; Agnes 494; Elizabeth, wife
    of **John** 519; George, uncle of **Nicholas**
    139; Hammond, son of **Nicholas** 139;
    Isabell, daughter of **Nicholas** 139; John,
    gent. 139; **John**, esq., of Northolme
    Wainfleet, son of **Nicholas** 139, **519**;
    Nicholas, esq., of Northolme by Wainfleet
    139; Nicholas, son of **John** 519; Nicholas,
    son of **Nicholas** 139
Urry, Jenet 293; John, of Stainton by
    Langworth 259, 293; Lucy 293; William
    293
Usher, Friar John 452
Usselby, Church, St. Margaret 407: St.
    Margaret 407
Ustwayt, William 333
Utterby 55; Church, St. Andrew 55, 215, 265:
    Banner cloth 55; Churchyard 55; High
    altar 55; Our Lady's gild 55
Utterby, Helen 358; John 220
Uttyng, Richard 60

Vassell, John, of Gosberton 12, 412, 454, 472,
    544; **Richard**, of Market Rasen **74**;
    Thomas, of Gosberton 296, 454
Vaudey Abbey: Abbot & convent 387
Vavasore, William, gent. 139
Vernon, Mrs. 284
Vincent, Anne 552; Richard 552; Sibyll 220

Vyrley, John 78

Wace, Geoffrey 308
Waddeslay *see* Wadeslay
Waddingham xi, 75; Church, St. Mary the
　Virgin 407: High altar 407
Waddingham, Church, St. Peter 407
Waddingworth, Church, St. Margaret 15
Wade, Alice, wife of William II 264; Sir Andrew
　222; Isabell 181; John 181; John, of
　Frieston 446; John, brother-in-law of
　William Wightman 73, 85, 87; **Sir John**,
　parson of Ruckland **181**; —, wife of
　Thomas 273; Margaret, servant of **Sir
　Robert Whyham** 470; Thomas 273; Walter
　181; William I 181; William II 264; Sir
　William III 181
Wadeslay, Abraham, son of **John** 154; Agnes,
　daughter of **John** 154; Agnes, wife of **John**
　154; Alice, goddaughter of **Robert Tulye**
　362; Elizabeth, daughter of **John** 154;
　Jenet, daughter of **John** 154; **John**, of
　South Willingham, husbandman **154**;
　John, son of **John** 154; Richard 362;
　Robert, son of **John** 154; Thomas, son of
　Richard 362; William, brother of **John**
　154, 362
Wadyngham, —, father of **John** 248; —
　(deceased), wife of **John** 248; Agnes,
　daughter of **John** 248; Isabell, daughter of
　John 248; **John**, of Aswarby 248; John, son
　of **John** 248; Maud, daughter of **John** 248;
　Robert, son of **John** 248; Thomas, son of
　John 248; William, son of **John** 248
Wadyngton, Sir Ranold, priest of Welbourn
　263, 320
Wainfleet 283
Wainfleet All Saints 20, 277, 345, 519, 528
　Church, All Saints 20, 139, 345:
　　Altars: – High altar 20, 277, 345, – Low
　　altars (2) 345, – Our Lady's altar 277, – St.
　　Nicholas' altar 277; Bells 20, 345;
　　Churchyard 277; Gilds: – St. James' gild
　　20, – St. Mary's gild 20; Middle aisle 20;
　　Repairs 20; Sacrament, ornament of 20;
　　St. John's chapel, maintenance of altar 20;
　　St. Mary of Bethlehem's light 20; St.
　　Nicholas' choir – St. Mary Magdalene,
　　burial before 345; Works 163
　Land:
　　– Bent Hill 20, – Key Lands 528, – St.
　　Mary's Field 345, Petcheller Toft 345
　Market place 20; Places:
　　– Newcroftes 20, – Redeberd 20
　Parson, *see* Ranson, Sir Richard
Wainfleet St. Mary 528
　Church, St. Mary's 139, 528:
　　Altars 528; Bells 528; High altar 30; Repairs
　　528; Sacrament 528; Sepulchre light 528

Land:
　– Gray Toft 528, – Gress Merff 528, –
　Hobtoft, arable land 528, – Holl Pasture
　528, – Lokmayn 528, – Muson Land 528, –
　North Moysse 528, – Schypyn Toft 528
　Parson 528; Properties:
　– Peper Thorpe, messuage 528, – Wye
　Pyngle 528
Wakefelde, **John**, of Ewerby **281**; Margery, wife
　of **John** 281
Wakelyng, Thomas 291
Walcot 104, 353
　Church, St. Andrew's 104:
　　All Saints' light 104, 353; Churchyard 353;
　　High altar 104, 353; St. John's gild 104,
　　353; St. Margaret's chapel 457
　Priest *see* Pell, Sir Thomas
Wales, William, of Greetham 218
Walgrave, Catherine, wife of William 181;
　William 181
Walhyll, Sir Robert, parson of Westborough
　480, 522
Walkeman, Alan 419
Walker, Agnes 431; Sir Christopher, vicar of
　Langton by Wragby 362; Helen, daughter
　of **Roger** 14; Henry 522; Humphrey 534;
　James 484; John, servant of Christopher
　Haghus 91; John, of Thurlby 405;
　Margery, goddaughter of John Kyngerby
　484; Robert 108; Robert 341; Sir Robert,
　parish priest of Wigtoft 17, 25, 78; **Roger**,
　of Bassingham **14**; Thomas 483; Thomas,
　of Doddington 493; William, son of **Roger**
　14; William, of Goxhill 195; William, of
　Alford 254
Walkewyd, *see* Walkwid
Walkwid, Agnes, wife of **Roger** 60; Elizabeth,
　daughter of **Roger** 60; Roger, of
　Luddington **60**; Thomas, son of **Roger** 60;
　William 60
Walkyngton, Sir Edmund 100
Wallys, Sir James, vicar of Tealby 247;
　Margaret 408, 570; Ralph 66; William 467
Walpole 8
Walpole, Mr. —, of Pinchbeck 474, 511; old
　Mrs. —, gossip of **Agens Clare** 511; John,
　of Ingoldmells 405, 461; Thomas, of
　Careby 168; Sir Thomas, priest 89, 511
Walpoll, Walpull *see* Walpole
Walsche *see* Walshe
Walshe, Agnes, servant of **Richard Trewe** 247;
　John 1; *alias* Ducheman, Thomas 247;
　William senior 450
Walsingham, Norfk., Our Lady xxvi, 34, 69, 82,
　117, 200, 227, 251, 256, 305, 484
Waltham 552, 555
　Church, All Saints 552:
　　Bells 552, 555; Chantry 552n; Churchyard
　　555; High altar 552, 555; Our Lady 555;

SUBJECT INDEX

Arabic numbers refer to the number of the individual document, Roman to the page number in the introduction.